LEGAL RESEARCH ILLUSTRATED

SIXTH EDITION

An Abridgment of
FUNDAMENTALS
OF
LEGAL RESEARCH

SIXTH EDITION

By

J. MYRON JACOBSTEIN
Professor of Law Emeritus and Law Librarian Emeritus
Stanford University

ROY M. MERSKY
Elton M. Hyder, Jr. and Martha Rowan Hyder Centennial
Professor of Law and Director of Research
University of Texas, Austin

DONALD J. DUNN
Law Librarian and Professor of Law
Western New England College

Westbury, New York
THE FOUNDATION PRESS, INC.
1994

Reprinted from
Jacobstein, Mersky and Dunn's Fundamentals of Legal Research, Sixth Edition

COPYRIGHT © 1994 By THE FOUNDATION PRESS, INC.
Library of Congress Catalog Card Number: 94–60946

ISBN 1–56662–167–4

*TEXT IS PRINTED ON 10% POST
CONSUMER RECYCLED PAPER*

PREFACE

This is an Abridgment of the sixth edition of *Fundamentals of Legal Research*. In preparing each edition of the parent work, we have been conscious of the many changes that have occurred since the publication of the previous edition. Frequent changes in legal research materials cause our text, as well as all other legal research texts, to become rapidly outdated.

Between editions, we will provide instructors information on changes publishers may have made in materials described in our book and on new publications.

This Abridgment is again designed to accomplish two purposes. The first objective is to introduce the fundamentals of legal resources to those law schools that do not have a formal course in legal research but attempt to integrate the techniques of legal research through a legal writing or other substantive law course. The Abridgment enables the law student to grasp the basic fundamental concepts of the materials in legal research in precise, readily comprehensive format.

Its second objective is to provide an introduction to legal resources for law-related courses and problems in the undergraduate or graduate curriculum. Dealing with the effective utilization of legal research and reference tools in a manner designed to meet the needs of the student in a non-law field, the Abridgment is a thorough guide to the scholar in interdisciplinary use of legal materials.

Law is a central concept in human society. Indeed, without law there would be no society. In our society, law is commonly defined in terms of the decisions of our various courts. It is the courts that fill out the bare bones of the statutes by specific applications and that fill in gaps in the statutory rules by creative judging. Especially since the 1954 decision by the Supreme Court of the United States in the now landmark case of *Brown vs. Board of Education of Topeka*,[1] popularly known as the School Segregation Case, our courts have been increasingly active in attacking social problems. As a result, an understanding of legal rules is a necessary requirement for scientists, technologists, as well as other professions.

This fact is part of a general trend toward interdisciplinary studies. With each passing year, our civilization increases in complexity. As an inevitable result, research in all fields becomes more interdisciplinarian in nature. Legal research, for example, has been substantially affected in recent years by the continued expansion of technological innovation and by a greater tendency to use legal solutions for a wide range of social problems. As these interdisciplinarian scholars have discovered that

---

1. 347 U.S. 483 (1954).

legal studies add valuable materials to their programs of instruction, a guide is needed to provide these non-lawyers who feel the impact of law upon their disciplines with an introduction to the essentials of legal research.

A few words are in order regarding the role of the computer in legal research. Both the West Publishing Company, with its WESTLAW System, and the Mead Data Central, with its LEXIS System, have made available online and in full text most of the materials that are covered in this text. These systems have greatly increased the techniques for doing legal research. We have, for several reasons, however, limited our treatment of computer-assisted research to references where it is discussed in our parent work, the *Fundamentals of Legal Research*. It is our belief that to become efficient in the use of computer-assisted legal research, it is necessary to have a sound understanding of the methodology of legal research using printed sources. Even when computer-assisted research is available, it is generally recommended that it be used in connection with traditional printed sources.

Chapters in this Abridgment on international law, legislative histories, administrative law, and computers and the law, are but a few of the subjects covered that will provide the interdisciplinarian professions an indispensable understanding of the legal duties and liabilities inherent in their practice.

Law is a well-indexed, well-organized body of materials, confusing and complex to the uninitiated, but easily accessible with the aid of a knowledgeable guide. This Abridgment is designed to be that guide.

But we wish to emphasize that this work is intended to provide only a bird's-eye view of legal research. For more intensive information on the use of law books, the parent work, *Fundamentals of Legal Research*, should be consulted.

In most instances, the summary of each chapter has been omitted in the Abridgment. The full edition should also be consulted for information on Computer-Assisted Legal Research, Court Rules and Procedure, Federal Tax Research, Legal Citation Form, Municipal Legislation, English Legal Research, and Table of Legal Abbreviations.

ASSIGNMENTS TO ACCOMPANY LEGAL RESEARCH ILLUS-TRATED is available as a separate pamphlet. These assignments are designed to help the student understand and examine in detail the research tools described in this book.

J. MYRON JACOBSTEIN
ROY M. MERSKY
DONALD J. DUNN

May, 1994

PREFACE

Since 1973, *Fundamentals of Legal Research* has been authored by J. Myron Jacobstein and Roy M. Mersky. We are pleased to announce that there is another coauthor, Donald J. Dunn, Law Librarian and Professor of Law, Western New England College School of Law. Don is a recognized authority on legal research, has written extensively in the area, and has lectured often about the subject. He has worked with us over the years on many projects, including the three previous editions of *Fundamentals*. In addition, he has been sole editor of *Noter Up* since 1986, and has assisted in compiling the *Index to Periodical Articles Related to Law* since 1991. With this Sixth Edition of *Fundamentals*, his contributions deserve to be fully recognized and, thus, he joins us as coauthor.

J. Myron Jacobstein
Roy M. Mersky

*

v

ACKNOWLEDGMENTS

We are pleased to have this opportunity to express our gratitude to the many people who have helped in the preparation of *Fundamentals of Legal Research*, Sixth Edition.

Much of the work for this edition took place at the University of Texas at Austin, Jamail Center for Legal Research, Tarlton Law Library and the Western New England College School of Law Library. The law library staffs at both institutions have earned our most sincere thanks for their collective expertise and, most of all, for their patience.

Specifically, at the University of Texas, David Gunn, Head of Reference Services; Kristin Cheney, Assistant Director for Public & Educational Services; and Brian Quigley, Assistant Director of Bibliographic Services, each proofread and contributed suggestions to the content of various chapters. David Gunn also assisted with the new section on researching the Supreme Court in Chapter 19. Jonathan Pratter, Foreign and International Law Librarian, greatly improved Chapter 20 "International Law" by providing a complete rewrite. He also revised Chapter 21 and Appendix C. Mark Giangrande, Tarlton Law Library Fellow, contributed the new discussion of the Internet to Chapter 22. Gwyn Anderson, Senior Administrative Associate, as she does with so many projects, maintained a calming presence that kept the project on track.

At Western New England College, the assistance of Associate Law Librarian Bonnie L. Koneski-White was enormous. In addition to meticulously proofreading many of the chapters and contributing significantly to the intellectual content of each, she substantially rewrote Chapter 9 "Federal Legislation" and Chapter 10 "Federal Legislative Histories", revised Chapter 13, and prepared the Index. Michele Dill LaRose, Head of Reader Services, and Christine Archambault, Head of Technical Services, were both invaluable in tracking down information on various sources. Research Assistants Lisa Mullin ('93) and Michelle Stover ('94) researched and verified much of the information in the text and read and critiqued the manuscript at various stages of its preparation. Donna Haskins, Secretary to the Law Librarian, assisted with manuscript preparation almost daily for a year, while always maintaining her joyful disposition. Special thanks also goes to Dean Howard I. Kalodner for his encouragement and support throughout this project.

We are also grateful to Daniel W. Martin, Director of the Pepperdine University Law Library, who shared his heavily-annotated teaching text from the Fifth Edition. It served as an excellent checklist for identifying areas needing improvement and inclusion.

ACKNOWLEDGMENTS

We are happy that for this edition Joan Howland, Director of the Law Library at the University of Minnesota, has assumed responsibility for the *Assignments* and the *Instructor's Manual*.

In the body of the text, credit is given to those who prepared individual chapters or sections. We want to acknowledge again these contributors: Steven M. Barkan, Associate Dean and Associate Professor of Law at Marquette University Law School; Eleanor DeLashmitt, Director of Educational Programs at Loyola Marymount University School of Law; Mark Giangrande, Tarlton Law Library Fellow at the University of Texas at Austin, Jamail Center for Legal Research, Tarlton Law Library; David Gunn, Head of Reference Services at the University of Texas at Austin, Jamail Center for Legal Research, Tarlton Law Library; Bonnie L. Koneski-White, Associate Law Librarian at Western New England College School of Law; Daniel W. Martin, Director of the Pepperdine University Law Library; Robert J. Nissenbaum, Director of the William M. Rains Library and Professor of Law at Loyola Marymount University School of Law; Jonathan Pratter, Foreign and International Law Librarian at the University of Texas at Austin, Jamail Center for Legal Research, Tarlton Law Library; and Fred R. Shapiro, Associate Librarian for Public Services and Lecturer in Legal Research at Yale Law School.

Each subsequent edition builds upon the prior one. Over the years many individuals have contributed advice, support, and technical assistance to the previous editions of *Fundamentals of Legal Research*. We have attempted to acknowledge this participation in the editions in which their major contributions appear. These previous good works continue to live in this new edition. To all our contributors through the six editions of this work, we express our most sincere appreciation.

We also want to thank the many publishers who provided updated information on their materials. Their Illustrations add immeasurably to this book's instructional purpose.

Finally, we want to thank the staff at The Foundation Press for their patience, advice, and publication expertise. One person, however, deserves special recognition. Harold Eriv, President of The Foundation Press for the past twenty years, has overseen the preparation and production of all six editions of this book. His consistent focus on quality and his fervor for deadlines always presented immense challenges. With his retirement in 1993, we lost a true leader in legal publishing. However, his friendship and his contributions to *Fundamentals of Legal Research* will endure.

SUMMARY OF CONTENTS

*

TABLE OF CONTENTS

TABLE OF CONTENTS

TABLE OF CONTENTS

*

GLOSSARY OF TERMS USED
IN LEGAL RESEARCH

This glossary of terms* is limited in scope, and the definitions of words are restricted in meaning to their legal or legal research context. Words whose meanings conform to general usage and are obvious are omitted from the list, *e.g.*, Index.

ACQUITTAL—

the verdict in a criminal trial in which the defendant is found not guilty.

ACT—

an alternative name for statutory law. When introduced into the first house of the legislature, a piece of proposed legislation is known as a *bill*. When passed to the next house, it may then be referred to as an *act*. After enactment the terms law and act may be used interchangeably. An act has the same legislative force as a joint resolution but is technically distinguishable, being of a different form and introduced with the words *Be it enacted* instead of *Be it resolved*.

ACTION—

the formal legal demand of one's rights from another person brought in court.

ADJUDICATION—

the formal pronouncing or recording of a judgment or decree by a court.

ADMINISTRATIVE AGENCY—

a governmental authority, other than a legislature or court, which issues rules and regulations or adjudicates disputes arising under its statutes and regulations. Administrative agencies usually act under authority delegated by the legislature.

ADMINISTRATIVE LAW—

law that affects private parties, promulgated by governmental agencies other than courts or legislative bodies. These administrative agencies derive their power from legislative enactments and are subject to judicial review.

---

* Revised for this edition by Fred R. Shapiro, Associate Librarian for Public Services and Lecturer in Legal Research, Yale Law School; Editor, *Oxford Dictionary of American Legal Quotations* (Oxford University Press, 1993).

ADVANCE SHEETS—

current pamphlets containing the most recently reported opinions of a court or the courts of several jurisdictions. The volume and page numbers usually are the same as in the subsequently bound volumes of the series, which cover several numbers of the advance sheets.

ADVISORY OPINION—

an opinion rendered by a court at the request of the government or an interested party and indicates how the court would rule on a matter should adversary litigation develop. An advisory opinion is thus an interpretation of the law without binding effect. The International Court of Justice and some state courts will render advisory opinions; the Supreme Court of the United States will not.

AFFIDAVIT—

a written statement or declaration of facts sworn to by the maker, taken before a person officially permitted by law to administer oaths.

AMICUS CURIAE—

means, literally, friend of the court. A party with strong interest in or views on the subject matter of the dispute will petition the court for permission to file a brief, ostensibly on behalf of a party but actually to suggest a rationale consistent with its own views.

ANNOTATIONS—

(1) Statutory: brief summaries of the law and facts of cases interpreting statutes passed by Congress or state legislatures that are included in codes; or (2) Textual: expository essays of varying length on significant legal topics chosen from selected cases published with the essays.

ANSWER—

the pleading filed by the defendant in response to plaintiff's complaint.

APPEAL PAPERS—

the briefs and transcripts of records on appeal filed by attorneys with courts in connection with litigation. A brief consists of a summary of the facts and circumstances or legal propositions as presented by a party to a pending action.

APPELLANT—

the party who requests that a higher court review the actions of a lower court. Compare with APPELLEE.

APPELLEE—

the party against whom an appeal is taken (usually, but not always, the winner in the lower court). It should be noted that a party's status as appellant or appellee bears no relation to his or her status as plaintiff or defendant in the lower court.

ARBITRATION—

the hearing and settlement of a dispute between opposing parties by a third party. This decision is often binding by prior agreement of the parties.

ASSAULT—

an unlawful, intentional show of force or an attempt to do physical harm to another person. Assault can constitute the basis of a civil or criminal action. See also BATTERY.

ASSAULT AND BATTERY—

See BATTERY.

ATTORNEY GENERAL OPINIONS—

opinions issued by the government's chief counsel at the request of some governmental body interpreting the law for the requesting agency in the same manner as a private attorney would for his or her client. The opinions are not binding on the courts but are usually accorded some degree of persuasive authority.

AUTHORITY—

that which can bind or influence a court. Case law, legislation, constitutions, administrative regulations, and writings about the law are all legal authority. See PRIMARY AUTHORITY; SECONDARY AUTHORITY; MANDATORY AUTHORITY; PERSUASIVE AUTHORITY.

AUTO–CITE—

the computerized citation verification service of Lawyers Cooperative Publishing. AUTO–CITE provides parallel citations and case-history information.

BAIL—

security given, in the form of a bail bond or cash, as a guarantee that released prisoners will present themselves for trial. This security may be lost if the released person does not appear in court at the appointed time.

BATTERY—

an unlawful use of force against another person resulting in physical contact (a tort); it is commonly used in the phrase *assault and battery*, assault being the threat of force, and battery the actual use of force. See also ASSAULT.

BILL—

a legislative proposal introduced in the legislature. The term distinguishes unfinished legislation from directly enacted law.

BLACK LETTER LAW—

an informal term indicating the basic principles of law generally accepted by the courts and/or embodied in the statutes of a particular jurisdiction.

BLUE BOOK—

a popular name for *A Uniform System of Citation*, which is published and distributed by the Harvard Law Review Association et al., and which is bound in a blue cover.

BOOLEAN LOGIC—

a form of search strategy used in databases such as LEXIS and WESTLAW. In a Boolean search, connectors such as AND, OR, and NOT are used to construct a complex search command. The LEXIS command *fungible and gasoline* for example, retrieves documents in which the term *fungible* and the term *gasoline* both appear. Compare with NATURAL LANGUAGE.

BREACH OF CONTRACT—

the failure to perform any of the terms of an agreement.

BRIEF—

(1) in American law practice, a written statement prepared by the counsel arguing a case in court. It contains a summary of the facts of the case, the pertinent laws, and an argument of how the law applies to the facts supporting counsel's position; (2) a summary of a published opinion of a case prepared for studying the opinion in law school.

BRIEFS AND RECORDS—

See APPEAL PAPERS.

CALENDAR—

can mean the order in which cases are to be heard during a term of court. *Martindale-Hubbell Law Directory* contains calendars for state

and federal courts, and includes the name of the court, the name of the judge, and the date of the term's beginning.

CALR—

an acronym for Computer-Assisted Legal Research. LEXIS and WESTLAW are CALR systems.

CAPTION—

See STYLE OF A CASE.

CASE IN POINT—

a judicial opinion which deals with a fact situation similar to the one being researched and substantiates a point of law to be asserted. (Also called *Case on All Fours*.)

CASE LAW—

the law of reported judicial opinions as distinguished from statutes or administrative law.

CASEBOOK—

a textbook used to instruct law students in a particular area of law. The text consists of a collection of court opinions, usually from appellate courts, and notes by the author(s).

CAUSE OF ACTION—

a claim in law and in fact sufficient to bring the case to court; the grounds of an action. (Example: breach of contract.)

CD–ROM—

an abbreviation for "compact disk/read only memory." A compact disk is a disk approximately 4³/₄ inches in diameter on which data is coded to be scanned by a laser beam and transmitted to a computer monitor. A large volume of data can be stored on such a disk.

CERTIORARI—

a writ issued by a superior to an inferior court requiring the latter to produce the records of a particular case tried therein. It is most commonly used to refer to the Supreme Court of the United States, which uses the writ of certiorari as a discretionary device to choose the cases it wishes to hear. The term's origin is Latin, meaning *to be informed of*.

CHARTER—

a document issued by a governmental entity that gives a corporation legal existence.

CHATTEL—

any article of personal property, as opposed to real property. It may refer to animate as well as inanimate property.

CHOSE—

any article of personal property. See PROPERTY.

CITATION—

the reference to authority necessary to substantiate the validity of one's argument or position. Citation to authority and supporting references is both important and extensive in any form of legal writing. Citation form is also given emphasis in legal writing, and early familiarity with *The Bluebook: A Uniform System of Citation* will stand the law student in good stead.

CITATORS—

a set of books that provide, through letter-form abbreviations or words, the subsequent judicial history and interpretation of reported cases, and lists of cases and legislative enactments construing, applying or affecting statutes. In America, the most widely used set of citators is *Shepard's Citations*.

CITED CASE—

a case that is treated by other cases.

CITING CASE—

the case that operates on the cited case.

CIVIL LAW—

(1) Roman law embodied in the *Code of Justinian,* which presently prevails in most countries of Western Europe other than Great Britain and that is the foundation of Louisiana law; (2) the law concerning noncriminal matters in a common law jurisdiction.

CLAIM—

(1) the assertion of a right, as to money or property; (2) the accumulation of facts that give rise to a right enforceable in court.

CLASS ACTION—

a lawsuit brought by a representative party on behalf of a group, all of whose members have the same or a similar grievance against the defendant.

CODE—

in popular usage, a compilation of statutes. Technically, in a code, the laws in force and judicial decrees having the force of law, are rewritten and arranged in classified order. Repealed and temporary acts are eliminated and the revision is reenacted.

CODIFICATION—

the process of collecting and arranging systematically, usually by subject, the laws of a state or country.

COMMON LAW—

the origin of the Anglo-American legal systems. English common law was largely customary law and unwritten, until discovered, applied, and reported by the courts of law. In theory, the common law courts did not create law but rather discovered it in the customs and habits of the English people. The strength of the judicial system in preparliamentary days is one reason for the continued emphasis in common law systems on case law. In a narrow sense, common law is the phrase still used to distinguish case law from statutory law.

COMPILED STATUTES—

in popular usage, a code. Technically, it is a compilation of acts printed verbatim as originally enacted but in a new classified order. The text is not modified; however, repealed and temporary acts are omitted.

COMPLAINT—

the plaintiff's initial pleading. Under *Federal Rules of Civil Procedure*, it is no longer full of the technicalities demanded by the common law. A complaint need only contain a short and plain statement of the claim upon which relief is sought, an indication of the type of relief requested, and an indication that the court has jurisdiction to hear the case.

CONNECTOR—

See BOOLEAN LOGIC.

CONSIDERATION—

something to be done, or abstained from, by one party to a contract in order to induce another party to enter into a contract.

CONSOLIDATED STATUTES—

in popular usage, a code. Technically, it is a compilation of acts rewritten, arranged in classified order and reenacted. Repealed and temporary acts are eliminated.

CONSTITUTION—

the system of fundamental principles by which a political body or organization governs itself. Most national constitutions are written; the English and Israeli constitutions are unwritten.

CONVERSION—

the wrongful appropriation to oneself of the personal property of another.

CONVEYANCE—

the transfer of title to property from one person to another.

COUNT—

a separate and independent claim. A civil petition or a criminal indictment may contain several counts.

COUNTERCLAIM—

a claim made by the defendant against the plaintiff in a civil lawsuit; it constitutes a separate cause of action.

COURT DECISION—

the disposition of the case by the court. See OPINION.

COURT RULES—

rules of procedure promulgated to govern civil and criminal practice before the courts.

DAMAGES—

monetary compensation awarded by a court for an injury caused by the act of another. Damages may be *actual* or *compensatory* (equal to the amount of loss shown), *exemplary* or *punitive* (in excess of the actual loss given to punish the person for the malicious conduct that caused the injury), or *nominal* (a trivial amount given because the injury is slight or because the exact amount of injury has not been determined satisfactorily).

DATABASE—

(1) a collection of information organized for rapid retrieval by computer. In legal research, it usually refers to a commercial service searched *online* by a user at a terminal connected to a communications network. A *full-text* database provides the complete text of documents such as court cases or newspaper articles. LEXIS and WESTLAW are full-text databases. A *bibliographic database* provides citations or abstracts of articles, books, reports, or patents. DIALOG is an example of a service with many bibliographic databases.

(2) in WESTLAW, a collection of documents that can be searched together.

DECISION—

See COURT DECISION.

DECREE—

a determination by a court of the rights and duties of the parties before it. Formerly, decrees were issued by courts of equity and distinguished from judgments, which were issued by courts of law. See EQUITY.

DEFENDANT—

the person against whom a civil or criminal action is brought.

DEMURRER—

a means of objecting to the sufficiency in law of a pleading by admitting the actual allegations made, but disputing that they frame an adequate legal claim.

DIALOG—

the information retrieval service of DIALOG Information Services, a subsidiary of Knight-Ridder, Inc. DIALOG is composed of hundreds of individual databases providing indexing, abstracting, or full text of publications relating to a wide range of academic, business, news, and law-related subjects.

DICTUM—

See OBITER DICTUM.

DIGEST—

an index to reported cases, providing brief, unconnected statements of court holdings on points of law, which are arranged by subject and subdivided by jurisdiction and courts.

DOCKET NUMBER—

a number, sequentially assigned by the clerk at the outset to a lawsuit brought to a court for adjudication.

DUE CARE—

the legal duty one owes to another according to the circumstances of a particular case.

DUE PROCESS OF LAW—

a term found in the Fifth and Fourteenth Amendments of the Constitution and also in the constitutions of many states. Its exact meaning varies from one situation to another and from one era to the next, but basically it is concerned with the guarantee of every person's enjoyment of his or her rights (e.g., the right to a fair hearing in any legal dispute).

EN BANC—

a session in which the entire bench of the court will participate in the decision rather than the regular quorum. In other countries, it is common for a court to have more members than are usually necessary to hear an appeal. In the United States, the Circuit Courts of Appeals usually sit in groups of three judges but for important cases may expand the bench to nine members, when they are said to be sitting *en banc*.

ENCYCLOPEDIA—

a work containing expository statements on principles of law, topically arranged, with supporting footnote references to cases in point.

EQUITY—

justice administered according to fairness as contrasted with the strictly formulated rules of common law. It is based on a system of rules and principles that originated in England as an alternative to the harsh rules of common law and that were based on what was fair in a particular situation. One sought relief under this system in courts of equity rather than in courts of law.

ESTATE—

(1) the interest or right one has in real or personal property; or (2) the property itself in which one has an interest or right.

EXECUTIVE AGREEMENT—

an international agreement, not a treaty, concluded by the President without senatorial consent on the President's authority as Commander-in-Chief and director of foreign relations. The distinction between treaty and executive agreement is complicated and often of questionable constitutionality, but the import of such agreements as that of Yalta or Potsdam is unquestionably great.

EXECUTIVE ORDERS—

an order issued by the President under specific authority granted to the President by Congress. There is no precise distinction between presidential proclamations and executive orders; however, proclama-

tions generally cover matters of widespread interest, and executive orders often relate to the conduct of government business or to organization of the executive departments. Every act of the President authorizing or directing the performance of an act, in its general context, is an executive order. See PRESIDENTIAL PROCLAMATIONS.

FICHE—

See MICROFICHE.

FORM BOOKS—

include sample instruments that are helpful in drafting legal documents.

FORMS OF ACTION—

governed common law pleadings and were the procedural devices used to give expression to the theories of liability recognized by the common law. Failure to analyze the cause of the action properly, to select the proper theory of liability and to choose the appropriate procedural mechanism or forms of action could easily result in being thrown out of court. A plaintiff had to elect his or her remedy in advance and could not subsequently amend the pleadings to conform to his or her proof or to the court's choice of another theory of liability. According to the relief sought, actions have been divided into three categories: real actions were brought for the recovery of real property; mixed actions were brought to recover real property and damages for injury to it; personal actions were brought to recover debts or personal property, or for injuries to personal, property, or contractual rights. The common law actions are usually considered to be eleven in number: trespass, trespass on the case, trover, ejectment, detinue, replevin, debt, covenant, account, special assumpsit, and general assumpsit.

FRAUD—

a deception that causes a person to part with his or her property or a legal right.

FREESTYLE—

is an associative retrieval natural language search protocol for use on LEXIS. FREESTYLE analyzes a natural language search strategy, eliminates irrelevant terms, and then ranks in importance the remaining terms in the strategy.

FULL TEXT—

See DATABASE.

GRAND JURY—

a jury of six to twenty-three persons that hears criminal accusations and evidence, and then determines whether indictments should be made. Compare with PETIT JURY.

HEADNOTE—

a brief summary of a legal rule or significant facts in a case, which, among other headnotes applicable to the case, precedes the printed opinion in reports.

HEARINGS—

proceedings extensively employed by both legislative and administrative agencies. Adjudicative hearings of administrative agencies can be appealed in a court of law. Investigative hearings are often held by congressional committees prior to enactment of legislation, and are important sources of legislative history.

HOLDING—

the declaration of the conclusion of law reached by the court as to the legal effect of the facts of the case.

HOLOGRAPH or OLOGRAPH—

a will, deed, or other legal document that is entirely in the handwriting of the signer.

HORNBOOK—

the popular reference to a series of treatises published by West Publishing Company each of which reviews a certain field of law in summary, textual form, as opposed to a casebook that is designed as a teaching tool and includes many reprints of court opinions.

INDEMNITY—

a contractual arrangement whereby one party agrees to reimburse another for losses of a particular type.

INDICTMENT—

a formal accusation of a crime made by a grand jury at the request of a prosecuting attorney.

INFORMATION—

an accusation based not on the action of a grand jury but rather on the affirmation of a public official.

INFOTRAC—

a self-contained microcomputer-based information storage and retrieval system developed by Information Access Company. The system consists of one or more terminals linked to an optical storage system that can support searching of several databases simultaneously.

INJUNCTION—

a judge's order that a person do or, more commonly, refrain from doing, a certain act. An injunction may be preliminary or temporary, pending trial of the issue presented, or it may be final if the issue has already been decided in court.

INSTACITE—

the computerized citation verification service of West Publishing Company. This service, which is available through WESTLAW, provides parallel citations and case-history information.

INTESTATE—

not having made a valid will.

JUDGMENT—

See COURT DECISION.

JURISDICTION—

the power given to a court by a constitution or a legislative body to make legally binding decisions over certain persons or property, or the geographical area in which a court's decisions or legislative enactments are binding.

JURISPRUDENCE—

(1) the science or philosophy of law; (2) a collective term for case law as opposed to legislation.

KEY NUMBER—

a building block of the major indexing system devised for American case law, developed by West Publishing Company. The key number is a permanent number given to a specific point of this case law.

LAW REVIEW or LAW JOURNAL—

a legal periodical. The term *law review* usually describes a scholarly periodical edited by students at a law school.

LEGALTRAC—

the legal periodical index of Information Access Company stored on CD–ROM and searched using IAC's InfoTrac system. The LegalTrac database is updated monthly by the replacement of the disk.

LEGISLATIVE HISTORY—

that information embodied in legislative documents that provides the meanings and interpretations (intent) of statutes. Citations and dates of legislative enactments, amendments, and repeals of statutes are sometimes imprecisely identified as legislative histories. More accurate designations of these citations of legislative changes, as included in codes, are historical notes or amendatory histories.

LEXIS—

the computerized legal research system of Mead Data Central, Inc. LEXIS is a database providing the full text of court decisions, statutes, administrative materials, *ALR* annotations, law review articles, reporter services, Supreme Court briefs, and other items. Documents are organized into *libraries* that are subdivided into *files*. *Key-word searches* and *segment searches* are available.

LIABILITY—

the condition of being responsible either for damages resulting from an injurious act or for discharging an obligation or debt.

LIBEL—

(1) written defamation of a person's character. Compare with SLANDER; (2) in an admiralty court, the plaintiff's statement of the cause of action and the relief sought.

LIEN—

a claim against property as security for a debt, under which the property may be seized and sold to satisfy the debt.

LITIGATE—

to bring a civil action in court.

LOOSELEAF SERVICES AND REPORTERS—

contain federal and state administrative regulations and decisions or subject treatment of a legal topic. They consist of separate, perforated leaves in special binders, simplifying frequent substitution and insertion of new leaves.

MALPRACTICE—

professional misconduct or unreasonable lack of skill. This term is usually applied to such conduct by doctors and lawyers.

MANDATORY AUTHORITY—

authority that a given court is bound to follow. Mandatory authority is found in constitutional provisions, legislation, and court cases. Compare with PERSUASIVE AUTHORITY.

MEMORANDUM—

(1) an informal record; (2) a written document that may be used to prove that a contract exists; (3) an exposition of all the points of law pertaining to a particular case (referred to as a *memorandum of law*); (4) an informal written discussion of the merits of a matter pending in a lawyer's office, usually written by a law clerk or junior associate for a senior associate or partner (referred to as an *office memorandum*).

MICROFICHE—

a sheet of film, usually 4 x 6 inches or 3 x 5 inches in size, containing miniaturized photographic images of printed text. The term *fiche* is synonymous with *microfiche*. *Ultrafiche* is a type of microfiche containing images that are reduced by a factor of 90 or more.

MICROFILM—

a film containing miniaturized photographic images of printed text. This is usually in a reel, but may also be in a cartridge or cassette form.

MICROFORM—

a general term describing miniaturized reproduction of printed text on film or paper. *Microfilm* and *microfiche* are specific types of microform.

MODEL CODES—

codes formulated by various groups or institutions to serve as model laws for legislatures, intended to improve existing laws or unify diverse state legislation.

MOOT POINTS—

points that are no longer subjects of contention and that are raised only for purposes of discussion or hypothesis. Many law schools conduct moot courts where students gain practice by arguing hypothetical or moot cases.

MOTION—

a formal request made to a judge pertaining to any issue arising during the pendency of a lawsuit.

NATIONAL REPORTER SYSTEM—

the network of reporters published by West Publishing Company, which attempt to publish and digest all cases of precedential value from all state and federal courts.

NATURAL LANGUAGE—

an online database search strategy using normal English-language sentences or phrases instead of Boolean commands. See BOOLEAN LOGIC. WESTLAW's natural language searching is called WIN (WESTLAW is Natural).

NEGLIGENCE—

the failure to exercise due care.

NEXIS—

the general and business news database of Mead Data Central, Inc. NEXIS provides the full text of newspaper, magazine and newsletter articles, wire-service stories, and other items.

NISI PRIUS—

generally, a court where a case is first tried, as distinguished from an appellate court.

NOTER–UP—

the term used in the British Commonwealth countries for a citator.

OBITER DICTUM—

an incidental comment, not necessary to the formulation of the decision, made by the judge in his or her opinion. Such comments are not binding as precedent.

OFFICIAL REPORTS—

court reports directed by statute. Compare with UNOFFICIAL REPORTS.

OPINION—

an expression of the reasons why a certain decision (the judgment) was reached in a case. A *majority opinion* is usually written by one judge and represents the principles of law that a majority of his or her colleagues on the court deem operative in a given decision; it has

more precedential value than any of the following. A *separate opinion* may be written by one or more judges in which he, she, or they concur in or dissent from the majority opinion. A *concurring opinion* agrees with the result reached by the majority, but disagrees with the precise reasoning leading to that result. A *dissenting opinion* disagrees with the result reached by the majority and thus disagrees with the reasoning and/or the principles of law used by the majority in deciding the case. A *plurality opinion* (called a *judgment* by the Supreme Court) is agreed to by less than a majority as to the reasoning of the decision, but is agreed to by a majority as to the result. A *per curiam* opinion is an opinion *by the court* that expresses its decision in the case but whose author is not identified. A *memorandum opinion* is a holding of the whole court in which the opinion is very concise.

ORAL ARGUMENT—

a spoken presentation of reasons for a desired decision directed to an appellate court by attorneys for the parties.

ORDINANCE—

the equivalent of a municipal statute, passed by the city council and governing matters not already covered by federal or state law.

PAMPHLET SUPPLEMENT—

a paperbound supplement to a larger bound volume usually intended to be discarded eventually.

PARALLEL CITATION—

a citation reference to the same case printed in two or more different reports.

PER CURIAM—

literally, by the court. Usually a short opinion written on behalf of the majority of the court. It may be accompanied by concurring or dissenting opinions.

PERIODICAL—

a publication appearing at regular intervals. Legal periodicals include law school publications, bar association publications, commercially published journals, and legal newspapers.

PERMANENT LAW—

an act that continues in force for an indefinite time.

PERSONAL PROPERTY—

See PROPERTY.

PERSUASIVE AUTHORITY—

that law or reasoning which a given court may but is not bound to follow. For example, decisions from one jurisdiction may be persuasive authority in the courts of another jurisdiction. Compare with MANDATORY AUTHORITY.

PETIT JURY—

a group of six, nine, or twelve persons that decides questions of fact in civil and criminal trials. Compare with GRAND JURY.

PETITION—

a formal, written application to a court requesting judicial action on a certain matter.

PETITIONER—

the person presenting a petition to a court, officer, or legislative body; the one who starts an equity proceeding or the one who takes an appeal from a judgment.

PLAINTIFF—

the person who brings a lawsuit against another.

PLEA BARGAINING—

the process whereby the accused and the prosecutor in a criminal case work out a mutually satisfactory disposition of the case. It usually involves the defendant's pleading guilty to a lesser offense or to only one or some of the counts of a multi-count indictment in return for a lighter sentence than that possible for the graver charge.

PLEADINGS—

technical means by which parties to a dispute frame the issue for the court. The plaintiff's complaint or declaration is followed by the defendant's answer; subsequent papers may be filed as needed.

POCKET SUPPLEMENT or POCKET PART—

a paper-back supplement to a book, inserted in the book through a slit in its back cover. Depending on the type of publication, it may have textual, case, or statutory references keyed to the original publication.

POPULAR NAME TABLE—

a table listing popular names by which some cases and statutes have become known, and identifying for each popular name the official name and citation of the case or statute.

POWER OF ATTORNEY—

a document authorizing a person to act as another's agent.

PRECEDENT—

See STARE DECISIS.

PRELIMINARY PRINTS—

the name given to the advance sheets of the official *United States Reports*.

PRESENTMENT—

in criminal law, a written accusation made by the grand jury without the consent or participation of a prosecutor.

PRESIDENTIAL PROCLAMATIONS—

a declaration issued under specific authority granted to the President by Congress. Generally, they relate to matters of widespread interest. Some proclamations have no legal effect but merely are appeals to the public, e.g., the observance of American Education Week. See EXECUTIVE ORDERS.

PRIMARY AUTHORITY—

statutes, constitutions, administrative regulations issued pursuant to enabling legislation, and case law. Primary authority may be either *mandatory* or *persuasive*. All other legal writings are *secondary authority* and are never binding on courts. See MANDATORY AUTHORITY; PERSUASIVE AUTHORITY.

PRIVATE LAW—

an act that relates to a specific person.

PROCEDURAL LAW—

that law which governs the operation of the legal system, including court rules and rules of procedure, as distinguished from substantive law.

PROPERTY—

ownership or that which is owned. *Real property* refers to land; *personal property* refers to moveable things or chattels; *chose in action*

refers to a right to personal property of which the owner does not presently have possession but instead has a right to sue to gain possession (e.g., a right to recover a debt, demand, or damages in a contractual action or for a tort or omission of a duty).

PUBLIC LAW—

an act that relates to the public as a whole. It may be (1) general (applies to all persons within the jurisdiction), (2) local (applies to a geographical area), or (3) special (relates to an organization that is charged with a public interest).

RATIO DECIDENDI—

the point in a case that determines the result—the basis of the decision.

REAL PROPERTY—

See PROPERTY.

RECORD—

the documentation, prepared for an appeal, of the trial court proceedings (pleadings, motions, transcript of examination of witnesses, objections to evidence, rulings, jury instructions, opinion, etc.

RECORDS AND BRIEFS—

See APPEAL PAPERS.

REGIONAL REPORTER—

a unit of the *National Reporter System* that reports state court cases from a defined geographical area.

REGULATIONS—

rules or orders issued by various governmental departments to carry out the intent of the law. Agencies issue regulations to guide the activity of their employees and to ensure uniform application of the law. Regulations are not the work of the legislature and do not have the effect of law in theory. In practice, however, because of the intricacies of judicial review of administrative action, regulations can have an important effect in determining the outcome of cases involving regulatory activity. United States Government regulations appear first in the *Federal Register*, published five days a week, and are subsequently arranged by subject in the *Code of Federal Regulations*.

RELIEF—

the remedy or redress sought by a complainant from the court.

REMAND—

to send back for further proceedings, as when a higher court sends back to a lower court.

REPORTS—

(1) *court reports*—published judicial cases arranged according to some grouping, such as jurisdiction, court, period of time, subject matter, or case significance; and (2) *administrative reports or decisions*—published decisions of an administrative agency.

RESOLUTION—

a formal expression of the opinion of a rule-making body adopted by the vote of that body.

RESPONDENT—

the party who makes an answer to a bill in an equity proceeding or who contends against an appeal.

RESTATEMENTS OF THE LAW—

systematic restatements of the existing common law in certain areas, published by the American Law Institute since 1923. The Restatements are valuable secondary research sources, but are not binding as law.

REVISED STATUTES—

in popular usage, a code. Technically, it is a compilation of statutes in the order and wording originally passed by the legislature, with temporary and repealed acts deleted.

RULES OF COURT—

the rules regulating practice and procedure before the various courts. In most jurisdictions, these rules are issued by the individual courts or by the highest court in that jurisdiction.

SANCTION—

(1) to assent to another's actions; (2) a penalty for violating a law.

SCOPE NOTE—

a notation appearing below a topic heading in a publication, that delimits and identifies the content of the topic.

SECONDARY AUTHORITY—

See PRIMARY AUTHORITY.

SECTION LINE—

the subject of a key number in West's Key Number digests, printed after the key number.

SESSION LAWS—

laws of a state enacted that are published in bound or pamphlet volumes after adjournment of each regular or special session.

SHEPARDIZING—

a trade-mark of Shepard's Citations, Inc., descriptive of the general use of its publications.

SLANDER—

oral defamation of a person's character. Compare with LIBEL.

SLIP LAW—

a legislative enactment published in pamphlet or single sheet form immediately after its passage.

SLIP OPINION—

an individual court case published separately soon after it is decided.

SQUIB—

a very brief rendition of a single case or a single point of law from a case. Compare with HEADNOTE.

STAR PAGINATION—

a scheme in reprint editions of court reports, that is used to show where the pages of the text of the official edition begin and end.

STARE DECISIS—

the doctrine of English and American law that states that when a court has formulated a principle of law as applicable to a given set of facts, it will follow that principle and apply it in future cases where the facts are substantially the same. It connotes the decision of present cases on the basis of past precedent.

STATUS TABLE—

gives the current status of a bill or court decision.

STATUTES—

acts of a legislature. Depending upon its context in usage, a statute may mean a single act of a legislature or a body of acts that are collected and arranged according to a scheme or for a session of a legislature or parliament.

STATUTES AT LARGE—

the official compilation of acts passed by the Congress. The arrangement is currently by Public Law number, and by chapter number in pre-1951 volumes. This is the official print of the law for citation purposes where titles of the *United States Code* have not been enacted into positive law.

STATUTES OF LIMITATIONS—

laws setting time limits after which a dispute cannot be taken to court.

STATUTORY INSTRUMENTS—

English administrative regulations and orders. The term applies especially to the administrative rules published since 1939, supplementing the English administrative code, *Statutory Rules and Orders*.

STATUTORY RULES AND ORDERS—

English administrative regulations and orders.

STYLE OF A CASE—

the parties to a lawsuit as they are written in the heading at the beginning of a written case. Also known as the *caption* of a case.

SUBPOENA—

a court order compelling a witness to appear and testify in a certain proceeding.

SUBSTANTIVE LAW—

that law which establishes rights and obligations, as distinguished from procedural law, which is concerned with rules for establishing their judicial enforcement.

SUMMONS—

a notice delivered by a sheriff or other authorized person informing a person that he or she is the defendant in a civil action, and specifying a time and place to appear in court to answer to the plaintiff.

SUPERSEDE—

to displace or to supplant one publication or its segment with another.

SUPREME COURT—

(1) the court of last resort in the federal judicial system (the Supreme Court of the United States also has original jurisdiction in some

cases); (2) in state judicial systems, except New York and Massachusetts, the highest appellate court or court of last resort.

SYLLABUS—

See HEADNOTE.

TABLE OF CASES—

a list of cases, arranged alphabetically by case names, with citations and references to the body of the publication where the cases are found or treated.

TABLE OF STATUTES—

a list of statutes with references to the body of the publication where the statutes are treated or construed.

TEMPORARY LAW—

an act that continues in force for a limited period of time.

TERM OF COURT—

signifies the space of time prescribed by law during which a court holds session. The court's session may actually extend beyond the term. The October Term of the Supreme Court of the United States is now the only term during which the Court sits, and lasts from October to June or July.

TORT—

a civil wrong that does not involve a contractual relationship. The elements of a tort are a duty owed, a breach of that duty, and the resultant harm to the one to whom the duty was owed.

TOTAL CLIENT–SERVICE LIBRARY—

a system of publications by Lawyers Cooperative Publishing, including, among others, *American Jurisprudence 2d, American Law Reports, United States Code Service,* and *United States Supreme Court Reports, Lawyers' Edition.*

TRANSCRIPT OF RECORD—

the printed record as made up in each case of the proceedings and pleadings necessary for the appellate court to review the history of the case.

TREATISE—

an exposition, which may be critical, evaluative, interpretative, or informative, on case law or legislation. Usually it is more exhaustive than an encyclopedia article, but less detailed and critical than a law review article.

TREATY—

an agreement between two or more sovereign nations.

TRESPASS—

an unlawful interference with one's person, property, or rights. At common law, trespass was a form of action brought to recover damages for any injury to one's person or property or relationship with another.

ULTRAFICHE—

See MICROFICHE.

UNIFORM LAWS—

statutes drafted for adoption by the several states in the interest of uniformity. A considerable number of uniform laws on various subjects have been approved by the National Conference of Commissioners on Uniform State Laws, and have been adopted in one or more jurisdictions in the United States and its possessions. The Uniform Commercial Code is now the law in forty-nine states.

UNIFORM SYSTEM OF CITATION—

See BLUE BOOK.

UNOFFICIAL REPORTS—

court reports published without statutory direction. They are not distinguished from official reports on grounds of varying quality or accuracy of reporting.

VENUE—

the particular geographical area where a court with jurisdiction may try a case.

WAIVER—

the voluntary relinquishment of a known right.

WESTLAW—

the computerized legal research system of West Publishing Company. WESTLAW provides the full text of court decisions, statutes, administrative materials, law review articles, reporter services, and other items. Documents are organized into *databases.* *Natural language searches, key-word searches, field searches* and *key-number searches* are available. See NATURAL LANGUAGE.

WRIT—

a written order, of which there are many types, issued by a court and directed to an official or party, commanding the performance of some act.

WRONGFUL DEATH—

a type of lawsuit brought by or on behalf of a deceased person's beneficiaries, alleging that the death was attributable to the willful or negligent act of another.

LEGAL RESEARCH ILLUSTRATED

*

Chapter 1

AN INTRODUCTION TO LEGAL RESEARCH [1]

Legal research is the investigation for information necessary to support legal decision-making. In its broadest sense, legal research includes each step of a process that begins with analyzing the facts of a problem and concludes with applying and communicating the results of the investigation.

Many types of information are needed to support legal decision-making. Although this book focuses on information sources that are concerned explicitly with law, legal decisions cannot be made out of their economic, social, historical, and political contexts. In a modern complex society, legal decisions are often dependent on business, scientific, medical, psychological, and technological information. Consequently, the process of legal research often involves investigation into other relevant disciplines.

This chapter is an introduction to legal research that is intended to explain why researchers seek certain types of information. After explaining the basic jurisprudential model upon which legal resources are designed, created, and collected, the chapter presents an introductory discussion of the materials of legal research that are discussed extensively in this book.

SECTION A. SOURCES OF LAW

American law, like the law of other countries, comes from a variety of sources. In the context of legal research, the term "sources of law" can refer to three different concepts that should be distinguished. One, sources of law can refer to the origins of legal concepts and ideas. Custom, tradition, principles of morality, and economic, political, philosophical, and religious thought may manifest themselves in law. On occasion, legal research must extend to these areas, especially when historical or policy issues are involved.

Two, sources of law can refer to the governmental institutions that formulate legal rules. The United States incorporates one national (federal) government, fifty autonomous state governments, and the local government of the District of Columbia. Although there are some variations in their structures, each of these governments has legislative, executive, and judicial components that interact with each other. Because all three branches of government "make law" and create legal

---

[1] This chapter was written by Steven M. Barkan, Associate Dean and Associate Professor of Law, Marquette University Law School.

1

information that is the subject of legal research, researchers must understand the types of information created by each branch.

Three, sources of law can refer to the published manifestations of the law. The books, computer databases, microforms, optical disks, and other media that contain legal information are all sources of law.

1. The Nature of Legal Authority

Legal authority is any published source of law setting forth legal rules, legal doctrine, or legal reasoning that can be used as a basis for legal decisions.[2] In discussions about legal research, the term *authority* is used to refer both to the types of legal information and to the degree of persuasiveness of legal information.

When the term is used to describe types of information, legal authority can be categorized as *primary* or *secondary*.[3] Primary authorities are authorized statements of the law by governmental institutions. Such documents include the written opinions of courts (*case law*); constitutions; legislation; rules of court; and the rules, regulations, and opinions of administrative agencies. Secondary authorities are statements about the law and are used to explain, interpret, develop, locate, or update primary authorities. Treatises, articles in law reviews and other scholarly journals, *American Law Reports (A.L.R.)* annotations, Restatements of the Law, and looseleaf services are examples of secondary authorities.[4]

When the term is used to describe the degree of persuasiveness of legal information, authority is an estimation of the power of information to influence a legal decision. In this sense, authority can be termed *binding* (also called *mandatory*), meaning that a court or other decision-maker believes the authority applies to the case before it and must be followed; or authority can be considered *persuasive,* meaning that a decision-maker can, if so persuaded, follow it. Only primary authority can be binding; but some primary authority will be merely persuasive, depending on the source of the authority and its content. Secondary authority can never be binding, but can be persuasive. Of course, the application of legal authority to individual problems is a complex and controversial process. Variations in the factual content of individual cases give judges, influenced by their own philosophies and perspectives, wide discretion in interpreting and applying legal authority.[5]

---

[2] THOMAS B. MARVELL, APPELLATE COURTS AND LAWYERS 129 (1978).

[3] When used in this sense, the terms *authority* and *source* are interchangeable.

[4] Other types of relevant information, such as historical, economic, and social science information, are sometimes referred to as secondary authorities. Such materials are often sources of law and thus used in legal argument.

[5] For an excellent, but dated, explanation of why courts cite authority and a discussion of the authority of various legal sources, see John Henry Merryman, *The Authority of Authority,* 6 STAN. L. REV. 613 (1954).

2. The Common Law Tradition

The American legal system, like those of most English-speaking countries, is part of the *common law* tradition. The common law is the body of law that originated and developed in England and spread to those countries that England settled or controlled. Historically, the common law was considered to be the "unwritten law" and was distinguished from the "written," or statutory, law. The common law was an oral tradition derived from general customs, principles, and rules handed down from generation to generation and was eventually reflected in the reports of the decisions of courts. The colonists carried the English common law with them to America and used it as a basis for developing their own law and legal institutions.[6] English common law is still cited as authority in American courts.[7]

The common law tradition should be contrasted with the *civil law* tradition, which is based on Roman law and predominates in continental Europe and other western countries. Common law and civil law systems differ in their theories about the sources of law, the relative persuasiveness of the sources, and the ways the sources are used in legal reasoning. For example, in legal systems that are part of the civil law tradition, the legislature creates a comprehensive code of legal principles that represents the highest form of law, and there is a presumption that code provisions apply to every legal problem.[8] In common law systems, there is no presumption that statutes or codes cover all legal problems; many legal principles are discoverable only through the "unwritten," or common law.

3. Case Law and the Doctrine of Precedent [9]

a. *Structure of the Court System.* On the federal level, and in the states, there are hierarchical judicial systems in which some courts have jurisdiction, or control, over other courts. The typical court structure consists of three levels,[10] and it is important to understand what types of information are created at each level and where that information may be found.

Trial courts are courts of original jurisdiction that make determinations of law and of fact, with juries often making the determinations of fact. Documents prepared by the parties called *pleadings* (complaint, answer, interrogatories, among others) and *motions* are filed before and

---

[6] For general histories of American law, see LAWRENCE M. FRIEDMAN, A HISTORY OF AMERICAN LAW (2d ed. 1985) and KERMIT L. HALL, THE MAGIC MIRROR: LAW IN AMERICAN HISTORY (1989).

[7] *See* Chapter 21, *infra,* for a discussion of basic English legal research.

[8] JOHN HENRY MERRYMAN, THE CIVIL LAW TRADITION 22–24 (2d ed. 1985).

[9] Case law is discussed extensively in the following chapters, *infra:* Chapter 3, Court Reports; Chapter 4, Federal Court Cases; Chapter 5, State Court Cases and the National Reporter System; Chapter 6, Digests for Court Reports; Chapter 7, Annotated Law Reports.

[10] A chart included in Chapter 3, *infra,* depicts the federal judicial system and a typical state judicial system.

during a trial; *exhibits* are submitted into evidence during the trial; and a *record* (or transcript) is made. Pleadings, motions, exhibits, and records are usually only available directly from the court in which the litigation was conducted; these documents are usually not collected by law libraries. The trial court issues a judgment or decision and sometimes a written opinion, which, however, is rarely published (or reported) or made generally available to the public.[11]

Intermediate appellate courts, often called circuit courts or courts of appeal,[12] have authority over lower courts in a specified geographical area or jurisdiction. Appellate courts will not review factual determinations made by lower courts, but will review claimed errors of law that are reflected in the record created in the lower courts. Appellate courts accept written *briefs* (statements prepared by the counsel arguing the case) and frequently hear *oral arguments*. Some large law libraries collect copies of the briefs filed in appellate courts. Intermediate appellate courts often issue written opinions that are sometimes published in volumes found in law libraries.

A court of last resort, often called the supreme court, is the highest appellate court in a jurisdiction. State courts of last resort are the highest authorities on questions of state law, and the Supreme Court of the United States is the highest authority on questions of federal law and federal constitutional law. Many libraries collect copies of the briefs and records filed in the Supreme Court of the United States and of the court of last resort in the state in which they are located. Transcripts of the oral arguments in these courts also are available in many law libraries. Courts of last resort usually issue written opinions that are almost always published and collected by libraries.

b. *Federal and State Jurisdiction.* There are some matters over which a state or federal court has exclusive jurisdiction and some matters over which a state court has concurrent jurisdiction with the federal courts. Federal courts can, in some instances, decide questions of state law; state courts can, in some instances, decide questions of federal law. For both the beginning law student and the experienced attorney, it can be difficult to determine which matters are questions of federal law, which are questions of state law, and which can be subjects of both. The point to be made here is that, with any particular problem, legal information of various types may be needed from both state and federal sources.

c. *Precedent.* In the early history of English law, the custom developed of considering the decisions of courts to be *precedents* that would serve as examples, or authorities, for decisions in later cases with similar questions of law. Under what has come to be called the *doctrine*

---

[11] Many inexperienced legal researchers are surprised to learn that written opinions are not issued in all cases, and that only a small percentage of written opinions are reported and published. For a more complete discussion of this subject, see Chapter 3, *infra*.

[12] Some states have no intermediate appellate courts; appeals go directly to the courts of last resort in these states.

of precedent, the decision of a common law court not only settles a dispute between the parties involved but also sets a precedent to be followed in future cases among other litigants.[13] According to an older, now discredited, theory, judges merely declared what had always been the law when they decided a case. It is now generally acknowledged that judges often create new law when applying precedent to current problems.

The doctrine of precedent encompasses three closely related concepts represented by the Latin terms *stare decisis, ratio decidendi,* and *dictum.*

Stare decisis, literally "to stand on what has been decided," is the principle that the decision of a court is binding authority on the court that issued the decision and on lower courts in the same jurisdiction for the disposition of factually similar controversies. In the hierarchical federal and state court systems, therefore, the decisions of a trial court can bind future decisions of that trial court, but they cannot bind other trial courts or appellate courts. Appellate courts can bind themselves and lower courts over which they have appellate jurisdiction, but appellate courts cannot bind each other by their decisions.

The *ratio decidendi* is the holding or the principle of law on which the case was decided. It is the *ratio decidendi* that sets the precedent and is binding on courts in the future. Unlike legislatures, American courts do not state general propositions of law, nor do they respond to hypothetical questions. Rather, courts decide actual cases and controversies, and they announce rules that are tied to specific fact situations. Therefore, the *ratio decidendi,* or rule of the case, must be considered in conjunction with the facts of the case.

---

[13] "The bare skeleton of an appeal to precedent is easily stated: The previous treatment of occurrence X in manner Y constitutes, *solely because of its historical pedigree,* a reason for treating X in manner Y if and when X again occurs." Frederick Schauer, *Precedent,* 39 STAN. L. REV. 571 (1987). For a discussion of the early development of the doctrine of precedent, see M. ETHAN KATSH, THE ELECTRONIC MEDIA AND THE TRANSFORMATION OF LAW 33–39 (1989).

For the views of a former U.S. Supreme Court Justice regarding the importance of *stare decisis,* see Lewis F. Powell, Jr., *Stare Decisis and Judicial Restraint,* 47 WASH. & LEE L. REV. 281 (1990). *See also* William N. Eskridge, Jr., *The Case of the Amorous Defendant: Criticizing Absolute Stare Decisis for Statutory Cases,* 88 MICH. L. REV. 2450 (1990); Lawrence C. Marshall, *Contempt of Congress: A Reply to the Critics of an Absolute Rule of Statutory Stare Decisis,* 88 MICH. L. REV. 2467 (1990).

For an extensive sociological inquiry into the importance of precedent, including the need for attention to computer technology, see Susan W. Brenner, *Of Publication and Precedent: An Inquiry into the Ethnomethodology of Case Reporting in the American Legal System,* 39 DE PAUL L. REV. 461 (1990). *But see* Michael Wells, *The Unimportance of Precedent in the Law of Federal Courts,* 39 DE PAUL L. REV. 357 (1990). For an attempt to describe precedent and its applications, see Ruggero J. Aldisert, *Precedent: What It Is and What It Isn't, When Do We Kiss It and When Do We Kill It?* 17 PEPPERDINE L. REV. 605 (1990). *See also* Lawrence C. Marshall, *"Let Congress Do It": The Case for an Absolute Rule of Statutory Stare Decisis,* 88 MICH. L. REV. 177 (1989); Note, *Constitutional Stare Decisis,* 103 HARV. L. REV. 1344 (1990); SUSAN W. BRENNER, PRECEDENT INFLATION (1991).

In contrast, *dictum* (or *obiter dictum*) is language in an opinion that is arguably not necessary to the decision. *Dictum* comes from the Latin verb *decire,* "to say," and refers to what is "said by the way," specifically, that which is not essential to the holding of the decision. Although language categorized as *dictum* is not binding on future courts, it might be persuasive. It is common for yesterday's *dictum* to develop into today's doctrine.

The *ratio decidendi* and *dictum* are sometimes easily identified, but more often the distinction is subject to interpretation. The determination of what is the *ratio decidendi,* and what is *dictum,* is a focus of legal analysis and is often the critical point of legal argument.

Courts have much leeway in interpreting cases put forth as binding precedent.[14] No two cases are exactly the same, and at some point every case can be distinguished from all others. Generally, a case will be considered binding if it shares the same significant facts with the case at issue and does not differ in any significant facts from the instant case. Furthermore, the issues presented in the two cases must be the same and must have been necessary to the decision in the previous case (otherwise, the words of the court would be *dictum*). Courts can reject cases put forth as binding authority by distinguishing the cases on their facts or issues, thus finding that the previous cases are different from the instant case in some significant way.[15] In some situations, a court can avoid being bound by a previous case by finding that the rule put forth in the previous case is no longer valid and by overruling it.

The doctrine of precedent assumes that decisions of common law courts should be given consideration even if they are not binding. It is for this reason that researchers often look for the relevant decisions of other states, jurisdictions, and even other common law countries. Cases that are not directly on point can contain principles on which to build legal arguments. Decisions that are not binding, either because they have different fact situations or because they are from another jurisdiction, can be persuasive because of the depth of analysis and quality of reasoning in the opinion. Among the other factors that can determine the persuasiveness of a non-binding opinion are the location and position of the court that issued the opinion, whether the opinion was issued by a unanimous or split court or written by a well-respected jurist, as well as subsequent judicial and academic approval of the opinion.

[14] In a chapter entitled "The Leeways of Precedent," Karl Llewellyn presented "a selection of [sixty-four] available impeccable precedent techniques" used by courts to follow, avoid, expand, or redirect precedent. KARL N. LLEWELLYN, THE COMMON LAW TRADITION: DECIDING APPEALS 77–91 (1960).

[15] *See generally* Kent Greenawalt, *Reflections on Holding and Dictum,* 39 J. LEGAL EDUC. 431 (1989). The practice of judges writing separately, generally in the hopes of laying the groundwork for a reversal or to demonstrate why one rationale may be better than another, is becoming commonplace. For some observations on this trend, see Laura Krugman Ray, *The Justices Write Separately: Uses of the Concurrence by the Rehnquist Court,* 23 U.C. DAVIS L. REV. 777 (1990); Ruth Bader Ginsburg, *Remarks on Writing Separately,* 65 WASH. L. REV. 133 (1990).

Policy considerations in favor of the doctrine of precedent are that it results in fairness because it encourages similar cases to be treated alike; it leads to predictability and stability in the legal system; and it saves time and energy because it enables us to make use of previous efforts and prior wisdom.[16] Critics argue that a reliance on precedent can result in a rigid and mechanical jurisprudence that can force us to treat unlike cases as if they were similar; that it can perpetuate outmoded rules; and that its inherently conservative nature can impede the law from being responsive to new social needs.[17]

Notwithstanding these criticisms, the doctrine of precedent remains the foundation upon which our models of legal research are constructed. The written opinions of courts, particularly appellate courts, are the "stuff" of legal argument and the major source of legal doctrine. Consequently, they are the primary, but certainly not the only, objects of legal research. Law libraries are filled with published court opinions, along with secondary sources and index tools to help researchers find, interpret, and update opinions that are relevant to particular fact patterns.

4. Legislation and the Interpretation of Statutes [18]

a. *Legislation.* A *statute,* sometimes referred to as legislation, is a positive statement of legal rules enacted by a legislature. In comparison, a constitution is the fundamental body of principles, most often written, by which a political body such as a nation or state governs itself. Because many of the basic concepts and techniques of statutory and constitutional research are similar, they can be discussed together at an introductory level. However, American constitutional law, both federal and state, is a pervasive and specialized subject; and including it in a general discussion of legislation should not obscure either its importance or its uniqueness.

In English law, the earliest statutes were enacted by the king with the concurrence of his council; later the role of statute-maker was assumed by Parliament. In America, statutes are enacted by the legislative branch and signed into law by the executive. The growth of statutory law reflected the impact of the industrial revolution, as it became apparent that a jurisprudence based only on judicial decisions could not meet the needs of a growing, dynamic society. Situations developed in which answers were needed that were not found in court reports, or the answers found in court reports no longer met current needs, or resulted in actions that were considered unjust.

[16] *See* John Henry Merryman, *The Authority of Authority, supra* note 5, for a discussion of the benefits of following precedent.

[17] *See* Steven M. Barkan, *Deconstructing Legal Research: A Law Librarian's Commentary on Critical Legal Studies,* 79 LAW LIBR. J. 617 (1987).

[18] Constitutions and legislation are discussed in the following chapters, *infra:* Chapter 8, Constitutions; Chapter 9, Federal Legislation; Chapter 10, Federal Legislative Histories; Chapter 11, State Legislation.

Statutes, and collections of statutes arranged by subject called *codes,* have become very important in common law systems; and American law is a combination of statutory law and case law. Statutes are used to create new areas of law, to fill gaps in the law, and to change court-made rules. However, unlike civil law systems, the American legal system has no presumptions that a statute will apply to every legal problem or that codes are comprehensive statements of the law.

b. *Statutory Interpretation.* Courts play predominant roles in interpreting and applying statutes and in extending the law to subjects not expressly covered by statutes. Judicial interpretations of statutes have the greatest authority for present controversies. In other words, the legislature can state a general legal rule in the form of a statute, but it is the judiciary that interprets the general rule and applies it to specific cases. Under the doctrine of precedent, it is the statute as *interpreted by the courts* that is applied in the next case. In theory, if the legislature disagrees with the way a court has interpreted a statute, the legislature must revise the statute.[19]

Statutory interpretation is an important part of legal research.[20] Researchers must not merely find the statutes applicable to a problem, but must also find information that will help determine what the statutes mean and how they should be applied. After looking for the "plain meaning" of the words of a statute,[21] and applying traditional canons or principles of statutory interpretation to the text of the statute,[22] researchers resort to a number of approaches to statutory interpretation.

An important method of statutory interpretation is to look for judicial opinions that have construed the specific statute. The persuasiveness of interpretive opinions will depend on the similarity of facts involved and on the courts issuing the opinions. Legislatures sometimes enact common law rules into statutes, and in such situations judicial opinions that pre-date the statute might be useful aids to interpretation.

Researchers often attempt to identify the legislature's purpose in passing the statute and the legislature's intended meaning for specific provisions of the statute. To do this, researchers will look at the *legislative history* of the statute—the documents such as revised versions of bills and legislative debates, hearings, and reports, among other materials, created by the legislature while the statute was under consid-

[19] GUIDO CALABRESI, A COMMON LAW FOR THE AGE OF STATUTES 31–34 (1982).

[20] On statutory construction in general see NORMAN J. SINGER, STATUTES AND STATUTORY CONSTRUCTION (5th ed. 1992).

[21] Some states have "plain meaning" statutes that attempt to limit courts in their interpretation of statutes that are unambiguous on their face. For an example, see OR. REV. STAT. § 174.010 *et seq.* (1987).

[22] Karl Llewellyn provided an extensive listing of canons of construction to demonstrate that, since legal arguments suggest that there can be only one correct meaning of a statute, there are two opposing canons on every point. KARL N. LLEWELLYN, THE COMMON LAW TRADITION: DECIDING APPEALS 521–35 (1960).

eration—for evidence of legislative purpose and intent.[23]   Although controversy exists over the proper uses of legislative histories,[24] legislative histories are often consulted by lawyers and judges and are frequently used in legal argument.

Researchers also search for cases from other jurisdictions that have interpreted similar statutes.   Although these opinions are not binding authority, well-reasoned opinions from other courts can be very persuasive.   This approach is consistent with the doctrine of precedent, under which the decisions of other common law courts may be considered, even if they are not binding.

5. Administrative Law [25]

The third major institutional source of law is the executive branch of government.   The President of the United States and the governors of the states issue orders and create other documents with legal effect. Executive departments and offices, and administrative agencies, establishments, and corporations all create legal information.

Administrative agencies, which exist on the federal and state levels, are created by the legislative branch of government and are usually part of the executive branch.   A number of independent agencies, establishments, and corporations exist that are within the executive branch but are not considered to be executive departments.[26]   For the most part, federal agencies handle matters of federal law and state agencies handle matters of state law, but there is often interaction between federal and state agencies.   Administrative agencies conduct activities that are in nature legislative and adjudicative, as well as executive.   Under the authority of a statute, they often create and publish rules and regulations that further interpret the statute.   Agencies may also make determinations of law and fact in controversies arising under the statute and, like courts, publish opinions.

Administrative law can be a very complex area to research.   Not only will researchers need to find, interpret, and update the rules, regulations, and decisions created by the administrative agency, but they will also need to find, interpret, and update the legislation the agency is

[23] The usual components of a legislative history are described in detail in Chapter 10, *infra.*

[24] *See* Peter C. Schanck, *An Essay on the Role of Legislative Histories in Statutory Interpretation,* 80 LAW LIBR. J. 391, 414 (1988); Philip P. Frickey, *From the Big Sleep to the Big Heat: The Revival of Theory in Statutory Interpretation,* 77 MINN. L. REV. 241 (1992). *But see* J. Myron Jacobstein & Roy M. Mersky, *Congressional Intent and Legislative Histories: Analysis or Psychoanalysis?,* 82 LAW LIBR. J. 297 (1990).   *See also* Chapter 10, *infra.*

[25] Administrative law is discussed in Chapter 12, *infra.*

[26] *See* 5 U.S.C. § 104 (1988).   The Federal Communications Commission, the Interstate Commerce Commission, and the Securities and Exchange Commission are among the many independent federal establishments and corporations.   The *United States Government Manual* contains a complete list of executive agencies, independent establishments, and government corporations.

administering and the judicial opinions interpreting the rules, administrative adjudications, and legislation.

SECTION B. THE MATERIALS OF LEGAL RESEARCH

Published legal resources can be divided into three broad categories: (1) primary sources or authorities,[27] (2) secondary sources, and (3) index, search, or finding tools. All of these "published" legal resources can appear in different media. They include printed books, computer databases, microforms, video and audio cassettes, and new technologies such as optical disks. Many resources contain more than one type of information and serve more than one function. For example, some computer databases and looseleaf services include both primary authority and secondary materials; and they are, at the same time, designed to be finding tools. An understanding of how legal materials are produced and organized will contribute to effective legal research.

1. Primary Sources

As noted earlier in this chapter, primary sources are authoritative statements of legal rules by governmental bodies. They include opinions of courts, constitutions, legislation, administrative regulations and opinions, and rules of court. Because many primary sources are published in the order they are issued with little or no subject access, secondary sources and indexing tools are needed to identify and retrieve them.

2. Secondary Sources [28]

Secondary sources are materials about the law that are used to explain, interpret, develop, locate, or update primary sources. The major types of secondary sources are treatises, Restatements, looseleaf services, legislative histories, law reviews and other legal periodicals, legal encyclopedias, *American Law Reports (A.L.R.)* annotations, and legal dictionaries. Secondary sources can be interpretive and contain textual analysis, doctrinal synthesis, and critical commentary of varying degrees of persuasiveness. Some secondary sources, such as Restatements, scholarly treatises, and journal articles, might be persuasive to a court, depending on the reputation of the author.[29] On the other hand, practice manuals and legal encyclopedias have little persuasive value but are useful for basic introductions to subjects, for concise or "black letter" statements of legal rules, and for practical advice. Secondary

---

[27] As noted earlier, the terms *authorities* and *sources* are interchangeable when referring to types of legal materials.

[28] Secondary sources are discussed in the following chapters, *infra:* Chapter 7, Annotated Law Reports; Chapter 10, Federal Legislative Histories; Chapter 14, Looseleaf Services; Chapter 16, Legal Encyclopedias; Chapter 17, Legal Periodicals and Indexes; Chapter 18, Treatises, Restatements, Model Codes, and Uniform Laws; Chapter 19, Other Research Aids.

[29] It should be noted, however, that the writings of legal scholars are generally not held in the same high levels of esteem in common law systems as in civil law systems. See JOHN HENRY MERRYMAN, THE CIVIL LAW TRADITION 56–60 (2d ed. 1985).

sources can be used as finding tools to locate other information. For example, cases cited in treatises, law review articles, and encyclopedias can lead to other cases.

3. Index, Search, and Finding Tools [30]

Index, search, and finding tools are intended to help locate or update primary and secondary sources. The major types of finding tools are *digests* (to locate cases discussing similar points of law), *annotations* in annotated statutes and codes,[31] *Shepard's Citators,* and legal periodical indexes. Index, search, and finding tools are *not* authority and should never be cited as such.

Looseleaf services and computer-assisted legal research systems such as WESTLAW and LEXIS are among the most valuable finding tools. They must be distinguished from other finding tools because they contain the full text of primary sources which, of course, can be cited as authority, as well as secondary information, which might also be cited as persuasive authority.

4. American Law Publishing

a. *Proliferation of Materials.* In the colonial period of American history, law books were extremely scarce and consisted mostly of English law reports. The most extensive law book collections numbered from fifty to one hundred volumes.[32] The situation did not continue for long. As the country spread westward and the economy changed from agrarian to industrial, greater demands were made upon courts and legislatures; and the body of American legal literature grew proportionately.[33]

There has been extraordinary growth in the quantity of primary legal materials. During the period from 1658 to 1896 American courts reported 500,000 decisions,[34] and by 1990 there were 4,000,000 reported decisions. In 1950, 21,000 cases were published, and it is estimated that over 130,000 cases are now published annually. Congress and the state legislatures produce about 50,000 pages of statutory law per year, and

---

[30] In this book, index, search, and finding tools are discussed in conjunction with the resources they are designed to locate. The following chapters, *infra,* however, are devoted to specific finding tools: Chapter 6, Digests for Court Reports; Chapter 15, Shepard's Citations.

[31] Do not confuse annotated statutes, which have brief annotations, or "squibs," describing cases that interpret statutory provisions, and annotated reports, such as *A.L.R.,* which have lengthy interpretive annotations of cases.

[32] ALBERT J. HARNO, LEGAL EDUCATION IN THE UNITED STATES 19 (1953); LAWRENCE M. FRIEDMAN, A HISTORY OF AMERICAN LAW 621–29 (2d ed. 1985). For thorough discussions of early American law book publishing, see ERWIN C. SURRENCY, A HISTORY OF AMERICAN LAW PUBLISHING (1990); Jenni Parrish, *Law Books and Legal Publishing in America, 1760–1840,* 72 LAW LIBR. J. 355 (1979).

[33] For an indication of the growth in size of academic law libraries, see J. Myron Jacobstein & Roy M. Mersky, *An Analysis of Academic Law Library Growth Since 1907,* 75 LAW LIBR. J. 212 (1982).

[34] 1 CENTURY DIGEST iii (1897).

federal and state administrative agencies produce thousands of pages of rulings and regulations.[35] Many of these primary materials are reproduced in multiple sources. The quantities of secondary sources and other law-related materials have expanded proportionately. The flood of legal publications has caused concern to the legal profession for over one hundred years; but the numbers continue to proliferate.[36]

b. *Official and Unofficial Publications.* American legal resources, whether books, computer databases, or other media, can be divided into those that are *official,* and those that are *unofficial.* This distinction is important but often misunderstood. An official publication is one that has been mandated by statute or governmental rule. It might be produced by the government, but does not have to be. Citation rules [37] require both official and unofficial citations, but the authority of official and unofficial publications is equivalent.

Unofficial publications of cases, statutes, and regulations are often more useful than official publications. Unofficial publications of primary authorities are published more quickly and usually include editorial features and secondary information that help interpret the primary sources, along with important locating or finding tools.

c. *Law Publishers.* American law publishing is dominated by the private publishing industry; and it is useful to learn something about these publishers, their philosophies, and the ways they structure their materials.

The largest private publisher of legal information is the West Publishing Company of Eagan, Minnesota. West produces the *National Reporter System* (the largest and most comprehensive collection of federal and state judicial opinions), the *American Digest System,* a computerized research system called WESTLAW, the *United States Code Annotated,* treatises, legal encyclopedias, law school textbooks, and many other resources. The company has played such an important role in legal publishing that some scholars claim West influenced the development of American law.[38] West has developed its resources around a theory of "comprehensive" reporting. Its *National Reporter System* includes all published cases, and West includes as many references to those cases as possible in its other books.

In contrast, Lawyers Cooperative Publishing of Rochester, New York, the next largest law publisher, follows a theory of "selective" reporting in its *Total Client Service Library.* Its publications, such as

---

[35] Recently, volumes of the *Federal Register* have exceeded 60,000 pages annually.

[36] For a discussion of the problems of excessive reporting, see J. Myron Jacobstein, *Some Reflections on the Control of the Publication of Appellate Court Opinions,* 27 STAN. L. REV. 791 (1975).

[37] For an explanation of how to read legal citations, see Chapter 23, *infra.*

[38] *See* GRANT GILMORE, THE AGES OF AMERICAN LAW 58–59 (1977); Robert C. Berring, *Full-Text Databases and Legal Research: Backing into the Future,* 1 HIGH TECH. L.J. 27 (1986); Steven M. Barkan, *Can Law Publishers Change the Law?* LEGAL REFERENCE SERVICES Q., Nos. 1/2, 1991, at 29.

the *United States Code Service, American Jurisprudence 2d,* and *American Law Reports (A.L.R.),* include what its editors feel are the most important or representative cases and references. These characterizations of the two largest publishers are broad generalizations, but they do reflect why one publisher's tools might be more, or less, useful for particular research problems.[39]

Other major commercial legal publishers include Commerce Clearing House (CCH); Research Institute of America; Bureau of National Affairs (BNA); Mead Data Central; Matthew Bender; Clark Boardman Callaghan; Warren Gorham & Lamont; Little Brown & Company; Shepard's; Michie; Butterworths; DIALOG Information Services; and Congressional Information Service (CIS), among others.[40]

5. Evaluating Legal Resources

When inspecting and evaluating legal resources, it is important to determine and understand the purposes the resources were designed to serve. The author or editor should be noted along with the types of authority (primary and secondary) included and the potential persuasiveness of the authority. Is the resource part of a set, or is it designed to be used with other resources? Does it have finding tools or special features, such as indexes and tables? How is the resource brought up to date? An awareness of the functions, features, interrelationships, strengths, and weaknesses of available resources will prove valuable for conducting legal research effectively.

SECTION C. AN ESSENTIAL SKILL

In 1992, a special task force of the American Bar Association on law schools and the legal profession issued a report that stated that "[i]t can hardly be doubted that the ability to do legal research is one of the skills that any competent practitioner must possess."[41] That report also stated: "[i]n order to conduct legal research effectively, a lawyer should have a working knowledge of the nature of legal rules and legal institutions, the fundamental tools of legal research, and the process of devising and implementing a coherent and effective research design."[42]

Furthermore, the ABA's *Model Rules of Professional Conduct* provide:

A lawyer shall provide competent representation to a client. Competent representation requires the legal knowledge, skill, thorough-

---

[39] *See A Symposium of Law Publishers,* 23 Am. L. Rev. 396 (1889), reprinted at Legal Reference Services Q., Wint. 1981, at 73.

[40] The reliance of lawyers on private law book publishers led the Federal Trade Commission to promulgate standards for the law book trade. *See* 16 CFR § 256 (1993).

[41] Legal Education and Professional Development: An Educational Continuum, Report of the Task Force on Law Schools and the Profession: Narrowing the Gap 163 (1992). The full text of the section of the report discussing legal research is reproduced in Appendix E, *infra.*

[42] *Id.*

ness, and preparation reasonably necessary for the representation.[43]

Clearly, a lawyer must be able to research the law to provide competent representation. In addition to issues of professional responsibility, questions relating to competency in legal research may arise in legal malpractice actions in which an attorney is sued for failing to know "those plain and elementary principles of law which are commonly known by well-informed attorneys, and to discover the additional rules which, although not commonly known, may readily be found by standard research techniques."[44] Issues relating to the competency of legal research are also raised in claims for malicious prosecution,[45] and in claimed violations of the Sixth Amendment rights to effective assistance of counsel.[46]

The knowledge and ability to use fundamental legal research tools and to implement an effective and efficient research plan must become part and parcel of every lawyer's training if she or he is to provide competent representation and uphold the standards of the legal profession.

[43] MODEL RULES OF PROFESSIONAL CONDUCT, Rule 1.1 (1983).

[44] Smith v. Lewis, 13 Cal. 3d 349, 530 P.2d 589, 118 Cal. Rptr. 621 (1975). In this case the plaintiff received a judgment of $100,000 in a malpractice action based on the negligence of the defendant lawyer in researching the applicable law.

[45] *See, e.g.,* Sheldon Appel Co. v. Albert & Oliker, 765 P.2d 498, 509 (Cal. 1989), a case in which the plaintiff in a malicious prosecution action unsuccessfully argued, among other things, that lack of probable cause for an action may be established by showing that the former adversary's attorney failed to perform reasonable legal research before filing a claim.

[46] *See, e.g.,* People v. Ledesma, 43 Cal. 3d 171, 729 P.2d 839, 233 Cal. Rptr. 404 (1987).

Chapter 2

THE LEGAL RESEARCH PROCESS[1]

Legal research is as much an art as a science. There are many approaches to legal research, and there is no single, or best, way to do legal research. Methods will vary according to the nature of the problem and will depend on the researcher's subject expertise and research skills.

Approaches to legal research may also be shaped by where the research is conducted. A knowledge of alternative research tools will prove to be valuable because every law library will not have all of the resources described in this book. Furthermore, sometimes the preferred resources do not produce the expected results.

The capacity to solve legal problems rapidly and accurately can best be developed by constructing a systematic approach to legal research. No matter how sophisticated you become in a field of law, you will encounter problems necessitating research into unfamiliar subjects. At these moments your basic approach developed as a novice becomes the artful technique of a trained professional.

The processes of legal research and legal writing are closely related. Legal research is often futile if the results are not communicated effectively. Legal research informs legal writing, and legal writing is meaningless unless its content is accurate. There are many differing viewpoints about how legal research and legal writing interrelate. Some researchers prefer to conduct most of their research before they begin to write. Others prefer to write as they conduct their research.

This chapter presents a general approach to legal research that can be modified and applied to most problems and can be merged with various approaches to legal writing. In the end, you must develop the research and writing methodology that you find most effective.

A GENERAL APPROACH TO LEGAL RESEARCH

A general approach to legal research, which can be modified to accommodate most problems, can be broken down into four basic steps. These are:

STEP 1. Identify and analyze the significant facts.

STEP 2. Formulate the legal issues to be researched.

STEP 3. Research the issues presented.

STEP 4. Update.

---

[1] This chapter was written by Steven M. Barkan, Associate Dean and Associate Professor of Law, Marquette University Law School.

This discussion will focus on each of these steps individually; however, each step is closely interrelated with the others. In the process of executing any one of the steps it will be necessary to revise and refine the work done in previous steps.

1. STEP 1: Identify and Analyze the Significant Facts

The researcher's first task is to identify and analyze the facts surrounding the particular problem. Some facts have legal significance; others do not. The process of legal research begins with compiling a descriptive statement of legally significant facts. It is often difficult for a beginner to identify the significant facts and to discard the insignificant ones. Consequently, when researching a problem in an unfamiliar area of the law, it is usually best to err on the side of over-inclusion rather than on the side of exclusion.

Factual analysis is the first step in formulating the legal issues to be researched. Another important purpose of factual analysis is to identify access points to the available resources. Which volumes do we pull off the shelf? Which subjects should be consulted in indexes and tables of contents? Which words should be used in an initial computer search? An experienced researcher will be able to identify issues and take a subject approach to the resources; but the beginning researcher, who does not have the experience to examine a fact pattern and readily categorize it and formulate legal issues, will need to devote more time and attention to this activity.

Inexperienced legal researchers tend to skim over the facts and begin researching. No productive research can be done outside a particular fact pattern. Most research, and controversy, is over facts, not law; and cases are most often distinguished on the facts. The rules stated by courts are tied to specific fact situations, and, in the future, must be considered in relation to those facts. Because the facts of a legal problem will control the direction of research, the investigation and analysis of facts must be incorporated into the research process. You will save time, and will achieve more accuracy, if you initially take the time to identify the relevant facts and write them down in some narrative form.

The TARP Rule. A useful technique is to analyze your facts according to the following factors:

T—Thing or subject matter;

A—Cause of action or ground of defense;

R—Relief sought;

P—Persons or **parties** involved.

Thing or subject matter. The place or property involved in a problem or controversy may be a significant element. Thus, when a passenger is injured in a skidding automobile, the automobile becomes an essential fact in the dispute.

Cause of action or ground of defense. Identify the claim that might be asserted or the defense that might be made. For example, the cause of action might be a breach of contract, negligence, or some other claim.

Relief sought. What is the purpose of the lawsuit? It might be a civil action in which the party bringing the suit is seeking monetary damages for an injury, or an action in which a party is asking the court to order another party to do a specific act or to refrain from doing a specific act; or it might be a criminal action brought by the state.

Persons or parties involved in the problem; their functional and legal status and relationship to each other. The parties or persons might be individuals, or might be a group that is significant to the solution of the problem or the outcome of the lawsuit. Similarly, the relationship between the parties, such as exists between husband and wife or employer and employee, might be of special importance.

2. STEP 2: Formulate the Legal Issues to Be Researched

This is the initial intellectual activity that presumes some knowledge of the substantive law. It is, therefore, the point at which inexperienced legal researchers are most likely to have trouble. The goal is to classify or categorize the problem into general, and increasingly specific, subject areas and to begin to hypothesize legal issues. For example, is this a matter of civil or criminal law? Federal or state law? Are we generally in the area of contracts or torts, or both? If torts, is it products liability or negligence? It should be noted that problems are not easily categorized and compartmentalized, problems can fall into more than one category, and categories affect each other.

a. *Get an Overview.* To assist in formulating issues, it is useful to consult general secondary sources for an overview of all relevant subject areas. These sources can include national legal encyclopedias, a state encyclopedia, treatises, looseleaf services, or one or more subject periodicals or journals. The best choice will vary according to your background, but start with the most general and work to the more detailed and specific. These sources can provide valuable background reading and can direct you to issues and to primary resources. Be sure to note any constitutional provisions, statutes, administrative regulations, and judicial and administrative opinions cited by these sources. The point to remember is that, at this stage, these secondary sources are used to provide background information and to help you formulate issues; they are the tools, not the objects of research.

Writing a clear, concise statement of each legal issue raised by the significant facts is an important and difficult task. Failure to frame all of the issues raised by a particular set of facts results in incomplete and inadequate research. It is better, when framing the issues, for a beginner to err on the side of too many issues. Insignificant issues can always be eliminated after they have been thoroughly investigated, and overlapping issues can be consolidated.

b. *Create an Outline.* Once statements of the issues have been drafted, they should be arranged in a logical pattern to form an outline. Logically related issues may be combined as sub-issues under a broader main issue. Issues which depend upon the outcome of other issues should be arranged accordingly. Your outline should be expanded, modified, and revised as your research progresses. As a particular issue is researched, it is often discovered to be overly broad, and it becomes evident that the statement of the issue should be narrowed. It may also be necessary at times to split an issue into two, or to divide an issue into two sub-issues. Similarly, it may develop that the original issue is too narrow and does not lead to any relevant information. In such instances, the issue should be broadened. Many times, during the process of research, it becomes apparent that issues not originally considered are relevant. For this reason, the task of framing issues may not be completed until the research project is finished.

3.   STEP 3: Research the Issues Presented [2]

After the facts have been analyzed and the issues have been framed, it is time to begin researching the first issue.

a. *Organize and Plan.* Although serendipity can play an important role in legal research, good legal researchers, as a rule, are systematic, methodical, and organized; and they keep good records. Every researcher must develop a system for taking notes.

For each issue, it is important to decide which sources to use, which sources not to use, and the order in which sources should be examined. The best practice is to write down all sources to be searched under each issue to be researched, even if sources are repeated. As you find information, record where you found it and why it is relevant. Expand your outline to include the information that you discover. Maintaining an accurate list of sources consulted, sources to be consulted, terms and topics checked, and updating steps taken will help prevent wasting time and overlooking crucial information.

As a general practice, it is best to research each issue completely before moving to the next issue. It will be necessary to revise issues along the way, but it is best to follow through with each issue before moving on, rather than moving back and forth from issue to issue. Dealing with each issue separately helps avoid backtracking or excessive interplay of issues, helps ensure that each issue and sub-issue will be distinct and logically complete, and helps avoid the temptation to stray into interesting but irrelevant areas.

There is sometimes a great temptation to include information that has taken many hours to develop but which you later determine is irrelevant to a proper analysis of the issues. You should expect to investigate a number of leads during the research process that prove to be irrelevant, and you must avoid the temptation to retain irrelevant

---

[2] After reading Step 3 it might also be useful to consult the "Chart on Legal Research Procedure" in Appendix F.

information that detracts from, and often masks, the legal analysis which is directly on point.

b. *Identify, Read, and Update All Relevant Constitutional Provisions, Statutes, and Administrative Regulations.* Identifying and reading relevant constitutional provisions, statutes, and administrative regulations will provide you with the framework on which the rest of your research will be built. These primary sources can be identified in several ways.

● *Statutory Compilations.* Statutory compilations almost always have tables of contents and indexes that list the subjects and topics covered by the statutes. Because relevant statutory provisions are often found in several places in the compiled statutes, consult both the table of contents and the index.

● *Computer–Assisted Legal Research.* The United States Code, the Code of Federal Regulations, the Federal Register, and the statutes of many states are available on LEXIS and WESTLAW. It is possible to search the full text of these documents for statutes and regulations that apply to your problem.

● *Secondary Sources.* Secondary sources such as encyclopedias, treatises, looseleaf services, and law review articles, commonly cite relevant constitutional provisions, statutes, and administrative regulations, particularly if those secondary sources focus on the law of one state or on federal law.

It will not always be easy to identify all relevant statutes at the onset of your research. Indexing problems sometimes make it difficult to match concepts with indexing terms. Sometimes your issues will be too vague or underdeveloped for you to realize that a statute applies. Accordingly, continue searching for relevant constitutional provisions, statutes, and administrative regulations as your research progresses; and be prepared to modify your issues and strategies accordingly.

c. *Identify, Read, and Update All Relevant Case Law.* After you have identified and read the relevant constitutional provisions, statutes, and administrative regulations, you must identify, read, and update the case law that has interpreted and applied those forms of enacted law, as well as other case law that is relevant to your fact situation.

Do not limit your search to cases that support your position. A competent researcher will anticipate both sides of an argument and identify the cases that indicate contrary conclusions. In many situations, these will be the same cases, and the argument will be over how the cases are to be interpreted, *e.g.,* whether the holding is to be broadly or narrowly applied, or whether the facts of the cases can be distinguished. Frequently, however, both sides will argue that entirely different lines of cases are controlling.

Your goal, at this stage of research, is to compile a comprehensive, chronological list of relevant opinions for each issue. Because no two cases are exactly alike, you should not expect to find cases with fact

patterns identical to yours. The most relevant judicial opinions will come from the same court or superior appellate courts in your jurisdiction because they are the only ones that are potentially binding. Next in importance will be judicial opinions, which might be persuasive, from other courts and jurisdictions dealing with similar facts, statutes, and issues. Even if you find cases that you consider to be binding authority, persuasive authority from other jurisdictions might help bolster your argument, particularly if the opinions you find are from well-known and respected judges. Reading the cases chronologically can reveal background information that is not necessarily repeated in each case, can show the development of the case law, and can point to the "lead" case that will be cited in other opinions.

Cases that interpret statutes can be identified in several ways.

● *Annotated Statutes and Codes.* Annotated statutes and codes list interpretive cases after each statutory provision.

● *Treatises and Looseleaf Services.* Treatises and looseleaf services, particularly if they are devoted to the law of one state or to federal law, cite cases that interpret the statutes they discuss.

● *Shepard's.* Shepardizing the statute will provide a list of cases that have cited the statute.

● *Computer–Assisted Legal Research (CALR).* Both WESTLAW and LEXIS can be searched for cases that have cited the statute.

Other relevant cases can be identified by subject searches of secondary sources and finding tools. Digests provide a subject arrangement of brief abstracts of cases that can be accessed through a table of contents and a descriptive word index. Also, the full text of court opinions can be searched in LEXIS and WESTLAW; treatises, *A.L.R.* annotations, looseleaf services, and encyclopedias should provide relevant case citations.

Once you have identified a relevant case, there are several techniques that can help you identify other cases on the same subject. These techniques include tracing the key numbers used in that case through the digests to find other cases with the same key numbers, shepardizing the case and using the CALR systems as citators to find other citing cases, and consulting the tables of cases in treatises, looseleaf services, encyclopedias, and digests.

As you read and brief each case, be sure to note its full citation, parallel citations, the judge and court issuing the opinion, the date of the decision, the relevant facts, the holding, a summary of the court's reasoning, key numbers assigned, and the sources cited by the court. Each of the sources cited should be read, briefed, and shepardized, and new cases should be added to your list. Each case you brief should be incorporated into your outline. There will likely be a great deal of redundancy, particularly when courts list a "string" of citations for each point of law.

d. *Refine the Search.* After you have identified, read, and organized the primary sources, go to secondary sources to refine the search

and expand your argument. Invariably, new cases and lines of argument will appear. Treatises, law review articles, and Restatements of the Law are not binding authority, but they can be persuasive and can provide ideas on how best to utilize the primary sources you have found. If the problem involves a statute, the legislative history might suggest the legislature's intent in passing the act and the problem the law was intended to remedy. Historical, social, economic, and political information can put legal arguments in their proper context and can support policy arguments.

4. STEP 4: Update

Although updating was discussed earlier as an integral part of researching the issues, its importance warrants special attention. Law changes constantly. Legislatures pass new statutes and modify old ones. Each appellate court decision either adds new law, refines the law, reaffirms the law, or changes the law; and researchers must be aware of the most recent decisions on the subject being researched. Research that is current today can be out of date tomorrow. Few lawyers would disagree that failure to update legal research is careless and negligent, sometimes leading to disastrous results.

Shepardize cases, statutes, and regulations; consult computerized databases such as WESTLAW, LEXIS, Insta–Cite, and Auto–Cite; and check pocket parts and supplements, looseleaf services, and advance sheets to determine whether the authorities have been interpreted or altered in any way, or whether new cases, statutes, or regulations have been published.

5. When to Stop

The question of when to stop researching is a difficult one. Obviously, there is no easy answer to the question: "Can I safely stop here?" With experience, researchers develop insight into when they can safely terminate their research. In many instances an obvious repetition of citations or absence of information will suggest that enough research has been done. However, there is no uniform rule on how extensive research should be, and knowing when to terminate research is a skill that can only be developed over time.

In some instances, carrying a problem through all the sources can be needless, unwarranted, or repetitious. It is possible to over-research your problem. All cases are not of equal importance; much information is redundant. Including too much information can obscure the important points you are trying to make. Furthermore, many simple problems do not call for exhaustive research. Common sense and professional insight, therefore, play significant roles in legal research.

In the last analysis, the skills of sophisticated researchers are measured as much by the knowledge of what can be omitted as by which research materials are used and how they are used. The attorney's

stock in trade is time; a skilled legal researcher knows how to use it wisely.[3]

---

[3] For an in-depth discussion of when to stop researching, see Christina L. Kunz, *Terminating Research,* 2 PERSPECTIVES: TEACHING LEGAL RES. & WRITING 2 (1993).

Chapter 3

COURT REPORTS

SECTION A. THE REPORTING OF COURT CASES

1. Introduction

The doctrine *stare decisis,* as discussed in Chapter 1, Section A–3, has as its premise that courts are to adhere to judicial precedent. Reliance on judicial precedent in American jurisprudence is derived from the common law. Researchers and the courts are expected to turn to established judicial authorities and rules of law as the foundation for formulating legal arguments and issuing opinions. Access to "case law"—the aggregate of reported cases that form a body of jurisprudence, as distinguished from statutory and administrative law—is, therefore, often crucial when one is asked to research a legal issue. Consequently, the editing, publishing, and ready availability of court cases have special characteristics in American law.

Court reports are compilations of judicially-decided cases, most often from state and federal appellate courts, arranged according to some grouping, such as jurisdiction, court, period of time, subject matter, or case significance. Today, the word "reporter" is often used synonymously with court reports.

When a court reaches a determination as to the outcome of a case, it issues an opinion in which it states the reason for its decision. Technically speaking, the *decision* of a court only signifies the action of the court and is indicated by the words *Affirmed,* or *Reversed,* or *Remanded,* or similar words and phrases. The *opinion* provides the explanation for the decision. In actual practice, the terms *opinion* and *decision* are often used interchangeably.[1]

The first volume of state appellate court reports was published in 1789, with the reports of the Supreme Court of the United States commencing officially in 1817. The numbers of published reports have proliferated dramatically since that time. Because these past court cases play such an important role in our law, the tremendous growth and inclusiveness of court reports are quite understandable.

More than 4,000,000 reported United States judicial cases are now in published form, and over 130,000 new American cases are reported each year from more than 600 courts. Most of these published cases are

---

[1] For a discussion of the difference between *decision of the court* and *opinion of the court,* see Rogers v. Hill, 289 U.S. 582, 587 (1933). *See also* Towley v. King Arthur Rings, Inc., 40 N.Y.2d 129, 351 N.E.2d 728, 386 N.Y.S.2d 80 (1976).

from the federal and state appellate courts. Justice Holmes observed that, "It is a great mistake to be frightened by the ever-increasing number of reports. The reports of a given jurisdiction in the course of a generation take up pretty much the whole body of law, and restate it from the present point of view. We could reconstruct the corpus from them if all that went before were burned." [2]

Computer technology has added yet another dimension to the storage and retrieval of legal information. The development and rapid expansion of two major electronic storage and retrieval systems, LEXIS and WESTLAW, both launched in the 1970s, allow full-text searching of court cases and numerous other databases of law-related materials. Even more recent technology, such as CD–ROMs (compact disk-read only memory) and electronic imaging, also provide computerized access to the full text of cases and to other materials for legal research. At times, a researcher's needs can be satisfied by relying exclusively on either computer-retrievable sources or bound court reporters; at other times the best results can be achieved by using both. Computer-assisted legal research (CALR) is discussed in detail in Chapter 22, J. Jacobstein, R. Mersky & D. Dunn, *Fundamentals of Legal Research* (6th ed.).

The massive quantity of available court cases in both bound volumes and computer-retrievable sources in turn creates problems for the legal profession—problems relating to locating relevant information within the published reports, keeping current in one's field, publication and subscription costs, space and technological considerations, and related issues.

Not all appellate court cases are published and publication procedures differ in the various appellate courts.[3] Justice Holmes' comments notwithstanding, the tremendous growth in the number of recently-decided cases has increased the attempts to restrict the number of those that are reported.[4] Many judges and lawyers believe that far too many

---

[2] OLIVER W. HOLMES, *The Path of the Law, in* COLLECTED LEGAL PAPERS 167, 169 (1920 & photo. reprint 1985).

[3] George M. Weaver, *The Precedential Value of Unpublished Judicial Opinions,* 39 MERCER L. REV. 477 (1988). *See also* William L. Reynolds & William M. Richman, *An Evaluation of Limited Publications in the United States Courts of Appeals: The Price of Reform,* 48 U. CHI. L. REV. 573 (1981).

[4] The practice of selective reporting of appellate court opinions has caused considerable debate as to its value. For an historical survey, see J. Myron Jacobstein, *Some Reflections on the Control of the Publication of Appellate Court Opinions,* 27 STAN. L. REV. 791 (1975). For more recent views, see Richard L. Neumeir, *Unpublished Opinions: Their Threat to the Appellate System,* BRIEF (A.B.A.), Spring, 1988, at 22; Keith H. Beyler, *Selective Publication Rules,* 21 LOY. U. CHI. L.J. 1 (1989); Jenny Mockenhaupt, Comment, *Assessing the Nonpublication Practice of the Minnesota Court of Appeals,* 19 WM. MITCHELL L. REV. 787 (1993).

For the current practice for some state supreme courts to "depublish" opinions of intermediate appellate courts, see Philip L. Dubois, *The Negative Side of Judicial Decision Making: Depublication as a Tool of Judicial Power and Administration of State Courts of Last Resort,* 33 VILL. L. REV. 469 (1988); Steven R. Barnett, *Making Decisions Disappear: Depublication and Stipulated Reversal in the California Supreme Court,* 26 LOY. L.A. L. REV.

opinions that do not merit the treatment of permanent publication are, nevertheless, written and reported. They argue that a significant number of reported cases relate merely to prosaic problems and make no doctrinal advancements. Although of value to the parties involved in the litigation, these cases add little or nothing to the existing law.

Ordinarily, cases decided by state trial courts are not reported. A few states, such as New York, Ohio, and Pennsylvania, do publish some trial court cases, but those selected are few in number and represent only a very small portion of the total cases heard by the trial courts. Moreover, cases decided by trial courts do not serve as mandatory precedents, and they do not play an important role in legal research.

2. The Structure and Operation of the Court System

Each jurisdiction has its own system of court organization, and although there may be differences in detail, the typical structure is the same. In general, there are trial courts and appellate courts. The former are the courts where the trial is held (courts of first instance). It is here the parties appear, witnesses testify, and the evidence is presented. The trial court usually determines any questions of fact in dispute and then applies the applicable rules of law.

Once the trial court reaches its decision, the losing party has a right of appeal to an appellate court. Each state has a final court of appeals or court of last resort. Thirty-eight states also have intermediate courts of appeals.[5] [See Illustration 1.] Generally, the appellate court can only decide questions of law and its decision in each case is based on the trial record from below, *e.g.,* pre-trial proceedings and trial transcript. Appellate courts do not receive new testimony or decide questions of fact, and in most jurisdictions only the appellate courts issue written opinions.

When a case is appealed to an appellate court, both parties submit written briefs that contain a summary of the facts and arguments on the points of law involved, and the court may hear oral arguments by the attorneys. The court then issues an opinion in which it states the reasons for its decision. If the case is decided by an intermediate appellate court and the losing party believes his or her position is legally correct, this lower court decision can frequently be appealed again, this time to the court of last resort for a further determination.

SECTION B. THE SEGMENTS OF COURT CASES

An American court case typically includes the following segments. [See Illustrations 2–3.]

1033 (1993); Gerald F. Uelman, *Publication and Depublication of California Court of Appeals Opinions: Is the Eraser Mightier Than the Pencil,* 26 Loy. L.A. L. Rev. 1077 (1993). *See infra* Chapter 4, note 12 for information on the federal court practices in this regard.

[5] For detailed information on the activities of state courts, see State Court Caseload Statistics: Annual Report, produced jointly by the Conference of State Court Administrators and the National Center for State Courts. *See also* latest Council of State Governments, Book of the States (biennial).

1. Name or Title of the Case

Cases generally are identified by the names of the parties to a lawsuit. This is sometimes referred to as the "caption." Examples are:

Gayle Payne, Plaintiff v. Richard M. Green, Defendant—in table of cases (a listing of cases typically arranged in alphabetical order) as *Payne v. Green.*

In re Payne—in table of cases as *Payne, In re.* These are judicial proceedings in which there are no adversarial parties. Such designations usually denote a bankruptcy case, a probate case, a guardianship matter, a contempt case, a disbarment, or a *habeas corpus* case.

Ex parte Payne—in table of cases as *Payne, Ex parte.* This is a special proceeding for the benefit of one party only.

State on the relation of Payne v. Green—in table of cases as *State ex rel. Payne v. Green.* These cases involve extraordinary legal remedies, *e.g., mandamus,* prohibition, *certiorari, quo warranto,* or *habeas corpus.*

State v. Payne—in table of cases as *State v. Payne.* Suit by the state in its collective capacity as the party wronged by a criminal act. In some reporters the criminal cases are arranged in alphabetical order under the names of the respective states. *People* or *Commonwealth* is used in some states instead of *State.* If the United States brings the suit, it is captioned, for example, as *United States v. Payne.* To aid with location, a case of this nature may also be listed in the table of cases as *Payne, State v.* or *Payne, United States v.*

In maritime law, a suit may be brought against the ship, *e.g., The Caledonia.*

Cases involving the seizure of commodities use the commodity as a party, *e.g., United States v. 37 Photographs.*

Usually the plaintiff-defendant names remain in that order when cases are appealed by the defendant; however, in some states, they are reversed, and the defendant on appeal becomes the plaintiff in error.

2. Citation

The citation to the case frequently appears near the name of the case in a published reporter. Often the parallel citation to another reporter in which the case is published is also provided.

3. Docket Number

A docket number is the numerical designation assigned to each case by a court, *e.g.,* No. 94–1145, or some similar numbering sequence. It is the means of identifying the case as the suit is in progress. Also, it is a convenient method commonly used by law libraries to organize the appellate briefs in the libraries' collections.

4. Date of Decision

This is the date on which the decision was rendered, and generally it appears after the docket number in the reported case.

5. Prefatory Statement

The prefatory statement explains the nature of the case, its disposition in the lower court, the name of the lower court and sometimes its judge, and the disposition of the case in the appellate court, *e.g.,* *Affirmed* or *Reversed.*

6. Syllabus or Headnote

Headnotes, or syllabi, are brief summaries of the rules of law or significant facts in a case. They are usually drafted by editors or reporters employed by the court, although in a few states they are prepared by the judges who rendered the decisions. Each headnote represents a point of law extracted from the case, and the number of headnotes will vary from case to case. However, headnotes cannot be relied on as authority; the actual case must be consulted.

The syllabi or headnotes are useful in allowing the reader to grasp quickly the legal issues discussed within the case and then to locate these issues within the case. They also serve a very useful function in the process of locating other cases on the same or similar points of law. This feature will be discussed in more detail in Chapter 6. [See Illustrations 2 and 4 for examples of headnotes.]

7. Names of Counsel

The names of counsel for both parties to a suit precede the opinion of the court.

8. Statement of Facts

A statement of the facts in the case usually follows the names of counsel.

9. Opinions of the Court

As previously mentioned, most court cases that are published are those of the appellate court. Every appellate court has at least three judges,[6] and in some jurisdictions the courts may have five, seven, nine, or more judges. The *opinion* of the court is the explanation of the court's decision, the latter being the conclusion or result in a controversy. The *majority opinion* is written by one member of the court and represents the principles of law that a majority of his or her colleagues on the court deem operative in a given decision.

---

[6] Many appellate courts sit in panels smaller than the full court. When the full court meets, it is referred to as an *en banc* proceeding. *See* Neil D. McFeeley, *En Banc Proceedings in the United States Courts of Appeals*, 24 IDAHO L. REV. 255 (1987–1988).

A member of the majority, while agreeing with a decision, may disagree with its reasoning. He or she then may write a *concurring opinion* elaborating his or her reasoning. When more judges join an opinion than any concurring opinion, but yet not a majority of the court, it is known as a *plurality opinion.*

The views of the minority generally are expressed by a *dissenting opinion,* which is written by one of the dissenting judges. An opinion, in *accord* with the dissent, is written by a dissenting judge when he or she agrees with the conclusions and results of the dissent, but disagrees with its reasoning. Or several dissenting opinions may be rendered independently by the judges, each expressing different views.

Dissenting opinions are not the law in a case; nor are they binding as precedent. They assume the characteristics of *dicta* and serve merely as persuasive or secondary authority. However, not infrequently the controlling opinion may later be overruled and the dissenting opinion might then be accepted as the correct statement of the law.

A *per curiam* opinion is an opinion of the entire majority as distinguished from an opinion written by a specific judge. In some courts, *e.g.,* New York Court of Appeals, a *per curiam* opinion may present a lengthy or a brief discussion of the issues in the case. In other courts, *e.g.,* Supreme Court of the United States, this type of opinion may only give the conclusion without any reasoning.[7] A *memorandum opinion* is a brief holding of the whole court in which the opinion is limited or omitted.

Two additional elements, mentioned in Chapter 1, merit reiteration. The first is the *ratio decidendi,* or the point in a case that determines the result. In other words, it is the basis of the decision, explicitly or implicitly, stated in the opinion. The second is *obiter dictum.* This is a collateral statement contained in the opinion that does not relate directly to the issues raised in the case. *Dictum,* therefore, is an official, incidental comment made by a judge in his or her opinion not necessary to the formulation of the decision and that is not binding as precedent.

10. Decision, with Judgment or Decree

This refers to the actual disposition of the case by the court. Thus, a decision is noted by such terms as *Affirmed, Reversed, Modified,* etc. Often the words *decision* and *judgment* are used synonymously. A decree, typically issued in equity or admiralty actions, announces the legal consequences of the facts found.

SECTION C. OFFICIAL AND UNOFFICIAL REPORTS

If the publication of a set of court reports is sanctioned by statute or court rule, the set is referred to as *official reports.* [See Illustration 2.]

---

[7] For discussion of the decline in the use of the *per curiam* opinion by the Supreme Court of the United States, see Stephen L. Wasby et al., *The Per Curiam Opinion: Its Nature and Functions,* 76 JUDICATURE 29 (1992). *See also* Stephen L. Wasby et al., *The Supreme Court's Use of Per Curiam Dispositions: The Connections to Oral Argument,* 13 No. ILL. U.L. REV. 1 (1992).

In some instances, these publications are produced under government supervision; in others the official report may have ceased and an existing commercial publication designated as the official source. This is discussed in more detail in Chapter 5. Those published without legislative or judicial authority are referred to as *unofficial reports, i.e.,* commercial or private publications. Neither term reflects superior quality or accuracy, because the language of the opinions reported in both is identical. [See Illustrations 2–6.]

1. Unofficially Reported Cases as Authority

Because court cases are not copyrighted,[8] numerous sets of court reports have been, or are currently, published by commercial publishers. These sets either duplicate the opinions in the official reports, or include cases not officially published, or both. Since the early nineteenth century, legal scholars have warned against the proliferation of court reports. In the past, courts and legislatures have attempted to control the publication of court cases by limiting the publication of cases in the official reports to those that (1) lay down a new rule of law or alter or modify an existing rule; (2) involve a legal issue of continuing public interest; (3) criticize existing law; or (4) resolve an apparent conflict of authority. But, inevitably, each such attempt has resulted in those cases that do not appear in the official reports being published in unofficial sets of reports. Furthermore, the availability of unreported cases has increased with the expansion of online legal databases.[9]

Only fairly recently have some courts attempted to control this proliferation by prohibiting the citing of opinions not specifically marked "For Publication." [10] This practice in turn has been severely criticized by some members of the bar. The final solution to the proliferation of court cases has still not been found. It is reasonable to conclude that so long as precedent plays a dominant role in American law, the number of published court cases will continue to grow. Always check local court rules before using unpublished cases as authority.

2. National Reporter System

The most exhaustive collection of bound court cases is in West Publishing Company's *National Reporter System.* The *National Reporter System,* which began in approximately 1880, is composed of numerous units that group together cases from the federal courts, state courts, and

[8] Wheaton v. Peters, 33 U.S. (8 Pet.) 591 (1834). *See also* Banks v. Manchester, 128 U.S. 244 (1988).

[9] The issue of copyright has also arisen between the two leading providers of online legal databases, particularly as it relates to the page numbers used in West Publishing Company's reporters. West Publishing Co. v. Mead Data Central, Inc., 616 F. Supp. 1571 (D. Minn. 1985) (grant of preliminary injunction on copyright issue), *aff'd,* 799 F.2d 1219 (8th Cir. 1986), *cert. denied,* 479 U.S. 1970 (1987).

[10] *E.g.,* CAL. R. P. 977. The treatment on non-publication of cases in the federal courts of appeals is discussed in Chapter 4.

specialized courts. The *National Reporter System* is discussed in detail in Chapter 5.

SECTION D. THE ELEMENTS OF JUDICIAL REPORTING

Several methods are used in publishing court cases. Generally, the order of their release is determined by their decision dates and not by other arrangements, such as subject. In states that still publish official reports, cases may be published separately as *slip opinions* soon after they are decided. Usually, each *slip opinion* is paged separately, contains no syllabus, and is not indexed.

The more common method of publishing cases is first as *advance sheets*. These pamphlets contain numerous recently-decided cases, are consecutively paged, are published as quickly as they can be assembled after the decisions are rendered, and when sufficient in size (typically three to five issues) are cumulated into a bound volume that uses the same page numbers as the *advance sheets*. These techniques permit prompt, permanent citations to cases. The features of the cases in the *advance sheets* are identical with those included in bound volumes. Some jurisdictions do not publish *advance sheets*. Online sources, of course, merge new cases with existing ones and, thus, can often eliminate the need for *slip opinions* and *advance sheets*.

1. Features of Bound Volumes of Reports

As indicated previously, cases are ultimately cumulated in bound volumes or incorporated into online versions. The bound volumes include most of the following significant features:

a. A table of cases contained in the volume.

b. A table of statutes interpreted in the cases reported in the volume.

c. Various types of opinions: (1) written by a judge (majority, plurality, dissenting, or concurring); (2) *per curiam;* and (3) memorandum.

d. The cases are cumulated from advance sheets and have the same volume and page numbers as the advance sheets.

e. Table of cases decided without opinions.

f. Subject index or digest of the cases reported.

g. Judicial definition of words and phrases used in the cases reported.

h. Changes in court rules.

i. A list of all judges sitting on the courts covered by the volume.

j. Unofficial reports generally contain cross-reference tables to the official reports.

SECTION E. ORGANIZATION OF COURT REPORTS

Court reports are organized in several different ways:

1. By Jurisdiction

The cases of a particular court are issued chronologically in a numbered series, such as the *New York Reports* or the *Illinois Appellate Court Reports* or the *United States Reports*. In some instances, the reports of both the highest state court and its intermediate appellate court are published in the same set of reports, such as in the *California Reporter*.

2. By Geography

The cases of a group of geographically adjacent states are published in one set of reports such as the *North Western Reporter,* which includes cases from the appellate courts of Iowa, Michigan, Minnesota, Nebraska, North Dakota, South Dakota, and Wisconsin. These various geographical groupings are discussed in Chapter 5.

3. By Subject

Standard sets of law reports contain cases arranged chronologically, and each volume may contain cases on subjects ranging from A to Z. Examples of these subject reports are *Labor Law Reports, United States Tax Reporter,* and *United States Patents Quarterly.*

SECTION F.   ILLUSTRATIONS

[Illustration 1]

BASIC COURT STRUCTURE IN THE UNITED STATES

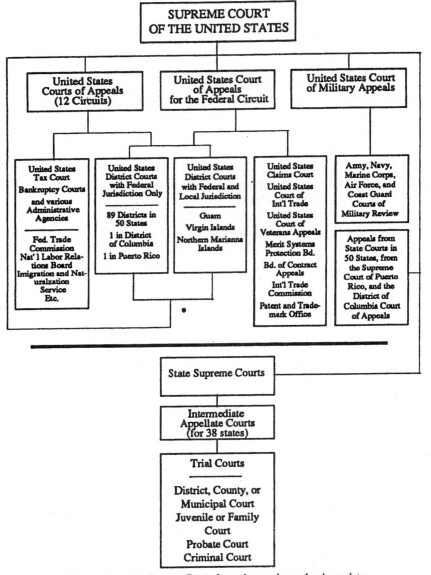

*Direct review of the Supreme Court of an order granting or denying an inter-locutory or permanent injunction in a civil action to be heard and determined by a district court of three judges, and from an interlocutory or final judgment of a court of the United States holding an Act of Congress unconstitutional in any civil proceeding to which the United States or any of its agencies, or any officer or employee, is a party. (28 U.S.C. §§ 1252, 1253)

[Illustration 2]

A TYPICAL CASE AS REPORTED IN AN OFFICIAL SET OF STATE COURT REPORTS (308 ARK. 439)

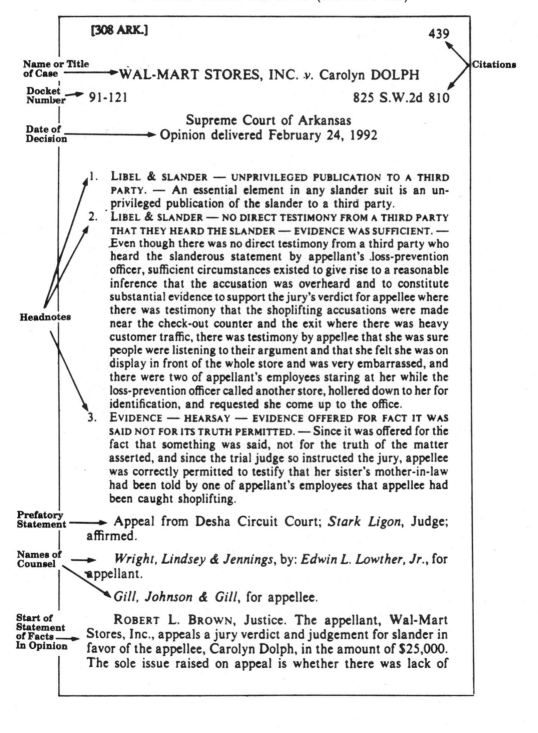

[308 ARK.]   **439**

Name or Title of Case ——→ WAL-MART STORES, INC. *v.* Carolyn DOLPH   Citations

Docket Number ——→ 91-121   825 S.W.2d 810

Date of Decision ——→ Supreme Court of Arkansas
Opinion delivered February 24, 1992

Headnotes

1. LIBEL & SLANDER — UNPRIVILEGED PUBLICATION TO A THIRD PARTY. — An essential element in any slander suit is an unprivileged publication of the slander to a third party.

2. LIBEL & SLANDER — NO DIRECT TESTIMONY FROM A THIRD PARTY THAT THEY HEARD THE SLANDER — EVIDENCE WAS SUFFICIENT. — Even though there was no direct testimony from a third party who heard the slanderous statement by appellant's loss-prevention officer, sufficient circumstances existed to give rise to a reasonable inference that the accusation was overheard and to constitute substantial evidence to support the jury's verdict for appellee where there was testimony that the shoplifting accusations were made near the check-out counter and the exit where there was heavy customer traffic, there was testimony by appellee that she was sure people were listening to their argument and that she felt she was on display in front of the whole store and was very embarrassed, and there were two of appellant's employees staring at her while the loss-prevention officer called another store, hollered down to her for identification, and requested she come up to the office.

3. EVIDENCE — HEARSAY — EVIDENCE OFFERED FOR FACT IT WAS SAID NOT FOR ITS TRUTH PERMITTED. — Since it was offered for the fact that something was said, not for the truth of the matter asserted, and since the trial judge so instructed the jury, appellee was correctly permitted to testify that her sister's mother-in-law had been told by one of appellant's employees that appellee had been caught shoplifting.

Prefatory Statement ——→ Appeal from Desha Circuit Court; *Stark Ligon*, Judge; affirmed.

Names of Counsel ——→ *Wright, Lindsey & Jennings*, by: *Edwin L. Lowther, Jr.*, for appellant.

Gill, Johnson & Gill, for appellee.

Start of Statement of Facts In Opinion ——→ ROBERT L. BROWN, Justice. The appellant, Wal-Mart Stores, Inc., appeals a jury verdict and judgement for slander in favor of the appellee, Carolyn Dolph, in the amount of $25,000. The sole issue raised on appeal is whether there was lack of

[Illustration 3]

LAST PAGE OF OPINION, 308 ARK. 439, 443

[308 ARK.]   WAL-MART STORES, INC. *v.* DOLPH   443
Cite as 308 Ark. 439 (1992)

Portion of Opinion

the testimony of Ms. Dolph as to what someone else told her — and you heard the linkage of where it came from — is not being offered for the truth of what Ms. Dolph said was told to Ms. Dolph, but merely for the purpose of showing that she did, in fact, receive some information, whether true or not. And my instruction to you is, you are not to consider it as being given or stated here for the truth of what Ms. Dolph said, but merely to show that she heard something.

Wal-Mart argues that the circuit court erred in permitting what amounted to triple hearsay into evidence. We do not agree.

The Eighth Circuit Court of Appeals resolved a similar question in a libel case and held that the testimony in question was not hearsay. *See Luster* v. *Retail Credit Company,* 575 F.2d 609 (8th Cir. 1978). In *Luster,* the plaintiff sued Retail Credit for a false statement made in a credit report which suggested arson on the plaintiff's premises. To prove publication, plaintiff used the testimony of a third-party insurance agent who heard from a deceased agent that a Dallas insurance firm believed Retail Credit's report implied arson. A hearsay objection was made and rejected by the trial court which gave a limiting instruction at the time of the disputed testimony. The Eighth Circuit affirmed the trial court's ruling on the basis that the testimony was admitted solely to prove the fact that the words were said — not to prove that they were true.

[3] The Eighth Circuit's reasoning in *Luster* is persuasive in this case which involves a comparable publication issue. Here, the testimony of the sister's mother-in-law about what the Wal-Mart employee said was not offered to prove the truth of what was said. It was offered to prove *the fact* that it was said, which then became some evidence of publication. The distinction is an important one, and we hold that the circuit court's ruling with the corollary instruction to the jury was appropriate in this case.

Decision ➤ Affirmed.

DUDLEY, J., not participating.

[Illustration 4]

A TYPICAL CASE AS REPORTED IN A SET OF UNOFFICIAL REPORTS, 825 S.W.2D (SAME CASE AS 308 ARK. 439)

810 Ark.   825 SOUTH WESTERN REPORTER, 2d SERIES

308 Ark. 439
WAL–MART STORES, INC., Appellant,

v.

Carolyn DOLPH, Appellee.

No. 91–121.

Supreme Court of Arkansas.

Feb. 24, 1992.

Customer brought suit against store for slander. The Desha County Circuit Court, Stark Ligon, J., rendered judgment for customer, and store appealed. The Supreme Court, Brown, J., held that: (1) there was sufficient evidence of publication, and (2) trial court did not permit inadmissible hearsay to support publication argument.

Affirmed.

1. Libel and Slander ⚖1

Central element in any slander suit is unprivileged publication of slander to third party.

2. Libel and Slander ⚖112(1)

Although there was no direct testimony from any third party who heard slanderous statement by store's loss-prevention officer that customer had been apprehended for shoplifting in another town the week before, sufficient circumstances existed to give rise to reasonable inference that officer's accusation was overheard and thus "published"; there was testimony of shoplifting accusations made by officer within a few feet of check-out counter and exit where there was heavy customer traffic and further testimony by customer that she was sure people were listening to the argument.

3. Evidence ⚖267

In customer's slander suit against store, customer's testimony that her sister's mother-in-law had been told by store employee that customer had been caught shoplifting was not hearsay; testimony was not offered to prove truth of what was said, but to prove fact that it was said, which then became some evidence of publication.

Edwin Lowther, Jr., Samuel Bird, Monticello, for appellant.

Brooks A. Gill, Dumas, for appellee.

BROWN, Justice.

The appellant, Wal-Mart Stores, Inc., appeals a jury verdict and judgment for slander in favor of the appellee, Carolyn Dolph, in the amount of $25,000. The sole issue raised on appeal is whether there was lack of sufficient proof of publication of the slander. We hold that there was substantial evidence of publication to support the judgment, and we affirm it.

The events leading to the complaint occurred on June 16, 1989, at the Wal–Mart

---

This is the same case as shown in Illustrations 2 & 4 as it appears in the *South Western Reporter 2d,* an unofficial set of court reports.

The prefatory statement and headnotes to the left in this Illustration are prepared by the publisher's editorial staff. Note that these are *not* the same as in the official *Arkansas Reports.*

Although the material preceding the opinion of the court may vary in the unofficial hard copy reports and computer-retrievable versions from that in the official reports, the text of the opinion itself is identical. [See Illustration 5.]

The differences between the official and unofficial reports, as well as other features of court reports, are further discussed in Chapters 4, 5, and 6.

See Appendix D for a list of states that have discontinued their official reports.

---

that she was not free to leave. McNeely then requested that Dolph come up to the office, but she refused and asked to see the manager. It turned out that McNeely was in error and that Dolph's sister—not

[Illustration 5]

LAST PAGE OF 825 S.W.2D 810, 812

812 Ark.   825 SOUTH WESTERN REPORTER, 2d SERIES

heavy customer traffic. There was further testimony by Dolph that she was sure people were listening to the argument between McNeely and her. She was on display in front of the whole store, Dolph stated, and was very embarrassed. Two Wal–Mart employees were specifically staring at her, Dolph testified, while McNeely was contacting the McGehee store and, then, hollering down at her for identification, and requesting that she come up to the office. We can make no clear distinction between this case and the foreign authorities cited above. The circumstances here were both sufficient to raise a reasonable inference of publication and also constitute substantial evidence to support the jury's verdict.

[3] Wal–Mart also raises a collateral hearsay issue relating to publication. At trial, Dolph testified that her sister's mother-in-law had been told by one of the Wal–Mart employees that Dolph had been caught shoplifting. The circuit court permitted the testimony into evidence but gave the following cautionary instruction:

However, I need to instruct you that in this particular case, the testimony of Ms. Dolph as to what someone else told her—and you heard the linkage of where it came from—is not being offered for the truth of what Ms. Dolph said was told to Ms. Dolph, but merely for the purpose of showing that she did, in fact, receive some information, whether true or not. And my instruction to you is, you are not to consider it as being given or stated here for the truth of what Ms. Dolph said, but merely to show that she heard something.

Wal–Mart argues that the circuit court erred in permitting what amounted to triple hearsay into evidence. We do not agree.

The Eighth Circuit Court of Appeals resolved a similar question in a libel case and held that the testimony in question was not hearsay. *See Luster v. Retail Credit Company*, 575 F.2d 609 (8th Cir.1978). In *Luster*, the plaintiff sued Retail Credit for a false statement made in a credit report which suggested arson on the plaintiff's premises. To prove publication, plaintiff used the testimony of a third-party insur-

ance agent who heard from a deceased agent that a Dallas insurance firm believed Retail Credit's report implied arson. A hearsay objection was made and rejected by the trial court which gave a limiting instruction at the time of the disputed testimony. The Eighth Circuit affirmed the trial court's ruling on the basis that the testimony was admitted solely to prove the fact that the words were said—not to prove that they were true.

The Eighth Circuit's reasoning in *Luster* is persuasive in this case which involves a comparable publication issue. Here, the testimony of the sister's mother-in-law about what the Wal–Mart employee said was not offered to prove the truth of what was said. It was offered to prove *the fact* that it was said, which then became some evidence of publication. The distinction is an important one, and we hold that the circuit court's ruling with the corollary instruction to the jury was appropriate in this case.

Affirmed.

DUDLEY, J., not participating.

> Compare this Illustration with Illustration 3. Note that all of page 433 of the *Arkansas Reports* (vol. 309) is contained on page 812 of the *South Western Reporter 2d* (vol. 825) and that the opinion in both sources is identical.

[Illustration 6]

TYPICAL STATUTORY PROVISIONS FOR PUBLICATION OF COURT REPORTS

Exerpt from West's Ann. Calif. Gov't Code

§ 68902. Publication of reports: Supervision by Supreme Court

Such opinions of the Supreme Court, of the courts of appeal, and of the appellate departments of the superior courts as the Supreme Court may deem expedient shall be published in the official reports. The reports shall be published under the general supervision of the Supreme Court.

Exerpts from McKinney's Consol. Laws of N.Y. Ann. Judiciary Law

§ 430. Law reporting bureau; state reporter

There is hereby created and established the law reporting bureau of the state of New York. The bureau shall be under the direction and control of a state reporter, who shall be appointed and be removable by the court of appeals by an order entered in its minutes. The state reporter shall be assisted by a first deputy state reporter and such other deputy state reporters and staff as may be necessary, all of whom shall be appointed and be removable by the court of appeals.

§ 431. Causes to be reported

The law reporting bureau shall report every cause determined in the court of appeals and every cause determined in the appellate divisions of the supreme court, unless otherwise directed by the court deciding the cause; and, in addition, any cause determined in any other court which the reporter, with the approval of the court of appeals, considers worthy of being reported because of its usefulness as a precedent or its importance as a matter of public interest.

Exerpt from Vernon's Ann. Mo. Stat.

§ 477.231. Designation of private publication as official reports

The supreme court may declare the published volumes of the decisions of the supreme court as the same are published by any person, firm or corporation, to be official reports of the decisions of the supreme court, and the courts of appeals may jointly make a similar declaration with respect to published volumes of the opinions of the courts of appeals. Any publication so designated as the official reports may include both the opinions of the supreme court and the courts of appeals in the same volume.

SECTION G. ABBREVIATIONS AND CITATIONS
OF COURT REPORTS

Court reports are published in numbered sets,[11] with the name of the set reflected in its title; for example, *Illinois Reports* (opinions of the Illinois Supreme Court) or *United States Reports* (opinions of the Supreme Court of the United States) or *Oil and Gas Reporter* (opinions from all U.S. jurisdictions dealing with the law of oil and gas). In all legal writing it is customary when referring to a court case to give both the name of the case and its citation in the appropriate court reports. But rather than citing to, for example, *Volume 132 of the Illinois Reports for the case starting at page 238,* a citation is given using a standard format and a standard abbreviation for the set of reports, *e.g.,* 132 Ill. 238, or 498 U.S. 103, or 18 Oil & Gas Rep. 1083.

It is extremely important in any legal writing to give a complete citation to the source or sources relied on in reaching one's conclusions. Tables of Abbreviations should be consulted for the proper method of abbreviation; and citation manuals for proper form of citation.[12]

To enable researchers to find and give citations to slip opinions and unreported cases, both WESTLAW and LEXIS provide a standard format for citation to recent cases and administrative decisions contained in their databases. These formats are called WESTLAW Cites and LEXIS Cites, respectively. In addition, WESTLAW includes in its online version of cases *star pagination* to the page numbers of cases appearing in West's *National Reporter System* and in the official *United States Reports.* Through a licensing agreement with West, LEXIS also has added *star pagination* to its databases for West's *National Reporter System.* *Star pagination* enables one to find where the language in the print version appears in the online version.

An extensive Table of Abbreviations with reference to the full name of court reports is set forth in J. Jacobstein, R. Mersky & D. Dunn, *Fundamentals of Legal Research,* Appendix A (6th ed.). Legal citation form is the subject of Chapter 21 of that text; computer-assisted legal research of that text describes computer-assisted legal research in detail.

---

[11] The first American cases were reported by private reporters and are cited to the name of the reporter. In Michigan, for example, the first volume of court reports was reported by Douglass and is cited as 1 Doug. The practice to citing to names or nominative reporters ceased in most jurisdictions during the middle of the nineteenth century.

[12] There is no universally accepted table of abbreviations or manual of citations. In addition to those abbreviations contained in Appendix A, tables of abbreviations may be located in law dictionaries and in other books on legal bibliography. The most widely used citation manual is *The Bluebook: A Uniform System of Citation* (15th ed. 1991), published by the Harvard Law Review Association, Columbia Law Review, University of Pennsylvania Law Review, and Yale Law Journal. Much newer is *The University of Chicago Manual of Legal Citation,* first published by Lawyers Cooperative Publishing and Mead Data Central, Inc. in 1989. This manual is often referred to as the "Maroon Book."

SECTION H. SUMMARY

To facilitate learning the essential features of the significant publications described in this and subsequent chapters, a summary is provided in the last section of some chapters. The summaries are generally arranged with the following points in mind: (1) scope—indicating coverage by subject matter and chronology, if any; (2) arrangements—for example, alphabetically by subject, by names or titles, or by chronology (following a time sequence); (3) index; and (4) supplementation.

1. Reporting of Court Cases

a. Court reports are compilations of judicial cases.

b. Most court reports contain only appellate court cases; trial court cases are rarely reported.

c. Court cases are available in both hard copy and computer-retrievable versions.

d. Not all appellate court cases that are decided are published.

2. Segments of a Court Case

a. Name of the case.

b. Citation.

c. Docket number.

d. Date of decision.

e. Prefatory statement—Synopsis, or summary, of the case.

f. Syllabus or headnote—brief summary of the legal rule or significant facts in a case.

g. Names of counsel.

h. Statement of facts.

i. Opinion or opinions and elements therein.

    (1) Opinion of the court—explanation of the court's decision written by a judge in the majority.

    (2) Concurring opinion—opinion that agrees with the decision of the majority but disagrees with the reasoning.

    (3) Plurality opinion—opinion where less than a majority join an opinion than any concurring opinion.

    (4) Dissent—expressed disagreement of one or more judges of a court with the decision reached by the majority.

    (5) Accord—opinion by a dissenting judge that agrees with the conclusions and results of the dissent, but not with its reasoning.

    (6) *Per curiam* opinion—opinion of the majority of the court as distinguished from an opinion written by a specific judge.

    (7) Memorandum opinion—a brief holding of the whole court in which the opinion (explanation) is very concise or totally absent.

(8) *Ratio decidendi*—the point in a case that determines the result.

(9) *Obiter dictum*—incidental comment made by a judge in his or her opinion, which is not necessary to the formulation of the decision nor binding as precedent.

j. Decision of the court—disposition of the case by the court.

3. Official and Unofficial Reports

a. Official reports—court reports authorized by statute or court rule.

b. Unofficial reports—court reports published without statutory authority or court direction, the most comprehensive of which being West's *National Reporter System.*

4. Elements of Judicial Reporting

a. *Slip opinion*—an individual court case published separately soon after it is decided.

b. Advance sheets—pamphlets that contain the most recently-decided cases by a court or the courts of several jurisdictions.

c. Order of release of cases is determined by their decision dates and not by other arrangements, such as subject.

d. A bound volume includes:

(1) Table of cases contained in the volume.

(2) Table of statutes interpreted in the cases reported in the volume.

(3) Cases cumulated from preceding advance sheets—written, *per curiam,* or memorandum.

(4) Subject index or digest of the cases reported.

(5) Judicial definitions of words and phrases used in the cases reported.

(6) Changes in court rules.

(7) A list of judges sitting on the court covered by the volume.

(8) Unofficial reports generally contain cross-reference tables to official reports and *star pagination* that show where pages in the official version appear in the unofficial version.

5. Organization of Court Reports

a. By jurisdiction. Cases of a specific court or several courts from the same state or jurisdiction and generally reported in chronological order.

b. By geography. Cases of the courts of adjacent states are reported in the same set of reports.

c. By subject. Cases only on a specific subject are included.

Chapter 4

FEDERAL COURT CASES

Section 1 of Article III of the Constitution of the United States provides that "The judicial Power of the United States, shall be vested in one supreme Court, and in such inferior Courts as the Congress may from time to time ordain and establish." Since the adoption of the Constitution in 1789, Congress has provided for various arrangements of the federal courts.[1]

Since 1880 the federal court system can be described as consisting of three main divisions: the Supreme Court of the United States (the highest court); the courts of appeals (intermediate courts); and the district courts (courts of original jurisdiction or trial courts).[2] [See Illustration 7 for a map of the lower federal courts.]

All written opinions of the Supreme Court of the United States are published in both official and unofficial reports. Most of its *per curiam* cases also are reported. All written opinions designated *for publication* by the courts of appeals are published in unofficial reports. Only selected cases of the federal district courts are reported unofficially. Unreported cases of the district courts generally are available through the court clerks, although the local court rules should be consulted before relying on any unreported cases as authority.

---

[1] CHARLES ALAN WRIGHT, THE LAW OF FEDERAL COURTS 1-8 (4th ed. 1983).

[2] For a description of the federal court system, see JAMES WILLIAM MOORE ET AL., MOORE'S FEDERAL PRACTICE §§ 0.1, 0.2 (2d ed. 1989) [hereinafter MOORE'S FEDERAL PRACTICE]. *See also* ERWIN C. SURRENCY, HISTORY OF THE FEDERAL COURTS (1987); ADMINISTRATIVE OFFICE OF THE UNITED STATES COURTS, THE UNITED STATES COURTS: THEIR JURISDICTION AND WORK (1989) [hereinafter THE UNITED STATES COURTS].

[Illustration 7]

GEOGRAPHICAL BOUNDARIES OF U.S. COURTS OF APPEALS AND U.S. DISTRICT COURTS
as set forth by 28 U.S.C. §§ 41, 81–131

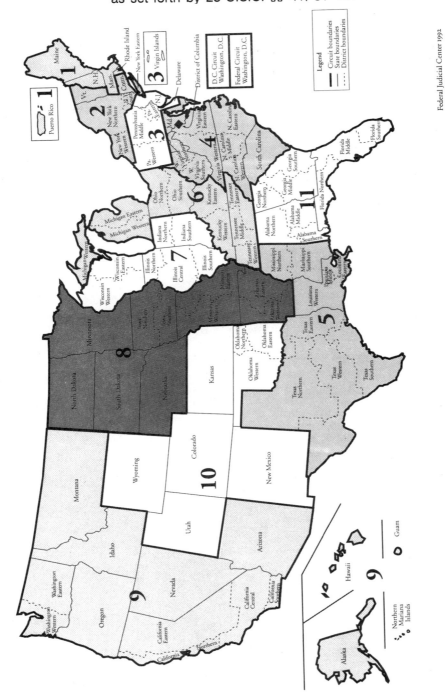

Federal Judicial Center 1992

SECTION A.   UNITED STATES SUPREME COURT REPORTS

Because of the preeminent role the Supreme Court of the United States holds in our system of jurisprudence, its discretion as to which cases it will review, and the significance of the limited cases it decides each year, access to the Court's cases is crucial. These cases are available in five current, printed sets and the two major computer-assisted legal research (CALR) services.

Bound reporters:

1. *United States Reports* (official edition) (Government Printing Office), cited *U.S.*

2. *West's Supreme Court Reporter* (West Publishing Company), cited *S. Ct.* or *Sup. Ct.*

3. *United States Supreme Court Reports, Lawyers' Edition* (Lawyers Cooperative Publishing), cited *L.Ed.* and *L.Ed.2d.*

Looseleaf Reporters:

4. *United States Law Week* (Bureau of National Affairs), cited *U.S.L.W.* or *U.S.L. Week.*

5. *U.S. Supreme Court Bulletin* (Commerce Clearing House), cited *S. Ct. Bull. (CCH).*

CALR Services:

6. WESTLAW (West Publishing Company), database identifier SCT for cases 1945 to date; SCT–OLD for cases 1790–1944.

7. LEXIS (Mead Data Central, Inc.), GENFED Library, US file.

1.   United States Reports (Official Edition)

The *United States Reports* are the official reports for cases decided by the Supreme Court of the United States. Prior to 1817, the *United States Reports* were published by private reporters. Since that date they have been published by official reporters.

The first 90 volumes are cited by the name of the individual ("reporter"), from Dallas through Wallace, who compiled the cases for publication. There were seven of these early reporters, and each time a new reporter was named the volume numbering began anew. Later, these volumes were renumbered consecutively from 1–90. Commencing with volume 91 (1875), the use of the name of the Reporter of Decisions of the Supreme Court for citation purposes was discontinued and consecutive numbering continued. 1 Dallas, although a volume of the *United States Reports,* contains only Pennsylvania cases. The other three volumes of Dallas contain both Supreme Court of the United States and Pennsylvania cases.[3] The seven early reporters, with their abbreviations and volumes and years of coverage, are as follows:

---

[3] Arthur John Keefe, *More Than You Want to Know About Supreme Court Reports,* 62 A.B.A. J. 1057 (1976). *See also* Craig Joyce, Wheaton v. Peters: *The Untold Story of the*

Dallas (Dall.)	4 v.	v. 1–4 U.S.	(1789–1800)
Cranch (Cranch)	9 v.	v. 5–13 U.S.	(1801–1815)
Wheaton (Wheat.)	12 v.	v. 14–25 U.S.	(1816–1827)
Peters (Pet.)	16 v.	v. 26–41 U.S.	(1828–1842)
Howard (How.)	24 v.	v. 42–65 U.S.	(1843–1860)
Black (Black)	2 v.	v. 66–67 U.S.	(1861–1862)
Wallace (Wall.)	23 v.	v. 68–90 U.S.	(1863–1874)

Until recently, it was the custom of the Supreme Court of the United States to have one term that started in October and ordinarily adjourned in June or July, with special terms held "whenever necessary." A rule, effective January 1, 1990, now requires the Court to "hold a continuous annual Term commencing on the first Monday in October."

The cases decided by the Supreme Court are officially printed and sold by the United States Government Printing Office and are issued in three formats. Initially, the cases are issued separately as *slip opinions*. Typically, each includes a syllabus and summary of facts prepared by the Reporter of Decisions, is individually paged, contains no index, and is subject to correction by the Court. These *slip opinions* are subsequently compiled, assigned a volume number, and published in consecutively-paged advance sheets known as *preliminary prints,* to which an index is added.

After two or three *preliminary prints* are published, which also are subject to correction, they are cumulated into a bound volume using the same volume and page numbers as in the *preliminary prints*. Three or four bound volumes are issued per term. Due to lengthy publication delays by the Government Printing Office, the bound volumes are usually two to three years behind schedule. As a result of the slower publication schedule for the *United States Reports,* and the editorial features in the unofficial reports discussed next, most researchers prefer the unofficial versions to the official one.

Sample pages from a case in the *United States Reports* are shown in Illustrations 8–11.

2. West's Supreme Court Reporter

This set, a unit of West's *National Reporter System,* reproduces verbatim the text of the opinion or opinions for each Supreme Court case. The publisher then adds the many editorial features common to its other sets of law reports, *e.g.,* syllabus, headnotes, topics, and key numbers. These various features are discussed in Chapters 5 and 6. *West's Supreme Court Reporter* begins with volume 106 (1882) of the

Early Reporters, 1985 SUP. CT. HIST. SOC'Y Y.B. 35. For a listing of the opinions by individual justices, see LINDA A. BLANDFORD & PATRICIA RUSSELL EVANS, SUPREME COURT OF THE UNITED STATES, 1789–1980: AN INDEX TO OPINIONS ARRANGED BY JUSTICE (1983). This two-volume set and a 1994 supplement lists opinions of all justices from October 1980 through 1990.

official set; therefore, it does not contain the cases reported in volumes 1–105 of the official reports.

Cases are first issued in advance sheets biweekly while the Court is in session and then compiled into interim volumes while the Court is making final corrections in its opinions. Once the corrections are made, these interim volumes are replaced by three bound, permanent volumes containing all the cases of the term.[4] The volume and page numbers used in the advance sheets and the interim volumes are the same as in the later permanent volumes. Because this set uses smaller type than is used in the official reports, two or three volumes of official reports are contained in one volume of *West's Supreme Court Reporter*.

Sample pages from *West's Supreme Court Reporter* are shown in Illustrations 12–14.

3. United States Supreme Court Reports, Lawyers' Edition

This set is privately published by Lawyers Cooperative Publishing and is in two series. The first series, which covers 1 U.S. through 351 U.S. (1789–1956), is in 100 volumes; the second series, which restarts its numbering with volume one, commences coverage with 350 U.S. (1956). Current cases are published twice a month in advance sheets while the Court is in session. The volume number and pagination of the advance sheets are the same as in subsequent bound volumes.

Until volume 78 of *Lawyers' Edition 2d*, two to three volumes of the official reports were in one volume of the unofficial set. The publisher then began to issue a single bound volume each time a volume of the official set was completed in advance sheet form. Both series reprint the opinions and syllabi in the *United States Reports*. These are supplemented with the editorial treatment given the cases by the publisher, including its own summary of cases and headnotes that precede the opinions.

In addition, and for selected important cases only, summaries of attorneys' briefs submitted to the Court and annotations written by the publisher's editorial staff are included in an appendix to each bound volume. Advance sheets do not contain annotations. Annotations are articles or essays on significant legal issues discussed in the reported cases. These are very useful in gaining an understanding of the impact and meaning of the cases. An increase in the number of annotations per volume occurred with volume 93 of the first series of *Lawyers' Edition*. Annotations are discussed in more detail in Chapter 7.

[4] Through volume 79 of *West's Supreme Court Reporter,* the volumes of the *United States Reports* covering a Term of the Court could be published in one volume of the West version. As the Court's opinions lengthened, commencing with the October 1959 Term, West began publishing the coverage of a Term in two books, *e.g.,* volumes 80 and 80A. Commencing with the October 1985 Term, coverage expanded to three books, *e.g.,* volumes 106, 106A, and 106B, owing in great part to the separate concurring and dissenting opinions issued by the justices.

A two-volume *Later Case Service* for volumes 1–31 of *Lawyers' Edition 2d*, updated with annual, cumulative pocket supplements, provides later cases relevant to the annotations in these 31 volumes. Beginning with volume 32, each volume of *Lawyers' Edition 2d* is updated with an annual pocket supplement in the back of each volume.

This supplement is in three parts: (1) *Citator Service*, consisting of brief summaries of the pertinent holdings from Supreme Court opinions subsequent to those reported in the volume; (2) *Later Case Service*, supplementing the annotations in the volume; and (3) *Court Corrections*, consisting of any corrections made by the Court after the bound *Lawyers' Edition* volumes were published. Since *Lawyers' Edition 2d* is prepared from the *preliminary prints* and not the final, bound *United States Reports*, the text of the opinions in this set may not be identical to the official version. Reference to the *Court Corrections* section is, therefore, essential.

A six-volume *General Index* (also published as part of *United States Supreme Court Digest, Lawyers' Edition* discussed in Chapter 6) provides a comprehensive topical index to cases decided by the Supreme Court of the United States. This index also includes a Table of Justices, statutory table, and a history table of past annotations. An annual *Quick Case Table* pamphlet contains an alphabetically-arranged table of cases for all the Court's decisions accompanied by opinions. It also includes references to annotations in *Lawyers' Edition 2d* [5] and the various *A.L.R.* series.

Sample pages from the *United States Supreme Court Reports, Lawyers' Edition 2d* are shown in Illustrations 15–19.

4. Looseleaf Reporters

Because cases decided by the Supreme Court of the United States are *the law of the land* and must be followed as precedent by all other American courts, both federal and state, it is obvious that lawyers, as well as lay persons, need immediate access to the Court's most recently-decided cases. Before cases can be published in the advance sheets mentioned previously, they must receive editorial treatment, such as preparation of the summary and the headnotes and then await enough cases to constitute a pamphlet, resulting in a delay of several weeks from the date a case is decided until it appears in an advance sheet.

More rapid access to current Supreme Court of the United States cases is available through the two looseleaf publications discussed below. The publishers receive the slip opinions on the day they are handed down, reproduce them, and mail them promptly to subscribers. These Supreme Court cases have few editorial features added to them, but they do allow cases to become available within a week or less after they are released by the Court and are most helpful for use during the current

---

[5] The *ALR Index*, discussed in Chapter 7, also indexes these annotations.

term. For older cases, it is preferable to use one of the three other sets previously discussed.

a. *United States Law Week.* This set, published by the Bureau of National Affairs, consists of two looseleaf binders—"Supreme Court Sections" and "General Law Sections." The Supreme Court Sections binder contains the complete text of all cases decided by the Supreme Court of the United States during its current term. In addition, this binder contains numerous other valuable features, although each feature is not necessarily in each issue published. These are:

(1) Summary of Orders: A summary of cases acted upon, as well as the lower court holdings that the Supreme Court consented to review, together with the questions presented for review by those cases.

(2) Journal of Proceedings: The minutes of all sessions of the Court held during the week.

(3) Cases Docketed: Includes citations to cases decided in the lower courts and to be heard by the Supreme Court, and the general subject matter of the cases.

(4) Summary of Cases Recently Filed.

(5) Hearings Scheduled: Includes docket number, caption, and brief statement of issues presented.

(6) Arguments Before the Court: A summary of the oral arguments of the more important cases argued each week.

(7) Table of Cases and the Case Status Report: Issued every three to four weeks. For most cases the user can determine the status of a case by consulting this table.

(8) Topical Index: Published at the outset of the Court's term and cumulated at frequent intervals, with a final cumulative index published shortly after the Court's last session of the term.

(9) Review of the Supreme Court's Term: A series of topical articles briefly summarizing and analyzing the most significant Court cases decided during the term and issued after the Court has completed its work for the term.

The "General Law Sections" deal with matters not connected with the Supreme Court of the United States. Included are the text of the more important recent federal statutes, a summary of federal legal trends, and accounts of significant lower federal court cases, federal agency rulings, and state cases. A topical index for materials in this binder is also provided.

b. *U.S. Supreme Court Bulletin.* This set, published by Commerce Clearing House, is also in looseleaf format. In addition to copies of the current cases, it includes an index to cases by case name, an index by docket numbers, and a status table of cases pending before the Court.

5. Electronic Access to Opinions

Both WESTLAW and LEXIS provide computerized access to the text of cases decided by the Supreme Court of the United States much faster than any of the publications discussed previously. The text of each case decided by the Court is transmitted electronically from the Court to these two information vendors almost simultaneously with the decision being announced from the bench. These cases frequently are available in these online sources within a day, and typically within a few hours, after being decided.

Later, when the *United States Reports* and *West's Supreme Court Reporter* are published, both vendors add *star pagination* to the text of the opinions in order for users to locate where the exact pages of these reporters appear on the screen. WESTLAW and LEXIS both provide comprehensive coverage dating from the Court's first term in 1790 to the present. In addition, *West's Supreme Court Reporter*, a part of the West CD-ROM Libraries family, covers from 1789 forward by including both the official *United States Reports* (volumes 1–105) and the complete *West's Supreme Court Reporter*.

Project Hermes, a project begun by the Supreme Court of the United States in 1990, transmits opinions to WESTLAW and LEXIS, wire services, and an educational consortium simultaneous with issuance of the opinion from the bench. As a result of the consortium arrangement, these Supreme Court cases are available through the Internet.

6. Chambers Opinions of the Supreme Court Justices

Each Supreme Court Justice is assigned at the beginning of each term the supervision of one or more federal judicial circuits. Frequently, when the Supreme Court is not in session, a petition may be directed to a Justice in his or her capacity as Circuit Justice. An opinion resulting from such a petition is known as a *Chamber Opinion*. Before the 1970 Term, these chambers opinions appeared only in *Lawyers' Edition* and *West's Supreme Court Reporter*. Starting with the 1970 Term, they also appear in the official *United States Reports*.[6] They are included as well in the two looseleaf reporters and the online services.

7. Preview of United States Supreme Court Cases

The *Preview of United States Supreme Court Cases*, published by the American Bar Association's Public Education Division, is not a reporter, but rather is composed of essays written by scholars on selected cases pending on the Court's calendar, but not yet argued. These essays provide excellent background and analysis of the cases the Court subsequently will decide.

---

[6] ROBERT L. STERN ET AL., SUPREME COURT PRACTICE 647–48 (7th ed. 1993) [hereinafter SUPREME COURT PRACTICE]. *See also* Frederick Bernays Wiener, *Opinions of Justices Sitting in Chambers*, 49 LAW LIBR. J. 2 (1956); Marian Boner, *Index to Chambers Opinions of Supreme Court Justices*, 65 LAW LIBR. J. 213 (1972).

8. Citing United States Supreme Court Cases

Proper citation practice calls for citing only to *United States Reports* after these are published. Therefore, the unofficial reporters, *West's Supreme Court Reporter* and *United States Supreme Court Reports, Lawyers' Edition,* which have their own distinct pagination, also show the pagination of the official reports in order for the proper citation to be made to the *United States Reports.* Like that used by the online services, this is known as *star pagination.* [See Illustration 17.] Both *West's Supreme Court Reporter* and *Lawyers' Edition* include in each volume a cross-reference table listing the cases in the *United States Reports* and showing where they are reported in their volumes.

SECTION B. LOWER FEDERAL COURT REPORTS

Although the Supreme Court of the United States is our country's highest court, it deals with only a small fraction of the total litigation within the federal court system. With certain exceptions, the Supreme Court selects only the cases it wishes to hear on appeal,[7] and these are relatively few in number. The bulk of the work of the federal courts occurs in the trial courts, *i.e.,* the federal district courts, and in the appeals from them to the United States courts of appeals. These appellate courts are divided geographically into twelve circuits, plus the United States Court of Appeals for the Federal Circuit. Each state and U.S. territory has one or more federal district courts. [See Illustration 7.]

In addition, there are federal courts with limited or specialized jurisdictions. The more important of these are the United States Court of Federal Claims,[8] the United States Court of Appeals Court for the Federal Circuit (mentioned above),[9] and the United States Tax Court.[10]

1. Privately Published Editions of the Lower Federal Court Reports

Only a few sets of official reports are published for lower federal court cases, and these are for specialized courts only. No official reports are published exclusively for cases of the federal district courts and the United States courts of appeals. West Publishing Company assumed the

[7] Technically, cases reach the Supreme Court either by writ of *certiorari* or by appeal. *See* SUPREME COURT PRACTICE, *supra* note 6.

[8] This court, originally named the United States Claims Court, was created by the Federal Courts Improvement Act of 1982, Pub. L. No. 97–164, 96 Stat. 25, effective on October 1, 1982. The United States Claims Court was renamed the United States Court of Federal Claims, as a result of certain provisions of the Federal Courts Administration Act of 1992, Pub. L. No. 102–572, 106 Stat. 4506, effective October 29, 1992.

[9] This court was created by Pub. L. No. 97–164, 96 Stat. 25, effective on October 1, 1982. It is a merger of the Court of U.S. Customs and Patent Appeals and the appellate division of the U.S. Court of Claims. For additional information on this court, see THE UNITED STATES COURT OF APPEALS FOR THE FEDERAL CIRCUIT: A HISTORY 1982–1990 (1991).

[10] For a more detailed description of specialized federal courts, see THE UNITED STATES COURTS, *supra* note 2; MOORE'S FEDERAL PRACTICE §§ 0.1, 0.2, *supra* note 2.

responsibility for publishing cases decided by these courts, primarily through the federal units of its *National Reporter System,* and until the arrival of CALR systems, West's reporters were the only comprehensive sources for these cases. These various West publications are discussed in this section. Additional information as to coverage is provided in Appendix E.

a. *Federal Cases.* Prior to 1880 and the development of the *National Reporter System,* the cases decided by the district courts and the circuit courts of appeals were published in many different sets of law reports. In the mid–1890s, West reprinted all previously reported lower federal court cases in one set of 31 volumes called *Federal Cases.* This set contains 18,313 cases reported between 1789 and 1879, accompanied by brief notes (annotations) to the cases. Unlike most sets of court reports, where the cases are arranged chronologically, the cases in this set are arranged alphabetically by case name and are numbered consecutively. Cases are cited by number. Volume 31 is the Digest volume and includes Blue Tables that cross reference from the citations of the original volumes of reports to *Federal Cases.*

Approximately 15 years before the compilation of *Federal Cases,* West commenced publication of its *National Reporter System,* which has grown to several units over the years. The features of these various units include the use of topic and key numbers and the issuance of cases first in advance sheets that are later cumulated into bound volumes that have the same volume and page numbers as the advance sheets. The remaining portions of this Section B–1 detail the content of the various federal units and an alerting service valuable for most recent case information. Broad discussion of the uses of and features in the *National Reporter System* are discussed in Chapter 5.

b. *Federal Reporter.* The *Federal Reporter* began in 1880. Although the *Federal Reporter* has contained cases from various federal courts over the years, it is most important to remember that it contains the cases of the United States Courts of Appeals (formerly the U.S. Circuit Courts of Appeals) from their organization in 1891, federal district court cases until 1932 when the *Federal Supplement* was started, and the Temporary Emergency Court of Appeals since 1972. Cases from other federal courts that have since been abolished or reorganized are also included in the *Federal Reporter,* namely the United States Circuit Court, Commerce Court of the United States, United States Emergency Court of Appeals, the United States Court of Claims, and the United States Court of Customs and Patents Appeals.[11]

The *Federal Reporter* is in three series. The First Series stopped with Volume 300 in 1924. The Second Series, consisting of volumes 1–

---

[11] Cases from the United States Court of Customs and Patents Appeals were reported in the *Federal Reporter,* beginning with volume 34 of the Second Series, until the court was abolished October 1, 1982. The function of that court, as well as that of the appellate division of the former United States Court of Claims, was transferred to the United States Court of Appeals for the Federal Circuit, whose cases are included in the *Federal Reporter.* *See supra* note 9 for additional information pertaining to this particular court.

999, covers cases reported in 1924 and continues coverage into 1993. The Third Series began in the fall of 1993.[12]

Under current practice, only those cases that are ordered to be published by the federal courts of appeals are included in the *Federal Reporter 2d* and *3d*. All of these courts have rules restricting the number of published cases.[13] To let researchers know the cases that were decided without written published opinions, the *Federal Reporter 2d* and *3d* periodically contain a list of *Decisions without Published Opinions*. [See Illustration 20.]

c. *Federal Supplement.* This set began in 1932 when West decided to cease including the federal district court cases and United States Court of Claims cases (from Volumes 1 to 181) in the *Federal Reporter* and to include them in this additional reporter. Coverage of United States Court of Claims cases returned to the *Federal Reporter* in 1960.

Since these are the trial courts within the federal court system, the cases reported in the *Federal Supplement* are exceptions to the general rule that only appellate court cases are reported. It must be emphasized, however, that only a very small percentage of the cases heard in the federal district courts are ever reported in the *Federal Supplement*. The decision whether or not to publish is made by the judge writing the opinion.

The *Federal Supplement,* in addition to its federal district court coverage, also reports cases of the United States Court of International Trade since 1980, from the United States Customs Court from 1956 to 1980 when it was replaced by the United States Court of International Trade, the Special Court under the Regional Rail Reorganization Act of 1973, and the Judicial Panel on Multidistrict Litigation since its inception in 1969.

Some cases not reported in the *Federal Supplement* may be printed in the subject reporters of other publications (discussed in Chapter 13) or may be available online.

---

[12] West provided very little by way of explanation as to why a *Federal Reporter 3d* started after almost seventy years and volume 999 of *Federal Reporter 2d*, other than to say it was "to avoid potential confusion that could arise from a four-digit case volume citation." Matthew Goldstein, *68 Years, 999 Volumes of F.2d End as New Era of F.3d Begins,* N.Y. L.J., October 14, 1993, at 1. No change in format or coverage occurred in this new series. Obviously, having volume numbers that are less than four digits in length saves, over an extended period of time, a tremendous amount of space in both printed citations and electronic storage.

[13] For discussion of these policies, see David Dunn, Note, *Unreported Decisions in the United States Courts of Appeals,* 63 Cornell L. Rev. 128 (1977); William L. Reynolds & William M. Richman, *The Non–Precedential Precedent—Limited Publication and No–Citation Rules in the United States Courts of Appeals,* 78 Colum. L. Rev. 1167 (1978); William L. Reynolds & William M. Richman, *An Evaluation of Limited Publication in the United States Courts of Appeals: The Price of Reform,* 48 U. Chi. L. Rev. 573 (1981); Donald R. Songer, *Criteria for Publication of Opinions in the U.S. Courts of Appeals: Formal Rules Versus Empirical Reality,* 73 Judicature 307 (1990). *See also supra* Chapter 3, notes 3 and 4.

d. *Federal Rules Decisions.* This set contains cases of the federal district courts since 1939 that construe the Federal Rules of Civil Procedure and cases since 1946 decided under the Rules of Criminal Procedure. These cases are not published in the *Federal Supplement.* Similar to other units of the *National Reporter System, F.R.D.* is issued in advance sheets and bound volumes, with headnotes that are classified to West's *Key Number System.* In addition to court cases, it also includes articles on various aspects of federal courts and federal procedure. A cumulative index to these articles is in every tenth volume, and a consolidated index for volumes 1–122 is in volume 122.

e. *Military Justice Reporter.* This set, which began in 1975, is the successor to the U.S. Court of Military Appeals *Decisions* and the *Court-Martial Reports* (1951–1975) by other publishers. This reporter includes cases of the United States Court of Military Appeals and the Courts of Military Review of the Army, Navy–Marine Corps, Air Force, and Coast Guard.

f. *Bankruptcy Reporter.* This set began in 1980 as a result of major changes in the bankruptcy laws enacted in 1978.[14] It reports cases from the United States Bankruptcy Courts and those cases from the federal district courts that deal with bankruptcy matters, no longer including these in the *Federal Supplement.* The *Bankruptcy Reporter* also reprints bankruptcy cases appearing in *West's Supreme Court Reporter* and *Federal Reporter 2d* and *3d,* retaining the paginations of these reporters.

g. *Federal Claims Reporter.* This set is a continuation of the *United States Claims Court Reporter,* which began in 1983 as a reporter of cases of the United States Claims Court, a trial-level federal court created in 1982. When the name of the United States Claims Court was changed to the United States Court of Federal Claims in 1992,[15] the *United States Claims Court Reporter* was renamed the *Federal Claims Reporter,* commencing with volume 27. This reporter also includes reprints from the *Federal Reporter 2d* and *3d* and *West's Supreme Court Reporter* of those cases that have reviewed cases of the United States Claims Court.

h. *West's Veterans Appeals Reporter.* Begun in October 1991, this set contains cases decided in the United States Court of Veterans Appeals [16] and cases of the United States Court of Appeals, Federal Circuit and the Supreme Court of the United States, which hear appeals from the decisions of the Court of Veterans Appeals.

i. *West's Federal Case News.* This is a weekly pamphlet, not a reporter, that summarizes recently-decided federal cases even before they are published in advance sheets. This alerting service includes the

---

[14] Bankruptcy Reform Act of 1978, Pub. L. No. 95–598, 92 Stat. 2549.

[15] *See supra* note 8.

[16] Veterans' Judicial Review Act of 1988, Pub. L. No. 100–687, 102 Stat. 4105. *See* Laurence R. Helfer, *The Politics of Judicial Structure: Creating the United States Court of Veterans Appeals,* 25 CONN. L. REV. 155 (1992).

case name, court, judge deciding the case, filing date, docket number, and the essential points of the case.

2. Officially Published Reports of Special Federal Courts

Cases Decided in the United States Court of Claims. Washington, Government Printing Office, 1863–1982. v. 1–231.

United States Court of International Trade Reports. Washington, Government Printing Office, 1980 to date. v. 1 *et seq.* This court was formerly the United States Customs Court, and its cases were reported in *United States Custom Court Reports,* 1938–1980, v. 1–85.

Reports of the United States Tax Court. Washington, Government Printing Office, Oct. 1942 to date. v. 1 *et seq.*

Cases Decided in the United States Court of Appeals for the Federal Circuit. Washington, Government Printing Office, 1982 to date. v. 1 *et seq.*

3. Electronic Access

Both WESTLAW and LEXIS provide comprehensive, full-text coverage of published federal cases, including those of the various specialized federal courts. These cases are being made available online with ever-increasing speed, and always prior to their publication in advance sheets. In addition, these two services include many cases found in looseleaf services and other publications but that may never be published in a West reporter. For these cases, the two services note at the start of the online version that this case may not be appropriate to rely on as authority.

In mid–1993, all federal courts of appeals began offering electronic public access via a bulletin board to their slip opinions through a system known either as Appellate Court Electronic Services (ACES) or Electronic Dissemination of Opinions System (EDOS).

SECTION C.   ILLUSTRATIONS

The case of *Peel v. Attorney Registration and Disciplinary Comm'n* [496 U.S. 91, 110 S. Ct. 2281, 110 L. Ed. 2d 83 (1990)] as it is published in:

8–11.   Advance Sheets (Preliminary Print) of the United States Reports (Official)

12–14.   Volume 110 of West's Supreme Court Reporter, interim volume

15–19.   Volume 110 of United States Supreme Court Reports, Lawyers' Edition, 2d Series (Lawyers Cooperative Publishing)

20.   Page from Federal Reporter, 2d Series

[Illustration 8]

PEEL V. ATTORNEY REGISTRATION AND DISCIPLINARY COMM'N AS REPORTED IN THE ADVANCE SHEETS OF THE UNITED STATES REPORTS 496 U.S. 91

PEEL *v.* ATTORNEY DISCIPLINARY COMM'N OF ILL.   91

Syllabus

PEEL *v.* ATTORNEY REGISTRATION AND DISCIPLINARY COMMISSION OF ILLINOIS

CERTIORARI TO THE SUPREME COURT OF ILLINOIS

No. 88–1775.   Argued January 17, 1990—Decided June 4, 1990

Petitioner Peel is licensed to practice law in Illinois and other States.   He also has a "Certificate in Civil Trial Advocacy" from the National Board of Trial Advocacy (NBTA), which offers periodic certification to applicants who meet exacting standards of experience and competence in trial work.   The Administrator of respondent Attorney Registration and Disciplinary Commission of Illinois filed a complaint alleging that Peel, by using a professional letterhead that stated his name, followed by the indented notation "Certified Civil Trial Specialist By the [NBTA]" and the unindented notation "Licensed: Illinois, Missouri, Arizona," was, *inter alia*, holding himself out as a certified legal specialist in violation of Rule 2–105(a)(3) of the Illinois Code of Professional Responsibility.   The Commission recommended censure.   The State Supreme Court adopted the Commission's recommendation, concluding that the First Amendment did not protect the letterhead because the public could confuse the State and NBTA as the sources of his license to practice and of his certification, and because the certification could be read as a claim of superior quality.

Held: The judgment is reversed, and the case is remanded.

126 Ill. 2d 397, 534 N. E. 2d 980, reversed and remanded.

JUSTICE STEVENS, joined by JUSTICE BRENNAN, JUSTICE BLACKMUN, and JUSTICE KENNEDY, concluded that a lawyer has a constitutional right, under the standards applicable to commercial speech, to advertise his or her certification as a trial specialist by NBTA.   Pp. 99–111.

(a) Truthful advertising related to lawful activities is entitled to First

---

This page is taken from the *Preliminary Prints* (advance sheets) to the *United States Reports*. As customary, indication is given to the court from which the case is being appealed.

Note that docket number, date of argument, and date of decision are also given.

---

no finding of actual deception or misunderstanding.   The state court's focus on the implied "claim" as to the "quality" of Peel's legal services confuses the distinction between statements of opinion or quality and statements of objective facts that may support an inference of quality. Even if NBTA standards are not well known, there is no evidence that

[Illustration 9]

SAMPLE PAGE FROM 496 U.S.

92　　　　　　　　OCTOBER TERM, 1989

Syllabus　　　　　496 U. S.

consumers, such as those in States with certification plans, are misled if they do not inform themselves of the precise standards of certification. There also has been no finding, and there is no basis for the belief, that Peel's representation generally would be associated with governmental action. The public understands that licenses are issued by governmental authorities and that many certificates are issued by private organizations, and it is unlikely that the public necessarily would confuse certification as a "specialist" by a national organization with formal state recognition. Moreover, other States that have evaluated lawyers' advertisements of NBTA certifications have concluded that they were not misleading and were protected by the First Amendment. Pp. 100–106.

(c) The State's interest in avoiding any potential that Peel's statements might mislead is insufficient to justify a categorical ban on their use; nor does the State Supreme Court's inherent authority to supervise its own bar insulate its judgment from this Court's review for constitutional infirmity. The need for a complete prophylactic rule against any

---

Each case is preceded by a summary and syllabus prepared by the Reporter of Decisions. See also previous Illustration.

Rule 2–105(a). Such information facilitates the consumer's access to legal services and better serves the administration of justice. To the extent that such statements could confuse consumers, the State might consider screening certifying organizations or requiring a disclaimer about the certifying organization or the standards of a specialty. Pp. 106–111.

JUSTICE MARSHALL, joined by JUSTICE BRENNAN, agreeing that the State may not prohibit Peel from holding himself out as a certified NBTA trial specialist because the letterhead is neither actually nor inherently misleading, concluded that the letterhead is potentially misleading and thus the State may enact regulations other than a total ban to ensure that the public is not misled by such representations. The letterhead is potentially misleading because NBTA's name could give the impression to nonlawyers that the organization is a federal governmental agency; the juxtaposition of the references to Peel's state licenses to practice law and to his certification by the NBTA may lead individuals to believe that the NBTA is somehow sanctioned by the States; and the reference to NBTA certification may cause people to think that Peel is necessarily a better trial lawyer than attorneys without certification, because facts as well as opinions may be misleading when they are presented without adequate information. A State could require a lawyer to provide additional information in order to prevent a claim of NBTA certification from being misleading. A State may require, for example, that the letterhead include a disclaimer stating that the NBTA is a private organization not affiliated with or sanctioned by the State or Federal Government, or

[Illustration 10]

SAMPLE PAGE FROM 496 U.S.

PEEL *v.* ATTORNEY DISCIPLINARY COMM'N OF ILL.   93

Opinion of STEVENS, J.

information about NBTA's requirements for certification so that any inferences drawn by consumers about the certified attorney's qualifications would be based on more complete knowledge of the meaning of NBTA certification.   Each State may decide for itself, within First Amendment constraints, how best to prevent such claims from being misleading.   Pp. 111–117.

STEVENS, J., announced the judgment of the Court and delivered an opinion, in which BRENNAN, BLACKMUN, and KENNEDY, JJ., joined. MARSHALL, J., filed an opinion concurring in the judgment, in which BRENNAN, J., joined, *post*, p. 111.   WHITE, J., filed a dissenting opinion, *post*, p. 118.   O'CONNOR, J., filed a dissenting opinion, in which REHNQUIST, C. J., and SCALIA, J., joined, *post*, p. 119.

Bruce J. Ennis, Jr., argued the cause and filed briefs for petitioner.

Stephen J. Marzen argued the cause for the Federal Trade Commission as *amicus curiae* urging reversal.   With him on the brief were *Solicitor General Starr, Assistant Attorney General Rill, Deputy Solicitor General Merrill, Kevin J. Arquit, Jay C. Shaffer,* and *Ernest J. Isenstadt.*

William F. Moran III argued the cause for respondent. With him on the brief was *James J. Grogan.* *

JUSTICE STEVENS announced the judgment of the Court and delivered an opinion, in which JUSTICE BRENNAN, JUSTICE BLACKMUN, and JUSTICE KENNEDY join.

The Illinois Supreme Court publicly censured petitioner because his letterhead states that he is certified as a civil trial specialist by the National Board of Trial Advocacy.   We

---

*Briefs of *amici curiae* urging reversal were filed for the American Advertising Federation, Inc., by *Philip B. Kurland* and *Alan S. Madans;* for the Association of National Advertisers, Inc., by *Burt Neuborne;* for the Association of Trial Lawyers of America et al. by *Jeffrey Robert White* and

---

This is the third page of the *Peel* case.   Note the indication as to which Justice wrote the majority opinion, which Justices joined the opinion, which Justices concurred, and which Justices dissented.

Note also how the names of the attorneys who were involved in the case before the Supreme Court of the United States are given.

[Illustration 11]

SAMPLE PAGE FROM 496 U.S.

118   OCTOBER TERM, 1989

WHITE, J., dissenting   496 U. S.

JUSTICE WHITE, dissenting.

I agree with JUSTICE MARSHALL that petitioner's letter-head is potentially misleading and with the reasons he gives for this conclusion.   Thus, there are four Justices—JUSTICE STEVENS and the three Justices joining his opinion—who believe that the First Amendment protects the letterhead as it is and that the State may not forbid its circulation.   But there are five Justices who believe that this particular letter-head is unprotected: JUSTICE O'CONNOR, THE CHIEF JUSTICE, and JUSTICE SCALIA believe the letterhead is inherently misleading and hence would uphold Rule 2–105(a)(3) of the Illinois Code of Professional Responsibility; at least two of us—JUSTICE MARSHALL and myself—find it potentially misleading and would permit the State to ban such letter-heads but only if they are not accompanied by disclaimers appropriate to avoid the danger.   This letterhead does not carry such a disclaimer.   The upshot is that while the State

> **First page of the dissenting opinion.**

affirm, rather than to reverse, the judgment below.

To reverse is to leave petitioner free to circulate his letter-head, not because it is protected under the First Amendment—indeed, it is not—but because five Justices refuse to enforce the Rule even as applied, leaving the State powerless to act unless it drafts a narrower rule that will survive scrutiny under the First Amendment.   This is nothing less than a

---

possibility that people would be misled.   Cf. *Zauderer* v. *Office of Disciplinary Counsel of Supreme Court of Ohio*, 471 U. S. 626, 663–664 (1985) (BRENNAN, J., concurring in part, concurring in judgment in part, and dissenting in part) ("[C]ompelling the publication of detailed fee information that would fill far more space than the advertisement itself . . . would chill the publication of protected commercial speech and would be entirely out of proportion to the State's legitimate interest in preventing potential deception").

[Illustration 12]

PEEL V. ATTORNEY REGISTRATION AND DISCIPLINARY COMM'N AS REPORTED IN 110 S. Ct. 2281 INTERIM VOLUME

PEEL v. ATTORNEY REG. & DISCIPLINARY COM'N **2281**
Cite as 110 S.Ct. 2281 (1990)

should be able to recover under any other law after the time for filing under § 210 has expired. The District Court reasoned, and respondent agrees, that if a state-law remedy is available after the time for filing a § 210 complaint has run, a whistleblower will have less incentive to bring a § 210 complaint. As a result, the argument runs, federal regulatory agencies will remain unaware of some safety violations and retaliatory behavior, and will thus be unable to ensure radiological safety at nuclear facilities. We cannot deny that there is some force to this argument, but we do not believe that the problem is as great as respondent suggests.

> This the first page of the *Peel* case as it appears in *West's Supreme Court Reporter*, an unofficial set. The summary is prepared by its editors.

ployee invokes the remedial provisions of § 210. Also, we are not so sure as respondent seems to be that employees will forgo their § 210 options and rely solely on state remedies for retaliation. Such a prospect is simply too speculative a basis on which to rest a finding of pre-emption. The Court has observed repeatedly that pre-emption is ordinarily not to be implied absent an "actual conflict." See, *e.g., Savage v. Jones,* 225 U.S. 501, 533, 32 S.Ct. 715, 725, 56 L.Ed. 1182 (1912). The "teaching of this Court's decisions ... enjoin[s] seeking out conflicts between state and federal regulation where none clearly exists." *Huron Cement Co. v. Detroit,* 362 U.S. 440, 446, 80 S.Ct. 813, 817, 4 L.Ed.2d 852 (1960).

III

We conclude that petitioner's claim for intentional infliction of emotional distress does not fall within the pre-empted field of nuclear safety as that field has been defined in prior cases. Nor does it conflict with any particular aspect of § 210. The contrary judgment of the Court of Appeals is reversed, and the case is remanded for

110B S.Ct.—3

further proceedings consistent with this opinion.

It is so ordered.

KEY NUMBER SYSTEM

Gary E. PEEL, Petitioner,

v.

ATTORNEY REGISTRATION AND DISCIPLINARY COMMISSION OF ILLINOIS.

No. 88–1775.

Argued Jan. 17, 1990.

Decided June 4, 1990.

Disciplinary proceedings were brought against attorney for violation of rule prohibiting attorney from holding himself out as specialist other than in fields of admiralty, trademark and patent law. The Supreme Court, Ryan, J., 126 Ill.2d 397, 128 Ill.Dec. 535, 534 N.E.2d 980, held that advertising rule did not violate attorney's First Amendment rights and imposed sanction. Attorney petitioned for writ of certiorari. The Supreme Court, Justice Stevens, held that attorney had First Amendment right, under standards applicable to commercial speech, to advertise certification as trial specialist by National Board of Trial Advocacy (NBTA).

Reversed and remanded.

Justice Marshall concurred in judgment and filed opinion, in which Justice Brennan joined.

Justice White dissented and filed opinion.

Justice O'Connor dissented and filed opinion, in which Chief Justice Rehnquist and Justice Scalia joined.

[Illustration 13]

SAMPLE PAGE FROM 110 S. Ct.

2282   **110 SUPREME COURT REPORTER**

1. Attorney and Client ⟳32(9)
  Constitutional Law ⟳90.2
  Attorney has First Amendment right, under standards applicable to commercial speech, to advertise certification as trial specialist by National Board of Trial Advocacy (NBTA), for which he cannot be disciplined. U.S.C.A. Const.Amend. 1; Code of Prof.Resp., DR 2–101(b), DR 2–105(a)(3), Ill.Rev.Stat.1989, ch. 110A, foll. ¶ 776.

2. Attorney and Client ⟳32(9)
  Truthful statement on attorney's letterhead, that he had been certified as trial specialist by National Board of Trial Advocacy (NBTA), was not actually or inherently misleading, in state which lacked its own certification program, as falsely suggesting that attorney had been recognized as specialist by state. (Per Justice Stevens, with three Justices concurring and one Justice concurring in result.) Code of Prof. Resp., DR 2–101(b), DR 2–105(a)(3), Ill.Rev. Stat.1989, ch. 110A, foll. ¶ 776.

3. Attorney and Client ⟳32(9)
  Constitutional Law ⟳90.2
  Alleged potentially misleading nature

The headnotes shown in this column have been prepared by the publisher's editorial staff. The significance of headnotes is discussed in Chapter 6.

The column at the right shows the syllabus as it appears in the official *United States Reports*. The majority, concurring, and dissenting opinions are then set forth exactly as in the official reports.

105(a)(3), Ill.Rev.Stat.1989, ch. 110A, foll. ¶ 776.

4. Federal Courts ⟳511
  Whether inherent character of statement places it beyond protection of First Amendment is question of law over which members of Supreme Court should exercise

---

de novo review, even on appeal from judgment of state Supreme Court exercising review over actions of its State Bar Commission. U.S.C.A. Const.Amend. 1.

Syllabus *

Petitioner Peel is licensed to practice law in Illinois and other States. He also has a "Certificate in Civil Trial Advocacy" from the National Board of Trial Advocacy (NBTA), which offers periodic certification to applicants who meet exacting standards of experience and competence in trial work. The Administrator of respondent Attorney Registration and Disciplinary Commission of Illinois filed a complaint alleging that Peel, by using professional letterhead that stated his name, followed by the indented notation "Certified Civil Trial Specialist By the [NBTA]" and the unindented notation "Licensed: Illinois, Missouri, Arizona," was, *inter alia*, holding himself out as a certified legal specialist in violation of Rule 2–105(a)(3) of the Illinois Code of Professional Responsibility. The Commission recommended censure. The State Supreme Court adopted the Commission's recommendation, concluding that the First Amendment did not protect the letterhead because the public could confuse the State and NBTA as the sources of his license to practice and of his certification, and because the certification could be read as a claim of superior quality.

Held: The judgment is reversed, and the case is remanded.

126 Ill.2d 397, 128 Ill.Dec. 535, 534 N.E.2d 980 (1989), reversed and remanded.

Justice STEVENS, joined by Justice BRENNAN, Justice BLACKMUN, and Justice KENNEDY, concluded that a lawyer has a constitutional right, under the standards applicable to commercial speech, to advertise his or her certification as a trial specialist by NBTA. Pp. 2287–2293.

---

* The syllabus constitutes no part of the opinion of the Court but has been prepared by the Reporter of Decisions for the convenience of the

reader. See *United States v. Detroit Lumber Co.,* 200 U.S. 321, 337, 26 S.Ct. 282, 287, 50 L.Ed. 499.

[Illustration 14]

SAMPLE PAGE FROM 110 S. Ct.

PEEL v. ATTORNEY REG. & DISCIPLINARY COM'N   **2293**
Cite as 110 S.Ct. 2281 (1990)

or inherently misleading, such as certification as a specialist by bona fide organizations such as NBTA. Cf. *In re Johnson,* 341 N.W.2d, at 283 (striking down the Disciplinary Rule that prevented statements of being " 'a specialist unless and until the Minnesota Supreme Court adopts or authorizes rules or regulations permitting him to do so' "). Information about certification and specialties facilitates the consumer's access to legal services and thus better serves the administration of justice.[18]

Petitioner's letterhead was neither actually nor inherently misleading. There is no dispute about the bona fides and the relevance of NBTA certification. The Commission's concern about the possibility of deception in hypothetical cases is not sufficient to rebut the constitutional presumption favoring disclosure over concealment. Disclosure of information such as that on petitioner's letterhead both serves the public interest and encourages the development and utilization of meritorious certification programs for attorneys. As the public censure of petitioner for violating Rule 2–105(a)(3) violates the First Amendment, the judgment of the Illinois Supreme Court is reversed and the case is remanded for proceedings not inconsistent with this opinion.

It is so ordered.

Justice MARSHALL, with whom Justice BRENNAN joins, concurring in the judgment.

Petitioner's letterhead is neither actually nor inherently misleading. I therefore concur in the plurality's holding that Illinois may not prohibit petitioner from holding himself out as a civil trial specialist certified by the National Board of Trial Advocacy. I believe, though, that petitioner's let-

terhead statement is potentially misleading. Accordingly, I would hold that Illinois may enact regulations other than a total ban to ensure that the public is not misled by such representations. Because Illinois' present regulation is unconstitutional as applied to petitioner, however, the judgment of the Illinois Supreme Court must be reversed and the case remanded for further proceedings.

The scope of permissible regulation depends on the nature of the commercial

> This is the last page of the majority opinion in *Peel.* All opinions in *West's Supreme Court Reporter* are identical to those in the official *United States Reports.* Only the editorial material preceding the majority opinion differs.
>
> Note the smaller type used in the West reporter. This allows this unofficial reporter to reproduce cases of each Term in fewer volumes.

contains no evidence that any recipient of petitioner's stationery actually has been misled by the statement. I also believe that petitioner's letterhead statement is not inherently misleading such that it may be banned outright. The Court has upheld such a ban only when the particular method by which the information is imparted to consumers is inherently conducive to deception and coercion. In *Ohralik v. Ohio State Bar Assn.,* 436 U.S. 447, 98 S.Ct. 1912, 56 L.Ed.2d 444 (1978), the Court upheld a prophylactic ban on a lawyer's in-person solicitation of clients for pecuniary gain because such solicitation "is inherently conducive to overreaching and other forms of misconduct." *Id.,* at 464, 98 S.Ct., at 1923. A statement on a letterhead, how-

---

18. See *Bates v. State Bar of Arizona,* 433 U.S. 350, 376, 97 S.Ct. 2691, 2705, 53 L.Ed.2d 810 (1977). A principal reason why consumers do not consult lawyers is because they do not know how to find a lawyer able to assist them with their particular problems. Federal Trade Commission, Staff Report on Improving Consumer Access to Legal Services: The Case for Remov-

ing Restrictions of Truthful Advertising 1 (1984). Justice O'CONNOR would extend this convenience to consumers who seek admiralty, patent, and trademark lawyers, *post,* at 2301, but not to consumers who need a lawyer certified or specializing in more commonly needed areas of the law.

[Illustration 15]

PEEL V. ATTORNEY REGISTRATION AND DISCIPLINARY COMM'N AS REPORTED IN 110 L. Ed. 2d

PEEL v ATTORNEY DISCIPLINARY COM.
(1990) 496 US 91, 110 L Ed 2d 83, 110 S Ct 2281

[496 US 91]
GARY E. PEEL, Petitioner

v

ATTORNEY REGISTRATION AND DISCIPLINARY COMMISSION OF
ILLINOIS

496 US 91, 110 L Ed 2d 83, 110 S Ct 2281

[No. 88-1775]

Argued January 17, 1990. Decided June 4, 1990.

Decision: Illinois held to have violated Federal Constitution's First Amendment by completely prohibiting lawyer from advertising his certification as trial specialist by private professional organization.

SUMMARY

The National Board of Trial Advocacy (NBTA), a private organization sponsored by various lawyers' groups, developed a set of standards and procedures for periodic certification of lawyers with experience and competence in trial work. A lawyer who practiced law in Illinois, and who was also licensed to practice in Arizona and Missouri, was issued a "Certificate in Civil Trial Advocacy" by the NBTA in 1981, which certificate was

---

This is the first page of the *Peel* case as it appears in the bound volume of *L. Ed. 2d*, an unofficial reporter. The Summary is prepared by Lawyers Cooperative Publishing's editorial staff.

Note the citations to the two other sets of reports of this case and the references to the Annotations and Briefs of Counsel.

Commission filed a complaint with the commission alleging that the lawyer, by use of this letterhead, was publicly holding himself out as a certified legal specialist in violation of a rule of the Illinois Code of Professional Responsibility, which rule—although allowing lawyers to claim specialization in patent, trademark, or admiralty practice—generally forbade lawyers from holding themselves out as "certified" or "specialists." A panel of the commission's hearing board recommended that the lawyer be censured for violating the rule, and the commission's review board affirmed the recommendation. The lawyer filed exceptions with the Supreme Court of Illinois,

---

SUBJECT OF ANNOTATION

Beginning on page 688, infra

Restrictions on attorneys' advertisements regarding legal services as violating Federal Constitution's First Amendment

---

Briefs of Counsel, p 685, infra.

83

[Illustration 16]

SAMPLE PAGE FROM 110 L. Ed. 2d

U.S. SUPREME COURT REPORTS　　　110 L Ed 2d

not completely ban commercial speech that is not actually or inherently misleading. [Per Stevens, Brennan, Blackmun, Kennedy, and Marshall, JJ. Dissenting: O'Connor, J., Rehnquist, Ch. J., and Scalia, J.]

Constitutional Law § 953 — lawyers' advertising — potentially misleading

6a-6e. For purposes of a rule that a state may—consistent with the Federal Constitution's First Amendment—regulate lawyers' advertising that is potentially misleading to con-

sumers, an attorney's professional letterhead is potentially misleading where it consists of (1) the attorney's name, (2) an indented notation, below the attorney's name, which states, "Certified Civil Trial Specialist By the National Board of Trial Advocacy," and (3) a second, unindented notation, beginning with the word "Licensed," which identifies three states as the source of the attorney's licensure. [Per Marshall, Brennan, White, and O'Connor, JJ., Rehnquist, Ch. J., and Scalia, J.]

[See annotation p 688, infra]

SYLLABUS BY REPORTER OF DECISIONS

Petitioner Peel is licensed to practice law in Illinois and other States. He also has a "Certificate in Civil

> The headnotes are prepared by the editorial staff of Lawyers Cooperative Publishing and differ from those in *West's Supreme Court Reporter.*
>
> *Lawyers' Edition* also reprints the syllabus as it appears in the *United States Reports.*

Peel, by using a professional letterhead that stated his name, followed by the indented notation "Certified Civil Trial Specialist By the [NBTA]" and the unindented notation "Licensed: Illinois, Missouri, Arizona," was, inter alia, holding himself out as a certified legal specialist in violation of Rule 2-105(a)(3) of the Illinois Code of Professional Responsibility. The Commission recommended censure. The State Supreme Court adopted the Commission's recommendation, concluding that the First Amendment did not protect the letterhead because the public could confuse the State and NBTA as the sources of his license to practice and of his certification, and be-

cause the certification could be read as a claim of superior quality.

Held: The judgment is reversed, and the case is remanded.

126 Ill 2d 397, 534 NE2d 980, reversed and remanded.

Justice Stevens, joined by Justice Brennan, Justice Blackmun, and Justice Kennedy, concluded that a lawyer has a constitutional right, under the standards applicable to commercial speech, to advertise his or her certification as a trial specialist by NBTA.

(a) Truthful advertising related to lawful activities is entitled to First Amendment protections. Although a State may prohibit misleading advertising entirely, it may not place an absolute prohibition on potentially misleading information if the information may also be presented in a way that is not deceptive. In re R. M. J. 455 US 191, 71 L Ed 2d 64, 102 S Ct 929.

(b) Peel's letterhead is not actually or inherently misleading. The facts stated on his letterhead are true and verifiable, and there has been no finding of actual deception or misunderstanding. The state court's focus

[Illustration 17]

SAMPLE PAGE FROM 110 L. Ed. 2d

PEEL v ATTORNEY DISCIPLINARY COM.
(1990) 496 US 91, 110 L Ed 2d 83, 110 S Ct 2281

however, completely ban statements that are not actually or inherently misleading, such as certification as a specialist by bona fide organizations such as NBTA. Cf. In re Johnson, 341 NW2d at 283 (striking down the Disciplinary Rule that prevented statements of being " 'a specialist unless and until the Minnesota Supreme Court adopts or authorizes rules or regulations permitting him to do so' "). Information about certification and specialties facilitates the consumer's access to legal services and thus better serves the administration of justice.[18]

[1d, 3c] Petitioner's letterhead was neither actually nor inherently misleading. There is no dispute about the bona fides and the
——————————▶ [496 US 111]

relevance of NBTA certification. The Commission's concern about the possibility of deception in hypothetical cases is not sufficient to rebut the constitutional presumption favoring disclosure over concealment. Disclosure of information such as that on petitioner's letterhead both serves the public interest and encourages the development and utilization of meritorious certification programs for attorneys. As the public censure of petitioner for violating Rule 2-105(a)(3) violates the First Amendment, the judgment of the Illinois Supreme Court is reversed, and the case is remanded for proceedings not inconsistent with this opinion.

It is so ordered.

Justice **Marshall,** with whom Justice **Brennan** joins, concurring in the judgment.

[1e, 3d, 6a] Petitioner's letterhead is neither actually nor inherently misleading. I therefore concur in the plurality's holding that Illinois may not prohibit petitioner from holding himself out as a civil trial specialist certified by the National Board of Trial Advocacy (NBTA). I believe, though, that petitioner's letterhead statement is potentially misleading. Accordingly, I would hold that Illinois may enact regulations other than a total ban to ensure that the public is not misled by such representations. Because Illinois' present regulation is unconstitutional as ap-

> This is the last page of the majority opinion in *Peel*.
>
> Note the references to the pages of the *United States Reports*. These cross references are also given in the bound volumes of *West's Supreme Court Reporter*.

speech entirely. In re R. M. J. 455 US 191, 203, 71 L Ed 2d 64, 102 S Ct 929 (1982). They may not, however, ban *potentially* misleading commercial speech if narrower limitations could be crafted to ensure that the information is presented in a non-misleading manner. Ibid.

[3e] I agree with the plurality that petitioner's reference to his NBTA certification as a civil trial specialist is not actually
[496 US 112] ◀——————
misleading. Ante, at

---

18. See Bates v State Bar of Ariz., 433 US 350, 376, 53 L Ed 2d 810, 97 S Ct 2691 (1977). A principal reason why consumers do not consult lawyers is because they do not know how to find a lawyer able to assist them with their particular problems. Federal Trade Commission, Staff Report on Improving Consumer Access to Legal Services: The Case for

Removing Restrictions of Truthful Advertising 1 (1984). Justice O'Connor would extend this convenience to consumers who seek admiralty, patent, and trademark lawyers, post, at 126, 110 L Ed 2d, at 111, but not to consumers who need a lawyer certified or specializing in more commonly needed areas of the law.

101

[Illustration 18]

FIRST PAGE OF ANNOTATION FOR PEEL V. ATTORNEY REGISTRATION AND DISCIPLINARY COMM'N, 110 L. Ed. 2d 688

PEEL v ATTORNEY DISCIPLINARY COM.
Reported p 83, supra

ANNOTATION

RESTRICTIONS ON ATTORNEYS' ADVERTISEMENTS REGARDING LEGAL SERVICES AS VIOLATING FEDERAL CONSTITUTION'S FIRST AMENDMENT—SUPREME COURT CASES

by

John F. Wagner Jr., J.D.

I. PRELIMINARY MATTERS

§ 1. Introduction
  [a] Scope
  [b] Related matters
§ 2. Background and summary

II. GENERAL PRINCIPLES

§ 3. View that complete prohibition of attorney advertising violates First Amendment
§ 4. View that restrictions must serve substantial state interest, generally
§ 5. View that disclosure requirements must be reasonably related to state interest in preventing deception

---

TOTAL CLIENT-SERVICE LIBRARY® REFERENCES

3 Am Jur 2d, Advertising § 18; 7 Am Jur 2d, Attorneys at Law § 66

Annotations: See the related matters listed in the annotation.

2B Am Jur Pl & Pr Forms (Rev), Attorneys at Law, Forms 11-28

Both sets of the *Lawyers' Edition* include in its bound volumes annotations on selected cases that bring together previous Supreme Court cases on a particular topic. Annotations are explained in more detail in Chapter 7.

The publisher also provides references to its other publications that contain information related to the topic of the annotation. These publications are discussed in subsequent chapters.

---

ney or Assistance of Attorney, Discipline and Disciplinary Actions; Freedom of Speech and Press

Auto-Cite®: Cases and annotations referred to herein can be further researched through the Auto-Cite® computer-assisted research service. Use Auto-Cite to check citations for form, parallel references, prior and later history, and annotation references.

Consult POCKET PART in this volume for later case service

[Illustration 19]

SAMPLE PAGE OF ANNOTATION FROM 110 L. Ed. 2d 83

ATTORNEY ADVERTISING §7
110 L Ed 2d 688

within the category of commercial speech protected by the Federal Constitution's First Amendment, may extend only as far as the interest such regulation serves.

§ 5. View that disclosure requirements must be reasonably related to state interest in preventing deception

The Supreme Court has held that a state's disclosure requirements with respect to attorney advertising do not violate the free speech provision of the Federal Constitution's First Amendment if such requirements are reasonably related to the state's interest in the prevention of deception.

Rejecting an attorney's contention that, in order for state disciplinary rules which imposed certain disclosure requirements on attorney advertising not to violate the Federal Constitution's First Amendment, the state must establish that such requirements directly advance a substantial governmental interest by the least restrictive means, the court ruled in Zauderer v Office of Disciplinary Counsel of Supreme Court (1985) 471 US 626, 85 L Ed 2d 652, 105 S Ct 2265, 17 Ohio BR 315, 1985-2 CCH Trade Cases ¶ 66645, that an attorney's rights as an advertiser are adequately protected as long as disclosure requirements are reasonably related to the state's interest in preventing the deception of consumers. Since the extension of First Amendment protection to commercial speech was justified principally by the value to consumers of the information such speech provides, the court observed, the attorney's constitutionally protected interest in not providing any particular factual information in his advertising was minimal. The court emphasized, however, that unjustified or unduly

burdensome disclosure requirements might offend the First Amendment by chilling protected commercial speech.

III. Restrictions as to General Nature or Effect of Advertisements

§ 6. Advertisements concerning illegal transactions

It has been recognized by the Supreme Court that attorney advertisements that involve illegal transactions may be prohibited, notwithstanding the free speech clause of the Federal Constitution's First Amendment.

The Supreme Court indicated in Bates v State Bar of Arizona (1977) 433 US 350, 53 L Ed 2d 810, 97 S Ct 2691, 51 Ohio Misc 1, 5 Ohio Ops 3d 60, 2 Media L R 2097, 1977-2 CCH Trade Cases ¶ 61573, reh den 434 US 881, 54 L Ed 2d 164, 98 S Ct 242, that advertising—including attorney advertising—which was a form of commercial speech protected by the Federal Constitution's First Amendment, may be suppressed where such advertising concerns transactions that are themselves illegal.

In Zauderer v Office of Disciplinary Counsel of Supreme Court (1985) 471 US 626, 85 L Ed 2d 652, 105 S Ct 2265, 17 Ohio BR 315, 1985-2 CCH Trade Cases ¶ 66645, the court observed that the states and the Federal Government are free, notwithstanding the Federal Constitution's First Amendment, to prevent the dissemination of commercial speech, including attorney advertisements, which proposes an illegal transaction.

§ 7. False, deceptive, or misleading advertisements

In the following cases, the Su-

693

[Illustration 20]

PAGE FROM 980 FEDERAL REPORTER, 2d SERIES

736   980 FEDERAL REPORTER, 2d SERIES

UNITED STATES COURT OF APPEALS

Ninth Circuit

DECISIONS WITHOUT PUBLISHED OPINIONS

Title	Docket Number	Date	Disposition	Appeal from and Citation (if reported)
Abate v. Walton	92–15613	12/2/92	AFFIRMED IN PART, VACATED IN PART	D.Ariz.
Anwiler, In re; Anwiler v. Anwiler	92–55034	12/2/92	DISMISSED	Bkrtcy.App. 9
Barter v. C.I.R.	92–70324	12/2/92	AFFIRMED	U.S.T.C.
Beagle v. Gooch	92–35304	12/2/92	AFFIRMED	W.D.Wash.
Beasley v. Carroll	91–16798	11/27/92	AFFIRMED IN PART, REMANDED IN PART	N.D.Cal.
Brown v. Sea–Land Service, Inc.	92–55194	12/1/92	AFFIRMED IN PART, REVERSED IN PART	C.D.Cal.
Callahan & Gauntlett v. Dearborn Ins. Co.	92–55137	12/2/92	AFFIRMED	C.D.Cal.
C & C Liberty Enterprises v. U.S.	91–16331,	11/30/92	AFFIRMED	N.D.Cal.

> A table illustrating how cases without published opinions that are decided in a Federal Court of Appeals are reported in the *Federal Reporter 2d.* Similar tables are published in *Federal Reporter 3d.*

Title	Docket Number	Date	Disposition	Appeal from and Citation (if reported)
Chuman v. Wright	92–55007	11/30/92	AFFIRMED	C.D.Cal.
Clark v. Rowland	91–16635, 92–15587	12/9/92	AFFIRMED IN PART, DISMISSED IN PART	E.D.Cal.
Coleman v. Mercy General of Sacramento	91–16201	12/9/92	AFFIRMED	E.D.Cal.
Colville Confederated Tribes, In re; Veeder v. Walton; Colville Confederated Tribes v. Walton	91–35490, 91–35755	11/13/92	AFFIRMED IN PART, VACATED IN PART	E.D.Wash.
Continental Cas. Co. v. Home Ins. Co.	91–35816	12/4/92	REVERSED	W.D.Wash.
Cox v. Brinderson Corp. v. Pioneer Const. Co.	91–35769	11/13/92	AFFIRMED	D.Mont.
Dawkins v. Crist	92–15357	12/2/92	AFFIRMED	D.Ariz.

Chapter 5

STATE COURT CASES AND THE NATIONAL REPORTER SYSTEM

SECTION A. STATE COURT REPORTS

As has been indicated in earlier chapters, the laws or court rules of the individual states provide for the method of publishing state court cases. Case reporters sanctioned by statutes are called *official reports*. [See Illustration 6.] Private companies also publish court cases, with or without legislative directives. The private publications of cases that are not legislatively endorsed are called *unofficial reports,* although they are no less accurate than the official reports. The unofficial reports may duplicate the opinions in the official reports or may be the only source of publication.

The unofficial reports fall into three categories. The first consists of those sets that were or are published to compete directly with the officially-published state reports. These reports, which collect cases decided by the courts and publish them in chronological order, usually have more helpful editorial features and a faster publication schedule than the official reports. In most states, the unofficial sets are units of the *National Reporter System,* which is discussed in the next section of this chapter. The other categories are annotated reports, discussed in Chapter 7, and special or subject reports, discussed briefly in this chapter and in more detail in subsequent chapters.

At one time, all states published their court cases in bound volumes of reports, such as the *Michigan Reports*.[1] Those states having intermediate courts of appeals[2] also may have separately bound sets of reports, such as the *Illinois Appellate Reports*. The cases are published chronologically by terms of court. An increasing number of states, however, have discontinued publishing official state reports and rely solely on the *National Reporter System* or reports of another commercial publisher as

---

[1] For additional references to early law reporting in America, see 1–3 Charles Evans, American Bibliography (1903); 4 Isaiah Thomas, History of Printing in America (2d ed. 1874); 1 Charles Warren, History of the Harvard Law School and of Early Legal Conditions in America 203–14 (1908); 1784 Conn. Pub. Acts 267; Mary R. Chapman, Bibliographical Index to the State Reports Prior to the National Reporter System (1977).

[2] For a listing of states with intermediate courts of appeals, see the latest edition of *Book of the States*.

the official source.[3] In a few instances, a state will not have a designated official set of reports.

Advance sheets or slip opinions often precede the publication of official bound reports in several states. The unofficial print publications always include advance sheets as part of the subscription.

A court or its reporter of decisions may have the power to select the cases for publication in the official state reports. In the exercise of that power some less important cases may be eliminated from the official reports.[4]

In a general survey, such as this, it is not possible to present a detailed study of the reporting system for each state. Legal research guides have been published for many states. These guides typically discuss a state's case law research in depth.[5]

SECTION B. NATIONAL REPORTER SYSTEM

The *National Reporter System*, which began in 1879, is published by West Publishing Company and is the largest and most comprehensive collection of state and federal cases in printed form. It consists of three main divisions: (1) cases of state courts; (2) cases of federal courts; and (3) cases of special courts. There are also subject reporters that extract cases from the various *National Reporter System* units. See Appendix E for a chart showing coverage of the *National Reporter System*.

The development of the *National Reporter System* has had a profound impact on the method of finding court cases and indeed on the development of American law.[6] At the inception of the *National Reporter System*, the states and territories in existence at the time, the various federal circuit courts, and the Supreme Court of the United States were all publishing court reports. In fact, some of these publications had been ongoing for almost a century. In the absence of a coherent, uniform means of accessing these materials, the difficulty of finding cases with similar points of law became immense. The *National Reporter System* brought organization to the chaos resulting from the rapid

[3] See Appendix C for a list of states that have discontinued their state reports and for a Table showing the year of the first case decided for each state or territory. For a state-by-state guide to published court reports and how they interrelate with the *National Reporter System*, see KEITH WIESE, HEIN'S STATE REPORT CHECKLIST (2d ed. 1990) [A.A.L.L. Legal Research Series, Title # 2, updated annually].

[4] Leah F. Chanin, *A Survey of the Writing and Publication of Opinions in Federal and State Appellate Courts,* 67 LAW LIBR. J. 362 (1974). *See also supra,* Chapters 3 and 4, notes 4 and 12, respectively, and accompanying text.

[5] A list of these state guides is published in Appendix A.

[6] See Thomas A. Woxland, *"Forever Associated with the Practice of Law": The Early Years of the West Publishing Company,* LEGAL REFERENCE SERVICES Q., Spring, 1985, at 115; Joe Morehead, *All Cases Great and Small: The West Publishing Company Saga,* SERIALS LIBRARIAN, 1988, at 3. *See also* Robert C. Berring, *Full–Text Databases and Legal Research: Backing into the Future,* 1 HIGH TECH. L.J. 27, 29–38 (1986); Robert C. Berring, *Legal Research and Legal Concepts: Where Form Molds Substance,* 75 CAL. L. REV. 15 (1987).

growth in published court reports by numerous sources. It continues to do so today.

1. State Court Coverage

The original idea of the *National Reporter System* was to group together the cases from several adjacent states. The first of these geographical groupings was the *North Western Reporter* begun in 1879. By 1887, an additional six groupings, *Pacific, North Eastern, Atlantic, South Western, Southern,* and *South Eastern* in that order, had been added and coverage was nationwide. [See Illustration 21 for a map of the regional groupings of the *National Reporter System.*]

These seven units are often referred to as regional reporters, although the states included in some groupings are not always what one might expect to find there, *e.g.,* Oklahoma in *Pacific Reporter,* Michigan in *North Western Reporter.* These early geographical groupings were likely based on the country's population at the time and with it the expectation that each regional unit would grow at approximately the same pace. Certainly this did not occur, but the regional groupings have remained unchanged since they were originally established. Today, each regional unit contains several hundred volumes and all are in a second series.

Population growth has, however, altered the coverage of two of the regional reporters. This occurred first in 1888 with the establishment of a separate reporter for New York, the *New York Supplement.* This reporter includes cases from the New York Court of Appeals, which is New York's court of last resort, as well as cases from the lower courts. The only New York cases currently reported in the *North Eastern Reporter* are those of the New York Court of Appeals. In 1960, West began publishing the *California Reporter.* It includes cases from the California Supreme Court and its intermediate appellate court. These intermediate appellate court cases from California are no longer in the *Pacific Reporter.* Both of these state units of the *National Reporter System* are in their second series.

The *National Reporter System* has, since its beginning, reported cases from each state's highest court. While it now also reports cases from all state intermediate appellate courts, the inclusion of these cases began at different times. For example, Missouri appellate cases are included in the *South Western Reporter,* beginning with 93 Mo.App. (1902); Illinois appellate cases are contained in the *North Eastern Reporter,* beginning with 284 Ill. App. (1936). The publisher notes that the *National Reporter System* also contains over 100,000 cases that are not in the official reports.

Often it is impractical for attorneys to acquire a regional reporter when what they most often need is access to cases from their particular state. Consequently, West publishes "offprint" reporters for individual states by reprinting a state's cases from a regional reporter and rebinding them under a new name, *e.g., Texas Cases, Missouri Decisions.*

There are approximately 30 publications of this type. These offprints retain the volume number and pagination of the regional reporter. The exception to this is the third state unit, *Illinois Decisions,* in which each volume is paged consecutively. Many states that no longer publish official state reports have adopted the regional reporter that covers their state and the offprint version as their official reports.

Both WESTLAW and LEXIS provide extensive state court case coverage. While there is no uniform date as to how far back this coverage extends, it is fair to say that coverage for most states is at least since the 1940s. For many states, the coverage is much more exhaustive, often dating from the late 1800s. Information as to the scope of coverage is available online and through publications of these two vendors. In addition, West has produced *State Case Law on CD ROM* for all states, *e.g., California Reporter 2d, Massachusetts Decisions,* and *New York Supplement 2d.* These products allow for hypertext linking whereby a researcher can highlight a case citation and jump automatically to a screen displaying the cited case.

2. Federal Court and Special Court Coverage

West's federal court coverage began only a year after its first regional reporter in 1879. Today, four units of the *National Reporter System* cover the various federal courts—*West's Supreme Court Reporter, Federal Reporter* (F., F.2d, F.3d), *Federal Supplement,* and *Federal Rules Decisions.* Another four units contain cases from specialized federal courts—*Bankruptcy Reporter, Military Justice Reporter, Federal Claims Reporter,* and *Veterans Appeals Reporter.* Like the regional reporters, the federal units are available online in both WESTLAW and LEXIS. These various federal units of the *National Reporter System* are discussed in Chapter 4.

3. Ultra Fiche Edition

West also publishes an ultra fiche edition of the *National Reporter System.* The reduction ratio is 75x and is compatible with lenses covering a range of 67x to 92x. The First Series and Second Series are available in this format. The Third Series is being filmed as the hard copy volumes are published, with very little lag time between issuance of the two formats. The shelf space savings allowed by the ultra fiche edition are enormous.

4. Coverage of Specialized Subjects

In addition to the federal, state, and regional reporters mentioned above, West also publishes the *Education Law Reporter, Social Security Reporting Service,* and *United States Merit Systems Protection Board Reporter.* While not units of the *National Reporter System,* these sets often reprint cases found in it.

5. Features of the National Reporter System

As has been shown, the full texts of cases decided by the various state and federal appellate courts are contained in the *National Reporter System*. West Publishing Company adds numerous enhancements in its reporters that facilitate use. These common features, discussed below, make possible a relatively simple method for researchers to find cases for all the states as well as those decided in the federal courts on the same or similar points of law.

When West receives cases decided by the courts, its editors prepare headnotes for these cases, which are Key Numbered to its *American Digest System,* and then issues these cases first in advance sheets, which are later cumulated into bound volumes. This Key Numbering is the crux of the *National Reporter System*'s indexing method, the nature of which is described in Chapter 6. Bound volumes retain the same volume and page numbers as the advance sheets.[7]

In addition to the opinions and headnotes, the advance sheets and bound volumes of the *National Reporter System* also include a synopsis of the case, a digest section containing the Key Numbered headnotes of the cases covered,[8] a Table of Cases arranged by state, a Table of Statutes interpreted by cases covered, a list of Words and Phrases defined in the cases reported, and a table showing cases that have cited the second edition of the American Bar Association's *Standards for Criminal Justice.* For all West reporters, except the *Military Justice Reporter,* there are tables listing all Federal Rules of Civil Procedure, Federal Rules of Criminal Procedure, Federal Rules of Appellate Procedure, and Federal Rules of Evidence that are interpreted by the cases covered. From time to time the various units also include proposed changes to or newly-approved versions of court rules.

The advance sheets to the reporters contain several current awareness features that are not incorporated into the bound volumes. For example, the state and regional reporters contain summaries of federal cases arising in each state covered by that reporter. "Judicial Highlights" and "Congressional and Administrative Highlights," found in all *National Reporter System* units except the *Federal Rules Decisions* and the *Bankruptcy Reporter* respectively, are monthly features that briefly describe cases, legislation, and administrative agency activities of special interest or significance.

---

[7] Occasionally after a case has been published in an advance sheet, the judge who wrote the opinion may, for one reason or another, decide it should not be published, and will recall the opinion. In such instances, another case is published in the appendix of a subsequent advance sheet with the same pagination as the withdrawn case. By this means, the original pagination is preserved in the bound volume.

[8] Features such as the digest section in individual volumes are current awareness devices and are repeated in the cumulations of digests on the state, regional, and national levels. Consequently, West does not reproduce these digest sections and some other features when reprinting older volumes.

[Illustration 21]

MAP OF THE NATIONAL REPORTER SYSTEM *
Showing the States in each Regional Reporter group

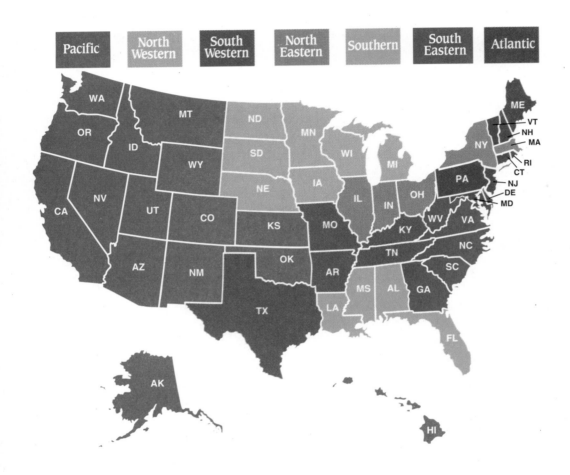

---

* The National Reporter System also includes:

Supreme Court Reporter	Federal Reporter
Federal Supplement	Federal Rules Decisions
West's Bankruptcy Reporter	New York Supplement
West's California Reporter	West's Illinois Decisions
West's Military Justice Reporter	Veterans Appeals Reporter
Federal Claims Reporter	

SECTION C. METHODS OF CITING

1. State Cases

a. *Name of Case.* Depending upon the court rules, a case cited, should contain the name of the case followed by the citation   the case either in the official reports if available, the citation to the corresponding unit or units of the *National Reporter System,* or both.[9] When both the official and unofficial citation are used, this is referred to as *parallel citation.* The full name of the case appears at its beginning, and then there is usually a short form of the case name at the top of each subsequent page of the case. Typically, it is the short form (or a slight variation) that is used in the citation, *e.g.,:*

> Josephine RAVO, an Infant, by Her Father and Natural
> Guardian, Antonio RAVO, Respondent
> v.
> Sol RAGATNICK, Respondent, and Irwin L. Harris,
> Appellant

Its short form title is *Ravo v. Ragatnick.*

b. *Parallel Citations.* When a case has been reported in an official state reporter and in a regional reporter, the citation to the state report is given first, followed by the parallel citation to the appropriate regional reporter or reporters, and, when available, its citation in the *American Law Reports.*[10] The year the case was decided is then given in parenthesis. Examples are:

> *Ravo v. Ragatnick,* 70 N.Y.2d 305, 514 N.E.2d 1104, 520 N.Y.S.2d 533, 9 A.L.R.5th 1170 (1987).

> *Izazaga v. Superior Court,* 54 Cal.3d 356, 285 Cal.Rptr. 231, 815 P.2d 304 (1991).

> *Commonwealth v. DiBenedetto,* 413 Mass. 37, 605 N.E.2d 811 (1992).

When there is no official set of state reports, citation is given first to where it is reported in the *National Reporter System* and then, if available, to the *American Law Reports,* with an indication of the court and year of decision in parenthesis. Examples are:

> *Tussey v. Commonwealth,* 589 S.W.2d 215 (Ky.1979).

> *Thompson v. State,* 318 So.2d 549, 90 A.L.R.3d 641 (Fla.Dist.Ct.App. 1975).

c. *Early State Reporters.* Where the name of a reporter is used in citing an early state report, the favored practice is to indicate the state and the date. An example is:

> *Day v. Sweetser,* 2 Tyl. 283 (Vt. 1803).

---

[9] For state court documents, the 15th edition of *The Bluebook: A Uniform System of Citation* requires parallel citations only for cases decided by courts of the state in which the documents are being submitted. For all other states, only the unofficial citation is required. However, courts do not necessarily follow *The Bluebook.* It is essential, therefore, to check the court rules to ascertain the proper citation form to be used.

[10] The *American Law Reports* are discussed in Chapter 7.

2. Federal Court Cases

a. *Supreme Court of the United States.* Since both *West's Supreme Court Reporter* and the *United States Supreme Court Reports, Lawyers' Edition* give cross references to the pages of the official *United States Reports,* it is customary to cite only to the official set, *e.g., University of California Regents v. Bakke,* 438 U.S. 265 (1978). If the case is so recent that it is not yet in the official reporter, the preferred practice is to cite to *West's Supreme Court Reporter.* For cases even more recent than *West's Supreme Court Reporter,* the preferred cite is to *U.S. Law Week.*

b. *Courts of Appeals and District Courts.* Since there are no official reports for the cases of these courts, citations are given to the appropriate unit of the *National Reporter System.* Examples are:

> *United States v. One 1987 27 Foot Boston Whaler,* 808 F.Supp. 382 (D.N.J.1992).

> *In re Ostaco, Inc.,* 981 F.2d 1166 (10th Cir.1992).

SECTION D.   CROSS–REFERENCE TABLES

1. State Court Citations

Frequently, a researcher has only the citation to a case in an official state report or a regional or state unit of the *National Reporter System* and needs to find the parallel citation. This can be accomplished in several ways.

a. *State Citation to National Reporter System Citation.* When only the state citation is available, refer to one of the following:

(1) *National Reporter Blue Book.* This set, published by West Publishing Company, lists all state citations, alphabetically by state, and gives for each state citation its parallel citation in the appropriate unit or units of the *National Reporter System.* This set consists of bound volumes that are kept current by annual cumulative pamphlets. [See Illustration 22.]

(2) *Shepard's Citations* for the state.

(3) The *Table of Cases* in the appropriate state or regional digest.

b. *National Reporter System Citation to State Citation.* When only the citation is available to a volume of the *National Reporter System,* refer to one of the following:

(1) *[State] Blue and White Book.* Another West publication, this volume is only sent to subscribers for the state in which the subscriber is located and is not available for all states. The blue pages repeat for the state the information available in the *National Reporter Blue Book* described above. The white pages give citations for the regional reporter or reporters to the official state reports. [See Illustration 22.] This publication is useful in locating state citations for the state where the research is taking place.

(2) *Shepard's Citations* for the appropriate regional and state reporter unit.

(3) *Table of Cases* in the appropriate state or regional digest, or *Table of Cases* volumes in the appropriate unit of the *American Digest System.*

(4) *Star Pagination in the National Reporter System.* As early as 1922, West provided star pagination or parallel pagination from the texts of opinions in its *New York Supplement* to the corresponding pages in the official *New York Reports.* This use of star pagination allows the researcher not only to find the official version of the case, but also to provide "jump cites" or "pinpoint cites" to textual matter within the body of the case. While this feature is still included for a few official reports in the unofficial reports, the delay of most states in publishing their official reports when coupled with West's speed in publishing their own, often renders star pagination impossible.

2. Federal Court Citations

a. *Supreme Court of the United States.* The general practice is to cite only to the official *United States Reports* because the unofficial sets include the official citations in their unofficial publications. [See Illustration 15.] When, however, the only citation available is to *West's Supreme Court Reporter* or the *United States Supreme Court Reports, Lawyers' Edition,* the citation to the other two sets can be obtained by referring to:

(1) *Shepard's United States Citations: Cases volumes.*

(2) *Table of Cases* in one of the digests for federal cases.

Tables of Cases and the American Digest System are discussed in Chapter 6. *Shepard's Citations* are discussed in Chapter 14.

b. *Lower Federal Court Cases.* Since there are no official reports for the federal courts of appeals and the federal district courts, citations are to the three series of the *Federal Reporter* and to the *Federal Supplement,* respectively.

3. Insta–Cite and Auto–Cite

Insta–Cite is an electronic case history and citation verification service available on WESTLAW. Auto–Cite, a similar service developed by Lawyers Cooperative Publishing, is available on LEXIS and displays citations with *The Bluebook* punctuation and abbreviations. Each service can be used to locate a parallel citation when only the official or unofficial citation is known. [See Illustration 23.] Both of these systems are discussed in more detail in Chapter 22, J. Jacobstein, R. Mersky & D. Dunn, *Fundamentals of Legal Research* (6th ed.).

[Illustration 22]

AN EXCERPT FROM THE NATIONAL REPORTER BLUE BOOK

20 CALIFORNIA REPORTS, THIRD SERIES

Cal.3d Page	Parallel Citation Vol. / Page	Cal.3d Page	Parallel Citation Vol. / Page	Cal.3d Page	Parallel Citation Vol. / Page	Cal.3d Page	Parallel Citation Vol. / Page
1.141	CalRptr 28 / 569 P2d 133	232.142	CalRptr 171 / 571 P2d 628	457.143	CalRptr 215 / 573 P2d 433	679.143	CalRptr 885 / 574 P2d 1237
10.141	CalRptr 20 / 569 P2d 125	238.142	CalRptr 279 / 571 P2d 990	476.143	CalRptr 205 / 573 P2d 423	→694.144	Cal.Rptr. 751 / 576 P.2d 466
25.141	CalRptr 315 / 569 P2d 1303	251.142	CalRptr 414 / 572 P2d 28	489.143	CalRptr 212 / 573 P2d 430	708.144	CalRptr 133 / 575 P2d 285
55.141	CalRptr 146 / 569 P2d 740	260.142	CalRptr 411 / 572 P2d 25	500.143	CalRptr 240 / 573 P2d 458	717.144	CalRptr 214 / 575 P2d 757
73.141	CalRptr 169 / 569 P2d 763	267.142	CalRptr 418 / 572 P2d 32	512.143	CalRptr 247 / 573 P2d 465	725.144	CalRptr 380 / 575 P2d 1162
90.141	CalRptr 157 / 569 P2d 751	285.142	CalRptr 429 / 572 P2d 43	523.143	CalRptr 609 / 574 P2d 425	765.144	CalRptr 758 / 576 P2d 473
109.141	CalRptr 177 / 569 P2d 771	300.142	CalRptr 286 / 571 P2d 997	550.143	CalRptr 253 / 573 P2d 472	788.144	CalRptr 404 / 575 P2d 1186
130.141	CalRptr 447[2] / 570 P2d 463[2]	309.142	CalRptr 439 / 572 P2d 53	552.143	CalRptr 408 / 573 P2d 852	798.144	CalRptr 408 / 575 P2d 1190
142.141	CalRptr 542 / 570 P2d 723	317.142	CalPptr 443 / 572 P2d 57	560.143	CalRptr 625 / 574 P2d 441	813.144	CalRptr 905 / 576 P2d 945
150.141	CalRptr 698 / 570 P2d 1050	327.142	CalRptr 904 / 572 P2d 1128	567.143	CalRptr 542 / 573 P2d 1369	844.143	CalRptr 695 / 574 P2d 766

The *National Reporter Blue Book* consists of a main bound volume, bound volume supplements, and an annual cumulative pamphlet. This *Blue Book* contains tables showing volume and page of the *National Reporter* volume for every case found in the corresponding state reports.

In this example, if one had only the citation to 20 Cal. 3d 694, the table may be used to locate the citation of this case in the *California Reporter* and the *Pacific Reporter 2d.*

AN EXCERPT FROM THE WHITE TABLES IN CALIFORNIA BLUE AND WHITE BOOK

1190 . . . . . 20 Cal.3d 798 144 Cal.Rptr. 408	**579 P.2d** Parallel Page Citation
576 P.2d Parallel Page Citation	1 . . . . 21 Cal.3d 337 146 Cal.Rptr. 352
92 [1]	7 . . . . 21 Cal.3d 471 146 Cal.Rptr. 358
Not officially published	441 . . . . . . 21 Cal.3d 322 146 Cal.Rptr. 550
92 [2] . . . . . 20 Cal.3d 878 144 Cal.Rptr. 609 [3]	449 . . . . . . 21 Cal.3d 386 146 Cal.Rptr. 558
93 . . . . 20 Cal.3d 888 144 Cal.Rptr. 610	476 . . . . . . 21 Cal.3d 431 146 Cal.Rptr. 585
→466 . . . . . . 20 Cal.3d 694 144 Cal.Rptr. 751	495 . . . . . 21 Cal.3d 349 146 Cal.Rptr. 604
473 . . . . 20 Cal.3d 765 144 Cal.Rptr. 758	505 . . . . . . 21 Cal.3d 497 146 Cal.Rptr. 614
945 . . . . . . 20 Cal.3d 813 144 Cal.Rptr. 905	514 . . . . . . 21 Cal.3d 482 146 Cal.Rptr. 623
963 . . . . . 20 Cal.3d 893 145 Cal.Rptr. 1	1043 . . . . . 21 Cal.3d 513 146 Cal.Rptr. 727
971 . . . . . 20 Cal.3d 906 145 Cal.Rptr. 9	1048 . . . . . 21 Cal.3d 542 146 Cal.Rptr. 732
1342 . . . . . . 21 Cal.3d 1 145 Cal.Rptr. 176	1053 . . . . . 21 Cal.3d 523 146 Cal.Rptr. 737

[Illustration 23]

USING INSTA–CITE OR AUTO–CITE TO FIND A PARALLEL CITATION

Type in: 496 U.S. 91

```
FOR EDUCATIONAL USE ONLY        INSTA-CITE            Page   1 of   2
CITATION: 496 U.S. 91
                             DIRECT HISTORY

    1  In re Peel, 126 Ill.2d 397, 128 Ill.Dec. 535, 534 N.E.2d 980,
           57 U.S.L.W. 2485 (Ill., Feb 02, 1989) (NO. 66771)
       Certiorari Granted by
    2  Peel v. Attorney Registration and Disciplinary Com'n of Illinois,
           492 U.S. 917, 109 S.Ct. 3240, 106 L.Ed.2d 588
           (U.S.Ill., Jul 03, 1989) (NO. 88-1775)
       AND Judgment Reversed by
=>  3  PEEL V. ATTORNEY REGISTRATION AND DISCIPLINARY COM'N OF ILLINOIS,
           496 U.S. 91, 110 S.Ct. 2281, 110 L.Ed.2d 83, 58 U.S.L.W. 4684,
           1990-1 Trade Cases  P 69,046 (U.S.Ill., Jun 04, 1990)
           (NO. 88-1775)

Note: This result is for the highlighted citation.  To view history for another
      case in this display, type IC and its NUMBER and press ENTER.  For
      indirect history prior to 1972 use Shepard's.  See SCOPE for more info.
(C) Copyright West Publishing Company 1993
```

```
Auto-Cite (R) Citation Service, (c) 1993 Lawyers Cooperative Publishing

496 US 91:                                        Screen 1 of 3

CITATION YOU ENTERED:

Peel v. Attorney Registration & Disciplinary Com.*1, 496 U.S. 91, 110 L. Ed. 2d
83, 1990 U.S. LEXIS 2909, 110 S. Ct. 2281, 58 U.S.L.W. 4684, 1990-1 Trade Cas.
(CCH) P 69046 (1990)

PRIOR HISTORY:

Re Peel, 126 Ill. 2d 397, 128 Ill. Dec. 535, 534 N.E.2d 980, 1989 Ill. LEXIS 14
(1989)

    mot. granted, cert. granted, Peel v. Attorney Registration & Disciplinary
    Com., 492 U.S. 917, 106 L. Ed. 2d 588, 1989 U.S. LEXIS 3386, 109 S. Ct.
    3240, 57 U.S.L.W. 3859 (1989)
```

SECTION E. SUMMARY

1. State Court Reports

a. Official reports are court reports published by statutory or court authority.

b. Unofficial reports are court reports published without statutory or court authority and often are available sooner than official publications.

c. Slip opinions and advance sheets are published officially for several states. Advance sheets are published for all unofficial reports.

d. Many states rely on unofficial advance sheets and bound volumes, *e.g., National Reporter System* or other commercial publications. Some states have adopted a commercial publication as their state's official publication.

e. Extensive coverage is provided in WESTLAW and LEXIS.

2. National Reporter System

a. Cases of all state appellate courts, arranged geographically into seven regional reporters and three state reporters.

b. Cases of the federal courts in four reporters, plus four reporters for special courts.

c. Three subject reporters that include cases reprinted from the *National Reporter System.*

d. Bound volumes retain the same pagination and volume number as the advance sheets.

e. Contains many editorial features, including headnotes, table of cases reported, table of statutes construed, words and phrases judicially defined, and key number digest section. Advance sheets often provide current awareness information.

3. Citations and Cross–Reference Tables

a. Depending upon the court rules, a citation may require inclusion of both the official and unofficial report.

b. *National Reporter Blue Book* refers the user from the official citation to the unofficial *National Reporter System* citation.

c. White Tables in *[State] Blue and White Book* refer the user from the unofficial *National Reporter System* citation to the official citation.

d. *Shepard's Citations* refer the user from the official citation to the unofficial citation and vice versa.

4. Insta–Cite and Auto–Cite

These are electronic case history and citation verification services that can be used to locate parallel citations in different sets of court reports.

Chapter 6

DIGESTS FOR COURT REPORTS

SECTION A. DIGESTS: IN GENERAL

Because our system of law follows the doctrine of *stare decisis,* the ability to locate earlier cases on the same or similar points of law is essential to sound legal research. As has been noted, cases are published in court reports in chronological order rather than being arranged by subject. For example, although a given volume of reports may contain cases dealing with diverse subjects ranging from *Abatement* to *Zoning,* their arrangement corresponds to the date of the decision. Without a method to search cases by subject, locating those cases with the same or similar points of law as the legal issue being researched would become unwieldy and unmanageable.

After cases are decided, editors for commercial publishers analyze the cases and write brief descriptive abstracts of the various points of law in the cases. These abstracts are typically referred to as headnotes or digest paragraphs. Later, these descriptive paragraphs are arranged by subject and published in sets known as *digests.* Digests are a very important means used in case finding. To demonstrate how digests can be used to research legal issues, assume the following problem, which will serve as the basis for discussion and most of the Illustrations used later in this chapter:

> Leslie was a voluntary outpatient of Dr. Seine, a psychiatrist, and was being treated for violent tendencies. One day during a scheduled appointment, Leslie was in an especially anxious state and, while making a stabbing motion with a pencil, yelled to Dr. Seine, "Dale is the cause of all my miseries and is going to pay real soon." Dr. Seine told no one of Leslie's outburst. The next day Leslie stabbed Dale in the back, causing Dale permanent physical injuries and great emotional distress.

Before beginning to research this inquiry, the researcher first must determine the important issues involved. One issue may be whether Dr. Seine is negligent for failing to warn Dale of Leslie's threat. Another may be whether Dr. Seine should have taken steps to have Leslie confined and, thus, prevent the injuries to Dale. A third may be whether the physician-patient privilege of confidentiality protects Dr. Seine from liability. Certainly, if liability against the psychiatrist is possible, one would also want to learn about the measures of damages that could be sought.

In order to find the law applicable to this situation, the researcher must search for appellate court cases with the same or similar facts. From these cases, the rules of law should be determined. If this incident had happened, for example, in California, and all that was available to the researcher were volumes of the reports of the California appellate courts, it would be necessary to examine individually hundreds of volumes of the California reports to determine if any cases were on point. If a California case on point could not be located, it then would be necessary to search for cases from other states. Because of their subject arrangement, digests alleviate the laborious task of having to search for cases in court reports volume by volume.

Digests provide various types of coverage. Some include only cases from the courts of a single state, one court, or a system of courts; others include cases from a group of neighboring states; some include only federal cases; and some include cases on only one broad subject. One includes cases from all appellate courts, federal and state.

In this chapter we will describe digests published primarily by the West Publishing Company. West's *Key Number Digests* consist of national, regional, state, federal, and subject units as is shown in Section I. Our focus will be on the *American Digest System,* the most extensive and comprehensive and also the most cumbersome of the many West's *Key Number Digests.* Since the methodology used in conducting research in the *American Digest System* is similar to that used with the other West's *Key Number Digests,* an understanding of the *American Digest System* can be transferred readily to the smaller, specialized West digests. Other digests, as well as different techniques for locating cases, are discussed in subsequent chapters.

SECTION B. WEST'S KEY NUMBER DIGESTS

1. Key Number System

When the *National Reporter System* began in the late-nineteenth century, West Publishing Company realized that users of their reporters needed a means to locate by subject the thousands of points of law made in the chronologically-arranged cases. To answer this need, West developed its own unique classification of law, created digest paragraphs containing the points of law made in the cases, and classified these digest paragraphs from all the cases to its system of classification.

West's classification system divides the subject of law into seven main classes: Persons; Property; Contracts; Torts; Crimes; Remedies; and Government. Each class is divided into subclasses and each subclass into Topics. Each of the over 400 Topics corresponds to a legal concept. [See Illustration 24.] The Topics are then divided into subdivisions in a given paragraph number called a Key Number. The Key Numbers vary from Topic to Topic from a few to many hundreds within a Topic. These digest paragraphs with their Topic and Key Numbers are cumulated and published in multi-volume sets of digests.

With this background in mind, it is necessary to examine the actual steps involved in developing West's *Key Number Digests*. Essentially, the process starts with a slip opinion. After a court case is decided, a copy of the slip opinion goes to the West Publishing Company and is assigned to an editor. Assume the editor receives a slip opinion for *Boynton v. Burglass,* a case with facts similar to the one used in our problem. The editor reads and analyzes the case and writes the headnotes, each headnote representing a particular point of law addressed in the case. Over 275,000 new headnotes are written each year. The editor takes each point of law that has been made into a headnote and assigns to it one or more Topics and Key Numbers, and determines the appropriate unit or units of the *National Reporter System* in which the case and its corresponding headnotes, Topics, and Key Numbers will be published.

For example, an editor decides that a particular headnote deals with negligence. The editor consults the list of over 400 Topics and assigns to the headnote the Topic *Negligence*. The next step is the assignment of a particular Key Number or Key Numbers. The editor examines a detailed outline (subdivisions) under the Topic *Negligence*. This outline, discussed more fully in Section D of this chapter, is referred to as the *Analysis*.

After consulting this outline, the editor determines that the headnote deals with acts or omissions constituting negligence and specifically with the second subdivision in the *Analysis*—duty to use care. The Topic *Negligence* receives Key Number 2. The same steps are followed for the next two paragraphs, both of which are assigned the Topic *Mental Health* and Key Number 414(2). Once the editorial work is complete, the case is published in the appropriate unit or units of the *National Reporter System*. [See Illustration 25.]

A set of brackets surrounding a number in the text of the published opinion, *e.g.,* [1], indicates the language that corresponds to the headnote. [See Illustration 26.] This enables a researcher interested in the point of law discussed in a particular headnote to go directly to that headnote's origin in the case. At times, a headnote is classified to more than one Topic. In such instances, all appropriate Topics and Key Numbers are shown.

2. The American Digest System

The *American Digest System* is a massive set of materials in several units and is described by West as a "master index to all of the case law of our country." It contains the headnotes, with their corresponding Topics and Key Numbers, from every unit of the *National Reporter System*. Once the process of creating headnotes for a case and assigning the case to a reporter is completed, the editors take the headnotes with their Topics and Key Numbers in the reporters and merge them into the proper locations in the appropriate sets of West's *Key Number Digests*.

In the *American Digest System,* this process of merging begins with a publication named the *General Digest.* This publication is issued in bound volumes, with a new volume issued approximately once a month. Each volume consists of *all* the headnotes taken from *all* the units of the *National Reporter System* for the period covered. These headnotes are arranged alphabetically by Topic, and then under each Topic numerically by Key Number.

If no further cumulation took place, digests of all the cases, arranged topically, would be in the bound volumes of the *General Digest.* Therefore, to find all the cases dealing with a particular Topic, *e.g., Negligence,* it would be necessary to examine each one of hundreds of bound volumes. Since this obviously is not practical, in 1906 West cumulated into one alphabetical arrangement all the Topics for all the *General Digest* volumes from 1897 to 1906. This set is called the *First Decennial Digest.* By examining a volume of the *First Decennial* containing a particular Topic and Key Number, all cases decided on that point during 1897–1906 can be located.

This process of systematically cumulating a set of the *General Digest* into a *Decennial* has taken place since 1897, with a new *Decennial* compiled every ten years. The latest is the *Tenth Decennial Digest, Part 1,*[1] covering 1986–1991. All digest paragraphs of cases decided from late 1991 through 1996 will be found in the *General Digest, 8th Series.* Thus, given a Topic and a Key Number, one can start with the *First Decennial* and proceed through the *Tenth, Part 1* and the available volumes of the *General Digest, 8th Series* to locate all cases on a point of law under a particular Topic and Key Number from 1897 to several weeks ago.[2] [See Illustrations 27–28.]

It is possible to find all cases from 1658, the date of the first reported American case, since cases from 1658 to 1896 are digested in a publication named the *Century Digest.* Since the *National Reporter System* did not exist during this period, the *Century Digest* does not contain Key Numbers. A different topical arrangement was used. For example, the Topic *Damages* Key Number 51 in the *Decennials* stands for *Mental Suffering Caused by Injury to the Person of Another,* whereas in the *Century Digest,* Damages 51 stands for *Damages Flowing Directly From Intervening Agency of Third Person,* and cases dealing with mental

---

[1] Starting with the *Ninth Decennial,* the publisher decided to issue it in two parts: *Part 1* covering 1976–81; *Part 2* covering 1981–86. This process of cumulating cases every five years has continued with the *Tenth Decennial.* One advantage of this new arrangement is that a researcher has fewer volumes of the *General Digest* to examine since it now ends, starts to be superseded by new part of a *Decennial,* and commences anew in five-year increments rather than the previous ten.

[2] In the *Decennials* and the *General Digest* cases are arranged hierarchically, beginning with those of the Supreme Court of the United States and followed by the lower federal courts, with the most recent case listed first in each grouping. These cases are followed by cases relating to the individual states. These cases are arranged alphabetically by state and hierarchically by court, with the most recent case listed first in each grouping.

suffering caused by injury to a third person are digested under Section Numbers 103, 255, and 256.[3]

The *American Digest System* consists of the following sets:

Century digest	1658–1896	50 vols.
First Decennial	1897–1906	25 vols.
Second Decennial	1907–1916	24 vols.
Third Decennial	1916–1926	29 vols.
Fourth Decennial	1926–1936	34 vols.
Fifth Decennial	1936–1946	52 vols.
Sixth Decennial	1946–1956	36 vols.
Seventh Decennial	1956–1966	38 vols.
Eighth Decennial	1966–1976	50 vols.
Ninth Decennial, Part 1	1976–1981	38 vols.
Ninth Decennial, Part 2	1981–1986	48 vols.
Tenth Decennial, Part 1	1986–1991	44 vols.
General Digest (8th Series)	1991–1996	in progress

3. Digest Paragraphs in WESTLAW

West Publishing Company includes the equivalent of its *American Digest System* in WESTLAW, the largest of its computer-assisted legal research services. It is, therefore, possible to search, for example, the Topic *Negligence,* Key Number 2 and retrieve all cases digested under this point of law, to restrict the search to a particular period of time, or to add a specific search term, such as *psychiatrist,* to the query. Key Number searching in WESTLAW eliminates the often laborious task of searching in the *Decennials.*[4]

WESTLAW includes the powerful hypertext feature in its headnotes. Each headnote for a case includes a triangle (>) for each level of hierarchy in its Key Numbers for that case. By use of the cursor or mouse on these symbols, a researcher can "jump" directly to the related text in the opinion or jump from the text directly to the related headnote. [See Illustration 29, Figure 1.] Computer-assisted legal research is discussed in more detail in Chapter 22, J. Jacobstein, R. Mersky & D. Dunn, *Fundamentals of Legal Research* (6th ed.).

4. Keeping the Key Number System Current

Law, of course, is constantly expanding or changing. For example, when the original Key Number classification was prepared in 1897, no

---

[3] In both the first and second *Decennials,* cross-references are made from the *Decennial* Key Numbers to the Section Numbers used in the *Century Digest,* with the one in the second being more complete. If one locates a point of law in the *Century Digest,* Key Numbers for later cases on the same point of law can be located by consulting a pink reference table in volume 21 of the *First Decennial.*

[4] In WESTLAW Topics are converted to a numerical equivalent that corresponds to the alphabetically-arranged Topics used in West digests. [See Illustration 24.] The Key number symbol is converted to the letter "k." [See Illustration 29, Figures 1 and 2.] Information showing the corresponding WESTLAW Topic number equivalent to use when searching WESTLAW is available online and in numerous print publications.

provisions were made for cases dealing with damages resulting from a jet breaking the sound barrier or for the control and regulation of nuclear energy. Consequently, to cover new areas of the law, at times West adds new Topics to the Key Number classification. In recent years these newly-added Topics include *Commodities Futures Trading Regulation* and *Racketeer Influenced and Corrupt Organizations* (RICO).

In addition to adding new Topics, Key Numbers are sometimes reclassified (revised) in order to adapt to changing circumstances. For example, the Topics *Bankruptcy* and *Federal Civil Procedure* were recently reclassified, *i.e.,* the existing Key Number classifications were changed to newly-renumbered ones to accommodate recent changes in the federal laws governing these areas. When this reclassification occurs, Key Number Translation Tables are provided near the start of the topic in the digest to show where the former Key Number is located in the new Key Number classification and vice versa. [See Illustration 30.] WESTLAW updates this information automatically for all Key Numbers since 1932. A researcher can retrieve all relevant cases under a current Key Number even though some of those cases may have been previously classified under a different Key Number. [See Illustration 29, Figure 2.]

At still other times, existing Topics are expanded as additional issues emerge in the area over time. For example, until recently all headnotes dealing with issues concerning liability of others for torts of mentally disordered persons, an issue relevant to our research problem, received the Topic *Mental Health* and the Key Number 414:

EXAMPLE FROM TOPIC *MENTAL HEALTH*, EIGHTH DECENNIAL DIGEST (1966–1976)

411. Liability of mentally disordered person in general.
412. Particular torts of mentally disordered persons.
413. Liability for torts of others.
414. Liability of others for torts of mentally disordered person.
415. Damages.

After a landmark California case in 1976 relating to a psychiatrist's liability for acts of a patient, other states began to address similar issues. It became necessary to expand *Mental Health* Key Number 414:

EXAMPLE FROM TOPIC *MENTAL HEALTH*, NINTH DECENNIAL DIGEST, PART 2 (1981–1986)

414. Liability of others for torts of mentally disordered person.
    (1) In general.
    (2) Mental health professionals and institutions.
    (3) Escape or release from custody.
    (4) Actions.

Thus, by adding new Topics, reclassifying older ones, and expanding existing ones, West's Key Number System attempts to keep current with the changing and dynamic aspects of law.

5. Table of Key Numbers

For cases more recent than those in the *Decennials,* it is necessary to examine the digest paragraphs under the same Topic and Key Number in the individual volumes of the latest *General Digest.* Since each volume contains digest paragraphs covering only a short period of time, there may be as many as sixty volumes to search before they are cumulated and replaced by a new *Decennial.* To avoid the necessity of examining a volume of the *General Digest* that does not include a particular Key Number, the publisher includes a *Table of Key Numbers* in every tenth volume of the *General Digest.* These tables indicate in which volumes of the *General Digest* cases are digested for a particular Key Number for that ten volume increment. [See Illustration 31.]

Illustrations in Section C show the development of headnotes from reported cases, the assignment of Topics and Key Numbers to the headnotes, how headnotes become a part of the various units of the *American Digest System,* and headnotes as they appear in WESTLAW.

Methods of determining under what Topics and Key Numbers to search are described in Section D & E *infra.*

SECTION C. ILLUSTRATIONS: KEY NUMBER CLASSIFICATION AND UNITS OF THE AMERICAN DIGEST SYSTEM

[Illustration 24]

SAMPLE PAGE FROM ALPHABETICAL LIST OF DIGEST TOPICS USED IN KEY NUMBER SYSTEM

DIGEST TOPICS

The topic numbers shown below may be used in WESTLAW searches for cases within the topic and within specified key numbers.

1	Abandoned and Lost Property	40	Assistance, Writ of	77	Citizens
2	Abatement and Revival	41	Associations	78	Civil Rights
		42	Assumpsit, Action of	79	Clerks of Courts
3	Abduction	43	Asylums	80	Clubs
4	Abortion and Birth Control	44	Attachment	81	Colleges and Universities
		45	Attorney and Client		
5	Absentees	46	Attorney General	82	Collision
6	Abstracts of Title	47	Auctions and Auctioneers	83	Commerce
7	Accession			83H	Commodity Futures Trading Regulation
8	Accord and Satisfaction	48	Audita Querela	84	Common Lands
		48A	Automobiles	85	Common Law
		48B	Aviation		

9	Accou				Scold
10	Accou				ding Offenses
11	Accou				ise and
11A	Accou				ent
12	Ackno				iium
13	Actio				of Goods
14	Actio				y
15	Adjoi				onal Law

> There are over 400 Topics in the *American Digest System.* These Topics are used in creating headnotes. See next Illustration.
>
> The numbers to the left of the Topics are used in accessing the Topics on WESTLAW. This is discussed in B–3 of this chapter.

15A	Administrative Law and Procedure	58	Bonds	92B	Consumer Credit
		59	Boundaries	92H	Consumer Protection
16	Admiralty	60	Bounties	93	Contempt
17	Adoption	61	Breach of Marriage Promise	95	Contracts
18	Adulteration			96	Contribution
19	Adultery	62	Breach of the Peace	97	Conversion
20	Adverse Possession	63	Bribery	98	Convicts
21	Affidavits	64	Bridges	99	Copyrights and Intellectual Property
22	Affray	65	Brokers		
23	Agriculture	66	Building and Loan Associations	100	Coroners
24	Aliens			101	Corporations
25	Alteration of Instruments	67	Burglary	102	Costs
		68	Canals	103	Counterfeiting
26	Ambassadors and Consuls	69	Cancellation of Instruments	104	Counties
				105	Court Commissioners
27	Amicus Curiae	70	Carriers	106	Courts
28	Animals	71	Cemeteries	107	Covenant, Action of
29	Annuities	72	Census	108	Covenants
30	Appeal and Error	73	Certiorari	108A	Credit Reporting Agencies
31	Appearance	74	Champerty and Maintenance		
33	Arbitration			110	Criminal Law
34	Armed Services	75	Charities	111	Crops
35	Arrest	76	Chattel Mortgages	113	Customs and Usages
36	Arson	76A	Chemical Dependents	114	Customs Duties
37	Assault and Battery	76H	Children Out-of- Wedlock	115	Damages
38	Assignments			116	Dead Bodies

VII

1–1

[Illustration 25]

SAMPLE PAGE FROM 590 So. 2d

---

446 Fla.   **590 SOUTHERN REPORTER, 2d SERIES**

> This is the first page of *Boynton v. Burglass*, a case relevant to our research problem. Three headnotes have been assigned to this case. Notice how each headnote has been assigned a Topic and a specific Key Number.
>
> **See next Illustration.**

Wayne BOYNTON, Sr., individually, as father and next best friend of Wayne Boynton, Jr., deceased, and as personal representative and survivor of the Estate of Wayne Boynton, Jr., and Dorothy Boynton, individually, as mother, next best friend, and survivor of the Estate of Wayne Boynton, Jr., Appellants,

v.

Milton BURGLASS, M.D., and Milton Burglass, M.D., P.A., Appellees.

No. 89–1409.

District Court of Appeal of Florida, Third District.

Sept. 24, 1991.

As Amended on Grant in Part of Motion for Rehearing or Certification Dec. 24, 1991.

Parents of murder victim brought action against psychiatrist for failure to hospitalize voluntary outpatient who murdered their son, failure to warn son, parents, or police that patient was violence-prone, and had threatened harm to son, and failure to prescribe proper medications for patient.

The Circuit Court, Dade County, George Orr, J., dismissed complaint for failure to state claim for relief. Parents appealed. The District Court of Appeal, Jorgenson, J., held that: (1) psychiatrist had no duty to control voluntary outpatient or to warn victim who patient killed or others about patient's behavior, and therefore psychiatrist was not liable for malpractice to victim's parents, and (2) psychiatrist did not have statutory duty to warn victim that patient posed threat to him.

Affirmed.

Cope, J., filed opinion specially concurring, in which Gersten, J., joined.

Schwartz, C.J., filed dissenting opinion, in which Baskin, Ferguson and Levy, JJ., joined.

1. Negligence ⬤2

Under common law, person had no duty to control conduct of another or to warn those placed in danger by such conduct; however, exception to that general rule can arise when there is special relationship between defendant and person whose behavior needs to be controlled or person who is foreseeable victim of that conduct.

2. Mental Health ⬤414(2)

Psychiatrist had no duty to control voluntary outpatient or to warn victim who patient killed or others about patient's behavior, and therefore psychiatrist was not liable to parents of victim.

3. Mental Health ⬤414(2)

Psychiatrist had no duty to warn potential victim of danger posed by voluntary outpatient under statute permitting psychiatrist to warn identifiable victims of threats of physical harm, given that cause

2. The complaint does not allege that Northwest Dade knew that Oscar had been committed to South Florida State Hospital and had escaped from custody. From Northwest Dade's point of view, Oscar was a walk-in outpatient and the *Paddock* analysis applies.

However, the result would not change as to these plaintiffs even if Northwest Dade did know of Oscar's committed but escaped status. Under the latter set of facts, Northwest Dade may have owed a duty to its own patient, Oscar,

to take some action in light of that information, a point not before us. The question presented here is whether Northwest Dade owed a duty to these plaintiffs, as third persons. We answer that question in the negative. Oscar was not committed to Northwest Dade and Northwest Dade had not taken charge of him within the meaning of the Restatement rule. A duty by Northwest Dade to these plaintiffs, as third persons, did not arise.

[Illustration 26]

SAMPLE PAGE FROM 590 So. 2d

448 Fla.   590 SOUTHERN REPORTER, 2d SERIES

followed the lead of the California Supreme Court in the landmark decision of *Tarasoff v. Regents of Univ. of California,* 17 Cal.3d 425, 131 Cal.Rptr. 14, 551 P.2d 334 (1976), we reject that "enlightened" approach.[7]

Florida courts have long been loathe to impose liability based on a defendant's failure to control the conduct of a third party. *See, e.g., Bankston v. Brennan,* 507 So.2d

---

This is the third page of *Boynton v. Burglass.* It illustrates how headnotes are developed. The bracketed numbers are inserted by the editors. Each section so bracketed has been condensed into a corresponding headnote for the point of law in each bracketed section.

See previous Illustration.

---

sought to be imposed is dependent upon standards of the psychiatric profession, we are asked to embark upon a journey that "will take us from the world of reality into the wonderland of clairvoyance." *Tarasoff,* 551 P.2d at 354, 131 Cal.Rptr. at 34 (Mosk, J., concurring and dissenting). Psychiatry "represents the penultimate grey area ... particularly with regard to issues of foreseeability and predictability of future dangerousness." *Lindabury v. Lindabury,* 552 So.2d 1117, 1118 (Fla. 3d DCA 1989) (Jorgenson, J., dissenting) (citations omitted); *Fischer v. Metcalf,* 543 So.2d 785, 787 n. 1 (Fla. 3d DCA 1989) ("Unlike other branches of medicine in which diagnoses and treatments evolve from objective, empirical, methodological foundations, 'psychiatry is at best an inexact science, if, indeed, it is a science....'") (citations omitted). It

Protect Third Persons Threatened by Patient, 83 A.L.R.3d 1201 (1978 & Supp.1990).

7. In *Tarasoff,* the California Supreme Court held that "[w]hen a therapist determines, or pursuant to the standards of his profession should determine, that his patient presents a serious danger of violence to another, he incurs an obligation to use reasonable care to protect the intended victim against such danger." 131 Cal.Rptr. at 20, 551 P.2d at 340. Four years later, the California Supreme Court narrowed the scope of its holding in *Tarasoff,* and held

---

is against the backdrop of this uncertain and inexact science that we address the legal issues presented by this appeal.

I. *The Duty to Warn*

Plaintiffs contend that Dr. Burglass had a duty, under the common law, to warn Boynton (or the police, or Boynton's family) that Blaylock intended to harm him. In our view, imposing on psychiatrists[8] the duty that plaintiffs urge is neither reasonable nor workable and is potentially fatal to effective patient-therapist relationships.

[1] Under the common law, a person had no duty to control the conduct of another or to warn those placed in danger by such conduct; however, an exception to that general rule can arise when there is a special relationship between the defendant and the person whose behavior needs to be controlled or the person who is a foreseeable victim of that conduct. *See Fischer v. Metcalf,* 543 So.2d 785, 787 n. 1 (Fla. 3d DCA 1989); *Department of Health & Rehab. Servs. v. Whaley,* 531 So.2d 723 (Fla. 4th DCA 1988); *Garrison Retirement Home Corp. v. Hancock,* 484 So.2d 1257 (Fla. 4th DCA 1985); *see also* Rest.2d Torts §§ 314–320. Implicit in the creation of that exception, however, is the recognition that the person on whom the duty is to be imposed has the ability or the right to control the third party's behavior. Restatement §§ 316–319. "Thus, in the absence of a relationship involving such control, the exception to the general rule, that there is no duty to control the conduct of a third party for the protection of others, should not be applicable." *Hasenei v. United States,* 541 F.Supp. 999, 1009 (D.Md.1982) (psychiatrist who had no right or ability to control voluntary outpatient's

that a county's duty to warn of the imminent release from confinement of a dangerous and violent individual "depends upon and arises from the existence of a prior threat to a specific identifiable victim." *Thompson v. County of Alameda,* 27 Cal.3d 741, 167 Cal.Rptr. 70, 80, 614 P.2d 728, 738 (1980).

8. Although we use the term "psychiatrist" throughout this opinion, our decision today applies equally to psychologists, psychotherapists, and other mental health practitioners.

[Illustration 27]

SAMPLE PAGE FROM GENERAL DIGEST, 8TH SERIES

817   **NEGLIGENCE** ⟾15

Ill.App. 1 Dist. 1991. Liability arises from "misfeasance," which is failure to exercise reasonable care when acting, regardless of whether duty to act exists, and not from "nonfeasance," which is failure to perform voluntary tasks in all instances, where there is no duty to act.—Lewis v. Razzberries, Inc., 165 Ill.Dec. 258, 584 N.E.2d 437, 222 Ill.App.3d 843.

Minn.App. 1991. In any negligence case, plaintiff must prove that defendant's act or failure to act breached duty to plaintiff and that such negligence was proximate cause of injury; if any of these elements is not proved, claim must be dismissed.—Lee v. State, Dept. of Natural Resources, 478 N.W.2d 237.

N.C.App. 1992. To sustain claim of actionable negligence, plaintiff must prove that defendant owed duty to plaintiff, defendant failed to exercise proper care in performance of that duty, and breach of that duty was proximate cause of plaintiff's injury, which person of ordinary prudence should have foreseen as probable under conditions as they existed.—Westbrook v. Cobb, 411 S.E.2d 651.

Tex.App.–Hous. [14 Dist.] 1991. There is no discernible difference between claim of failure to perform in good and workmanlike manner and claim of negligent performance.—Sears, Roebuck and Co. v. Nichols, 819 S.W.2d 900.

⟾**2. Duty to use care.**

C.A.5 (La.) 1992. Duty-risk analysis, under Louisiana law, resolves into three inquiries: was the affirmative conduct a cause-in-fact of the resulting harm, was there a duty to protect this plaintiff from this type of harm arising in this manner, and was that duty breached.—Ellison v. Conoco, Inc., 950 F.2d 1196.

Under Louisiana law, an employer generally has no duty to insure that an independent contractor performs its obligations in a safe manner; however, an employer who retains control over the operative details of the independent contractor's work has a duty to discover or remedy hazards created by the contractor.—Id.

D.D.C. 1991. Under District of Columbia law, defendant can be held liable for damages resulting from intervening criminal acts of third parties only if the event is foreseeable and the defendant has a duty to take measures to guard against it.—Cebula v. Bush, 778 F.Supp. 567.

S.D.Iowa 1991. Under Iowa law, prerequisite to establishing claim of negligence is existence of legal duty.—Jackson v. Drake University, 778 F.Supp. 1490.

N.D.W.Va. 1991. To establish cause of action in negligence, complainant must first show that alleged tort-feasor was under duty or obligation, recognized by law, requiring person to conform to certain standard of conduct for protection of others against unreasonable risks.—Hartman v. Bethany College, 778 F.Supp. 286.

Fla.App. 3 Dist. 1991. Under common law, person had no duty to control conduct of another or to warn those placed in danger by such conduct; however, exception to that general rule can arise when there is special relationship between defendant and person whose behavior needs to be controlled or person who is foreseeable victim of that conduct.—Boynton v. Burglass, 590 So.2d 446, amended on denial of rehearing.

Ill. 1991. In absence of a showing from which court can infer existence of a duty, no recovery for negligence is possible as a matter of law.—Vesey v. Chicago Housing Authority, 164 Ill.Dec. 622, 583 N.E.2d 538, 145 Ill.2d 404.

La.App. 3 Cir. 1991. Duty-risk analysis requires that court inquire first as to whether defendant's action was cause-in-fact of accident, and second whether defendant owed duty

to plaintiff.—Shafer v. State, Through Dept. of Transp. and Development, 590 So.2d 639.

Minn.App. 1991. At common law, person owed no duty to warn those endangered by the conduct of another, but case law has carved out an exception to that rule where defendant stands in some special relationship to either the person whose conduct needs to be controlled or to the foreseeable victim of that conduct.—N.W. by J.W. v. Anderson, 478 N.W.2d 542, review denied.

Mo.App. 1991. Surveyor owed no duty of care to adjoining landowners with whom he was not in privity of contract and who had not relied on survey.—Gipson v. Slagle, 820 S.W.2d 595.

⟾**3. Degrees of care in general.**

N.D.W.Va. 1991. Obligation to exercise due care under circumstances does not arise absent duty at law to protect others against unreasonable risks.—Hartman v. Bethany College, 778 F.Supp. 286.

Ill. 1991. Pursuant to the voluntary-undertaking theory of liability, one who gratuitously renders services to another is subject to liability for bodily harm caused to the other by one's failure to exercise due care or such competence and skill as one possesses.—Vesey v. Chicago Housing Authority, 164 Ill.Dec. 622, 583 N.E.2d 538, 145 Ill.2d 404.

⟾**4. Ordinary or reasonable care.**

> When the Topic and Key Number are known, sets of digests can be consulted to locate cases with the same or similar points of law. The text of these cases should then be read. The digest paragraphs from the *Boynton* case were first published in the *General Digest 8th* and will later be cumulated into the *Tenth Decennial, Part 2.* In these sets of digests, federal court cases are listed first, followed by state court cases arranged alphabetically by state and starting with the most recent case.
>
> Notice how digest paragraphs are reprinted as they originally appeared as headnotes in the reported cases. Notice also how citations are given after the digest paragraph to where the case is reported.
>
> After selecting the relevant paragraphs and noting citations, one should then check under the same Topic and Key Number in other *General Digest* volumes for additional cases. One can check the prior *Decennials* under this Topic and Key Number for earlier cases.

against surveyor who was employed by owners of adjoining land to survey boundary of the properties; owners were not within class of persons that standards regulating land surveyors were designed to protect since they were not the employers. V.A.M.S. §§ 327.041, 327.291, 327.441, 327.451.—Id.

Ohio App. 10 Dist. 1989. Negligence per se does not equate liability per se; simply because law may presume negligence from person's violation of statute or rule does not mean that law presumes that such negligence was proximate cause of harm inflicted.—Perkins v. Ohio Dept. of Transp., 584 N.E.2d 794, 65 Ohio App.3d 487, cause dismissed 566 N.E.2d 673, 57 Ohio St.3d 612, rehearing denied 570 N.E.2d 281, 58 Ohio St.3d 711.

Pa.Cmwlth. 1991. Duty may be established by statute, and violation of statute may further establish breach of that duty, giving rise to negligence per se.—Gilson v. Doe, 600 A.2d 267.

Wis.App. 1991. Violation of safety regulation is generally negligence.—James v. Heintz, 478 N.W.2d 31.

⟾**10. Unintended consequences.**

D.D.C. 1991. Under District of Columbia law, defendant can be held liable for damages resulting from intervening criminal acts of third parties only if the event is foreseeable and the defendant has a duty to take measures to guard against it.—Cebula v. Bush, 778 F.Supp. 567.

Under District of Columbia law, foreseeability of harm must be more precisely shown where there is intervening criminal conduct than in the typical negligence situation.—Id.

⟾**11. Willful, wanton, or reckless acts or conduct.**

Bethany College, 778 F.Supp. 286.

⟾**15. Joint and several liability.**

W.Va. 1991. Under the "rule of joint and several liability" for plaintiffs, where plaintiffs are injured by concurrent negligence of several defendants, plaintiffs may elect to sue one or

For subsequent case history information see Table of Cases Affirmed, Reversed or Modified

[Illustration 28]

SAMPLE PAGE FROM TENTH DECENNIAL DIGEST, PART 1

29 10th D Pt 1—1135   **NEGLIGENCE**   ⊜2

negligent.—Lucas v. Godfrey, 467 N.W.2d 180, 161 Wis.2d 51, review denied 471 N.W.2d 509.

Wis.App. 1990. Public policy reasons for denying recovery, even if negligence has been proven include injury too remote from negligence, injury too wholly out of proportion to culpability of negligent tort-feasor, or fact that allowance of recovery would enter field that has no sensible or just stopping point.—Johnson v. Grzadzielewski, 465 N.W.2d 503, 159 Wis.2d 601.

Wis.App. 1987. Liability does not necessarily follow even when negligence and negligence as cause-in-fact of injury are present; public policy considerations may preclude liability.—Becker v. State Farm Mut. Auto. Ins. Co., 416 N.W.2d 906, 141 Wis.2d 804.

Public policy reasons for not imposing liability despite finding of negligence as substantial factor producing injury are: injury is too remote from negligence; injury is too wholly out of proportion to culpability of negligent tort-feasor; in retrospect it appears too highly extraordinary that negligence should have brought about harm; allowance of recovery would place too unreasonable a burden on negligent tort-feasor; allowance of recovery would be too likely to open way for fraudulent claims; or allowance for recovery would enter field that has no sensible or just stopping point.—Id.

Wis.App. 1986. There is no inherent cause of action for every negligent performance of contractual obligation.—McDonald v. Century 21 Real Estate Corp., 390 N.W.2d 68, 132 Wis.2d 1, review denied 393 N.W.2d 544, 132 Wis.2d 484.

Wyo. 1990. The elements of negligence duty, a violation of that duty, which proximate cause of an injury to the pl MacKrell v. Bell H₂S SAFETY, 795 P

Wyo. 1989. Intent is not factor gence, since negligence precludes inten duct.—Kobos By and Through Kobos v. 768 P.2d 534.

⊜2. Duty to use care.

Library references

C.J.S. Architects §§ 27, 47, 48, 51; Negligence § 4 et seq.

C.A.11 (Ala.) 1987. Staff safety engineer, area construction manager, and transmission line construction foreman had legal duty to lineman, who was injured when he fell from pole while erecting high power transmission line for Tennessee Valley Authority project, to maintain safe working conditions, primarily by fulfillment of safety standards as indicated by the Occupational Safety and Health Administration regulations and the TVA standards; job descriptions for such coemployees involved safety responsibilities.—Andrews v. Benson, 809 F.2d 1537, rehearing granted and vacated 817 F.2d 1471, vacated, reinstated 845 F.2d 255.

C.A.7 (Ill.) 1989. As general rule, Illinois does not impose duty to protect others from criminal attacks by third parties; however, exception is recognized where criminal attack was reasonably foreseeable and parties had special relationship such as carrier-passenger, innkeeper-guest, business invitor-invitee, or voluntary custodian-protectee.—Figueroa v. Evangelical Covenant Church, 879 F.2d 1427, rehearing denied.

Under Illinois law, showing of reliance or of increased risk is not required to meet "voluntary undertaking" exception to general rule that party owes no duty to protect others from criminal attacks by third parties; however, any duty assumed must be strictly limited to scope of undertaking and injuries sustained must be reasonably foreseeable.—Id.

C.A.7 (Ill.) 1989. There is no duty to warn against obvious danger, for obvious danger is no danger to reasonably careful person.—Pomer v. Schoolman, 875 F.2d 1262.

C.A.7 (Ill.) 1986. Duty is essential element of negligence and is question of law to be decided by trial court; foreseeability is necessary, but not sufficient requirement before imposing duty.—Homer v. Pabst Brewing Co., 806 F.2d 119.

Liability may arise from negligent performance of voluntary undertaking, but scope of duty is limited by extent of undertaking.—Id.

Employer which maintained medical department to provide first aid and palliative care to its employees did not owe duty of care to persons injured in collision with employee, who lost consciousness when driving home after his shift was completed, as employer did not volunteer to protect general public from illnesses that may befall its employees.—Id.

C.A.7 (Ind.) 1989. Charter tour operator had no duty under Indiana law to make specific inquiries into guest safety or security at hotel which provided accommodations as an option in tour package, where nothing indicated hotel was located in a high-crime area, that hotel experienced more safety and security problems than other resort hotels on island, or that level of criminal activity involving guests at hotel was unusually high for large beach resort.—Wilson v. American Trans Air, Inc., 874 F.2d 386.

Under Indiana law, charter tour operator did not gratuitously assume a duty to conduct a reasonable inquiry into safety of proposed hotel accommodations and to warn prospective pa

One can check the *Decennials* under Negligence 2 for cases with the same or similar points of law that are earlier than those in the *General Digest*.

chase order, breach of which would give rise to tort liability, based on reliance by owner of the compressor.—McGowan v. Cooper Industries, Inc., 863 F.2d 1266, rehearing denied.

C.A.5 (La.) 1989. Surveyor employed by private inspection firm did not owe a duty to engineer employed by owner of semi-submersible drilling rig to warn the engineer of the possibility of deadly gases in a particular compartment being inspected where the rig owner had supplied a "competent person" to test the atmosphere in each compartment before it was entered by the three men.—Miller-Schmidt v. Gastech, Inc., 864 F.2d 1181.

Absent legal duty, a cause of action for negligence must necessarily fail.—Id.

C.A.8 (Minn.) 1990. Under Minnesota law, there is no duty to protect another from injury or harm which might befall him or her; nevertheless, in some circumstances one who gratuitously accepts responsibility of acting to protect another must utilize due care even though no duty would exist otherwise.—Kruchten v. U.S., 914 F.2d 1106.

C.A.3 (N.J.) 1991. Liability for negligence can never arise absent some duty.—Matute v. Lloyd Bermuda Lines, Ltd., 931 F.2d 231, certiorari denied 112 S.Ct. 329, 116 L.Ed.2d 270.

C.A.2 (N.Y.) 1989. Trademark registration agents had duty to meet foreign standards in effecting trademark renewals promptly in foreign countries and maintaining appropriate and orderly files in effort to do so.—William Wrigley Jr. Co. v. Waters, 890 F.2d 594.

C.A.10 (Okl.) 1988. Company which agreed to develop a distillate desulfurizer for use in plaintiff's oil refinery owed duty of due care to plaintiff, apart from any duties specifically enumerated in parties' contract, to warn plaintiff of

hazards associated with desulfurizer that allegedly resulted in fire at refinery.—Hess Oil Virgin Islands Corp. v. UOP, Inc., 861 F.2d 1197.

C.A.5 (Tex.) 1991. Under Texas law, there is no duty to warn when danger is obvious or actually known to injured person.—Stout v. Borg-Warner Corp., 933 F.2d 331, rehearing denied 940 F.2d 657, certiorari denied 112 S.Ct. 584, 116 L.Ed.2d 609.

C.A.5 (Tex.) 1990. One cannot be liable for negligence unless one first has duty to act.—Randolph v. Laeisz, 896 F.2d 964, rehearing denied.

C.A.10 (Utah) 1990. Generally, Utah law does not impose upon party affirmative duty to care for another; it does impose upon party affirmative duty to act only when there are certain special relationships such as assumption of responsibility for another's safety or deprivation of normal opportunities for self-protection.—Flynn v. U.S., 902 F.2d 1524.

C.A.10 (Utah) 1990. Under Utah law, burden involved in eliminating risk is relevant to court's duty of care analysis.—Shute v. Moon Lake Elec. Ass'n, Inc., 899 F.2d 999, rehearing denied.

E.D.Ark. 1989. Absent a duty, there can be no breach of duty and there can be no negligence liability.—Federal Sav. and Loan Ins. Corp. v. Smith, 721 F.Supp. 1039.

N.D.Cal. 1988. Even if a defendant has acted negligently, if he owes no duty to plaintiff, he may not be held liable.—In re Rexplore, Inc. Securities Litigation, 685 F.Supp. 1132.

D.Colo. 1991. Negligence claim fails if under

in order to show negligence by reason of nonfeasance, plaintiff must show existence of special relationship imposing duty to act.—Id.

D.Colo. 1991. In determining existence of duty to particular defendant, court must consider factors of risk involved, foreseeability or likelihood of injury as weighed against social utility of conduct, magnitude of burden of guarding against injury or harm, and consequences of placing such burdens on defendants in these circumstances; other considerations may also be relevant, and no one factor controls.—Cottam v. First Baptist Church of Boulder, 756 F.Supp. 1433, affirmed 962 F.2d 17.

D.Colo. 1987. Determination of duty of care requires consideration of risk involved, the foreseeability and likelihood of injury as weighed against social utility of actor's conduct, the magnitude of burden of guarding against injury or harm, and the consequences of placing burden upon actor.—Shewmake v. Badger Oil Corp., 654 F.Supp. 1184.

D.Conn. 1990. Negligence cannot be predicated upon failure to perform an act which actor was under no duty or obligation to perform.—Cumis Ins. Soc., Inc. v. Windsor Bank & Trust Co., 736 F.Supp. 1226.

D.D.C. 1987. Under District of Columbia law, lender owed duty of care to loan applicants, and thus incurred negligence liability, where lender accepted applicants' "processing fees" and acknowledged duty toward applicants when it extended assurances that there were "no problems" with application.—High v. McLean Financial Corp., 659 F.Supp. 1561.

C.D.Ill. 1990. Under Illinois law, consultant hired for purpose of administering employee benefit plans and performing necessary paper work did not owe duty to plans regarding provision of investment advice.—Branch-Hess Vending Ser-

For references to other topics, see Descriptive-Word Index

[Illustration 29]

SAMPLE SCREENS FROM WESTLAW SHOWING HEADNOTES

Figure 1. Case Headnote Showing > Feature

```
                    COPR. (C) WEST 1993 NO CLAIM TO ORIG. U.S. GOVT. WORKS
AUTHORIZED FOR EDUCATIONAL USE ONLY
590 So.2d 446
(CITE AS: 590 SO.2D 446)
Boynton v. Burglass
  > [1]
  > 272      NEGLIGENCE           This is the first headnote in Boynton v. Bur-
  > 272I     Acts or Omis         glass as it appears in WESTLAW.  The > can
  > 272I(A)  Personal C           be used to hypertext or "jump" directly to the
                                  related text in the opinion.  Note that in
                                  WESTLAW the Topic name is replaced with a
  > 272k2  k. Duty to use         number and the Key Number symbol is re-
Fla.App. 3 Dist.,1991.            placed with the letter "k."
Under common law, person had no duty to control conduct of another or to warn
those placed in danger by such conduct; however, exception to that general
rule can arise when there is special relationship between defendant and person
whose behavior needs to be controlled or person who is foreseeable victim of
that conduct.
```

Figure 2. Case Headnote with *Formerly* Line

```
                    COPR. (C) WEST 1993 NO CLAIM TO ORIG. U.S. GOVT. WORKS
AUTHORIZED FOR EDUCATIONAL USE ONLY
619 F.2d 216       R 1 OF 14        P 8 OF 25        FBKR-CS        T
(CITE AS: 619 F.2D 216)
In re Adamo
  > [5]
  > 51       BANKRUPTCY          The Topic Bankruptcy was recently revised.
  > 51I      In General          This headnote from WESTLAW illustrates how
  > 51I(B)   Constitut.          a search of a new Key Number also identifies
                                 the Topic's former Key Number.  See next Il-
  > 51k2026  k. Repeal.          lustration.
```

```
Formerly 51K8
C.A.N.Y., 1980.
Premature repeal of the Higher Education Act provision pertaining to the
dischargeability of student loans had no effect in proceedings in bankruptcy
commenced prior to the effective date of the Bankruptcy Reform Act.  Higher
Education Act of 1965, s 439A, > 20 U.S.C. (1976 Ed.) s 1087-3; Bankr.Code,
> 11 U.S.C.A. s 523(a)(8); s 402(a), 11 U.S.C.A. note preceding section 101.
```

[Illustration 30]

KEY NUMBER TRANSLATION FROM THE TENTH
DECENNIAL DIGEST, PART 1

◄ 10th D Pt 1—943 **BANKRUPTCY**

TABLE 3

KEY NUMBER TRANSLATION TABLE

FORMER KEY NUMBER TO PRESENT KEY NUMBER

The topic BANKRUPTCY has been extensively revised in consideration of the Bankruptcy Reform Act of 1978.

This table indicates the location, in the revised topic, of cases formerly classified to the earlier key numbers.

In many instances there is no one-to-one relation between the key numbers, new and old. This table recognizes only significant correspondence, and the user who has found a particular case classified to an old key number is advised to consult the Table of Cases, where its present classification may be found.

The absence of a key number indicates that there is no useful parallel.

Former Key Number	Present Key Number	Former Key Number	Present Key Number
1	2012–2018	44.5	2255, 2256, 2311
2, 3	2013–2025	47	2258
4	2001, 2021, 2022	48	2252–2254, 2259–2264
5	2023	49	2264(1)
6	2023–2025	50	2252–2254, 2259–2264
7	2023	51	2251
8	2026	52	2281, 2293
9	2002, 2513, 2534, 2762–2765, 2826	54	2234
		55–64	2281
10	2341	65	2282, 2284, 2288
11(1)	2001, 2016, 2041–2082, 2102, 2104, 2122–2126,	67	2222–2231, 2311
		68	2229

> This illustrates one of the ways the Key Number classification is kept current. The Topic *Bankruptcy* has been revised. This table translates an old key number to a new one. For example, if one had reference to Key Number 8 from an older *Decennial*, the point of law covered by that Key Number is now digested under Key Number 2026. See previous Illustration, Figure 2.
>
> A similar Table translates the current Key Numbers to older ones.

Former	Present	Former	Present
24	2127	81	2290, 2293
25	2201	82, 83	2290
27	2321–2325	84(1)	2204, 2292
28	2321	85, 86	2290
29	2322	87	2131
30	2323	88	2204
31	2324	89	2294
32	2325	90	2290
33	2127	91	2294
35	2127, 2131	91(1, 2)	2296
36	2133	92	2282–2289, 2295
37	2121	93	2130; Jury ⊕19(9)
38	2001, 2251	94–96	2295
39	2235	97	3040–3048
41	2222–2231	98	3761 et seq.
42	2227	99	2295
43	2224–2228	100	2297
44	2257, 2311	101	3061

[Illustration 31]

TABLE OF KEY NUMBERS FROM VOLUME 10
OF THE GENERAL DIGEST, 8TH SERIES

729

MECHANICS' LIENS—Cont'd	MECHANICS' LIENS—Cont'd	MENTAL HEALTH—Cont'd	MENTAL HEALTH—Cont'd
☞	☞	☞	☞
137(1)—3	271(15)—9	130—2	475—3
137(2)—3	273—8	132—5	476—2
139(1)—8	276—8	133—3, 5, 7, 9	482—6
139(3)—6, 7	276(2)—2	135—3, 4, 5, 6, 8, 9	485—3, 6
141—6	277(1)—2	137—1, 3	486—4, 8, 9
144—4	279—3, 4, 7, 9	144—3	488—4
147—4, 8	281(1)—1, 5, 7, 9	146—5, 9	495—2, 3
149(1)—6	281(4)—2, 9	151—8	496—2
149(3)—3, 6	281(5)—4, 7	153—6	499—6
149(4)—8	302—9	154—8	506—5
153—2	303(1)—8, 9	155—5	508—5
154(2)—4	303(2)—3, 4	156—3, 6, 9	514—6, 9
154(3)—10	304(3)—9	158—5	517—6
154(5)—10	309—1, 2	159—4, 5, 7, 8	
154(6)—3, 4	310(1)—5, 6, 10	160—2	MILITARY JUSTICE
156—1, 3, 4	310(2)—9	161—2	☞
157(1)—3, 8, 10	310(3)—1, 2, 6, 7, 8, 10	167—5	500—2
157(3)—3, 6, 7	310(4)—6	175—9	503—6
157(5)—2, 6		176—6, 8	504—3, 9
158—4, 6	MENTAL HEALTH	177—8	505—3
160—1, 6, 8	☞		
161(1)—6, 7, 8, 9	3—2, 3		
161(3)—6	10—1		
161(4)—1	19—2		
163—9	20—1, 6,		
164(1)—1, 8, 9	21—1, 2,		
166—6	31—4, 5		
167—2	32—2, 3		
168—1, 4, 6	36—3, 5		
172—6, 7	37—2, 3		
173—3, 4, 6, 7	38—2, 4		
178—1	39—3, 5,		
180—4	40—2, 5,		
183—5, 7, 10	41—1, 2,		
184—7	42—2, 6		
186—7	43—1, 3,		

> This Table, published in every tenth volume of the *General Digest*, allows a researcher to determine which of the volumes 1–10 contain a particular Topic and Key Number.
>
> In this example, one would only have to consult four of the ten volumes for cases dealing with the Topic *Mental Health* and Key Number 414(2).

187—3, 4	44—2, 4, 5, 8	300—3	552—8
189—8	45—1, 2, 3, 4, 5, 6, 7, 9	301—2	554—6, 9
191—8	46—3, 6	302—2	556—9
195—7	48—5	305—2	560—1, 3, 4, 7, 10
196—6	50—2, 3, 9	309—3	563—1, 4, 7, 8, 10
197—7	51—3, 4, 5	371—3	564—1, 9
198—2, 3, 6	51.5—1, 2, 3, 4, 8, 9, 10	372—6	565—2
208—1, 3, 6, 8, 10	51.15—3, 6, 7, 8	375—1	566—2, 10
216(1)—6	51.20—1, 2, 3, 4, 5, 6, 7, 9	377—8	569—4, 6, 8, 9
226—7	52—2, 5	379—6	572—5, 6, 8, 9, 10
228—3, 6	53—2, 5	411—1	575—1, 3, 8
237—10	54—4	412—1	578—9
238—7	55—4	414(1)—4	581—1, 5
239—6	56—3, 5, 9	414(2)—1, 2, 7, 9	596—3, 6, 7, 8, 9
245(1)—1	57—3	414(3)—1	599—3, 6, 7, 8, 9
245(2)—9	59—5, 6, 8	414(4)—2	600—3
245(3)—9	60—5, 6, 8, 9	415—5	605—3
246—9	73—8	432—1, 2, 3, 4, 5, 6, 7, 8, 9, 10	606—3
249—8, 9	76—6	433—2, 5, 7, 8, 9	614—9
253—5, 6	78—3, 8, 10	434—1, 2, 3, 4, 5, 6, 7, 8, 9, 10	632—6
254(2)—1, 9	79—2, 3, 6	435—7	635—10
255—9	82—7, 8	436—4, 6, 7, 9, 10	638—6, 10
260(1)—2, 6	85—2	437—5, 7, 10	641—4, 10
260(2)—5	101—2, 5, 6, 8	438—8, 9, 10	642—2, 6
260(4)—1, 8, 9	102—5	439—1, 2, 3, 4, 5, 6, 9	644—5, 7
260(6)—2, 7	105—5, 6, 7	440—2, 5, 6, 7, 8, 9	650—3, 5
263(1)—1	110—5	441—10	653—3
263(3)—2	114—5	442—1, 3, 5, 9	671—9
263(7)—3, 8	116—4, 5, 6, 7, 8	444—2	681—3, 8, 9
263(9)—9	117—4, 8, 9	445—8	684—10
263(10)—3	118—7, 9	446—8	686—1
264(2)—7	120—6	447—5, 7	688—4
265—1, 6	124—5, 6	448—1, 2, 9	691—6
268—1, 3, 6, 8	128—5	449—8, 9	700—5
271(7)—4	129—5	472—5	706—1, 5
271(14)—4		473—2	709—1, 7, 9

SECTION D. FINDING TOPICS AND KEY NUMBERS

The *American Digest System,* as classified to the *Key Number System,* provides a means to locate all cases on the same or similar point of law. Once it is determined to what Topic and Key Number a particular point of law has been classified, searching for cases can commence in the various units of the *American Digest System.*

Learning how to find the appropriate Topics and Key Numbers is very important for successful case finding. Four common methods are provided for finding Topics and Key Numbers within the *American Digest System.*

1. The Descriptive Word Method

The *Descriptive–Word Index* is a highly-detailed, alphabetically-arranged subject index to the contents of the digests. This index is often the best starting point for research, unless a relevant case or the particular Topic and Key Number being researched is already known. It includes *catch words* or descriptive words relating to the legal issues digested and all the Topics of the digest classification system. There is a separate *Descriptive–Word Index,* often in several volumes, for each of the *Decennial* units. Each volume of the *General Digest* contains its own *Descriptive–Word Index,* which is cumulated in every tenth volume.

Using the *Descriptive–Word Indexes* successfully requires analysis of the legal issues and often the ability to think in both broad and narrow terms or from the general to the specific. It might prove helpful at this point to review the *TARP Rule* discussed in Chapter 2.

Let us examine the problem described in Section A to see how the *Descriptive–Word Indexes* to the *Decennial* units of the *American Digest System* are used to locate Topics and Key Numbers for finding cases dealing with a psychiatrist's duty to warn someone of possible injury by a patient.

In starting the search, it is best to begin in a recent *Decennial* or in the *General Digest.* When using an index, the first entry to consult should be a specific word or phrase relevant to the fact situation under research.

In our fact situation, the most specific word is *psychiatrist.* An examination of this word in the *Tenth Decennial, Part 1* reveals the following entry:

PSYCHIATRISTS

LIABILITY—

Torts of mentally disordered persons.

Mental H 414(2)

[See Illustrations 32 and 35.]

An examination of the cumulative volumes of the *General Digest* reveals the following additional entry:

PSYCHIATRISTS

DUTY to warn third parties—

    Readily identifiable victim.

Mental H 414(2)

These references indicate that under the Topic *Mental Health,* Key Number 414(2) in both the *Tenth Decennial Digest, Part 1* and the *General Digest* are digest paragraphs that address the legal issue being researched.

2. Analysis or Topic Method

As mentioned in Section B–1, over 400 Topics are used in West's *Key Number Digests.* Once an editor assigns a Topic to a headnote, the next step is assignment of the Key Number. Each Topic is arranged in outline form with main heading and subdivisions. Often these subdivisions are further subdivided into minute detail. These various breakdowns under a broad Topic are assigned Key Numbers. After analyzing the legal issue contained in a particular headnote, the editor uses these outlines to establish the most specific Key Number for the point of law in the headnote. On occasion, and in order to assure that a headnote receives the necessary topical coverage, it may be assigned to more than one Topic.

These outlines are published at the start of each Topic in the *American Digest System.* Two preliminary sections, "Subjects Included" and "Subjects Excluded and Covered in Other Topics," are published immediately before the detailed outline. Reading this "scope note" is often helpful in determining if the research is being conducted in the proper Topic. The topical outline that follows immediately thereafter, actually West's Key Number classification scheme, is entitled the *Analysis.*

The *Analysis* sections under the Topics *Negligence* and *Mental Health* were used in establishing the Key Numbers for the headnotes in *Boynton v. Burglass,* the case used in our problem. By rereading these headnotes, one can see that the headnote pertaining to negligence covers a broad general principle of law, whereas the two relating to mental health are much more specific. By carefully scanning the *Analysis,* a researcher can often see details in coverage that might not have come to mind in initial assessment of a legal issue and, thus, identify the most specific Key Number to use. [See Illustrations 33–35.]

Use of the *Analysis* method generally requires certainty that the Topic selected is the proper one, as well as a thorough understanding of West's Key Number classification. Therefore, use of this method is often most successful when used in connection with the *Descriptive-Word Index* method.

3. Table of Cases Method

Each *Decennial* unit and each volume of the *General Digest* have an alphabetical *Table of Cases* by plaintiff. The *Table of Cases* is cumulated in every tenth volume of the *General Digest*. Each case listing includes the citation and the Topics and Key Numbers under which the case has been digested. For example, if one knows that the case of *Boynton v. Burglass* is pertinent to the issue being researched and the case citation is not available, the *Table of Cases* will provide both the citation and the Topics and Key Numbers assigned to that case. [See Illustration 36.] Once the Topic and Key Numbers are known, the *Analysis* can be consulted for other relevant Key Numbers.

Defendant–Plaintiff volumes are published for the *Decennials* commencing with the *Ninth Decennial Digest, Part 1*. These volumes enable a researcher to locate a case when only the name of the defendant, *e.g.,* *Burglass,* is known.

4. An Alternative Method for Locating Topics and Key Numbers

Frequently, in the course of one's research, a citation to a case will be located that suggests that it contains a relevant point of law. Such citations may be found in almost any legal source, *e.g.,* a law review article, another case, a set of annotated statutes, a treatise, an encyclopedia. Rather than attempting to find similar cases using any of the three methods described *supra,* it is sometimes more practical to go immediately to the unit of the *National Reporter System* containing the cited case that has been identified. If after reading the case, a determination is made that it is important to the research being conducted, one should note all relevant Topics and Key Numbers. A researcher can then go directly to any of West's *Key Number Digests* and look under the same Topics and Key Numbers and find other digest paragraphs with these same Topics and Key Numbers.

SECTION E. ILLUSTRATIONS: FINDING TOPICS AND KEY NUMBERS

[Illustration 32]

PAGE FROM DESCRIPTIVE–WORD INDEX TO THE
TENTH DECENNIAL DIGEST, PART 1

39–10th D Pt 1—345   **PSYCHIATRISTS**

PROXIMATE CAUSE—Cont'd
AUTOMOBILES—Cont'd
  Questions for jury—
    Injuries from defects or obstructions in
      highway. **Autos 308(10)**
    Speed. **Autos 201(2)**
AVIATION, see this index **Aviation**
BRIDGES, injuries from defects or obstruc-
  tions. **Bridges 43, 46(11)**
CARGO, improper stowage as proximate
  cause of injury to or loss of. **Ship
  123(5)**
CARRIERS—
  Goods, loss or injury. **Carr 123**
  Baggage of passenger. **Carr 397**
  Warehouseman, liability of carrier as.
    Carr 144
  Livestock, loss or injury. **Carr 217(2)**
  Passengers, injuries to. **Carr 305**
  Instructions. **Carr 321(19)**

PROXIMATE CAUSE—Cont'd
INSTRUCTIONS to jury—Cont'd
  Negligence in general. **Neglig 140**
  Railroad accidents. **R R 485(9)**
  Street railroads. **Urb R R 30**
INSURANCE loss—
  Automobiles—
    Injuries from operation or use of high-
      ways. **Autos 201(9)**
    Questions for jury. **Autos 245(65)**
  Life insurance—
    Accidental death. **Insurance 515.5**
  Marine insurance. **Insurance 413**
  Property and title insurance. **Insurance
    427**
INTERVENING efficient cause. **Neglig 62**
  Fright of horses. **Neglig 62(2)**
  Third person's act or omission. **Neglig
    62(3)**
INTOXICATING liquors, injury from sale

PROXIMATE CAUSE—Cont'd
REMOTE consequences. **Neglig 60**
SEWERS or drains, injuries from defects or
  obstructions in. **Mun Corp 840**
SPECIAL findings. **Trial 350.5**
SPEED, see this index **Speed**
STORED goods, loss of or injury to. **Wareh
  24(5)**
STREET, injury on. **Mun Corp 705(11),
  800, 821(19)**
  Automobiles, generally, ante
  Contractor's liability. **Mun Corp 809(2)**
  Contributory negligence or assumption of
    risk of person injured. **Mun Corp
    802–807**
  Evidence. **Mun Corp 819(4)**
  Liabilities of abutting owners. **Mun Corp
    808**
STREET railroads, injuries. **Urb R R 27**

> This page illustrates how Topics and Key Numbers can be located by using the *Descriptive-Word Index* to a unit of the *American Digest System*. In this instance, we begin with the most specific word in our fact situation, "psychiatrist." Notice in the two sub-entries that we should consult *Mental Health*, Key Number 414(2).
>
> Many times, one will not find an index entry under a particular word or phrase. In such instances, one should search in the *Index* under another appropriate word or phrase.

ligence
DAMAGE—
  Nature and extent. **Neglig 64**
  Proximate or remote consequences.
    Damag 17–19
DEATH. **Death 17**
  Instructions. **Death 104(2)**
  Question for jury. **Death 103(2)**
DEFINITIONS and distinctions, efficient
  cause of injury. **Neglig 56(1.4, 1.5)**
DIRECTLY and indirectly, act produces
  event. **Neglig 56(1.6–1.13)**
EFFICIENT cause of injury in general.
  Neglig 56
  Intervening efficient cause. **Neglig 62**
  Violation of statute, ordinance or munici-
    pal regulation. **Neglig 56(3)**
  Wrongful acts in general. **Neglig 56(2)**
ELECTRICITY, injuries from. **Electricity
  16(7)**
EVIDENCE, direct or circumstantial. **Neg-
  lig 134(2)**
EXISTENCE of. **Neglig 56(1.14–1.16)**
EXPERT testimony, basis of opinion—
  Crim Law 486(10)
  Evid 555.5
FRAUD. **Fraud 25**
HIGHWAYS. **High 196, 197(6), 213(3)**
  Automobiles, generally, ante
INACTION as proximate cause. **Neglig
  56(1.16)**
INEVITABLE accident. **Neglig 63**
INFANTS—
  Generally, see this index **Infants**
INJURIES to employee, see this index **Em-
  ployers' Liability**
INSTRUCTIONS to jury—
  Contributory negligence—
    Neglig 141(8)
    R R 351(13)

misconduct. **Phys 15(4)**
PLEADING. **Neglig 111(3)**
PRESUMPTIONS and burden of proof.
  Neglig 121.5
PRODUCTS liability. **Prod Liab 15**
  Automobiles. **Prod Liab 38**
PUBLIC buildings or other property, inju-
  ries from condition or use. **Mun Corp
  854**
PUBLIC housing. **Mun Corp 854**
PUPIL injured while being transported.
  Schools 89.18
QUESTIONS for jury in general. **Neglig
  136(25)**
RAILROADS, injuries—
  Accidents to train. **R R 296**
  Animals on or near tracks. **R R 425,
    446(13)**
  Construction or maintenance, injuries
    from. **R R 113(10)**
  Contributory negligence as proximate
    cause. **R R 278**
  Crossing accidents. **R R 337**
    Evidence. **R R 348(2)**
    Instructions to jury. **R R 351(2)**
    Pleading. **R R 344(7)**
    Presumptions and burden of proof. **R
      R 346(7)**
    Questions for jury. **R R 350(32)**
  Fires on or near tracks. **R R 463–465**
    Instructions to jury. **R R 485(9)**
    Pleading. **R R 478(6)**
  Licensees or trespassers on railroad prop-
    erty. **R R 279**
  Persons on or near tracks. **R R 389**
    Contributory negligence, question for
      jury. **R R 400(10)**
    Instructions. **R R 401(1)**
    Question for jury. **R R 400(1)**

railroads, injuries. **Urb R R 27**
WEIGHT and sufficiency of evidence in
  general. **Neglig 134(11)**
WORKERS' compensation—
  Consequences of injury for which com-
    pensation may be had. **Work Comp
    597–603**
  Questions of law and fact. **Work Comp
    1717**

PRUDENT MAN RULE
INVESTMENT, trustees. **Trusts 217.3(5)**

PRURIENT INTEREST
INDIGENTS—
  Criminal defendant's right to appoint-
    ment to assist in defense, see this
    index **Indigent Persons**
OBSCENITY, element of, see this index
  Lewdness or Obscenity

PSYCHIATRIC EXAMINATION
WARNINGS, necessity of. **Crim Law
  412.2(3)**

PSYCHIATRISTS
DUTY to warn third parties—
  Readily identifiable victim. **Mental H
    414(2)**
LIABILITY—
  Judicial determinations—
    Competency to stand trial. **Judges 36**
  Torts of mentally disordered persons.
    Mental H 414(2)
MALPRACTICE—
  Patient's husband—
    Cause of action. **Phys 7**
MARRIAGE, causing patient to pursue dis-
  solution—
  Alienation of affections. **Hus & W 324**

[Illustration 33]

TOPIC: MENTAL HEALTH FROM TENTH DECENNIAL DIGEST, PART 1

28 10th D Pt 1—678

MENTAL HEALTH

SUBJECTS INCLUDED

Promotion of mental health

Care and treatment of persons affected by mental disorder of any kind not merely temporary in nature

Custody and protection of such persons and their property

Rights and disabilities of mentally disordered persons in general

Legal proceedings affecting such persons

SUBJECTS EXCLUDED AND COVERED BY OTHER TOPICS

Asylums and hospitals for the mentally disordered. see ASYLUMS, HOSPITALS

This illustrates the "Analysis" method of locating Topics and Key Numbers. If a researcher knows that a particular issue deals with *Mental Health*, that Topic can be consulted immediately in the appropriate volume or volumes of a digest. After reading the "scope note" for information included, excluded, or covered elsewhere, the next step is to find a relevant Key Number.

Note that in the initial broad outline under IV. Disabilities and Privileges of Mentally Disordered Persons is subheading (D) Torts, which covers Key Numbers 411–430. This broad outline enables a researcher to narrow a search to a range of Key Numbers.

See next Illustration.

Analysis

I. IN GENERAL, ☞1–30.

II. CARE AND SUPPORT OF MENTALLY DISORDERED PERSONS, ☞31–100.
　　(A) CUSTODY AND CURE, ☞31–70.
　　(B) SUPPORT, ☞71–100.

III. GUARDIANSHIP AND PROPERTY OF ESTATE, ☞101–330.
　　(A) GUARDIANSHIP IN GENERAL, ☞101–210.
　　(B) PROPERTY AND MANAGEMENT OF MENTALLY DISORDERED PERSON'S ESTATE, ☞211–290.
　　(C) ACCOUNTING AND SETTLEMENT, ☞291–330.

IV. DISABILITIES AND PRIVILEGES OF MENTALLY DISORDERED PERSONS, ☞331–470.
　　(A) IN GENERAL, ☞331–350.
　　(B) CAPACITY TO TAKE AND HOLD PROPERTY, ☞351–370.
　　(C) CONTRACTS AND TRANSFERS OF PROPERTY, ☞371–410.
➤　　(D) TORTS, ☞411–430.
　　(E) CRIMES, ☞431–470.

V. ACTIONS, ☞471–518.

[Illustration 34]

TOPIC: MENTAL HEALTH FROM TENTH DECENNIAL DIGEST, PART 1

---

28 10th D Pt 1—681   **MENTAL HEALTH**

III. GUARDIANSHIP AND PROPERTY OF ESTATE.—Cont'd

(B) PROPERTY AND MANAGEMENT OF MENTALLY DISORDERED PERSON'S ESTATE.—Cont'd

249. —— Nature of allowances to family; conditions.
250. —— Services in general.
251. —— Counsel fees and costs.
252. —— Evidence.
253. —— Presentation and allowance of claims in general.
254. —— Jurisdiction.
255. —— Limitations and laches.
256. —— Hearing and determination.
257. —— Priorities and payment.
258. Sales, transfers, and encumbrances by guardian; order of court.
259. —— Authority to sell or convey in general.
260. —— Necessity of court approval.
261. —— Purposes of, and grounds for, sale, and objections.
262. —— Property or interests subject to disposal.
263. —— Jurisdiction.
264. —— Proceedings for sale in general.
265. —— Parties and application.
266. —— Notice.
267. —— Hearing, order or decree, and record.
268. —— Validity of sale.
269. —— Confirmation.
270. —— Vacating or setting aside.
271. —— Title, rights, and liabilities of purchasers.
272. —— Collateral attack.
273. —— Proceeds.

274. —— Lease.
275. —— Mortgage or pledge.

(C) ACCOUNTING AND SETTLEMENT.

⚷291. In general.
292. Duty to account.
293. Persons entitled to accounting, and persons liable to account.
294. Jurisdiction of courts.
295. Proceedings for accounting.
296. Actions for accounting.
297. Charges.
298. Credits.
299. Form and requisites of account.
300. Objections and exceptions.
301. Evidence.
302. Hearing or reference, and determination.
303. Order or decree.
304. Opening or vacating.
305. Review.
306. —— Scope of review and trial de novo.
307. —— Determination and disposition.
308. Costs and expenses.
309. —— Attorneys' fees.
310. Operation and effect.
311. —— Collateral attack.
312. —— Intermediate accounts.
313. Private accounting and settlement.

IV. DISABILITIES AND PRIVILEGES OF MENTALLY DISORDERED PERSONS.

(A) IN GENERAL.

⚷331. Disabilities and privileges in general.

384. —— Effect of adjudication, commitment, or guardianship.
385. —— Bona fide purchasers.

After a narrow range of Key Numbers is identified, these Key Numbers can be consulted for the most appropriate one to use for locating cases on the issue being researched. See next Illustration.

---

352. Adverse possession.

(C) CONTRACTS AND TRANSFERS OF PROPERTY.

⚷371. Transactions in general.
372. Contracts in general.
373. —— Contracts before adjudication or appointment of guardian.
374. —— Effect of adjudication, commitment, or guardianship.
375. Necessaries.
376. Sale, purchase, exchange, or lease.
377. Services.
378. Loans and advances.
379. Bills and notes.
380. Compromise, settlement, and release
381. Insurance.
382. Conveyances.
383. —— Before adjudication or guardianship.

393. —— Persons as to whom transactions may be avoided.
394. —— Time for avoidance and laches.
395. —— Operation and effect.
396. Ratification.

(D) TORTS.

⚷411. Liability of mentally disordered persons in general.
412. Particular torts of mentally disordered persons.
413. Liability for torts of others.
414. Liability of others for torts of mentally disordered persons.
    → (1). In general.
    (2). Mental health professionals and institutions.
    (3). Escape or release from custody.
    (4). Actions.
415. Damages.

[Illustration 35]

PAGE FROM GENERAL DIGEST, 8TH SERIES
TOPIC: MENTAL HEALTH

---

791   **MENTAL HEALTH**   ⟜432

hearing, to reduce any award that patient or ex-patient might receive in suit against state violated due process. U.S.C.A. Const.Amend. 14; 42 U.S.C.A. § 1983.—Id.

III. GUARDIANSHIP AND PROPERTY OF ESTATE.

(A) GUARDIANSHIP IN GENERAL.

⟜**104. Persons subject to guardianship.**

⟜**105. —— Mental incompetency or incapacity in general.**

Ohio Prob. 1991. Prospective ward who was alleged to be "comatose due to pontine hemorrhage" qualified for appointment of guardian.—In re Guardianship of McInnis, 584 N.E.2d 1389, 61 Ohio Misc.2d 790.

⟜**116. Persons who may be appointed.**

Ohio App. 8 Dist. 1990. In evaluating applications for appointment of a guardian, probate court must engage in a two-part determination: it must first determine that a guardian is required, and must also determine who shall be appointed guardian.—In re Medsker, 583 N.E.2d 1091, 66 Ohio App.3d 219.

To be effective as a nomination of a guardian, a writing shall be signed by the person making the nomination in the presence of two witnesses, signed by the witnesses, contain an attestation of the witnesses that the person making the nomination signed in their presence, and be acknowledged by the person making the nomination before a notary public. R.C. § 2111.121.—Id.

⟜**118. —— Heirs, next of kin, and relatives in general.**

Ohio App. 8 Dist. 1990. Daughter, who was

gal interests. West's C.R.S.A. §§ 15–14–308, 15–14–314.—Id.

Probate court's determination that incapacitated person's various interests would best be served by appointing legal counsel, in addition to guardian ad litem, in guardianship proceeding instituted to gain permission to withhold life sustaining treatment from incapacitated person did not constitute abuse of discretion where it was undisputed that incapacitated person did not understand nature and significance of proceedings, could not make decisions on her own behalf, and did not possess ability to communicate with and act on advice of counsel, and that her guardian ad litem did not undertake representation of her legal interests.—Id.

⟜**158. Costs.**

⟜**159. —— Attorneys' fees.**

Colo.App. 1991. Trial court's assessment of attorney fees against Department of Institutions did not constitute abuse of discretion where probate court appointed attorney to represent incapacitated person's legal interests in proceeding instituted by Department to gain permission to withhold life sustaining treatment from incapacitated person at request of person's parents, even though Department believed that, in light of its requirement to render treatment to its residents, it had no option but to file petition requesting special instructions concerning withholding of life sustaining treatment.—Department of Institutions, Grand Junction Regional Center v. Carothers, 821 P.2d 891.

In guardianship proceeding, probate court possesses authority to determine reasonable compensation and method of payment for any court-appointed attorney. West's C.R.S.A. § 15–14–303(6).—Id.

⟜**178. Appointment of successor.**

have a medical malpractice action against the center as they were not patients of the medical staff there.—Santa Cruz v. Northwest Dade Community Health Center, Inc., 590 So.2d 444.

There was no affirmative obligation on the part of psychiatrist or mental health center to detain voluntary patient or to have him involuntarily committed, and they could not be held liable for failing to do so to those subsequently injured by the patient.—Id.

Even if mental health center knew that patient whom it was treating had escaped from another institution to which he had been involuntarily committed, that did not give rise to duty of center to third parties to prevent the patient from harming them.—Id.

(E) CRIMES.

⟜**432. Mental disorder at time of trial.**

C.A.D.C. 1991. Individual cannot be prosecuted on criminal charges unless he is competent to stand trial; he is generally considered to be incompetent if he is unable to understand the nature and consequences of the proceedings against him or to assist properly in his defense. 18 U.S.C.A. § 4241(a).—U.S. v. Weissberger, 951 F.2d 392.

C.A.9 (Ariz.) 1991. It is possible to be found incompetent to plead but competent to stand trial, as the applicable standards are different.—U.S. v. Hoskie, 950 F.2d 1388.

In order for defendant to be found competent to stand trial, it is not enough to find that he is oriented in time and place and has some recollection of events; he must have sufficient present ability to consult with his lawyer with a reasonable degree of rational understanding and must have a rational as well as a factual under-

---

> Using either the *Descriptive-Word Index* method or the "Analysis" method can lead a researcher to cases under the Topic *Mental Health* and Key Number 414(2), which deals with a psychiatrist's liability for the acts of a patient.

---

court a writing which failed to meet the statutory requirements and where there was no indication that mother consented to his appointment in any fashion; furthermore, court erred in failing to consider daughter for the position where she was nominated as guardian in a power of attorney executed by her mother. R.C. §§ 1337.09(D), 2111.121.—Id.

⟜**133. Appearance and representation by attorney; guardian ad litem.**

Colo.App. 1991. In guardianship proceeding involving incapacitated person who is not represented by counsel, probate court is required to appoint visitor to investigate and evaluate circumstances giving rise to petition, and court possesses broad discretion to appoint attorney for incapacitated person if it determines that his rights and interests cannot otherwise be adequately protected or represented. West's C.R.S.A. § 15–14–303.—Department of Institutions, Grand Junction Regional Center v. Carothers, 821 P.2d 891.

Authority to appoint legal counsel does not limit probate court's power to appoint guardian ad litem. West's C.R.S.A. § 15–14–303(5)(c).—Id.

Visitor functions as disinterested investigator and evaluator on behalf of probate court, guardian ad litem's primary obligation is to act as special fiduciary and to make informed decisions for incapacitated person, and attorney must counsel and represent incapacitated person's le-

conservator.—Id.

IV. DISABILITIES AND PRIVILEGES OF MENTALLY DISORDERED PERSONS.

(D) TORTS.

⟜**414. Liability of others for torts of mentally disordered persons.**

⟜**414(2). Mental health professionals and institutions.**

Fla.App. 3 Dist. 1991. Psychiatrist had no duty to control voluntary outpatient or to warn victim who patient killed or others about patient's behavior, and therefore psychiatrist was not liable to parents of victim.—Boynton v. Burglass, 590 So.2d 446, amended on denial of rehearing.

Psychiatrist had no duty to warn potential victim of danger posed by voluntary outpatient under statute permitting psychiatrist to warn identifiable victims of threats of physical harm, given that cause of action against psychiatrist for alleged failure to warn arose prior to effective date of statute, and statute merely permitted psychiatrist to make disclosure, but did not require it. (Per Jorgenson, J., with four judges concurring and two judges specially concurring). West's F.S.A. § 455.2415.—Id.

Fla.App. 3 Dist. 1991. Persons who were shot by patient of mental health center did not

content of that standard is question of law reviewed de novo in federal habeas proceeding. 28 U.S.C.A. § 2254; U.S.C.A. Const.Amend. 14.—Lafferty v. Cook, 949 F.2d 1546.

Defendant must have rational as well as factual understanding of proceedings against him to be competent to stand trial.—Id.

Defendant lacks rational understanding required for competency to stand trial if his mental condition precludes him from perceiving accurately, interpreting, and/or responding appropriately to world around him.—Id.

Showing that defendant had factual understanding of proceedings against him was not by itself sufficient to establish defendant's competency to stand trial; it was improper to make finding of competency under view that defendant who was unable to accurately perceive reality due to paranoid delusional system had only to act consistently with his paranoid delusion to be competent.—Id.

Cal. 1992. Defendant's appeal in capital case could proceed even if defendant had become incompetent, despite defendant's claim that his right to meaningful appellate review and to effective assistance under State and Federal Constitutions precluded proceeding with appeal if he was incompetent; issues on appeal are limited to appellate record, appeal involves only legal issues based on that record and attorneys need not rely on defendant to decide what issues are worthy of pursuing. U.S.C.A. Const.Amend. 6;

For subsequent case history information see Table of Cases Affirmed, Reversed or Modified

[Illustration 36]

PAGE FROM TABLE OF CASES IN VOLUME 10
OF THE GENERAL DIGEST, 8TH SERIES

825   **TABLE OF CASES**   `BRADFORD

References are to Digest Topics and Key Numbers

Box v. Ferrellgas, Inc., CA5 (Tex), 942 F2d 942.—Fed Civ Proc 2212, 2214, 2337; Fed Cts 823; Gas 20(4).

Box v. French Market Corp., LaApp 4 Cir, 593 So2d 836.—App & E 73(2), 339(4), 344, 874(2).

Boyan, Matter of, NJ, 604 A2d 98, 127 NJ 266.—Const Law 62(5); Judges 22(5); Statut 223.4.

Boyar, In re Estate of, FlaApp 4 Dist, 592 So2d 341.—Contracts 221(1); Wills 58(1), 66.

Boyd, Ex parte, Ala, 582 So2d 484. See AMI West Alabama General Hosp., Ex parte.

Boyd v. Briarwood Ford, Inc., BkrtcyWDMich, 133 BR 392. See Check Reporting Services, Inc., In re.

Boyd v. Dock's Corner Associates, BkrtcyWDMich, 135 BR 46. See Great Northern Forest Products, Inc., Matter of.

Boyd v. Employees' Retirement System of Georgia, GaApp, 408 SE2d 157, 200 GaApp 345.—Offic 101.5(1); States 64.1(3).

Boyd v. Eugene Heikkila Inc., BkrtcyWDMich, 187 BR 653. See Check Reporting Services, Inc., In re.

Boyd v. Ford Motor Co., CA6 (Mich), 948 F2d 283.—Fed Civ Proc 2544; Fed Cts 776, 915; Seamen 2.

Boyd v. L.G. DeWitt Trucking Co., Inc., NCApp, 405 SE2d 914, 103 NCApp 396.—App & E 946, 1026; Autos 193(...

ag 199...

139

Boyd

Co.

den

Boyd v. North End Auto Sales, Inc., BkrtcyWDMich, 137 BR 653. See Check Reporting Services, Inc., In re.

Boyd v. Permian Servicing Co., Inc., NM, 825 P2d 611.—Judgm 183; Work Comp 2084, 2097.

Boyd v. Sanitary Dist. of Decatur, Ill., IllApp 4 Dist, 158 IllDec 707, 574 NE2d 820, 215 IllApp3d141.—App & E 356; Judgm 276, 284.

Boyd v. Schildkraut Giftware Corp., CA2 (NY), 936 F2d 76.—Fed Civ Proc 2557; Jury 31(8); Pat 211(1), 218(1), 222, 224, 324.2.

Boyd v. State, AlaCrApp, 590 So2d 344.—Crim Law 637, 649, 829(5), 847, 867, 961, 1043(2), 1155, 1172.1(5); Jury 90, 149; Witn 388(7), 389, 390.

Boyd v. State, GaApp, 409 SE2d 44, 200 GaApp 591, cert den.—Crim Law 577.-10(10), 1043(1), 1159.2(7); Tel 362.

Boyd v. State, MoApp, 816 SW2d 19. See State v. Boyd.

Boyd v. State, TexCrApp, 811 SW2d 105.—Crim Law 394.1(2), 519(8), 641.-13(7), 730(3), 790, 1028, 1035(6), 1077.3, 1208.1(6); Homic 286(3), 289, 309(3), 311, 343, 351, 357(1), 357(3); Ind & Inf 69, 144.1(1), 184; Jury 131(4), 131(15), 131(17).

Boyd Co. v. Boston Gas Co., DMass, 775 FSupp 435. See John Boyd Co. v. Boston Gas Co.

Boyd Enterprises v. Fireman's Fund Ins. Co., CalApp 2 Dist, 2 CalRptr2d 548. See William Boyd Enterprises v. Fireman's Fund Ins. Co.

Boyd, McComb on Behalf of, v. Regan, NYAD 3 Dept, 579 NYS2d 240. See McComb on Behalf of Boyd v. Regan.

Boyd Motors, Inc. v. Employers Ins. of Wausau, DKan, 766 FSupp 998.—Insurance 675.

Boyea v. Fiore, NYAD 3 Dept, 575 NYS2d 171.—Lim of Act 130(5); Pretrial Proc 695.

Boyer v. Boyer, FlaApp 5 Dist, 588 So2d 615.—Costs 264; Divorce 182, 186.

Boyer v. Derwinski, VetApp, 1 VetApp 531.—Armed S 143, 156.

Boyer v. State, Md, 594 A2d 121, 323 Md 558.—Autos 175(1), 175(2), 196; Counties 59, 146; Mun Corp 745, 747(3); States 79, 112.2(2).

Boyett Coffee Co. v. U.S., WDTex, 775 FSupp 1001.—Fed Civ Proc 2465, 2544; Int Rev 3123.

Boyette v. State, FlaApp 5 Dist, 585 So2d 1115.—Crim Law 412.2(2), 721(4).

Boykin v. State, TexCrApp, 818 SW2d 782.—Const Law 70.1(2); Drugs & N 69; Statut 181(1), 184, 188, 189, 212.3, 214, 217.4, 219(1).

Boylan v. Town of Yorktown, NYAD 2 Dept, 579 NYS2d 126.—Interest 22(1); Mun Corp 185(15).

Boyle v. Chicago Housing Authority, CA7 (Ill), 946 F2d 54.—Fed Civ Proc 2311, 2641, 2643, 2658; Fed Cts 657, 658, 666.

Boyle v. Division of Community Services, Me, 592 A2d 489.—Const Law 318(7); Records 62, 65, 66.

Boyle v. MTV Networks, Inc., NDCal, 766 FSupp 809.—Fed Cts 287. 340; ... 1031(1), 1133, 1169.1(5), Cr July 66. 4(1); Homic 18(1), 163(2), 285, 357(6); Kidnap 5; Searches 174, 184; Witn 17, 36, 52(7).

Boyle v. Titus, NYAD 4 Dept, 578 NYS2d 6.—Autos 251.19.

Boyle, Camden County Bd. of Social Services on Behalf of, v. Yocavitch, NJSuperCh, 596 A2d 769, 251 NJSuper 24. See Camden County Bd. of Social Services on Behalf of Boyle v. Yocavitch.

Boyles v. City of Kennewick, WashApp, 813 P2d 178.—Assault 7, 10, 21, 24(1); Lim of Act 189.

Boynton v. Burglass, FlaApp 3 Dist, 590 So2d 446, am on denial of reh.—Mental H 414(2); Negllg 2.

Bozarth, Matter of, NJ, 604 A2d 100, 127 NJ 271.—Judges 11(4).

Bozarth, McCord and McCrary v. Oklahoma Dept. of Transp., OklApp, 812 P2d 815.—Admin Law 763; Em Dom 2(1); High 153.5; Mand 12, 87; R R 73(1), 73(4).

Bozeman v. Sloss Industries Corp., NDAla, 138 FRD 590.—Fed Civ Proc 2252.

Bozeman v. State, SC, 414 SE2d 144.—Crim Law 586, 590(1), 593, 641.13(1), 641.13(2), 814(20), 998(3), 1151; Homic 309(6).

Bozzelli v. Hollenbaugh, IndApp 5 Dist, 582 NE2d 905.—App & E 842(1); Brok 66.

Bozzelli v. Wayne's Realty, IndApp 5 Dist, 582 NE2d 905. See Bozzelli v. Hollenbaugh.

B.P. v. State, FlaApp 5 Dist, 588 So2d 39.—Contempt 70.

BP America, Inc. v. Cimcast Corp., NDOhio, 768 FSupp 208. See Baker v. BP America, Inc.

BP Oil Co. v. Jefferson County, Ala., Ala, 589 So2d 725.—App & E 1216.

BPS Guard Services, Inc. v. N.L.R.B., CA8, 942 F2d 519, reh den.—Courts 96(4); Labor 202, 598.

B.R., Matter of, PaSuper, 596 A2d 1120.—Infants 154, 172, 177, 179, 193, 250. 252.

B.R., Matter of, TexApp-Tyler, 822 SW2d 103.—Infants 155, 178, 179.

Braat, In re, CAFed, 937 F2d 589.—Pat 120, 328(2).

Braatz v. Mathison, NYAD 3 Dept, 581 NYS2d 112.—Labor 219.

Brace, In re, BkrtcyWDMich, 131 BR 612.—Bankr 2836, 3411; Interest 31, 39(2.5), 39(2.20).

Bracey v. Helene Curtis, Inc., NDIll, 780 FSupp 568.—Civil R 141, 153, 373, 383.

Bracey v. King, GaApp, 406 SE2d 265.—Costs 263; Waters 53.

Bracey v. Monsanto Co., Inc., Mo, 823 SW2d 946.—App & E 1177(6); Contracts 1; Pretrial Proc 558, 624, 643, 690.

Bracey v. State ex rel. Jones, AlaCivApp, 591 So2d 95.—Drugs & N 185.10, 195; Searches 27.

Brackin v. King, Ala, 585 So2d 37.—Adv Poss 114(1); App & E 931(1), 931(2), 1008.1(7), 1010.2, 1012.1(1).

Brackin v. Sumner County By and ...ld. of ... d 57.— ..), 395;

Mont, Phys

Walls, GaApp, 412 SE2d 603, 201 GaApp 822.—Guar 53(2); Sec Tran 240.

Bracy v. Scott, Ala, 589 So2d 145.—Estop 68(2); Ex & Ad 39.

Bradbury v. Kaiser, CalApp 2 Dist, 5 CalRptr2d 325, 3 CA4th 1257.—Tax 301(4), 510.

Braddy v. State, FlaApp 4 Dist, 593 So2d 1225.—Crim Law 980(1), 1177.

Braden v. Braden, IndApp 1 Dist, 575 NE2d 293.—Divorce 101, 139; Plead 4, 146.

Braden v. Downey, Tex, 811 SW2d 922.—Mand 153; Pretrial Proc 44, 245, 248, 249, 276, 286.

Bradenton, City of, v. Amerifirst Development Corp., FlaApp 2 Dist, 582 So2d 166. See City of Bradenton v. Amerifirst Development Corp.

Bradford v. American Federal Bank, F.S.B., NDTex, 783 FSupp 283.—Banks 505; Bills & N 158; Fed Civ Proc 2487; Fed Cts 414.

Bradford v. Crozier, CA5 (Tex), 958 F2d 72. See Laymon, Matter of.

Bradford v. State, Ark, 815 SW2d 947, 306 Ark 590.—Crim Law 412.2(4), 412.-2(5), 438(6).

Bradford v. State, Ga, 412 SE2d 534.—Const Law 268(11); Crim Law 510, 511.1(3), 511.1(6), 511.1(9), 511.3, 789(4), 789(8).

Bradford v. Whitley, CA5 (La), 953 F2d 1008.—Const Law 268(8); Crim Law 641.13(1), 641.13(2), 662.7, 720(5), 1213.8(2); Searches 78; Witn 372(1), 392(1).

Bradford v. Workers' Compensation Com'r, WVa, 408 SE2d 13.—Work Comp 600, 604, 1357, 1530.

For Later Case History Information, see INSTA-CITE on WESTLAW

When a case is known to deal with a topic of law, Key Numbers assigned to that Topic can be located by use of the Table of Cases. See, for example, the listing for *Boynton v. Burglass.*

SECTION F.   OTHER WEST'S KEY NUMBER DIGESTS

1.   In General

As has been noted, the *American Digest System* with its Key Number classification is made up of the headnotes from all the units of the *National Reporter System*.   Because it is all-inclusive, it is most useful when one is interested in locating cases from all American jurisdictions.   More typically, however, when one is engaged in legal research, the interest is primarily in locating cases from a particular state or group of states, or in only those cases decided in the federal courts.   In such instances, it is better and easier to use a specialized West's *Key Number Digest* that is less comprehensive than the *American Digest System*.   These consist of state, regional, federal, and subject digests.

Before describing the actual contents of these specialized digests, it is important to understand how their content is determined and to realize that a Topic and Key Number that appear in the *American Digest System* also appear in identical form in at least one of the other West's *Key Number Digests*.   For example, assume that a state appellate case is appealed to the Supreme Court of the United States and a decision is issued.   The digest paragraphs and Topics and Key Numbers used for the Supreme Court case are published in identical form in the appropriate state digest, the appropriate regional digest (if one is published covering that state), the most recent federal digest, a digest dealing with only Supreme Court of the United States cases, and possibly in subject matter digests as well.

2.   Common Features

West's *Key Number Digests* have the following common features in addition to Topics and Key Numbers:

a.   *Descriptive–Word Index* volume(s) used in the same manner as was described for the *American Digest System*.

b.   *Table of Cases* volume(s) for plaintiff-defendant and used in the same manner as was described for the *American Digest System*.

c.   *Words and Phrases* volume(s) that contain in alphabetical order words and phrases that have been judicially defined.   Volumes of this type are not provided for the units of the *American Digest System* or for the regional digests.

d.   *Defendant–Plaintiff* volume(s) used to locate a case when only the name of the defendant is known.   Volumes of this type are not provided for the regional digests, except for the latest *Pacific Digest*. They were first provided for the *American Digest System* commencing with the *Ninth Decennial Digest, Part 1*.

e.   Updating, consisting of replacement volumes, pocket supplements, interim pamphlet supplements, and later bound volumes and advance sheets of the West reporters.

f. References in the pocket supplements and recently published volumes to Topics that may be used in WESTLAW searches for cases with the Topic and within specified Key Numbers.

3. State Digests

West Publishing Company publishes a *Key Number Digest* for almost every state.[5] A typical state Key Number digest consists of digest paragraphs for all reported appellate cases of the particular state, including federal court cases that arose in or were appealed from that jurisdiction. [See Illustrations 37–38 for examples of a state digest.] Some of the West state digests have special features unique to a particular state, such as a reference to law review articles from law schools within the state. Researchers should examine carefully the state digest available for their state and familiarize themselves with any special features.

4. Regional Digests

Four sets of regional digests are published that correspond to four sets of the regional reporters of the *National Reporter System*. Other regional digests have ceased over time, likely due to an inadequate subscription base. Regional digests are arranged under the Key Number classification and include digests of all reported cases for each of the states in the region, including federal court cases that arose in or were appealed from those jurisdictions. The digest paragraphs under each Key Number are arranged alphabetically by the states included within the digest. The regional digests still being published are:

Atlantic Digest, First and Second Series

North Western Digest, First and Second Series

Pacific Digest, Five series [6]

South Eastern Digest, First and Second Series

5. Digests for Federal Court Cases

Whenever a researcher is aware that the problem being researched is one under the jurisdiction of a federal court, it is quicker and more accurate to confine the research to a federal digest. Numerous digests are published for federal court cases.

a. *West's Federal Practice Digest, 4th.*[7] This set includes digests of cases from December 1975 to date for all federal courts. Its special features are:

---

[5] The West Publishing Company publishes Key Number digests for every state except Delaware, Nevada, and Utah. Additionally, a few states have digests available from other publishers.

[6] Volumes in these series are not connoted as 1st, 2d, etc. Rather each series shows the first volume of the *Pacific Reporter* or *Pacific Reporter 2d* included in the set.

[7] Publication of West's *Federal Practice Digest, 4th* began in 1989 and was completed in 1993. There is no "bright line" as to its scope of coverage or to West's *Federal Practice*

(1) Under each Key Number, cases are arranged chronologically, first for the Supreme Court of the United States, then the courts of appeals, and then the district courts arranged alphabetically by jurisdiction.

(2) The digest paragraphs include information as to whether a case has been *affirmed, reversed,* or *modified.*

(3) A complete numerical listing of all patents adjudicated for the period covered by this digest is found under the Topic, *Patents,* Key Number 328.

(4) An alphabetical table of all *Trade–Marks and Trade Names Adjudicated* is included in the *Trade Regulations* volume at Key Number 736.

(5) References to Topics that may be used in WESTLAW searches for cases with the Topic and within specified Key Numbers.

b. *Earlier Federal Digests.* Federal cases prior to 1984 are available in the following:

(1) *West's Federal Practice Digest, 3rd,* December 1975 to *West's Federal Practice Digest 4th.*

(2) *West's Federal Practice Digest, 2nd,* 1961–November 1975.

(3) *Modern Federal Practice Digest,* 1939–1960.

(4) *Federal Digest,* all federal cases prior to 1939.

c. *U.S. Supreme Court Digest.* Because the Supreme Court of the United States plays such a significant role within the American legal system, a digest that contains only its cases is extremely useful. West publishes a multi-volume set for this purpose. It duplicates the Supreme Court digest paragraphs in the *American Digest System* and in the various West federal digests.

6. Other Specialized West Digests

a. *West's Bankruptcy Digest.* This Key Number digest includes cases from *West's Bankruptcy Reporter* and selected bankruptcy cases from the *Federal Reporter 2d* and *3d* and the West's *Supreme Court Reporter.*

b. *West's Military Justice Digest.* This set digests cases from *West's Military Justice Reporter* and is a Key Number digest.

Digest, 3rd, which it continues. For example, some volumes of the *3rd,* issued in 1975 when this set began, covered cases through November 1975 and were never revised. These volumes contained pocket supplementation that included cases decided from December 1975 and into 1983. Other volumes of the *3rd* were revised at various times, the last being issued in 1983. As new volumes of the *4th* were published, they incorporated the supplementation to the *3rd.* This means that some volumes in the *4th* contain cases from December 1975, while others have coverage commencing in 1983. Therefore, specifically for the period December 1975 through 1983, both the *3rd* and *4th must* be consulted to assure comprehensive coverage. For cases from 1984 forward, only the *4th* needs to be consulted.

c. *United States Federal Claims Digest.* This is a Key Number digest that includes cases from volumes 1–26 of the *United States Claims Court Reporter* and volume 27 and forward of the *Federal Claims Reporter.*

d. *West's Education Law Digest.* This publication provides Key Number digest paragraphs from all cases in the *National Reporter System* on Topics relating to education law.

e. *United States Merit System Protection Board Digest.* This publication digests cases involving federal employees and the federal merit system. It uses a classification scheme different from the Key Number digests.

SECTION G.   UPDATING WEST'S KEY NUMBER DIGESTS

Because digest paragraphs originate as headnotes in the advance sheets of the *National Reporter System,* to update paper research to its most current point one must engage in a systematic process. After locating an appropriate Topic and Key Number in the bound volume of a digest, next check under the same Topic and Key Number in the pocket supplement in that volume and in any interim pamphlets. Note the information in the table usually entitled *Closing with Cases Reported in* located in the front of the latest supplementation, typically on the back of the title page. This "closing table" indicates the last volume from each *National Reporter System* unit covered.

For example, a recent closing table in *West's Federal Practice Digest 4th* might include references similar to the following:

Closing with Cases Reported in

Supreme Court Reporter	113 S.Ct. 1438
Federal Reporter, Second Series	985 F.2d 1074
Federal Supplement	812 F.Supp. 236
Federal Rules Decisions	145 F.R.D. 613
Bankruptcy Reporter	150 B.R. 486
Federal Claims Reporter	27 Fed.Cl. 638
Court of Claims	231 Ct.Cl.
Court of Customs and Patent Appeals	60 C.C.P.A.
Military Justice Reporter	36 M.J. 316
Veterans Appeals Reporter	4 Vet.App. 131

Once you have determined the coverage of the digest, the next step is to check under this Topic and Key Number in the digest section found in the *back* of any later bound volumes of reporters covering the jurisdiction being researched. The last step is to check the digest paragraphs found in the *front* of each advance sheet to these reporters. Only *West's Supreme Court Reporter* cumulates its digest paragraphs in the last advance sheet for a volume.

SECTION H.   ILLUSTRATIONS USING A STATE DIGEST

37.   Page from Descriptive–Word Index to Florida Digest 2d
38.   Page from Florida Digest 2d

[Illustration 37]

SAMPLE PAGE FROM DESCRIPTIVE–WORD
INDEX TO FLORIDA DIGEST 2d

36 Fla D 2d—7 **PUBLIC**

References are to Digest Topics and Key Numbers

PROPERTY—Cont'd
INJUNCTIONS—
  See this index Injunction
  Preliminary injunctions—
    Grounds and objections. Inj 138.30
    Proceedings. Inj 139–159½
MENTAL suffering—
  Injury to property. Damag 55

PROPERTY INSURANCE
  See also, this index Insurance, passim
EXTENT of loss. Insurance 493–508.2
PROPERTY covered. Insurance 161–166
RISKS covered. Insurance 417.5–429.2

PROSECUTION
DISCRIMINATORY, see this index Discrimination
SELECTIVE, see this index Selective Prosecution

PUBLIC CONTRACTS—Cont'd
PUBLIC contracts—
  Public policy—
    Particular contracts. Contracts 108(2)
STATES, contracts with—
  Bids or proposals, see also, Proposals or bids, post
  Highway construction, see also, this index Highways
  Injunctions—
    Preliminary injunctions—
      Grounds and objections. Inj 138.63
      Proceedings. Inj 139–159½
UNITED States—
  Advertisement for proposals or bids, see this index Advertisement
UNITED States, contract with—
  Award on competitive bidding. U S 64.45
  Bids or proposals, and bidders' remedies—
    Preparation costs, recovery of. U S 64.60(6)

Frequently, when engaged in legal research, the researcher is interested in finding cases from the courts of a particular state. In such instances, it may be best to start the research in a state digest. As this Illustration indicates, this is much less complex than using the *Descriptive-Word Index* to a *Decennial* as shown in Illustration 32.

State digests are kept current with replacement volumes, annual pocket supplements, interim pamphlets, and later bound volumes and advance sheets of West reporters covering cases from the particular state for which research is being conducted.

PROXIMATE CAUSE
CIVIL rights, persons protected and entitled to sue. Civil R 203

PSYCHIATRISTS
INDIGENTS—
  Criminal defendant's right to appointment to assist in defense, see this index Indigent Persons
LIABILITY—
  Torts of mentally disordered persons. Mental H 414(2)

PSYCHOANALYSIS
INJURIES to persons not patients—
  Child abuse, failure to report. Infants 13

PUBLIC AGENCY
CLASS actions—
  Decl Judgm 305
  Fed Civ Proc 184.30

PUBLIC AID
FEDERAL aid—
  State and local agencies, see also, State and local agencies, post

PUBLIC ASSISTANCE
Generally, see this index Public Aid

PUBLIC CONTRACT BONDS
UNITED States contracts—
  Deposit or security on making proposal or bid. U S 64.35

PUBLIC CONTRACTS
INJUNCTIONS—
  Preliminary injunctions—
    Grounds and objections. Inj 138.63
    Proceedings. Inj 139–159½

CIVIL rights liability, privilege or immunity. Civil R 213
DISQUALIFICATION. Atty & C 19
FEES. Atty & C 132
LIEN. Costs 325
WITHDRAWAL—
  Juvenile proceedings. Infants 205

PUBLIC EMPLOYEES
ARMED services—
  Civilian employees of, see this index Armed Services
INJUNCTIONS—
  Preliminary injunctions—
    Grounds and objections. Inj 138.69
    Proceedings. Inj 139–159½
OUSTER—
  Misconduct. Offic 66
PENSIONS, see this index Retirement and Pensions

PUBLIC FUNDS
INJUNCTIONS—
  Preliminary injunctions—
    Grounds and objections. Inj 138.66
    Proceedings. Inj 139–159½

PUBLIC IMPROVEMENTS
INJUNCTIONS—
  Preliminary injunctions—
    Contracts—
      Grounds and objections. Inj 138.63
      Proceedings. Inj 139–159½

PUBLIC INTEREST
ATTORNEY fees as costs—
  Costs 194.42
  Fed Civ Proc 2737.2

[Illustration 38]

SAMPLE PAGE FROM FLORIDA DIGEST 2d

24 Fla D 2d—9   **MENTAL HEALTH** ⬅432

Fla.App. 5 Dist. 1986. Liability for compensatory damages of insane persons for their acts or omissions is based on public policy rather than on traditional tort concepts of fault, but the liability of insane persons does not extend to punitive damages, nor can it be extended to any tort requiring wanton misconduct.—Preferred Risk Mut. Ins. Co. v. Saboda, 489 So.2d 768, review denied 501 So.2d 1283.

⬅**412. Particular torts of mentally disordered persons.**

Fla.App. 3 Dist. 1991. Institutionalized Alzheimer's patient owed no duty of care to her custodian, and was not liable in tort for injuries sustained by custodian while attempting to prevent patient from committing suicide, when patient pushed custodian and caused her to fall and injure herself.—Mujica v. Turner, 582 So.2d 24, review denied 592 So.2d 681.

Fla.App. 3 Dist. 1991. Violently insane mental institution resident...

voluntary patient or to have him involuntarily committed, and they could not be held liable for failing to do so to those subsequently injured by the patient.—Id.

Even if mental health center knew that patient whom it was treating had escaped from another institution to which he had been involuntarily committed, that did not give rise to duty of center to third parties to prevent the patient from harming them.—Id.

Fla.App. 3 Dist. 1989. Psychiatrist had neither right nor ability to control behavior of voluntary outpatient, so as to render psychiatrist liable for failure to prevent patient's physical and mental abuse of his daughters.—Fischer v. Metcalf, 543 So.2d 785.

Fla.App. 3 Dist. 1988. County mental health agency appointed by court owed no duty to protect citizen injured by mentally disturbed woman and was not negligent due to alleged failure to insure that woman received medication and psychiatric...

After locating a Topic and Key Number as demonstrated in the previous Illustration, the next step is to consult the digest paragraphs under the appropriate Key Number.

Cases from other jurisdictions may be located by switching to other sets of Key Number digests and consulting the same Topic and Key Number.

...innocent of any wrongdoing.—Anicet v. Gant, 580 So.2d 273, review denied 591 So.2d 181.

⬅**414. Liability of others for torts of mentally disordered persons.**
  (1). In general.
➤ (2). Mental health professionals and institutions.
  (3). Escape or release from custody.
  (4). Actions.

⬅**414(1). In general.**

Fla.App. 3 Dist. 1988. County law enforcement officials owed no duty to protect citizen by executing arrest warrant and investigating location of mentally disturbed woman before she attacked citizen and, therefore, were not negligent.—Bradford v. Metropolitan Dade County, 522 So.2d 96.

⬅**414(2). Mental health professionals and institutions.**

See also Physicians and Surgeons ⬅7.

Fla.App. 3 Dist. 1991. Psychiatrist had no duty to control voluntary outpatient or to warn victim who patient killed or others about patient's behavior, and therefore psychiatrist was not liable to parents of victim.—Boynton v. Burglass, 590 So.2d 446, amended on denial of rehearing.

Psychiatrist had no duty to warn potential victim of danger posed by voluntary outpatient under statute permitting psychiatrist to warn identifiable victims of threats of physical harm, given that cause of action against psychiatrist for alleged failure to warn arose prior to effective date of statute, and statute merely permitted psychiatrist to make disclosure, but did not require it. (Per Jorgenson, J., with four judges concurring and two judges specially concurring). West's F.S.A. § 455.-2415.—Id.

Fla.App. 3 Dist. 1991. Persons who were shot by patient of mental health center did not have a medical malpractice action against the center as they were not patients of the medical staff there.—Santa Cruz v. Northwest Dade Community Health Center, Inc., 590 So.2d 444, review denied 599 So.2d 1278.

There was no affirmative obligation on the part of psychiatrist or mental health center to detain

...damages of insane persons for their acts or omissions is based on public policy rather than on traditional tort concepts of fault, but the liability of insane persons does not extend to punitive damages, nor can it be extended to any tort requiring wanton misconduct.—Preferred Risk Mut. Ins. Co. v. Saboda, 489 So.2d 768, review denied 501 So.2d 1283.

(E) CRIMES.

Research Notes

Federal criminal procedure; appointment of psychiatrist, see West's Federal Practice Manual. See Wright & Miller, Federal Practice and Procedure: Civil.

Library references
C.J.S. Insane Persons § 127 et seq.

⬅**432. Mental disorder at time of trial.**

C.A.11 (Fla.) 1992. Treatment with antipsychotic drugs does not per se render a defendant incompetent to stand trial; administration of drugs is merely a relevant factor in determination of competence.—Sheley v. Singletary, 955 F.2d 1434.

C.A.11 (Fla.) 1989. Competency to stand trial means ability to cooperate with counsel and participate in one's own defense.—Futch v. Dugger, 874 F.2d 1483.

C.A.11 (Fla.) 1987. Test for determining competence to stand trial is whether defendant has sufficient present ability to consult with lawyer with reasonable degree of rational understanding and whether he has rational, as well as factual, understanding of proceedings against him.—Agan v. Dugger, 835 F.2d 1337, rehearing denied 840 F.2d 25, certiorari denied 108 S.Ct. 2846, 487 U.S. 1205, 101 L.Ed.2d 884.

C.A.11 (Fla.) 1987. Amnesia alone does not automatically render defendant incompetent to stand trial, but trial court should evaluate the facts and circumstances of defendant's amnesia in light of usual standard for determining competency. 18 U.S.C.A. § 4241(e); U.S.C.A. Const.Amends. 5, 14. —U.S. v. Rinchack, 820 F.2d 1557.

Defendant with amnesia was competent to stand trial, even though codefendants riding in truck with defendant were acquitted, where Government had more evidence tying defendant to plane load of

SECTION I.   CHART ILLUSTRATING
WEST'S KEY NUMBER DIGESTS

MASTER INDEX TO ALL CASE LAW

American Digest System

Cases from: U.S. Supreme Court, all lower
  federal courts, all specialized federal
  courts, and all state courts.

Use:	Chronological Coverage
*Century Digest	1658-1896
First Decennial	1896-1906
Second Decennial	1907-1916
Third Decennial	1916-1926
Fourth Decennial	1926-1936
Fifth Decennial	1936-1946
Sixth Decennial	1946-1956
Seventh Decennial	1956-1966
Eighth Decennial	1966-1976
Ninth Decennial (Part 1)	1976-1981
Ninth Decennial (Part 2)	1981-1986
Tenth Decennial (Part 1)	1986-1991
General Digest (8th Series)	1991-1996
(in progess)	

*The Century Digest indexes cases prior
to the start of the National Reporter System.
Therefore, digest coverage is more inclusive than reporter coverage.

FEDERAL COURT COVERAGE

Complete Supreme Court coverage

Cases from: *Supreme Court Reporter*
Use: *U.S. Supreme Court Digest*

Complete Federal Court coverage

Cases from: U. S. Supreme Court, all
  lower federal courts, and all specialized
  federal courts.

Use: *Federal Practice Digest, 4th*
      (Dec. 1975 to date)
    Federal Practice Digest, 3rd
      (Dec. 1975 to *Fed. Prac. Dig. 4th*)
    Federal Practice Digest, 2nd
      (1961 - Nov. 1975)
    Modern Federal Practice Digest
      (1939 - 1960)
    Federal Digest
      (all federal cases through 1938)

STATE COURT COVERAGE

Individual State Digests

Coverage corresponds to regional digest
  in which the state appears. Note: Some
  state digests are in a 2d, 3d, or 4th series.

Published for all states except:
  Del. (Use: *Atlantic Digest*);
  Nev. and Utah (Use: *Pacific Digest*)

Regional Reporter Digests

Cases from: The seven regional reporters,
  Calif. & N.Y., plus pre-reporter cases

Use as appropriate:
Atlantic (CT, DE, MD, ME, NH, NJ, PA, RI,
  VT, DC)
  1st (to 1938)
  2d (1938 to date)
North Western (IO, MI, MN, NE, ND, SD, WI)
  1st (to 1941)
  2d (1941 to date)
Pacific (AK, AZ, CA*, CO, HI, ID, KA, MT,
  NM, NV, OK, OR, UT, WA, WY)
  1850-1931 (California & Pacific)
  1-100 P.2d
  101-366 P.2d
  367-584 P.2d
  585-to date
South Eastern (GA, NC, SC, VA, WV)
  1st (to 1938)
  2d (1938 to date)
           *   *   *   *
North Eastern (IL, ID, MA, NY, OH)
  (to 1968)
  CEASED PUBLICATION
  Use: appropriate state digest
Southern (AL, FL, LA, MS)
  (to 1988)
  CEASED PUBLICATION
  Use: appropriate state digest
South Western
  NOT PUBLISHED
  Use: state digests for AR, KY, MO, TN, TX

*Covers all Calif. courts to 1960 and only
Cal. Sup. Ct. thereafter. For full coverage
since 1960, use *California Digest* Series.

SECTION J.   OTHER DIGESTS

Digests are not unique to the West Publishing Company.   In fact,
digests on a variety of topics are prepared by numerous publishers.
Researchers frequently will encounter these in the course of their
research and should take the time to become familiar with their format
and special features.   Some deserve special mention and are discussed
below.

(1) *Digest of United States Supreme Court Reports, Lawyers' Edition* (Lawyers Cooperative Publishing). This is a multi-volume digest, with annual pocket supplements, to all cases of the Supreme Court of the United States. The digest paragraphs used are collected from those published in the *U.S. Supreme Court Reports, Lawyers' Edition.* This digest provides references to other publications of Lawyers Cooperative Publishing.

(2) *Digests for Looseleaf Services, Topical Reporters, and Other Types of Publications.* Frequently looseleaf services, topical reporters, multi-volume treatises, and, on occasion, legal periodicals, provide digests of particular subjects or of cases arranged alphabetically. At other times, materials are grouped under state or federal code sections. Still others use a hybrid of these methods. Since digests are useful finding aids for identifying like-kind materials, it is always useful to check sets for separate bound digest volumes and for digest sections within volumes.

(3) *A.L.R. Digests.* These publications are discussed in Chapter 7.

(4) *Taxes.* See Chapter 24, J. Jacobstein, R. Mersky & D. Dunn, *Fundamentals of Legal Research* (6th ed.).

SECTION K. CITING DIGESTS

Because digests are finding aids that serve as a means of locating cases by subject, they have no legal authority and are never cited for such. Do not rely on the text of the digest paragraphs for the theory of a case, but merely as a means for obtaining citations to cases. Digest paragraphs are necessarily brief and can fail to suggest a nuance or shading of a case or may omit an element that may have a specific bearing on the problem being researched.

In all instances, the actual opinion from which the digest paragraph was obtained should be read.

SECTION L. WORDS AND PHRASES
AND POPULAR NAME TABLES

1. Words and Phrases

Sometimes a problem in legal research involves the definition of certain words or phrases as, for example, *income or reasonable attorney's fee.* Courts frequently must define the meaning of such words and phrases. In cases reported in the units of the *National Reporter System,* these definitions are often included as headnotes, as in the following example from 111 S. Ct. 2597 (1991):

> **17. Courts** ☜89
>
> "Stare decisis" is the preferred course because it promotes evenhanded, predictable and consistent development of legal principles, fosters reliance on judicial decisions, and contributes to the actual and perceived integrity of judicial process.
>
> See publication Words and Phrases for other judicial constructions and definitions.

Headnotes that contain judicial definitions are subsequently reprinted in *Words and Phrases,* a multi-volume set containing approximately 500,000 alphabetically-arranged judicial definitions of legal and non-legal terms. *Words and Phrases* is kept up to date by annual cumulative pocket supplements, which are further supplemented by *Words and Phrases* tables in later bound volumes and advance sheets of the various units of the *National Reporter System.* Many of the digests discussed in Section F also contain such tables. [See Illustration 39 for an example of a page from *Words and Phrases.*]

2. Popular Name Tables

Frequently, a case becomes better known by a popular name rather than by its actual name. For example, *Cruzan v. Director, Missouri Dept. of Health* is popularly known as the *"Right to Die"* Case. At other times, a group of cases may come to be known collectively by a popular name, such as the *Right to Counsel Cases.* When only the popular name of a case or a group of cases is known, it is necessary to consult a table of cases by popular name in order to obtain citations to the actual case or cases. These tables may be located in the following sources:

a. *First through Sixth Decennial Digests.* The Table of Cases volume contains a cumulative *List of Popular Name Titles* in the *American Digest System.* This feature was discontinued with the *Seventh Decennial.*

b. *Tables of Cases by Popular Names* in the various special digests.

c. *Shepard's Acts and Cases by Popular Names.* [See Illustration 40.]

SECTION M.   ILLUSTRATIONS

39. Page From Words and Phrases
40. Page From Shepard's Acts and Cases by Popular Name

[Illustration 39]

SAMPLE PAGE FROM VOLUME OF WORDS AND PHRASES

PSYCHOCALISTHENICS

PSYCHIATRIC EVIDENCE

Statute defining psychiatric evidence as evidence of a mental disease or defect which is offered in connection with the affirmative defense of lack of criminal responsibility [McKinney's CPL § 250.10, subd. 1(a)] does not limit "psychiatric evidence" to opinions of psychiatrists and psychologists and may be read as including opinions of certified social workers. People v. Scala, 491 N.Y.S.2d 555, 562, 128 Misc.2d 831.

Properly qualified certified social workers appointed to examine a defendant in relation to a potential defense of lack of criminal responsibility may provide expert opinions that may serve as the sole "psychiatric evidence" in relation to the affirmative defense. Id.

PSYCHIATRIC EXAMINATION

Requiring a criminal defendant to undergo an involuntary "psychiatric examination" once the question of insanity is raised as a defense is not inconsistent with the Standards for Criminal Justice, Discovery and Procedure Before Trial of the American Bar Association providing that a judicial officer may require the accused to submit to a reasonable physical or "medical inspection" of his body. State v. Seehan, Iowa, 258 N.W.2d 374, 378.

PSYCHIATRIC EXAMINER

A properly qualified certified social worker may act as a "psychiatric examiner" under the dangerousness statute [McKinney's CPL § 330.20

PSYCHIATRIC THERAPY

For purpose of determining whether medical expenses exceeded the $500 threshold under the Insurance Law, neurological evaluation, X rays and laboratory procedures did not constitute excludable "psychiatric therapy"; fact that procedures were performed at the request of a psychiatrist or in a psychiatric hospital did not change their nature. Shorey v. LaRocca, 399 N.Y.S.2d 771, 772, 59 A.D.2d 1030.

PSYCHIATRIST
See, also,
    Competent Psychiatrist.
    Qualified Psychiatrist.

"Psychiatrist" specializes in the treatment of mental, emotional and behavioural disorders. Nick v. Colonial Nat. Bank of Garland, Tex.Civ.App., 517 S.W.2d 375, 377.

A "psychiatrist" is a medical doctor who usually has completed at least three years of post graduate training in psychiatry (the branch of medicine concerned with the diagnoses and treatment of mental illness) at a recognized training hospital. U.S. v. Cortes-Crespo, ACMR, 9 MJ 717, 721.

PSYCHIATRY

"Psychiatry" is branch of medicine that relates to mental diseases. Wallach v. Monarch Life Ins. Co., 295 N.Y.S.2d 109, 111, 58 Misc.2d 202.

A page from *Words and Phrases*. The paragraphs are essentially the same as they appeared as headnotes in the volumes of the *National Reporter System*. The pocket supplements of the volumes of *Words and Phrases* should always be checked.

This Illustration shows definitions that could be important to our research problem.

---

misconduct, that principal's damages included lost reputation, humiliation, stress, loss of sleep, and impaired enjoyment of life, did not rise to level of "psychiatric impairment" caused by willful conduct, but instead were more in nature of humiliation and other emotional harm which were incidental claims in action, and therefore principal's action did not implicate statute stating that district court shall order that personal injury tort and wrongful death claims shall be tried in district court in which bankruptcy case is pending. Bertholet v. Harman, Bkrtcy.D.N.H., 126 B.R. 413, 415.

PSYCHIATRIC OR MEDICAL EVIDENCE

For purposes of proceeding brought by county department of social services seeking guardianship and custody of child on ground that mother was unable, by reason of mental illness, to provide proper and adequate care for child, proof proposed by mother dealing with competence and expertise of psychiatrists constituted "psychiatric or medical evidence" as provided in statute giving parent "the right to submit other psychiatric, psychological or medical evidence" in such a proceeding. Matter of Roth, 412 N.Y.S.2d 568, 569, 97 Misc.2d 834.

PSYCHOANALYSIS

"Psychoanalysis" is a specialized form of psychotherapy. Markham v. U.S., D.C.N.Y., 245 F.Supp. 505, 507.

PSYCHOCALISTHENICS

Term "psychocalisthenics," as employed by defendant in brochures, advertisements, and promotions for its courses in a series of physical exercises combining various yoga systems, dance, and calisthenics, was not merely "descriptive" but was sufficiently fanciful to be entitled to registration as a "suggestive term" without proof of a secondary meaning, where it was an odd and unusual term which suggested a number of things, but which did not describe any one thing in particular and, though it could indicate a system of purely mental exercises such as those employed by plaintiff, it could also indicate a system of physical exercises such as defendant's which were designed to create specific mental, emotional, and physical results, or even a traditional exercise program merely designed to improve mental fitness and alertness. West & Co., Inc. v. Arica Institute, Inc., C.A.N.Y., 557 F.2d 338, 342.

[Illustration 40]

SAMPLE PAGE FROM SHEPARD'S ACTS AND CASES BY POPULAR NAMES

FEDERAL AND STATE CASES CITED BY POPULAR NAME | Rol

Rights of Pretrial Detainees Case
441 US 520, 60 LE2d 447, 99 SC 1861

Right to Appoint Counsel Case
440 US 367, 59 LE2d 383, 99 SC 1158

Right to be Heard Case
415 US 452, 39 LE2d 505, 94 SC 1209

Right to Counsel Cases
315 US 791, 86 LE 1194, 62 SC 639; 316 US 455, 86 LE 1595, 62 SC 1252
469 US 91, 83 LE2d 488, 105 SC 490
51 LE2d 424, 97 SC 1232
116 F2d 690; 313 US 551, 85 LE 1222, 61 SC 835; 315 US 60, 86 LE 680, 62 SC 457; 315 US 827, 86 LE 1222, 62 SC 629, 62 SC 637

"Right to Die" Case
111 LE2d 224, 110 SC 2841

Right-To-Reply Case

Roane-Anderson Case
192 Tenn 150, 239 SW2d 27; 342 US 847, 96 LE 639, 72 SC 74; 342 US 232, 96 LE 257, 72 SC 257

Roanoke Rapids Case
345 US 153, 97 LE 918, 73 SC 609; 191 F2d 796; 343 US 941, 96 LE 1346, 72 SC 1034

Robertson Case
89 Fed 504

Rochester Telephone Case
307 US 125, 83 LE 1147, 59 SC 754; 23 FS 634; 59 SC 252

Rochin Case
342 US 165, 96 LE 183, 72 SC 205; 101 CalApp2d 140, 225 P2d 1, 225 P2d 913

Rockaway Rolling Mill Case
101 NJEq 192, 137 At 650; 103 NJEq 297, 143 At

This is a typical page from the "Cases" section of *Shepard's Acts and Cases by Popular Names*. This set is kept current by publication of a periodic pamphlet supplement.

Other Tables of Popular Names are in many of the state, regional, and other special digests.

---

20 F2d 873; 275 US 552, 72 LE 421, 48 SC 115; 275 US 555, 72 LE 423, 48 SC 116
121 Tex 515, 50 SW2d 1065; 25 SW2d 706

River Rights Cases
199 AppDiv 539, 192 NYSupp 211; 235 NY 351, 139 NE 474; 236 NY 579, 142 NE 291; 271 US 364, 70 LE 992, 46 SC 569
199 AppDiv 552, 192 NYSupp 222; 235 NY 364, 139 NE 477; 236 NY 578, 142 NE 291; 271 US 403, 70 LE 1009, 46 SC 581

River Road Case
353 US 30, 1 LE2d 622, 77 SC 635; 353 US 948, 1 LE2d 857, 77 SC 823; 229 F2d 926

Riverside Mills Case
168 Fed 987; 168 Fed 990; 219 US 186, 55 LE 167, 31 SC 164

Million Dollar Road Bond Case
207 Iowa 923, 223 NW 737

Road Cases
30 Tex 503
30 Tex 506

294 US 648, 79 LE 1110, 55 SC 595

Rockne Case
115 US 600, 29 LE 477, 6 SC 201

Rodin's Hand of God Case
177 FS 265, 394 FS 1390

Rogers Lumber Company Case
117 NLRB 1732, No. 230

Rogers Silverware Cases
285 US 247, 76 LE 740, 52 SC 387
11 Fed 495
70 Fed 1017
110 Fed 955
17 PQ 32
39 Conn 450
66 NJEq 119, 57 At 1037; 66 NJEq 140, 57 At 725; 67 NJEq 646, 60 At 187; 71 NJEq 560, 63 At 977; 72 NJEq 933, 67 At 105

Roller Miller Patent Case
43 Fed 527; 156 US 261, 39 LE 417, 15 SC 333

Chapter 7

ANNOTATED LAW REPORTS

As has been shown in the previous three chapters, one means of case finding is through the comprehensive publishing of court reports, together with the sophisticated digest methodology used for locating these cases by subject. *Annotations,* as the term is used in this chapter, are encyclopedic essays or memoranda that collect cases germane to a particular point of law and then, through use of these cases, discuss and analyze in depth that particular point of law.

The leading publisher of *annotations* is Lawyers Cooperative Publishing (and its related company Bancroft–Whitney Company). Lawyers Cooperative Publishing believes that only a small portion of the total number of cases decided each year is of interest to most lawyers, as most cases deal with either strictly local matters or cover an area of the law so well settled that they add very little to the understanding of the law.

Unlike West Publishing Company, which publishes all reported cases and provides finding aids to help one locate all cases on point, Lawyers Cooperative Publishing, founded shortly after West, identifies points of law not previously resolved, or that indicate a change in the law, or that indicate an emerging trend in legal thinking. The publisher then selects and reports one contemporary case representative of that legal issue, collects all the relevant cases, and uses them in providing a detailed critique of that point of law. Through this method of *selective law reporting,* this publisher feels that lawyers can have access to all important cases and not have to burden their libraries with thousands of cases that add nothing to the corpus of the law.

Although selective law reporting was the basis for its first venture into publishing court reports, Lawyers Cooperative Publishing also realized that researchers must be able to locate cases not reported in its publications and to have a method of locating current cases. It began to publish auxiliary sets, all related to each other, and all aimed to assist researchers in finding answers to legal questions through these publications. These sets gradually grew into what is now called the *Total Client–Service Library (TCSL),*[1] which consists of twelve distinctive units that are national in scope. In addition to these national units, there are

[1] The *Total Client–Service Library* consists of: *American Law Reports (A.L.R., A.L.R.2d, A.L.R.3d, A.L.R.4th, A.L.R.5th, A.L.R. Fed.); American Jurisprudence 2d; American Jurisprudence Legal Forms 2d; American Jurisprudence Pleading and Practice Forms, Revised; American Jurisprudence Proof of Facts (1st, 2d, 3d); American Jurisprudence Trials; United States Code Service; United States Supreme Court Reports, Lawyers' Edition; Federal Procedure, Lawyers' Edition; Federal Procedural Forms, Lawyers' Edition; Federal Rules Service;* and *Federal Rules of Evidence Service.*

numerous state units and several specialized publications that interrelate with the *TCSL* by means of extensive cross referencing. This chapter will discuss Lawyers Cooperative Publishing's annotated law reports.

SECTION A. AMERICAN LAW REPORTS

I. Introduction

Lawyers Cooperative Publishing's *American Law Reports (A.L.R.)* series, which began in 1919, is a selective reporter of appellate court cases. Its attorney-editors scan all current cases looking for points of law that warrant *Annotations*. Once they identify a point of law deserving of an *Annotation,* they then select a case to illustrate the point of law to be annotated. This case and the accompanying monographic *Annotation* are published in *A.L.R.*

2. A.L.R. and its Series

The *American Law Reports* are in six series.[2]

(a) Federal (cited *A.L.R. Fed.*), 1969 to date. This series discusses federal topics only and is a consequence of the increasing importance and growth of federal case law. From volumes 1–110 the illustrative case immediately preceded the related *Annotation.* Commencing with volume 111 (1993), the illustrative cases reported in the volume follow all the *Annotations* in that volume. Also starting with volume 111, this set includes for the first time references to West's *Key Number System* and to West's legal encyclopedia *Corpus Juris Secundum (C.J.S.),* electronic search queries compatible with LEXIS and WESTLAW, a jurisdictional table of cited statutes and cases, and references to secondary sources such as law reviews and texts and looseleaf services from other publishers.

(b) Fifth Series (cited *A.L.R.5th*), 1992 to date. This series covers state topics only and includes numerous enhancements not found in some of the earlier series discussed below. For example, it includes references to West's *Key Number System* and to *C.J.S.,* electronic search queries, a jurisdictional table of cited statutes and cases, and references to secondary sources such as law reviews and texts and looseleaf services from other publishers. It also includes the features traditional of most *A.L.R.* series, such as the illustrative cases, outlines, *Annotations* and their various sections, indexes, and references to other *TCSL* publications. The illustrative cases reported in the volume follow all the *Annotations* in that volume.

(c) Fourth Series (cited *A.L.R.4th*), 1980–1992, 90 volumes. This set covers state topics only and contains the traditional *A.L.R.* series features, including the illustrative cases, outlines, *Annotations* and their

---

[2] The *American Law Reports* replace the *Lawyers' Reports Annotated (L.R.A.).* For information about this set, three sets collectively known as the *Trinity Series,* and other earlier sets of annotated reports, see Ervin H. Pollack, Fundamentals of Legal Research 116–17 (3d ed. 1967).

various sections, indexes, and references to other *TCSL* publications. The illustrative case immediately precedes the related *Annotation*. The same enhancements included in *A.L.R.5th* and in *A.L.R. Fed.* are being added to the pocket supplements of *A.L.R.4th*. *Electronic Search Queries and West Digest Key Numbers for Annotations in ALR 4th* is provided as a separate paperback book.

(d) Third Series (cited *A.L.R.3d*), 1965–1980, 100 volumes. For the period 1965 to 1969 this series covers both state and federal topics. After *A.L.R. Fed.* began in 1969, coverage in *A.L.R.3d* was limited to state topics. It includes the traditional features found in the more recent *A.L.R.* series.

(e) Second Series (cited *A.L.R.2d*), 1948–1965, 100 volumes. This series covers both state and federal topics and includes the traditional features found in the later *A.L.R.* series.

(f) First Series (cited *A.L.R.*), 1919–1948, 175 volumes. Coverage and features are the same as in *A.L.R.2d*.

3. The Value of A.L.R. Annotations

The usefulness of locating a relevant *A.L.R. Annotation* should be evident, since it presents in an organized fashion a commentary and discussion of all previously reported cases and saves the researcher the task of locating the cases and then analyzing and synthesizing them. Approximately 15–20 separate *Annotations* are published in each volume of *A.L.R.* [See Illustration 41.]

SECTION B. FINDING A.L.R. ANNOTATIONS

Finding *A.L.R. Annotations* and demonstrating their value can best be made clear with an example and illustrations.

In the case of *Regalado v. United States,* decided in the District of Columbia Court of Appeals,[3] an individual was convicted of cruelty to an animal, specifically the beating of a puppy. The editors at Lawyers Cooperative determined that this six-page case was illustrative of the modern view with respect to cruelty to animals. Thereafter, an editor prepared a 150 page *Annotation* entitled *What Constitutes Offense of Cruelty to Animals—Modern Cases.*

In preparing this *Annotation,* the editor researched the entire area of the law covered by the topic of the *Annotation,* collected all cases from all jurisdictions from 1950 forward that related to the *Annotation,* and wrote the *Annotation,* incorporating the many editorial features common to the *A.L.R.* series. This *Annotation,* as with all *A.L.R. Annotations,* discusses all the cases and all sides of the issue, presents general principles deduced from the cases, and gives their exceptions, qualifications, distinctions, and applications. [See Illustrations 41–48.]

[3] 572 A.2d 416, 6 A.L.R.5th 1178 (D. C. Ct. App. 1990).

1. Index Method

The first step in locating an *A.L.R. Annotation* is to consult the multi-volume *ALR Index*. This set indexes all *Annotations* in all the *A.L.R.* series, except the First Series. (There is also a separate, one volume *ALR Federal Quick Index* that reproduces the federal references found in the *ALR Index*.) The *ALR Index* is kept current by annual pocket supplements.

In our example, the terms to use would probably be "animals" or "dogs" or perhaps even "cruelty."

Under the first two terms suggested are the following [see also Illustration 49]:

ANIMALS

Cruelty
> defamation, liability for statement or publication representing plaintiff as cruel to or killer of animals, 39 ALR2d 1388

> what constitutes offense of cruelty to animals, 6 ALR5th 733; 82 ALR2d 794

DOGS

Cruelty
> experiments or tests, applicability of state animal cruelty statute to medical or scientific experimentation employing animals, 42 ALR4th 860

> what constitutes offense of cruelty to animals, 6 ALR5th 733; 82 ALR2d 794

2. Digest Method

There are separate sets of digests for *A.L.R.* and *A.L.R.2d*. However, *A.L.R.3d, A.L.R.4th, A.L.R.5th,* and *A.L.R.Fed.* are combined in one set of digests.

The *Digests* are classified into over four hundred topics arranged alphabetically. Under each topic are headnotes from cases reported in the entire *A.L.R.* family, along with a listing of the *Annotations* that deal with the particular subject in question. [See Illustration 50.]

3. Electronic Format Method

The almost 13,000 *Annotations* in *A.L.R.2d* through *5th, A.L.R.Fed.,* and *Lawyers' Edition 2d* are available exclusively on LEXIS, in its ALR library, the ALR file. *Annotations* can be located through Boolean and FREESTYLE searches, with additional means of access provided for the features common to the *A.L.R.* series. They are retrieved automatically when one searches all federal cases or all state cases. Updating these citations through *Auto–Cite* is discussed in D–3–b of this chapter.

ALR on LawDesk is a CD–ROM product containing the contents of all of *A.L.R.3d, 4th,* and *5th.* It enables a user to "jump" directly to the articles and sections needed.

4. Shepard's Citations Method

Shepard's Citations for Annotations, a set that covers *A.L.R.3d, 4th, 5th, Federal,* and *U.S. Supreme Court Reports, Lawyers' Edition 2d,* contains references to annotations citing to cases and references to cases citing to annotations. Other units of *Shepard's Citations* also provide references to *A.L.R. Annotations. Shepard's Citations* are discussed in Chapter 14.

SECTION C.   ILLUSTRATIONS: A.L.R. ANNOTATIONS AND HOW TO FIND THEM

[Illustration 41]

SAMPLE PAGE OF SUBJECTS ANNOTATED IN AN A.L.R. VOLUME

6 ALR5th　　　Subjects Annotated　　　xi

CONTRIBUTION

Release of one joint tortfeasor as discharging liability of others under Uniform Contribution Among Tortfeasors Act and other statutes expressly governing effect of release, 6 ALR5th 883

CONTROLLED SUBSTANCES

Delay in setting hearing date or in holding hearing as affecting forfeitability under Uniform Controlled Substances Act or similar statute, 6 ALR5th 711

Seizure [...] de [...] st [...] wl [...] stance seized is small, 6 ALR5th 652

> *A.L.R. Annotations* are written on many different topics. A subject guide is published in each *A.L.R.* volume.

CRUELTY TO ANIMALS

Actions constituting offense of cruelty to animals—modern cases, 6 ALR5th 733

CUSTODY OF CHILDREN

Default jurisdiction of court under § 3(a)(4) of the Uniform Child Custody Jurisdiction Act (UCCJA) or the Parental Kidnapping Prevention Act (PKPA), 28 USCS § 1738A(c)(2)(D), 6 ALR5th 69

Home state jurisdiction of court under § 3(a)(1) of the Uniform Child Custody Jurisdiction Act (UCCJA) or the Parental Kidnapping Prevention Act (PKPA), 28 USCS § 1738A(c)(2)(A), 6 ALR5th 1

DAMAGES

Insurer's liability to insurance agent or broker for damages suffered as result of insurer's denial of coverage or refusal to pay policy proceeds to insured, 6 ALR5th 611

Release of one joint tortfeasor as discharging liability of others under Uniform Contribution Among Tortfeasors Act and other statutes expressly governing effect of release, 6 ALR5th 883

DEATH AND DEATH ACTIONS

Childbirth: liability of hospital, physician, or other medical personnel for death or injury to mother or child caused by improper treatment during labor, 6 ALR5th 490

Postdelivery diagnosis, care and representations: liability of hospital, physician, or other medical personnel for death or injury to mother caused by improper postdelivery diagnosis, care and representations, 6 ALR5th 534

[...] r as [...] thers [...] ution [...] other statutes expressly governing effect of release, 6 ALR5th 883

DEFAULT JURISDICTION

Child custody: default jurisdiction of court under § 3(a)(4) of the Uniform Child Custody Jurisdiction Act (UCCJA) or the Parental Kidnapping Prevention Act (PKPA), 28 USCS § 1738A(c)(2)(D), 6 ALR5th 69

DELAY

Hearing: delay in setting hearing date or in holding hearing as affecting forfeitability under Uniform Controlled Substances Act or similar statute, 6 ALR5th 711

DENIAL OF COVERAGE

Insurance: insurer's liability to insurance agent or broker for damages suffered as result of insurer's denial of coverage or refusal to pay policy proceeds to insured, 6 ALR5th 611

DISCHARGE

Joint tortfeasor: release of one joint tortfeasor as discharging liability of others under Uniform Contribution Among Tortfeasors Act and other statutes expressly governing effect of release, 6 ALR5th 883

DISQUALIFICATION

Attorneys: disqualification of member of law firm as requiring disqualification of entire firm—state cases, 6 ALR5th 242

[Illustration 42]

HEADNOTES AND START OF OPINION IN A.L.R.5th

REGALADO v UNITED STATES 6 ALR5th
(Dist Col App) 572 A2d 416, 6 ALR5th 1178

proof not of specific intent to harm but of general intent with malice, such a standard reflecting the growing concern in the law for the

cruelty to animals, where a neighbor observed the defendant angrily holding a 12-week-old German Shepherd suspended in the air by a

A case representative of the subject of each *A.L.R. Annotation* in a volume is also reported in that volume. When citing an *A.L.R. Annotation*, reference is to the *Annotation*, not the representative case.

of their animals.
[Annotated]

Animals § 44 — statutes outlawing animal cruelty — sufficiency of evidence to support conviction

3. The evidence was sufficient to support a jury's finding that the defendant acted willfully in an attempt to harm a puppy, supporting a verdict of guilty in a prosecution for violating a statute outlawing

lesions about the left eye which were too recent to have occurred 2 days before treatment, when the defendant claimed the dog had been hit by a taxi, and the defendant seriously undermined his own credibility by first claiming that the puppy's injuries occurred in the taxi mishap and then asserting that the animal whose injuries where displayed in photographs was not the animal in question.
[Annotated]

APPEARANCES OF COUNSEL

Janell M. Wolfe, Falls Church, Va., appointed by the court, was on the brief, for appellant.

Jay B. Stephens, U.S. Atty.,

and **John R. Fisher, Thomas J. Tourish, Nancy Woodward**, Washington, D.C., and **Oscar S. Mayers, Jr.**, Asst. U.S. Attys., were on the brief, for appellee.

Before ROGERS, Chief Judge, and SCHWELB, Associate Judge, and KERN, Senior Judge.

OPINION OF THE COURT

ROGERS, Chief Judge:

Appellant Peter Regalado appeals from his conviction by a jury of cruelty to animals, D.C.Code § 22-801 (1989 Repl.)[1] on the

---

1. D.C.Code § 22-801 defines cruelty to animals as:

Whoever overdrives, overloads, drives when overloaded, overworks, tortures, torments, deprives of necessary sustenance, cruelly beats, mutilates, or cruelly kills or causes or procures to be so overdriven, over-

loaded, driven when overloaded, overworked, tortured, tormented, deprived of necessary sustenance, cruelly beaten, mutilated, or cruelly killed any animal, and whoever, having the charge or custody of any animal, either as owner or otherwise, inflicts unnecessary cruelty upon the

[Illustration 43]

FIRST PAGE OF ANNOTATION, 6 A.L.R.5th 733

---

6 ALR5th 733

WHAT CONSTITUTES OFFENSE OF CRUELTY TO ANIMALS—MODERN CASES

by
Sonja A. Soehnel, J.D.

> This is the first page of the *Annotation* for 6 A.L.R.5th 733 (1992). This prefatory paragraph, new to *A.L.R.5th*, briefly describes the subject of the *Annotation*. For *A.L.R.5th*, the illustrative cases used with the *Annotations* are published toward the rear of the volume following all *Annotations* in that volume. For earlier *A.L.R.* series, the case immediately precedes the *Annotation*.

Prosecutions for the offense of cruelty to animals have been instituted for shooting, burning, or beating an animal, failure to provide necessary care to an animal, and for acts relating to organized fights between animals. Whether a conviction results may turn on a variety of factors—evidence presented by the prosecution that the alleged act occurred; evidence presented by the defendant that the alleged act was a necessary act of discipline or was in protection of a person or of property; and the court's ruling on the statutory wording as to the degree of intent with which the defendant must have acted. In the recent case of Regalado v United States (1990, Dist Col App) 572 A2d 416, 6 ALR5th 1178, a prosecution for beating a puppy, the court held that the evidence supported an inference of discipline crossing over the line to cruelty and held that the statute under which the plaintiff was charged did not require proof of specific intent to injure or abuse an animal but required only proof of general intent with malice. This annotation collects and analyzes the cases decided in or after 1950 that discuss what constitutes the offense of cruelty to animals.

Regalado v United States is fully reported at page 1178, infra.

733

[Illustration 44]

FIRST PAGE OF OUTLINE TO ANNOTATION, 6 A.L.R.5th 733

CRUELTY TO ANIMALS 6 ALR5th
6 ALR5th 733

Table of Contents

Research References

Index

Jurisdictional Table of Cited Statutes and Cases

ARTICLE OUTLINE

I. PRELIMINARY MATTERS

II. GENERAL CONSIDERATIONS

This is the first page of a detailed outline of the *Annotation* that follows the prefatory paragraph. Note that while this *Annotation* covers the point specific to *Regalado v. United States*, it covers numerous other issues as well. The outline enables a researcher to turn immediately to a section being researched and find relevant cases. See Illustration 48.

III. AFFIRMATIVE ACT

[Illustration 45]

PAGE SHOWING RESEARCH REFERENCES
FOR ANNOTATION, 6 A.L.R.5th 733

---

6 ALR5th   CRUELTY TO ANIMALS
                          6 ALR5th 733

1 Am Jur Pl & Pr Forms (Rev), Animals, Forms 171-198

37 Am Jur Proof of Facts 711, Justifiable Destruction of Animal

Federal Statutes

7 USCS §§ 2131-2156 (Animal Welfare Act); 15 USCS §§ 1821-1831
(Horse Protection Act)

Digests and Indexes

L Ed Digest, Animals § 14

ALR Digests, Animals §§ 43-45

Index to Annotations, Animals; Birds; Bulls; Cats; Dogs; Horses; Pets;
Poultry; Veterinarians; Zoos ·

Auto-Cite®

Cases and annotations referred to herein can be further researched
through the Auto-Cite® computer-assisted research service. Use
Auto-Cite to check citations for form, parallel references, prior and
later history, and annotation references.

RESEARCH SOURCES

The following are the research sources that were found to be
helpful in compiling this annotation:

Encyclopedias

4 Am Jur 2d, Animals §§ 27-29

3A CJS Animals §§ 100-112

Law Reviews

Goodkin, The Evolution of Animal Rights, 18 Colum Hum Rts L Rev
259 (Spring, 1987)

Electronic Search Query

(animal w/3 (cruel! or mistreat)) and name (people or state or commonwealth) and date aft 1949

West Digest Key Numbers

Animals 38, 40-43, 45, 52, 78, 84,
86, 87, 94, 96, 101, 102, 108-
110, 113

A.L.R. Annotations include references to other *TCSL* publications,
as well as to sources by other publishers. In earlier series, the
TCSL references are in a box on the first page of the *Annotation.*

737

[Illustration 46]

FIRST PAGE OF INDEX TO ANNOTATION, 6 A.L.R.5th 733

CRUELTY TO ANIMALS   6 ALR5th
6 ALR5th 733

INDEX

Abandonment of animal, §§ 6, 8, 16[a], 18[a]

Abscess, § 17[a]

Accusations, required specificity, § 18[b]

Admission to fight involving animal, §§ 21-23, 25[d], 26[a, b], 27

Affirmative act, §§ 12-15

Affirmative defenses, §§ 28-31

Agent and principal, § 16[b]

Chain, dog training, § 15[a]

Circus, §§ 15[a], 16[b]

Cockfight, §§ 6, 23-26

Cold weather, § 16

Colts, §§ 12[a], 29[a]

Conducting fight involving animals, §§ 21, 25, 27

Confinement, poor maintenance of fences, § 16[a]

Constructive design to cause harm, § 4

> **A.L.R.5th Annotations** include a detailed index that can lead to specific points in the *Annotation*. Lengthy *Annotations* in earlier series also contain an index.

27

Association, right of, § 26[b]

Australian shepherd dogs, § 12[a]

Automobile, confining dog in, § 16[a]

Award in game, live animal as, § 15[a]

Baseball bat, beating dog, § 14[a]

Beagles, §§ 15[b], 25[c], 28[b], 29[b]

Beating, §§ 3, 4, 11[b], 14, 15, 17[a], 28[b], 29[b], 30, 31[b]

Bedsores, § 16[a]

Betting in connection with animal fights, §§ 21[a], 22[b, c], 24[a, c], 25[c-e], 26[a]

Birds, §§ 6, 16, 23-26, 29[a]

Bladder stone, § 17[a]

Blind dogs, §§ 16[a], 17[a]

Bovine animals, §§ 7, 10, 12, 13, 15, 16[a], 17[a]

Boxer mix, § 12[a]

Brittany, §§ 12, 29

Bucking straps, § 15[a]

Bullfights, § 27

Bulls, §§ 15[a], 27

Burning, § 13

Cages, size of, § 16

Car, confining dog in, § 16[a]

Castration of dogs, § 15[b]

Cats, §§ 12[b], 13, 15[a], 16, 18[b], 29[a]

Cattle, §§ 7, 10, 12, 13, 15-17[a]

Cattle prods, dog training, § 15[a]

Criminal negligence, §§ 8, 11[a], 16[b]

Cumulative penalties, § 16[a]

Deer, dogs chasing, §§ 29[a], 31[a]

Dehydration, §§ 16[a], 17[a]

Design or intent, generally, §§ 3-11, 17[a], 22[b]

Discipline or training, §§ 3, 4, 14, 15, 30

Diseases, §§ 16[a], 17[a]

Display window, unventilated, § 16[a]

Distemper, dogs, §§ 16[a], 17[a]

Doberman pinschers, §§ 15[a], 17[a]

Dog bite, §§ 12, 14[b], 18[a], 28

Dogfight, §§ 5, 19-22

Dogs, §§ 3-6, 9-22, 28-31

Dog training business, §§ 10, 14[a], 15[a]

Dog warden, §§ 14[b], 16[a], 28[b], 31[b]

Dolphins, § 26[d]

Dragging dog behind car, § 15[a]

Drink, failure to provide, §§ 8, 10, 11[b], 16, 17[a]

Driver of horse, reliance on owner's statements as to fitness, § 17[b]

Ducks, § 16[a]

Due process, §§ 14[a], 16[a], 25[a, c-e], 26[b]

Dwarf cattle, § 16[b]

Ear infections, § 17[a]

738

[Illustration 47]

FIRST PAGE OF JURISDICTIONAL TABLE
TO ANNOTATION, 6 A.L.R.5th 733

CRUELTY TO ANIMALS   6 ALR5th
6 ALR5th 733

Jurisdictional Table of Cited Statutes and Cases*

ALABAMA

Ala Code § 3-1-12 (1975). See § 13
Ala Code § 3-1-29 (1975). See §§ 5, 20
Ala Code § 13A-11-14 (1975). See §§ 7, 16[a], 17[a]

Anderton v State (1980, Ala App) 390 So 2d 1083—§ 13
Jones v State (1985, Ala App) 473 So 2d 1197—§§ 2, 5, 20
La Rue v State (1985, Ala App) 478 So 2d 13—§§ 2, 7, 16[a], 17[a]
Williams v State (1984, Ala App) 462 So 2d 771—§ 5

ARIZONA

This jurisdictional table, found in *A.L.R.5th*, provides citations to statutes and cases relevant to the *Annotation*. This information is much more detailed than in earlier series.

ARKANSAS

Ark Code Ann § 5-2-202(2). See §§ 16[a], 18[a]
Ark Code Ann § 5-62-101 (1987). See §§ 6, 16[a], 18[a]
Ark Stat Ann §§ 41-2918.1, 41-2918.2 (Supp 1985). See §§ 21[a], 22[a]

Ash v State (1986) 290 Ark 278, 718 SW2d 930—§§ 2, 21[a], 22[a]
Norton v State (1991) 307 Ark 336, 820 SW2d 272—§§ 6, 16[a], 18[a]

CALIFORNIA

Cal Penal Code § 7 subd 4 cl 2. See § 12[a]
Cal Penal Code § 597. See §§ 11[b], 16[b]
Cal Penal Code § 597 subd (a). See §§ 3, 12[a], 29[a]
Cal Penal Code § 597(b). See §§ 11[a], 16[b]
Cal Penal Code § 597b. See §§ 6, 26[a]
Cal Penal Code § 597f. See §§ 11[b], 16[a], 18[a]

People v Brian (1980) 110 Cal App 3d Supp 1, 168 Cal Rptr 105—§§ 2, 11[a], 16[b]
People v Dunn (1974, 1st Dist) 39 Cal App 3d 418, 114 Cal Rptr 164—§§ 2, 3, 12[a], 29[a]

---

* Statutes, rules, regulations, and constitutional provisions bearing on the subject of the annotation are included in this table only to the extent, and in the form, that they are reflected in the court opinions discussed in this annotation. The reader should consult the appropriate statutory or regulatory compilations to ascertain the current status of relevant statutes, rules, regulations, and constitutional provisions.

For federal cases involving state law, see state headings.

742

[Illustration 48]

PAGE FROM ANNOTATION, 6 A.L.R.5th 733

defendant had admitted placing the cat in the oven, turning the oven on, and

only co⌐
might h
The cou
inferenc⌐
easily dr⌐

⌐ Notice how § 14 brings together and discusses all cases dealing with beating of animals. § 1 always gives the scope of the *Annotation* and then lists related *Annotations*. ⌐

railing of steps in a manner so tangled that the puppy could not

.hat the
ieverely
d swol-
id told
)uppy's
puppy

§ 14. Beating

[a] Ruling for prosecution

In the following cases in which the defendant was charged with beating a dog in violation of a statute prohibiting some type of cruelty to animals, the courts ruled in favor of the prosecution.

→In Regalado v United States (1990, **Dist Col** App) 572 A2d 416, 6 ALR5th 1178, the court held that the evidence was sufficient to sustain the defendant's conviction under an animal cruelty statute (DC Code § 22-801 (1989 Repl)) for beating a puppy. Rejecting the defendant's contention that the government had failed to prove that he had had the specific intent to harm the puppy, the court held that § 22-801 required only proof of general intent with malice. Section 22-801 prohibited cruelly beating an animal or inflicting unnecessary cruelty on an animal in one's custody. The defendant's neighbor testified that he had seen the defendant hitting the puppy very hard while the puppy was being held suspended in the air by a tied rope, that the defendant had been very angry and out of control, and that the neighbor had yelled at the defendant to stop, but the defendant had refused. A humane society officer who had responded to the neighbor's call testified that she had seen the puppy tied to the

being hit by a car a week earlier; that while she and the defendant had tried to extricate the puppy, the defendant had slapped the puppy on the face to show the humane officer what he had done earlier; and that, fearing for the puppy's safety, she had transported it to an animal hospital. A veterinarian testified that the puppy had a swollen left eye with hemorrhage of the conjunctiva and a less swollen right eye and that the lesions around the puppy's eyes had occurred within 12 to 24 hours before his treatment of the puppy. The court stated that these three witnesses had offered evidence to support a finding of malice. The court noted the neighbor's description of the defendant's state of mind and the effect on the puppy and noted that the humane officer's reaction to the defendant's demonstration of how he had beaten the puppy and the veterinarian's testimony of the extent and nature of the injuries supported an inference of discipline crossing over the line to cruelty. The court affirmed the conviction.

The court, in People v McKnight (1980) 102 **Mich** App 581, 302 NW2d 241, affirmed the defendant's conviction for kicking to death a dog. After the defendant had broken into a home with intent to steal, he had kicked to death the absent owner's dog. The dog had died 12 hours later. The statute

[Illustration 49]

EXAMPLE FROM ALR INDEX

CRUEL AND UNUSUAL PUNISHMENT—Cont'd

Tax returns, validity, construction, and application of provisions for assessment and review of civil penalty against taxpayer who files frivolous income tax return, 84 ALR Fed 433,' § 4

Torture (this index)

Traffic offenders, validit̲ tion of statute or or ing imprisonment repeated traffic offe 618

Vacating or setting asid after remarriage ᴏɪ party, ALR4th 1153, §§ 3[b-d], 4, 5[b], 8[a], 14

Visitation, state regulation of conjugal or overnight familial visits in penal or correctional institutions, 29 ALR4th 1216

CRUELTY

As to abuse of persons. **Abuse of Persons** (this index)

Animals

– defamation, liability for statement or publication representing plaintiff as cruel to or killer of animals, 39 ALR2d 1388

– what constitutes offense of cruelty to animals, 6 ALR5th 733; 82 ALR2d 794

Attorneys' fees, amount in matters involving domestic relations and divorce, 32 ALR3d 1227, §§ 5[b], 7[a, b], 10; 59 ALR3d 152, §§ 3[b-d], 4[b], 5[b], 7[a-d]

Children

– abuse. **Abuse of Persons** (this index)

– mistreatment of children as ground for divorce, 82 ALR2d 1361

Condonation of cruel treatment as defense to action for divorce or separation, 32 ALR2d 107

Criminal misconduct, charging spouse with criminal misconduct as cruelty constituting ground for divorce, 72 ALR2d 1197

Decedents' estates, estoppel or laches precluding lawful spouse from asserting rights in decedent's estate as against putative spouse, 81 ALR3d 110, § 17

> In using the *ALR Index, Annotations* generally are indexed under two or more terms. Note citations to the *Annotation* for the problem being researched.

CRUELTY—Cont'd

Divorce

– condonation of cruel treatment as defense to action for divorce or separation, 32 ALR2d 107

– criminal misconduct, charging spouse with criminal misconduct as cruelty constituting ground for di- t2d 1197

children as ground 2 ALR2d 1361

e, insistence on sex cruelty or indignity ground for divorce, 3

– single act of cruelty as basis, 7 ALR3d 761

Dogs

– experiments or tests, applicability of state animal cruelty statute to medical or scientific experimentation employing animals, 42 ALR4th 860

– what constitutes offense of cruelty to animals, 6 ALR5th 733; 82 ALR2d 803

Drunkenness, habitual intemperance, or use of drugs as constituting cruelty as a ground for divorce, 76 ALR2d 419

Juvenile courts, liability of parent for support of child institutionalized by juvenile court, 59 ALR3d 636, § 5

Mental Cruelty (this index)

Mistreatment of children as ground for divorce, 82 ALR2d 1361

Sexual intercourse, insistence on sex relations as cruelty or indignity constituting ground for divorce, 88 ALR2d 553

Suicide, threats or attempts to commit suicide as cruelty or indignity constituting a ground for divorce, 86 ALR2d 422

CRUISING

Validity, construction, and effect of statutes or ordinances forbidding automotive cruising—practice of driving repeatedly through loop of public roads through city, 87 ALR4th 1110

CRUSHING

Accident insurance, what is loss of body member for purposes of accident insurance, 51 ALR4th 156, §§ 5, 21[a]

[Illustration 50]

PAGE FROM ALR DIGEST TO 3d, 4th, 5th, Fed.

ANIMALS § 1

Consult pocket part for later cases

III. KILLING OR INJURING

(A) IN GENERAL

§ 8 Generally
§ 9 Injury to animals trespassing or running at large
§ 10 —Failure to fence
§ 10.5 Contributory or comparative negligence

(B) KILLING OR INJURING DOGS

§ 11 Generally
§ 12 Dogs running at large or trespassing
§ 13 Barking dogs
§ 14 Dogs attacking other animals
§ 15 By person assaulted by dog
§ 16 By police officers

IV. LIABILITY FOR INJURY OR DAMAGE BY

(A) IN GENERAL; STOCK

§ 17 Generally
§ 18 While trespassing or running at large
§ 19 —Knowledge of breachy or vicious disposition
§ 20 Vicious animals; knowledge of disposition
§ 21 Wild ar
§ 22 Bees
§ 23 Contrib risk;
§ 24 To who
§ 25 —To h
§ 26 Liabilit

§ 27 Generally
§ 28 Liability of owner or operator of place of public resort
§ 29 Vicious disposition
§ 30 —Knowledge of
§ 31 Acts or negligence contributing to injury

V. RUNNING AT LARGE; ESTRAYS; IMPOUNDING

§ 32 Generally
§ 33 Pounds; impounding or distraining

VI. DISEASED ANIMALS

§ 34 Generally
§ 35 Restrictions on importation of
§ 36 Tuberculin test
§ 37 Liability of owner
§ 38 Liability of seller
§ 39 Liability of carrier
§ 40 Liability for killing infected animal

VII. REGULATIONS CONCERNING; LICENSE AND TAX LAWS

§ 41 Generally
§ 41.5 Animal Welfare Acts
§ 42 Tax on dogs

VIII. CRUELTY TO; CRIMINAL LIABILITY FOR INJURING

§ 43 Generally
§ 44 Dogs
§ 45 Shooting birds

IX. VETERINARIANS

§ 46 Generally; licensing and regulation
§ 47 Liability to and of veterinarians

I. IN GENERAL

§ 1 Generally

Text References:

4 Am Jur 2d, Animals §§ 1–4

Practice References:

1B Am Jur Pl & Pr Forms (Rev), Animals, Forms 1 et seq.

2 Am Jur Legal Forms 2d, Animals, §§ 20:1 et seq; 20 Am Jur Legal Forms 2d, Veterinarians, §§ 256:1 et seq.

2 Am Jur Trials 1, Investigating Particular Civil Actions § 9

7 USCS §§ 1 et seq; 16 USCS §§ 1 et seq; 21 USCS §§ 151 et seq., 321 et seq.

L Ed Digest, Animals § 1

Annotations:

Products liability; animal feed or medicines, 29 ALR4th 1045

ecticides, pes... d the like, or f, 12 ALR4th

t of damages th 1287

spraying or

cation of Endangered Species Act of 1973 (16 USCS §§ 1531–1543), 32 ALR Fed 332

Auto-Cite®: Cases and annotations referred to herein can be further researched through the Auto-Cite® computer-assisted research service. Use Auto-Cite to check citations for form, parallel references, prior and later history, and annotation references.

Once a federal agency has had meaningful consultation with the Secretary of Interior concerning actions that may affect an endangered species, the final decision whether to proceed with the action lies with the agency itself. Endangered Species Act of 1973 § 7 does not give the Department of Interior a veto power over the actions of other federal agencies, provided the required consultation has occurred. *National Wildlife Federation v Coleman (1976, CA5 Miss) 529 F2d 359, 32 ALR Fed 306,* reh den *(CA5 Miss) 532 F2d 1375* and cert den *429 US 979, 50 L Ed 2d 587, 97 S Ct 489.*

[Annotated]

After consulting with the Secretary of Interior concerning actions that may affect an endangered species, the federal agency involved must determine whether it has taken all necessary action to insure that its actions will not jeopardize the continued existence of the endangered species, or destroy or modify habitat

325

> Notice how the outline at the start of the topic *Animals* directs the researcher to the proper location in the digest. Notice also the references to other sources, including *Annotations.*

SECTION D.   HOW A.L.R. IS KEPT CURRENT

1. Upkeep Service

Once an *A.L.R. Annotation* is found, further steps must be taken to locate cases subsequent to those found in the *Annotation*. Over the years the publisher has developed several different ways to keep its various *A.L.R.* series up to date.

a. *A.L.R.3d, 4th, 5th, Federal.* Each volume of these series has an annual cumulative pocket supplement. After reading an *Annotation* in any of these series, it is necessary to check the pocket supplement for later cases. Digests of cases are keyed directly to each section of the *Annotation*. [See Illustration 51.] Also, as new volumes continue to be published for *A.L.R.5th* and *A.L.R. Federal,* to assure complete coverage it is necessary to examine the contents page or "subjects annotated" section in all bound volumes published after the pocket supplement.

b. *A.L.R.2d.* This series is kept current with a multi-volume *A.L.R.2d Later Case Service,* with each volume covering two to four volumes of the 100 volumes in *A.L.R.2d.* This *Later Case Service* provides digests of cases and then keys them directly to each section of the *A.L.R.2d Annotations.* [See Illustration 52.] This set is kept up to date with annual pocket supplements and occasional revised volumes. Thus, to update an *A.L.R.2d Annotation,* both the bound *Later Case Service* and its supplement must be checked.

c. *A.L.R. (First Series).* This series is kept current through a cumbersome seven volume set entitled the *A.L.R. Blue Book of Supplemental Decisions.* Each "permanent" volume covers a different span of years, with the latest being for 1984–1989. Each volume lists citations to all cases on the same topic as the *Annotations,* but provides no discussion of the cases. [See Illustration 53.] The set is supplemented with an annual pamphlet, making it necessary to consult eight separate sources to fully update an *Annotation* in *A.L.R. (First Series).*

2. Superseding and Supplementing Annotations

a. *Superseding Annotations.* Frequently, a topic of law of an *A.L.R. Annotation* is completely changed by later cases. For example, an *Annotation* in an early volume of *A.L.R.* might show that there is little likelihood that one would be convicted of cruelty to animals. Subsequently, statutes are enacted, cases interpret those statutes, and the law changes. The editors may then decide to rewrite and publish in a later *A.L.R.* volume a *superseding* (replacement) *Annotation.* Sometimes only a part of a previous *Annotation* will be superseded.

b. *Supplementing Annotations.* This method was used most frequently in *A.L.R.* and *A.L.R.2d.* In such instances, a new *Annotation* was written that supplemented the original one. Therefore, for comprehensive coverage both *Annotations* must be read together as if they are one *Annotation.*

3. Locating the Most Recent Annotations

a. *Annotation History Table.* Whenever a researcher has a citation to an *A.L.R. Annotation,* to avoid a waste of time by reading an obsolete *Annotation* or one not fully covering a topic, the researcher should always first check to see if an *Annotation* has been *superseded* or *supplemented.* This is done either by checking the citation in the appropriate *A.L.R.* upkeep volume, or by using the *Annotation History Table* located in the T–Z volume of the *ALR Index.* This *Table* gives the history of *Annotations* in all of the *A.L.R.* series. Its use can best be shown with the excerpt below:

ANNOTATION HISTORY TABLE

12 ALR 111	13 ALR 17	13 ALR 1465
Supplemented 37 ALR2d 453	Supplemented 39 ALR2d 782	Superseded 3 ALR5th 370
12 ALR 333	13 ALR 151	14 ALR 240
Superseded 7 ALR2d 226	Superseded 46 ALR2d 1227	Superseded 51 ALR2d 331
12 ALR 596	13 ALR 225	14 ALR 316
Superseded 57 ALR2d 379	Superseded 13 ALR4th 1060	Superseded 11 ALR3d 1074

This example means that 12 *A.L.R.* 111 and 37 *A.L.R.2d* 453 should be read together as if they are a single *Annotation,* and then updated for later cases using the *A.L.R.2d Later Case Service* as previously described.

Suppose, however, that the researcher has found a citation to 82 *A.L.R.2d* 794, an *Annotation* on cruelty to animals. By checking the *Annotation History Table* in the *ALR Index,* it would be noted that this *Annotation* is *superseded* as indicated below:

ANNOTATION HISTORY TABLE

78 ALR2d 412	79 ALR2d 431	82 ALR2d 794
Superseded 69 ALR Fed 600	¶ 29, 36 Superseded 46 ALR4th 1197	Superseded 6 ALR5th 733
	¶ 35 Superseded 63 ALR4th 105	
78 ALR2d 429	¶ 37 Superseded 54 ALR4th 574	82 ALR2d 1183
Superseded 96 ALR Fed 778		¶ 3-5 Superseded 53 ALR4th 282
		63 ALR4th 221
78 ALR2d 446	79 ALR2d 990	
Superseded 25 ALR3d 383	Superseded 20 ALR3d 1127	82 ALR2d 1429
	38 ALR4th 200	Superseded 44 ALR4th 271
	79 ALR2d 1005	
	Superseded 54 ALR4th 391	

b. *Auto–Cite. Auto–Cite,* available on LEXIS, is an electronic system of citations and is a trade name of Lawyers Cooperative Publishing. By typing an *A.L.R.* citation into *Auto–Cite* the system retrieves citations to all supplementing or superseding annotations. For example, entering 82 *A.L.R.2d* 794, the same citation as used with the *Annotation History Table,* the result reproduced below is obtained:

Auto–Cite (R) Citation Service, (c) 1994 Lawyers Cooperative Publishing

82 ALR2D 794:   Screen 1 of 2

CITATION YOU ENTERED:

What constitutes statutory offense of cruelty to animals, 82 A.L.R.2d 794 (superseded by What constitutes offense of cruelty to animals—modern cases, 6 A.L.R.5th 733).
* * *

c. *Latest Case Service Hotline.* Each pocket supplement lists a toll free number that can be used to obtain citations to any relevant cases decided since the last supplement.

SECTION E.   ILLUSTRATIONS: A.L.R. UPKEEP SERVICES

51.   **Page from an A.L.R.5th volume pocket supplement**
52.   **Page from A.L.R.2d Later Case Service**
53.   **Excerpts from A.L.R. Blue Book of Supplemental Decisions**

[Illustration 51]

PAGE FROM POCKET SUPPLEMENT TO 6 A.L.R.5th

6 ALR5th 652–710   ALR5th

Auto-Cite®: Cases and annotations referred to herein can be further researched through the Auto-Cite® computer-assisted research service. Use Auto-Cite to check citations for form, parallel references, prior and later history, and annotation references.

§ 3. Trace, residue, debris, or the like
[a] Forfeiture allowed
Also allowing forfeiture of property in question where amount of controlled substance was unweighed or unweighable:

NY—Property Clerk, New York City Police Dept. v Larouche (1992, 1st Dept) 187 App Div 2d 289, 589 NYS2d 459.

[b] Forfeiture not allowed
Small amount of marijuana found in car coupled with police dog's detecting of odor of controlled substance on cash found in car did not provide substantial evidence connecting cash with drug dealing; forfeiture of cash was reversed. Re Daniels (1991, Iowa) 478 NW2d 622.

§ 11. Less than 1 ounce
[a] Forfeiture allowed
Also allowing forfeiture of property in question where amount of controlled substance was less than one ounce:

Utah—State v One 1988 Chevrolet Camaro (1991, Utah) 813 P2d 1186, 164 Utah Adv Rep 25.

6 ALR5th 711–732

§ 1. Introduction
[b] Related annotations
Forfeitability of property under Uniform Controlled Substances Act or similar statute where amount of controlled substance seized is small. 6 ALR5th 652.

Auto-Cite®: Cases and annotations referred to herein can be further researched through the Auto-Cite® computer-assisted research service. Use Auto-Cite to check citations for form, parallel references, prior and later history, and annotation references.

§ 5. —30-day period
[a] Hearing timely
Under statute providing for hearing within 30 days of filing of petition following criminal trial, third-party interested in frozen bank account was not deprived of due process by delay of hearing for approximately 10 to 11 months following freezing of account. Protective Order on Intergroup Invest. Corporation's Account at Mega Bank v Arboleda-Hurtado (1992, SD Fla) 790 F Supp 1140, 6 FLW Fed D 124.

Under pre-1989 forfeiture statute requiring hearing to be conducted within 30 days after answer was filed, time provision was mandatory and would give parties right, by mandamus, to compel court to hear case promptly; nevertheless, where State filed notice on February 22, subject of forfeiture answered March 10, and case was set for trial on May 7, dismissal of action for delay was improper. State v $435,000.00 (1992, Tex) 842 SW2d 642, rehg of cause overr (Dec 16, 1992).

6 ALR5th 883–1030

§ 7. Limited release as extending only to express terms
[b] Release reserving rights against tortfeasor claiming benefit
Plaintiff, who executed covenant not to sue pizza delivery driver or driver's insurer, and expressly reserved right to sue employer, had right to action against employer on theory of vicarious liability, under NC Gen Stat § 1B-4(1), where employer was "tortfeasor" within meaning of act. Yates v New South Pizza, Ltd. (1992) 330 NC 790, 412 SE2d 666, reh den 331 NC 292, 417 SE2d 73.

Annotations in *A.L.R.3d, A.L.R.4th, A.L.R.5th* and *A.L.R. Federal* are kept current by annual pocket supplements. Citations to cases later than the supplement can be obtained by calling the publisher's toll free number.

Notice that no new material has been added for Annot., 6 A.L.R.5th 733 (1992).

8

[Illustration 52]

PAGE FROM POCKET SUPPLEMENT TO
A.L.R.2d LATER CASE SERVICE

LATER CASE SERVICE   **82 ALR2d 863–867**

marriage following their divorce because they had resumed cohabitation, where even under relaxed standard of proof man and woman failed to show common-law marriage in that they had considered their obligations under common law to be more relaxed than those under civil marriage, they had filed separate tax returns, and woman had eventually moved out and resumed her maiden name. Re Frawley (1990, DC Colo) 112 BR 32 (applying Col law).

In proceeding in which former husband was held in contempt for failure to comply with property settlement

cree, husband failec
vincing evidence t
established commo
divorce when wife c
residence, and that
sion therefore did t
and wife filed separ
husband did not see
and former wife t
together. Fields v Fields (1987, Montgomery Co) 39 **Ohio** App 3d 187, 530 NE2d 933.

> To locate later cases for an *Annotation* in *A.L.R.2d*, the *A.L.R. Later Case Service* can be used. This page from the pocket supplement illustrates that the *Annotation* being researched has been superseded by a later one.

82 ALR2d 726–740

§ 1. **Scope and related matters, p. 727.**

Liability of mobile vendor for injury to child. 8 Am Jur Proof of Facts 3d 477.

Auto-Cite®: Cases and annotations referred to herein can be further researched through the Auto-Cite® computer-assisted research service. Use Auto-Cite to check citations for form, parallel references, prior and later history, and annotation references.

82 ALR2d 750–756

§ 1. **Scope and background, p. 750.**

Auto-Cite®: Cases and annotations referred to herein can be further researched through the Auto-Cite® computer-assisted research service. Use Auto-Cite to check citations for form, parallel references, prior and later history, and annotation references.

§ 3. **Withdrawal held effective, p. 753.**

Borough police officer would be reinstated with pay until date of discharge where officer, who had tendered resignation on March 27 to be effective April 13, withdrew resignation on April 10, prior to borough council's acceptance of resignation. California v Horner (1989, **Pa** Cmwlth) 565 A2d 1250, reh den (Pa Cmwlth) 1990 Pa Commw LEXIS 58 and app den (Pa) 577 A2d 891 and app den (Pa) 577 A2d 892.

82 ALR2d 764–769

§ 1. **Scope and introduction, p. 764.**

Auto-Cite®: Cases and annotations referred to herein can be further researched through the Auto-Cite® computer-assisted research service. Use Auto-Cite to check citations for form, parallel references, prior and later history, and annotation references.

§ 3. **Circumstances excusing use; paramountcy of navigation rules, p. 767.**

Nonuse of radar by cargo vessel's crew,
ation of rule govern-
t contribute to colli-
g vessel where cargo
ling vessel about 50
and periodically esti-
ed, and collision was
essel's sudden sharp
1. Slobodna Plovidba
) 688 F Supp 1226,
hout op (CA6 Mich)
870 F2d 658.

82 ALR2d 794–853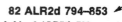

Superseded by 6 ALR5th 733.

82 ALR2d 858–859

What constitutes "family farmer" entitled to relief under Chapter 12 of Bankruptcy Code (11 USCS §§ 1201 et seq.). 101 ALR Fed 502.

Auto-Cite®: Cases and annotations referred to herein can be further researched through the Auto-Cite® computer-assisted research service. Use Auto-Cite to check citations for form, parallel references, prior and later history, and annotation references.

82 ALR2d 863–867

Auto-Cite®: Cases and annotations referred to herein can be further researched through the Auto-Cite® computer-assisted research service. Use Auto-Cite to check citations for form, parallel references, prior and later history, and annotation references.

Competent evidence existed to allow jury reasonably to find that lessee with option to buy intended to deprive lessor of stereo, where (1) lessee only made two lease payments, (2) in spite of lease conditions that lessor retained ownership of property and title thereto, that lessee would keep and use stereo only at home address, and that lessee had no right to transfer or in any way encumber stereo, lessee pawned stereo approximately two months after commencement of lease at time when investment in stereo was quite small, and (3) lessee failed to redeem

37

[Illustration 53]

EXCERPTS FROM A.L.R. BLUE BOOK OF SUPPLEMENTAL DECISIONS

VOL. 1

24 A.L.R. 1002–1016.
Brede v. P. 263 U.S. 4, 68 L ed. 132, 44 S.Ct. 8.
Duke v. U. S. 301 U.S. 492, 81 L.ed. 1243, 57 S.Ct. 835.
Cleveland v. M. 287 F. 048, 52 App. Cas. (D.C.) 374.
U. S. v. I. 288 F. 039.
U. S. v. S. 289 F. 123.
Remus v. U. S. 291 F. 513.
Rossini v. U. S. 6 F.(2d) 350
Christian v. U. S. 8 F.(2d) 732.
U. S. v. T. 15 F.(2d) 207.
Orban v. U. S. 18 F.(2d) 874.
Beland v. US, 128 F(2d) 795.
U. S. v. S. 31 FSupp 327.

VOL. 2

24 ALR 977–978
Supplementing 17 ALR 1005.
Superseded in 166 ALR 1118.✦

24 ALR 1002–1016
Kempe v. U. S. 151 F2d 680.
United States v. K. (CCA NJ) 159 F2d 058.
Barkman v. S. (CCA Ga) 162 F2d 592.
Baldwin v. C. (Ky) 235 SW2d 771.

24 ALR 1137–1148
U. S. v. R. (CA NY) 191 F2d

VOL. 3

24 ALR 973–974
Re Brener's Estate. 155 Neb 836, 54 NW2d 75.

24 ALR 977–978
Superseded 166 ALR 1118.✦

24 ALR 1002–1016
Green v U. S. 356 US 165, 2 L ed 2d 672, 78 S Ct 632.
U. S. v G. (DC NY) 140 F Supp 117
State v McK. (NC) 94 SE2d 853 (citing anno).
Elder v C. E. B. (Okla) 326 P2d

VOL. 4

24 ALR 1002–1016
U. S.—Goldfine v U. S. (CA Mass) 268 F2d 941
Yates v U. S. (CA Kan) 316 F2d 718
Berman v L. 107 I. B. of T. Inc. (DC Pa) 237 F Supp 767 (citing anno)
Cal.—P. v Douglas, 187 Cal App 2d 802, 10 Cal Rptr 188
Fla.—Duff v S. (App) 171 So 2d 55
Ky.—Elsner v Com. 375 SW2d 825
Ohio—Cleveland v B. 168 Ohio St 386, 7 Ohio Ops 2d 151, 154 NE2d 917

VOL. 5

24 ALR 962–964
Ark.—Craig v Il. 447 SW2d 120
N. C.—Burns v B. (App) 167 SE2d 82
Tex.—Eddie v L. 412 SW2d 811 (citing anno)

24 ALR 977–978
Superseded 166 ALR 1118✦

24 ALR 1002–1016
U. S.—Hampton v S. (CA Okla) 368 F2d 9
U. S. v Funk (CA Minn) 412 F2d 452

VOL. 6

24 ALR 1002–1016
U.S.—U. S v Pandilidis (CA Ohio) 524 F2d 644
U. S. v Kahl (CA5 Tex) 583 F2d 1351
U. S. v Moss (CA8 Neb) 604 F2d 569
U. S. v Driscoll (CA9 Mont) 612 F2d 1155
U. S. v Armored Transport, Inc. (CA9 Cal) 629 F2d 1313, 1980–81 CCH Trade Cas ¶ 63626
U. S. v Yellow Freight System, Inc. (CA9 Cal) 637 F2d 1248

VOL. 7

24 ALR 1002-1016
U.S.—U. S v Coachman (App DC) 752 F2d 685
U. S. v Rivera (CA10 Okla) 837 F2d 906, 24 Fed Rules Evid Serv 827
Ind.—Pettery v G. (App) 491 NE2d 583
Neb.—S. v Burchett, 224 Neb 444, 399 NW2d 258
R.I.—S. v Padula, 551 A2d 687

24 ALR 1025-1038
Supplemented 64 ALR 436✦

LATEST PAM. SUPP.

24 ALR 1002-1016
U.S.—U.S. v Celestine (CA5 Tex) 905 F2d 59
U.S. v Williams (CA5 Tex) 919 F2d 266
U.S. v L. (CA9 Cal) 921 F2d 841, 90 CDOS 8960
U.S. v Mandell (ED Pa) 722 F Supp 1208
Resnover v P. (ND Ind) 754 F Supp 1374
Alaska—Michael v S., 805 P2d 371
Cal.—Faubel v S. C. (5th Dist) 228

Note how the *A.L.R. Blue Book of Supplemental Decisions* also indicates when an *Annotation* has been supplemented or superseded. It is simpler to use the *Annotation History Table* in the *ALR Index.*

After using an *Annotation* in *A.L.R. (First Series)*, later cases may be found in the *A.L.R. Blue Book of Supplemental Decisions.* There are seven *Blue Books* that may contain references to cases decided after the original *Annotation* was written. Vol. 1 covers 1919–45; vol. 2, 1946–52; vol. 3, 1953–58; vol. 4, 1959–67; vol. 5, 1968–75; vol. 6, 1976–83; vol. 7, 1984–89. An annual pamphlet lists citations since 1989. Note that 24 A.L.R. 1002–1016 has been updated with additional cases in each *Blue Book* and the supplemental pamphlet.

SECTION F.　UNITED STATES SUPREME COURT REPORTS, LAWYERS' EDITION

Chapter 4 discusses the *United States Supreme Court Reports, Lawyers' Edition*. It was pointed out that a significant aspect of this set is the *Annotations* that are provided for selected important cases. [See Illustrations 19–20.] These *Annotations* are published only in the bound volumes. These *Annotations* can be located using the *ALR Index* or *Auto–Cite*.

SECTION G.　SUMMARY

1.　Annotated Law Reports

a.　*Annotations.*　Often lengthy, encyclopedic essays on a particular point of law.

b.　*Selective law reporting.*　Used extensively by Lawyers Cooperative Publishing.　A representative case is selected that is illustrative of a point of law discussed in an *Annotation*.

2.　American Law Reports (A.L.R.)

a.　*Scope*

(1) Began in 1919 and is now in six series—*A.L.R.* through *A.L.R.5th* and *A.L.R. Federal,* with *A.L.R.5th* and *A.L.R. Federal* currently being published.

(2) Federal topics are included in *A.L.R. Federal, A.L.R., A.L.R.2d,* and volumes 1–21 of *A.L.R.3d.*

(3) State topics are included in *A.L.R.* through *A.L.R.5th.*

b.　*Features*

(1) *Annotations* and illustrative case; citations are to the *Annotation,* not the illustrative case.

(2) Detailed outline of topic annotated.

(3) Index accompanying each *Annotation* in *A.L.R.5th* and lengthy *Annotations* in other series.

(4) Jurisdictional references.

(5) References to other *Total Client–Service Library* publications, and, commencing with *A.L.R.5th,* volume 111 of *A.L.R. Fed.,* and *A.L.R.4th* pocket supplements, references to sources by other publishers, West *Key Number System* references, and electronic search queries.

3.　How A.L.R. Is Kept Current

a.　*Upkeep Service*

(1) *A.L.R.3d, 4th, 5th, Federal.*　These sets are kept current with annual pocket supplements in which digests of cases are keyed directly to each section of the *Annotation.*

(2) *A.L.R.2d.* A *Later Case Service,* with annual pocket supplements, digests cases and keys them to each section of the *Annotation.*

(3) *A.L.R. (First Series).* A seven volume *A.L.R. Blue Book of Supplemental Decisions* and an update pamphlet lists citations to more recent cases than those in the *Annotation.* All eight sources must be used for complete updating.

b. *Superseding and Supplementing Annotations.* A superseding *Annotation* replaces an existing one; a supplementing *Annotation* updates an existing one and both must be read as if they are one *Annotation.*

c. *Locating the Most Recent Annotations.* Use the *Annotation History Table* in the T–Z volume of *ALR Index,* the appropriate *A.L.R.* upkeep service, *Auto–Cite,* or the toll free "hotline."

4. United States Supreme Court Reports, Lawyers' Edition.

This set contains *Annotations* for selected important cases. These *Annotations* can be located using the *ALR Index* and the General Index to the *United States Supreme Court Reports, Lawyers' Edition,* as discussed in Chapter 4, A–3.

Chapter 8

CONSTITUTIONS

This chapter will discuss the role of constitutions for the federal and state governments. As these documents are the charters adopted by the people, they are the highest primary authority.

SECTION A. FEDERAL CONSTITUTION

The Constitution of the United States of America, in a formal sense, is the written document that was drafted at Philadelphia in the summer of 1787, plus the amendments that have since been added. The framers of the Constitution did not intend it to be a static document, but rather, as stated by Chief Justice Marshall, "to endure for ages to come, and, consequently, to be adapted to various *crises* of human affairs." [1] A noted twentieth century scholar has commented that "[t]he proper point of view from which to approach the task of interpreting the Constitution is that of regarding it as a living statute, palpitating with the purpose of the hour, reenacted with every waking breath of the American people, whose primitive right to determine their institutions is its sole claim to validity as law and as the matrix of laws under our system." [2]

It follows from these famous observations that to research problems in constitutional law, one must not only consult the document itself,[3] but also sources that assist in the interpretation of the Constitution. These sources include the background and record of the Constitutional Convention, the interpretation of the Constitution by the Supreme Court of the United States in the over 500 volumes of its reports, and the commentaries on the Constitution in treatises, legal periodicals, encyclopedias, and other secondary sources. This chapter will discuss how to locate and use these various sources.

1. Judicial Interpretations

a. *Annotated Editions of the Federal Constitution*

The courts, and especially the Supreme Court of the United States, are frequently called upon to interpret provisions of the Constitution of

[1] McCulloch v. Maryland, 17 U.S. (4 Wheat.) 316, 415 (1819).

[2] Edwin S. Corwin, *Constitution V. Constitutional Theory: The Question of the State V. the Nation,* 19 Am. Pol. Sci. Rev. 290, 303 (1925). For more recent commentary on constitutional interpretation, see *Symposium: In Celebration of Our Constitution,* 70 Marq. L. Rev. 351 (1987); *Symposium: "To Endure for Ages to Come"—A Bicentennial View of the Constitution,* N.C. L. Rev. 881 (1987).

[3] The text of the Constitution and its amendments are readily available. In addition to being included with the official *United States Code* and the annotated federal codes (discussed in this section), it is typically included in sets of state annotated codes, as well as in constitutional law texts and casebooks, law dictionaries, and in pamphlets frequently distributed at annual May 1 "Law Day" events across the country.

the United States. Some of the most useful sources for these interpretations are the various annotated editions of the Constitution. These publications set forth each article, section, and clause of the Constitution and its amendments and provide digests of the cases interpreting that part of the Constitution or its amendments and, in some instances, commentary as to the provisions and their interpretations.

(1) *United States Code Annotated, Constitution of the United States Annotated* (West Publishing Company). This set, published as part of the *United States Code Annotated (U.S.C.A.)* consists of ten unnumbered volumes [4] and two tables volumes. An index to the Constitution is included at the end of the last volume of the set, *i.e.*, the volume that also contains Amendments 14 to End. After each article, section, and clause of the Constitution and for each of its 27 amendments are cross references to pertinent sections in *U.S.C.A.* and references to encyclopedias, law reviews, texts, and treatises.

Notes of Decisions, which are digest paragraphs from all cases that have interpreted a constitutional provision or amendment, follow these various references. For example, Article I, Section 1 is followed by 85 notes of decisions, while Article I, Section 8, Clause 3 is followed by 1,560 notes. These notes are preceded first by references to West's *Key Number System* and relevant encyclopedia section numbers and then by numbered topics, which enable a user to go directly to the cases digested under those topics. Additional notes of decisions are in the annual pocket and subsequent pamphlet supplements. [See Illustrations 54–56 for the means of locating a constitutional provision and the notes of decisions that accompany it.]

(2) *United States Code Service, Constitution* (Lawyers Cooperative Publishing). These four volumes are a separate unit of the *United States Code Service (U.S.C.S.)*. As such, they are a part of the Lawyers Cooperative Publishing's *Total Client–Service Library* [5] and include references to this publisher's other publications. These *Constitution* volumes are organized and updated in much the same way as the *United States Code Annotated* and are used in a like manner, with volume four containing an index.

(3) *The Constitution of the United States of America* (Library of Congress ed. 1987, and latest supplement). This annotated, one volume edition of the Constitution [6] is prepared by the Congressional Research Service of the Library of Congress, as authorized by a Joint Congression-

---

[4] This set, published in 1987 and referred to by the publisher as the "Bicentennial Edition," is a comprehensive revision of all earlier volumes in this set.

[5] See Chapter 7, Section A.

[6] THE CONSTITUTION OF THE UNITED STATES OF AMERICA, S. DOC. NO. 16, 99th Cong., 1st Sess. (1987).

al Resolution.[7] This publication sets forth each article, section, and clause of the Constitution and its amendments. Immediately following each of them, in smaller typeface, is an analysis and commentary prepared by the editorial staff. Important cases decided by the Supreme Court of the United States are discussed in the analysis, and citations to the cases are given in the footnotes. [See Illustrations 57–58.] Frequently, the commentary quotes from the proceedings of the Constitutional Convention, the opinions of dissenting justices, and other documents. This volume, unlike the ones discussed above, does not attempt to cite or comment on all cases of the Supreme Court of the United States, but refers only to the more significant ones. It has a detailed index and includes the following useful tables:

Proposed Amendments Pending Before the States.

Proposed Amendments Not Ratified by the States.

Acts of Congress Held Unconstitutional in Whole or in Part by the Supreme Court of the United States.

State Constitutional and Statutory Provisions and Municipal Ordinances Held Unconstitutional on Their Face or As Administered.

Ordinances Held Unconstitutional.

Supreme Court Decisions Overruled by Subsequent Decisions.

Table of Cases.

This is a very useful volume, and even as it becomes somewhat dated, it is often the preferred starting point for research on constitutional questions.

b. *Digests of Federal Court Cases*

Digests of federal cases provide access to additional interpretations of the Constitution.[8] The following publications are discussed in detail in Chapter 6.

(1) *Digest of United States Supreme Court Reports, Lawyers' Edition* (Lawyers Cooperative Publishing). Volume 17 contains the text of the Constitution together with references to this publisher's relevant headnote topics and sections.

(2) *U.S. Supreme Court Digest* (West Publishing Company).

(3) *Federal Digest, Modern Federal Practice Digest,* and *West's Federal Practice Digest, 2nd, 3rd, 4th,* and *5th* (West Publishing Company).

---

[7] 2 U.S.C. § 168 (1988). This Joint Resolution provides for a new hard-bound volume every ten years with pocket supplements to be issued biennially. Regrettably, there have been serious problems with the publication schedule. The previous edition was published in 1972. The present 2,308 page edition, which covers to July 2, 1982, has a 1987 imprint date but did not reach libraries until mid–1988. Although a biennial supplement is published, it typically only supplements the volume to within two to three years of the date at the time of its issuance.

[8] It is important to remember that state and regional digests also contain digest paragraphs for federal cases arising within their jurisdictional coverage.

c. *Annotations.* The *Annotations* in *A.L.R. Federal, U.S. Supreme Court Reports, Lawyers' Edition, A.L.R., A.L.R.2d,* and *A.L.R.3d* (pre-1969) may contain discussions of constitutional issues, in which case these *Annotations* will provide case references.

d. *Online Access.* The text of the *United States Code* is available on LEXIS; *U.S.C.A.* is available exclusively on WESTLAW; and *U.S.C.S.* is exclusively on LEXIS. All three sets contain the text of the Constitution. For the two annotated sets, search terms can be used with sections and clauses in the Constitution and with the amendments to retrieve relevant cases.

e. *Shepard's Citations.* *Shepard's United States Citations* and the state units of Shepard's citators provide references to cases citing or construing the Constitution. *Shepard's Citations* are discussed in Chapter 14.

2. Secondary Sources

The constitutional commentary by legal scholars is voluminous. Research in constitutional law can seldom be completed successfully without consulting the secondary sources, such as texts, treatises, encyclopedias, and periodical articles, as these sources may provide exhaustive analysis of constitutional concerns being researched. Some of these sources deserve special mention.

The 200th anniversary of the U.S. Constitution celebrated in 1987 seemed to spawn significant scholarship that is especially useful in constitutional analysis. The four volume *Encyclopedia of the American Constitution* [9] contains approximately 2,100 articles written by 262 authors, typically lawyers, historians, and political scientists. Arrangement is alphabetical with either cases or subjects forming the basis of the discussion. Some of the articles contain useful bibliographic references.

The Founders' Constitution [10] is a five volume set containing an extensive collection of documents that bear on the text of the Constitution, from the Preamble through the Twelfth Amendment. Volume 1 is arranged by theme and highlights the debate over the principles embodied in the Constitution; volumes 2–4 are arranged to correspond to the text of the Constitution; and volume 5 is devoted to Amendments I–XII.

Researchers seeking an extensive listing of sources on the Constitution will want to consult Kermit L. Hall's *A Comprehensive Bibliography of American Constitutional and Legal History, 1896–1979.* [11] This five volume set contains over 68,000 entries for books, journal articles, and doctoral dissertations. It is divided into seven chapters: general surveys and texts; institutions; constitutional doctrine; legal doctrine; bio-

---

[9] Leonard W. Levy, Editor-in-Chief, Macmillan Publishing Co. (1986). *Supplement I* was published in 1992.

[10] Philip B. Kurland & Ralph Lerner eds., University of Chicago Press (1987).

[11] Krauss International Pubs. (1984). A two volume supplement covers 1980–1987.

graphical; chronological; and geographical. Also useful in this regard is the one volume *The Constitution of the United States: A Guide and Bibliography to Current Scholarly Research.*[12]

While all law dictionaries provide definitions of terms bearing on constitutional law, the two volume *Constitutional Law Dictionary*[13] is intended specifically for this purpose. Volume 1 is subtitled *Individual Rights;* volume 2 *Governmental Powers.* Each volume contains a summary of approximately 300 cases organized in a subject-matter chapter format whereby cases are grouped under topics. This arrangement is followed by several hundred definitions.

The most highly-regarded contemporary treatises in the area of constitutional law are Laurence H. Tribe's one volume *American Constitutional Law*[14] and the four volume *Treatise on Constitutional Law: Substance and Procedure,*[15] by Ronald D. Rotunda and John E. Nowack. Constitutional law casebooks[16] and legal periodicals[17] also often provide constitutional analysis.

3. Historical Sources

When faced with the task of interpreting the meaning of a provision or clause of the Constitution, it is frequently useful to ascertain the meaning of the words used by the framers. This may make it necessary to consult sources that preceded the adoption of the Constitution, such as documents of the Continental Congress or the Articles of Confederation. These sources can be readily located in the Library of Congress Legislative Reference Service's *Documents Illustrative of the Formation of the Union of the American States.*[18] Also useful is *Documentary History of the Constitution of the United States of America, 1786–1870.*[19]

---

[12] Bernard D. Reams, Jr. & Stuart D. Yoak eds., Oceana Pubs. (1988). This volume is also published as volume 11 of *Sources and Documents of United States Constitutions.*

[13] Ralph C. Chandler et al., ABC–Clio Information Sources (1985 & 1987). These volumes are updated periodically with bound supplements.

[14] 2d ed., Foundation Press (1988).

[15] 2d ed., West Publishing Co. (1992). An abridged version is published as *Constitutional Law* (4th ed. 1991) and is a part of West's Hornbook Series.

[16] The best example is GERALD GUNTHER, CONSTITUTIONAL LAW (12th ed., Foundation Press, 1991). An annual supplement is published.

[17] Almost any legal periodical will, at times, publish articles on constitutional issues. Some, however, are devoted to these topics, such as the University of Minnesota's *Constitutional Commentary,* Seton Hall University's *Constitutional Law Journal, George Mason University Civil Rights Law Journal, Harvard Civil Rights–Civil Liberties Law Review, Hastings Constitutional Law Quarterly,* and *William and Mary Bill of Rights Journal.* Legal periodicals are discussed in detail in Chapter 16.

[18] H.R. Doc. No. 398, 69th Cong., 1st Sess. (1935). *See also* SOL BLOOM, FORMATION OF THE UNION UNDER THE CONSTITUTION (1935). For background on the Articles of Confederation, see William F. Swindler, *Our First Constitution: The Articles of Confederation,* 67 A.B.A. J. 166 (1961). For documents pertaining to the adoption of the Bill of Rights, see BERNARD SCHWARTZ, THE BILL OF RIGHTS: A DOCUMENTARY HISTORY, Chelsea House (2 vols., 1971).

[19] U.S. Bureau of Rolls and Library of the Department of State (1894–1905; reprinted in 1965 by Johnson Reprint Corp.).

Indispensable are the essays of Madison, Jay, and Hamilton published as *The Federalist*.[20] The sources mentioned in this paragraph, as well as other sources on the historical development of the Constitution, are available on WESTLAW in the *Bicentennial of the Constitution* (BICENT) database.

While the Constitutional Convention did not keep official records of its secret sessions, the most widely-accepted source for insights into the debates that took place is Max Farrand's three volume *Records of the Federal Constitution of 1787*.[21] For understanding the ratification process by the states, a valuable source is *Elliot's Debates*.[22] When complete, by far the most comprehensive and up-to-date source of the history of the ratification of the U.S. Constitution will be *Documentary History of the Ratification of the Constitution*.[23] The courts, at times, also turn to these historical sources for support in their opinions.[24]

SECTION B. ILLUSTRATIONS: FEDERAL CONSTITUTION

Problem: What protection is given in the Constitution to speeches of the members of Congress?

Illustrations

54. **Page from volume containing Index to Constitution: U.S.C.A.**
55. **Page from Constitution volume: U.S.C.A.**
56. **Page showing Notes of Decisions: Constitution volume: U.S.C.A.**
57–58. **Pages from The Constitution of the United States of America (Library of Congress ed. 1987)**

[20] *The Federalist* has been published in many editions. *See also* JAMES MADISON, THE PAPERS OF JAMES MADISON (Henry D. Gilpin ed. 1840).

[21] Yale University Press (1911). A supplement was prepared in 1987 by James H. Hutson. *See also* THE FOUNDERS' CONSTITUTION, *supra* note 10; WILBOURN E. BENTON, 1787: DRAFTING THE U.S. CONSTITUTION, Texas A & M University Press (2 vols., 1986).

[22] JONATHAN ELLIOT, THE DEBATES, RESOLUTIONS, AND OTHER PROCEEDINGS, IN CONVENTION, ON THE ADOPTION OF THE FEDERAL CONSTITUTION (1827). This set has appeared in many editions with different titles and somewhat different content, all known generally as *Elliot's Debates*. The most complete edition was published in five volumes in 1937.

[23] Merrill Jensen ed. (State Historical Society of Wisconsin). This set, which began in 1976 and is projected for 16 volumes, is over one-half complete.

[24] *See, e.g.,* Morrison v. Olson, 487 U.S. 654, 674 (1988) (citing RECORDS OF THE FEDERAL CONVENTION OF 1787 (Max Farrand ed. 1966); Welch v. Texas Dept. of Highways, 483 U.S. 468, 481 n. 10 (1987) (citing ELLIOT'S DEBATES, 2d ed. 1861); Atascadero State Hosp. v. Scanlon, 473 U.S. 234, 271 (1985) (Brennan, J., dissenting) (citing DOCUMENTARY HISTORY OF THE RATIFICATION OF THE CONSTITUTION).

[Illustration 54]

PAGE FROM VOLUME CONTAINING INDEX
TO CONSTITUTION: U.S.C.A.

CONGRESS   INDEX

CONGRESS—Cont'd
Privilege of Members from arrest except for
    treason, felony and breach of the peace,
    Art. 1, § 6, cl. 1
Prize vessels, power to make rules concern-
    ing, Art. 1, § 8, cl. 11
Prohibitions,
    Assemblage, abridgment of right, Am. 1
    Freedom of speech and press, abridgment,
        Am. 1
    Petitions for redress of grievances, abridg-
        ment, Am. 1
    Religion, laws regarding, Am. 1
Promotion of science by granting exclusive
    rights, Art. 1, § 8, cl. 8
Provision for common defense by, Art. 1,
    § 8, cl. 1
Public officers and employees, titles, gifts,
    etc., from foreign princes, consent of,
    required for acceptance, Art. 1, § 9, cl. 8
Punishment,
    Members for disorderly behavior, Art. 1,
        § 5, cl. 2
    Offenses against law of nations, Art. 1,
        § 8, cl. 10
    Powers of Members, ante, this heading
    Treason, power to declare, Art. 3, § 3, cl. 2
Qualifications of Members, Art. 1, § 6, cl. 2
    Each House to be judge of, Art. 1, § 5, cl.
        1
Quorum, majority in either House to consti-
    tute, Art. 1, § 5, cl. 1
Ratio, representation,
    Apportioned among several States, Am. 14,
        § 2
    Until first enumeration under, Art. 1, § 2,
        cl. 3

CONGRESS—Cont'd
Seat of Government, exclusive legislation
    over, Art. 1, § 8, cl. 17
Secrecy, not to publish what may require,
    Art. 1, § 5, cl. 3
Senate, generally, this index
Sessions, frequency and time, Art. 1, § 4, cl.
    2; Am. 20, § 2
Shall make necessary laws, Art. 1, § 8, cl. 18
Ships of war, no State to keep without con-
    sent of, Art. 1, § 10, cl. 3
Slave traffic, taxes, power to impose, Art. 1,
    § 9, cl. 1
Slaves, limitation on Congressional power,
    Art. 1, § 9, cl. 1
South Carolina, five Representatives in first
    Congress, Art. 1, § 2, cl. 3
Speeches, etc., immunity of Members from
    questioning, Art. 1, § 6, cl. 1
State legislature to exercise authority over
    places purchased for erection of forts,
    magazines, arsenals, or dockyards, Art.
    1, § 8, cl. 17
State not to be deprived of equal suffrage
    in Senate without consent, Art. 5
State not to keep troops or ships of war in
    time of peace without consent of, Art. 1,
    § 10, cl. 3
State of Union, President to give Congress
    information of, Art. 2, § 3
State traffic, power to impose duties, Art. 1,
    § 9, cl. 1
Succession to Presidency and Vice Presiden-
    cy, disability of President, Am. 25
Sundays excepted from ten days allowed
    President to return bill, Art. 1, § 7, cl. 2

> The first step in researching a problem involving the U.S. Constitution is
> to look in the volume containing the index to the Constitution. For the
> problem under research, Article 1, Section 6, Clause 1 should be examined.
> See next Illustration.

reserved to States or to people, Am. 10
Resignation of President, may by law pro-
    vide for officer in case of, Art. 2, § 1,
    cl. 5
Resolutions of Congress, generally, this in-
    dex
Returns, each House to be judge of, Art. 1,
    § 5, cl. 1
Revenue bills, origin and amendments, Art.
    1, § 7, cl. 1
Revenues, regulations, port preferences for-
    bidden, Art. 1, § 9, cl. 6
Rhode Island, one Representative in first
    Congress, Art. 1, § 2, cl. 3
Right of petition, prohibition on abridge-
    ment, Am. 1
Rules,
    Adjournment during session, Art. 1, § 5, cl.
        4
    Of capture, power relating to, Art. 1, § 8,
        cl. 11
    Powers of Members, ante, this heading
Salaries of Members, Art. 1, § 6, cl. 1

to make rules respecting, Art. 4, § 3, cl.
    2
To be in session every year, Art. 1, § 4, cl. 2
To promote progress in science and useful
    arts, Art. 1, § 8, cl. 8
Treason,
    Members not privileged from arrest for,
        during session, Art. 1, § 6, cl. 1
    Punishment, power to declare, Art. 3, § 3,
        cl. 2
Tribunals inferior to Supreme Court, power
    to create, Art. 1, § 8, cl. 9
Troops, maintenance without consent of,
    prohibited, Art. 1, § 10, cl. 3
Two-thirds vote,
    Disability incurred by participation in in-
        surrection or rebellion removed by,
        Am. 14, § 3
    Expulsion of Member by, Art. 1, § 5, cl. 2
    Succession to Presidency and Vice Presi-
        dency, disability of President, Am. 25
Virginia, ten Representatives in first Con-
    gress, Art. 1, § 2, cl. 3

[Illustration 55]

PAGE FROM A CONSTITUTION VOLUME: U.S.C.A.

Sec. 5, cl. 3   THE CONGRESS   Art. 1
Note 2

Congress. Field v. Clark, Ill.1892, 12   not conclusive in determining whether
S.Ct. 495, 143 U.S. 670, 36 L.Ed. 294.   bill had been returned by President with-
                                          in 10–day period allowed by Constitu-
3. Failure to publish Items   tion, since President had no control over
   That the Journal of the House may not entries upon Journal. Prevost v. Mor-
have shown objections of the President   genthau, 1939, 106 F.2d 330, 70 App.D.C.
to an appropriation bill when bill was   306.
returned by president's messenger was

This shows the text of the constitutional provision covering speeches by members of Congress as it appears in a Constitution volume of the *United States Code Annotated*. Note the references to additional useful sources. This set and the *United States Code Service* are kept current by annual pocket supplements and subsequent pamphlets.

CROSS REFERENCES

Convening of Congress by President on extraordinary occasions, see section 3 of
   article 2.

WESTLAW ELECTRONIC RESEARCH

See WESTLAW guide following the Explanation pages of this volume.

Section 6, Clause 1. Compensation of Members; Privilege From Arrest

The Senators and Representatives shall receive a Compensation for their Services, to be ascertained by Law, and paid out of the Treasury of the United States. They shall in all Cases, except Treason, Felony and Breach of the Peace, be privileged from Arrest during their Attendance at the Session of their respective Houses, and in going to and returning from the same; and for any Speech or Debate in either House, they shall not be questioned in any other Place.

CROSS REFERENCES

Compensation and allowances of members of Congress, see 2 USCA § 31 et seq.

LIBRARY REFERENCES

Administrative Law

   Legislative immunity, see Administrative Law and Practice § 10.79.

Law Reviews

   Congressional papers, judicial subpoenas, and the Constitution. David Kaye, 24
      UCLA L.Rev. 523 (1977).
   The immunity of congressional speech—Its origin, meaning, and scope. Leon R.
      Yankwich, 99 U.Pa.L.Rev. 960 (1951).

Texts and Treatises

   Congressional action and the separation of powers: the Speech or Debate
      Clause, see Tribe, American Constitutional Law § 5-18.
   "Extortion" defined, see Federal Jury Practice and Instructions § 56.03.
   Immunity from arrest granted senators and representatives, see Wright & Miller,
      Federal Practice and Procedure: Civil § 1077.

[Illustration 56]

PAGE SHOWING NOTES OF DECISIONS (DIGEST PARAGRAPHS) FROM A CONSTITUTION VOLUME: U.S.C.A.

Art. 1 COMPENSATION, ETC.   **Sec. 6, cl. 1**
                                                      Note 1

Judicial power over political questions, see Wright, Miller & Cooper, Federal
    Practice and Procedure: Jurisdiction 2d § 3534 et seq.
Legislative immunity, see Criminal Law Defenses § 204

After the text of each clause are digest paragraphs of all cases that have
interpreted the clause. These paragraphs are preceded by an index to these
paragraphs.

NOTES OF DECISIONS

I.   GENERALLY 1–30
II. SPEECH OR DEBATE PROTECTION—GENERALLY 31–60
III.   ACTIVITIES PROTECTED 61–87

For Detailed Alphabetical Note Index, see the Various Subdivisions.

I. GENERALLY

Subdivision Index

Compensation of members 4
Construction 1
Construction with other Constitutional
    provisions 2
Privilege from arrest
    Generally 5
    Civil arrest or process within privi-
        lege 7
    Duration of privilege 8
    Offenses within privilege 6
    Waiver of privilege 9
Purpose 3

American Digest System
    Compensation of members of Con-
gress, see United States ☞7, 39(1).

    Privilege from arrest of members of
Congress, see United States ☞12.

Encyclopedias
    Compensation of members of Con-
gress, see C.J.S. United States § 17.

    Representatives and Senators as privi-
leged from arrest, see C.J.S. United
States § 18.

1. Construction
    The speech or debate provision of this
clause must be read broadly to effectu-
ate its purposes. Doe v. McMillan, Dist.
Col.1973, 93 S.Ct. 2018, 412 U.S. 306, 36
L.Ed.2d 912, motion denied 95 S.Ct. 614,
419 U.S. 1043, 42 L.Ed.2d 637. See, also,
McSurely v. McClellan, 1976, 553 F.2d

1277, 180 U.S.App.D.C. 101, certiorari
dismissed 98 S.Ct. 3116, 438 U.S. 189, 57
L.Ed.2d 704, certiorari denied 106 S.Ct.
525, 88 L.Ed.2d 457; U.S. v. Eilberg,
D.C.Pa.1979, 465 F.Supp. 1080; U.S. v.
Meyers, D.C.Pa.1977, 432 F.Supp. 456.

    This clause that for any speech or de-
bate in either House, Senators and Representatives shall not be questioned in
any other place is to be interpreted liberally and not narrowly. U.S. v.
Johnson, C.A.Md.1964, 337 F.2d 180, affirmed 86 S.Ct. 749, 383 U.S. 169, 15
L.Ed.2d 681, certiorari denied 87 S.Ct.
44, 134, 385 U.S. 846, 889, 17 L.Ed.2d 77,
117.

    Privilege or immunity to be afforded
senators and representatives by this
clause should be read broadly to provide
some practical security against interference or intimidation by the executive
and accountability before a possibly hostile judicial branch. U.S. ex rel. Hol-
lander v. Clay, D.C.D.C.1976, 420 F.Supp.
853.

    This clause, providing that congress-
men should, except for treason, felony,
and breach of peace, be privileged from
arrest, and that they should not be questioned for any speech in either House, is
to be liberally construed to free congressman from fear of prosecutions for
words spoken, votes cast, or actions tak-
en in pursuit of their lawful functions
but is not to be construed as shield from
bribery or conspiracy prosecution involving acceptance of money for making
a speech on floor of House of Represent-

[Illustration 57]

PAGE FROM THE CONSTITUTION OF THE UNITED STATES
OF AMERICA (LIBRARY OF CONGRESS, 1987 Ed.)

---

122   ART. I—LEGISLATIVE DEPARTMENT

Sec. 6—Rights of Members   Journal

House had been voting to expel they would still have cast an affirmative vote in excess of two-thirds.[5]

Duty To Keep a Journal

The object of the clause requiring the keeping of a Journal is
"to insure publicity to the proceedings of the legislature, and a cor-
respondent responsibility of the members to their respective con-
stituents."[6] When the Journal of either House is put in evidence
for the purpose of determining whether the yeas and nays were ordered, and what the vote was on any particular question, the Journal must be presumed to show the truth, and a statement therein
that a quorum was present, though not disclosed by the yeas and
nays, is final.[7] But when an enrolled bill, which has been signed by
the Speaker of the House and by the President of the Senate, in
open session receives the approval of the President and is deposited

---

This one-volume edition sets forth the full text of each Article, Section, and
Clause of the Constitution and its amendments. Analysis and commentary
immediately follow, in smaller type.

SECTION 6. Clause 1. The Senators and Representatives
shall receive a Compensation for their Services, to be ascertained by Law, and paid out of the Treasury of the United
States. They shall in all Cases, except Treason, Felony and
Breach of the Peace, be privileged from Arrest during their Attendance at the Session of their respective Houses and in going
to and returning from the same; and for any Speech or Debate
in either House, they shall not be questioned in any other
Place.

---

[5] Id., 506–512.
[6] 2 J. Story, *Commentaries on the Constitution of the United States* (Boston:
1833), § 840, quoted with approval in *Field v. Clark,* 143 U.S. 649, 670 (1892).
[7] *United States v. Ballin,* 144 U.S. 1, 4 (1892).
[8] *Field v. Clark,* 143 U.S. 649 (1892); *Flint v. Stone Tracy Co.,* 220 U.S. 107, 143
(1911). A parallel rule holds in the case of a duly authenticated official notice to the
Secretary of State that a state legislature has ratified a proposed amendment to the
Constitution. *Leser v. Garnett,* 258 U.S. 130, 137 (1922); *see also Coleman v. Miller,*
307 U.S. 433 (1939).

[Illustration 58]

PAGE FROM THE CONSTITUTION OF THE UNITED STATES OF AMERICA (LIBRARY OF CONGRESS, 1987 Ed.)

ART. I—LEGISLATIVE DEPARTMENT 123

Sec. 6—Rights of Members Cl. 2—Disabilities

Clause 2. No Senator or Representative shall, during the Time for which he was elected, be appointed to any civil Office under the Authority of the United States, which shall have been created, or the Emoluments whereof shall have been in

Analysis of the Disabilities Clause by the editors of the volume. Footnotes contain citations to cases mentioned in the analysis.

during his Continuance in Office.

COMPENSATION, IMMUNITIES AND DISABILITIES OF MEMBERS

When the Pay Starts

A Member of Congress who receives his certificate of admission, and is seated, allowed to vote, and serve on committees, is *prima facie* entitled to the seat and salary, even though the House subsequently declares his seat vacant. The one who contested the election and was subsequently chosen to fill the vacancy is entitled to salary only from the time the compensation of such "predecessor" has ceased.[1]

Privilege From Arrest

This clause is practically obsolete. It applies only to arrests in civil suits, which were still common in this country at the time the Constitution was adopted.[2] It does not apply to service of process in either civil[3] or criminal cases.[4] Nor does it apply to arrest in any criminal case. The phrase "treason, felony or breach of the peace" is interpreted to withdraw all criminal offenses from the operation of the privilege.[5]

Privilege of Speech or Debate

Members.—This clause represents "the culmination of a long struggle for parliamentary supremacy. Behind these simple phrases lies a history of conflict between the Commons and the Tudor and Stuart monarchs during which successive monarchs utilized the criminal and civil law to suppress and intimidate critical legislators. Since the Glorious Revolution in Britain, and through-

---

[1] *Page* v. *United States,* 127 U.S. 67 (1888).
[2] *Long* v. *Ansell,* 293 U.S. 76 (1934).
[3] Id., 83.
[4] *United States* v. *Cooper,* 4 Dall. (4 U.S.) 341 (C.C. Pa. 1800).
[5] *Williamson* v. *United States,* 207 U.S. 425, 446 (1908).

SECTION C.   STATE CONSTITUTIONS

Each of the fifty states has adopted its own constitution, and many states have adopted several different constitutions at different times over the years.   A state's constitution, except for those issues covered by the supremacy clause of the Constitution of the United States,[25] is the highest primary legal authority for the state.   The procedure for adopting a new constitution is usually accomplished by the convening of a state constitutional convention.   *State Constitutional Conventions, Commissions, and Amendments,* a microfiche collection of Congressional Information Service covering 1776 through 1978, is the most comprehensive source for documents for the fifty states.[26]

When doing research involving a state constitution, it also may be necessary to check the historical documents that led to its adoption and to consult the state and federal court cases interpreting it.

1.   Texts of State Constitutions

a.   The most common source for the text of a state constitution is the constitution volume of the state code.[27]   This constitution volume ordinarily contains the current text, the text of previously-adopted versions, and digest paragraphs similar in annotated version format to those discussed in Section A–1 of this chapter.   Many states also print and distribute an unannotated edition of the state constitution in pamphlet form.

b.   Columbia University, Legislative Drafting Research Fund.   *Constitutions of the United States: National and State* (2d ed. 1974 to date).

This multi-volume looseleaf set collects the texts of the constitutions for the United States, the fifty states, and all U.S. territories and is kept current by supplements.[28]

2.   Judicial Interpretations of State Constitutions

Court cases interpreting provisions of a state's constitution can be

[25] U.S. Const. art. VI, cl. 2. *See* digest paragraphs in *U.S.C.A.* and *U.S.C.S.* for cases on the supremacy clause.

[26] Two bibliographies provide access to this set: Cynthia E. Browne, State Constitutional Conventions From Independence to the Completion of the Present Union, 1776–1959: A Bibliography, Greenwood Press (1973); Congressional Information Service, State Constitutional Conventions, 1959–1978: An Annotated Bibliography (2 vols., 1981).

[27] An increasing number of state codes are being made available on WESTLAW and LEXIS and with them the state's constitutions. This development greatly improves the ability to conduct comparative research of state constitutional provisions. State codes are discussed in Chapter 11.

[28] For a listing of over 2,100 entries relating to the literature of state constitutions, see Bernard D. Reams, Jr. & Stuart D. Yoak, The Constitutions of the States: A State-by-State Guide and Bibliography to Current Scholarly Research, Oceana Pubs. (1987). This volume is also published as volume 5 of *Sources and Documents of United States Constitutions, Second Series.*

located in ways similar to those discussed in Section A–1.[29]   These include the digest paragraphs accompanying the annotated version of the state constitution, state digests, state Shepard's citators, computer-assisted legal research, and *A.L.R. Annotations.*   Likewise, treatises,[30] legal periodical articles, and state legal encyclopedias can assist with constitutional interpretation.

3.   Historical Sources of State Constitutions

The records, journals, proceedings, and other documents relating to state constitutional conventions provide valuable information on the intended meanings and interpretations given to state constitutions by their framers.   *State Constitutional Conventions, Commissions, and Amendments,* discussed earlier, makes available most of these materials. *Sources and Documents of United States Constitutions,*[31] compiled by William F. Swindler, reprints in chronological order the major constitutional documents of each state.

4.   Comparative Sources of State Constitutions

Frequently, a provision of a particular state constitution may not have received any judicial interpretation.   In such instances, cases on similar provisions in other state constitutions may be useful.   One method of locating comparative state constitutional provisions is through *Index Digest of State Constitutions* [32] (Columbia University, Legislative Drafting Research Fund), a companion to *Constitutions of the United States: National and State,* discussed in Section C–1–b.   It is arranged alphabetically by subject and under each subject are listed references to the various constitutional provisions of the states.   Although this volume has only been updated through 1967, it is still useful, as many provisions

---

[29] Recent articles have focused on the roles of state constitutions.   *See, e.g.,* James A. Gardner, *The Failed Discourse of State Constitutionalism,* 90 MICH. L. REV. 761 (1992); Hans A. Linde, *Are State Constitutions Common Law?* 34 ARIZ. L. REV. 215 (1992).

[30] *Reference Guides to the State Constitutions of the United States* is a series begun in 1990 by Greenwood Press, Westport, CT.   The series, due for completion in 1995, will cover each of the 50 states in a separate volume.   Each volume contains an historical overview of the state's constitutional development, the text of the state's constitution and a section-by-section analysis, a bibliographic essay, a table of cases, and an index.   A separate volume will be prepared on common themes and variations in constitutional development. A separate index to the 51 volumes will complete the set.

[31] Oceana Pubs. (11 vols. in 12, 1973–79).   Volume 11, a bibliography, was added to this set in 1988.   *See supra* note 12.   A Second Series began in 1982.   Older, but still useful titles for tracing the historical development of state constitutions are BENJAMIN PEARLEY POORE, CHARTERS AND CONSTITUTIONS (1877); FRANCIS NEWTON THORPE, FEDERAL AND STATE CONSTITUTIONS (1909); NEW YORK CONSTITUTIONAL CONVENTION COMMITTEE, 3 REPORTS: CONSTITUTIONS OF THE STATES AND UNITED STATES (1938).   Although the Poore and Thorpe volumes are out of date, they are helpful for their parallel study of state constitutions.   The last item, although never brought up to date, is still useful for its index volume to the constitutions of all of the states.   *See also* ALBERT LEE STRUM, A BIBLIOGRAPHY ON STATE CONSTITUTIONS AND CONSTITUTIONAL REVISION, 1945–1975 (1975).

[32] Oceana Pubs. (2d ed. 1959).

of state constitutions do not change with great frequency.[33]

SECTION D. FOREIGN CONSTITUTIONS

There are occasions when it is necessary to locate the constitutions of foreign countries. This can be accomplished by consulting *Constitutions of the Countries of the World*.[34] This multi-volume set is published in looseleaf format, with a separate pamphlet for each country. The constitutions for each country are preceded by a constitutional chronology and followed by an annotated bibliography. For countries where there is not an official English version, an English translation is provided. The introduction in Chapter 1 of this set should be consulted for bibliographical references to previous compilations of constitutions. Supplements are issued periodically, keeping each constitution up to date.

A companion set is *Constitutions of Dependencies and Special Sovereignties*.[35] This multi-volume set contains pamphlets on the world's associated states, dependent territories, and areas of special sovereignty. Each pamphlet contains constitutional status data and an annotated bibliography. When a *territory* in this set achieves the status of a nation-state, its constitution is incorporated into *Constitutions of the Countries of the World*.

---

[33] An attempt to provide a comprehensive subject index to all state constitutions began in 1980 when Columbia University's Legislative Drafting Research Fund issued "Fundamental Liberties and Rights: A Fifty State Index" as part of its *Constitutions of the United States: National and State*. This was followed in 1982 by "Laws, Legislature, Legislative Procedure: A Fifty State Index." Since no further indexes have been published, it would seem that this ambitious project has been abandoned.

[34] Albert P. Blaustein & Gisbert H. Flanz eds., Oceana Pubs. (1971 to date).

[35] Albert P. Blaustein & Eric B. Blaustein eds., Oceana Pubs. (1975 to date).

Chapter 9

FEDERAL LEGISLATION *

Article I, Section 8, of the United States Constitution enumerates the powers of Congress, and provides the authority for Congress to make all laws necessary and proper for carrying into execution the enumerated powers, as well as other powers vested in Congress.

The Senate and the House of Representatives, collectively known as Congress, meet in two-year periods. Each year is a session and the two-year period is known as a Congress. The period in which Congress met, for example, during 1992–93, is known as the 102nd Congress, the 1st Congress being 1789–91. Under the Constitution, Congress must meet at least once a year.[1]

This chapter is devoted exclusively to a discussion of enacted legislation and the sources for locating these materials. Chapter 10, Federal Legislative Histories, discusses the various documents generated during the legislative process, the sources to use to locate these documents, and the sources containing the documents themselves.

SECTION A. THE ENACTMENT OF FEDERAL LAWS

Before discussing the various ways federal legislation is published, a brief description of the legislative process is necessary.[2] At the beginning of each Congress, Representatives and Senators may introduce legislation in their respective branch of Congress. Each proposed law is called a *bill* or a *joint resolution* [3] when introduced. The first bill in the House of Representatives in each Congress is labeled *H.R. 1,* with all

* Revised for this edition by Bonnie L. Koneski–White, Associate Law Librarian, Western New England College.

[1] U.S. CONST. art. I, § 4, cl. 2.

[2] For more detailed statements on the enactment of federal laws, see EDWARD F. WILLETT, JR., HOW OUR LAWS ARE MADE, H.R.DOC. No. 139, 101st Cong., 2d Sess. (1990) [hereinafter HOW OUR LAWS ARE MADE]; ROBERT B. DOVE, ENACTMENT OF A LAW: PROCEDURAL STEPS IN THE LEGISLATIVE PROCESS, S. DOC. No. 20, 97th Cong., 1st Sess. (1982). *See also* CONGRESSIONAL QUARTERLY, INC., CONGRESSIONAL QUARTERLY'S GUIDE TO CONGRESS (4th ed. 1991) [hereinafter CONGRESSIONAL QUARTERLY'S GUIDE]; ROBERT U. GOEHLERT & FENTON S. MARTIN, CONGRESS AND LAW-MAKING: RESEARCHING THE LEGISLATIVE PROCESS (2d ed. 1989); JUDITH MANION ET AL., A RESEARCH GUIDE TO CONGRESS: HOW TO MAKE CONGRESS WORK FOR YOU (2d ed. 1991).

[3] A *bill* is the form used for most legislation. A *joint resolution* may also be used, but there is no practical difference between the two, and the two forms are used indiscriminately. *Concurrent resolutions* are used for matters affecting the operations of both houses, but are not legislative. *Simple resolutions* are used for matters concerning the operation of either house and are not legislative. The first three forms are published in the *United States Statutes at Large,* the latter in the *Congressional Record.* HOW OUR LAWS ARE MADE, *supra* note 2, at 5–7.

subsequent bills numbered sequentially. Similarly, the first bill introduced in the Senate is labeled *S. 1.* After a bill passes the house in which it was introduced, it is sent to the other house for consideration. If approved in identical form, it is then sent to the President for signing. If the President signs it, the bill becomes a law. If the President vetoes it,[4] it becomes law only if the veto is overridden by two-thirds of both houses of Congress.[5] Under the Constitution, a bill sent to the President also becomes law if the President does not either sign or veto it within ten days of receiving it.[6] Bills introduced, but not passed during a specific Congress, do not carry over to the next Congress. If the sponsors wish the bill to be considered by the new Congress, it must be submitted as a new bill.

After a bill becomes law, it is sent to the Archivist, who is directed to publish all laws so received.[7] The Archivist classifies each law as either a public law or a private law. A *public law* affects the nation as a whole, or deals with individuals as a class and relates to public matters. A *private law* benefits only a specific individual or individuals. Such laws deal primarily with matters relating to claims against the government or with matters of immigration and naturalization.[8]

The first law to pass a Congress is designated as either Public Law No. 1, *e.g.,* Pub. L. No. 103–1, or Private Law No. 1, *e.g.,* Priv. L. No. 103–1, with 103 designating the Congress. Each succeeding public or private law is then numbered in sequence throughout the two-year life of a Congress.

SECTION B.   PUBLICATION OF FEDERAL LAWS

1.   Recent Public Laws

The first official publication of a law is issued by the United States Government Printing Office in the form of a *slip law.* [See Illustration 59.] Each law is separately published and may be one page or several hundred pages in length. Slip laws are available in all libraries that are depositories for U.S. government publications [9] and in other libraries that subscribe to these publications. Other sources that are commonly consulted for the text of recent public laws are:

a. *United States Code Congressional and Administrative News.* This set, which began in 1941 with the 77th Congress, 1st Session, is published by West Publishing Company. During each session of Con-

---

[4] For a list of Presidential vetoes, see GREGORY HARNESS, PRESIDENTIAL VETOES, 1789–1988 (1992); GREGORY HARNESS, PRESIDENTIAL VETOES, 1989–1991 (1992).

[5] U.S. CONST. art. I, § 7, cl. 2.

[6] *Id.*

[7] 1 U.S.C. § 106(a) (1988), Exec. Order No. 10,530, 3 C.F.R. 55, 58 (1954 Supp.), *reprinted in* 3 U.S.C. § 301, at 397 (1988). *See also* 44 U.S.C. §§ 709–711 (1988).

[8] For a complete discussion of private bills and laws, see CONGRESSIONAL QUARTERLY'S GUIDE, *supra* note 2, at 359–68.

[9] There are approximately 1,400 depository libraries. For a complete listing, see JOINT COMM. ON PRINTING, A DIRECTORY OF U.S. GOVERNMENT DEPOSITORY LIBRARIES (annual).

gress, it is issued in monthly pamphlets and prints the full text of all public laws. Each issue contains a cumulative subject index and a cumulative *Table of Laws Enacted.* After each session of Congress, the pamphlets are reissued in bound volumes.

   b. *United States Code Service Advance Service.* These monthly pamphlets, containing newly-enacted public laws, are published by Lawyers Cooperative Publishing in connection with the *United States Code Service.* This *Service* contains a cumulative index arranged in alphabetical order.

   c. *United States Law Week.* This Bureau of National Affair's weekly looseleaf service, discussed more fully in Chapter 4, Section A–4–a, includes the text of selected public laws passed during the previous week.

   d. *WESTLAW* and *LEXIS.* Both online systems include the text of public laws. Current public laws are available in WESTLAW in the US–PL database. Historical databases date to the 101st Congress, 1st Session. LEXIS contains public laws starting with the 100th Congress, 2nd Session in the LEGIS, GENFED, and CODES libraries, PUBLAW file.

   e. *Specialized Looseleaf Services.* For selected "important" legislation that relates to the subject covered by the looseleaf service, publishers often provide pamphlet reproductions of public laws.

2. United States Statutes at Large

   At the end of each session of Congress, all the slip laws, both public and private, are published in numerical order as part of the set entitled *United States Statutes at Large.* Public and private laws are in separate sections of the volumes. Thus, all the laws enacted since 1789 are contained in the many volumes of this set. [See Illustration 62.] The *United States Statutes at Large* (Stat.) is the source for the authoritative text of federal laws.

   Because this set did not commence until 1846, it was necessary to publish retrospectively the legislation up to that point. Consequently, volumes 1–5 cover the public laws and volume 6 the private laws for the 1st through 28th Congresses (1789–1845), with volumes 7 and 8 devoted exclusively to treaties. See Chapter 19, for a discussion of treaties. The publication pattern for volumes 9 through 49 differs from the one used now. Volume 9 covers the 29th–31st Congresses; volumes 10 through 12 cover two Congresses each (32nd–37th); and volumes 13 to 49 cover one Congress each (38th–74th). The current pattern of one numbered volume per session began in 1936 with the 75th Congress, 1st Session.[10]

---

[10] For a concise historical explanation of the development of the United States Statutes at Large, its significance, and a complete bibliographic listing of the set, see CURT E. CONKLIN & FRANCIS ACLAND, A BIBLIOGRAPHIC INTRODUCTION TO THE UNITED STATES STATUTES AT LARGE (1992). *See also* LARRY M. BOYER, CHECKLIST OF U.S. SESSION LAWS, 1789–1873 (1976).

It is important to keep in mind that the laws in the *United States Statutes at Large* are arranged in chronological order rather than by subject. Moreover, amendments to a prior law may appear in different volumes from the law being amended. For example, a law passed in 1900 is in volume 31 of the *United States Statutes at Large*. If Congress amended it in 1905, the amendment will appear in the volume for that year. Some laws have been amended numerous times. To obtain the full and current text of such a law, the *United States Statutes at Large* volume containing the original law must be examined in conjunction with subsequent volumes in which amendments to that law appear.

Each volume of the *United States Statutes at Large* has its own subject index. Beginning in 1991, a popular name index was added. From 1957 through 1976, each volume contained tables listing how each public law in that volume affected previous public laws. Marginal notes since volume 33 give House or Senate bill numbers, Public Law numbers, and dates. The *United States Statutes at Large* also contain interstate compacts. Regrettably, publication of the bound *United States Statutes at Large* runs about two years, or one Congress, behind in its schedule. When published, it supersedes the slip laws for that volume.

SECTION C. CODIFICATION OF FEDERAL LAWS

The chronological method of publication of congressional laws creates obvious problems for the process of determining the statutory provisions on any given subject. Therefore, the laws passed by Congress have to be rearranged in a manner that will do three things: (1) collate the original law with all subsequent amendments by taking into consideration the deletion or addition of language made by the amendments; (2) bring all laws on the same subject or topic together; and (3) eliminate all repealed, superseded, or expired laws. This process is called codification.[11]

1. United States Revised Statutes

The first codification of the *United States Statutes at Large* resulted in the publication of the *Revised Statutes of the United States*.[12] This first codification is also known either as the Revised Statutes of 1873, reflecting the last year of laws contained in this code, as the Revised Statutes of 1874, reflecting the date of enactment of this code, or as the Revised Statutes of 1875, reflecting its date of publication. Throughout this chapter, this codification will be called the "Revised Statutes of 1875."

Because the *United States Statutes at Large* have no cumulating subject index, the difficulty in research was apparent. In 1866, Presi-

---

[11] For a discussion of the process involved in codification, see Charles S. Zinn, *Revision of the United States Code,* 51 LAW LIBR. J. 388 (1958).

[12] Ralph H. Dwan & Ernest R. Feidler, *The Federal Statutes—Their History and Use,* 22 MINN. L. REV. 1008, 1012–13 (1938) [hereinafter Dwan & Feidler].

dent Andrew Johnson, pursuant to congressional authorization, appointed a commission to extract from the volumes of the *United States Statutes at Large* all public laws that met the following criteria: (1) they were still in force, and (2) they were of a general and permanent nature. The next step was to take each public law and all its amendments and rewrite the law in one sequence by incorporating amending language and eliminating deleted language. All the laws were then arranged by topics in chapters, or *Titles*. Title 14, for example, contained all legislation passed by Congress, and still in force, on the judiciary; Title 64, all legislation in force on bankruptcy. All the Titles were then bound in one volume, a subject index prepared, and the volume issued as the *Revised Statutes of 1875*.

The *Revised Statutes of 1875* was submitted to Congress, introduced as a bill, and went through the legislative process of becoming a public law. Incorporated in the bill before Congress was a Title specifically repealing each previously passed public law that had been incorporated into the *Revised Statutes of 1875*.[13]

Thus, when it passed Congress and was signed by the President, all the public laws passed between 1789 and 1873, in force and of a general and permanent nature, were codified in the *Revised Statutes of 1875*. Moreover, as the act of codification repealed all pertinent *United States Statutes at Large,* the *Revised Statutes of 1875* became *positive law*, and it was no longer necessary to refer to the *United States Statutes at Large*.

Unfortunately, this volume, known as the first edition, was subsequently discovered to contain many inaccuracies and unauthorized changes in the law.[14] In 1878, a second edition of the *Revised Statutes* was authorized to be published that would include legislation passed since 1873, delete sections that were repealed since 1873, and correct the errors inadvertently incorporated into the first edition.

The second edition indicated changes to the text of the first edition by the use of brackets and italics. It is important to note, however, that the second edition of the *Revised Statutes* was never reenacted by Congress, and all changes indicated in it are only *prima facie* evidence of the law. Although several attempts were made to adopt a new codification, it was not until 1924 that Congress authorized the publication of a codification of federal laws.[15]

2. United States Code (U.S.C.)

Prior to 1926, the positive law for federal legislation was contained in one volume of the *Revised Statutes of 1875* and then in each of the twenty-four subsequent volumes of the *United States Statutes at Large*. In 1926, the *United States Code,* prepared under the auspices of special

[13] Revised Statutes of the United States, 1873–74, Act of June 22, 1874, tit. LXXIV, §§ 5595–5601, at 1085 (1878).

[14] Dwan & Feidler, *supra* note 12, at 1014–15.

[15] For a discussion and bibliography of federal laws before 1926, see Erwin C. Surrency, *The Publication of Federal Laws: A Short History,* 79 Law Libr. J. 469 (1987).

committees of the House and Senate, was published. In this codification, all sections of the *Revised Statutes of 1875* that were not repealed were extracted, and then all the public and general laws still in force from the *United States Statutes at Large* since 1873 were included.

These laws were then arranged into fifty Titles and published as the *United States Code,* 1926 edition.[16] Between 1927 and 1933 cumulated bound supplements were issued each year. In 1934 a new edition was issued that incorporated the cumulated supplements to the 1926 edition, and this became the *United States Code,* 1934 edition. Every six years a new edition is published with cumulative supplements issued during the intervening years. The *U.S.C.* is thus the "official" edition of the codification of federal public laws of a general and permanent nature, which are in effect at the time of publication.

Unlike the *Revised Statutes of 1875,* the *U.S.C.* was never submitted to Congress and reenacted in its entirety. Instead Congress created the Office of the Revision Counsel[17] and directed that Office to revise the *U.S.C.* Title by Title. Each Title is submitted to Congress for enactment into law. To date, less than one half of the Titles have been enacted into law.[18] Thus, in using the *U.S.C.,* it is important to ascertain if the Title being consulted has been enacted into positive law. Those Titles not yet enacted are *prima facie* evidence of the law.[19] Should there be a conflict between the wording in the *U.S.C.* and the *United States Statutes at Large,* the latter will govern.[20] The *United States Statutes at Large* citations, the original enactment, and any amendments are provided after each section of the *U.S.C.* These parenthetical references lead to

[16] *See* Preface at 44, Pt. 1 Stat. at v (1926).

[17] The principal duty of this Office is "to develop and keep current an official and positive codification of the laws of the United States," 2 U.S.C. § 285a (1988), and "to prepare ... one title at a time, a complete compilation, restatement, and revision of the general and permanent laws of the United States ...." 2 U.S.C. § 285b(1) (1988).

[18] Titles reenacted as positive law are 1, 3, 4, 5, 9, 10, 11, 13, 14, 17, 18, 23, 28, 31, 32, 35, 37, 38, 39, 44, 46, 49, and the Internal Revenue Code (Title 26). Title 34 was eliminated by Title 10; and the enactment of Title 31 repealed Title 6. A list of Titles reenacted as positive law is in the following sources: (1) after the title page of, and in the preface to, the volumes of the *U.S.C.;* (2) after Section 204(e) of Title 1 in the *U.S.C.,* the *United States Code Annotated,* and the *United States Code Service (U.S.C.S.);* and (3) inside the front cover of bound volumes of the *U.S.C.S.*

[19] 1 U.S.C. § 204(a) (1988) provides that:

The matter set forth in the edition of the Code of Laws of the United States current at any time shall, together with the then current supplement, if any, establish *prima facie* the laws of the United States, general and permanent in their nature, in force on the day preceding the commencement of the session following the last session the legislation of which is included: *Provided, however,* That whenever titles of such Code shall have been enacted into positive law the text thereof shall be legal evidence of the laws therein contained, in all the courts of the United States, the several States, and the Territories and insular possessions of the United States.

[20] For an interpretation of 1 U.S.C. § 204(a), see United States v. Welden, 377 U.S. 95, 98 n. 4 (1964). *See also* North Dakota v. United States, 460 U.S. 300 (1983); United States v. Wodtke, 627 F. Supp. 1034, 1040 (N.D. Iowa 1985), *aff'd,* 871 F.2d 1092 (8th Cir. 1988).

the positive law for those Titles of the *U.S.C.* that have not yet been reenacted by the Congress. [See Illustrations 66–67.]

Some additional features of the *U.S.C.* are as follows:

a. A multi-volume general index.

b. Historical notes that provide information on amendments or other public laws' effect on sections of the *U.S.C.*

c. Cross references to other sections of the *U.S.C.* that contain related matter or that refer to the section of the *U.S.C.* being researched.

d. A table of "Acts Cited by Popular Name," in which public laws are listed alphabetically by either the short titles assigned by Congress or by the names by which the laws have become known. Citations are provided to the *U.S.C.* and to the *United States Statutes at Large.*

e. Tables volumes that provide the following information:

(1) Table 1 shows where Titles of the *U.S.C.* that have been revised and renumbered since the 1926 edition appear in the current edition of the *U.S.C.*

(2) Table 2 provides references to the current edition of the *U.S.C.* from the *Revised Statutes of 1878.*

(3) Table 3 lists the public laws in the *United States Statutes at Large* in chronological order and indicates where each section of a public law is contained in the current edition of the *U.S.C.*

(4) Another table provides information on internal cross references within the *U.S.C.*

(5) There are additional tables that indicate where other documentation, *e.g.,* Presidential executive orders, are referenced in the current edition of the *U.S.C.*

The Tables volumes are updated by the annual cumulative supplements to the *U.S.C.*

3. Annotated Editions of the United States Code

Because the *U.S.C.* is printed and sold by the U.S. Government Printing Office, it is often slow in being published, particularly in the issuance of the supplements, which are seldom available until several months after a session of Congress is over. Furthermore, the meaning of a law passed by a legislative body is not always clear and the language used must frequently be interpreted by a court. Consequently, access to the court cases interpreting statutes is frequently as important as the text of the statute itself. This has led to the publication of annotated codes where digests of court cases interpreting or deciding the constitutionality of a *Code* section are given. Two annotated editions of the *U.S.C.* are published privately.

The annotated editions have many advantages over the official edition of the *U.S.C.* and are usually consulted in preference to it. These advantages are: (1) each Title is published in one or more

separate volumes; (2) the entire set is kept up to date by annual cumulative pocket supplements and, when necessary, by recompiled volumes; (3) pamphlets are issued during the year bringing the pocket supplements up to date; (4) more detailed indexing is provided in bound volumes and supplements [see Illustration 60]; (5) each *Code* section contains annotations of court cases that have interpreted it; and (6) when applicable, citations to the *Code of Federal Regulations*[21] are given.

a. *United States Code Annotated (U.S.C.A.).* This set is published by West Publishing Company. *U.S.C.A.* uses the text as it appears in the official version, the *U.S.C.* Thus, it contains the same features as were listed in Section C–2, *supra.*

Many enhancements have been added by the publisher to supplement those features found in the official version of the *U.S.C.* Most important are the Notes of Decisions, which provide digests of cases that have interpreted a particular section of the *Code.* This feature is popularly referred to as annotations. Notes of Decisions are organized under an alphabetical subject index, which precedes the actual annotations.

Other features of the *U.S.C.A.* are as follows:

(1) References to other West publications and to Topic and Key Numbers that can assist the users in finding additional cases and other materials pertinent to their research.

(2) A multi-volume General Index is issued annually in paperback form. In addition, each Title of the *U.S.C.A.* has a separate index in the last volume containing sections of the particular Title of the *U.S.C.A.*

(3) Public laws that have been enacted since the last supplementation was prepared for a specific Title and that affect sections of that Title can be located in *U.S.C.A.*'s supplementary pamphlets. The public laws are classified to particular *Code* sections. The most recent Notes of Decisions are included for *Code* sections that have been construed by the courts since the last pocket supplements were published. The most recent court cases that have interpreted public laws can be located by using the Tables of Statutes Construed in the bound volumes and advance sheets of the units of the *National Reporter System.*

(4) A "Popular Name Table for Acts of Congress" is located in the last volume of the General Index. [See Illustration 69.] The listing is alphabetical by popular name, with references provided to the *United States Statutes at Large* and to the *Code.* This Popular Name Table is cumulatively updated by means of the pamphlets discussed in 3, *supra.* Also, many Titles of the *U.S.C.A.* contain tables entitled "Popular Name Acts," which provide an alphabetical listing of public laws within that Title and references to sections of that specific Title. [See Illustration 70.] These tables are located in the first volume of the Title, if there is more than one volume.

[21] This publication is discussed in Chapter 13.

The General Index also includes, in the proper alphabetical location, the public law by popular name. Most frequently, the researcher is referred to the Popular Name Table for Acts of Congress in the last volume of the *U.S.C.A.*'s General Index. Occasionally, a direct reference is given to the *Code*.

(5) The *U.S.C.A.* contains many of the same tables as described for the *U.S.C.* These tables are contained in separate volumes labeled as such and are updated by means of pocket and pamphlet supplementation as described *supra*.

b. *United States Code Service (U.S.C.S.).* This set is published by Lawyers Cooperative Publishing and is a unit of its *Total Client–Service Library*. Like *U.S.C.A.*, *U.S.C.S.* provides the same features of *U.S.C.*, *e.g.*, historical notes, cross references in a section entitled "History; Ancillary Laws and Directives," which follows each section of the *Code*.

A major difference between *U.S.C.S.* and *U.S.C.A.* is that *U.S.C.S.* follows the text of the public laws as they appear in the *United States Statutes at Large*. Therefore, if a Title has not been reenacted into positive law, the user will have the language that is needed. If the editors of *U.S.C.S.* believe that clarification of the language of the public laws in the set is necessary, this information will be shown by the use of brackets (inserting words or references) or by use of explanatory notes.

Because it is an annotated *Code, U.S.C.S.* provides "pertinent" digests of not only court cases but also of federal administrative agency decisions that have interpreted or construed a public law or a particular section of a public law by means of Interpretative Notes and Decisions.

An "analytical" index, which precedes the actual digest of cases and administrative decisions, enables users to focus their research. The Later Case and Statutory Service pamphlets, issued three times a year, update the Interpretative Notes and Decisions between the time of the issuance of the annual pocket supplements.

Other features of the *U.S.C.S.* are as follows:

(1) *U.S.C.S.* provides references to other publications in its *Total Client–Service Library* and to relevant law review articles. These references are in a section entitled Research Guide.

(2) A multi-volume Revised General Index, which is kept current by a General Index Update pamphlet.

(3) Public laws that have been enacted since the last supplementation has been prepared for a specific Title and that affect sections of that Title can be located in *U.S.C.S.*'s Cumulative Later Case and Statutory Service, issued three times a year. The public laws are classified to particular *Code* sections.

(4) A "Table of Acts by Popular Name," is located in the Tables volumes of *U.S.C.S.* The listing is alphabetical by popular name, with references provided to the *United States Statutes at Large* and to

U.S.C.S. This Table is updated by the *United States Code Service Advance Service* discussed in Section B–1–b, *supra.*

The General Index also includes, in the proper alphabetic location, the public law by popular name. References are given to a *U.S.C.S.* citation or a cross reference is given to a subject in the General Index when the specific sections of the public law are contained in the *U.S.C.S.*

(5) *U.S.C.S.* contains many of the same tables as described for the *U.S.C.* These tables are contained in separate volumes labeled as such and are updated by means of pocket and pamphlet supplementation as described *supra.*

c. *Summary and Comparison: Annotated Editions of the United States Code.* Both the *U.S.C.A.* and the *U.S.C.S.* follow the same citation pattern as the official *U.S.C.* and, therefore, a citation to *U.S.C.* can be located in either of the two annotated sets.[22] As noted in Section C–2, *supra,* only certain Titles of the *U.S.C.* have been reenacted. The *U.S.C.A.* uses the text as it appears in the *U.S.C.,* while the *U.S.C.S.* follows the text as it appears in the *United States Statutes at Large.* Thus, when using the *U.S.C.A.,* it may be necessary at times to check the text of the *United States Statutes at Large* for those Titles that are still only *prima facie* evidence of the law.

Both *U.S.C.A.* and *U.S.C.S.* contain digests of cases that have interpreted a section of the *U.S.C.* Each set is kept up to date by annual pocket supplements, monthly pamphlets, and, when necessary, by issuance of replacement volumes. Each has editorial matter that refers to other publications by the same publisher. The *U.S.C.A.* contains more annotations than the *U.S.C.S.;* the *U.S.C.S.* frequently cross references to *Annotations* in *A.L.R. Fed.* or in *United States Supreme Court Reports, Lawyers' Edition* for additional cases in lieu of providing annotations. Each set is easier to use, more current, and better indexed than the *U.S.C.* However, when only the text of the *Code* is needed, it may be simpler to consult the official, unannotated edition. [See Illustrations 60–67, which show the use of the various sets of the *Code.*]

Both annotated codes include volumes containing the United States Constitution and the various court rules. These components are discussed in Chapters 8 and 12, respectively.

4. Access to the Code in Electronic Format

a. *LEXIS.* LEXIS contains the *Code* as published in the *U.S.C.S.* in its GENFED, CODES, and LEGIS libraries, USCODE file. Each section of a *Code* Title contains the full text of the law, a complete history of the *Code* section showing source and derivations of the law plus any amendments, and a list of research references and interpretative notes. Each *Code* section is updated to include the new material in

---

[22] For a discussion of these two sets, *see* Jeanne Benioff, *A Comparison of Annotated U.S. Codes,* Legal Reference Services Q., Spring 1982, at 37.

the paper supplementation. Information regarding each section's currency is included.

b. *WESTLAW.* WESTLAW contains the *Code* as published in the *U.S.C.A.* The USC database provides the unannotated version. A related materials directory enables the user to update the *Code* section, to view historical notes, references and tables, and to find Notes of Decisions. The USCA database contains the text of the *Code,* annotations, and a popular name table. The *Code* section can be updated and notes, references, and tables can be viewed by using the related materials directory.

c. *CD–ROM Products.* West Publishing Company, Lawyers Cooperative Publishing, and the Government Printing Office each have a CD–ROM version of the *Code* they publish.

SECTION D. ILLUSTRATIONS

[Illustration 59]

SLIP LAW—103d CONGRESS

①

107 STAT. 6   PUBLIC LAW 103–3—FEB. 5, 1993

Public Law 103–3
103d Congress
                                        An Act

Feb. 5, 1993
②→ [H.R. 1]   To grant family and temporary medical leave under certain circumstances.

Family and   *Be it enacted by the Senate and House of Representatives of*
Medical Leave   *the United States of America in Congress assembled,*
Act of 1993.   **SECTION 1. SHORT TITLE; TABLE OF CONTENTS.**
③→29 USC 2601
note.   (a) SHORT TITLE.—This Act may be cited as the "Family and
                              Medical Leave Act of 1993".
                                  (b) TABLE OF CONTENTS.—The table of contents is as follows:

> This is a typical *slip law*. At the end of a session, laws are published in a bound volume of the *United States Statutes at Large.*
>
> Marginal notes are not part of the law but editorial aids. The *Code* citations in the margin indicate where the text is found in the *United States Code.*
>
> Notes: 1. *United States Statutes at Large* citation.
>   2. Bill number in House.
>   3. *United States Code* sections.

③→ 29 USC 2601.   **SEC. 2. FINDINGS AND PURPOSES.**

                              (a) FINDINGS.—Congress finds that—
                                  (1) the number of single-parent households and two-parent
                              households in which the single parent or both parents work
                              is increasing significantly;

[Illustration 60]

PAGE FROM VOLUME OF GENERAL INDEX TO THE U.S.C.A.

GRAZING   700

GRAZING—Cont'd
→ Districts—Cont'd

Mineral resources, development, **43 § 315e**
Mineral title, application for, **43 § 315j**
Mining rights, **43 § 315b**
Natural resources, **43 § 315d**
Notice, creation of districts in States, hearing, **43 § 315**
Offenses, **43 § 315a**
Partition fences, **43 § 315c**
Permits, **43 § 315b**
Preference in issuance of permit, **43 § 315b**
Protection, **43 § 315a**
Range improvements, use of moneys received, **43 § 315i**
Refunds, **43 § 315b**
Regulation, **43 § 315a**
Reservoirs, **43 § 315c**
Restrictions, etc., prior rights, **43 § 315**
Rights of way, **43 §§ 315, 315e**

GRAZING—Cont'd
Lands,

Coos Bay Wagon Road grant lands, reconveyed lands, **43 § 1181d**
Field employees of Bureau of Land Management to furnish horses and equipment, **43 § 315o–2**
Grazing Districts, generally, this index
Inapplicability, provisions concerning Federal civil defense transactions to lease of Government realty for grazing, **50 Ap § 2285**
Leases, isolated or disconnected tracts, **43 § 315m**
Mining activities causing damage, liability, **30 § 54**
National defense, payment for use for national defense purposes, **43 § 315q**
National Forest Administration land under, **43 §§ 315k, 315l**

FINDING A FEDERAL LAW

Problem: Find the statutory section dealing with water rights in grazing districts.

Step 1. Check index to either *U.S.C.*, *U.S.C.A.*, or *U.S.C.S.*

This will indicate that this topic is covered at 43 U.S.C. § 315b.

State police power, **43 § 315n**
States,

Appropriations, moneys received by State, **43 § 315j**
Police power, **43 § 315n**

Stone, use for domestic purposes, **43 § 315d**
→ Water rights, **43 § 315b**
Wells, **43 § 315c**
Wildlife, cooperation in conservation or propagation, **43 § 315h**
Domestic livestock on public rangelands. Public Lands, generally, this index
El Malpais National Conservation Area, continuance of, **16 § 460uu–22**
El Malpais National Monument, **16 § 460uu–3**
Federal civil defense, applicability of section concerning leases of Government realty for grazing purposes, **50 Ap § 2285**
Federal land policy and management. Public Lands, this index
Grand Canyon National Park, **16 §§ 221e, 228f, 228i**
Great Basin National Park, appropriate limit or control of land with respect to, **16 § 410mm et seq.**
Helium gas, issuance of leases to surface of lands or structures for grazing purposes without interfering with production, **50 § 167a**
Hells Canyon National Recreation Area, valid use of, **16 § 460gg–10**
Indian lands, **25 § 179**
Kings Canyon National Park, dedication affecting grazing permits, **16 § 80**
Lake Mead National Recreation Area, **16 § 460n–3**

Withdrawal of grazing lands for war or national defense purposes, **43 § 315q**
Lassen Volcanic National Park, **16 § 202**
Leases,

Defined, Federal land policy and management, **43 § 1702**
Glen Canyon National Recreation Area, **16 § 460dd–5**

Military departments, real property transactions, applicability of section to real property for grazing purposes, **10 § 2662**
National Parks, generally, **16 § 3**
Oregon and California railroad grant lands, lease of revested lands for grazing, **43 § 1181d**
Oregon Cascades Recreation Area, allowance of limited activities, etc., for livestock grazing, **16 § 460oo**
Permits,

Arches National Park, **16 § 272b**
Capitol Reef National Park,
Generally, **16 § 273b**
Renewals, occupied lands, period involved, protection of resources, etc., **16 § 273b**

Defined, Federal land policy and management, **43 § 1702**
Grazing districts, **43 § 315b**
Kings Canyon National Park, effect of dedication of land, **16 § 80**
Mono Basin National Forest Scenic Area, **16 § 543c**
Paiute Indian Tribe of Utah, trust lands, **25 § 766 nt**
Sequoia National Park, **16 § 45c**

[Illustration 61]

PAGE FROM UNITED STATES CODE, 1988 EDITION

REFERENCES IN TEXT

The Stock Raising Homestead Act, referred to in text, is act Dec. 29, 1916, ch. 9, 39 Stat. 862, as amended, which was classified generally to subchapter X (§ 291 et seq.) of chapter 7 of this title and was repealed by Pub. L. 94–579, title VII, §§ 702, 704(a), Oct. 21, 1976, 90 Stat. 2787, 2792, except for sections 9 and 11 which are classified to sections 299 and 301, respectively, of this title. For complete classification of this Act to the Code, see Short Title note set out under section 291 of this title and Tables.

Section 471 of title 16, referred to·in text, was repealed by Pub. L. 94–579, title VII, § 704(a), Oct. 21, 1976, 90 Stat. 2792.

AMENDMENTS

1954—Act May 28, 1954, struck out of first sentence provision limiting to one hundred and forty-two million acres the area which might be included in grazing districts.

1936—Act June 26, 1936, increased acreage which could be included in grazing districts from 80 million to 142 million acres.

time in accordance with governing law. Grazing permits shall be issued only to citizens of the United States or to those who have filed the necessary declarations of intention to become such, as required by the naturalization laws, and to groups, associations, or corporations authorized to conduct business under the laws of the State in which the grazing district is located. Preference shall be given in the issuance of grazing permits to those within or near a district who are landowners engaged in·the livestock business, bona fide occupants or settlers, or owners of water or water rights, as may be necessary to permit the proper use of lands, water or water rights owned, occupied, or leased by them, except that until July 1, 1935, no preference shall be given in the issuance of such permits to any such owner, occupant, or settler, whose rights were acquired between January 1, 1934, and December 31, 1934, both dates, inclusive, except that no permittee complying with

---

> **Step 2.** Locate the title and section referred to in the Index. Ordinarily, one would consult the latest edition of *U.S.C.* and its cumulative supplement, or one of the two annotated codes.
>
> This Illustration shows how this law appears in the *U.S.C.*
>
> Note how at the end of § 315b (as is the case with all *U.S.C.* sections) citations are given to where the section originally appeared in the *United States Statutes at Large*. § 315b was first passed in 1934 and amended in 1947 and 1976.

---

section 315 of this title, and he shall make such rules and regulations and establish such service, enter into such cooperative agreements, and do any and all things necessary to accomplish the purposes of this subchapter and to insure the objects of such grazing districts, namely, to regulate their occupancy and use, to preserve the land and its resources from destruction or unnecessary injury, to provide for the orderly use, improvement, and development of the range; and the Secretary of the Interior is authorized to continue the study of erosion and flood control and to perform such work as may be necessary amply to protect and rehabilitate the areas subject to the provisions of this subchapter, through such funds as may be made available for that purpose, and any willful violation of the provisions of this subchapter or of such rules and regulations thereunder after actual notice thereof shall be punishable by a fine of not more than $500.

(June 28, 1934, ch. 865, § 2, 48 Stat. 1270.)

§ 315b. Grazing permits; fees; vested water rights; permits not to create right in land

The Secretary of the Interior is authorized to issue or cause to be issued permits to graze livestock on such grazing districts to such bona fide settlers, residents, and other stock owners as under his rules and regulations are entitled to participate in the use of the range, upon the payment annually of reasonable fees in each case to be fixed or determined from time to

in whole or in part, or authorize postponement of payment of grazing fees for such depletion period so long as the emergency exists: *Provided further,* That nothing in this subchapter shall be construed or administered in any way to diminish or impair any right to the possession and use of water for mining, agriculture, manufacture, or other purposes which has heretofore vested or accrued under existing law validly affecting the public lands or which may be hereafter initiated or acquired and maintained in accordance with such law. So far as consistent with the purposes and provisions of this subchapter, grazing privileges recognized and acknowledged shall be adequately safeguarded, but the creation of a grazing district or the issuance of a permit pursuant to the provisions of this subchapter shall not create any right, title, interest, or estate in or to the lands.

(June 28, 1934, ch. 865, § 3, 48 Stat. 1270; Aug. 6, 1947, ch. 507, § 1, 61 Stat. 790; Oct. 21, 1976, Pub. L. 94–579, title IV, § 401(b)(3), 90 Stat. 2773.)

AMENDMENTS

1976—Pub. L. 94–579 substituted provisions authorizing fees to be fixed in accordance with governing law, for provisions authorizing fees to take into account public benefits to users of grazing districts over and above benefits accruing to users of forage resources and provisions requiring fees to consist of a grazing fee and a range-improvement fee.

1947—Act Aug. 6, 1947, provided for method to be used by Secretary of the Interior in fixing amount of

[Illustration 62]

PAGE FROM 90 UNITED STATES STATUTES AT LARGE

PUBLIC LAW 94-579—OCT. 21, 1976   90 STAT. 2773

of all moneys received by the United States as fees for grazing domestic livestock on public lands (other than from ceded Indian lands) under the Taylor Grazing Act (48 Stat. 1269; 43 U.S.C. 315 et seq.) and the Act of August 28, 1937 (50 Stat. 874; 43 U.S.C. 1181d), and on lands in National Forests in the eleven contiguous Western States under the provisions of this section shall be credited to a separate account in the Treasury, one-half of which is authorized to be appropriated and made available for use in the district, region, or national forest from which such moneys were derived, as the respective Secretary may direct after consultation with district, regional, or national forest user representatives, for the purpose of on-the-ground range rehabilitation, protection, and improvements on such lands, and the remaining one-half shall be used for on-the-ground range rehabilitation, protection, and improvements as the Secretary concerned directs. Any funds so appropriated shall be in addition to any other appropriations made to the respective Secretary for planning and

> **As noted in the previous Illustration, 43 U.S.C. § 315b has been amended twice, most recently in 1976. As is frequently the case, a public law may amend different Titles and sections of the same Title of the *U.S.C.***

tive Secretary may direct after consultation with user representatives. The annual distribution and use of range betterment funds authorized by this paragraph shall not be considered a major Federal action requiring a detailed statement pursuant to section 4332(c) of title 42 of the United States Code.

(2) The first clause of section 10(b) of the Taylor Grazing Act (48 Stat. 1269), as amended by the Act of August 6, 1947 (43 U.S.C. 315i), is hereby repealed. All distributions of moneys made under section 401(b)(1) of this Act shall be in addition to distributions made under section 10 of the Taylor Grazing Act and shall not apply to distribution of moneys made under section 11 of that Act. The remaining moneys received by the United States as fees for grazing domestic livestock on the public lands shall be deposited in the Treasury as miscellaneous receipts.   `43 USC 1751.`   `43 USC 315j.`

(3) Section 3 of the Taylor Grazing Act, as amended (43 U.S.C. 315), is further amended by—   `43 USC 315b.`

    (a) Deleting the last clause of the first sentence thereof, which begins with "and in fixing," deleting the comma after "time", and adding to that first sentence the words "in accordance with governing law".

    (b) Deleting the second sentence thereof.

GRAZING LEASES AND PERMITS

SEC. 402. (a) Except as provided in subsection (b) of this section, permits and leases for domestic livestock grazing on public lands issued by the Secretary under the Act of June 28, 1934 (48 Stat. 1269, as amended; 43 U.S.C. 315 et seq.) or the Act of August 28, 1937 (50 Stat. 874, as amended; 43 U.S.C. 1181a–1181j), or by the Secretary of Agriculture, with respect to lands within National Forests in the eleven contiguous Western States, shall be for a term of ten years subject to such terms and conditions the Secretary concerned deems appropriate and consistent with the governing law, including, but not limited to, the authority of the Secretary concerned to cancel, suspend, or modify a grazing permit or lease, in whole or in part, pursuant to the terms and conditions thereof, or to cancel or suspend a grazing permit or   `43 USC 1752.`

[Illustration 63]

PAGE FROM TITLE 43 U.S.C.A.

Ch. 8A　　GRAZING LANDS　　　　　　　　　43 § 315b

West's Federal Practice Manual

Grazing in grazing districts, see § 5587 et seq.

Code of Federal Regulations

Criminal law enforcement, see 43 CFR 9260.0–1 et seq.
Gifts, see 43 CFR 2110.0–1 et seq.
Leases, see 43 CFR 2120.0–2 et seq.
National Wildlife Refuge System, see 50 CFR Chap. I, Subchap. C.
Off-road vehicles, see 43 CFR 8340.0–1 et seq.
Visitor service, see 43 CFR 8360.0–3 et seq.
Wild horse and burro management, see 43 CFR 4700.0–1 et seq.

Notes of Decisions

Cooperative agreements　2
Fines　3
Rules and regulations　1

1. Rules and regulations

The Federal Range Code for Grazing Districts promulgated under this chapter is the law of the range and the activities of Federal range agents are controlled by its provisions. Hatahley v. U.S., Utah 1956, 76 S.Ct. 745, 351 U.S. 173, 100 L.Ed. 1065.

Rights to the use of the public domain must be determined in accordance with provisions of this chapter and the Range Code. U.S. v. Morrell, C.A.Utah 1964, 331 F.2d 498, certiorari denied 85 S.Ct. 146, 379 U.S. 879, 13 L.Ed.2d 86.

State Grazing Dist. v. Tysk, D.C.Mont.1968, 290 F.Supp. 227.

Rules and regulations respecting issuance and effect of grazing permits as promulgated by Secretary of the Interior have the force and effect of law, and the law existing at the time and place of making of permit agreement is as much a part thereof as though it were expressed therein. Wilkinson v. U.S., D.C.Or.1960, 189 F.Supp. 413.

2. Cooperative agreements

Under agreement, authorized by this chapter, between state cooperative grazing district and federal Bureau of Land Management whereby Bureau agreed to establish and fix, in cooperation with state grazing district, grazing capacity of federal and district land,

The U.S.C.A. has the same text as it appears in the official edition of the Code, the U.S.C.

did not assess adequately the individual district or area situations to provide the local decision maker with the necessary data to analyze alternatives open to him and their consequences. Natural Resources Defense Council, Inc. v. Morton, D.C.D.C.1974, 388 F.Supp. 829, affirmed 527 F.2d 1386, 174 U.S.App.D.C. 77, certiorari denied 96 S.Ct. 3201, 427 U.S. 913, 49 L.Ed.2d 1204.

Regulations issued pursuant to this chapter, have effect of law. Buffalo Creek Co-op.

Buffalo Creek Co-op. State Grazing Dist. Tysk, D.C.Mont.1968, 290 F.Supp. 227.

3. Fines

$500 fine limitation under this chapter refers only to the penalty which can be imposed upon a criminal prosecution for a violation of this chapter or its implementing regulations; in no way does it limit the administrative sanctions otherwise available to the Secretary of the Interior. Diamond Ring Ranch, Inc. v. Morton, C.A.Wyo.1976, 531 F.2d 1397.

§ 315b. Grazing permits; fees; vested water rights; permits not to create right in land

The Secretary of the Interior is hereby authorized to issue or cause to be issued permits to graze livestock on such grazing districts to such bona fide settlers, residents, and other stock owners as under his rules and regulations are entitled to participate in the use of the range, upon the payment annually of reasonable fees in each case to be fixed or determined from time to time in ac-

[Illustration 64]

PAGE FROM TITLE 43 U.S.C.A.

43 § 315b   PUBLIC LANDS   Ch. 8A

cordance with governing law. Grazing permits shall be issued only to citizens of the United States or to those who have filed the necessary declarations of intention to become such, as required by the naturalization laws, and to groups, associations, or corporations authorized to conduct business under the laws of the State in which the grazing district is located. Preference shall be given in the issuance of grazing permits to those within or near a district who are landowners engaged in the livestock business, bona fide occupants or settlers, or owners of water or water rights, as may be necessary to permit the proper use of lands, water or water rights owned, occupied, or leased by them, except that until July 1, 1935, no preference shall be given in the issuance of such permits to any such owner, occupant, or settler, whose rights were acquired between January 1, 1934, and December 31, 1934, both dates inclusive, except that no permittee complying with the rules and regulations laid down by the Secretary of the Interior shall be denied the renewal of such permit, if such denial will impair the

> **This Illustration shows the references to the *United States Statutes at Large* and the Historical Notes summarizing the effect of the amendments on the original public law.**

range depletion due to severe drought or other natural causes, or in case of a general epidemic of disease, during the life of the permit, the Secretary of the Interior is hereby authorized, in his discretion to remit, reduce, refund in whole or in part, or authorize postponement of payment of grazing fees for such depletion period so long as the emergency exists: *Provided further,* That nothing in this subchapter shall be construed or administered in any way to diminish or impair any right to the possession and use of water for mining, agriculture, manufacturing, or other purposes which has heretofore vested or accrued under existing law validly affecting the public lands or which may be hereafter initiated or acquired and maintained in accordance with such law. So far as consistent with the purposes and provisions of this subchapter, grazing privileges recognized and acknowledged shall be adequately safeguarded, but the creation of a grazing district or the issuance of a permit pursuant to the provisions of this subchapter shall not create any right, title, interest, or estate in or to the lands.

(June 28, 1934, c. 865, § 3, 48 Stat. 1270; Aug. 6, 1947, c. 507, § 1, 61 Stat. 790; Oct. 21, 1976, Pub.L. 94–579, Title IV, § 401(b)(3), 90 Stat. 2773.)

Historical Note

1976 Amendment. Pub.L. 94–579 substituted provisions authorizing fees to be fixed in accordance with governing law, for provisions authorizing fees to take into account public benefits to users of grazing districts over and above benefits accruing to users of forage resources and provisions requiring fees to consist of a grazing fee and a range-improvement fee.

1947 Amendment. Act Aug. 6, 1947, provided for method to be used by the Secretary of the Interior in fixing the amount of grazing fees and by assessing a separate grazing fee and a range-improvement fee.

Savings Provisions. Amendment by Pub.L. 94–579 not to be construed as terminating any valid lease, permit, patent, etc., existing on Oct. 21, 1976, see section 701 of Pub.L. 94–579 set out as a note under section 1701 of this title.

Legislative History. For legislative history and purpose of Act Aug. 6, 1947, see 1947 U.S.Code Cong.Service, p. 1638. See, also, Pub.L. 94–579, 1976 U.S.Code Cong. and Adm.News, p. 6175.

[Illustration 65]

PAGE FROM TITLE 43 U.S.C.A.

Ch. 8A   GRAZING LANDS   **43 § 315b**
                                                  Note 2

Cross References ◄————

Disposition of moneys received, see section 315i of this title.

————► **West's Federal Practice Manual**

Permits and licenses, see § 5588.

Library References ◄————

Public Lands ⬤—17.
C.J.S. Public Lands §§ 19 to 23.

————► **Notes of Decisions**

Death of permittee, termination of permits
    11
Denial of application 4
Drought conditions, termination of permits
    10
Grazing fees 5
Grazing preference 6
Indispensable parties 17
Injunction 20
Interest in lands 7
Issuance of permits 3
Jurisdiction 14
Mandamus 23
Nature and scope of permits 2

other lands under regulation providing that transfer of base property or part thereof would entitle transferee, if qualified, to so much of grazing privilege as was based thereon, and that original license or permit would be terminated or decreased to extent of such transfer, such regulation became a part of permit agreement between Government and decedent. Wilkinson v. U.S., D.C.Or.1960, 189 F.Supp. 413.

2. Nature and scope of permits

Secretary of Interior properly granted grazing permit to extent of number of animal

---

> The important difference in the annotated sets of the *Code* is the digest of court cases that appear after each section of the *Code*. These digests assist in interpreting the meaning of the *Code* section.
>
> Also illustrated are other research aids available in the *U.S.C.A.*

Review 22
Rights, title, or interest in lands 7
Rules and regulations 1
Safeguard of grazing privileges
    Generally 12
    Trespass on grazing lands 13
Termination of permits
    Generally 9
    Death of permittee 11
    Drought conditions 10
Trespass on grazing lands, safeguard of grazing privileges 13
Withdrawal of permits 8

————

1. Rules and regulations

A regulation that permit for grazing within National Forests shall have the full force and effect of a contract between the United States and the permittee means only that the United States will regard the terms of its permit as binding between it and other permit seekers. Osborne v. U.S., C.C.A.Ariz.1944, 145 F.2d 892.

Where deceased as owner of land was issued grazing permit with respect to certain

Udall, 1964, 340 F.2d 801, 119 U.S.App.D.C. 276, certiorari denied 85 S.Ct. 1448, 381 U.S. 904, 14 L.Ed.2d 285.

The grant of grazing permits is a use of the public domain for the benefit of the United States which receives a fee from the holders of preferential permits, and of those holding grazing permits. U.S. v. Morrell, C.A.Utah 1964, 331 F.2d 498, certiorari denied 85 S.Ct. 146, 379 U.S. 879, 13 L.Ed.2d 86.

Stock raisers qualifying for grazing permits under this chapter acquire rights which are something of real value and have their source in an enactment of Congress. McNeil v. Seaton, 1960, 281 F.2d 931, 108 U.S.App. D.C. 296.

A permit, granted owners of land in grazing district by district grazer, to graze additional number of cattle after they leased adjacent state land and two ranches, did not impliedly grant them exclusive right to graze livestock on public domain simply because it decreased lessor's grazing permit by equivalent number of sheep, in view of evidence that district grazer and advisory board did not intend to grant such owners exclusive grazing

[Illustration 66]

PAGE FROM TITLE 43 U.S.C.S.

GRAZING LANDS   **43 USCS § 315b**

life of the permit, the Secretary of the Interior is hereby authorized, in his discretion to remit, reduce, refund in whole or in part, or authorize postponement of payment of grazing fees for such depletion period so long as the emergency exists: Provided further, That nothing in this Act shall be construed or administered in any way to diminish or impair any right to the possession and use of water for mining, agriculture, manufacturing, or other purposes which has heretofore vested or accrued under existing law validly affecting the public lands or which may be hereafter initiated or acquired and maintained in accordance with such law. So far as consistent with the purposes and provisions of this Act, grazing privileges recognized and acknowledged

This illustrates the cross references and "Research Guide" (continued next Illustration) of the *U.S.C.S.* *U.S.C.S.* uses the text of the public law as it appears in the *United States Statutes at Large.*

law. for , and in fixing the amount of such fees the Secretary of the Interior shall take into account the extent to which such districts yield public benefits over and above those accruing to the users of the forage resources for livestock purposes. Such fees shall consist of a grazing fee for the use of the range, and a range-improvement fee which, when appropriated by the Congress, shall be available until expended solely for the construction, purchase, or maintenance of range improvements."

Other provisions:
Savings provisions. Act Oct. 21, 1976, P. L. 94-579, Title VII, § 701(a), 90 Stat. 2786, located at 43 USCS § 1701 note, provided that nothing in Act Oct. 21, 1976, shall be construed as terminating any valid lease, permit, patent, right-of-way, or other land use right or authorization existing on Oct. 21, 1976.

CODE OF FEDERAL REGULATIONS

Nondiscrimination in federally-assisted programs of Department of Interior; effectuation of Title VI of Civil Rights Act of 1964, 43 CFR Part 17.
Grazing administration, exclusive of Alaska, 43 CFR Part 4100.
Grazing administration; Alaska; livestock, 43 CFR Part 4200.
Grazing administration; Alaska; reindeer, 43 CFR Part 4300.
Wild free-roaming horse and burro protection, management and control, 43 CFR Part 4700.

CROSS REFERENCES

National Environmental Policy Act, 42 USCS §§ 4321–4347.
Lease of isolated or disconnected tracts for grazing, 43 USCS § 315m.
Range management, grazing leases and permits, 43 USCS § 1752.

RESEARCH GUIDE

Am Jur:
26 Am Jur 2d, Eminent Domain § 276.

253

[Illustration 67]

PAGE FROM TITLE 43 U.S.C.S.

---

43 USCS § 315b   PUBLIC LANDS

Forms:

5 Federal Procedural Forms L Ed, Condemnation of Property § 13:204.

14 Federal Procedural Forms L Ed, Public Lands and Property §§ 55:2, 55:7.

15 Am Jur Legal Forms 2d, Public Lands § 212:18.

Annotations:

Construction and application of Taylor Grazing Act [43 USCS §§ 315 et seq.] 42 ALR Fed 353.

Federal Tort Claims Act: Construction of provision excepting claims involving "discretionary function or duty." 99 ALR2d 1016.

INTERPRETIVE NOTES AND DECISIONS ◄───────

I. IN GENERAL

1. Generally
2. Relation to other laws

II. ISSUANCE, REVOCATION, RENEWAL, AND MODIFICATION OF PERMITS

3. Issuance as discretionary
4. Fees

Annotations:

Construction and application of Taylor Grazing Act [43 USCS §§ 315 et seq.] 42 ALR Fed 353 (see, especially § 4 on Federal Supremacy).

2. Relation to other laws

Congress did not desire that restrictions contained in 43 USCS § 315b should be applicable to grazing leases in 43 USCS § 315m since if it

---

> **This Illustration shows the remainder of the Research Guide and the annotations, which are editorial enhancements to the annotated sets of the *Code*.**

III. OTHER CONSIDERATIONS AFFECTING PERMITS

10. Grazing privileges on isolated tracts
11. Binding nature of permits
12. Preferences
13. Temporary licenses
14. Protection of permit rights
15. Grazing trespass

IV. PRACTICE AND PROCEDURE

16. Jurisdiction
17. Secretary as indispensable party
18. Pleadings
19. Representation at hearings
20. Evidence, generally
21. —Grazing trespass
22. Burden of proof
23. Review

I. IN GENERAL

1. Generally

Congress intended to grant to Secretary of Interior exclusive power over granting permits to use of public domain, and this power supersedes police power or regulations of state as to right of use of federal public domain. Noh v Babcock (1937, DC Idaho) 21 F Supp 519, revd on other grounds (CA9 Idaho) 99 F2d 738.

Grazing clearly may have severe impact on local environments so that grazing permit program of Bureau of Land Management is subject to requirement of filing environmental impact statements under National Environmental Policy Act (42 USCS §§ 4321-4347); plaintiffs have standing in federal court in action alleging that Bureau of Land Management's grazing permit program does not comply with National Environmental Policy Act's requirements regarding filing of environmental impact statements where all but one of plaintiffs are environmental organizations whose general objectives are to enhance and protect environment and insure proper resource management, and where remaining plaintiff is specialist in study of bighorn sheep, whose scientific, conservation and esthetic interests are allegedly jeopardized; motion for summary judgment was granted against Department of Interior officials where Bureau of Land Management's programmatic environmental impact statement was insufficient to comply with National Environmental Policy Act in that specific environmental effects of permits issued or renewed in each district must be assessed. Natural Resources Defense Council, Inc. v Morton (1974, DC Dist Col) 388 F Supp 829, affd without op 174 App DC 77, 527 F2d 1386, and affd without op 174 App DC 77, 527 F2d 1386, cert den 427 US 913, 49 L Ed 2d 1204, 96 S Ct 3201.

254

SECTION E. POPULAR NAMES FOR FEDERAL LAWS

It is common practice to refer to a publication by a popular name. With respect to federal legislation, this is generally the name that the public or media gives to a statute and it may describe its subject matter, *e.g.*, Gold Clause Act, or refer to its authors, *e.g.*, Taft–Hartley Act.

The tables of popular names of federal laws are designed to provide citations to acts when only the popular names are known. In addition to the popular name tables already discussed in this chapter in connection with *U.S.C.*, *U.S.C.A.*, and *U.S.C.S.*, the following sources also provide popular name tables:

1. *Shepard's Acts and Cases by Popular Names*. This source is discussed in Chapter 14. [See Illustration 68.]

2. *United States Code Congressional and Administrative News*. Since the 77th Congress, 2d Session, 1942, this source contains a table of "Popular Name Acts" for each session of Congress.

SECTION F. TABLES FOR FEDERAL LAWS

As has been noted, federal laws are first published in chronological order in the volumes of the *United States Statutes at Large*. A particular law may be on one topic, or may include matters on several different topics. Another law may amend one or several previous laws. Some are public laws of a general and permanent nature and are codified in the *U.S.C.*

This method of enacting and publishing laws makes it necessary to have tables that enable a researcher to trace each section of a law as it appears in the *United States Statutes at Large* and find out if it has been codified and, if so, its citation in the *U.S.C.* For example, assume a researcher has a citation to Section 3(2) of Pub. L. No. 101–376 and needs to find out where this section is in the *U.S.C.* To do so, the appropriate table of public laws has to be consulted. [See Illustration 71.]

From time to time, a particular Title of *U.S.C.* is completely revised with entirely new section numbers. One having a citation to the old Title must then consult a table to find out the section number in the new Title. [See Illustration 72.]

Each of the three sets containing the *Code* described *supra* has a volume or volumes that include cross-reference tables that serve various purposes. These include the following:

1. *Revised Title*. These tables show where sections of former Titles of the *U.S.C.* that have been revised are now incorporated within the *Code*.

2. *Revised Statutes of 1878*. This table shows where *Revised Statutes* citations are found in the *Code*.

3. *United States Statutes at Large.* This table shows where public laws as they appear in the *United States Statutes at Large* are found in the *Code*.

SECTION G. ILLUSTRATIONS: POPULAR NAMES AND TABLES

[Illustration 68]

PAGE FROM SHEPARD'S ACTS AND CASES BY POPULAR NAMES

FEDERAL AND STATE ACTS CITED BY POPULAR NAME   Tra

Tracy-Copps Act (Vocational Rehabilitation)
Ohio Laws Vol. 109, p. 310

Trade Act (Aleutian)
See U.S. Code tables
Nov. 16, 1990, P.L. 101-595, 104 Stat. 2979, §
601 et seq.

Trade Act of 1974
U.S. Code 1988 Title 19, §2101 et seq.
Jan. 3, 1975, P.L. 93-618, 88 Stat. 1978

Trade Act (Monopoly or Restraint of)
N.Y. General Business Law (Consol. Laws Ch.
20) §340 et seq.

Trade Act (Philippine)
U.S. Code 1970 Title 22, §1251 et seq.
Apr. 30, 1946, c. 244, 60 Stat. 141

Trade Adjustment Assistance Reform and
Extension Act of 1986
See U.S. Code tables

Trade and Competitiveness Act
See U.S. Code tables
U.S., Aug. 23, 1988, P.L. 100-418, 102 Stat.
1107

Trade and Customs Act
See U.S. Code tables
Aug. 20, 1990, P.L. 101-382, 104 Stat. 629

Trade and Development Enhancement Act of 1983
U.S. Code 1988 Title 12, §650 et seq.
U.S. Code 1988 Title 19, §§1671a, 1671b, 1671g
Nov. 30, 1983, P.L. 98-181, 97 Stat. 1153, §1,
Subsecs. 641 to 650

Trade and Export Policy Commission Act
(Agriculture)
U.S., Aug. 30, 1984, P.L. 98-412, 98 Stat.
1576, §1217 et seq.

Trade and Industrial Competitiveness Act
(International)
N.Y. Agriculture and Markets (Consol. Laws.
Ch. 69) §16

Frequently, a public law will become known by a popular name. When only
the popular name is known, popular name tables enable one to locate the actual
citation(s). *See, e.g.,* Trade Act of 1974.

See next two Illustrations.

Trade Agreements Act
U.S. Code 1988 Title 19, §1351 et seq.
June 12, 1934, c. 474, 48 Stat. 943

Trade Agreements Act of 1979
U.S. Code 1988 Title 19, §2501 et seq.
July 26, 1979, P.L. 96-39, 93 Stat. 144

Trade Agreements Extension Act
U.S. Code 1988 Title 19, §1351 et seq.
Mar. 1, 1937, c. 22, 50 Stat. 24
Apr. 12, 1940, c. 96, 54 Stat. 107
June 7, 1943, c. 118, 57 Stat. 125
July 5, 1945, c. 269, 59 Stat. 410
June 26, 1948, c. 678, 62 Stat. 1053
Sept. 26, 1949 c.585, 63 Stat. 697
June 16, 1951, c 141, 65 Stat. 72
Aug. 7, 1953, c. 348, 67 Stat. 472
July 1, 1954, c. 445, 68 Stat. 360
June 21, 1955, c 169, 69 Stat. 162
Aug. 20, 1958, P.L. 85-686, 72 Stat. 673

Trade and Agricultural Development Act
See U.S. Code tables
Nov. 28, 1990, P.L. 101-624, 104 Stat. 3359, §§
1501 to 1578

U.S. Code 1988 Title 25, §§177, 179, 180, 193,
194, 201, 229, 230, 251, 263
July 22, 1790, c. 33, 1 Stat. 137
Mar. 1, 1793, c. 19, 1 Stat. 329
Mar. 3, 1799, c. 46, 1 Stat. 743
June 30, 1834, c. 161, 4 Stat. 729

Trade and Investment Act
U.S. Code 1988 Title 19, §§2112, 2114, 2114a,
2138, 2155, 2171, 2241, 2411 et seq.
U.S. Code 1988 Title 22, §§3101, 3103, 3104
Oct. 30, 1984, P.L. 98-573, 98 Stat. 2948, Title
3

Trade and Manufacturing Site Act
Alk. Comp. Laws Anno. 1949, §47-2-71

Trade and Tariff Act of 1984
See U.S. Code tables
Oct. 30, 1984, P.L. 98-573, 98 Stat. 2948

Trade Center Act
Wash. Rev. Code 1989, 53.29.010 et seq.

363

[Illustration 69]

PAGE FROM POPULAR NAME TABLE IN U.S.C.A.

1501   **ACTS OF CONGRESS**

Trade Act of 1974—Continued

Pub.L. 99–272, Title XIII, §§ 13002 to 13008, 13023, Apr. 7, 1986, 100 Stat. 300 to 305, 307 (Title 19, §§ 2171, prec. 2271 note, 2271, 2272, 2291, 2292, 2293, 2296, 2297, 2311, 2317, 2319, 2341 to 2344, 2346)

Pub.L. 99–514, § 1887, Oct. 22, 1986, 100 Stat. 2923 (Title 19, §§ 2112, 2138, 2155, 2171, 2462, 2464)

Pub.L. 99–570, Title IX, §§ 9001, 9002, Oct. 27, 1986, 100 Stat. 3207–164, 3207–166 (Title 19, §§ 2462, 2491 to 2495, 2702)

Pub.L. 100–203, Title IX, § 9504, Dec. 22, 1987, 101 Stat. 1330–382 (Title 19, § 2171)

Pub.L. 100–204, Title VIII, § 806(a), (b), Dec. 22, 1987, 101 Stat. 1398 (Title 19, § 2492)

Pub.L. 100–418, Title I, §§ 1104, 1107(b), 1111(a), 1213(a), 1214(j), 1215, 1301(a), (b), 1302, 102 Stat. 1132, 1135, 1163, 1176 (Title 19, § 1 et. seq.)

Pub.L. 100–647, Title IX, §§ 9001(a)(1), (2)(A), (8), (10), (20), Nov. 10, 1988, 102 Stat. 3806 to 3808 (Title 19, §§ 2131, 2212, 2253, 2254, 2296)

Pub.L. 100–690, Title IV, § 4408, Nov. 18, 1988, 102 Stat. 4281 to 4284 (Title 19, § 2492)

Pub.L. 101–179, Title III, § 301, Nov. 28, 1989, 103 Stat. 1311 (Title 19, § 2462)

Pub.L. 101–207, § 1(a), Dec. 7, 1989, 103 Stat. 1833 (Title 19, § 2171)

Pub.L. 101–382, Title I, §§ 103(a), 131, 132(a) to (c), 136, Title II, § 226, Aug. 20, 1990, 104 Stat. 134, 643 to 647, 652, 660 (Title 19, §§ 2171, 2191 to 2194, 2318, 2432, 2435, 2437, 2462, 2463)

Pub.L. 102–145, § 121, as added Pub.L. 102–266, § 102, Apr. 1, 1992, 106 Stat. 95 (Title 19, § 2487)

Pub.L. 102–318, Title I, § 106(a), July 3, 1992, 106 Stat. 294 (Title 19, § 2291)

Trade Adjustment Assistance Reform and Extension Act of 1986

Pub.L. 99–272, Title XIII, §§ 13001 to 13009, Apr. 7, 1986, 100 Stat. 300 (Title 19, §§ 2101 note, prec. 2271 note, 2271, 2272, 2291, 2291 note, 2292, 2293, 2296, 2297, 2311, 2317, 2319, 2341 to 2344, 2346)

Pub.L. 99–272, Title XIII, §§ 13024, 13032, Apr. 7, 1986, 100 Stat. 308, 310 (Title 19, § 58b)

Trade Agreements Act

June 12, 1934, ch. 474, §§ 1–4, 48 Stat. 943 (Title 19, §§ 1001, 1201, 1351–1354)

Trade Agreements Act of 1979

Pub. L. 96–39, July 26, 1979, 93 Stat. 144 (Title 5, § 5315; Title 13, § 301; Title 19, §§ 993, 1202, 1303, 1311, 1315, 1332, 1336, 1337, 1351, 1352, 1401a, 1466, 1514–1516a, 1671–1671f, 1673, 1673a–1673i, 1675, 1677–1677g, 1872, 2033, 2101 note, 2111 note, 2112, 2119, 2131, 2135 note, 2155, 2192, 2194, 2211, 2251, 2253, 2411–2416, 2432, 2434, 2435, 2462, 2463, 2464, 2481, 2486, 2501–2504, 2511–2518, 2531–2533, 2541–2547, 2551–2554, 2561, 2562, 2571–2573, 2581, 2582; Title 26, §§ 1 note, 5001–5008, 5043, 5061, 5064, 5066, 5116, 5171, 5172, 5173, 5175–5178, 5180, 5181, 5201, 5202, 5203, 5204, 5205, 5207, 5211, 5212, 5213–5215, 5221, 5222, 5223, 5231, 5232, 5235, 5241, 5273, 5291, 5301, 5352, 5361–5363, 5365, 5381, 5391, 5551, 5601, 5604, 5610, 5612, 5663, 5681, 5682, 5691; Title 28, §§ 1582, 2632, 2633, 2637)

Pub. L. 96–467, § 14(a), Oct. 17, 1980, 94 Stat. 2225

Pub. L. 96–609, title II, § 203(a), Dec. 28, 1980, 94 Stat. 3561

Pub. L. 98–67, Title II, § 214(d), Aug. 5, 1983, 97 Stat. 392 (Title 19, § 2582)

Pub.L. 98–573, Title VI, § 611(c), Oct. 30, 1984, 98 Stat. 3033 (Title 19, § 1671 note)

Pub.L. 99–47, § 7, June 11, 1985, 99 Stat. 84 (Title 19, § 2518)

Pub.L. 100–418, Title I, § 1214(k), (t); Title VII, §§ 7003, 7005(e), Aug. 23, 1988, 102 Stat. 1158, 1548, 1153 (Title 19, §§ 2511, 2515, 2581)

Pub.L. 100–449, Title III, § 306, Sept. 28, 1988, 102 Stat. 1876 (Title 19, §§ 2112 note, 2518)

Trade Agreements Extension Act of 1948

June 26, 1948, ch. 678, 62 Stat. 1053 (Title 19, § 1351 note, 1354, 1357, 1357 note, 1358, 1359)

Trade Agreements Extension Act of 1949

Sept. 26, 1949, ch. 585, 63 Stat. 697 (Title 19, §§ 1351, 1352, 1354, 1645 note)

Trade Agreements Extension Act of 1951

June 16, 1951, ch. 141, 65 Stat. 72 (Title 7, § 624; Title 19, §§ 1352, 1354, 1360, 1360 note, 1361–1367, 1516 note)

Aug. 7, 1953, ch. 348, title I, § 102, 67 Stat. 472 (Title 19, §§ 1364, 1364 note)

June 21, 1955, ch. 169, §§ 4–7, 69 Stat. 165, 166 (Title 19, §§ 1352a, 1363, 1364)

Aug. 20, 1958, Pub. L. 85–686, §§ 4, 5(a), (b)(1), (c), 6, 72 Stat. 675 (Title 19, §§ 1360, 1364)

Trade Agreements Extension Act of 1953

Aug. 7, 1953, ch. 348, 67 Stat. 472 (Title 7, § 624; Title 19, §§ 1330, 1351 note, 1352, 1364, 1366 note, 1654 note)

[Illustration 70]

POPULAR NAME TABLE FROM TITLE 19, U.S.C.A.

POPULAR NAME ACTS

Popular Name	Sections
Tariff Act of 1930	1551, 1552 to 1565, 1581 to 1588, 1592, 1594 to 1595a, 1599, 1602 to 1615, 1617 to 1624, 1641, 1643 to 1645, 1648, 1649, 1651 to 1653, 1654
Tariff Classification Act of 1962	prec. 1202 notes, 1202, 1312, 1351 note
Tariff Schedules of the United States	1202
Tariff Schedules Technical Amendments Act of 1965	prec. 1202 notes, 1202, 1981 note
Trade Act of 1974	2101, 2102, 2111 to 2119, 2131 to 2137, 2151 to 2155, 2171, 2191 to 2194, 2211 to 2213, 2231, 2232, 2251 to 2253, 2271 to 2274, 2291 to 2298, 2311 to 2322, 2341 to 2354, 2371 to 2374, 2391 to 2394, 2411, 2412, 2431 to 2441, 2461 to 2465, 2481 to 2487
Trade Agreements Act	1351, 1352, 1353, 1354
Trade Agreements Extension Act of 1937	1352
Trade Agreements Extension Act of 1940	1352
Trade Agreements Extension Act of 1943	1351, 1352
Trade Agreements Extension Act of 1945	1351, 1352, 1354
Trade Agreements Extension Act of 1949	1351, 1352, 1354
Trade Agreements Extension Act of 1951	1352, 1354, 1360, 1361, 1366
Trade Agreements Extension Act of 1953	1330, 1352
Trade Agreements Extension Act of 1954	1352
Trade Agreements Extension Act of 1955	1351, 1352
Trade Agreements Extension Act of 1958	1333, 1335 to 1337, 1351, 1352, 1360
Trade Expansion Act of 1962	prec. 1202 note, 1323, 1351, 1352, 1352 note, 1801, 1806, 1821, 1823, 1862, 1863, 1872, 1881, 1885, 1887, 1888, 1916, 1918 to 1920, 1981, 1982
Trade Fair Act of 1959	1751 to 1756
Underwood Tariff Act	124, 128, 130, 131
Unfair Practices in Imports Acts	1337, 1337a

XXXI

[Illustration 71]

PAGE FROM TABLES VOLUME—U.S.C.S.

103 Stat			STATUTES AT LARGE						101st Cong	
Pub. L.	**Section**	**Stat. Page**	**USCS Title**	**Section**	**Status**	**Pub. L.**	**Section**	**Stat. Page**	**USCS Title Section**	**Status**
		1990 August—Cont'd						**1990 August—Cont'd**		
101-366—Cont'd						101-371		453	Spec.	Un-class.
	102(b)	431	38	prec. 4141	Added					
			38	4141	Added	101-372		454	Spec.	Un-class.
		435	38	4142	Added					
	102(c)	436	38	4107(e)(1)	Amd.	101-373		455	Spec.	Un-class.
	102(d)		38	prec. 4101	Amd.					
	103	437	38	4107(e)(5)	Amd.	101-374	1	456	42 201 nt.	New
	104		38	4141 nt.	New		2(a)		42 290aa-12(a)	Amd.
	201(a)(1)		38	620C	Added		2(b)(1)		42 290aa-12(d)	Rpld.
	201(a)(2)	438	38	prec. 601	Amd.		2(b)(2)		42 290aa-12(e)- (g)	
	201(b)		38	620C nt.	New				[(c), (e), (f)]	Redes.
	2*2(a)		38	5051	Amd.		2(b)(3)		42 290aa-12(c),	
	202(b)(1)		38	5053(a)	Amd.				(d)	Added
	202(b)(2)		38	5053(b)	Amd.		2(c)(1)		42 290aa-12(g)(1)	Amd.
	203(1)	439	38	4114(a)(3)(A)	Amd.		2(c)(2)		42 290aa-12(g)(3)	Amd.
	203(2)		38	4114(a)(3)(C)	Amd.		2(c)(3)	457	Appn.	Un-class.
	204		38	612A nt.	Amd.		2(d)		Spec.	Un-class.
	205(a)(1)		38	prec. 4351	Amd.					
			38	4351	Added		2(e)		42 290aa-12 nt.	New
		440	38	4352	Added		3(a)		42 290cc-2	Amd.
			38	4353	Added					
			38	4354	Added					

> This Table lists all Public Laws and indicates where each section has been codified in the *U.S.C.*
>
> For example, Section 3(2) of Pub. L. No. 101–376 can be located in Title 5 § 7701(j) in the *U.S.C.*, or the *U.S.C.A.*, or the *U.S.C.S.*

	205(c)(2), (b)		38	4302(a)(1), (b)	Amd.					class.
	205(c)(3)		38	4304(1)(A), (2) (D), (5)	Amd.				**1990 August 17**	
	206(a)		38	1784A	Added					
	206(b)	442	38	1434 nt.	New	101-376	1	461	5 7501 nt.	New
	206(c)		38	prec. 1770	Amd.		2(a)		5 7511	Amd.
	206(d)		5	552a nt.	New		2(b)	462	5 4303(e)	Amd.
	207		38	1622 nt.	New		2(c)		5 4303 nt.	New
	208(a)	443	38	1791(b)	Amd.		3(1)		5 7701(k)(j)]	Redes.
	208(b)		38	1791 nt.	New		3(2)		5 7701(j)	Added
	209		Spec.		Un-class.		4	463	5 4303 nt.	New
101-367	1, 2	445	Spec.		Un-class.	101-377	1	464	16 430g-4	New
							2		16 430g-5	New
101-368	1	446	42	201 nt.	New		3	465	16 430g-6	New
	2(a)(1)		42	247b(j)(2)	Amd.		4		16 430g-7	New
	2(a)(2)		42	247b(k)(2)(A)- (D)	Amd.		5	466	16 430g-8	New
	2(b)		42	247b(l)	Added		6	467	16 430g-9	New
	2(c)		42	247b(j)(2)	Amd.		7		16 430g-10	New
101-369	1	448	9	prec. 301	Amd.	101-378	Title I			
			9	301	Added		101	468	Spec.	Un-class.
			9	302	Added		Title II			
			9	303	Added		201		Spec.	Un-class.
		449	9	304	Added		202		Spec.	Un-class.
			9	305	Added					
			9	306	Added		203	469	Spec.	Un-class.
			9	307	Added		204		Spec.	Un-class.
	2	450	9	prec. 1	Amd.					
	3		9	301 nt.	New		205(a)	470	16 1132 nt.	Amd.
101-370	1	451	49				205(b)		Spec.	Un-class.
			Appx.	1475(d)(4)	Added		Title III			
	2		49				301(1)	471	43 1629c(d)(1)(A)	Amd.
			Appx.	1357(g)	Amd.		301(2)		43 1629c(d)(2)(B)	Redes.
	3	452	49						(i)](d)(2)(B)]	
			Appx.	1482 nt.	New					

400

[Illustration 72]

PAGE FROM TABLES VOLUME—U.S.C.S.

T 38   REVISED TITLES

TITLE 38—VETERANS' BENEFITS

[This title was enacted into law by Act Sept. 2, 1958, P. L. 85-857, § 1, 72 Stat. 1105. This table shows where sections of former Title 38 are incorporated in revised Title 38]

Title 38 Former Sections	Title 38 New Sections	Title 38 Former Sections	Title 38 New Sections
1–3	Omitted	16b	5203
4	214	16c	5204
5–9	Omitted	16d	5205
10	215	16e	5206
11	201, 210(b)	16f	5207
11a	101(1), 210(a), 210(b)	16g	5208
11a-1	Omitted	16h	601(4), 5209
11a-2	211(a)	16i	5210
11a-3	233	16j	Omitted
11b	5006	17	5220
11c–11d-1	Omitted	17a	5221
11e	214	17b	5222
11f	Omitted	17c	5223
11g	202	17d	5224
11h	3303	17e	5225
11i	5014	17f	5226
11j	233(1), (2)	17g	5227
11k	233(4)	17h	5228
11*l*	3204	17i	Omitted
12	Omitted	17j	210(c)

> **When a Title of the *U.S.C.* is revised with new section numbering, a table similar to this one is prepared and can be consulted in the Tables Volumes of the various sets containing the *Code*.**

Former	New	Former	New
13e	4206	34	902
13f	4207	35	Omitted
13g	4208	36	3102(b)
14	5101	37	101(4)
14a	5102	38	107(a)
14b	5103	39, 39a	505
14c	5104	41	3002
14d	5105	42–49	Omitted
14e	214	49a	3107
15	4101	50	3020
15a	4102	51–57	Omitted
15b	4103	58	See 3011
15c	4104	71–75	Omitted
15d	4105	76	111(a)–(c)
15e	4106	77	111(d)
15f	4107	91–95	Omitted
15g	4108	96	See 3021
15h	4109	97	Omitted
15i	4110	101	3402, 3403
15j	4111	102	3404
15k	4112	103	3405
15*l*	4113	104	Omitted
15m	4114	111	3404
15n	4115	112–116	Omitted
16	5201	121–124	Omitted
16a	5202	125	3301

92

SECTION H.   FEDERAL LEGISLATION: RESEARCH PROCEDURE

1. Public Laws in Force

To determine whether there are any *Code* sections on any given topic, the following procedures may be used:

a. *Index Method.* Check first the general index to one of the sets of the *Code.* As both *U.S.C.A.* and *U.S.C.S.* have more current indexes, it is usually better to start with either of these rather than the official *U.S.C.* The index will lead to the *Code* Title under which the subject being researched will be found. Next, check the index to the individual *Code* Title in either of the annotated editions. The individual *Code* Title indexes may provide a better guide to the subject matter of the Title than the entries located in the general index.

b. *Topic or Analytic Method.* If one is familiar with a *Code* Title that includes the topic under research, *e.g.,* bankruptcy or copyright, it may be useful to obtain the volumes covering the Title and consult the outline or "table of contents" preceding each Title. This listing will provide the headings for each section and, therefore, can narrow the research path.

c. *Definition Method.* The general indexes of all three sets of the *Code* have a main entry, "Definitions," and list under it all terms that have been defined within the *Code.* This method may be a quick entry into the *Code.* For example, if one were doing research in labor relations and wanted to determine if the term *supervisor* is defined in the *Code,* the following relevant entries would be noted in the *U.S.C.A.:*

SUPERVISOR

Labor management relations, 29 § 142.

Federal employees, 5 § 7103

Federal Service, 5 § 7101 nt, EON 11491

National Labor Relations Act, 29 § 152.

Similar information can be found in the *U.S.C.* and the *U.S.C.S.*

2. Public Laws No Longer in Force

When interested in locating public laws that are no longer in force, the following indexes should be consulted:

a. Middleton G. Beaman & A.K. McNamara, *Index Analysis of the Federal Statutes, 1789–1873* (1911).

b. Walter H. McClenon & Wilfred C. Gilbert, *Index to the Federal Statutes, 1874–1931* (1933).

To locate the text of public laws no longer in force, the superseded editions of the *U.S.C.* may be consulted. As indicated, the *U.S.C.* began in 1926 and since 1934 has been published every six years with cumulative supplements issued between editions. Many law libraries keep the

superseded editions or have them in microform.   A microfiche collection of historical compilations of federal laws, *Hein's Early Federal Laws* (1992–) can be consulted to locate federal laws from the 18th and 19th centuries.

3. Private, Temporary, and Local Laws

Occasionally, there is the need to locate a private or temporary or local law that was never included in the *U.S.C.*   These laws are in the *United States Statutes at Large* and can be consulted if the date of enactment is known.   If this date is not known, it becomes more difficult to locate such laws.   The *Consolidated Index to the Statutes at Large of the United States of America from March 4, 1789 to March 3, 1903,* may be used to find laws within the time frame covered.   After that period the volumes of the *United States Statutes at Large* must be checked individually.

The *United States Code Service* has a volume, *Notes to Uncodified Laws and Treaties,* that contains interpretive notes and decisions for laws that were not classified to the *U.S.C.* or that were classified to the *U.S.C.* but subsequently eliminated.   The text of the law is not included.

4. Shepard's Citations

Shepard's United States Citations can be used to determine the history and treatment of a federal statute.   This unit of Shepard's is discussed in detail in Chapter 14.

Chapter 10

FEDERAL LEGISLATIVE HISTORIES *

SECTION A. LEGISLATIVE HISTORIES
IN LEGAL RESEARCH

A law is the means by which a legislative body expresses its intent to declare, command, or prohibit some action. In the traditional sense, a *legislative history* is the term used to designate the documents that contain the information considered by the legislature prior to deciding whether or not to enact a law. Therefore, one purpose of a legislative history is to facilitate one's understanding of the reasons behind an enactment of a law or the failure of a bill to become law. For pending legislation, researchers may need to find the current status of the proposed legislation and to locate documents generated during the progress of this legislation through Congress. Often, the status of pending legislation is important to certain groups and to their representatives to influence whether or not pending legislation becomes a public law.

Because an act of the legislature is usually prospective and is not always drafted in the most precise language, a legislative history most frequently will be used to determine the purpose of a law or to ascertain the meaning of specific language used in the law. Courts often look to certain legislative documents to determine the intent of a legislative body in passing a law or to determine the meaning of specific language used in a law.[1] Some differences of opinion exist as to the extent to which legislative histories should be used to determine the meaning of a law.[2] This conflict has led to a re-examination of legislative histories as

* Prepared for this edition by Bonnie L. Koneski–White, Associate Law Librarian, Western New England College.

[1] "But, while the clear meaning of statutory language is not to be ignored, 'words are inexact tools at best,' . . . and hence it is essential that we place the words of a statute in their proper context by resort to the legislative history." Tidewater Oil Co. v. United States, 409 U.S. 151, 157 (1972).

[2] *See, e.g.,* Schwegmann Bros. v. Calvert Distillers Corp., 341 U.S. 384, 395 (1951) (Justice Jackson in a concurring opinion indicating that "we should not go beyond Committee reports"); National Small Shipments Traffic Conference, Inc. v. Civil Aeronautics Board, 618 F.2d 819, 828 (D.C. Cir. 1980) (court warns against the manufacture of legislative histories). *But see* Schwenke v. Secretary of Interior, 720 F.2d 571, 575 (9th Cir. 1983) (reversing the lower court for failure to consider legislative history of the statute in question). *See also Conference on Statutory Interpretation: The Role of Legislative History in Judicial Interpretation: A Discussion Between Kenneth W. Starr and Judge Abner J. Mikva,* 1987 Duke L.J. 361.

a subject in law school legal research courses.[3] However, these conflicts are more academic than practical because the use of legislative histories is an essential component of contemporary litigation.

Investigation into the success or failure of a bill to become law, research to find the current status of pending legislation, and questions concerning the purpose of a law or the meaning of specific language used in legislation may be found in the language of the bill introduced into the legislature, the subsequent amendments to the bill, the reports of legislative committees to which the bill was assigned, the debates about the bill, and other documents issued in consideration of the bill.

In this chapter, legislative history will be discussed in terms of identifying which documents are pertinent to one's research, becoming familiar with finding aids that will provide citations and references to such documents, and obtaining the documents themselves.

Once the concept of what is contained in a legislative history is understood, the location and compilation of the history of a federal law

---

An increasingly vocal group of federal judges led by Justice Antonin Scalia of the Supreme Court of the United States argue that legislative history has become an unreliable guide to congressional intent because it is so often distorted by lobbyists and congressional staff members. *See, e.g.,* Charles Rothfeld, *Read Congress's Words, Not Its Mind, Judges Say,* N.Y. TIMES, Apr. 14, 1989, at B5, col. 3. *See generally* U.S. DEPARTMENT OF JUSTICE, OFFICE OF LEGAL POLICY, USING AND MISUSING LEGISLATIVE HISTORY: A RE-EVALUATION OF THE STATUS OF LEGISLATIVE HISTORY IN STATUTORY INTERPRETATION 120 (1989), which offers four basic principles intended to "reinforce certain traditional axioms of statutory analysis, consistent with original meaning jurisprudence."

For discussions of the use, misuse, abuse, or appropriateness of legislative histories in judicial decision making, *see* Anthony D'Amato, *Can Legislatures Constrain Judicial Interpretation of Statutes?,* 75 VA. L. REV. 561 (1989); George Costello, *Sources of Legislative History as Aids to Statutory Construction* (1989); Jeffrey J. Soles, *Changing the Past: The Role of Legislative History in Statutory Interpretation,* United States ex rel. Bergen v. Lawrence, 6 COOLEY L. REV. 361 (1989); George A. Costello, *Reliance on Legislative History in Interpreting Statutes,* CRS REV., Jan.–Feb. 1990, at 29; Louis Fisher, *Statutory Interpretations by Congress and the Courts,* CRS REV., Jan.–Feb. 1990, at 32; Patricia M. Wald, *The Sizzling Sleeper: The Use of Legislative History in Construing Statutes in the 1988–89 Term of the United States Supreme Court,* 39 AM. U.L. REV. 277 (1990); Nicholas S. Zeppos, *Legislative History and the Interpretation of Statutes: Toward a Fact–Finding Model of Statutory Interpretation,* 76 VA. L. REV. 1295 (1990); Leigh Ann McDonald, *The Role of Legislative History in Statutory Interpretation: A New Era After the Resignation of Justice William Brennan?* 56 MO. L. REV. 121 (1991); Stephen Breyer, *On the Uses of Legislative History in Interpreting Statutes,* 65 S. CAL. L. REV. 845 (1992); William T. Mayton, *Law Among the Pleonasms: The Futility and Aconstitutionality of Legislative History in Statutory Interpretation,* 41 EMORY L.J. 113 (1992); W. David Slawson, *Legislative History and the Need to Bring Statutory Interpretation Under the Rule of Law,* 44 STAN. L. REV. 383 (1992).

[3] *See, e.g.,* Peter C. Schanck, *An Essay on the Role of Legislative Histories in Statutory Interpretation,* 80 LAW LIBR. J. 391 (1988); J. Myron Jacobstein & Roy M. Mersky, *Congressional Intent and Legislative Histories—Analysis or Psychoanalysis?,* 82 LAW LIBR. J. 297 (1990); Peter C. Schanck, *The Only Game in Town: Contemporary Interpretive Theory, Statutory Construction, and Legislative Histories,* 82 LAW LIBR. J. 419 (1990).

becomes easier.[4] The techniques for identifying and locating legislative documents should provide assistance for all purposes.

As the term "legislative history" denotes, the true components of a legislative history are the documents that contain the words expressing the intent of the members of Congress. However, ancillary documents, such as Presidential messages, testimony of witnesses at hearings, etc., often provide assistance in accomplishing the purposes of doing a legislative history. Therefore, these sources are also included in the discussion in this chapter.

Chapter 9, Federal Legislation, should be consulted for a discussion of enacted legislation and for the sources containing those laws.

SECTION B. DOCUMENTS RELEVANT TO A FEDERAL LEGISLATIVE HISTORY

Before compiling a federal legislative history, it is necessary to be familiar with the documents that may be relevant to establishing legislative intent.[5] These documents can typically be found in federal government depository libraries and are available for purchase from the Government Printing Office.

1. Congressional Bills

Prior to its enactment as a law, a proposed piece of legislation is introduced as a bill or a joint resolution into either the House of Representatives, where it is assigned an H.R. or H.J. Res. number, or the Senate, where it is assigned either an S. or S.J. Res. number.[6] This number stays with the bill until it is passed or until the end of the Congress in which it was introduced. When a bill is amended, it is usually reprinted with the amending language, or the amendment or amendments are printed separately. The comparison of the language of the bill as introduced and its subsequent amendments, with the final language of the bill as passed (the public law), may reveal legislative intent since the insertion or deletion of language may indicate a legislative choice.[7] [See Illustrations 81–84.]

Therefore, the researcher will need to identify and obtain each of the following documents that exist for the research being done:

a. The bill as originally introduced in the House or Senate.

---

[4] This Chapter is devoted exclusively to a discussion of federal legislative histories. The documents for compiling a state legislative history are often more difficult to obtain and rarely are as extensive as those of the federal government. Chapter 11, Section G discusses state legislative histories.

[5] Because legislative histories consist primarily of documents produced during the consideration of the bill by Congress, the sources cited in Chapter 9, note 2, should be consulted.

[6] *See* Chapter 9, note 3.

[7] United States v. St. Paul M. & M. Ry. Co., 247 U.S. 310, 318 (1918). *See also* Donovan v. Hotel, Motel & Restaurant Employees and Bartenders Union, Local 19, 700 F.2d 539, 543, n.4 (9th Cir. 1983).

b.   The bill with any amendments.

c.   The bill as it passed in the originating body and as introduced into the other house.

d.   The bill as amended by the second house.

e.   The bill as it is passed by the second chamber.

f.   The bill as amended by a conference committee of the House and Senate.

g.   The public law.

2.   Committee Reports

After a bill is introduced into either the House or the Senate, it is assigned to one or more committees that have jurisdiction over the subject matter of the bill.   The committee's obligation is to consider the bill and to decide whether or not to recommend its passage.   If passage is not recommended or if no action is taken during the Congress in which the bill was introduced, the bill "dies in committee."   If the committee recommends passage, it does so in a written committee report that usually sets forth: the revised text of the bill, if any; the changes made in committee; an analysis of the intent and the content of the proposed legislation; and the rationale behind the committee's recommendation.

When the bill is approved by the house in which it was introduced, it is then sent to the other house and again assigned to an appropriate committee or committees where it receives similar consideration.[8]   When a bill is passed by both houses, but in different versions, a conference committee is convened, which consists of Representatives and Senators who are restricted to reconciling differing language in the respective versions of the bill.   The conference committee issues a conference committee report, which contains recommendations for reconciling the differences between the two bills and a statement explaining the effect of the actions.

Committee reports are usually considered the most important documents in determining the legislative intent of Congress because the reports reflect the understanding of those members of Congress closely involved in studying the subject matter of and then drafting the proposed legislation.[9]   [See Illustration 73.]

Therefore, the researcher will need to identify and obtain each of the following documents that exist for the research being done:

---

[8] After a bill passes one house, it is thereafter referred to as an *act*.   An act only becomes a law when it successfully makes its way through the entire legislative process as described in this chapter.

[9] GWENDOLYN B. FOLSOM, LEGISLATIVE HISTORY: RESEARCH FOR THE INTERPRETATION OF LAWS 33 (1972). *See also* Zuber v. Allen, 396 U.S. 168, 186 (1969); Stevenson v. J.C. Penney Co., 464 F. Supp. 945, 948–49 (N.D. Ill. 1979).

a. The reports of the committees of both houses to which the bill was assigned.

b. The report of the conference committee of the House and Senate. This report is usually issued as a House report.[10]

3. Committee Hearings

Hearings, which may be held by the committees of the House and Senate, are generally of two types. A hearing may be held to investigate matters of general concern, *e.g.,* AIDS. The second type is the most prevalent, that is, hearings related to proposed legislation. These hearings are held after a bill is assigned to a Congressional committee.

The primary function of this type of hearing is to provide committee members with information that may be useful in their consideration of the bill. Interested persons or experts on the subject of the bill may be requested to express their opinions on the bill's purpose or effect and may suggest changes or amendments to the bill. In most instances, transcripts of the hearings are published. When published, hearings contain the transcript of testimony, the questions of committee members and the answers of the witnesses, statements and exhibits submitted by interested parties, and occasionally the text of the bill that is the subject of the hearing.

It is important to remember that hearings are not held on all legislation and that not all hearings are published. In addition, hearings that are pertinent to the intent of a public law may have been held during a session of Congress prior to the one in which the law was enacted. Hearings also might have been held on proposed legislation that contains similar provisions to the law being researched. Therefore, it may be beneficial to extend the search for hearings beyond a particular session, or for legislation other than the law being researched. The last caveat is especially beneficial if either no hearings were held or if the hearings were not published for the legislation being researched.

Committee hearings are technically not part of a legislative history since they do not contain Congressional deliberations but rather the views of non-legislators of what the bill under consideration should accomplish. Often senators and members of the House of Representatives may present testimony. Therefore, hearings should be consulted when available because they frequently contain information helpful to understanding why Congress adopted or did not adopt certain language based on the testimony heard and to find the testimony of legislators.

Therefore, the researcher will need to identify and obtain each of the following documents that exist for the research being done:

[10] Under the rules of Congress, the conference report is also to be printed as a Senate report. This requirement frequently is waived by the unanimous consent of the Senate. ENACTMENT OF A LAW: PROCEDURAL STEPS IN THE LEGISLATIVE PROCESS, S. DOC. No. 20, 97th Cong., 1st Sess. (1981).

a. The hearings held by the committees to which the bill was assigned.

b. The hearings from previous Congressional sessions concerning the subject matter of the bill being researched.

c. The hearings on related bills or bills containing similar provisions that may have been held in prior Congresses.

4. Congressional Debates

Debate on the floor of the House or Senate on a bill can take place at almost any time during the legislative process, but most frequently the debate occurs after a bill has been reported out of the committee to which it was assigned.[11] During the debates, amendments may be proposed, arguments for and against the pending bill and amendments are made, and discussion and explanation of ambiguous or controversial provisions occur. Some authorities claim that floor statements of legislators on the substance of a bill under discussion are not to be considered by courts as determinative of Congressional intent.[12] The courts, however, generally do give some weight to such statements, especially when they are made by the bill's sponsors, whose stated intention is to clarify or explain the bill's purpose.[13] Such statements are published in the *Congressional Record* and are usually included as an integral part of legislative histories.[14]

Therefore, the researcher will need to identify and obtain the debates, if any, on the floor of both houses of Congress for the research being done. [See Illustration 85.]

[11] Most public laws are passed without ever being debated on the floor of Congress. Usually, only bills of great public interest receive such debate.

[12] S. & E. Contractors, Inc. v. United States, 406 U.S. 1, 13 n.9 (1972).

[13] Federal Energy Admin. v. Algonquin SNG, Inc., 426 U.S. 548, 564 (1976). *But see* State of Ohio v. United States Environmental Protection Agency, 997 F.2d 1520, 1532 (D.C. Cir. 1993).

[14] The *Congressional Record* may not truly reflect what was actually said on the floor of either house of Congress, since members have the right to correct their remarks before publication. Studies have shown that this privilege generally is not abused since the majority of revisions are syntactical or otherwise within the bounds of propriety. Prior to 1978, members of Congress were allowed to insert remarks into the *Congressional Record* that were not delivered on the floor of either house without any indication that this was the process followed. Effective March 1, 1978, Congress changed its rules to provide that statements in the *Congressional Record* were to be identified when no part of them was spoken on the floor of either house of Congress. In such instances, a *bullet* symbol (●) precedes and follows the statement. If, however, any part of a statement was delivered orally, the entire statement appears without the symbol. 124 CONG. REC. 3852 (1978). *See also* Donald J. Dunn, *Letter to the Editor*, 14 GOV'T PUBLICATIONS REV. 113 (1987) (updating a part of Michelle M. Springer, *The Congressional Record: "Substantially a Verbatim Report"?*, 13 GOV'T PUBLICATIONS REV. 371 (1986)). *Note:* Commencing with vol. 132, no. 115 of the *Congressional Record* (September 8, 1986), the House of Representatives abolished the *bullet* symbol and substituted instead the use of a different style of typeface to indicate material inserted or appended. The Senate, however, has retained the *bullet* symbol. *See* Joe Morehead, *Into the Hopper: Congress and the Congressional Record: A Magical Mystery Tour*, 13 SERIALS LIBR. 59 (1987).

5. Committee Prints

Committee prints are special studies in specific subject areas prepared for the use and reference of Congressional committees and their staffs. These publications are of a varied nature, from bibliographies, analyses of similar bills on a subject, excerpts from hearings, etc.[15]

Therefore, the researcher will need to identify and obtain those documents that may have some relation to the present legislation under consideration for the research being done.

6. Presidential or Executive Agency Documents

Occasionally, other documents are relevant to developing a legislative history but since the documents are not developed by Congress, they are not primary sources for legislative intent. These may consist of Presidential messages [16] or reports and documents of federal agencies. The President of the United States or members of an executive agency, who usually act through the President, often send proposed legislation to Congress for consideration. Presidential messages or executive agency memoranda may accompany the proposal to Congress. These documents explain the purpose and describe the President's or agency's intent of the legislation.

After a bill passes Congress, it is sent to the President. If the President signs or vetoes the legislation, the President may add a signing statement or veto message, which incorporates the President's rationale for the action taken on the legislation.

Therefore, the researcher will need to identify and obtain each of the following documents that exist for the research being done:

a. Presidential or executive agency reports accompanying proposed legislation sent to Congress by the President.

b. Presidential signing statements or veto messages.

---

[15] Often, only a limited number of committee prints, for the use of the committee members, are printed. Recently, they have become more available through the Depository Program, though indexing is often incomplete. See Chapter 9, note 2.

[16] The role of presidential signing statements in a legislative history is discussed in Frank B. Cross, *The Constitutional Legitimacy and Significance of Presidential Signing Statements,* 40 Admin. L. Rev. 209 (1988); Brad Waites, Note, *Let Me Tell You What You Mean: An Analysis of Presidential Signing Statements,* 21 GA. L. REV. 755 (1987); Kathryn M. Dressayer, Note, *The First Word: The President's Place in 'Legislative History',* 89 MICH. L. REV. 399 (1990); William D. Popkin, *Judicial Use of Presidential Legislative History: A Critique,* 66 IND. L.J. 699 (1990).

SECTION C. FEDERAL LEGISLATIVE HISTORY DOCUMENTATION

The possible documents that can result as part of the legislative process and that may be relevant to a federal legislative history are illustrated on the chart that follows.

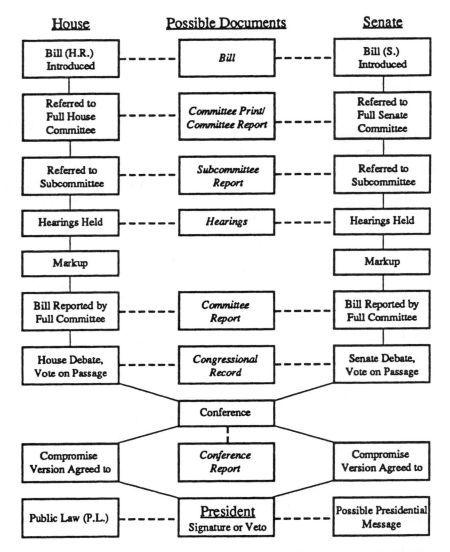

House	Possible Documents	Senate
Bill (H.R.) Introduced	*Bill*	Bill (S.) Introduced
Referred to Full House Committee	*Committee Print/ Committee Report*	Referred to Full Senate Committee
Referred to Subcommittee	*Subcommittee Report*	Referred to Subcommittee
Hearings Held	*Hearings*	Hearings Held
Markup		Markup
Bill Reported by Full Committee	*Committee Report*	Bill Reported by Full Committee
House Debate, Vote on Passage	*Congressional Record*	Senate Debate, Vote on Passage
	Conference	
Compromise Version Agreed to	*Conference Report*	Compromise Version Agreed to
Public Law (P.L.)	President Signature or Veto	Possible Presidential Message

A bill must be passed by both houses of Congress before it can be sent to the President for action. A straight line shows a simple path a bill may take in Congress. At times, a bill may also go to the Rules Committee, to more than one subcommittee, and be debated more than once. A bill may be amended as it goes through these steps. A broken line leads to possible documents that can be generated in the legislative process.

SECTION D. SOURCES FOR LOCATING COMPILED FEDERAL LEGISLATIVE HISTORIES

The process of identifying and then locating the various documents that are needed for a legislative history can be a time-consuming and laborious task. As compiled legislative histories may be available for some public laws, researchers may save considerable time and effort by ascertaining if one is available for the law involved in their research.

This section is divided into three areas. The first division, Finding Aids, lists sources that provide references to print or online publications that can contain: a listing of documents that need to be obtained for a federal legislative history; the text of some or all of the documents needed; or a combination of both. These sources do not contain either the list of the necessary documents nor the documents themselves but merely alert the researcher to other sources that include this information.

The second division of this section, Finding Aids and Documents, includes sources that contain some or all of the following: finding aids; texts of documents; or citations to documents not reproduced in the source itself.

The third division, Compiled Legislative Histories, provides general informational sources for compiled legislative histories.

1. Finding Aids

The following sources provide information on whether a compiled legislative history exists. These sources do not contain the text of the documents comprising a legislative history.

a. *Sources of Compiled Legislative Histories: A Bibliography of Government Documents, Periodical Articles, and Books.*[17] This looseleaf service provides references to other publications or online services that contain compiled legislative histories for major laws. The definition of compiled legislative history, as provided by the compiler, is the collection in one place of "either the texts of legislative documents pertaining to a statute or citations to the necessary legislative documents."[18] Coverage began with the first Congress in 1789 and is current through the 101st Congress in 1990. This checklist, which is arranged chronologically by Congress and then by Public Law number, indicates which legislative documents are contained or referenced in the publication or online service listed. Indexes are provided for author-title and for Public Law by name.

b. *Union List of Legislative Histories: 47th Congress, 1881–101st Congress, 1990.*[19] This publication, compiled by the Law Librarians'

---

[17] NANCY P. JOHNSON, SOURCES OF COMPILED LEGISLATIVE HISTORIES: A BIBLIOGRAPHY OF GOVERNMENT DOCUMENTS, PERIODICAL ARTICLES, AND BOOKS (1979) (updated periodically).

[18] *Id.* at i.

[19] (Rothman, 6th ed., 1991).

Society of the District of Columbia, provides information on compiled legislative histories commercially produced or compiled in-house by librarians in the Washington, D.C. area.

    c. *Monthly Catalog of United States Government Publications.* Legislative histories may be compiled by agencies of the federal government. Access to these publications may be through *Sources of Compiled Legislative Histories, supra,* cr through the *Monthly Catalog of United States Government Publications,* a comprehensive index to publications of the federal government.

    d. *CIS On–Line.* The *CIS Indexes* as discussed *infra,* containing the index and abstract volumes since 1970, are available through DIALOG Information Services, Inc.

2. Finding Aids and Documents

    The sources described below contain components that list, identify, or cite to documents that are generated as a bill travels through Congress and also have a component (usually microfiche) that reproduces some of the documents themselves.

    a. *Congressional Information Service, Inc. (CIS).* The publication of a set commencing in 1970 by CIS has simplified the method of compiling a federal legislative history. CIS provides indexes to locate legislation where some action has occurred after the introduction of the bill. Abstracts also are provided that give a brief synopsis of the document resulting from a specific step in the progress of the bill. If the bill is enacted as a public law, this set provides a compiled legislative history providing citations to documents comprising the legislative history. A companion microfiche component reproduces many of the documents needed to determine the intent of the public law.

    Since 1970, the CIS service is the quickest and most efficient method of locating citations to documents and many of the documents that make up a legislative history because of the frequency of publication, the thoroughness of the indexing, the citation to all relevant documents, and the microfiche component. Each of the components of the set is described below.

    (1) *CIS/Index.* This monthly component is in two parts, an abstract and an index pamphlet. The abstract pamphlet of the *CIS/Index* contains entries that briefly describe the format and scope of the hearings, reports, committee prints, and other Congressional publications such as House and Senate Documents included in the *Index.* For hearings, the abstract provides not only a synopsis of the testimony but also the name, affiliation, and perspective of the witness. The abstract pamphlet to the *CIS Index* is cumulated yearly as the *CIS Annual/Abstracts.*

    This index pamphlet contains detailed indexes by subject, title, bill, report, document, hearing, and print number. Each index entry includes an accession number that provides access to a specific publication in the abstract volume. [See Illustrations 76–77.] The index pamphlet

of the *CIS/Index* is cumulated quarterly and annually as the *CIS Annual Index* and then quadrennially.

(2) *Legislative Histories of U.S. Public Laws.* From 1970 to 1983, each CIS Annual volume contained a section on legislative histories for public laws passed during the year. Starting in 1984 this section expanded into a separate volume, *Legislative Histories of U.S. Public Laws.* Each public law is listed and citations are given to the bill number, the committee reports, hearings, the *Congressional Record,* and other documents that may be relevant to a legislative history, such as committee prints and other Congressional documents. Through the use of indexes and the annual *Legislative Histories of U.S. Public Laws,* references to public laws may be found by the name or title of a public law, by the subject matter of the law, or by bill number.

The Legislative History volumes contain histories in two formats. For laws identified as major legislation (based on the criteria that the law may be the subject of litigation in which interpretation of its provisions may be important), the citations for Congressional committee publications also include the CIS abstracts. Additional citations are provided to all relevant bills and debates. [See Illustrations 74–75.]

For the other laws, citations do not include the full abstract but instead references to the abstracts are provided. Related bills are not cited, and debate citations are limited to those provided from the slip law.

Both formats provide citations to Presidential Signing Statements or veto messages.

(3) *CIS/Microfiche Library,* 1970 to date. For bills that have become public laws, this component provides a microfiche reprint of the bills, hearings, reports, committee prints, and Congressional documents related to the enacted legislation.

(4) *Congressional Masterfile 2.* This CD–ROM product provides access to each *CIS Index, Abstract,* and *Legislative History* volume published since 1970. The *Index* and *Abstracts* are updated quarterly and the *Legislative History* component is updated annually. *Congressional Masterfile 1* is a CD–ROM product which provides access to the indexes published by CIS to locate other Congressional documents pre–1970. The CIS print indexes to hearings, the *Serial Set,* and committee prints are discussed *infra.*

b. *Public Laws—Legislative Histories on Microfiche.*[20] From the 96th Congress through the 100th Congress, this set made available the House and Senate bill as introduced; the reported House bill, Senate bill, or both; committee reports; conference reports, if any; committee prints; slip laws; and relevant legislative debate as reported in the *Congressional Record.* All enactments are indexed by subject, by Public

---

[20] This set, which ceased publication in 1988, was published by Commerce Clearing House and covered 1979–1988.

Law number, and by bill number. This set includes a compiled legislative history for every public law.

c. *GAO Legislative History Collection.* This collection, reproduced in microfiche by Information on Demand, Inc., is comprised of selected legislative histories of public laws beginning with 1921 as compiled by the General Accounting Office. Each legislative history contains: prints of all relevant bills and amendments; committee reports; debates; hearings; and related Congressional material.

The *GAO Legislative History Collection Register of Public Laws* contains a listing by Public Law number and title of all legislative histories that are a part of the collection.

d. *United States Code Congressional and Administrative News (USCCAN).* Besides the tables in the *United States Code Congressional and Administrative News,* which are discussed *infra, USCCAN* contains a finding aid list and the text of some documents relevant to a federal legislative history.

This set is published by the West Publishing Company and is issued in monthly pamphlets during each session of Congress. After each session of Congress, it is reissued in bound volumes. It contains the public laws for each session of Congress and has separate volumes for legislative histories.

Immediately before the reprint of the selected committee reports and other documents, if applicable, *USCCAN*'s legislative history section provides the researcher with: citations to all committee and conference reports; references to the dates of consideration and passage of the bill in both houses; and to the President's Signing Statement, if any. [See Illustration 73.]

Prior to the 99th Congress (1985–86), *USCCAN* usually printed only a House report or a Senate report. Starting with the 99th Congress, it expanded its coverage, usually including the House or Senate report and the conference report. It also now includes any statement that the President made upon signing the law. Recently, *USCCAN* began to include joint explanatory statements and statements by legislative leaders for laws that the editors view as major legislation. These statements often contain citations to the *Congressional Record.*

USCCAN is available in many law libraries and provides a simple method of obtaining one of the most important documents of a legislative history, the committee reports.

The committee reports and Presidential Signing Statements included in *USCCAN* also are available online through WESTLAW in the Legislative History (LH) database. Coverage for committee reports begins in 1948. Presidential Signing Statements are available from 1986.

e. *The United States Congressional Serial Set.* The *Serial Set* has been known by various titles since its inception in 1789. It is published by the Government Printing Office.

Although the *Serial Set* includes numerous publications of the federal government and even from some non-governmental organizations, the relevant publications for legislative history are the committee reports and the Presidential messages relevant to legislation.

From the 84th through the 95th Congresses, House and Senate reports on public and private bills were available in bound volumes entitled "Miscellaneous Reports" for each type of bill. Beginning with the 96th Congress, all reports are compiled and arranged in numerical sequence in bound volumes. Presidential messages can be found in the House and Senate Documents section of the *Serial Set*. Occasionally, a committee print may be classified as a House or Senate document and can be found in this set.

Congressional Information Service, Inc. publishes the *CIS US Serial Set Index,* covering 1789–1969, along with microfiche files that provide access to the documents located through the *Index.*

3. Compiled Legislative Histories

The following sources provide access to many documents needed for a legislative history. Because of the variety of publishers and online vendors that provide these sources, methods of gaining access to the documents vary with each source.

a. *Looseleaf Services, Treatises, and Other Compiled Legislative Histories.* Many looseleaf services and treatises dealing with specific areas of the law, *e.g.,* securities, tax, and labor, may contain compiled legislative histories for laws related to their subject. Other publications may have as their sole purpose the compilation of a federal legislative history. Some of these sources will be covered in *Sources of Compiled Legislative Histories, supra.*

b. *Online Sources.*

(1) *LEXIS.* This online service provides legislative histories for selected bankruptcy, estates, tax, securities, environmental, and banking statutes and for appropriation laws for various agencies. The documents included vary with each legislative history as does the Library and File where the legislative history may be found.

(2) *WESTLAW.* WESTLAW contains selective legislative histories for recent major public laws. The legislative histories were prepared by the law firm of Arnold & Porter. Some areas covered are pensions, environment, banking, bankruptcy, and securities. The documents included vary with each legislative history.

(3) LEGI–SLATE is an online service of the Washington Post Company. It includes the text of bills, committee reports, and the issues of the *Congressional Record* from the current Congress.

Supplementary information is provided, including citations to articles discussing a bill in selected commercial publications, such as the *Washington Post.*

SECTION E.   HOW TO IDENTIFY/FIND CITATIONS TO DOCUMENTS RELEVANT TO A FEDERAL LEGISLATIVE HISTORY

Frequently, a legislative history has to be compiled during the course of one's research. This may be necessary because the sources described in Section C are not available, or because the public law in question does not have a previously-compiled history. As mentioned previously, it may be necessary to examine Congressional documents for a bill considered by Congress but not enacted into a public law, or to track pending legislation.

The first step in this process is to obtain a list of documents related to the public law, the legislation that was not enacted, or the pending bill.

The sources described below will provide information, references, or citations to the documents generated during the bill's progress.

1.   Slip Laws/United States Statutes at Large

Since 1975, at the end of each slip law there is a legislative history summary, which provides citations to the bill that became the public law, to the committee reports, to the dates of consideration and passage of the bill by both houses of Congress, and to Presidential statements, if any. Although the volume number of the *Congressional Record* is provided for dates of consideration and passage of the bill, there are no page references. When the slip laws are compiled as the *United States Statutes at Large* this information is retained. [See Illustration 84.]

From 1963 to 1974, the *United States Statutes at Large* contains a Guide to Legislative History of Bills Enacted into Public Law, which includes the same references now provided at the end of the slip law, except that references to Presidential statements began to be included in 1971 for the 91st Congress, 2d Session.

Each slip law contains the bill number that was enacted into the specific public law reprinted in this format. Since the 58th Congress in 1903, each public law reprinted in the *United States Statutes at Large* gives the bill number that became the public law.[21] [See Illustration 83.]

The slip laws and *United States Statutes at Large* provide information for bills that have become public laws.

2.   United States Code Congressional and Administrative News (USCCAN)

The monthly pamphlets of *USCCAN* contain a Legislative History Table that provides information on bills that have become public laws. The tables are cumulated in the annual bound volume. The Table, which is arranged by Public Law number, provides the citation to the *United States Statutes at Large,* the bill number, citations to the commit-

---

[21] Bill numbers for laws passed prior to 1903 may be located in EUGENE NABORS, LEGISLATIVE REFERENCE CHECKLIST: THE KEY TO LEGISLATIVE HISTORIES FROM 1789–1903 (1982).

tee reports, and references to dates of consideration and passage of the bill. Beginning with the 1992 volumes, the dates of consideration of bills were eliminated. The information for committee reports includes the Committee report number and an abbreviated reference to the committees of the House and Senate, and the conference committee, if any. For dates of consideration and passage of the bill, the volume of the *Congressional Record* is provided along with the dates when the House and Senate took these actions.

3. Digest of Public General Bills and Resolutions

The *Digest of Public General Bills and Resolutions* has been published by the Congressional Research Service of the Library of Congress from 1936 until publication ceased with the 102nd Congress in 1990. Thus, this resource is primarily helpful for historical research. The *Digest* was issued annually in two volumes. The *Digest* is divided into three parts.

One part provides summaries of the provisions of the legislation on which some action occurred after the bill was introduced. A brief legislative history lists, as appropriate, dates reported from committee, report numbers, dates for consideration and passage, conference actions, and the date of Presidential action. This part is further divided into Public Laws and Other Measures Receiving Action. [See Illustration 79.]

The second part provides digests for bills and resolutions where no action was taken after the measure was introduced and assigned to a committee. Indexes by sponsor and co-sponsor, short title, subject, and identical bills comprise the third part.

As noted above, this publication provides information on bills enacted into public law, and those that were pending, or that were not enacted as a public law.

4. Congressional Record

This publication will be discussed in detail later in this chapter, however, there are several features that are highlighted here because of their usefulness in identifying documents that are part of a federal legislative history.

(a) *History of Bills and Resolutions.* The *History of Bills and Resolutions* is a section of the bi-weekly index to the daily edition of the *Congressional Record*. It is divided by chamber and is arranged in order by bill number. Information available in this section includes a brief digest of the legislation, the name of the sponsor, the committee to which the legislation was referred, and references to debates, committee reports, and passage. Page references are provided to the daily *Congressional Record* where the activity is reported. Although this section only covers bills acted upon during the two weeks covered by the index, coverage is complete back to the date of the bill's introduction. A cumulative "History of Bills and Resolutions" for each session of Con-

gress is a part of the annual Index to the bound set of the *Congressional Record*. [See Illustration 80.]

(b) *History of Bills Enacted into Public Law*. This table appears in the annual Daily Digest volume of the bound *Congressional Record*. It includes the same information as the History of Bills and Resolutions, with the exception of entries for the sponsor and for the debates. As the name implies, it only covers bills that have become public laws.

Both History tables in the *Congressional Record* provide citations to bill numbers. The History table in the bi-weekly index can provide information on pending bills, on bills that have not become public law, and on bills that were enacted into public law.

5. Congressional Index

This two-volume looseleaf service is published by Commerce Clearing House, Inc. (CCH) and is updated weekly while Congress is in session and for several weeks thereafter until all public bills and resolutions sent to the President have been acted upon. New volumes are issued for each Congress.

A digest provides the contents of each bill introduced in Congress. There are status tables for pending bills in the Senate and in the House. The status tables set forth actions taken on the bill and provide committee report numbers and most importantly note if hearings were held and on what date. [See Illustration 78.]

Subject and sponsor indexes are provided for bills and public laws. An Enactment—Vetoes section contains tables by Public Law number and by the name of the law. The set also contains a table of companion bills, tables of voting records of Congressional members by bill and resolution number, and a list of treaties, reorganization plans, and nominations pending.

Because of its weekly supplementation, the *Congressional Index* is an excellent source to use in obtaining information about pending legislation and for those bills that became public law. Older volumes can be consulted to gather information on bills that failed to reach the enactment stage.

6. House and Senate Calendars

The *Calendars* chronicle the activity of bills as they travel through Congress.

(a) *Calendars of the United States House of Representatives and History of Legislation*. This is the "calendar" of the House of Representatives, but it actually consists of five calendars to which House bills may be assigned. It is printed each day that the House is in session. Although the *Calendars* title refers only to the House, it serves as an index to all legislation that has been reported by the committees and acted upon by either or both chambers, with the exception of Senate resolutions not of interest to the House and special House reports.

Each issue of the *Calendar* is cumulative. A subject index for both House and Senate legislation that have been reported by the committees and acted upon by either or both of the chambers is printed in the *Calendar* on the first legislative day of the week that the House is in session. It does not list hearings and debates comprehensively.

The section of this *Calendar* entitled "History of Bills and Resolutions: Numerical Order of Bills and Resolutions Which Have Been Reported to or Considered by Either or Both Houses," divides the pending legislation by chamber and then again by the form of legislation. It provides the current status and legislative history of all activity on each piece of legislation on which some action has been taken. Information on hearings is not provided. It is arranged by bill or resolution number.

(b) *Senate Calendar of Business.* This *Calendar* is less useful in tracing the current status of Senate legislation. It does not cumulate and has no index. However, a separate section entitled "General Orders" covers all legislation by bill number, title, and report number.

These sources provide bill numbers and can be used to trace action on pending legislation on public laws and on bills that did not become public laws.

7. House and Senate Journals

The *Journals,* unlike the *Congressional Record,* are constitutionally mandated and as such are the official documents for the proceedings of Congress. Both *Journals* are published at the end of each session; they have subject indexes and "History of Bills and Resolutions" actions.

SECTION F.   ILLUSTRATIONS: IDENTIFYING DOCUMENTS

Compiling legislative history for S.2516, 101st Cong., 2d Sess.

[Illustration 73]

PAGE FROM 1990 USCCAN LEGISLATIVE HISTORY VOLUME

FOREIGN DIRECT INVESTMENT AND INTERNATIONAL FINANCIAL DATA IMPROVEMENTS ACT OF 1990

P.L. 101–533, see page 104 Stat. 2344

———→ DATES OF CONSIDERATION AND PASSAGE

Senate: October 18, 1990 House: October 23, 1990

——→ Senate Report (Commerce, Science, and Transportation Committee) No. 101–443, Aug. 30, 1990
[To accompany S. 2516]

——→ House Report (Foreign Affairs Committee) No. 101–855(I), Oct. 12, 1990
[To accompany H.R. 4520]

——→ House Report (Energy and Commerce Committee) No. 101–855(II), Oct. 17, 1990
[To accompany H.R. 4520]

Cong. Record Vol. 136 (1990)

The Senate bill was passed in lieu of the House bill. | *The Senate Report (this page) is set out below, and the President's Signing Statement (page 3335-1) follows.*

SENATE REPORT NO. 101–443

[page 1]

The Committee on Commerce, Science, and Transportation, to which was referred the bill (S. 2516) to augment and improve the quality of international data compiled by the Bureau of Economic

---

Legislative Histories are in a separate section or volume in *USCCAN*. This is the first page of the legislative history for Pub. L. No. 101-533. Notice how at the top of the page, reference is made to Committee Reports and to the Dates of Consideration and Passage.

While *USCCAN* is useful and widely available, it does not set forth the texts of all the documents of a legislative history. *USCCAN* reprints the House or Senate report and the Conference report, if any. Since 1986, it includes the text of Presidential Signing Statements.

---

access will improve the accuracy and analysis of BEA's reports to the public and to Congress on foreign direct investment in the United States. In addition, the bill requires BEA to submit a report on foreign investment to the Committee on Foreign Investment in the United States (CFIUS) upon request. This data exchange will ensure a more thorough and informed analysis by CFIUS of the impact of certain foreign takeovers.

3331

[Illustration 74]

PAGE FROM 1990 CIS/ANNUAL LEGISLATIVE HISTORIES VOLUME

Public Law 101-533   **104 Stat. 2344**

Foreign Direct Investment and International Financial Data Improvements Act of 1990

November 7, 1990

Public Law

1.1   Public Law 101-533, approved Nov. 7, 1990. (S. 2516)

③

b. Require the Department of Commerce to issue an annual report on foreign direct investment in the U.S., and authorize a GAO critique of the report.

c. Increase penalties for unlawful access to or disclosure of confidential business information provided to Federal statistical agencies or collect-

"To augmer the Bureau Trade in Se establishme for other pu Requires th reign direct report.
Authorizes the Bureau
Increases ci ment and T for unlawfu provided to Internation

This the first page of CIS Legislative History for Pub. L. No. 101–533. It is important to note that CIS does not reproduce in full the various documents that are part of a legislative history. Rather, it gives only abstracts with full citations to the actual documents. But it is most useful, as it cites all relevant Congressional documents for each public law.

CIS gives the following information, either in abstract or citation to:

1. all House, Senate, and conference reports issued in reference to the enacted public law;

2. other committee reports that may have been issued that are relevant to the public law;

3. the bill that was enacted and companion bills; and

4. debates on bills in the *Congressional Record.*

101st Col

①

2.1   S. Rpt. 101-443 on S. 2516, "International Data Improvement Act of 1990," Aug. 30, 1990.

(CIS90:S263-38   ii+8 p.)
(Y1.1/5:101-443.)

Recommends passage with amendments of S. 2516, the International Data Improvement Act of 1990, to amend the International Investment and Trade in Services Survey Act to allow the Bureau of Economic Analysis access to Bureau of Census information on foreign direct investment in the U.S.

②

2.2   H. Rpt. 101-855, pt. 1 on H.R. 4520, "Foreign Direct Investment and International Financial Data Improvements Act of 1990," Oct. 12, 1990.

(CIS90:H383-7   15 p.)
(Y1.1/8:101-855/pt.1.)

Recommends passage, with an amendment in the nature of a substitute, of H.R. 4520, the Foreign Direct Investment and International Financial Data Improvements Act of 1990, to amend the International Investment and Trade in Services Survey Act (ITTSSA) to improve the capability of the Bureau of Economic Analysis (BEA) to coordinate and analyze data on foreign direct investment in the U.S. and its impact on the economy.
Includes provisions to:
a. Allow BEA to exchange information with the Bureau of Census and BLS on foreign direct investment in the U.S.

P.L. 101-533 Debate ◄── ④

133 Congressional Record
100th Congress, 1st Session - 1987

4.1   Apr. 30, House consideration and rejection of the Lent amendment to H.R. 3.

134 Congressional Record
100th Congress, 2nd Session - 1988

4.2   Oct. 5, House consideration and passage of H.R. 5410.

136 Congressional Record
101st Congress, 2nd Session - 1990

4.3   Oct. 18, Senate consideration and passage of S. 2516.

4.4   Oct. 23, House consideration and passage of S. 2516.

[Illustration 75]

PAGE FROM 1990 CIS/ANNUAL LEGISLATIVE HISTORIES VOLUME

Public Law 101-533   Item 5.1

① ➤ **P.L. 101-533 Hearings**   ② ➤ **P.L. 101-533 Miscellaneous**

99th Congress

5.1   "Disclosure of Foreign Investment in the U.S.," hearings before the Subcommittee on Telecommunications, Consumer Protection, and Finance, House Energy and Commerce Committee, May 8, 1986.

(CIS87:H361-22   iii+364 p.)
(Y4.En2/3:99-125.)

100th Congress

5.2   "Federal Collection of Information on Foreign Investment in the U.S.," hearings before the Senate Commerce, Science, and Transportation Committee, Mar. 24, 1988.

(CIS88:S261-48   iii+148 p.)
(Y4.C73/7:S.hrg.100-650.)

5.3   "Foreign Investment in the U.S.," hearings before the Subcommittee on International Economic Policy and Trade, House Foreign Affairs Committee, Sept. 22, 1988.

8.1   Weekly Compilation of Presidential Documents, Vol. 26 (1990): Nov. 7, Presidential statement.

CIS also gives information, either in abstract or citation, to:

101st Congress

1. all hearings held on or related to the public law;

5.4   "Foreign Ir
        Senate Con
        mittee, July

2. Presidential messages; and

3. committee prints (not illustrated.)

(Y4.C73/7:S.hrg.101-336.)

5.5   Hearings on H.R. 4520 and H.R. 4608 before the Subcommittee on Commerce, Consumer Protection, and Competitiveness, House Energy and Commerce Committee, June 13, 1990. (Not available at time of publication.)

5.6   "Foreign Investment in the U.S.," hearings before the Subcommittee on Foreign Commerce and Tourism, Senate Commerce, Science, and Transportation Committee, July 19, 1990.

(CIS91:S261-2   iii+163 p.)
(Y4.C73/7:S.hrg.101-919.)

5.7   Hearings on data collection and analysis of foreign direct investment in the U.S. before the Subcommittee on International Economic Policy and Trade, House Foreign Affairs Committee, Oct. 3, 1990. (Not available at time of publication.)

[Illustration 76]

PAGE FROM 1991 CIS/INDEX

Index of Subjects and Names

Foreign relations legislation and docs, texts, S382-7

Intelligence agencies activities and covert ops, Pres notification of Congress, PL102-88

Latin Amer and Caribbean countries economic dev initiatives estab, H381-63

Latin Amer and Caribbean countries economic dev initiatives estab, Pres message, H240-1

Money laundering through financial instns, Fed regulatory and enforcement measures, H383-3

State Dept and related agencies programs, FY92-FY93 authorization, H383-4, H383-10

Trade promotion and technology dev programs, reorganization, S401-6

Foreign Bank Supervision Act
Foreign banks US activities, regulations revision, S243-5

Foreign Bank Supervision Enhancement Act
Foreign banks US activities, regulation revision, H241-92, H243-6, H243-13, H243-16, PL102-242

Foreign Broadcast Information Service
"Gorbachev's Report to the USSR Supreme Soviet, June 12, 1990", H382-14

Foreign Claims Settlement Commission
Approp, FY92, H181-36.5
Members term of office extension, H523-25

Foreign Claims Settlement Commission Amendments Act

Financial instns ops in foreign mkts, foreign govts natl treatment of US firms, negotiation and regulatory measures estab, H241-71, S241-1

Financial instns regulation revisions, H243-6, H243-13, S243-5, PL102-242

Food products imported by US Govt, fair labor standards requirement estab, H521-27

Foreign corporations controlled by US shareholders, tax on import profits, H782-39

Foreign govts procurement from US sources, barriers and US response, H401-4

Intl aviation policy issues, negotiations, and agreements, review, H641-46.4, H641-46.12

Japan anticompetitive business practices, impact on US industry; antitrust law enforcement against foreign corporations, S261-7

Japanese corp acquisition of US semiconductor mfg equipment co, Fed interagency review committee actions, S261-39

Mexico-US free trade agreement, prospects and implications, H781-10.7

Mfg technologies impact on US industry intl competitiveness, economic and Govt policy issues, J952-91

Military weapons and technology intl production and trade, OTA rpt, J952-63, J952-64

Foreign economic relations

Middle East devs, review and regional implications, H381-35.2

Military sales to Egypt, debt cancellation, H181-62.3

Military sales to Egypt, debt cancellation, Pres communic, H380-6

Panama economic sanctions status rpt, Pres message, H380-17, H380-34

UN programs, US payment of arrearages, H381-75.2

see also International debts

Foreign diplomats and missions in U.S.
Chinese students in US, alleged intimidation and harassment by Chinese diplomats, H381-52

Congressional directory, 102d Congress, list of heads of missions and consular offices, J872-4

see also Embassy security

see also Protection of foreign visitors

Foreign Direct Investment and International Financial Data Improvements Act ◄
Foreign direct investment in US, Fed data coordination improvement, H381-63, H381-70 ◄

Foreign Dredge Act
Maritime Admin programs, FY92 authorization, H563-12

Foreign economic relations
Agric programs issues and proposals, H161-35.5

Banking industry intl competitiveness issues, H241-11

In the 1991 *CIS/Index*, the Index of Subjects and Names, one can locate references under the Title of Public Law 101-533. One of these references provides the abstracts of hearings that were not available at the time of publication of the 1990 *CIS/Annual Legislative Histories* volume.

Auto parts trade deficit with Japan, S721-1.2

Bank loans to Iraq from Banca Nazionale del Lavoro Atlanta agency, Eximbank programs role, H241-81

Bank loans to Iraq from Banca Nazionale del Lavoro Atlanta agency, investigation, H241-74

Bank loans to Iraq from Banca Nazionale del Lavoro Atlanta agency, investigation; foreign bank brs and agencies in US, regulatory supervision responsibilities, H241-44

Banking industry intl competitiveness issues, H242-3

Biotechnology applications and policy issues, contractor docs, J952-84

Biotechnology applications and policy issues, OTA rpt, J952-82, J952-83

Chemical and biological weapons production and use by foreign countries, US sanctions and controls estab, H383-9, H783-22, PL102-138

Corporate income tax revenues decline, issues and impact, S361-14.2

Electronics industry intl competitiveness issues, S261-35.1

Europe economic policies and devs, implications for US trade and investments, H781-7.10

Export control programs revision, H701-27.3

promotion programs assessment and policy issues, H701-29.2, H701-29.4

Technology dev and technical info programs, extension and revision, S263-24

Uranium enrichment corp estab, S313-9

see also Multinational corporations

Foreign Corrupt Practices Act
Criminal justice laws and programs, revision, H523-12, H523-32

Foreign debts
Agric export credit to emerging democracies, program revisions, H163-18

Economic policies and trade practices worldwide, State Dept 1991 rpt, H382-3

Intl environmental issues, CRS briefing book, H382-21

Latin Amer and Caribbean countries economic dev and conservation initiatives estab, H381-39

Latin Amer and Caribbean countries economic dev initiatives estab, H241-42, H241-90, H383-6, S381-20, S381-40, S381-40.2, S383-5

Latin Amer and Caribbean countries economic dev initiatives estab, Pres message, H240-1

Latin Amer and Caribbean countries economic dev initiatives programs, FY92 approp, H181-27, H181-62.4

Mexico-US Interparliamentary Group, 31st annual meeting, background materials, H382-10

China economic reforms assessment, study papers compilation, J842-9

Def Production Act programs, extension and revision, S241-7

Eastern Europe economic devs, US policy issues, S381-42

Economic competitiveness of US, review and tax policy issues, H782-17

Economic summit meeting in Houston, issues review, J841-18

Educ and cultural exchange programs, oversight, H381-7.3

Employee health insurance costs, impact on US business intl competitiveness, J841-2

"Energy for America and World Economic Cooperation: The First, Foremost Challenge of the 1990's", H241-67

Europe and Soviet Union economic conditions and relations with US, Congressional study mission rpt, H782-41

Europe-US relations, H381-4.1

European Community mkt integration plans, product standards and testing requirements implications for US labs, H701-18

Financial instns ops in foreign mkts, foreign govts natl treatment of US firms, negotiation and regulatory measures estab, H241-71, S241-1

Financial instns ops in foreign mkts, GATT negotiations status, H241-53

[Illustration 77]

PAGE FROM 1991 CIS/ABSTRACTS

H381–68   Foreign Affairs

H381–68   FOREIGN ASSISTANCE LEGISLATION FOR FY92-FY93 (Part 1).
Feb. 6, 7, 21, 26, Mar. 12, 19, Apr. 17, 1991. 102-1.
v + 508 p. GPO $15.00
S/N 552-070-10746-1.
CIS/MF/8
•Item 1017-A; 1017-B.
°Y4.F76/1:F76/57/992-93/pt.1.
MC 91-22487. LC 91-601425.
Hearings to consider Administration FY92 authorization request for foreign assistance and Peace Corps programs.
Apr. 17 hearing was held as a roundtable discussion.
Supplementary material (p. 429-508) includes witnesses' written statements and correspondence.
H381–68.1: Feb. 6, 1991. p. 2-66, 429-453.

Statement and Discussion: Overview of EPA international environmental programs; perspectives on international environmental issues.
H381–68.7: Mar. 19, 1991. p. 281-332, 487-505.
Witness: CHENEY, Richard B., Secretary, DOD.
Statement and Discussion: Impact of changes in the Soviet Union on U.S. military strategy; views on military strategy and security issues relating to 1990 Persian Gulf War; perspectives on military assistance policies.
H381–68.8: Apr. 17, 1991. p. 333-428.
Witnesses: KURATOWSKA, Zofia, Deputy Speaker, Polish Senate.
KURIA, Gibson K., human rights activist; attorney.

H381–69.1: May 2, 1991. p. 3-60.
Witness: LEVITSKY, Melvyn, Assistant Secretary, Bureau of International Narcotics Matters, Department of State.
Statement and Discussion: Clarification of Administration proposals to revise international drug control programs; aspects of Administration international drug control policies and programs.
Insertion:
– Department of State, "Counternarcotics Andean Strategy: The Fifth Objective" cable (p. 37-60).

H381–70   FEDERAL GOVERNMENT'S DATA COLLECTION AND ANALYSIS OF FOREIGN DIRECT INVESTMENT IN THE U.S.

> By using the accession number in the *CIS/Index*, one can refer to the CIS/Abstract volume to find a synopsis of hearings held on Public Law 101–533. Notice that it provides the (1) names of the witness and (2) internal page references to the hearings where the specific witness' testimony may be located.

tions and U.S. foreign policy concerns; perspectives on U.S. foreign policy issues involving various countries.

H381–68.2: Feb. 7, 1991. p. 67-138.
Witness: ROSKENS, Ronald W., Administrator, AID.
Statement and Discussion: Need to refocus concept of foreign aid to establish new international partnerships better suited to post-Cold War era; explanation of AID initiatives undertaken in response to new international challenges; presentation of AID budget request for FY92; update on AID programs and activities.

H381–68.3: Feb. 21, 1991. p. 140-181, 468-486.
Witness: COVERDELL, Paul D., Director, Peace Corps.
Statement and Discussion: Overview of Peace Corps programs; explanation of Peace Corps budget request for FY92; issues relating to Peace Corps volunteer recruitment.

H381–68.4: Feb. 21, 1991. p. 181-207.
Witness: GRAY, Linda H., Executive Director, National Council of Returned Peace Corps Volunteers.
Statement and Discussion: Merits of Peace Corps programs; review of issues raised in House Government Operations Committee 1990 report recommending Peace Corps program improvements.

H381–68.5: Feb. 26, 1991. p. 209-236.
Witness: CROWDER, Richard T., Under Secretary, International Affairs and Commodity Programs, USDA.
Statement and Discussion: Explanation of USDA FY92 budget request for international food assistance programs, including P.L. 480; perspectives on food assistance needs and activities.

H381–68.6: Mar. 12, 1991. p. 239-279.
Witness: REILLY, William K., Administrator, EPA.

LOWENTHAL, Abraham F., Executive Director, Inter-American Dialogue.
MURAVCHIK, Joshua, Resident Scholar, American Enterprise Institute for Public Policy.
Statements and Discussion: Views on democratic movements in various countries; perspectives on U.S. role in promoting democracy abroad; recommendations to improve U.S. democracy promotion programs, including initiatives in Latin America; perspectives on human rights issues associated with democratic movements.
Insertion:
– Regan, Ralph E. (Yale Univ), "Interview, Gibson Kamuau Kurai: The Rule of Law in Kenya and the Status of Human Rights" Yale Journal of International Law, Vol. 16 No. 1, 1991 (p. 344-360).

H381–69   REVIEW OF THE PRESIDENT'S NARCOTICS CONTROL LEGISLATIVE REQUEST: SHOULD CERTIFICATION BE REPEALED?
May 2, 1991. 102-1.
iii + 60 p. GPO $2.00
S/N 552-070-10879-3.
CIS/MF/3
•Item 1017-A; 1017-B.
°Y4.F76/1:P92/9.
MC 91-22492. LC 91-601317.
Hearing before the Task Force on International Narcotics Control to review Administration proposals to simplify and revise international drug control programs, including proposal to effectively revoke certification process currently used to assess and report foreign governments cooperation with U.S. anti-narcotics efforts.
Supplementary material (p. 37-60) includes correspondence.

1990, the Foreign Direct Investment and International Financial Data Improvements Act of 1990 to amend the International Investment and Trade in Services Survey Act to improve Federal coordination of information on foreign investment in the U.S.
Includes transcript (p. 39) of Subcom markup session on H.R. 4520 (text, p. 40-56). Bill was favorably reported.
Supplementary material (p. 12, 27-38) includes correspondence and submitted statements.

H381–70.1: Congressional Testimony.
Witnesses: SHARP, Philip R., (Rep, D-Ind) p. 5-13.
JOHNSON, Nancy L., (Rep, R-Conn) p. 14-15.
Statements and Discussion: Support for H.R. 4520.

H381–70.2: Oct. 3, 1990. p. 15-26.
Witness: PLANT, Mark W., Deputy Under Secretary, Economic Affairs, Department of Commerce.
Statement and Discussion: Opposition to H.R. 4520; concerns about protecting the confidentiality of foreign investment data.

H381–71   U.S. INTEREST IN POST-COLD WAR LATIN AMERICA AND THE CARIBBEAN.
Feb. 19, 1991. 102-1.
iii + 82 p. GPO $2.50
S/N 552-070-10878-5.
CIS/MF/3
•Item 1017-A; 1017-B.
°Y4.F76/1:P84/2.
MC 91-22490. LC 91-601582.
Hearing before the *Subcom on Western Hemisphere Affairs* to examine recent developments in U.S. policy toward Latin America, in light of political developments in Eastern Europe and the Soviet Union and changing U.S. foreign policy objectives.

[Illustration 78]

PAGE FROM SENATE STATUS TABLE FROM CONGRESSIONAL INDEX

---

92   12-7-90   **Status of Senate Bills**   **21,053**
See also Status at pages 20,101 and 20,501.
For digest, see "Bills" and "Resolutions" Divisions.

2494
Introduced 4/23/90
Ref to S Commerce Com 4/23/90
Hrgs begun by Consumer Subcom 5/2/90
Ordered reptd w/amdts by Com 6/27/90
Amdts adopted (Voice) 10/22/90
Passed by S (Voice) 10/22/90

2498
Introduced 4/24/90
Ref to S Commerce Com 4/24/90
Ordered reptd w/o amdts by Com 5/22/90
Reptd w/o amdts, S Rept 101-324, by Com .....
.................................6/8/90

2499
Introduced 4/24/90
Ref to S Veter~~~~~~~~~~~~~~~~~
Hrgs begun by~~~~~~~~~~~~~~~~~~~~~~~~~~

Introduced ..~~~~~~~~~~~~~~~~~~~~~~~
Ref to S Comr~~~~~~~~~~~~~~~~~~~~~~~~
Commerce Co~~~~~~~~~~~~~~~~~~~~~~~~~
Ref to S Envir~~~~~~~~~~~~~~~~~~~~~~~
Ordered reptd w/o amdts by Environment Com ..
.................................9/25/90
Reptd w/o amdts, S Rept 101-532, by Environment Com 10/16/90

2513
Introduced 4/25/90
Ref to S Govt Affairs Com 4/25/90
Govt Affairs Com discharged 5/8/90
Ref to S Rules Com 5/8/90

2515
Introduced 4/25/90
Ref to S Labor Com............./......4/25/90
Hrgs begun by Com........ ....7/26/90

★ 2516
Introduced 4/25/90
Ref to S Commerce Com 4/25/90
Hrgs begun by Com..................7/19/90
Ordered reptd w/amdts by Com 7/31/90
Reptd w/amdts, S Rept 101-443, by Com .....
.................................8/30/90
Amdts adopted (Voice) 10/18/90
Passed by S (Voice) 10/18/90
Passed under suspension of rules by 2/3 vote
(Voice) 10/23/90
Signed by President.................11/7/90
Public Law 101-533 (104 Stat 2344) 11/7/90

2521
Introduced 4/25/90
Ref to S Energy Com 4/25/90
Hrgs begun by Public Lands Subcom 7/27/90
Ordered reptd w/amdts by Com 9/26/90
Reptd w/amdts, S Rept 101-538, by Com ....
.................................10/18/90

Indef postponed and H 4630 passed in lieu ......
.................................10/25/90

2527
Introduced 4/26/90
Ref to S Energy Com................4/26/90
Hrgs begun by Public Lands Subcom 7/27/90
Ordered reptd w/o amdts by Com 9/19/90
Reptd w/o amdts, S Rept 101-492, by Com .....
.................................10/3/90
Passed by S (Voice) 10/12/90
Ref to H Interior Com...............10/16/90

2530
Ref to S Finance Com 4/26/90

2532
~~~~~~~~~~~~~~~~~~~~~~~~~~~~~~~.....4/26/90
~~~~~~~~~~~~~~~~~~~~~~~~~~~~~~~.....4/26/90
~~~~~~~~~~~~~~~~~~~~~~~~~~~~~~~.....6/14/90

~~~~~~~~~~~~~~~~~~~~~~~~~~~~~~~.....4/26/90
~~~~~~~~~~~~~~~~~~~~~~~~~~~~~~~.....4/26/90
~~~~~~~~~~~~~~~~~~~~~~~~~~~~~~~ y 2/3 vote
.................................5/1/90
Signed by President.................5/4/90
Public Law 101-281 (104 Stat 164) 5/4/90

2537
Introduced 4/27/90
Ref to S Veterans Affairs Com 4/27/90
Hrgs begun by Com..................5/11/90

2539
Introduced 4/27/90
Ref to S Rules Com 4/27/90
Ordered reptd w/amdts by Com 6/13/90
Reptd w/amdts, S Rept 101-341, by Com .....
.................................6/27/90
Passed by S (Voice) 7/10/90

★ 2540
Introduced 4/27/90
Ref to S Rules Com 4/27/90
Ordered reptd w/o amdts by Com 6/13/90
Reptd w/o amdts, S Rept 101-342, by Com .....
.................................6/27/90
Passed by S (Voice) 7/10/90
Ref to H Administration; Public Works Coms....
.................................7/12/90
Passed by H in lieu of H 4463 (Voice) ..10/10/90
Sent to President 10/16/90
Signed by President.................10/24/90
Public Law 101-455 (104 Stat 1067) ...10/24/90

2542
Introduced 4/30/90
Ref to S Veterans Affairs Com 4/30/90
Hrgs begun by Com..................6/14/90

2543
Introduced 4/30/90

> This Status Table in the *Congressional Index* (CCH) for 1989–90 lists all bills introduced during the 101st Congress and gives citations to committee reports. Date references for hearings and debates are provided.

[Illustration 79]

PAGE FROM DIGEST OF PUBLIC GENERAL BILLS AND RESOLUTIONS

DIGESTS WITH HISTORY

Public Law 101-535

10-18-90	Call of calendar in Senate
10-18-90	Measure considered in Senate
10-18-90	Measure passed Senate
10-25-90	Measure enrolled in House
10-25-90	Measure enrolled in Senate
11-07-90	Measure presented to President
11-07-90	Public Law 101-532

Public Law 101-533   Approved 11/7/90; S. 2516.

Foreign Direct Investment and International Financial Data Improvements Act of 1990 - Requires the Secretary of Commerce (Secretary) to submit to specified congressional committees a report concerning the role and significance of foreign direct investment in the United States.

Authorizes the Comptroller General to review the report and submit to specified congressional committees an analysis of it with recommendations. Provides for the confidentiality of information used in such analysis.

Requires the Bureau of the Census to exchange with the Bureau of Economic Analysis of the Department of Commerce information relating to any business enterprise that operates in the United States if the Secretary determines such information is appropriate to augment and improve the quality of data collected under the International Investment and Trade in Services Survey Act.

Amends such Act to authorize the collection and use of information on direct investments owned or controlled directly by foreign governments or persons.

Requires the President to publish for the general p agencies information on foreign investment in the with tables listing certain businesses (50 percent of percent or less, of whose voting securities are owned by foreign persons).

Authorizes the President to request from the Bure ic Analysis a report on foreign investment in any giv try.

Authorizes the Bureau of the Census and the Bu Statistics, with respect to augmenting and improving data they collect, to have access to data relating to prises and international services transactions.

Requires: (1) affirmation under oath of certain reports made pursuant to the International Investment and Trade in Services Survey Act by the officer directly responsible for maintenance and compilation of such information; and (2) certification of their substantial accuracy, except when estimates are provided because accurate data are unavailable or cannot be obtained without undue burden.

Increases, and makes mandatory, the civil penalties for failure to provide information under such Act.

Sets forth requirements and penalties with respect to the confidentiality of and access to information collected under this Act.

08-30-90	Reported to Senate from the Committee on Commerce, Science, and Transportation with amendment, S. Rept. 101-443
10-19-90	Measure called up by unanimous consent in Senate
10-19-90	Measure considered in Senate
10-19-90	Measure passed Senate, amended
10-23-90	Measure called up under motion to suspend rules and pass in House
10-23-90	Measure considered in House
10-23-90	Measure passed House
10-26-90	Measure enrolled in House
10-26-90	Measure enrolled in Senate
10-30-90	Measure presented to President
11-07-90	Public Law 101-533

Public Law 101-534   Approved 11/7/90; H.R. 3911.

Attendant Allowance Adjustment Act - Increases the maximum amount the Secretary of Labor may pay for compensation for services of attendants for disabled Federal employees receiving workers' compensation.

10-15-90	Measure called up under motion to suspend rules and pass in House

10-15-90	Measure considered in House
10-15-90	Measure passed House
10-25-90	Measure called up by unanimous consent in Senate
10-25-90	Measure considered in Senate
10-25-90	Measure passed Senate, amended
10-25-90	House agreed to Senate amendment
10-30-90	Measure enrolled in House
10-31-90	Measure enrolled in Senate
10-31-90	Measure presented to President
11-07-90	Public Law 101-534

Public Law 101-535   Approved 11/8/90; H.R. 3562.

Nutrition Labeling and Education Act of 1990 - Amends the Federal Food, Drug, and Cosmetic Act (FDCA) to deem a food misbranded unless its label bears nutrition information that provides: (1) the serving size or other common household unit of measure customarily used; (2) the number of servings or other units per container; (3) the number of calories per serving and derived from total fat and saturated fat; (4) the amount of total fat, saturated fat, cholesterol, sodium, total carbohydrates, complex carbohydrates, sugars, total protein, and dietary fiber per serving or other unit; and (5) subject to conditions, vitamins, minerals or other nutrients. Authorizes the Secretary of Health and Human Services to: (1) require certain information to be highlighted; (2) require

> In the Public Law section of Actions Taken During the Congress part of the *Digest of Public General Bills and Resolutions* a substantive digest of the Public Law is included in addition to information on actions that may result in legislative history documents, except hearings.   Citations are given for committee reports.

ided for frequently consumed varieties of vegetables, fruit, and raw fish. Regulates the location, content, and manner of presentation of the information. Prohibits prosecution for minor violations if there has been substantial compliance.

Exempts from the labeling requirements food: (1) sold for immediate consumption in restaurants, or sold to restaurants for sale or use in restaurants; (2) processed and prepared primarily in a retail establishment and not for immediate consumption in the establishment; (3) including certain infant formulas; (4) which is a medical food; (5) which is customarily processed, labeled, or repacked in substantial quantities at establishments other than those where it was originally processed or packed; (6) in small packages containing no nutrition information; (7) which contains insignificant amounts of all the nutrients and does not make any claim with respect to the nutritional value of the food; (8) sold by certain small businesses, unless the label provides nutrition information or makes a nutrition claim; and (9) sold by a distributor to restaurants or certain other establishments. Allows the Secretary to require, if a food contains insignificant amounts of more than half the nutrients required to be included in the labeling, that the amounts of such nutrients be stated in a simplified form.

Requires certain vitamins and minerals to include nutrient information in their labeling as appropriate and as specified by the Secretary.

Directs the Secretary to issue regulations which: (1) require the nutrition information on labels to be conveyed in a manner which enables the public to readily observe and comprehend it and to understand its relative significance in the context of a total daily diet; (2) establish standards to define serving size or other unit of measure; (3) permit the inclusion of certain information beyond that which is required; and (4) permit single statements or ranges when there are minor variations in the nutritional value or the food is comprised of an assortment of similar foods which have variations in nutritional value.

Directs the Secretary to carry out consumer education regarding nutrition labeling.

271

[Illustration 80]

EXCERPT FROM 1990 CONGRESSIONAL RECORD BI–WEEKLY INDEX

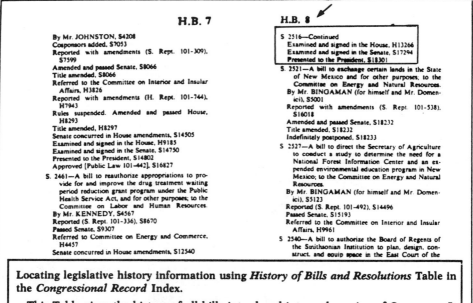

H.B. 7

By Mr. JOHNSTON, S4208
Cosponsors added, S7053
Reported with amendments (S. Rept. 101–309), S7599
Amended and passed Senate, S8066
Title amended, S8066
Referred to the Committee on Interior and Insular Affairs, H3826
Reported with amendments (H. Rept. 101–744), H7943
Rules suspended. Amended and passed House, H8293
Title amended, H8297
Senate concurred in House amendments, S14505
Examined and signed in the House, H9185
Examined and signed in the Senate, S14750
Presented to the President, S14802
Approved [Public Law 101–442], S16827

S. 2461—A bill to reauthorize appropriations to provide for and improve the drug treatment waiting period reduction grant program under the Public Health Service Act, and for other purposes; to the Committee on Labor and Human Resources.
By Mr. KENNEDY, S4567
Reported (S. Rept. 101–336), S8670
Passed Senate, S9307
Referred to Committee on Energy and Commerce, H4457
Senate concurred in House amendments, S12540

H.B. 8

S 2516—Continued
Examined and signed in the House, H13266
Examined and signed in the Senate, S17294
Presented to the President, S18301

S. 2521—A bill to exchange certain lands in the State of New Mexico and for other purposes; to the Committee on Energy and Natural Resources.
By Mr. BINGAMAN (for himself and Mr. Domenici), S5001
Reported with amendments (S. Rept. 101–538), S16018
Amended and passed Senate, S18232
Title amended, S18232
Indefinitely postponed, S18233

S 2527—A bill to direct the Secretary of Agriculture to conduct a study to determine the need for a National Forest Information Center and an expended environmental education program in New Mexico; to the Committee on Energy and Natural Resources.
By Mr. BINGAMAN (for himself and Mr. Domenici), S5123
Reported (S. Rept. 101–492), S14496
Passed Senate, S15193
Referred to the Committee on Interior and Insular Affairs, H9961

S 2540—A bill to authorize the Board of Regents of the Smithsonian Institution to plan, design, construct, and equip space in the East Court of the

---

Locating legislative history information using *History of Bills and Resolutions* Table in the *Congressional Record* Index.

This Table gives the history of all bills introduced into each session of Congress. It refers to all relevant documents, except hearings.

These Tables are located in the bound annual Index volumes of the *Congressional Record*, and in the bi-weekly index of the unbound issues. H.B. in this Illustration stand for History of Bills and Resolutions.

---

mitted in connection with sales made with a telephone, and for other purposes; to the Committee on Commerce, Science, and Transportation.
By Mr. BRYAN, S4829
Cosponsors added, S8763
Reported with amendment (S. Rept. 101–396), S10841
Amendments, S16472, S16482, S16484
Debated, S16482
Amended and passed Senate, S16488

S. 2500—A bill to amend title 23, United States Code, to control billboard advertising adjacent to interstate Federal-aid primary highways, and for other purposes; to the Committee on Commerce, Science, and Transportation.
By Mr. CHAFEE (for himself, Mr. Bentsen, Mr. Hatfield, Mr. Jeffords, Mr. Pell, Mr. Wilson, Mr. Moynihan, and Mr. Wirth), S4924
Cosponsors added, S5022, S5723, S8903, S9657
Referred to the Committee on Environment and Public Works, S10404
Reported (S. Rept. 101–532), S15410

S. 2516—A bill to augment and improve the quality of international data compiled by the Bureau of Economic Analysis under the International Investment and Trade in Services Survey Act by allowing that agency to share statistical establishment list information compiled by the Bureau of the Census and for other purposes; to the Committee on Commerce, Science, and Transportation.
By Mr. EXON (for himself and Mr. Hatch), S5001
Amendments, S6619, S16055, S16076
Cosponsors added, S7904, S9985
Reported with amendments (S. Rept. 101–443), S12725
Amended and passed Senate, S16075
Rules suspended. Amended and passed House, H11911

and Natural Resources.
By Mr. McCAIN, S5575
Reported (S. Rept. 101–310), S7599
Passed Senate, S8066
Referred to the Committee on Interior and Insular Affairs, H3826
Debated, H13045
Amendments, H13046
Committee discharged. Amended and passed House, H13050
Title amended, H13050
Senate concurs in House amendment, S17717

S 2570—A bill to amend title 5, United States Code, to provide higher rates of basic pay for Federal employees within the consolidated metropolitan statistical areas of which the District of Columbia and the city of Baltimore, MD, is a part; to the Committee on Governmental Affairs.
By Ms. MIKULSKI (for herself and Mr. Sarbanes), S5651
Amendments, S17891

S 2575—A bill to urge the Secretary of State to negotiate a ban on mineral resource activities in Antarctica, and for other purposes; to the Committee on Foreign Relations
By Mr. KERRY (for himself, Mr. Gore, and Mr. Pell), S5651
Cosponsors added, S13641
Reported (no written report), S13817
Amendments, S15419, S15430
Amended and passed Senate, S15429

S 2588—A bill to amend section 5948 of title 5, United States Code, to reauthorize physicians comparability allowances; to the Committee on Governmental Affairs.
By Mr. STEVENS (for himself, Mr. Glenn, Mr. Pryor, and Mr. Sasser), S5822
Committee discharged. Passed Senate, S14020

SECTION G. ILLUSTRATIONS: DOCUMENTS

[Illustration 81]

FIRST PAGE OF S.2516—101st CONGRESS, 2d SESSION

101st CONGRESS
2D SESSION

S. 2516

To augment and improve the quality of international data compiled by the Bureau of Economic Analysis under the International Investment and Trade in Services Survey Act by allowing that agency to share statistical establishment list information compiled by the Bureau of the Census and for other purposes.

IN THE SENATE OF THE UNITED STATES

APRIL 25 (legislative day, APRIL 18), 1990

Mr. EXON (for himself and Mr. HATCH) (by request) introduced the following bill; which was read twice and referred to the Committee on Commerce, Science, and Transportation

---

A BILL

To augment and improve the quality of international data compiled by the Bureau of Economic Analysis under the International Investment and Trade in Services Survey Act by allowing that agency to share statistical establishment list

---

From the indexes or tables shown in previous Illustrations the researcher should now have citations to (1) bill number, (2) reports, and (3) *Congressional Record*. These must all be separately obtained and examined.

This Illustration shows the first page of S.2516 as introduced during the 101st Congress, 2d Session.

---

3 SECTION 1. SHORT TITLE.

4   This Act may be cited as the "International Data

5 Improvement Act of 1990."

★(Star Print)

[Illustration 82]

SECOND PAGE OF S.2516—101st CONGRESS, 2d SESSION, AS AMENDED

2

1 *Be it enacted by the Senate and House of Representa-*

2 *tives of the United States of America in Congress assembled,*

3 **SECTION 1. SHORT TITLE.**

4 This Act may be cited as the "International Data

5 Improvement Act of 1990".

6 **SEC. 2. AMENDMENT TO THE INTERNATIONAL INVESTMENT**

7 **AND TRADE IN SERVICES SURVEY ACT.**

8 Section 4(a) of the International Investment and Trade

9 in Services Survey Act (22 U.S.C. 3103(a)) is amended by

10 striking ~~the~~ "and" at the end of paragraph (4); *by* striking the

11 ~~:~~ *period* at the end of paragraph (5) and inserting in lieu

12 thereof ~~;~~ "; *and*"; and by adding ~~a new paragraph (6) to~~

13 ~~read as follows:~~ *at the end the following new paragraph:*

14 "(6) report to Congress on *(A)* the progress of the

When a bill is amended, it is frequently reprinted with the new version indicating the new language added by the amendments in italics, and the deleted words indicated by the lines drawn through the amended language.

---

17 national Data Improvement Act of 1990 with data col-

18 lected pursuant to this Act and *(B)* the extent to

19 which such integration permits a higher level of accu-

20 racy and a greater degree of analysis on direct invest-

21 ment and United States services trade.".

[Illustration 83]

FIRST PAGE OF PUB. L. NO. 101–533 AS PRINTED IN THE UNITED STATES STATUTES AT LARGE

104 STAT. 2344   PUBLIC LAW 101-533—NOV. **7, 1990**

Public Law 101-533
101st Congress

An Act

①

Nov. 7, 1990
[S. 2516]

②

Foreign Direct
Investment and
International
Financial Data
Improvements
Act of 1990.
Business and
industry.
22 USC 3141
note.
22 USC 3141.

To augment and improve the quality of international data compiled by the Bureau of Economic Analysis under the International Investment and Trade in Services Survey Act by allowing that agency to share statistical establishment list information compiled by the Bureau of the Census, and for other purposes.

Be it enacted by the Senate and House of Representatives of the United States of America in Congress assembled,

SECTION 1. SHORT TITLE.

This Act may be cited as the "Foreign Direct Investment and International Financial Data Improvements Act of 1990".

SEC. 2. FINDINGS.

The Congress makes the following findings:

(1) The United States Government collects substantial amounts of information from foreign owned or controlled business enterprises or affiliates operating in the United States.

(2) Additional analysis and presentation of this information is desirable to assist the public debate on the issue of foreign

---

Note how the laws in the *United States Statutes at Large* refer to (1) the date the bill became law and (2) the bill which became public law.

The text of the public law as it appears here can be compared against the bill, as amended, to determine legislative intent.

---

foreign owned or controlled businesses operating within the United States with other business enterprises operating within the same industry can be accomplished under sections 2(b) and 5(c) of the International Investment and Trade in Services Survey Act, and under Executive Order Numbered 11961, without the need to collect additional information, by sharing with other authorized Government agencies the employer identification numbers maintained by the Bureau of Economic Analysis.

(5) Public disclosures of confidential business information collected by the United States Government relating to international direct investment flows could cause serious damage to the accuracy of the statistical data base.

(6) The General Accounting Office may have limited access to Government data on foreign direct investment.

22 USC 3142.   SEC. 3. REPORT BY SECRETARY OF COMMERCE.

(a) ANNUAL REPORT ON FOREIGN DIRECT INVESTMENT IN THE UNITED STATES.—Not later than 6 months after the date of the enactment of this Act, and not later than the end of each 1-year period occurring thereafter, the Secretary of Commerce shall submit to the Committee on Energy and Commerce, the Committee on Ways and Means, and the Committee on Foreign Affairs of the House of Representatives, to the Committee on Commerce, Science,

[Illustration 84]

LAST PAGE OF P.L. NO. 101–533 AS PRINTED IN THE UNITED STATES STATUTES AT LARGE

PUBLIC LAW 101–533—NOV. 7, 1990   104 STAT. 2351

Bureau of Economic Analysis and the Bureau of Labor Statistics, except that the Director shall not construe this section in a manner which would prevent the augmentation and improvement of the quality of international data collected under the International Investment and Trade in Services Survey Act.

SEC. 9. CONSTRUCTION OF THE ACT.   22 USC 3145.

(a) IN GENERAL.—Nothing in this Act or the amendments made by this Act shall be construed to require any business enterprise or any of its officers, directors, shareholders, or employees, or any other person, to provide information beyond that which is required before the enactment of this Act.

(b) IMPLEMENTATION.—All departments and agencies implementing this Act and the amendments made by this Act shall, with respect to surveys or questionnaires used in such implementation—

(1) eliminate questions that are no longer necessary,

(2) cooperate with one another in order to ensure that questions asked are consistent among the departments and agencies, and

(3) develop new questions in order to obtain more refined statistics and analyses,

consistent with the purposes of the provisions of law amended by this Act and the Paperwork Reduction Act of 1980.

SEC. 10. DEFINITIONS.   22 USC 3146.

For purposes of this Act—

(1) the terms "foreign", "direct investment", "international investment", "United States", "business enterprise", "foreign person", and "United States person" have the meanings given those terms in section 3 of the International Investment and Trade in Services Survey Act (22 U.S.C. 3102); and

(2) the term "foreign direct investment in the United States" means direct investment by foreign persons in any business enterprise that is a United States person.

Approved November 7, 1990.

Since 1975 at the end of each slip law separately-published and then cumulated in the *United States Statutes at Large* is a brief summary providing references or citations to some documents that may be relevant to the legislative history of a public law.

LEGISLATIVE HISTORY—S. 2516 (H.R. 4520):

HOUSE REPORTS: No. 101-855, Pt. 1 (Comm. on Foreign Affairs) and Pt. 2 (Comm. on Energy and Commerce), both accompanying H.R. 4520.
SENATE REPORTS: No. 101-443 (Comm. on Commerce, Science, and Transportation).
CONGRESSIONAL RECORD, Vol. 136 (1990):
    Oct. 18, considered and passed Senate.
    Oct. 23, considered and passed House.
WEEKLY COMPILATION OF PRESIDENTIAL DOCUMENTS, Vol. 26 (1990):
    Nov. 7, Presidential statement.

[Illustration 85]

PAGE FROM DEBATES ON S.2516—101st CONGRESS, 2d SESSION—CONGRESSIONAL RECORD

October 18, 1990   **CONGRESSIONAL RECORD — SENATE**   **S 16079**

plementation of the exchange of information under this Act between the Bureau of the Census and the Bureau of Economic Analysis, and shall resolve any questions on access to information, data, or methodology that may arise between the Bureau of the Census and the Bureau of Economic Analysis, except that the Secretary shall not construe this section in a manner which would prevent the augmentation and improvement of the quality of international data collected under the International Investment and Trade in Services Survey Act. The Bureau of Economic Analysis and the Bureau of the Census shall agree in writing to the data to be shared under this Act.

(2) The Director of the Office of Management and Budget shall be responsible for the implementation of the exchange of information under this Act between the Bureau of Economic Analysis and the Bureau of Labor Statistics, and shall resolve any questions on access to information, data, or methodology that may arise between the Bureau of Economic Analysis and the Bureau of Labor Statistics, except that the Director shall not construe this section in a manner which would prevent the augmentation and improvement of the quality of international data collected under the International Investment and Trade in Services Survey Act.

SEC. 8. CONSTRUCTION OF THE ACT.

(a) IN GENERAL.—Nothing in this Act or the amendments made by this Act shall be construed to require any business enterprise

1974, the seminal legislation in this field was written by the Senate Commerce Committee, Public Law 93-479, which authorized the Secretary of Commerce to conduct surveys on foreign direct and portfolio investment in the United States. In 1976, the Commerce Committee again passed legislation, Public Law 94-472, the International Investment Survey Act [Survey Act], to supplement the authority already granted to the Secretary of Commerce to collect regular and periodic information on foreign direct and portfolio investment in the United States and on U.S. investment abroad.

Again in 1978, the Commerce Committee acted on Public Law 95-381, to increase the authorization of appropriations for the Survey Act. In 1979, the committee reported legislation with an authorization for the Survey Act for fiscal years 1980 and 1981. In 1981, the committee passed legislation reauthorizing the Survey Act and directing the Secretary of Commerce to do benchmark surveys on foreign direct investment in 1980, 1987 and every 5 years thereafter.

Since 1987, the Commerce Committee has been examining the U.S. Government's collection and analysis of

islative proposals with some changes, embodied in H.R. 5 and S. 289, respectively. The most significant changes related to the limits on disclosure of individual investor information. Instead of being publicly available, the information was limited to several specific groups of people.

Senator MURKOWSKI also introduced legislation in 1989 to permit DOC's Bureau of Economic Analysis [BEA], the office within DOC that does the surveys on foreign investment, to share information with the Committee on Foreign Investment in the United States [CFIUS] and to require BEA to collect and disseminate information on foreign governments' direct investments in the United States. The Commerce Committee held hearings on these bills in July 1989.

In April 1990, Senator EXON introduced legislation to require BEA to share data with the Census Bureau [Census]. This had been an idea strongly supported in testimony before the committee over the years. This data exchange would allow BEA to report data at a more detailed level and would allow BEA to check its enterprise, or companywide, data against

---

The discussion of a pending bill by members of Congress may be useful in determining Congressional intent. The researcher should ascertain such discussion in both houses of Congress.

---

(1) eliminate questions that are no longer necessary,

(2) cooperate with one another in order to ensure that questions asked are consistent among the departments and agencies, and

(3) develop new questions in order to obtain more refined statistics and analyses, consistent with the purposes of the provisions of law amended by this Act and the Paperwork Reduction Act of 1980.

SEC. 10. DEFINITIONS.

For purposes of this Act—

(1) the terms "foreign", "director investment", "international investment", "United States", "business enterprise", "foreign person", and "United States person" have the meanings given those terms in section 3 of the International Investment and Trade in Services Survey Act (22 U.S.C. 3102); and

(2) the term "foreign direct investment in the United States" means direct investment by foreign persons in any business enterprise that is a United States person.

Mr. HOLLINGS. Mr. President, today the Senate is considering an amendment in the nature of a substitute to S. 2516, a bill reported by the Commerce Committee on August 30, 1990. I take this opportunity to review the committee's work as it relates to the Federal Government's collection of data on foreign direct investment.

The Senate Committee on Commerce, Science, and Transportation has a long record of legislative activity and oversight in the area of foreign investment in the United States. Under the able leadership of Senator INOUYE, the committee passed several bills in the 1970's and 1980's on this topic. In

Committee had passed, in 1987, an amendment offered by Congressman JOHN BRYANT, which required the filing of additional information of foreign investment with the Department of Commerce [DOC] and disclosure of investment information to the public. In July 1987, Senator HARKIN offered a similar amendment to the trade bill on the Senate floor. I opposed that amendment because the committee had not held hearings on the issue. The amendment was tabled, and the committee held hearings on the Bryant and Harkin amendments in March 1988.

Later, we faced the issue in a House-Senate conference on the trade bill. At that time, a compromise was suggested to the Bryant language—that compromise was suggested to the Bryant language—that compromise provided access by the General Accounting Office [GAO] to the information collected by DOC. I supported that compromise, but it failed because a majority of the conferees could not reach agreement. Ultimately, the Bryant amendment was dropped in conference. After the conference, the Bryant amendment was passed by the House as separate legislation. It came over to the Senate in the closing days of the 100th Congress and was referred to the Commerce Committee.

At the beginning of the 101st Congress, Congressman BRYANT and Senator HARKIN again introduced their leg-

for Senator MURKOWSKI. This amendment requires BEA to do reports on investments in particular sectors upon the request of CFIUS. If CFIUS requests such a report during a review of a takeover under the Exon-Florio amendment, embodied in section 721 of the Defense Production Act, the report must be provided within 14 days. If the request is not made within that context, it must be provided within 60 days. This amendment reflected Senator MURKOWSKI's longstanding desire that CFIUS have the benefit of BEA's analysis, when needed, in an Exon-Florio review and investigation.

At the same time that the Senate Commerce Committee was working on S. 2516, the House Energy and Commerce Committee was considering several bills pending before that committee. One bill was introduced by Congressman LENT, the companion bill to S. 2516; another bill was introduced by Congressman SHARP and HAMILTON; and a third bill was introduced by Congressman BRYANT. Congressman SHARP and LENT have been in negotiations for several weeks with the administration to come up with compromise language acceptable to the administration. H.R. 4520, the Sharp-Lent compromise, was ordered reported by the House Commerce Committee on October 2. After further talks with the administration, additional changes were made by the House For-

SECTION H. HOW TO OBTAIN THE LEGISLATIVE HISTORY DOCUMENTS

After using the sources previously described, the bills with amendments, the committee reports, the debates on the bills, and the committee hearings now have to be located and examined. Ancillary sources such as committee prints, Presidential messages, and hearings on related bills should also be located and examined. In prior sections of this chapter, sources were discussed that allow a researcher to identify which documents exist and that often provide references or citations to the documents. This section explains where the full text of these documents may be located. Also, additional sources for locating hard-to-find legislative documents are highlighted.

1. Public Bills

a. *United States Congress Public Bills and Resolutions*. This microfiche set, published by the United States Government Printing Office, contains the text of all public bills and resolutions, including amendments introduced in both houses of Congress since the 96th Congress. Access to this set is provided by the *Microfiche Users Guide/Bill Finding Aid*. It should be noted that recently the *Guide* may refer to a public bill or resolution that has not yet been provided in the microfiche set.

b. *CIS/Microfiche Library*. From 1970, CIS provides reprints of the bills that have become public laws.

c. *Public Law—Legislative Histories on Microfiche*. From 1979 through 1988, bills can be located in this collection.

d. *GAO Legislative History Collection*. For selected legislation that has become public law, reprints of relevant bills and amendments are available on microfiche.

e. *Looseleaf Services*. As previously discussed, looseleaf services for specific areas of the law may issue legislative documents, including bills as introduced and as amended, as special releases (usually as pamphlets). Other publications of the government or commercial entities may include the text of bills in their compilations.

f. *Congressional Record*. Occasionally, the text of a bill, especially if amended on the floor of either house during discussion or debate, may be printed in the *Congressional Record*. However, it should be noted that this is not a usual circumstance.

g. *Committee Reports*. Often, the bill as amended by a committee will be included in a report if the bill in fact is reported out of committee.

The committee reports reprinted in the *United States Code Congressional and Administrative News* do not include the text of the bill even if it was a part of the report reprinted in that set.

h. *Online Services.*

(1) *LEXIS.* The text of current public bills, including amendments can be found in the LEGIS, CODES, and GENFED libraries, BILLS and BLTXT (Billtext) files. Historical material is available in the same libraries, with individual designations for each Congress, *e.g.,* the bills for the 101st Congress (the first available) are in the BLT101 file.

(2) *WESTLAW.* The Congressional Quarterly's Washington Alert— Text of Congressional Bills (CQ–BILLTXT) database includes the text of all available versions of bills introduced in the 103rd Congress.

(3) *LEGI–SLATE.* The text of bills introduced in the current Congress are available through this service.

2. House, Senate, and Conference Committee Reports

a. *CIS.* Reports from 1970 to date that have been issued for bills that have become public law can be found in the *CIS Microfiche Library.*

b. *United States Code Congressional and Administrative News.* From 1941, *USCCAN* selectively reprints committee reports for public bills that became law. Beginning with the 99th Congress, the House or the Senate committee reports are reprinted as are the Conference committee reports.

c. *Serial Set.* The Committee reports are reprinted in the official series and the commercial set published by CIS.

d. *GAO Legislative Histories.* For selected laws, committee reports for bills that became public laws are available.

e. *Public Laws—Legislative Histories on Microfiche.* This set makes available Senate, House, and Conference committee reports for public laws enacted during the 96th–100th Congresses.

f. *Looseleaf Services, Treatises, and Other Compiled Legislative Histories.* Committee reports for specialized areas of legal research may be available in these sources.

g. *Congressional Record.* This publication may contain committee reports, although this is not the standard method of publication.

h. *Online Services.*

(1) *WESTLAW.* As noted previously, WESTLAW includes in its LH database since 1948 all committee reports printed in USCCAN. From 1990, the LH database contains all committee reports, as they are available, even for bills that did not become law.

(2) *LEXIS.* In the LEGIS library, CMTRPT file, House and Senate reports for legislation since 1990 are available.

(3) *LEGI–SLATE.* Committee reports for bills from the current Congress are available through this online service.

3. Congressional Debates

Although the *Congressional Record* contains much more than the debates that occur on proposed legislation, it is the primary source for the transcripts of debates and votes on pending legislation. When using the *Congressional Record,* the researcher should be acquainted with its history and pattern of publication.

a. *Predecessors to the Congressional Record.* The predecessors to the *Congressional Record* are the *Annals of Congress,* 1789–1824 (1st to 18th Cong., 1st Sess.); the *Register of Debates,* 1824–1837 (18th Cong., 2d Sess. to 25th Cong., 1st Sess.); and the *Congressional Globe,* 1833–1873 (25th Cong., 2d Sess. to 42d Cong., 2d Sess.). The early volumes of the *Congressional Globe* contain abridged versions of the proceedings of Congress. The *Congressional Record* began in 1873 with the 43d Cong., 1st Sess.

b. *Congressional Record Daily Edition.* The *Congressional Record* is published daily while either chamber is in session. It consists of four sections: the proceedings of the House of Representatives and the Senate (including debates) in separate sections; the Extension of Remarks (reprints of articles, editorials, book reviews, and tributes); and the Daily Digest (since the 80th Congress, each issue contains a "Daily Digest," which summarizes the day's proceedings, lists actions taken and laws signed by the President that day, and provides very useful committee information). [See Illustration 85.]

Each section of the daily *Congressional Record* is paginated consecutively and separately during each session of Congress. Each page in each section is preceded by the following letter prefix: S–Senate; H–House; E–Extension of Remarks; and D–Daily Digest.

An index to the *Congressional Record* is published every two weeks and provides access in a single alphabetical listing by subject, name of legislator, and title of legislation. These indexes are noncumulative.

c. *Congressional Record Permanent Edition.* A permanent, bound edition of the *Congressional Record* is slated to be published after the end of each session of Congress. Due to contract problems with printers, the paper and microfiche copies of this edition are behind schedule and are often issued in the order of printing, not always in chronological order. However, the permanent edition is generally the accepted source for most research.

The permanent edition differs from the daily edition in that it does not use the same method of pagination but rather integrates all material into one sequence. Additionally, the permanent edition does not contain the Extension of Remarks from 1955 to 1968.

The permanent edition has an index that provides access by subject, sponsor, and bill number. The "Daily Digest" section of each of the daily editions of the *Congressional Record* is cumulated in one volume of the permanent edition.

d. *Congressional Record Online.* The *Congressional Record* is available through these commercial online sources:

(1) *LEXIS.* Since 1985, the House and Senate debates and proceedings are in the GENFED and LEGIS libraries, HOUSE or SENATE files, respectively.

(2) *WESTLAW.* Coverage is available in the Congressional Record (CR) database beginning in 1985.

(3) *LEGI–SLATE.* The *Congressional Record* for the current Congress is included in this online service.

4. Hearings

The hearings relating to bills can be difficult to locate. In addition to the references provided *supra,* the following may provide information for locating reprints of the published and unpublished texts of these documents:

a. *Congressional Information Service (CIS).*

(1) Since 1970, the CIS publications have provided citations to, and a microfiche copy of the full text of, all Senate and House hearings.

(2) *CIS US Congressional Committee Hearings Index.* This *Index* provides access to published hearings from 1833 to 1969. The microfiche component provides the text of published hearings within the time frame covered by this *Index.*

(3) *CIS Index to Unpublished US Senate Committee Hearings.* The volumes of this *Index* provide coverage for Senate hearings from 1823 to 1968 that were not published. The microfiche component to the set allows access to the text of the hearings. Supplements are planned for coverage beyond 1968.

(4) *CIS Index to Unpublished US House of Representative Hearings.* Along with the microfiche portion, this *Index* enables a researcher to find the citation to an unpublished hearing and to locate the text. Coverage is from 1833 to 1946, with planned supplementation.

b. United States. Congress. Senate. Library. *Index of Congressional Committee Hearings (not confidential in character) prior to January 3, 1935 in the United States Senate Library.*

c. United States. Congress. Senate. Library. *Cumulative Index of Congressional Committee Hearings (not confidential in character) from Seventy–Fourth Congress (January 3, 1935) Through Eighty–Fifth Congress (January 3, 1959) in the United States Senate Library.*

d. United States. Congress. Senate. Library. *Shelflist of Congressional Committee Hearings (not confidential in character) in the United States Senate Library from Eighty–Sixth Congress (January 7, 1959) through Ninety–First Congress (January 2, 1971).*

e. *Congressional Hearings Calendar: An Index to Congressional Hearings by Date, Committee/Subcommittee, Chairman, and Title,* 1985

to date. The purpose of these compilations is to provide a current means to identify recently held hearings that may not yet be covered by government document indexes. It also provides different access points than *CIS*, for example, by date of hearing, by name of committee and subcommittee, and by name of the chair presiding over the hearing. This is especially helpful for multi-part hearings, making only one look-up necessary.

f. *Monthly Catalog of United States Government Publications.* This index provides references to hearings held on a particular piece of legislation.

5. Committee Prints

The sources that follow can provide access to committee prints:

a. *CIS US Congressional Committee Prints Index* and microfiche component. This multi-volume Index covers committee prints from 1830 to 1969. The microfiche component reprints these documents.

b. *CIS.* From 1970 forward, the *CIS Index and Abstracts* volumes enable the researcher to locate committee prints published since 1970. The CIS microfiche library provides reprints of the documents.

c. *Serial Set.* If a committee print is designated as a House or Senate document, it is available in the official *Serial Set* or in the CIS commercial component of this set. The commercial series is complete through 1969 and is then continued by the CIS microfiche library, *supra.*

6. Presidential Documents

The statements that the President uses when sending proposed legislation to Congress or when signing or vetoing a bill can be located in the following sources.

a. *Weekly Compilation of Presidential Documents.* The *Weekly Compilation* is issued each Monday and includes the text of many Presidential documents. Of particular importance to compilers of legislative histories are the veto messages, signing statements, messages to Congress, and a list of acts approved by the President. Each issue contains an index to all material in the previous issues for the current quarter. Semi-annual and annual cumulative indexes also are published. This publication is discussed in more detail in Chapter 12.

The *Weekly Compilation* is available through LEXIS in the GENFED and LEGIS libraries, PRESDC file from 1981.

b. *Public Papers of the Presidents of the United States.* This annual series began with the 1957 volume covering the Eisenhower administration. The series is being compiled contemporaneously and retrospectively. Prior to 1977, *Public Papers* was an edited version of the *Weekly Compilation.* However, beginning with the administration of Jimmy Carter and continuing through the volume for 1988–89, the first year of President Reagan's administration, the set includes all of the material printed in the *Weekly Compilation of Presidential Documents.*

Beginning in 1989, the first year of the administration of President Bush, Proclamations and Executive Orders are not reproduced. Rather a table refers the user to the appropriate issue of the *Federal Register* in which the documents are published.

The set contains an annual index for each year of an administration. A cumulative index for each administration is commercially published under the title *Cumulated Indexes to the Public Papers of the Presidents of the United States.* This publication is discussed in Chapter 12.

Public Papers is available through LEXIS in the GENFED and LEGIS libraries, PRESDC file from 1981.

c. *United States Code Congressional and Administrative News.* Since 1986, *USCCAN* reprints the text of Presidential Signing Statements in the legislative history volumes of the set. The Signing Statements as reprinted by *USCCAN* are available through WESTLAW in the LH database.

d. *Additional Sources.* Presidential messages can also be found in the *Congressional Record,* the House and Senate *Journals,* and in the *Serial Set* if considered as a House or Senate document.

SECTION I.   FINDING AIDS AND SOURCES FOR DOCUMENTS

This chart identifies a document; its finding aids; and sources where the document itself may be located. For specific information on the items in these categories, the reader should refer back to the narrative in this chapter.

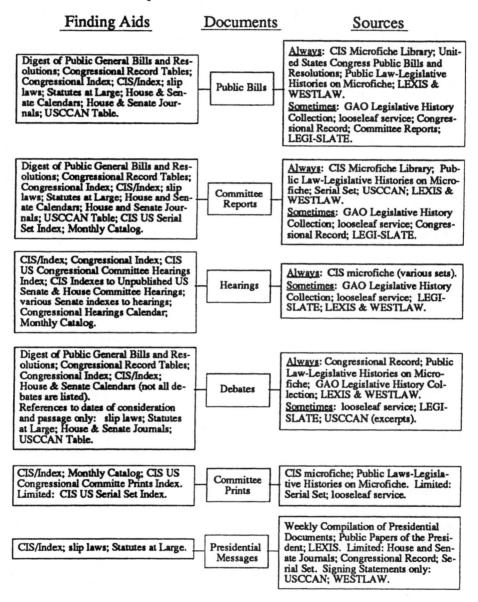

Finding Aids	Documents	Sources
Digest of Public General Bills and Resolutions; Congressional Record Tables; Congressional Index; CIS/Index; slip laws; Statutes at Large; House & Senate Calendars; House & Senate Journals; USCCAN Table.	Public Bills	Always: CIS Microfiche Library; United States Congress Public Bills and Resolutions; Public Law-Legislative Histories on Microfiche; LEXIS & WESTLAW. Sometimes: GAO Legislative History Collection; looseleaf service; Congressional Record; Committee Reports; LEGI-SLATE.
Digest of Public General Bills and Resolutions; Congressional Record Tables; Congressional Index; CIS/Index; slip laws; Statutes at Large; House and Senate Calendars; House and Senate Journals; USCCAN Table; CIS US Serial Set Index; Monthly Catalog.	Committee Reports	Always: CIS Microfiche Library; Public Law-Legislative Histories on Microfiche; Serial Set; USCCAN; LEXIS & WESTLAW. Sometimes: GAO Legislative History Collection; looseleaf service; Congressional Record; LEGI-SLATE.
CIS/Index; Congressional Index; CIS US Congressional Committee Hearings Index; CIS Indexes to Unpublished US Senate & House Committee Hearings; various Senate indexes to hearings; Congressional Hearings Calendar; Monthly Catalog.	Hearings	Always: CIS microfiche (various sets). Sometimes: GAO Legislative History Collection; looseleaf service; LEGI-SLATE; LEXIS & WESTLAW.
Digest of Public General Bills and Resolutions; Congressional Record Tables; Congressional Index; CIS/Index; House & Senate Calendars (not all debates are listed). References to dates of consideration and passage only: slip laws; Statutes at Large; House & Senate Journals; USCCAN Table.	Debates	Always: Congressional Record; Public Law-Legislative Histories on Microfiche; GAO Legislative History Collection; LEXIS & WESTLAW. Sometimes: looseleaf service; LEGI-SLATE; USCCAN (excerpts).
CIS/Index; Monthly Catalog; CIS US Congressional Committe Prints Index. Limited: CIS US Serial Set Index.	Committee Prints	CIS microfiche; Public Laws-Legislative Histories on Microfiche. Limited: Serial Set; looseleaf service.
CIS/Index; slip laws; Statutes at Large.	Presidential Messages	Weekly Compilation of Presidential Documents; Public Papers of the President; LEXIS. Limited: House and Senate Journals; Congressional Record; Serial Set. Signing Statements only: USCCAN; WESTLAW.

SECTION J.   PENDING LEGISLATION

In addition to the sources previously described, the following online sources allow researchers to track the progress of pending legislation and in most cases to identify documents generated during the bill's progress.

1. BILLCAST

BILLCAST, published by Information for Public Affairs, Inc., provides a forecast report for public bills pending in the current Congress. The report gives a brief summary of the bill's purpose and predictions of the bill's chance of passing in committee and on the floor. BILLCAST for the current Congress is available through WESTLAW in the BC database and in LEXIS in the LEGIS, CODES, and GENFED libraries, BLCAST file. Both online services also include archives for BILLCAST.

2. Bill Tracking Reports

a. *WESTLAW.* The US–BILLTRK database contains summaries and status information relating to current federal legislation. A public bill is covered through each step of the legislative process.

b. *LEXIS.* Bill tracking summaries providing an ongoing update of the status of bills pending in both houses of the current Congress are available in the LEGIS, CODES, and GENFED libraries, Billtrack file (BLTTRCK). Each summary contains a synopsis of the bill, its introduction date, committee referrals, and a complete legislative chronology including references to the *Congressional Record*.

c. *LEGI–SLATE.* In addition to the full-text documents available through this online service, LEGI–SLATE tracks legislative action on pending bills.

d. *Electronic Legislative Search System (ELSS).* This online bill tracking service, offered by Commerce Clearing House, summarizes pending legislation and provides daily information on the progress of the legislation as it proceeds through Congress.

SECTION K.   CONGRESSIONAL QUARTERLY MATERIALS

Congressional Quarterly, Inc. is a prolific publisher of materials that provide current information and reference works that deal with all branches of the federal government. Some of these publications particularly relevant to federal legislative histories are highlighted in this section.

1. Congressional Quarterly Weekly Report

This magazine of Congressional news contains summaries of major legislation and issues. Although coverage is not as complete as the sources previously described, *CQ Weekly Report* is valuable because of its extensive analysis and background discussion of laws and legislative issues.

Chapter 11

STATE LEGISLATION

The enactment, organization, and publication of federal and of state statutes are very similar. The differences that do exist among the statutes of the fifty states are mostly in nomenclature rather than substance. Each state has a state legislature and, with the exception of Nebraska, each has an upper and lower house similar to the Senate and the House of Representatives of the United States Congress. In general, the legislative process for the passage of state laws is similar to that previously described for federal laws.[1]

State legislatures meet in either annual or biennial sessions.[2] Information for individual states as to nomenclature, frequency of session, and other pertinent information on state legislatures can be obtained by consulting the latest edition of *The Book of the States*.[3]

SECTION A. SESSION LAWS

Each state publishes all of the laws passed during each session of its legislature in volumes with the generic name, *session laws*, although in some states these may have other names, such as *acts and resolves*, or *statutes*, or *laws*.[4] These include public laws, as well as private, temporary, local, and appropriation acts. The session laws are published in chronological order comparable to those in the *United States Statutes at Large* and are issued in bound form after the session is over. Several states also publish their laws in *slip* form soon after they are passed. In addition, current laws are frequently provided by private publishers in advance sheets a part of a subscription to an annotated state code.[5] [See Illustration 86.]

SECTION B. CODIFICATION OF STATE LAWS

Each volume of the session laws for a state contains the public laws passed by the legislature during an annual, biennial, or special session.

---

[1] The primary purpose of this Chapter is to present information on how to locate state statutes. It must be noted, however, that after the relevant statute has been found, it is frequently necessary to determine its proper application. For this latter purpose, see Norman Singer, STATUTES AND STATUTORY CONSTRUCTION (5th ed. 1992).

[2] COUNCIL OF STATE GOVERNMENTS, THE BOOK OF THE STATES 128 (1992–93).

[3] *Id.* at 123–208.

[4] SESSION LAWS OF AMERICAN STATES AND TERRITORIES (William S. Hein & Co., Inc.) is a comprehensive microfiche collection covering 1775 to date. It contains both operative and inoperative law. *See also infra* note 8 and accompanying text.

[5] For information pertaining to the availability of slip laws, advance legislative services, and advance annotation services, see MARY L. FISHER, GUIDE TO STATE LEGISLATIVE AND ADMINISTRATIVE MATERIALS (4th ed. 1988).

Since the laws passed are arranged chronologically in each volume, in order to facilitate access it is necessary to have the laws rearranged by title or subjects as they are in the *United States Code*. Each state does, in fact, have a set of statutes that have been extracted from the session laws and then reorganized topically for ease of use. [See Illustration 87.] The terms *revised, compiled, consolidated,* and *code* are often used indiscriminately to describe such sets of books.[6]

In some instances, compilations are accomplished under the official auspices of a state, in others by private publishers, and in some states there are both official and unofficial sets of codes.[7] Some state codes have been enacted into positive law; others are only *prima facie* evidence of the law with the positive law being in the volumes of the session laws. The important thing to note is that each state has a set of session laws and at least one current code. The set being used should be examined carefully to note its features, its method of publication, and the way it is kept up to date. Since state codes contain only public acts, the private, temporary, local, and appropriation acts must be located in the session laws.

The following features are common to many sets of state codes:

1. Constitutions

Each state code contains the constitution of the state that is currently in force, usually with annotations, as well as the text of previous constitutions. The text of the Constitution of the United States, typically unannotated, is usually included as well.

2. Tables

Each state code has tables, usually in a separate volume, that cross reference from the session law to the code section, and many will have tables that refer from the older codification to the current one. [See Illustration 88.]

---

[6] Methods of compilation differ from state to state. One state may simply reissue the session laws in chronological order but with temporary and repealed acts not included. A second may arrange the laws still in effect in a classified order but with the text kept intact as originally arranged. A third may rewrite, rearrange, and reenact the laws in a new classified order. For additional information, consult the sources *infra* note 7.

[7] For articles dealing with the codification of state laws, see Barbara C. Salken, *To Codify or Not to Codify—That Is the Questions: A Study of New York's Efforts to Enact an Evidence Code*, 58 BROOK. L. REV. 641 (1993); Kelly Kunsch, *Statutory Compilations of Washington*, 12 U. PUGET SOUND L. REV. 285 (1989); Vincent C. Henderson, *The Creation of the Arkansas Code of 1987 Annotated*, 11 U. ARK. LITTLE ROCK L.J. 21 (1988–89); Terry A. McKenzie, *The Making of a New Code: The Official Code of Georgia Annotated: Recodification in Georgia*, 18 GA. ST. B.J. 102 (1982); Dennis R. Bailey et al., Comment, *1975—A Code Odyssey, A Critical Analysis of the Alabama Recodification Process*, 10 CUMB. L. REV. 119 (1979); Diana S. Dowling, *The Creation of the Montana Code Annotated*, 40 MONT. L. REV. 1 (1979); John H. Tucker, Jr., *Tradition and Technique of Codification in the Modern World: The Louisiana Experience*, 25 LA. L. REV. 698 (1965).

3. Indexes

All sets of state codes contain a separate subject index for use in locating materials within the entire set. [See Illustration 89.] These indexes will occasionally provide the popular names of state acts. In addition, most of these sets also contain an index at the completion of each subject grouping within the set.

4. Text of Statutes

Each state code contains the public laws of a general nature and still in force, arranged by subject. [See Illustrations 87 and 90.]

5. Historical Notes

Historical references, which follow the text of the statute, provide citations to the session laws from which the statute was derived. Since many states have had several codifications of their laws over time, citations frequently are given to the present provision in a previous codification.

6. Annotations

At least one annotated code is published for each state and in some instances there are two, each by a different publisher. Some are very similar in appearance to the *U.S.C.A.* or the *U.S.C.S.*, including such information as notes of decisions, citations to law review articles, legal encyclopedias, and other research aids, and cross references to related code provisions. [See Illustration 90.] Some codes include pamphlet "advance annotation services" containing the latest topically-arranged materials prior to their incorporation into the pocket supplements.

7. Rules of Court

State codes typically contain the rules of court, which detail the procedural requirements for presenting matters before the various courts within the state. Frequently, a separate "rules" pamphlet, issued annually, accompanies the set. Court rules are discussed in Chapter 12, J. Jacobstein, R. Mersky & D. Dunn, *Fundamentals of Legal Research* (6th ed.).

SECTION C. DATABASE ACCESS TO STATE CODES

WESTLAW has reached comprehensive coverage for the annotated codes for the 50 states, the District of Columbia, and the territories, and LEXIS, likewise, is moving toward having an annotated code available online for each state. The unannotated versions for all states are already available online. These statutory sources can be searched individually or collectively for all states. Similarly, the advance legislative services, which contain the most recently-enacted legislation, are being added to these online services, and these too are nearing complete coverage. Also, an increasing number of state codes are becoming available on CD–ROM, often in conjunction with case law databases.

SECTION D. FINDING STATE LEGISLATION

1. Current State Law

When researching state legislation, one is usually attempting to ascertain if there is a current state statutory provision on a particular subject, *e.g.*, at what age may one be issued a driver's license? The first step in the research process is to examine carefully the code for the state in question and become familiar with the way the code is organized. Consulting the index should lead to the citation of a provision in the code that sets forth the current statutory law on the subject. Next, if the set is annotated, the notes of decisions and other references set forth below the statutory provision should be consulted. The method of supplementation should also be noted, *e.g.*, revised replacement volumes, pocket supplements, bound cumulative supplements, or advance pamphlets, and these sources should be checked for the most recent enactments.

At times, a state statute may become known by its popular name rather than by its actual name. Citations to acts can often be located in the "Table of Acts by Popular Names or Short Title" in the appropriate state unit of *Shepard's Citations* [See Illustration 91.] or in the national *Shepard's Acts and Cases by Popular Name*. The state units of *Shepard's Citations* can also be helpful for locating citations when only the actual name of the act is known. These sources are discussed in Chapter 14.

2. Inoperative State Law

At times the problem being researched may involve an act that has been repealed or is no longer in force. In these instances consult the code that was available when the law was in force or the session law volume that contains the text of the act as originally passed by the legislature. These sources are often available in microform.[8]

SECTION E. ILLUSTRATIONS FOR STATE LEGISLATION

86. **Page from the 1992 Vernon's Missouri Legislative Service (session law)**

87. **Page from 1993 pocket supplement to Vernon's Annotated Missouri Statutes (code)**

88. **Page from the Tables volume, Vernon's Annotated Missouri Statutes**

89. **Page from an Index volume, Massachusetts General Laws Annotated**

90. **Page from Chapter 187, Massachusetts General Laws Annotated**

91. **Page from Shepard's Missouri Citations**

---

[8] HEIN'S SUPERSEDED STATE STATUTES AND CODES (William S. Hein & Co., Inc.) is a comprehensive microfiche collection that contains volumes of annotated codes that have been replaced by later volumes in sets that are currently being published. "Superseded," as used in this collection, does not suggest that all laws in a replaced volume are inoperative; however, some of them will be. *See also supra* note 4.

[Illustration 88]

PAGE FROM THE TABLES VOLUME, VERNON'S ANNOTATED MISSOURI STATUTES

TABLE OF SESSION LAWS

LAWS 1992
Second Regular Session
SENATE BILLS

S.B. No.	Sec.	V.A.M.S. Sec.
	B	Emergency
867	A	334.044
	B	Emergency
870	1	no class
	2	no class

LAWS 1992
Second Regular Session
HOUSE BILLS

H.B. No.	Sec.	V.A.M.S. Sec.
852	A	43.200
	(A)1	43.541
878	A	268.011
		268.031
		268.041
		268.101
		268.131
		268.141
		269.010
		269.020
		269.021
		269.022
		269.023
		269.025
		269.030
		269.032

LAWS 1992
Second Regular Session
HOUSE BILLS

H.B. No.	Sec.	V.A.M.S. Sec.
	(A)2	340.202
	(A)3	340.204
	(A)4	340.206
	(A)5	340.208
	(A)6	340.210
	(A)7	340.212
	(A)8	340.214
	(A)9	340.216
	(A)10	340.218
	(A)11	340.220
	(A)12	340.222
	(A)13	340.224
	(A)14	340.226
	(A)15	340.228
	(A)16	340.230
	(A)17	340.232
	(A)18	340.234
	(A)19	340.236
	(A)20	340.238
	(A)21	340.240
	(A)22	340.244
	(A)23	340.246
	(A)24	340.248
	(A)25	340.250
	(A)26	340.252

> When only a citation to a state session law is available, a transfer table, usually included in a volume of the state's codification, must be consulted to locate where a particular section of a session law is within the state's code. For example, this Illustration shows that House Bill (H.B.) No. 852 is incorporated into Section 43.200 of *Vernon's Annotated Missouri Statutes (V.A.M.S.)*.
>
> Sometimes an individual session law may deal with several different matters as does H.B. 878 also shown in this table. In these instances, notice how the session law may be incorporated into several sections of the code.

	269.140
	269.145
	269.150
	269.160
	269.170
	269.200
	269.210
	269.220
	340.010 Rep.
	340.020 Rep.
	340.030 Rep.
	340.060 Rep.
	340.080 Rep.
	340.120 Rep.
	340.130 Rep.
	340.140 Rep.
	340.141 Rep.
	340.142 Rep.
	340.145 Rep.
	340.150 Rep.
	340.160 Rep.
	340.170 Rep.
	340.180 Rep.
(A)1	340.200

(A)39	340.278
(A)40	340.280
(A)41	340.282
(A)42	340.284
(A)43	340.286
(A)44	340.288
(A)45	340.290
(A)46	340.292
(A)47	340.294
(A)48	340.296
(A)49	340.298
(A)50	340.300
(A)51	340.302
(A)52	340.304
(A)53	340.306
(A)54	340.308
(A)55	340.310
(A)56	340.312
(A)57	340.314
(A)58	340.316
(A)59	340.318
(A)60	340.320
(A)61	340.322
(A)62	340.324

[Illustration 89]

PAGE FROM AN INDEX VOLUME, MASSACHUSETTS GENERAL LAWS ANNOTATED

EASEMENTS

EASEMENTS—Cont'd

Low-level radioactive waste management, site selection, 111H § 23

Massachusetts bay transportation authority, 161A § 1 et seq.

Massachusetts turnpike, acquisition, 81 App. § 1–7

Natural gas pipe line companies, eminent domain, requisites, 164 § 75C

Nominal damages for disturbing, allowance of costs, 187 § 4

Notice,
  Disturbance of easement, 187 § 4
  Herbicide spraying by public utilities, 132B § 6B
  Prevent acquisition of, 187 § 3

Posting notice preventing acquisition of easement, 187 §§ 3, 4

Prescription, 187 § 2

Preservation restrictions, 184 § 31 et seq.

Prevention of easements by notice, 187 §§ 3, 4

Private ways, public utilities, 187 § 5

Public Utilities, this index

Quieting title, 240 § 1

Discharge of mortgages, 240 § 15

EASEMENTS—Cont'd

Time, acquisition by prescription, twenty year use, 187 § 2

Trails, construction and maintenance by department of natural resources, 132 § 38A

Turnarounds, way not connected with another way, subdivision control law, 41 § 81Q

Urban renewal projects, 121B § 23

Use, light and air, 187 § 1

Use for twenty years, acquisition by prescription, 187 § 2

Water companies,
  Authority to acquire, 165 § 4B
  Private ways, 187 § 5

Water resources division, impoundment sites, acquisitions of lands and waters, 21 § 9A

Watershed preservation restrictions, 184 § 31 et seq.

Waterworks, lands no longer needed, 40 § 15B

Windows, light and air, acquisition by use, 187 § 1

When research involves locating a statute, the search is started in the index volume of the state code.

Assume the problem under research is whether a property owner in Massachusetts can gain an easement to light and air through the use of windows.

This Illustration shows how the relevant statute is located in the *Massachusetts General Laws Annotated* at Chapter 187, § 1.

Registration, examination of due, fee, 262 § 39

Registry of deeds, notice to prevent acquisition of easement, 187 § 3

Sewers and drains,
  Abandonment, 83 § 4
  Construction and maintenance, 83 § 1

Solar energy, 187 § 1A

Solid waste disposal, 16 § 19

State forests,
  Public utilities, etc., 132 § 34A
  Trails, 132 § 38

State highways. Highways and Streets, this index

State recreation areas, public utilities, 132A § 3

State tidelands, access, scuba and skin diving, 91 § 10D

Subdivision Control Law, turnaround, termination, 41 § 81Q

Superior court actions, costs, 261 § 4

Tax deed, conveyance subject to benefit of easement, 60 § 45

Tax title subject to, 60 § 54

Telephone and telegraph companies, 166 § 37
  Herbicide spraying notices, 132B § 6B
  Private ways, 187 § 5

See, also, Cities and Towns, generally, this index

Brockton regional transit authority, 161B § 1 et seq.

Congressional districts, 57 § 1

District court, 218 § 1

Medical examiners, 38 § 1

Senatorial districts, 57 § 3

EAST BROOKFIELD, TOWN OF

See, also, Cities and Towns, generally, this index

Congressional districts, 57 § 1

District court, 218 § 1

Senatorial districts, 57 § 3

EAST LONGMEADOW, TOWN OF

See, also, Cities and Towns, generally, this index

Congressional districts, 57 § 1

District court, 218 § 1

Lower Pioneer Valley regional transit authority, 161B § 1 et seq.

Senatorial districts, 57 § 3

EAST NORFOLK, TOWN OF

District court,
  Assistant clerks, 218 § 10

[Illustration 90]

PAGE FROM CHAPTER 187, MASSACHUSETTS GENERAL LAWS ANNOTATED

TITLE TO REAL PROPERTY

After locating the citation to the statute in the Index, the section cited must be read carefully.

Always check any supplement that may be available. In this set, annual pocket supplements and advance annotation pamphlets are published.

Following the text of each section of a statute, citations are provided to: (1) historical and statutory sources; (2) articles from law reviews published in the state; (3) encyclopedias, digests, and treatises; and (4) notes of decisions from all federal and state cases and Attorney General opinions that have cited and interpreted this section of the statute.

➤ § 1. Right to light and air

Whoever erects a house or other building with windows overlooking the land of another shall not, by the mere continuance of such windows, acquire an easement of light or air so as to prevent the erection of a building on such land.

Historical and Statutory Notes ◄— ①

St.1852, c. 144.   P.S.1882, c. 122, § 1.
G.S.1860, c. 90 § 32.   R.L.1902, c. 130, § 1.

② ——➤ Law Review Commentaries

Air space utilization. (1971) 5 Suffolk U.L. Rev. 1009.
Easements of light and air over streets. (1901) 15 Harvard L.Rev. 305.

Solar access: Transferable development rights. (1978) 13 New England L.Rev. 835.

Library References ◄— ③

Easements ⊜11.
WESTLAW Topic No. 141.
C.J.S. Easements § 19.

Comments.
  Conditions and covenants, see M.P.S. vol. 14A, Simpson and Alperin, § 1431 et seq.

Damnum absque injuria, see M.P.S. vol. 14A, Simpson and Alperin, § 1683; vol. 17, Bishop, § 543.
Easement of light or air, see M.P.S. vol. 28, Park, § 290.

WESTLAW Electronic Research

See WESTLAW Electronic Research Guide following the Preface.

④ ——➤ Notes of Decisions

In general 1
Acquisition of easements 2
Deeds and conveyances 4
Injunctions 6
Intention of parties 3
Windows overlooking another's land 5

---

1. In general

One has no right to have adjacent premises remain open for the admission of light and air. In re Opinion of the Justices (1911) 94 N.E. 849, 208 Mass. 603.

2. Acquisition of easements

Easement of light and air is acquired only by express grant, by covenant, or by implication. Novello v. Caprigno (1931) 176 N.E. 809, 276 Mass. 193.

Easement of light and air can be acquired only by express grant, by covenant, or by implication where light or air is actually and absolutely necessary. Hampe v. Elia (1925) 146 N.E. 730, 251 Mass. 465.

Easement of light and air can exist only by express grant, covenant, or absolute necessity, and cannot be created by prescription. Tidd v.

608

[Illustration 91]

PAGE FROM SHEPARD'S MISSOURI CITATIONS—TABLE OF MISSOURI ACTS (POPULAR NAMES)

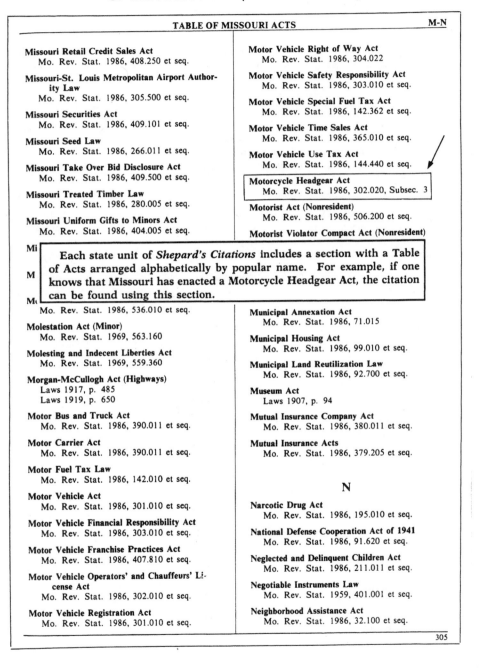

TABLE OF MISSOURI ACTS   M-N

Missouri Retail Credit Sales Act
Mo. Rev. Stat. 1986, 408.250 et seq.

Missouri-St. Louis Metropolitan Airport Author-ity Law
Mo. Rev. Stat. 1986, 305.500 et seq.

Missouri Securities Act
Mo. Rev. Stat. 1986, 409.101 et seq.

Missouri Seed Law
Mo. Rev. Stat. 1986, 266.011 et seq.

Missouri Take Over Bid Disclosure Act
Mo. Rev. Stat. 1986, 409.500 et seq.

Missouri Treated Timber Law
Mo. Rev. Stat. 1986, 280.005 et seq.

Missouri Uniform Gifts to Minors Act
Mo. Rev. Stat. 1986, 404.005 et seq.

Motor Vehicle Right of Way Act
Mo. Rev. Stat. 1986, 304.022

Motor Vehicle Safety Responsibility Act
Mo. Rev. Stat. 1986, 303.010 et seq.

Motor Vehicle Special Fuel Tax Act
Mo. Rev. Stat. 1986, 142.362 et seq.

Motor Vehicle Time Sales Act
Mo. Rev. Stat. 1986, 365.010 et seq.

Motor Vehicle Use Tax Act
Mo. Rev. Stat. 1986, 144.440 et seq.

Motorcycle Headgear Act
Mo. Rev. Stat. 1986, 302.020, Subsec. 3

Motorist Act (Nonresident)
Mo. Rev. Stat. 1986, 506.200 et seq.

Motorist Violator Compact Act (Nonresident)

> Each state unit of *Shepard's Citations* includes a section with a Table of Acts arranged alphabetically by popular name. For example, if one knows that Missouri has enacted a Motorcycle Headgear Act, the citation can be found using this section.

Mo. Rev. Stat. 1986, 536.010 et seq.

Molestation Act (Minor)
Mo. Rev. Stat. 1969, 563.160

Molesting and Indecent Liberties Act
Mo. Rev. Stat. 1969, 559.360

Morgan-McCullogh Act (Highways)
Laws 1917, p. 485
Laws 1919, p. 650

Motor Bus and Truck Act
Mo. Rev. Stat. 1986, 390.011 et seq.

Motor Carrier Act
Mo. Rev. Stat. 1986, 390.011 et seq.

Motor Fuel Tax Law
Mo. Rev. Stat. 1986, 142.010 et seq.

Motor Vehicle Act
Mo. Rev. Stat. 1986, 301.010 et seq.

Motor Vehicle Financial Responsibility Act
Mo. Rev. Stat. 1986, 303.010 et seq.

Motor Vehicle Franchise Practices Act
Mo. Rev. Stat. 1986, 407.810 et seq.

Motor Vehicle Operators' and Chauffeurs' Li-cense Act
Mo. Rev. Stat. 1986, 302.010 et seq.

Motor Vehicle Registration Act
Mo. Rev. Stat. 1986, 301.010 et seq.

Municipal Annexation Act
Mo. Rev. Stat. 1986, 71.015

Municipal Housing Act
Mo. Rev. Stat. 1986, 99.010 et seq.

Municipal Land Reutilization Law
Mo. Rev. Stat. 1986, 92.700 et seq.

Museum Act
Laws 1907, p. 94

Mutual Insurance Company Act
Mo. Rev. Stat. 1986, 380.011 et seq.

Mutual Insurance Acts
Mo. Rev. Stat. 1986, 379.205 et seq.

N

Narcotic Drug Act
Mo. Rev. Stat. 1986, 195.010 et seq.

National Defense Cooperation Act of 1941
Mo. Rev. Stat. 1986, 91.620 et seq.

Neglected and Delinquent Children Act
Mo. Rev. Stat. 1986, 211.011 et seq.

Negotiable Instruments Law
Mo. Rev. Stat. 1959, 401.001 et seq.

Neighborhood Assistance Act
Mo. Rev. Stat. 1986, 32.100 et seq.

305

SECTION F. COMPARATIVE STATE STATUTORY RESEARCH

State statutes do not have a comprehensive indexing service comparable to West's *Key Number System*. When one must compare a particular law of one state with that of another or must compare similar laws of all fifty states, it may be necessary to consult the indexes for all state codes being researched. This process can perhaps be circumvented through a well-constructed search query used in one of the CALR services. Regardless of whether the research is conducted in an online service or in hard copy, it is tedious and time-consuming. It is important to remember that the various state codes do not have a national thesaurus. Consequently, the words or concepts used in one state code may differ from those used by other states.

Naturally, if someone has already done the research for you, do not attempt to recreate the effort. The following sources provide citations to or digests of all state statutes on a particular subject.

1. Looseleaf Services

Many looseleaf services provide either full texts, digests, or tables of citations on a specific subject. For example, Commerce Clearing House's *All–State Tax Reporter* provides charts and digests of comparative tax provisions; Lawyers Cooperative Publishing's *Estate Planning* provides the text of state laws from all states on wills, trusts, and estates.

2. Martindale–Hubbell Law Directory

This annual publication, discussed more fully in Chapter 18, includes a two-volume *United States Law Digest* that provides a digest of state laws on many subjects.

3. Sources for Locating State Statutory Compilations

Treatises, legal periodical articles, and other secondary sources are often good sources for multistate comparisons of state laws. Especially helpful is the subject-arranged volume by Lynn Foster & Carol Boast, *Subject Compilations of State Laws* (1981), which covers compilations published between 1960 and summer 1979, and its various supplements: Cheryl Rae Nyberg & Carol Boast, *Subject Compilations of State Laws, 1979–1983* (1984); Cheryl Rae Nyberg, *Subject Compilations of State Laws, 1983–1985* (1986); *1985–1988* (1989); *1988–1990* (1991); *1990–1991* (1992). Effective with the *1990–1991* volume, this source became an annual publication. A cumulative index is available to the first five volumes.

Also helpful is Jon S. Schultz, *Statutes Compared: A U.S., Canadian, Multinational Research Guide to Statutes by Subject* (1991) and Richard A. Leiter, *National Survey of State Laws* (1993). This latter title allows users to make basic state-by-state comparisons of current

state laws for 42 frequently-requested and controversial legal topics in the United States.

SECTION G. STATE LEGISLATIVE HISTORIES

Attempting to compile a legislative history for a state law in a manner similar to that described in Chapter 10 for federal laws is often difficult and, at times, is impossible. As a general rule, state legislatures do not publish their debates, committee reports, or transcripts of hearings held before legislative committees. Yet the need for these sources are often just as great, since state laws can contain provisions that are vague and ambiguous.[9]

The most accessible official documents are the Senate and House Journals. These Journals usually contain only brief minutes of the proceedings and final votes on legislation.[10] A few states may have reports of a State Law Revision Commission or the reports of special committees of the legislature for selected laws. If a state has an annotated code, the notes should be carefully examined to see if reference is made to such documents.

Often, guidance for research in state legislative history is available in the state legal research guides listed in Appendix B or from librarians with extensive experience within the state. Some states maintain "working documents" or copies of legislative history materials that are only available through a visit to the state's legislative library in the capital. In many instances, however, extrinsic aids for determining legislative intent are not available and one must rely on the language of the act by using the ordinary rules of statutory construction.

---

[9] To determine those state documents that are available, see FISHER, *supra* note 5. For information on the legislative process for each state, see LYNN HELLEBUST, STATE LEGISLATIVE SOURCEBOOK: A RESOURCE GUIDE TO LEGISLATIVE INFORMATION IN THE FIFTY STATES (annual).

[10] Maine and Pennsylvania, however, have legislative journals that record actual legislative debate and parallel the *Congressional Record* in form of content. Alaska has the most comprehensive collection of legislative history materials, including online access to a majority of its documents.

Chapter 12

ADMINISTRATIVE LAW *

SECTION A. FEDERAL ADMINISTRATIVE REGULATIONS AND DECISIONS: INTRODUCTION

Administrative law has been defined as:

> [T]he law concerning the powers and procedures of administrative agencies, including especially the law governing judicial review of administrative action. An administrative agency is a governmental authority, other than a court and other than a legislative body, that affects the rights of private parties through either adjudication, rulemaking, investigating, prosecuting, negotiating, settling, or informally acting. An administrative agency may be called a commission, board, authority, bureau, office, officer, administrator, department, corporation, administration, division or agency.[1]

The principal purpose of this chapter is to explain the manner in which the regulations, rules, and adjudications of federal administrative bodies are published and how they can be located. Also discussed are Presidential documents and state administrative materials.

The power to issue regulations [2] and to adjudicate disputes is delegated to administrative bodies by Congress.[3] The increasing complexity of American society, industry, and government in the last fifty years brought about a tremendous increase in the number of administrative agencies and in the documents produced by them for publication. The normal procedure is for Congress to delegate to an administrative office or agency the power to issue rules or regulations, and in some instances the power to hear and settle disputes arising from the statute. Once an administrative body has been established, the issuance of rules or regulations is fairly simple, unlike the enactment of a statute which

---

* Revised for this edition by Bonnie L. Koneski–White, Associate Law Librarian, Western New England College School of Law.

[1] 1 KENNETH DAVIS, ADMINISTRATIVE LAW AND GOVERNMENT 6 (2d ed. 1975).

[2] A summary of all the procedures that affect the rulemaking process is contained in ADMINISTRATIVE CONFERENCE OF THE UNITED STATES, A GUIDE TO FEDERAL AGENCY RULEMAKING (2d ed. 1991).

[3] For a discussion of Congressional authority to delegate legislative power to administrative agencies, *see* 1 JACOB A. STEIN ET AL., ADMINISTRATIVE LAW § 3.03 (1988). For example, 16 U.S.C. §§ 1600–1687 (1988) deal with the nation's forest preserves and § 1613 provides that "[t]he Secretary of Agriculture shall prescribe such regulations as he determines necessary and desirable to carry out the provisions of this subchapter."

must go through the legislative process in Congress. Some agencies, such as the National Labor Relations Board, not only promulgate regulations, but are also authorized to adjudicate disputes between management and labor unions; the results of their adjudications are published in a format similar to court reports.

All regulations by administrative agencies are issued either under authority delegated to them by a federal statute or by a Presidential Executive Order.

The types of actions taken by federal agencies may be classified as: rules or regulations; orders; licenses; advisory opinions; and decisions. These are defined as follows:

(1) *Rules or regulations.* The words *rules* and *regulations* are used interchangeably. These are statements of general or particular applicability made by an agency and are designed to implement, interpret, or prescribe law or policy. Properly promulgated rules and regulations have the same legal effect as statutes.

(2) *Orders.* These are used to describe the final dispositions of any agency matters (other than rulemaking, but including licensing).

(3) *Licenses.* These include any permits, certificates, or other forms of permission.

(4) *Advisory opinions.* Although containing advice regarding contemplated action, these are not binding and serve only as authoritative interpretations of statutes and regulations.

(5) *Decisions.* Federal agencies authorized by law adjudicate controversies arising out of the violation or interpretation of statutes and administrative regulations or rules. The results of these adjudications are issued as decisions of the agencies. The adjudication function is performed by special boards of review, hearing examiners, or other officers.

SECTION B. PUBLICATION OF FEDERAL REGULATIONS: HISTORICAL BACKGROUND

Prior to 1936, no official source for publication of rules and regulations of federal agencies existed, nor indeed were such agencies required to make their rules and regulations available to the public. This resulted in much confusion, since there was no way to determine if a proposed action by a person or company was prohibited by some federal agency. In fact, in one well-known instance, the federal government prosecuted a corporation for violations of an administrative regulation. This case, *Panama Refining Co. v. Ryan,*[4] reached the Supreme Court of the United States before the Attorney General realized that the action was based on a regulation that had been revoked prior to the time the original action had begun.[5]

---

[4] 293 U.S. 388 (1935).

[5] *See* Note, *The Federal Register and the Code of Federal Regulations—A Reappraisal,* 80 HARV. L. REV. 439 (1966).

As a result of the *Panama Refining* case, in 1935 Congress passed the Federal Register Act[6] providing for the publication of the *Federal Register*. The *Federal Register* was first published in 1936. Any administrative rule or regulation that has general applicability and legal effect must be published in the *Federal Register*. The definition of a document that has "general applicability and legal effect" is as follows:

> ... [A]ny document issued under proper authority prescribing a penalty or course of conduct, conferring a right, privilege, authority, or immunity, or imposing an obligation, and relevant or applicable to the general public, members of a class, or persons in a locality, as distinguished from named individuals or organizations ....[7]

Thus, since 1936, the *Federal Register* has contained, in chronological order, every regulation having general applicability and legal effect, and amendments thereto, issued by federal agencies authorized by Congress or the President to issue rules or regulations.

Had the *Federal Register* continued year after year with no compilation of its regulations, the ability to locate regulations would have become unmanageable and researchers virtually would have been back to the point that existed at the time of the *Panama Refining* case. Fortunately, in 1937, Congress amended the Act[8] and provided for a systematic method of codification of and subject access to these regulations in a set entitled the *Code of Federal Regulations (CFR)*. The *CFR*, first published in 1939, bears the same relationship to the *Federal Register* as the *United States Code* bears to the *United States Statutes at Large*. Over the years the *CFR* has been published at different intervals and in different formats, but since 1968 the *CFR* has been issued annually, in quarterly installments.

Despite the fact that by 1937 a regular vehicle had been mandated for publication and compilation of agency rules and regulations by the Federal Register Act, as amended, the process and procedures of agency rulemaking remained an enigma to the public. In 1946, Congress remedied this situation by passing the Administrative Procedure Act,[9] which granted the public the right to participate in the rulemaking process by requiring agencies to publish notice of their proposed rulemaking in the *Federal Register* and by providing the public with the opportunity to comment on these proposed rules.

Subsequently, three additional laws were enacted to enhance the public's access to agency information. The Freedom of Information Act

---

[6] Ch. 417, 49 Stat. 500 (1935) (codified as amended at 44 U.S.C. §§ 1501–1511 (1988)).

[7] 1 C.F.R. § 1.1 (1993). It is often difficult to determine precisely which documents the government should be required to publish in the *Federal Register*. For a discussion of this problem, see Randy S. Springer, Note, *Gatekeeping and the* Federal Register: *An Analysis of the Publication Requirement of Section 552(a)(1)(D) of the Administrative Procedure Act*, 41 ADMIN. L. REV. 533 (1989).

[8] Ch. 369, 50 Stat. 304 (1937) (codified as amended at 44 U.S.C. § 1510 (1988)).

[9] Ch. 324, 60 Stat. 237 (1946) (codified as amended in scattered sections of 5 U.S.C.).

of 1966 [10] requires that agencies publish in the *Federal Register* (1) descriptions of their organizations including the agency employees from whom the public may obtain information, (2) rules of procedure and general applicability, and (3) policy statements and interpretations. The Government in the Sunshine Act of 1976 [11] requires agencies to publish in the *Federal Register* notices of most meetings.

In 1980, the Regulatory Flexibility Act [12] was passed which dictates that agencies publish in the *Federal Register* during October and April an agenda briefly detailing (1) the subject area of any rule that the agency expects to propose or promulgate which would have a significant economic impact, (2) a summary of the rules being considered, their objectives, and the legal basis for issuance, and (3) an approximate schedule for finishing action on rules for which the agency issued notices of proposed rulemaking.

SECTION C. SOURCES OF FEDERAL REGULATIONS

1. The Federal Register [13]

The *Federal Register* is published daily (except Saturday, Sunday, and official federal holidays) and its contents are required to be judicially noticed.[14] All issues in a given year constitute a single volume with consecutive pagination throughout the year. In recent years an annual volume of the *Federal Register* has exceeded 60,000 pages. In addition to the chronologically-arranged publication of the rules and regulations of federal agencies [see Illustration 101], issues of the *Federal Register* contain the following features.

a. *Contents.* At the front of each issue is a table of contents in which agencies are listed alphabetically. Under the name of each agency, the documents appearing in that issue are arranged by category and page references are provided. A database (FR–TOC), available on WESTLAW, contains the daily *Federal Register*'s table of contents. Coverage begins in January, 1993.

b. *CFR Parts Affected In This Issue.* Discussed in Section E–1–b *infra.*

c. *Presidential Documents.* Discussed in Section H *infra.*

d. *Proposed Rules.* This section contains notices of proposed issuance of rules and regulations. Its purpose is to give interested persons

---

[10] Pub. L. No. 89–487, 80 Stat. 250 (1966) (codified as amended at 5 U.S.C. § 552 (1988)).

[11] Pub. L. No. 94–409, 90 Stat. 1241 (1976) (codified as amended at 5 U.S.C. §§ 551–52, 556–57; 5 App. U.S.C. § 10; 39 U.S.C. § 410 (1988)).

[12] Pub. L. No. 96–354, 94 Stat. 1164 (1980) (codified as amended at 5 U.S.C. §§ 601–612 (1988)).

[13] Additional information on this publication is provided in OFFICE OF THE FEDERAL REGISTER, THE FEDERAL REGISTER: WHAT IT IS AND HOW TO USE IT (1992).

[14] 44 U.S.C. § 1507 (1988).

an opportunity to participate in the rulemaking process prior to the adoption of final rules.

e. *Notices.* This section of the *Federal Register* contains documents other than rules or proposed rules that are applicable to the public, *e.g.,* grant application deadlines, filing of petitions and applications.

f. *Sunshine Act Meetings.* Notices of meetings required by the Government in the Sunshine Act are in this section.

g. *Unified Agenda of Federal Regulations.* The Regulatory Flexibility Act requires that agencies publish in April and October regulatory agenda describing the regulatory actions they are developing. Each agency lists its rules in four groups: (1) Prerule Stage; (2) Proposed Rule Stage; (3) Final Rule Stage; and (4) Completed Actions.

h. *Reader Aids.* This section appears at the end of the *Federal Register* and contains telephone numbers for information and assistance, a parallel table of *Federal Register* pages for the month, a cumulative table of *CFR Parts Affected* during the month, and a List of Public Laws, which lists those bills from the current session of Congress that have recently become law. The Monday issue contains a "CFR Checklist" of the current *CFR* Parts.

i. *Special Sections.* To accommodate the duplication and distribution needs of issuing agencies, some agency documents are published in separate sections near the end of each issue rather than in the appropriate sections.

2. The Code of Federal Regulations (CFR) [15]

This set is a codification of rules and regulations first published in the *Federal Register,* in which all regulations and amendments in force are brought together by subject. The *Code of Federal Regulations* is *prima facie* evidence of the text of the documents.[16] The *CFR* is in fifty Titles (similar to, but not parallel to, the arrangement of the *United States Code*). Each Title is subdivided into Chapters, Subchapters, Parts, and Sections and is cited by Title and Section, *e.g.,* 42 C.F.R. § 405.501. [See Illustrations 95 and 96.] Each year the pamphlet volumes of the *Code of Federal Regulations* are issued in a different colored binding from the previous year (except Title 3, which has had a white cover since 1985) and on a quarterly basis approximately as follows:

Title 1 through Title 16 .... as of January 1
Title 17 through Title 27 .... as of April 1
Title 28 through Title 41 .... as of July 1
Title 42 through Title 50 .... as of October 1

---

[15] For a detailed history of the publication of the earlier editions of the *Code of Federal Regulations,* see ERVIN H. POLLACK, FUNDAMENTALS OF LEGAL RESEARCH 366–72 (3d ed. 1967).

[16] 44 U.S.C. § 1510(e) (1982).

Each new volume contains the text of regulations in force, incorporating those promulgated during the preceding twelve months and deleting those revoked. Through this process, all regulations first published chronologically in the *Federal Register* and currently in force are rearranged by subject and agency in the fifty Titles of the *CFR*. For example, all regulations issued by the Federal Communications Commission, and still in force, are in Title 47 of the *CFR* and are up to date through October 1.

3. Looseleaf Services

Looseleaf services, discussed in Chapter 13, often contain documents published in the *Federal Register* and the *CFR*. These services usually are better indexed than the government publications and contain other features facilitating the location of information.

Consequently, when it is necessary to research a problem of administrative law, it is good practice to ascertain if a looseleaf service covering the topic under research exists and to use that service as a starting point rather than the official publications.

4. Electronic Research

The following electronic sources can be extremely helpful in locating regulations, especially when a particular word or phrase cannot be found in the print indexes to the *Federal Register* or the *Code of Federal Regulations*.

a. *LEXIS.* The *Federal Register* is available in many LEXIS libraries including the CODES, GENFED, and EXEC libraries in the FEDREG file from July 1980. The current *Code of Federal Regulations* is available in the CODES, GENFED, and EXEC libraries in the CFR file. The archived *CFRs* beginning in 1981 are available in the GENFED library. The CFR and FEDREG files can be searched in a combined file, ALLREG.

b. *WESTLAW.* In the Federal Register (FR) database in WESTLAW, rules and regulations, proposed rules, notices and Unified Agenda documents published in the *Federal Register* can be accessed beginning from July 1, 1980. The current *Code of Federal Regulations* is available in the CFR database. Once a CFR section is located it can be brought current by using UPDATE to locate revisions appearing in the *Federal Register* after the latest CFR database revision. A historical database of *CFRs* beginning with 1984 also is available.

Federal Register Abstracts (FRA), a DIALOG database available through WESTLAW, provides coverage, in summary form, of federal administrative and regulatory activity. Coverage begins in March 1977.

c. *LEGI–SLATE.* This service, which is published by Legislate, Inc., an information subsidiary of the *Washington Post,* contains the *Federal Register* and the *Code of Federal Regulations.* A database,

DAILY, incorporates the promulgated final rules and regulations directly into the *CFR* in the appropriate Title each weekday.

d. *DIALOG.* The *Federal Register* is available through DIALOG from 1988. Federal Register Abstracts, available from 1977, provides, in summary form, coverage of federal administrative and regulatory activity.

e. *Internet.* Counterpoint Publishing Inc. of Cambridge, Massachusetts, provides same-day availability of the complete *Federal Register* through the Internet. Backfile issues of the *Federal Register* are available from January 1993. Titles of the *Code of Federal Regulations* are being added as produced by the government.

f. *CD–ROMS.* A number of CD–ROM products have recently been developed that facilitate access to federal regulations.

(1) *Compact Disc Federal Register.* This CD–ROM product is re-compiled and issued weekly and provides the complete text of the previous week's *Federal Register* and the past six months of *Federal Register*s on one disk. The disk is updated monthly, bi-monthly, quarterly, and semi-annually. Searching can be done by table of contents, agency name, words and phrases, and by using Boolean logic. Coverage begins with July 1, 1990.

(2) *OnDisc Federal Register.* This CD–ROM product, produced by Dialog Information Services, Inc., contains the full-text of the *Federal Register* including the print copy page number. Each disk contains each issue of the *Federal Register* from the first of the current year to the time the disk is produced. It is updated monthly. Historical coverage is available from 1990.

There are ten options for searches including words, *Federal Register* dates, *CFR* sections affected, page numbers, etc.

(3) *Compact Disc Code of Federal Regulations.* The 50 Titles of the *CFR* are available on CD–ROM from Counterpoint Publishing. Update disks are provided according to the rotating publishing schedule of the Government Printing Office. A monthly update disk incorporates the final rules and regulations and presidential documents into the appropriate Titles of the *CFR*. Subscriptions for any grouping of titles can also be purchased. Titles that relate to specific areas of interest are available as "bundle" subscriptions.

(4) *Code of Federal Regulations.* This CD–ROM product from CD Book Publishers, Fullerton, California, offers the 50 Titles of the *CFR*. It is updated quarterly as the revised Titles are issued by the government.

5. Other Sources

Selected regulations also are published in the monthly pamphlets to the *United States Code Congressional and Administrative News* and in the *United States Code Service* Advance Service.

SECTION D. FINDING FEDERAL REGULATIONS

Because the *Federal Register* and the *Code of Federal Regulations* are the official sources of agency regulations, these two sources are emphasized in this discussion.

The key to knowing whether to start one's research in the *Federal Register* or the *CFR* is the date of the regulation. If the regulation was recently issued, that is, later than the scope of the coverage of the *CFR* volume on the same subject, the research should commence in the *Federal Register*. If, however, the regulation is not very recent, or if the date is not known, the starting point is the *CFR*. These two sources are accessed differently.

1. Access to the Federal Register

a. *Federal Register Index.* This official index, arranged alphabetically by agency, is issued monthly. Each issue of this *Index* cumulates that year's previous monthly indexes, with the December issue being the final annual index. Because this *Index* is not distributed until several weeks after the month covered, the Contents in each issue of the *Federal Register* subsequent to the last *Index* should be consulted. The *Index* and Contents, however, are not adequately detailed and, at times, it is difficult to locate a regulation if one does not know the agency that issued it.

b. *CIS Federal Register Index.* This publication, which started in 1984, comprehensively indexes each issue of the *Federal Register*. It is issued weekly with monthly cumulative indexes and permanent semi-annual bound volumes. It includes indexes by subject and name, *CFR* Section numbers affected, federal agency docket number, and Calendar of Effective Dates and Comment Deadlines.

2. Access to the Code of Federal Regulations

a. *CFR Index and Finding Aids.* This single volume accompanies the *CFR* and is revised annually.[17] It provides several access points to the *CFR*.

(1) *Index.* The index includes in one alphabet both subject entries and the names of administrative agencies. Consequently, one can consult it either under the name of an agency or under a specific subject heading. Since January 1980, the subject terms used are taken from a thesaurus developed by the Office of the Federal Register.[18] This now assures that the same subject headings are used in the index if two or more agencies use different terms covering the same concept. For example, in its regulations one agency may use the word *compensation,* another *pay,* and a third *salaries.* By use of the thesaurus, references to

[17] Lawyers Cooperative Publishing publishes a copy of the *CFR Index and Finding Aids* volume as a part of the *United States Code Service.*

[18] Thesaurus of Indexing Terms, 45 Fed. Reg. 2998 (1980).

all three of these regulations will appear in the index under the subject heading *Wages*.

The index refers to the appropriate Title of the *CFR* and then to the specific Part within the Title. [See Illustration 92.] Because the references are to Parts and not to Sections, specificity is reduced.

(2) *Parallel Table of Authorities and Rules.* This table appears as Table I in the *CFR Index and Finding Aids* volume. [See Illustration 94.] If the citation is known to a law or Presidential document that authorized an agency or administrator to issue regulations, this table indicates where administrative regulations promulgated under such authority are found in the *CFR*. The table also includes citations to laws that are interpreted or applied by regulations codified in the *CFR*. The citations in Table I are divided into four segments: U.S.C.; Statutes at Large; public law; and Presidential documents. Within each segment the citations are arranged in numerical order.

For Presidential documents included or cited in regulations in the *CFR*, one should use Table II. However, Table II has not been revised since January 1, 1976, and was last published in the *Index* for that year.

(3) *List of Agency–Prepared Indexes Appearing In Individual CFR Volumes.* This list provides information to locate agency-prepared indexes that are published in various volumes of the *CFR*.

b. *Index to the Code of Federal Regulations.*[19] Published since 1984, this annual, private publication provides access by subject and geographic location. The references are to *CFR* Title and Part. [See Illustration 93.]

c. The Index portion of the 1990 CFR *Index and Finding Aids* volume is available online through LEXIS in the GENFED library, INDEX file.

3. Regulations No Longer in Force

It is often necessary to determine what regulations were in force at some prior date. Where prior editions of the *CFR* are available, one simply can consult the edition that was current at the applicable time. Some libraries keep superseded editions of the *CFR* in paper copy or in microform.[20] Regulations no longer in force can also be located in the electronic sources listed in Section C–4, *supra*.

One also can begin by locating the applicable subject matter in the current edition of *CFR*, which gives the date and *Federal Register* citation for the adoption of each section, and the same information for each subsequent amendment of that section. This allows the researcher to determine whether the present language of the section was in effect at the applicable time and to find the original language in the *Federal Register* if the section has been amended.

[19] Congressional Information Service, Inc. Earlier editions of the *Index* were published by Information Handling Services (1977–79) and Capitol Services Annotated (1980).

[20] Some libraries may have a cumulation of each Title on microfilm or microfiche.

The following official publications also provide *CFR* citations to allow one to find the precise text of regulations that were in force on any given date during the years covered: *Code of Federal Regulations List of Sections Affected, 1949–1963; List of CFR Sections Affected, 1964–1972* (2 volumes); and *List of CFR Sections Affected, 1973–1985* (4 volumes). For changes from January 1, 1986, each volume of the *CFR* contains a *List of CFR Sections Affected.* The *List* appears at the end of the volume and is arranged by year.

SECTION E. UPDATING REGULATIONS

After one has located a regulation, further research is necessary to determine whether the regulation has been amended or revoked. If the regulation was amended or revoked or if a new regulation has been promulgated, the *Federal Register* contains the documentation. The sources described below are essential tools to locate citations to the *Federal Register* where changes to regulations are published.

1. Sources

a. *LSA: List of CFR Sections Affected.* This publication is issued monthly and indicates finalized and proposed changes made since the latest publication of the *CFR.* The December issue cumulates all changes for Titles 1–16; the March issue contains all changes for Titles 17–27; the June issue lists changes for Titles 28–41; and the September issue indicates changes for Titles 42–50. [See Illustration 97.] For changes to regulations which have become final, the *LSA* is arranged by *CFR* Title and Section and sets forth the nature of the changes, *e.g.,* "revised," and provides page number references to the *Federal Register.* [See Illustration 98.] For proposed changes, the *LSA* is arranged by Title and Part with reference to the applicable *Federal Register* page numbers. [See Illustration 99.] A separate section of the *LSA* updates the *Parallel Table of Authorities and Rules.*

LEXIS contains the *LSA* from March, 1991 in the GENFED library, LSA file. Changes for each Title can be searched cumulatively or by each month. The *LSA* online is not as current as the print version.

b. *CFR Parts Affected.* Each issue of the *Federal Register* contains a section near the front that lists *CFR Parts Affected in This Issue.* However, this section is incorporated in the cumulative list in the Reader Aids section. The section in the front of the *Federal Register* would be used if one must review each issue of the *Federal Register* to ascertain if any changes occur to a specific regulation being monitored.

Each issue of the *Federal Register* also includes a list of *CFR Parts Affected* in the Reader Aids section. The list is cumulative for one calendar month. [See Illustration 102.] Both lists give page number references to the *Federal Register.*

c. *Converting Page Number References to Specific Issues of the Federal Register.* If the regulation one is researching has been affected, a reference to the *Federal Register* is provided in the *LSA* and/or the list

of *CFR Parts Affected*. This reference is to the page number of the *Federal Register* on which the amendment, proposed amendment, or removal appears. To find the issue of the *Federal Register* in which the change appears, use the conversion table in the *Federal Register Index* or the *LSA*, whichever is more current. [See Illustration 100.] If the page number does not appear in the *Index*'s or *LSA*'s conversion table, one must turn to the last issue of each month of the *Federal Register* published since the *Index* or the *LSA* and use the conversion tables, which appear in the Reader Aids section. [See Illustration 102.]

d. *Shepard's Code of Federal Regulations Citations.* To ascertain whether a federal court has ruled on the constitutionality or validity of a regulation, this unit of *Shepard's Citations* should be consulted. In addition to updating regulations, a researcher may be interested in locating cases and other materials that have cited a regulation. *Shepard's Code of Federal Regulations Citations* provides a method for locating citations to court cases, selected law review articles, and *A.L.R. Annotations* that have cited regulations published in the *CFR*. The use of *Shepard's Citations* is explained in Chapter 14.

2. Research Methodology

The need to refer to the sources to update a regulation described *supra* is dictated by where the regulation being updated was found and the recency of the publication containing the regulation.

If the regulation was found in the *CFR*, the researcher should first use the most current *LSA*. It is important to note the publication date on the cover of the *CFR* volume in which the regulation was found in order to cover the appropriate time period. Since the *LSA* is issued monthly, a further check must be made in the cumulative list of *CFR Parts Affected* in the *Federal Register* for any later changes. Therefore, note the coverage of the *LSA* used, and check the list of *CFR Parts Affected* in the last issue of each subsequent month, including the current month, of the *Federal Register*.

If the regulation was found in the *Federal Register* and if the latest issue of *LSA* is for a month *later* than the month of the issue of the *Federal Register* in which the regulation appears, first use the *LSA* that covers the period from the date of the issue of the *Federal Register* in which the regulation was found. Since the *LSA* is issued monthly, a further check must be made for any later changes in the cumulative list of *CFR Parts Affected* in the *Federal Register*. Therefore, note the coverage of the *LSA* used, and check the list of *CFR Parts Affected* in the last issue of each subsequent month, including the current month, of the *Federal Register*.

If the regulation was found in an issue of the *Federal Register* and if the latest *LSA* available is for a month *prior* to the month of the issue of the *Federal Register* in which the regulation appears, check the list of *CFR Parts Affected* in the last issue of the month of the *Federal Register* in which the regulation was found and the list of *CFR Parts Affected* in

the last issue of each subsequent month, including the current month, of the *Federal Register*.

If the regulation appears in an issue of the *Federal Register* for the current month, check the list of *CFR Parts Affected* in the last available issue of the current month's *Federal Register* to be as up to date as possible.

SECTION F.   ILLUSTRATIONS OF FEDERAL REGISTER AND CODE OF FEDERAL REGULATIONS

Problem: **Find regulations pertaining to determination of reasonable charges for federal health insurance for the aged and disabled.**

[Illustration 92]

EXCERPTS FROM PAGES FROM CFR INDEX
AND FINDING AIDS VOLUME

Health professions	**CFR Index**
Federal Acquisition Regulations System, 48 CFR 1601	Medicare
Forms, 48 CFR 1653	*See also* Peer Review Organizations (PRO)
Improper business practices and personal conflicts of interest, 48 CFR 1603	Exclusions from Medicare and limitations on Medicare payment, 42 CFR 411
Protection of privacy and freedom of information, 48 CFR 1624	→Federal health insurance for aged and disabled, 42 CFR 405
Protests, disputes, and appeals, 48 CFR 1633	Ambulatory surgical services, 42 CFR 416
Publicizing contract actions, 48 CFR 1605	Appeals procedures for determinations that affect participation, 42 CFR 498
Quality assurance, 48 CFR 1646	Conditions for coverage of particular services, 42 CFR 494
Sealed bidding, 48 CFR 1614	Conditions for payment, 42 CFR 424
Subcontracting policies and procedures, 48 CFR 1644	Conditions of participation, home health agencies, 42 CFR 484
Termination of contracts, 48 CFR 1649	General administrative requirements, official records confidentiality and disclosure, 42 CFR 401
Types of contracts, 48 CFR 1616	
Special programs and projects, Medicare, 42 CFR 403	
Health insurance for aged	Health maintenance organizations, competitive medical plans, and health care prepayment plans, 42 CFR 417
→*See* Medicare	
Health maintenance organizations (HMO)	Health facilities certification, 42 CFR 491
Medicaid, contracts, 42 CFR 434	Hospice, 42 CFR 418
Medicare Health care maintenance organizations,	

Step 1

Consult the Index in the current *CFR Index and Finding Aids* volume. Health insurance for the aged refers one to Medicare. Note the sub-entry Federal health insurance for aged and disabled, 42 CFR 405. This refers to Title 42, Part 405.

See next Illustration.

...ces, appointment of doctors of osteopathy as medical officers, 32 CFR 74	Introduction; definitions, 42 CFR 400
	Laboratory requirements, 42 CFR 493
Construction of teaching facilities, educational improvements, scholarships and student loans, grants, 42 CFR 57	Long term care facilities, conditions of participation and requirements, 42 CFR 483
Drugs used for treatment of narcotic addicts, 21 CFR 291	Payment on reasonable charge basis, end-stage renal disease, 42 CFR 414
Emergency health and medical occupations, 44 CFR 325	Physicians' services, fee schedule, 42 CFR 415
Family planning services, grants, 42 CFR 59	Principles of reasonable cost reimbursement, end-stage renal disease services payment, 42 CFR 413
Federal Aviation Administration, representatives of Administrator to	

[Illustration 93]

PAGE FROM THE INDEX TO THE CODE OF FEDERAL REGULATIONS (CIS)

HEALTH INSURANCE PROGRAM

Step 1a

This privately-published Index of the Congressional Information Service provides much more detailed indexing. Notice how it leads directly to reimbursement for reasonable charges.

[Illustration 94]

PAGE FROM PARALLEL TABLE OF AUTHORITIES AND RULES, CFR INDEX AND FINDING AIDS VOLUME

CFR Index		

42 U.S.C.—Continued	CFR
	20 Parts 350, 363
	32 Part 818
663—682	5 Part 581
663—664	45 Part 303
664	45 Parts 301, 302, 307
665	15 Part 15b
	32 Parts 54, 818
	33 Part 54
	42 Part 21
666—667	45 Parts 301-303, 307
670 et seq	45 Parts 1355-1357
681—687	45 Parts 240, 250
684	45 Part 251
701 et seq	45 Part 96
702	42 Part 51a
907	45 Part 204
1070b	34 Part 676
1102	20 Part 615
1141 note	24 Part 581
1202—1203	45 Part 1393
1202	45 Part 233
1203	45 Part 201
1232c	34 Part 676
1301	45 Parts 201, 301, 1355
→ 1302	20 Parts 401, 404, 409, 410, 416, 417, 422, 601, 602, 603, 625, 640, 650
	29 Part 56
	40 Part 484
	42 Parts 51a, 400, 401, 403, 405-418, 420, 421, 424, 430-436, 440-442, 447, 455-456, 462, 466, 473, 476, 482, 483, 485, 488, 489, 491, 493, 498, 1000-1006
	45 Parts 75, 95, 201, 204-206, 212, 213, 224, 225, 232-235, 237-240, 250, 251, 255-257, 282, 301-307, 1355-1357, 1397
1302c-3	42 Part 466
1304 note	45 Part 96
1305	45 Part 96
1305 note	20 Part 404
1306	20 Parts 401, 410, 416, 422

42 U.S.C.—Continued	CFR
1320c—1320c-2	42 Part 462
1320c	42 Part 405
1320c-1—1320c-2	42 Part 462
1320c-3—1320c-4	42 Part 473
1320c-3	42 Parts 405, 466, 476
1320c-5	42 Parts 455, 476, 1004, 1005
1320c-8	42 Part 466
1320c-9	42 Part 476
1327	20 Part 416
1331a	20 Part 416
1338	42 Part 482
1341	20 Part 401
1345hh	42 Part 403
1352—1353	45 Part 1393
1352	45 Part 233
1353	45 Part 201
1381—1381a	20 Part 416
1382—1382e	20 Part 416
1382	45 Parts 233, 1393, 1397
1382c	20 Parts 404, 416
1382f	20 Part 416
1382g—1382h	20 Part 416
1382j	20 Part 416
1383	20 Parts 404, 416
	45 Parts 205, 1393
1383 note	45 Part 201
1383a	20 Part 416
1383b—1382c	20 Part 416
1385x	42 Part 411
1394hh	42 Part 412
1394ww	42 Part 412
1395 et seq	20 Part 404
1395	42 Parts 405, 421, 489
1395-1	42 Part 421
1395a	42 Part 414
1395b-1	42 Part 421
1395b-4	42 Part 403
1395d—1395f	42 Part 418
1395d—1395e	42 Part 409
1395f—1395v	42 Part 405
1395f—1395g	42 Parts 413, 424
1395f	42 Parts 482, 488

Step 1b

An alternative method of finding regulations in the *CFR*.

There are times when the U.S.C. citation to the statute that delegated the authority to issue regulations is known. In such instances, the Parallel Table of Authorities and Rules in the *CFR Index and Finding Aids* volume can be used to locate citations to regulations in the *CFR*. For example, the statutory authorization for determination of reasonable charges under Medicare is found at 42 U.S.C. § 1302.

1320a-7	42 Parts 1001, 1002, 1006
1320a-7a	42 Parts 405, 1006
1321a-7b	42 Part 1001
1320b-2	45 Part 95
1320b-2 note	45 Part 95
1320b-6	42 Part 482
1320b-7	42 Part 433
1320b-10	42 Part 1003
1320b-13	20 Part 422

1395p—1395s	42 Part 408
1395u—1395w-4	42 Part 414
1395u	42 Parts 411, 415, 421, 424, 1001, 1003
1395v	42 Part 408
1395w-4	42 Parts 405, 415
1395x—1395z	42 Part 405
1395x	40 Parts 411,

[Illustration 95]

PAGE FROM TITLE 42 OF CFR

Health Care Financing Administration, HHS   **Pt. 405**

SUBCHAPTER B—MEDICARE PROGRAM

PART 405—FEDERAL HEALTH INSURANCE FOR THE AGED AND DISABLED

Step 2

Refer to Title 42, Part 405 of the *CFR* as located using Step 1. After each Part, a detailed list of Sections is given. In this instance, Section 405.501 seems relevant.

41

[Illustration 96]

PAGE FROM TITLE 42 OF CFR

§ 405.501

[48 FR 8936, Mar. 2, 1983, as amended at 48 FR 39829, Sept. 1, 1983]

Subpart E—Criteria for Determination of Reasonable Charges; Payment for Services of Hospital Interns, Residents, and Supervising Physicians

AUTHORITY: Secs. 1102, 1814(b), 1832, 1833(a), 1834(b), 1842(b) and (h), 1848, 1861(b), (v), and (aa), 1862(a)(14), 1866(a), 1871, 1881, 1886, 1887, and 1889 of the Social Security Act as amended (42 U.S.C. 1302, 1395f(b), 1395k, 1395l(a), 1395m(b), 1395u(b) and (h), (1395w-4, 1395x(b), (v), and (aa), 1395y(a)(14), 1395cc(a), 1395hh, 1395rr, 1395ww, 1395xx, and 1395zz)

SOURCE: 32 FR 12599, Aug. 31, 1967, unless otherwise noted. Redesignated at 42 FR 52826, Sept. 30, 1977.

§ 405.501 Determination of reasonable charges.

(a) Except as specified in paragraphs (b), (c), and (d) of this section, Medicare pays no more for Part B medical and other health services than the "reasonable charge" for such service. The reasonable charge is determined by the carriers (subject to any deductible and coinsurance amounts as specified in §§ 410.152 and 410.160 of this chapter).

(b) Part B of Medicare pays on the basis of "reasonable cost" (see part 413 of this chapter) for certain institutional services, certain services furnished

42 CFR Ch. IV (10-1-92 Edition)

(1) Actual charge;

(2) Prevailing charge that would be recognized if the services had been performed by an anesthesiologist; or

(3) Fee schedule amount, as described in §§ 414.451 and 414.452.

(e) Carriers will determine the reasonable charge on the basis of the criteria specified in § 405.502, and the customary and prevailing charge screens in effect when the service was furnished. (Also see §§ 405.480 through 405.482 and §§ 405.550 through 405.557, which pertain to the determination of reimbursement for services performed by hospital-based physicians.) However, when services are furnished more than 12 months before the beginning of the fee screen year (January 1 through December 30) in which a request for payment is made, payment is based on the customary and prevailing charge screens in effect for the fee screen year that ends immediately preceding the fee screen year in which the claim or request for payment is made.

[47 FR 63274, Dec. 31, 1981, as amended at 51 FR 34978, Oct. 1, 1986; 51 FR 37911, Oct. 27, 1986; 54 FR 9003, Mar. 2, 1989; 57 FR 24975, June 12, 1992; 57 FR 33896, July 31, 1992]

§ 405.502 Criteria for determining reasonable charges.

(a) *Criteria.* The law allows for flexibility in the determination of reasonable charges to accommodate reim-

---

Step 3

Note how at the end of Subpart E the statutory authorization is noted and how at the end of Part 405.501 citations are given to where the regulation and amendments appeared in the *Federal Register*. Next the researcher would read § 405.501.

April 1, 1989, payment under Medicare Part B for radiologist services is governed by radiology fee schedules that are determined in accordance with the provisions of §§ 405.530 through 405.533.

(d) For services furnished on or after January 1, 1989 and before January 1, 1991, by a certified registered nurse anesthetist or an anesthesiologist's assistant, payment is made after the Part B deductible is met based on 80 percent of the least of the—

physician or other person furnishing such services.

(2) The prevailing charges in the locality for similar services.

(3) In the case of physicians' services, the prevailing charges for such services for fiscal year 1973 adjusted to reflect the cumulative economic index since calendar year 1971 but only if the charges so determined are not more than the prevailing charges determined under § 405.504(a)(2). The data used in determining the cumula-

[Illustration 97]

TITLE PAGE FROM LSA: LIST OF CFR SECTIONS AFFECTED PAMPHLET

LSA

List of CFR Sections Affected

September 1993

**Save this issue for Titles
42–50 (Annual)**

Title 1–16
Changes January 4, 1993
through September 30, 1993

Title 17–27
Changes April 1, 1993
through September 30, 1993

Title 28–41
Changes July 1, 1993
through September 30, 1993

Title 42–50
Changes October 1, 1992
through September 30, 1993

Step 4

   Title 42 of the *CFR* is revised annually as of October 1. Hence, it must be ascertained if any changes have subsequently occurred.

   This is accomplished by using this List. It is issued monthly, the December, March, June, and September issues consisting of an annual cumulation as indicated on the title page.

[Illustration 98]

PAGE FROM LSA: LIST OF CFR SECTIONS AFFECTED PAMPHLET

SEPTEMBER, 1993   **129**

CHANGES OCTOBER 1, 1992 THROUGH SEPTEMBER 30, 1993

	Page
57.4001 Amended	45746
57.4002 Amended	45746
57.4003 Amended; Footnote 1 removed	45746
57.4005 (a) introductory text amended	45746
57.4007 (c) amended	45746
57.4008 Amended	45746
57.4009 OMB number	45746
57.4102 Amended	45746
57.4103 Footnote 1 removed; OMB number	45746
57.4104 Amended	45746
57.4105 (i) amended	45746
57.4107 (a) amended	45746
57.4111 Amended	45746

	Page
406.30 Redesignated as 406.50	58717
406.31 Redesignated as 406.52	58717
406.32 Transferred to Subpart C; (c) amended	58717
406.34 Redesignated from 406.24; (a)(1) and (b)(1) amended	58717
406.38 Transferred to Subpart C	58717
406.50 Redesignated from 406.30	58717
406.52 Redesignated from 406.31	58717
409.5 Amended	30666

Step 4a

Note that a subsection of 405.501 has been added. This addition was first printed at page 57688 of the 1992 *Federal Register*. This should be read for the text of the addition.

	Page
59.9 Suspended	7463
59.10 Suspended	7463
62.25 (a) amended	56996
110.101—110.103 (Subpart A) Appendix A nomenclature change	30123

Chapter IV—Health Care Financing Administration, Department of Health and Human Services (Parts 400—499)

	Page
400.200 Amended	55912
400.202 Amended	30666
400.310 Revised (OMB numbers)	56997
401.601 (b) and (c) revised	56998
405.374 (c) revised	56998
405.501—405.580 (Subpart E) Authority citation revised	57688
➤405.501 (f) added	57688
405.502 (a)(3) revised	55912
405.504 (a)(3)(i) introductory text and (iii) revised; (d) added	55912
405.514 Removed	57688
405.701—405.750 (Subpart G) Authority citation revised	56504
405.705 (c) and (d) revised; (e) and (f) added	56504
406.24 Redesignated as 406.34	58717

	Page
heading, (1)(iii) and (3)(ii) revised	30666
409.12 (b) amended	30666
Heading and (a) revised	30667
409.13 (a) introductory text, (1), (2), (3) and (b) amended	30666
409.14 (a) introductory text, (1), (2), (b) introductory text, (1) and (2) amended	30666
409.15 Introductory text amended	30666
409.16 Introductory text, (a), (b) and (c) amended	30666
409.20 (a) introductory text revised; (c)(3) added	30667
409.27 Revised	30667
409.30 Introductory text, (a)(2), (b)(1) and (2) amended	30666
(a)(1) revised	30667
409.31 (b)(2)(i) and (ii) amended	30666
409.60 (a) and (b)(1) revised	30667
409.61 (a)(2) and (c) amended	30666
(a) heading, (3) heading and (b) heading revised; (a)(1)(i) and (b) amended	30667
409.64 (a)(2)(ii) amended	30667
409.65 (a)(1), (3), (4), (d)(1), (2), (e)(1), (2) introductory text, (i) and (ii) amended	30666

NOTE: Boldface page numbers indicate 1992 changes.

[Illustration 99]

PAGE FROM LSA: LIST OF CFR SECTIONS AFFECTED PAMPHLET

144   **LSA—LIST OF CFR SECTIONS AFFECTED**

CHANGES OCTOBER 1, 1992 THROUGH SEPTEMBER 30, 1993

TITLE 42 Chapter IV—Con.   Page
(e)(4) corrected..............................39156
493.1806 (d) amended....................5237
493.1814 (b)(3) revised.................. 5237
493.1834 (b) and (f)(2)(iii) re-
vised..5237
493.1836 (c)(2) and (3) re-
vised..5237
493.2001 (e) revised......................5237
498.2 Amended...............................30677

Chapter V—Office of Inspector General–Health Care, Department of Health and Human Services (Parts 1000—1999)

1001 Authority citation re-
vised..52729
Authority citation revised..........40753
1001.1 Existing text designated
as (a); (b) added...........................5618
1001.952 (k)(1)(iii) revised; (l)
and (m) added; interim.............52729
Regulation at 57 FR 52729
comment period extended;
interim..2989
1001.1301 (a)(3) amended............40753
1005.4 (c)(1) revised......................5618
1005.7 (e)(1) revised......................5618

Title 42—Proposed Rules:

51a 38995
59 .... 7464, 34024
63 42039
65 50897
100 49055
→ 400—499 (Ch. IV) 47587
→ 405 .... 37994, 43832
412 .... 30222, 34742
413 .... 30222, 34742, 43832
414 .... 37994, 43832

                         Page
442 46362
447 43832
456 61614
482 34977
483 61614
488 46362
489 46362
498 46362
1001 49008
1003 59024
....8568

TITLE 43—PUBLIC LANDS: INTERIOR

Subtitle A—Office of the Secretary of the Interior (Parts 1—199)

Subtitle A Policy statement
and advisory guidelines............52730
2 Appendix B amended...............48973
4.21 (a) in part, (b) and (c) redesignated as (b), (c) and
(d); new (c) revised....................4942
20 Authority citation revised......32447
20.735–1 (a)(8) through (11) re-
vised...32447
20.735–6 Removed; new 20.735–
6 redesignated from 20.735–
8...32447
20.735–7 Removed; new 20.735–
7 redesignated from 20.735–
9...32447
20.735–8 (d)(2)(ii) and (3)(ii)
amended; redesignated as
20.735–6; new 20.735–8 redesignated from 20.735–12.............32447
20.735–9 Redesignated as
20.735–7; new 20.735–9 redes-

Step 4b

This *LSA* should also be consulted to ascertain if proposed rules may be pertinent.

....23652
433 49272
434 59024
....8568
435 .... 56294, 57403
....42041
436 56294
....42041
440 46362
441 42041

designated as (d) through
(n); (a)(3)(ii) revised; (k)
amended.......................................32447
20.735–11 Removed........................32447
20.735–12 (c)(3) amended; redesignated as 20.735–8.............32447
20.735–13 Removed........................32447
20.735–14 Redesignated as
20.735–9..32447
20.735–15 Removed........................32447

NOTE: Boldface page numbers indicate 1992 changes.

[Illustration 100]

PAGE FROM LSA'S TABLE OF FEDERAL REGISTER ISSUE PAGES AND DATES

206   **TABLE OF FEDERAL REGISTER ISSUE PAGES AND DATES**

1992

57 FR Page

45261–45558	Oct. 1
45559–45707	2
45709–45972	5
45973–46078	6
46079–46294	7
46295–46476	8
46477–46746	9
46747–46948	13
46949–47252	14
47253–47398	15
47399–47554	16
47555–47754	19
47755–47974	20
47975–48160	21
48161–48304	22
48305–48434	23
48435–48556	26
48557–48710	27

Pages	Date
61249–61556	24
61557–61758	28
61759–62144	29
62145–62465	30
62467–62919	31

1993

58 FR Page

Pages	Date
1–211	Jan. 4
213–465	5
467–2964	6
2965–3192	7
3193–3483	8
3485–3823	11
3825–4057	12
4059–4294	13
4295–4568	14
4569–4890	15
4891–5252	19
5253–5560	21

Step 5

This Table lists pages of the *Federal Register* and shows the date of the *Federal Register* in which the pages are located.

Page 57688 is found in the December 7, 1992 *Federal Register*.

Pages	Date
53211–43430	9
53431–53536	10
53537–53846	12
53537–53846	13
53981–54164	16
54165–54284	17
54285–54484	18
54485–54678	19
54677–54894	20
54895–55042	23
55043–55436	24
55437–56230	25
56231–56432	27
56433–56802	30
56803–56962	Dec. 1
56963–57093	2
57095–57320	3
57321–57644	4
57645–57873	7
57875–58119	8
58121–58397	9
58399–58696	10
58697–58960	11
58691–59274	14
59275–59800	15
59801–59894	16
59895–60071	17
60073–60448	18
60449–60713	21
60715–60973	22
60975–61248	23

Pages	Date
6875–7041	3
7043–7184	4
7185–7475	5
7477–7713	8
7715–7860	9
7861–7951	10
7953–8199	11
8201–8515	12
8517–8689	16
8691–8892	17
8893–9106	18
9107–9516	19
9517–10935	22
10937–11184	23
11185–11359	24
11361–11495	25
11497–11781	26
11783–11950	Mar. 1
11951–12144	2
12145–12328	3
12329–12536	4
12537–12900	5
12901–12996	8
12997–13188	9
13189–13400	10
13401–13528	11
13529–13694	12
13695–14144	15
14145–14302	16
14303–14493	17
14495–15070	18

[Illustration 101]

PAGE FROM VOLUME 57, FEDERAL REGISTER

57688   Federal Register / Vol. 57, No. 235 / Monday, December 7, 1992 / Rules and Regulations

PART 405—FEDERAL HEALTH INSURANCE FOR THE AGED AND DISABLED

Subpart E—Criteria for Determination of Reasonable Charges; Radiology Fee Schedules; and Reimbursement for Services of Hospital Interns, Residents, and Supervising Physicians

A. The authority citation for subpart E is revised to read as follows:

Authority: Secs. 1102, 1814(b), 1832, 1833(a), 1834 (a) and (b), 1842 (b) and (h), 1848, 1861 (b), (v), and (aa), 1862(a)(14), 1866(a), 1871, 1881, 1886, 1887, and 1889 of the Social Security Act as amended (42 U.S.C. 1302, 1395f(b), 1395k, 1395l(a), 1395m (a) and (b), 1395u (b) and (h), 1395w–4, 1395x (b), (v), and (aa), 1395y(a)(14), 1395cc(a), 1395hh, 1395rr, 1395ww, 1395xx, and 1395zz).

B. Section 405.501 is amended by adding a new paragraph (f) to read as follows:

§ 405.501   Determination of reasonable charges.

*   *   *   *   *

(f) For services furnished on or after January 1, 1989, payment under Medicare Part B for durable medical equipment and prosthetic and orthotic devices is determined in accordance with the provisions of subpart D of part 414 of this chapter.

§ 405.514   [Removed]

C. Section 405.514 is removed.

II. Part 410 is amended as follows:

PART 410—SUPPLEMENTARY MEDICAL INSURANCE (SMI) BENEFITS

A. The authority citation for part 410 is revised to read as follows:

Author
1835, 18
and 1881
U.S.C. 1
1395x(r),
1395rr).

Subpart B—Medical and Other Health Services

B. In § 410.36, the undesignated introductory text is redesignated as paragraph (a); paragraphs (a), (b), and (c) are redesignated as paragraphs (a)(1), (a)(2), and (a)(3) and are republished, and new paragraph (b) is added to read as follows:

§ 410.36   Medical supplies, appliances and devices: Scope.

(a) Medicare Part B pays for the following medical supplies, appliances and devices:

(1) Surgical dressings, and splints, casts, and other devices used for reduction of fractures and dislocations.

(2) Prosthetic devices, other than dental, that replace all or part of an internal body organ, including colostomy bags and supplies directly related to colostomy care, including—

(i) Replacement of prosthetic devices; and

(ii) One pair of conventional eyeglasses or conventional contact lenses furnished after each cataract surgery during which an intraocular lens is inserted.

(3) Leg, arm, back, and neck braces and artificial legs, arms, and eyes, including replacements if required because of a change in the individual's physical condition.

(b) As a requirement for payment, HCFA may determine through carrier instructions, or carriers may determine, that an item listed in paragraph (a) of this section requires a written physician order before delivery of the item.

C. In § 410.38, in paragraph (b), the phrase "1861(j)(1)" is revised to read "1819(a)(1)"; paragraph (c) is revised; and new paragraphs (d), (e), (f), and (g) are added to read as follows:

§ 410.38   Durable medical equipment: Scope and conditions.

*   *   *   *   *

(c) Wheelchairs may include a power-operated vehicle that may be appropriately used as a wheelchair, but only if the vehicle—

(1) Is determined to be necessary on the basis of the individual's medical and physical condition;

(2) Meets any safety requirements specified by HCFA; and

(3) Except as provided in paragraph (c)(2) of this section, is ordered in writing by a specialist in physical medicine, orthopedic surgery,

(4) A written prescription from the beneficiary's physician is acceptable for ordering a power-operated vehicle if a specialist in physical medicine, orthopedic surgery, neurology, or rheumatology is not reasonably accessible. For example, if travel to the specialist would be more than one day's trip from the beneficiary's home or if the beneficiary's medical condition precluded travel to the nearest available specialist, these circumstances would satisfy the "not reasonably accessible" requirement.

(d) Medicare Part B pays for medically necessary equipment that is used for treatment of decubitus ulcers if—

(1) The equipment is ordered in writing by the beneficiary's attending physician, or by a specialty physician on referral from the beneficiary's attending physician, and the written order is furnished to the supplier before the delivery of the equipment; and

(2) The prescribing physician has specified in the prescription that he or she will be supervising the use of the equipment in connection with the course of treatment.

(e) Medicare Part B pays for a medically necessary seat-lift if it—

(1) Is ordered in writing by the beneficiary's attending physician, or by a specialty physician on referral from the beneficiary's attending physician, and the written order is furnished to the supplier before the delivery of the seat-lift;

(2) Is for a beneficiary who has a diagnosis designated by HCFA as requiring a seat-lift; and

(3) Meets safety requirements specified by HCFA.

(f) Medicare Part B pays for transcutaneous electrical nerve stimulator units that are—

(1) Determined to be medically necessary; and

(2) Ordered in writing by the beneficiary's attending physician, or by a specialty physician on referral from the beneficiary's attending physician, and the written order is furnished to the supplier before the delivery of the unit to the beneficiary.

(g) As a requirement for payment, HCFA may determine through carrier instructions, or carriers may determine that an item of durable medical equipment requires a written physician order before delivery of the item.

III. Part 414 is amended to read as follows:

FOR PART B HEALTH

... on for part 414 is revised to read as follows:

Authority: Secs. 1102, 1833(a), 1834 (a) and (h), 1871, and 1881 of the Social Security Act (42 U.S.C. 1302, 1395l(a), 1395m (a) and (h), 1395hh and 1395rr).

B. Subpart D is amended by adding new §§ 414.200 through .222, §§ 414.226 through .229, and § 414.232 to read as follows:

Subpart D—Payment for Durable Medical Equipment and Prosthetic and Orthotic Devices

Sec.
414.200   Purpose.
414.202   Definitions.
414.210   General payment rules.

> This is the page from the *Federal Register* on which the addition to 405.501 is published.

[Illustration 102]

PAGE FROM VOLUME 58, FEDERAL REGISTER—
LISTING OF CFR PARTS AFFECTED

Reader Aids

Federal Register

Vol. 58, No. 208

Friday, October 29, 1993

INFORMATION AND ASSISTANCE

Federal Register

Index, finding aids & general information	202–523–5227
Public inspection desk	523–5215
Corrections to published documents	523–5237
Document drafting information	523–3187
Machine readable documents	523–3447

Code of Federal Regulations

Index, finding aids & general information	523–5227
Printing schedules	523–3419

Laws

Public Laws Update Service (numbers, dates, etc.)	523–6641
Additional information	523–5230

CFR PARTS AFFECTED DURING OCTOBER

At the end of each month, the Office of the Federal Register publishes separately a List of CFR Sections Affected (LSA), which lists parts and sections affected by documents published since the revision date of each title.

1 CFR

305,	54271
310	54271

3 CFR

Proclamations:

6598	51559
6599	51561
6600	51721
6601	51723
6602	52205

EO 12869	51751
12382 (Continued by EO 12869)	51751
12498 (Revoked by EO 12868)	51735
12675 (Revoked in part EO 12869)	51751
12667 (Revoked by EO 12869)	51751
12696 (Revoked by EO 12869)	51751

Step 6

The *LSA: List of CFR Sections Affected* as shown in Illustration 108 indicates changes made during the year to the *CFR*. To ascertain further changes, one should check the *CFR Parts Affected* table in the last issue of the *Federal Register* for months subsequent to the most recent *LSA*. Note the table of *Federal Register* pages and dates.

Guide to Record Retention Requirements	523–3187
Legal staff	523–4534
Privacy Act Compilation	523–3187
Public Laws Update Service (PLUS)	523–6641
TDD for the hearing impaired	523–5229

ELECTRONIC BULLETIN BOARD

Free **Electronic Bulletin Board** service for Public Law numbers, and Federal Register finding aids.   **202–275–1538, or 275–0920**

▶ **FEDERAL REGISTER PAGES AND DATES, OCTOBER**

51211–51664	1
51665–51756	4
51757–51972	5
51973–52206	6
52207–52396	7
52397–52628	8
52629–52874	12
52675–53096	13
53097–53392	14
53393–53634	15
53635–53832	18
53833–54024	19
54025–54270	20
54271–54484	21
54485–54924	22
54925–57534	25
57535–57716	26
57717–57950	27
57951–58096	28
58097–58254	29

6614	54027
6615	54269
6616	54909
6617	57535
6619	57715

Executive Orders:

July 9, 1910 (Revoked in part by PLO 7004)	53429
3053 (Revoked in part by PLO 7004)	53429
3406 (Revoked in part by PLO 7001)	52683
5327 (Revoked in part by PLO 7002)	52684
8578 (See PLO 7005)	54049
11145 (Continued by EO 12869)	51751
11183 (Continued by EO 12869)	51751
11287 (Continued by EO 12869)	51751
11776 (Continued by EO 12869)	51751
12002 (See EO 12867)	51747
12131 (Continued by EO 12869)	51751
12197 (Continued by EO 12869)	51751
12214 (See EO 12867)	51747
12216 (Continued by EO 12869)	51751
12291 (Revoked by EO 12866)	51735
12345 (Continued by EO 12869)	51751
12367 (Continued by	

EO 12869	51751
12775 (See notice of September 30)	51563
12775 (See EO 12872)	54029
12775 (See DOT rule of Oct. 15)	54024
12779 (See EO 12872)	54029
12779 (See notice of September 30)	51563
12779 (See DOT rule of Oct. 15)	54024
12792 (Revoked by EO 12869)	51751
12780 (Revoked by EO 12873)	54911
12813 (Revoked by EO 12869)	51751
12853 (See notice of September 30)	51563
12853 (See EO 12872)	54029
12853 (See DOT rule of Oct. 15)	54024
12866	51735
12866 (Supplemented by EO 12875)	58093
12867	51747
12868	51749
12869	51751
12870	51753
12871	52201
12872	54029
12873	54911
12874	54921
12875	58093

Administrative Orders:

Memorandums:

August 19, 1993	52397

SECTION G. SOURCES OF ADDITIONAL INFORMATION ON ADMINISTRATIVE AGENCIES

1. The United States Government Manual

This handbook, published by the Office of the Federal Register, is revised annually and contains general information about Congress and the federal judiciary. However, the major emphasis of this publication is on the executive branch and regulatory agencies. Each department and agency is described in concise form with citations to the statutes creating the department or agency. A description of functions and authority, names and functions of officials, and listings of major publications are provided.

The *Manual* includes several appendices. One appendix lists all abolished and transferred agencies with an indication of what has happened to the functions for which they had responsibility. For example, under *Civil Service Commission, U.S.* it is noted that the agency has been redesignated as the *Merit Systems Protection Board* and its functions transferred to the *Board* and to the *Office of Personnel Management* by the Reorganization Plan No. 2 of 1978.

Other appendices list: commonly used abbreviations and acronyms; *Standard Federal Regions* and *Federal Executive Boards;* and all agencies, in alphabetical order, that appear in the *CFR*. Separate indexes for name and agency/subject also are available.

It is frequently useful to consult *The United States Government Manual* before starting research on an administrative law problem.

2. Federal Regulatory Directory [21]

The *Directory* can be used to augment the information in *The United States Government Manual*. Discussion of the topic of regulation and of the current issues involving federal administrative agencies and extensive profiles of the largest and most important agencies are included. Summary information on most of the other federal agencies is provided. The 6th edition, published in 1990, is the most recent.

SECTION H. PRESIDENTIAL DOCUMENTS

Most rules or regulations are the result of the activities of federal agencies operating under powers delegated by Congress. The President also has the authority to issue documents that have legal effect. This authority is either constitutional, statutory, or both. This section describes the types of Presidential documents and describes sources in which documentation of Presidential activities may be located.

[21] Published by Congressional Quarterly, Inc.

1. Proclamations and Executive Orders [22]

Proclamations and executive orders have been widely used by presidents to exercise their authority. Proclamations are generally addressed to the entire nation and their content frequently relates to ceremonial or celebratory occasions. [See Illustration 103.] Executive orders generally are used by the President to direct and govern the activities of government officials and agencies. [See Illustration 104.]

Proclamations and Executive Orders appear in:

a. *Federal Register*

b. *Weekly Compilation of Presidential Documents*

c. Title 3 of *CFR* and compilation volumes of Title 3

d. *Public Papers of the Presidents* to January 1989

e. *United States Code Congressional and Administrative News* Advance Pamphlets

f. *United States Code Service,* Advance Service pamphlets

g. *CIS Presidential Executive Orders & Proclamations on Microfiche*

h. LEXIS and WESTLAW as described in Section C–4 *supra.* WESTLAW in its Presidential Documents (PRES) database contains Executive Orders since 1936 and Proclamations, Administrative Orders, Trade Agreements, and Reorganization Plans or Designations from the *Federal Register* since 1984.

LEXIS has the full text of the *Weekly Compilation of Presidential Documents* and the *Public Papers of the Presidents* in the GENFED and LEGIS libraries, PRESDC file from January 20, 1981.

In addition, the other electronic research sources described in Section C–4 contain the Presidential documents that are in the *Federal Register* and the *CFR.*

i. Proclamations also may be found in the *United States Statutes at Large.*

2. Codification of Presidential Proclamations and Executive Orders

This publication was started in 1979 by the Office of the Federal Register. Its purpose is to provide in one source Proclamations and Executive Orders that have general applicability and continuing effect.

---

[22] For a detailed study, see HOUSE COMM. ON GOVERNMENT OPERATIONS, 85TH CONG., 1ST SESS., EXECUTIVE ORDERS AND PROCLAMATIONS: STUDY OF A USE OF PRESIDENTIAL POWERS (Comm. Print 1957). *See also* Donna Bennett & Philip Yannarella, *Locating Presidential Proclamations and Executive Orders—A Guide to Sources,* LEGAL REFERENCE SERVICES Q., Sum./Fall 1985, at 177; Mary Woodward, *Executive Orders: A Journey,* LEGAL REFERENCE SERVICES Q., No. 3, 1990, at 125. To locate Executive Orders issued prior to the publication of the *Federal Register,* see NEW YORK CITY HISTORICAL RECORDS SURVEY, PRESIDENTIAL EXECUTIVE ORDERS, NUMBERED 1–8030, 1862–1938 (1944); NEW JERSEY HISTORICAL RECORDS SURVEY, LIST AND INDEX OF PRESIDENTIAL EXECUTIVE ORDERS: UNNUMBERED SERIES (1789–1941) (1944).

This codification takes all the previously-published Proclamations and Executive Orders still in force and arranges them by subject. Amendments to the original documents are incorporated in the text.

This codification is arranged in 50 titles corresponding to those of the *Code of Federal Regulations* and covers the period April 13, 1945— January 20, 1989. A "Disposition Table" at the back of the volume lists all Proclamations and Executive Orders issued during 1945–1989, with their amendments, and indication of their current status and chapter designations, where applicable.

3. Reorganization Plans

By the provisions of 5 U.S.C. §§ 901–912 (1988), the President is authorized to examine the organization of all agencies and make changes that provide for the better management of the executive branch of the government. The President is authorized to submit proposed reorganization plans to both houses of Congress. Proposed reorganization plans are published in the *Congressional Record*. The reorganization plan becomes effective if the President accepts the joint resolution passed by the House and the Senate approving the plan submitted by the President.

Reorganization plans are published, as approved, in the *Federal Register,* Title 3 of the *CFR, United States Statutes at Large,* and in 5 *U.S.C.* Appendix. The *Congressional Record* is a source for plans not approved by Congress.

4. Other Presidential Documents

In addition to the documents discussed *supra,* the President issues Administrative Orders, such as findings, determinations, and memoranda; Executive Agreements (discussed in Chapter 19); and messages to Congress and signing statements [see Chapter 10]. Administrative Orders are published in the *Federal Register* and in Title 3 of the *Code of Federal Regulations.*

5. Presidential Nominations

At the end of each issue of the *Weekly Compilation of Presidential Documents* is a list of Presidential nominations submitted to the Senate. The *Congressional Record's Daily Digest* for the Senate contains in each issue the names of those nominated and of those confirmed by the Senate.

An up-to-date cumulative list of Executive branch (but not judicial) nominations is published in Volume 1 of the *CCH Congressional Index.*[23]

---

[23] For a directory of judicial nominations, see IRIS J. WILDMAN, FEDERAL JUDGES AND JUSTICES: A CURRENT LISTING OF NOMINATIONS, CONFIRMATIONS, ELEVATIONS, RETIREMENTS (1987, periodically supplemented).

6. Compilations of Presidential Documents

The following sources provide comprehensive collections of presidential documents:

a. *Weekly Compilation of Presidential Documents.* This Office of the Federal Register publication is published every Monday and contains statements, messages, and other Presidential materials released by the White House during the preceding week. It includes an index of Contents at the beginning of each issue for documents in that issue. Each issue also contains a cumulative subject index and name index for the previous issues of the current quarter. An annual index, divided into names and subjects, is published. Other finding aids are: lists of laws approved by the President; nominations submitted to the Senate; and a checklist of White House releases.

b. *Public Papers of the Presidents.* This series starts with the administration of President Hoover. It is published annually in one or more volumes and includes a compilation of the Presidents' messages to Congress, public speeches, news conferences, and public letters. The final volume for each year contains a cumulative index to the volumes published during the year. After all the volumes for an administration are published, a cumulative index for that President is published by a commercial publisher.[24] The papers of President Franklin Roosevelt and certain earlier Presidents have been published commercially.

Beginning with the 1977 volumes, which cover the first year of President Carter's administration and continuing through the volume for 1988–89, the last year of President Reagan's administration, the set includes all of the material printed in the *Weekly Compilation of Presidential Documents.* Beginning in 1989, the first year of the administration of President Bush, Proclamations and Executive Orders are not reproduced. Rather a table refers the user to the appropriate issues of the *Federal Register* in which the documents are published.

c. *Title 3 of the Code of Federal Regulations.* Presidential documents that were required to be published in the *Federal Register* are compiled in Title 3 of the *CFR.* Prior to 1976, compilation volumes of Title 3 were published covering various time periods. Since 1976, a compilation volume has been published annually. Unlike the other yearly codifications of agency regulations, each compilation of Title 3 is a unique source of Presidential documents and not an updated codification. Thus, each compilation of Title 3 is a permanent reference source. Since 1985, most yearly compilations of Title 3 have a white cover to distinguish them from other volumes of the *CFR* and to emphasize the permanent value of each edition.

d. *Inaugural Addresses of the Presidents of the United States from George Washington 1789 to George Bush 1989* [Bicentennial Edition], Washington, DC: Government Printing Office, 1989.

---

[24] THE CUMULATED INDEXES TO THE PUBLIC PAPERS OF THE PRESIDENTS OF THE UNITED STATES (KTO Press, 1977–79; Krauss International Publications, 1979).

7. Updating Presidential Documents

The use of *Shepard's Code of Federal Regulations Citations,* described in Section E–1–d *supra,* also applies to Presidential Proclamations, Executive Orders, and Reorganization Plans. Presidential documents included in Title 3 can be updated using the *LSA.*

SECTION I. ILLUSTRATIONS FOR PRESIDENTIAL DOCUMENTS

103. Example of Presidential Proclamation
104. Example of Presidential Executive Order

[Illustration 103]

EXAMPLE OF PRESIDENTIAL PROCLAMATION

Federal Register / Vol. 58, No. 197 / Thursday, October 14, 1993 / Presidential Documents   **53101**

Presidential Documents

Proclamation 6609 of October 8, 1993

National School Lunch Week, 1993

By the President of the United States of America

A Proclamation

Since 1946, the National School Lunch Program has demonstrated a partnership between Federal, State, and local officials in providing nutritious low-cost and free meals to America's schoolchildren. Our commitment to the National School Lunch Program reflects our recognition of the importance of nutrition to our children's health and to our Nation's future.

Currently, the National School Lunch Program operates in more than 90 percent of the Nation's public schools and serves about 25 million lunches a day. Many of our children receive their only nutritious meal of the day at sch[   ]ion span and l[Proclamation issued by the President   ]. School lunch[   ]learning laboratories, putting into practice the classroom lessons learned by the students on the importance of nutrition to health and well-being.

There is no longer any question that diet is related to good health, and school meal programs should meet the Dietary Guidelines for Americans so that children get nutritious meals. Like preventive medicine, the value of school lunches will multiply and the benefits will last a lifetime. National School Lunch Week affords us the opportunity to take a fresh look at the National School Lunch Program to determine what changes are necessary in order to meet these dietary guidelines. We also can recognize health professionals, school food service personnel, teachers, principals, parents, community leaders, and others for their commitment to ensuring that the lunches served in their schools will provide the nutrition so important to young students.

In recognition of the contributions of the National School Lunch Program to the nutritional well-being of children, the Congress, by joint resolution of October 9, 1962 (Public Law No. 87–780), has designated the week beginning the second Sunday in October in each year as "National School Lunch Week" and has requested the President to issue a proclamation in observance of that week.

NOW, THEREFORE, I, WILLIAM J. CLINTON, President of the United States of America, do hereby proclaim the week beginning October 10, 1993, as National School Lunch Week. I call upon all Americans to recognize those individuals whose efforts contribute to the success of this valuable program.

IN WITNESS WHEREOF, I have hereunto set my hand this eighth day of October, in the year of our Lord nineteen hundred and ninety-three, and of the Independence of the United States of America the two hundred and eighteenth.

William J. Clinton

[FR Doc. 93–25411
Filed 10–12–93; 4:09 pm]
Billing code 3195–01–P

[Illustration 104]

EXAMPLE OF PRESIDENTIAL EXECUTIVE ORDER

Presidential Documents

Executive Order 12848 of May 19, 1993

Federal Plan To Break the Cycle of Homelessness

By the authority vested in me as President by the Constitution and the laws of the United States of America, including title II of the Stewart B. McKinney Homeless Assistance Act, as amended (42 U.S.C. 11311–11320), and section 301 of title 3, United States Code, and in order to provide for the streamlining and strengthening of the Nation's efforts to break the cycle of homelessness, it is hereby ordered as follows:

Section 1. Federal member agencies acting through the Interagency Council on the Homeless, established under title II of the Stewart B. McKinney Homeless Assistance Act, shall develop a single coordinated Federal plan for breaking the cycle of existing homelessness and for preventing future homelessness.

Sec. 2. The plan shall recommend Federal administrative and legislative in~~~~~~oposed
sc **Executive Order issued by the President** ng any
nlegisla-
tiappro-
priate, existing programs designed to assist homeless individuals and families.

Sec. 3. The plan shall make recommendations on how current funding programs can be redirected, if necessary, to provide links between housing, support, and education services and to promote coordination and cooperation among grantees, local housing and support service providers, school districts, and advocates for homeless individuals and families. The plan shall also provide recommendations on ways to encourage and support creative approaches and cost-effective, local efforts to break the cycle of existing homelessness and prevent future homelessness, including tying current homeless assistance programs to permanent housing assistance, local housing affordability strategies, or employment opportunities.

Sec. 4. To the extent practicable, the Council shall consult with representatives of State and local governments (including education agencies), nonprofit providers of services and housing for homeless individuals and families, advocates for homeless individuals and families, currently and formerly homeless individuals and families, and other interested parties.

Sec. 5. The Council shall submit the plan to the President no later than 9 months after the date of this order.

William J Clinton

THE WHITE HOUSE,
May 19, 1993.

[FR Doc. 93-12224
Filed 5-19-93; 12:22 pm]
Billing code 3195-01-P

SECTION J. FEDERAL ADMINISTRATIVE DECISIONS

1. Agency Decisions

Many federal administrative agencies also serve a quasi-judicial function and, in performing this function, issue decisions.[25] The Federal Communications Commission, for example, is authorized by statute to license radio and television stations. It also has the authority to enforce its regulations covering the operations of these stations. When stations allegedly violate the terms of the statute or the regulations, the Federal Communications Commission can hear charges and issue decisions.

Decisions of administrative agencies are published, not in the *Federal Register,* but in separate sources.[26] They are often in two formats: (1) official publications of administrative agencies published by the U.S. Government Printing Office, and (2) unofficial publications of commercial publishers, including LEXIS and WESTLAW.

a. *Official Publications of Decisions of Federal Administrative Agencies.* These are available in most law libraries and in public and university libraries that are official depositories of the U.S. Government Printing Office. The format, frequency, and method of publication vary from agency to agency. Generally, they are issued on an infrequent schedule and are poorly indexed. Some sets have indexes and digests in the back of each volume. For other sets, separate indexes and digests are published. Some sets of federal administrative decisions have an advance sheet service.

b. *Unofficial Publications of Decisions of Federal Administrative Agencies.* Commercially published agency decisions are reproduced in looseleaf services, which often are accompanied by bound, sequentially numbered volumes. For example, Pike and Fischer's *Radio Regulation* contains decisions of the Federal Communications Commission. LEXIS and WESTLAW have topical databases that contain FCC decisions. Looseleaf services are discussed in Chapter 13.

2. Judicial Review of Agency Decisions

After an agency has issued a decision, the decision may, in most instances, be appealed to the federal courts. The decisions resulting from these appeals may be found by consulting the following sources:

a. *West's Federal Practice Digest 4th* and its predecessor sets.

b. *United States Supreme Court Digest, Lawyers' Edition* or *U.S. Supreme Court Digest.*

[25] Many of the mysteries about various administrative law courts are explained in Harold H. Bruff, *Specialized Courts in Administrative Law,* 43 ADMIN. L. REV. 329 (1991).

[26] For a detailed discussion of sources (official, unofficial, and databases) to consult for decisions of 33 agencies, *see* Veronica Maclay, *Selected Sources of United States Agency Decisions,* 16 GOV'T PUBLICATIONS REV. 271 (1989).

c. *American Digest System* if the preceding digests are not available.

d. *Shepard's United States Administrative Citations* (discussed in Chapter 14).

e. *Treatises on administrative law* (discussed in Chapter 17).

f. *Looseleaf services* (Chapter 13 contains a general discussion).

g. *LEXIS* and *WESTLAW.*

3. Representative Examples of Currently Published Official Decisions of Federal Administrative Agencies

a. Federal Communications Commission. *Reports* [1st Series], vol. 1–45 (1934–1965); [2d Series], vol. 1–104 (1965–1986). Continued by: *FCC Record,* vol. 1 *et seq.* (1986 to date).

b. Federal Trade Commission. *Decisions,* vol. 1 *et seq.* (1915 to date).

c. Interstate Commerce Commission. *Reports* [1st Series], vol. 1–366 (1887–1983); [2d Series], vol. 1 *et seq.* (1984 to date).

d. National Labor Relations Board. *Decisions and Orders,* vol. 1 *et seq.* (1935 to date).

e. Occupational Safety and Health Review Commission. *Decisions,* vol. 1 *et seq.* (1971 to date).

f. Securities and Exchange Commission. *Decisions and Reports,* vol. 1 *et seq.* (1934 to date).

SECTION K. STATE ADMINISTRATIVE REGULATIONS AND DECISIONS

1. State Regulations

The regulations of state agencies are published in a variety of formats. In some states the administrative regulations are officially codified and published in sets similar to the *Code of Federal Regulations.*[27] These may be supplemented by a publication similar to the *Federal Register.* In other states, each agency issues its own regulations, and it is necessary that inquiries be directed to the pertinent agency. Increasingly, state regulations are being added to WESTLAW and LEXIS and are being produced as CD–ROM products.

2. State Administrative Decisions

Many state agencies also publish their decisions. Most commonly, the decisions of unemployment compensation commissions, tax commissions, and public utility commissions are published. Increasingly, state

---

[27] KAMLA J. KING & JUDITH SPRINGBERG, BNA'S DIRECTORY OF STATE ADMINISTRATIVE CODES AND REGISTERS (1993), provides comprehensive coverage for the 50 states and the territories of American Samoa, Guam, Puerto Rico, Northern Mariana Islands, and Virgin Islands, including the contents pages from each published administrative code.

agency decisions are being added to WESTLAW and LEXIS and are being produced as CD–ROM products.

3. Research in State Administrative Law

a.   Check the state code to determine if the state has an Administrative Procedure Act and if the method for publication of regulations is prescribed therein.

b.   Check the state's organization manual to determine the agencies that issue regulations or decisions.

c.   Consult a legal encyclopedia or administrative law treatise if published for a state.

d.   Consult a state legal research manual, if available (see Appendix B).

e.   Consult the various electronic sources to determine if state regulations or agency decisions are available.

SECTION L.   SUMMARY

1. Federal Register

a.   Types of documents published are:

(1) Regulations and rules of federal agencies.

(2) Proposed regulations and rules of federal agencies.

(3) Agency notices.

(4) Presidential documents.

b.   Indexes.

(1) *Federal Register Index.*

Cumulative index published monthly and annually.

(2) *CIS Federal Register Index.*

c.   Cumulative *List of Parts Affected.*

This table updates the monthly issues of the *LSA: List of CFR Sections Affected.*

d.   Frequency of publication.

Began in 1936.   Published Monday through Friday, except on an official federal holiday.

e.   Contents of the *Federal Register* must be judicially noticed.

2. Code of Federal Regulations

a.   Contains all regulations that first appeared in the *Federal Register* that are of a general and permanent nature and are still in force.

b.   Arranged by subject in 50 Titles.

c.   Each Title is subdivided into Chapters, Subchapters, Parts, and Sections.   The *CFR* is cited by Title and Section.

d. Each Title is in a separate pamphlet or pamphlets. Each Title is republished once a year, at which time new material is added, and repealed or obsolete material is deleted.

e. Regulations published in the *CFR* are *prima facie* evidence of the official text.

f. Indexes.

(1) *CFR Index and Finding Aids.*

Annual subject and agency index. The *Finding Aids* section in the annual index volume has a *Parallel Table of Authorities and Rules* and other aids for locating regulations and Presidential documents.

(2) CIS *Index to the Code of Federal Regulations.*

g. *LSA: List of CFR Sections Affected.*

This list indicates any changes to the annual volumes of the *CFR*.

3. The United States Government Manual

a. Annual handbook.

b. Describes administrative organizations whose regulations are published in the *Federal Register*.

c. Information on Congress, the federal judiciary, and important agency personnel.

d. Subject/agency index and name/agency index.

4. Presidential Documents

a. Issued pursuant to constitutional or statutory authority, or both.

b. Types of documents:

(1) Proclamations

(2) Executive Orders

(3) Reorganization Plans

(4) Administrative orders, executive agreements, messages to Congress, and signing statements.

c. Official comprehensive sources of Presidential documents.

(1) *Weekly Compilation of Presidential Documents*

Published each Monday and contains Presidential materials released by the White House during the preceding week.

(2) *Public Papers of the Presidents*

Coverage begins with the administration of President Hoover. Papers of Franklin Roosevelt are excluded. Volumes are issued annually and from 1977 to January 1989 include all material in the *Weekly Compilation*.

(3) Title 3 of *Code of Federal Regulations*

Since 1976, an annual compilation providing Proclamations, Executive Orders, and other Presidential documents. Prior to 1976, compilation volumes for various time periods were published. Since each compilation is a unique source of one year's documents, each compilation has permanent reference value.

d.   Sources of selective types of documents:

(1) *Federal Register*

(2) Codification of Presidential Proclamations and Executive Orders

Subject arrangement of all previously-published Proclamations and Executive Orders still in force.

(3) *United States Code Congressional and Administrative News,* Advance pamphlets

(4) *United States Code Service,* Advance Service pamphlets

(5) *CIS Presidential Executive Orders & Proclamations on Microfiche*

(6) LEXIS and WESTLAW

(7) *United States Statutes at Large*

(8) 5 *U.S.C.* Appendix

(9) *Congressional Record.*

5. Federal Administrative Decisions

a.   Official publications published by U.S. Government Printing Office.

b.   Unofficial publications by commercial publishers.

c.   Electronic resources, including WESTLAW and LEXIS.

6. State Administrative Regulations and Decisions

a.   Some states have codified the regulations of their administrative agencies.

b.   Some states publish the decisions of their administrative agencies.

Chapter 13

LOOSELEAF SERVICES

SECTION A. INTRODUCTION TO LOOSELEAF SERVICES

Law publishers have always been concerned with keeping their publications current. Traditionally, this has been accomplished by the issuance of pocket supplements, usually on an annual basis, together with supplemental pamphlets and occasional revised volumes. This is still the most common method of keeping sets of statutes, digests, and encyclopedias up to date. Some other types of materials, most notably those in the area of administrative law, often require much more frequent updating, and thus a different method of supplementation.

For example, to research adequately a problem in the law of taxation, a researcher must locate not only relevant statutes and court cases but also regulations of the Internal Revenue Service and the Treasury Department, rulings of the Commissioner of Internal Revenue, news releases, technical information bulletins, U.S. Tax Court cases, and other agency documents. A researcher attempting to find the answer to a tax problem using only the *United States Code,* the digests, the *Federal Register,* and the *Code of Federal Regulations* would find it not only cumbersome but, at times impossible, to accomplish. Publishers have responded to the problems of inaccessibility, complexity, and the sheer bulk of rapidly-changing information by developing looseleaf services.

1. Special Characteristics

As the name indicates, looseleaf services consist of special binders that simplify the insertion, removal, and substitution of individual pages. This characteristic allows the publisher to update material frequently and systematically through a process of constant editing, introducing what is new, and removing what is superseded. The speed and accuracy afforded by this ongoing revision are two of the looseleaf services greatest assets.

This looseleaf format also allows for creativity in the ways materials are organized. Most services, however, attempt to consolidate into one source the statutes, regulations, court cases and administrative agency decisions, and commentary on a particular legal topic and then facilitate access to this material through detailed indexes and other finding aids. By these means a researcher can find the relevant material, both primary and secondary, in one place. Further, most services include current awareness information, which can include news of proposed legislation, pending agency regulations and agency decisions, and even

informed rumor. They also frequently contain forms, summaries of professional meetings, calendars of forthcoming events, and other news deemed relevant to the researcher or practicing attorney.

Looseleaf services are of three types: (1) those, as previously described, in which pages are *interfiled* with existing materials; (2) those in *newsletter* format whereby each issue is added to a binder sequentially and chronologically; and (3) a combination of the two formats. Traditionally, those prepared by a publisher's editorial staff, regardless of the publication's format, have a standardized publication schedule, typically weekly, biweekly, or monthly. By contrast, looseleaf services by named authors usually are updated with interfiled materials less frequently and on an "as needed" basis.

The convenience, currency, frequency, and excellent indexing of looseleaf services often make them the best place to begin researching administrative law problems. In many rapidly-developing areas of the law, such as privacy, the environment, and consumer protection, the looseleaf service may be the only exhaustive research tool available.[1]

2. Publishers of Looseleaf Services

Looseleaf services vary in content and coverage, reflecting both the subject area of the service and the editorial policy of the publisher. Historically, three publishers—Commerce Clearing House (CCH), Bureau of National Affairs (BNA), and Prentice Hall (PH)—were the leading publishers of looseleaf services prepared by editorial staffs. Recently, Prentice Hall was sold and subdivided and its publications either have been taken over by others or discontinued, leaving CCH and BNA as the dominant players.

Meanwhile, other publishers, especially divisions of Thomson Legal Publications, *e.g.,* Lawyers Cooperative Publishing and Research Institute of America, have increased their activity in the editorial staff-produced looseleaf services market.[2] Matthew Bender & Company, Inc. continues to be the largest publisher of treatises by named authors, including such notable works as *Moore's Federal Practice, Benedict on Admiralty,* and *Powell on Real Property,* with Shepard's/McGraw–Hill, Inc., Butterworth, Little, Brown & Company, and Thomson division

---

[1] A tremendous number of looseleaf services by various publishers on many different subjects are currently published. *See, e.g.,* LEGAL LOOSELEAFS IN PRINT (Arlene L. Eis comp. & ed.), which is an annual publication that lists approximately 4,000 titles by over 300 publishers. This source includes information on the number of volumes in a looseleaf set, price, frequency, cost of supplementation, and Library of Congress classification number. It is arranged alphabetically by title and includes publisher, subject, and electronic format indexes.

[2] For example, Lawyers Cooperative Publishing produces the multi-volume *Americans With Disabilities—Practice and Compliance Manual.* Research Institute of American (RIA) publishes the *United States Tax Reporter,* a remodeled version of what was once Prentice Hall's *Federal Taxes.* RIA also publishes a number of other looseleaf services in the tax, estate planning, and business areas.

companies, *e.g.,* Clark Boardman Callaghan and Warren Gorham & Lamont, also playing prominent roles.

Perhaps the most remarkable development in recent years with respect to looseleaf services is the extent to which they are being added full-text to the online services, WESTLAW and LEXIS, and being published in CD–ROM versions. This electronic availability allows precision searching of these services that heretofore was impossible.

This Chapter focuses on only those features that are common to most interfiled and newsletter looseleaf services. Particular attention is given to representative publications from CCH and BNA. When using any looseleaf service, one should be alert to its individual characteristics, and special attention should be paid to the introductory and prefatory materials supplied by the publisher. This is particularly necessary when using looseleaf services on taxation [3] or labor law because the magnitude of materials on these subjects makes the looseleaf service very complex.

SECTION B. USING LOOSELEAF SERVICES

1. Interfiled Looseleafs in General

Most topical looseleaf services in which new material replaces older pages rather than supplementing existing ones have the following common elements:

a. Full text of the statutes on the topic, often with significant legislative history

b. Either full text or digests of relevant court cases or administrative agency decisions

c. Editorial comment and explanatory notes

d. Topical indexes

e. Tables of cases and statutes

f. Finding lists for statutes, cases, and administrative materials

g. Indexes to current materials and cumulative indexes

h. Current reports summarizing recent developments

i. A weekly, biweekly, or monthly publication schedule.

2. Newsletter Looseleafs in General

Most topical looseleaf services in the newsletter format, whereby pamphlets are filed sequentially and chronologically, have the following common elements:

a. News and editorial comments of general interest

b. Recent state and federal developments and recent developments in particular topics within the broad subject covered

---

[3] For more detailed information on federal taxation, see Chapter 24, J. Jacobstein, R. Mersky & D. Dunn, *Fundamentals of Legal Research* (6th ed.).

c. Text of or excerpts from major legislation, court cases, and administrative regulations and agency decisions

d. Subject and table of cases indexes

e. A weekly, biweekly, or monthly publication schedule.

3. Using Commerce Clearing House Looseleaf Services

Commerce Clearing House, Inc. (CCH) is one of the two major publishers of looseleaf services, and its publications are typically of the type in which pages are interfiled. Examples of these include the *U.S. Supreme Court Bulletin, Copyright Law Reporter, Federal Securities Law Reporter, Products Liability Reporter,* and *Trade Regulation Reporter.* CCH publications range from those complete in one binder to those that fill a dozen or more.

Regardless of size, these publications begin with an introductory section that discusses the use and organization of the service. The importance of this feature cannot be over-emphasized. A careful reading of it may save the researcher both time and frustration. The volumes are divided into sections by tabcards. These offer quick access to major topic headings. Typically, there will be a comprehensive Topical Index to the entire service. In addition, some services have special indexes to particular topics or volumes. The quality of the indexing is generally quite high, as the publisher strives to provide as many access points as possible.

The indexes are made more useful by the unique, dual numbering system employed by the publisher. Under this system, in addition to normal pagination, there is a paragraph number assigned to each topic area. These numbers may encompass as little as one textual paragraph or as much as fifty or more pages. This flexibility of format allows for frequent additions and deletions to the text without a total disruption of the indexing system. Research can begin by consulting one of the indexes, which will refer to the appropriate paragraph number. By then turning to the correct paragraph number, one can locate the pertinent material. In looseleaf services, page numbers often are used only as guides for filing new pages and removing old ones. The volumes containing the CCH editorial explanations of the topic of the reporter, various reference materials, laws and regulations, and forms are typically referred to as "compilation" volumes.

The full texts of new court cases and agency rulings, often supplied as part of the looseleaf service, generally are placed in a separate volume or section from the contents of the compilation volume(s). Each case or ruling is commonly assigned its own paragraph number, and can be located in any one of several ways. Most services have tables of cases, statutes, and administrative regulations. When a citation to one of these is encountered, research can begin by consulting the appropriate table and obtaining the paragraph number where the cited material is discussed. Special indexes cross reference from materials found under the paragraph numbers to materials concerning current developments.

Materials summarizing current developments generally are presented in the form of weekly bulletins that accompany the pages to be filed. These bulletins are often retained as part of the service, and constitute valuable research tools in themselves. [See Illustrations 105–109 for examples of how a typical CCH looseleaf service is used.]

Some services include state laws sections. These are generally arranged by state, with the same paragraph number being assigned uniformly to the same topic for each state. In some instances, *all-state* charts are published that give citations to the various state codes. [See Illustration 110.]

Often a CCH service that systematically reports court cases or agency decisions will have a separate, bound reporter that results from the looseleaf subscription.[4] For example, CCH's widely-used *Standard Federal Tax Reporter* includes a binder labeled "U.S. Tax Cases— Advance Sheets." These advance sheets are cumulated into bound volumes twice a year, with the "Advance Sheet" volume always containing only the most recent materials.

In general, the successful use of CCH looseleaf services requires the researcher to use the following three steps:

a. Locate the topic or topics under research by consulting the Topical Index to the service.

b. Read carefully all materials under paragraph numbers referred to by the Topical Index. When digests of cases are given, note citations to cases so that the full text can be read.

c. Consult the appropriate index or indexes to current materials.

4. Using Bureau of National Affairs Looseleaf Services

The Bureau of National Affairs, Inc. (BNA) is the second major publisher of looseleaf services. As a general rule, its organizational principles differ from those of CCH. BNA's typical format consists of one or more three-ring binders in which periodic issues (or releases) are filed. Unlike CCH, the issues do not contain individual pages to be interfiled with existing text, but instead consist of pamphlet inserts numbered sequentially and filed chronologically. Thus, there is no provision for revision of earlier issues. This format allows for the service to be issued quickly, at the expense of the comprehensiveness guaranteed by the interfiling system. Examples of these publications are *Antitrust & Trade Regulation Report, Securities Regulation & Law Report,* and *Patent, Trademark & Copyright Journal.*

A slight variation of the self-contained publications are those that include several separate components, usually including a summary and analysis of major developments, the text of pertinent legislation, and the

---

[4] As was noted in Chapter 4, federal district court cases are reported selectively. Some cases not reported in the *Federal Supplement* are published in one or more of the subject looseleaf services. Consequently, it is frequently worthwhile to check the Table of Cases of these services for cases not reported in the *Federal Supplement.*

text or a digest of court actions. Such features as important speeches, government reports, book reviews, and bibliographies also may be included. Each of these components is generally filed behind its own tabcard. Examples of these services include *United States Law Week, Criminal Law Reporter,* and *Family Law Reporter,* with the latter also including a monograph section that provides detailed treatments of timely, practice-related issues.

BNA services feature cumulative indexes that offer topical access to the material. Since current issues supplement earlier ones, there is no need for paragraph numbers, and simple pagination is used. There are also case tables for each service. For some of its sets, BNA periodically supplies special storage binders for old issues, so that the main volumes can always contain current material. Regardless of whether the service is issued as a single newsletter or in several pamphlet-type components, each is an attempt to keep the researcher fully informed of all developments in the subject area of the service.

BNA has long published one large service that differs significantly in arrangement from its other looseleaf services described above. This is its *Labor Relations Reporter.* This set has separate looseleaf volumes for the following areas of labor relations:

Labor Management Relations (federal)
Labor Arbitration and Dispute Settlement
Wages and Hours
Fair Employment Practices
State Labor Laws
Individual Employment Rights
Americans with Disabilities

Each of the looseleaf volumes for these units of the *Labor Relations Reporter* contains relevant statutes, regulations, and court cases. Periodically, court cases are removed from the looseleaf volumes and reprinted in bound series, *e.g., Labor Arbitration Reports, Wage and Hour Cases.* Each set of cases also has its own index and digest where the cases are classified according to BNA's classification scheme.

The entire set is unified by a two-volume looseleaf "Master Index" and a two-volume looseleaf "Labor Relations Expediter." [See Illustrations 111–114 for how one component of the *Labor Relations Reporter* is used.]

BNA also publishes other services, including *Environment Reporter* and *Occupational Safety & Health Reporter,* in a format similar to *Labor Relations Reporter.*[5]

5. Looseleaf Services in Electronic Format

The concept of a looseleaf service as exclusively a paper product has disappeared. These services are being made available on LEXIS and

---

[5] A useful source for learning more about the various publications and services of the Bureau of National Affairs, Inc. is BNA's Reporter Services and Their Use (3d ed. 1992).

WESTLAW with increasing frequency. Having a full-text, interfiled-type version of a looseleaf service available online may provide the most convenient means yet discovered for updating materials, while offering the most precise searching capabilities. Rather than subscribers having to file new pages, the online versions are updated electronically by the vendors as new language is added, deleted, or changed. Obviously, the sequentially-published newsletter-type looseleaf services are even easier to include in databases.

Almost all Bureau of National Affairs' publications are available online in LEXIS or NEXIS and WESTLAW, with coverage for many services dating back to 1982. Some services issued more frequently than their online counterparts are available only online. These include *Law Week Daily Edition* and *BNA Tax Updates,* the latter being updated twice daily. Several Research Institute of America publications are likewise available in the CALR services. While CCH services are less likely to be available in the two major CALR services, *Standard Federal Tax Reporter* and its companion volumes are on WESTLAW, and the state securities *Blue Sky Law Reporter* is on both LEXIS and WEST-LAW.

In addition, numerous looseleaf treatises are in online versions, such as those from Matthew Bender, Lawyers Cooperative Publishing, Clark Boardman Callaghan, and Warren Gorham & Lamont. Because of their less frequent updating, these looseleaf treatises also lend themselves well to CD–ROM technology. For example, Matthew Bender has several CD–ROM products containing looseleaf treatises, and BNA publishes its *Tax Management Portfolio* series as a CD–ROM product. The availability of looseleaf services in electronic format will continue to expand in the years ahead.[6]

---

[6] The best means to determine whether a particular publication is available in electronic format is to consult the online and paper content guides of both WESTLAW and LEXIS or a particular publisher's catalog. Also helpful is the "Electronic Format Index" in LEGAL LOOSELEAFS IN PRINT, note 1 *supra.*

SECTION C. ILLUSTRATIONS

Illustrations Using CCH Copyright Law Reporter

Problem: Does copyright law prohibit the copying of the pagination from law reporters?

105.   Page from the Topical Index
106–108.   Pages from compilation volume
109.   Page from the Cumulative Index
110.   Page from CCH Food Drug Cosmetic Law Reporter

Illustrations Using BNA Fair Employment Practices (FEP) Division of Labor Relations Reporter

Problem: Can attorneys' fees be collected for the work of paralegals and law clerks?

111.   Page from Master Index volume containing FEP Outline of Classifications
112.   Page from a Master Index volume containing FEP Cumulative Digest and Index (CDI)
113–114.   Pages from Fair Employment Cases

[Illustration 105]

PAGE FROM TOPICAL INDEX, CCH COPYRIGHT LAW REPORTER

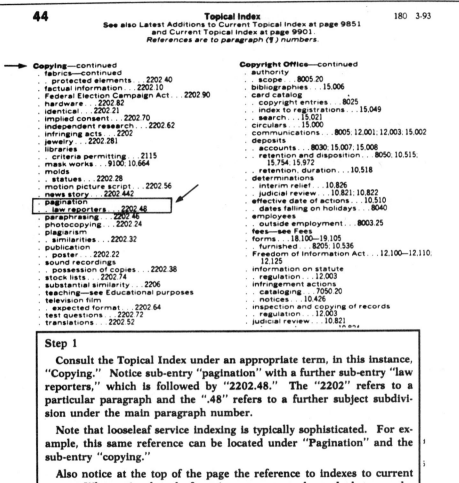

44   **Topical Index**   180   3-93

See also Latest Additions to Current Topical Index at page 9851
and Current Topical Index at page 9901.
References are to paragraph (¶) numbers.

Copying—continued
. fabrics—continued
. . protected elements . . . 2202.40
. factual information 2202.10
. Federal Election Campaign Act . . . 2202.90
. hardware . . . 2202.82
. identical . . . 2202.21
. implied consent . . . 2202.70
. independent research . . . 2202.62
. infringing acts . . . 2202
. jewelry . . . 2202.281
. libraries
. . criteria permitting . . . 2115
. mask works . . . 9100; 10,664
. molds
. . statues . . . 2202.28
. motion picture script . . . 2202.56
. news story . . . 2202.442
. pagination
. . law reporters . . . 2202.48
. paraphrasing . . . 2202.46
. photocopying . . . 2202.24
. plagiarism
. . similarities . . . 2202.32
. publication
. . poster . . . 2202.22
. sound recordings
. . possession of copies . . . 2202.38
. stock lists . . . 2202.74
. substantial similarity . . . 2206
. teaching—see Educational purposes
. television film
. . expected format . . . 2202.64
. test questions . . . 2202.72
. translations . . . 2202.52

Copyright Office—continued
. authority
. . scope . . . 8005.20
. bibliographies . . . 15,006
. card catalog
. . copyright entries . . . 8025
. . index to registrations . . . 15,049
. . search . . . 15,021
. circulars . . . 15,000
. communications . . . 8005; 12,001; 12,003; 15,002
. deposits
. . accounts . . . 8030; 15,007; 15,008
. . retention and disposition . . . 8050; 10,515; 15,754; 15,972
. . retention, duration . . . 10,518
. determinations
. . interim relief . . . 10,826
. . judicial review . . . 10,821; 10,822
. effective date of actions . . . 10,510
. . dates falling on holidays . . . 8040
. employees
. . outside employment . . . 8003.25
. fees—see Fees
. forms . . . 18,100—19,105
. . furnished . . . 8205; 10,536
. Freedom of Information Act . . . 12,100—12,110; 12,125
. information on statute
. . regulation . . . 12,003
. infringement actions
. . cataloging . . . 7050.20
. . notices . . . 10,426
. inspection and copying of records
. . regulation . . . 12,003
. judicial review . . . 10,821

Step 1

Consult the Topical Index under an appropriate term, in this instance, "Copying." Notice sub-entry "pagination" with a further sub-entry "law reporters," which is followed by "2202.48." The "2202" refers to a particular paragraph and the ".48" refers to a further subject subdivision under the main paragraph number.

Note that looseleaf service indexing is typically sophisticated. For example, this same reference can be located under "Pagination" and the sub-entry "copying."

Also notice at the top of the page the reference to indexes to current cases. When using looseleaf services, one must always look to supplementary indexes for current information.

See next Illustration for Step 2.

Copyright Clearance Center
. library association position . . . 16,073
. publishers/authors guidelines . . . 16,055; 16,070

Copyright notice—see Notice of copyright

Copyright Office
. actions reviewable . . . 10,825
. administration . . . 8005; 10,500
. . catalog of registrations . . . 15,755; 15,973
. . effect of postal problems . . . 15,757; 15,974
. . retention of deposits . . . 15,754; 15,972
. Administrative Procedure Act
. . actions . . . 10,503; 16,030
. annual report of Register . . . 8055

. . comments on . . . 13,000
. . proposed . . . 14,000
. . text . . . 12,000
. special handling of requests . . . 8030
. visual arts registry
. . submissions . . . 12,047

Copyright owner
. definition . . . 4110; 10,007
. exclusive rights—see Exclusive rights
. government contractor
. . technical data . . . 10,849
. interests
. . divisibility . . . 2050
. jukeboxes
. . access to players . . . 3250; 10,137

STA

[Illustration 106]

PAGE FROM COMPILATION VOLUME, CCH
COPYRIGHT LAW REPORTER

---

178   1-93   **1775**

ELEMENTS OF INFRINGEMENT

¶ 2200   **In General**

Infringement of a copyright is the violation of any of the exclusive rights conferred to the copyright owner or to the author of a work of visual art or it is the importation of copies or phonorecords into the United States without the copyright owner's consent (.01). The exclusive rights protected against violation are the rights (1) to make copies and phonorecords, (2) to distribute copies and phonorecords by sale or otherwise (3) to make derivative works based on a copyrighted work, (4) to perform a copyrighted work, and (5) to display such a work (.02).

Questions immediately arise as to what constitutes a reproduction by a copy or phonorecord, what constitutes a derivative work, what is a performance, and what is a display constituting an infringement of a copyrighted work. These problems are discussed in the paragraphs that follow.

The 1976 Copyright Act codified, for the first time in U.S. copyright history, the concept of "fair use" as a defense to a complaint of infringement of a copyrighted work. Under the statute, "fair use" is a limitation on the exclusive rights conferred on a

---

Step 2

Consult the paragraph number referred to in the Topical Index, *e.g.*, 2202. Most CCH looseleaf services provide a brief discussion of the subject of the paragraph, in this instance "Direct Copying as Infringement."

See next Illustration.

.04 **Legislative History.** The statement of the fair use doctrine in section 107 offers some guidance to users in determining when the principles of the doctrine apply. However, the endless variety of situations and combinations of circumstances that can rise in particular cases precludes the formulation of especially during a period of rapid technological change. Beyond a very broad statutory explanation of what fair use is and some of the criteria applicable to it, the courts must be free to adapt the doctrine to particular situations on a case-by-case basis. *Senate Report No. 94-473.*

→ **¶ 2202**   **Direct Copying as Infringement**

Since the exclusive right to reproduce copies or phonorecords of a copyrighted work is reserved to the author of a work or the copyright owner by the 1976 Act (.01), copying a copyrighted work, unless permitted by one of the specific limitations on that right or by the doctrine of "fair use," is an infringement (.02). Fair use is discussed at ¶ 2235—2260.

In *WhiteSmith Music Co. v. Apollo Co.* (1908), 209 U.S.1, the United States Supreme Court said a copy is "that which comes so near to the original as to give every person seeing it the idea created by the original."

To establish a case of infringement, it must be shown that the plaintiff owns a valid copyright in the work and that it was copied. Infringing copying may be established by either (1) direct proof or (2) when such proof is unavailable, by showing that the alleged infringer had access to the copyrighted work (see ¶ 2204) and created substantially similar material (see ¶ 2206). Unauthorized photocopying (.24), video taping (.26), or use of molds of copyrighted works (.28) have established direct copying,

Copyright Law Reports   **¶ 2202**

[Illustration 107]

PAGE FROM COMPILATION VOLUME, CCH
COPYRIGHT LAW REPORTER

: **1776**　　**Scope of Protection—Limitations—Fair Use**　　178　1-93

as has incorporating copyrighted computer programs in other software (.30) without consent. Direct copying has been inferred from the duplication of errors (.34), misspellings (.341) from a preexisting work (.34), and from possession of the items necessary to manufacture infringing articles (.38).

To constitute infringement, protected elements of copyrighted work must be appropriated (.40). Copying factual information is generally permitted (.42).

In 1991, the U.S. Supreme Court held that the copying of names, towns, and telephone numbers from a telephone company's white pages directory did not consti-

> Following the general discussion under the paragraph number, there is frequently an alphabetical listing of "Annotations by Topic." Note that there is a topic for "Pagination," *i.e.*, ".48."
>
> See next Illustration.

digital or analog audio recording devices or media.

See ¶ 2180 for a discussion of copying of computer programs by users.

Annotations by Topic

Actionable Copies	.20	Hidden legend	.36
Citations	.01	Identical copying	.21
Commencement of infringement	.77	Implied consent	.70
Commercial significance	.51	Independent research	.62
Common law copyright	.92	Molds	.28
Compilations (Pre *Feist Publications*)	.50	1909 Copyright Act	.96
Computer programs	.30	Pagination	.48
Copying by state	.98	Photocopying	.24
Different medium	.54	Plagiarism	.32
Dominance in the field	.72	Protected elements	.40
Errors	.34	Publication	.22
Estoppel	.78	Quoting and paraphrasing	.46
Excerpts	.44	Record piracy	.38
Expected format	.64	Same source	.60
Evidence of copying	.68	Sufficiency of changes	.56
Factual information	.10	Translations	.52
Familiarity with other media	.66	Utilitarian works	.74
Federal Election Campaign Act	.90	Videotaping	.26
Findings on copying	.82	Willfullness	.76

Citations

.01 17 U.S.C. § 106, ¶ 10,040.

.02 17 U.S.C. § 501(a), ¶ 10,385.

.10 Factual information.—A publisher did not infringe a telephone company's copyright in its combined white and yellow pages directory by copying names, addresses, and telephone numbers from the telephone company's white pages, because the work copied was uncopyrightable facts that the telephone company did not select, coordinate, or arrange in an original manner. (*Feist Publications, Inc. v. Rural Telephone Service Company, Inc.* (US SCt 1991) 1991 Copyright Law Decisions ¶ 26,702.

.101 Copying factual information from a publisher's copyrighted used car guide to create lists of assessed values of motor vehicles did not constitute infringement, because the defendants used the information for the purpose for which it was intended, to assess values of vehicles. *N.A.D.A. Services Corporation v. Business Data of Virginia, Inc. (DC ED Va. 1986) 1987* Copyright Law Decisions ¶ 26,031, 651 F.Supp. 44.

.102 A book by an art critic on one of the paintings of Claude Monet did not infringe a biography of Monet, because the material copied was uncopyrightable facts. *Mount v. The Viking Press,*

Inc., Publishers (CA-2 1979) 1978-81 Copyright Law Decisions ¶ 25,073.

.20 Actionable copies.—The script, story board, story reel, and promotional reel constituted actionable copies capable of infringing another studio's copyrights even before completion of the motion picture. *Disney Productions, Walt v. Filmation Associates* (DC CD Cal. 1986) 1986 Copyright Law Decisions ¶ 25,948, 628 F.Supp. 871.

.201 Plaintiff's inability to produce copies of infringing television commercials after six years of intensive discovery proceedings required dismissal of his infringement action. *Gero v. Seven-Up Co.* (DC ED N.Y. 1982) 1982 Copyright Law Decisions ¶ 25,404, 535 F.Supp. 212.

.21 Identical copying.—Copying the format and general appearance of copyrighted advertisements was infringement, even though the infringing advertisement was not identical with the one infringed It is not necessary that a copy be identical to be improper. Paraphasing or copying with evasion is an infringement *Ansehl v. Puritan Pharmaceutical Co.* (CA-8 1932) 61 F.2d 131, 20 COBull 32.

.211 A group of convenience stores, along with its president and 50 percent shareholder, was guilty of infringing the valid copyright in plaintiffs' employ-

¶ **2202**

[Illustration 108]

PAGE FROM COMPILATION VOLUME, CCH
COPYRIGHT LAW REPORTER

. **1778** Scope of Protection—Limitations—Fair Use 158 5-91

Minn. 1986) 1986 COPYRIGHT LAW DECISIONS ¶ 26,015.

.341 The defendant copied editorial selections of food terms, individual dishes, and translations from the plaintiffs' copyrighted menu translator books, including the plaintiffs' translation errors. *Marling v. Ellison* (DC SD Fla. 1982) 1983 COPYRIGHT LAW DECISIONS ¶ 25,586.

.36 **Hidden legend.**—Direct evidence showed that the defendant copied a ROM that was a copy of the plaintiff's ROM. A hidden legend contained in the plaintiff's program appeared in the defendants' program, and differences between the programs were studied efforts to create minor distinctions between the two works. *Kramer Manufacturing, Co., Inc., M. v. Andrews* (CA-4 1986) 1986 COPYRIGHT LAW DECISIONS ¶ 25,891, 783 F.2d 421.

.38 **Record piracy.**—Infringement of recording companies' sound recordings was inferred because the defendants, who were not authorized to copy any of the companies' sound recordings, possessed copies of the companies' records and tapes as well as items necessary to manufacture recordings. *RSO Records v. Peri (* ...
DECISION ...

.40 P ...
fabric pa ...
because ...
portions ...
ied. *Kent* ...
SD N.Y. ...
¶ 25,679, ...

.44 E: ...
mailer co ...
in a mo: ...
summary ...
right infringement count. *Chicago Lawyer, Ltd. v. Forty-Sixth Ward Regular Democratic Organization* (DC ND Ill. 1982) 1983 COPYRIGHT LAW DECISIONS ¶ 25,472.

.441 Similar treatment, organization, and content in a subsequent work on valuation in condemnation proceedings was infringement of a copyrighted work, although no more than 35% of the original text was copied in the infringing work. The first work was entirely original, with no antecedent text on the subject. *Orgel v. Clark Boardman Co.* (DC SD N.Y. 1960) 33 COBull 431; affirmed (CA-2 1961) 301 F.2d 119, 33 COBull 449.

.442 A newspaper that excerpted portions of a news story from another newspaper infringed the original story. The story was written in more than a straight factual style and with fairly obvious literary qualities that distinguished it from mere reporting. *Chicago Record-Herald Co. v. Tribune Association* (CA-7 1921) 275 F. 797, 19 COBull 40.

.46 **Quoting and paraphrasing.**—Preparation of a college text on child psychology by paraphrasing chapter by chapter a copyrighted work in the same field was substantial copying and an infringement justifying an injunction. *Meredith Corp. v. Harper & Row, Publishers, Inc.* (DC SD N.Y. 1974) 378 F.Supp 686, 39 COBull 571.

.461 Paraphrase for a television script of a copyrighted play derived from the novel "Ethan Frome" was an infringement of the copyright on the play. It was immaterial that the television producer had been authorized to make a film of the novel. *Davis v.*

¶ **2202**

E.I. *DuPont de Nemours & Co.* (DC SD N.Y. 1965) 240 F.Supp. 612, 35 COBull 116.

.48 **Pagination.**—Use of the page numbers of a publisher's copyrighted law reporters in the defendant's computer-assisted legal research system would constitute infringement because it would have supplanted part of the normal market for the publisher's reporters. The page numbers for the publisher's reporters created internal page citations or "jump cites" that would have given the defendant's subscribers the precise location of opinions in the publisher's reporters and eliminated their need to buy the publisher's law reporters. *West Publishing Co. v. Mead Data Central, Inc.* (CA-8 1986) 1986 COPYRIGHT LAW DECISIONS ¶ 25,998, 799 F.2d 1219, cert. denied (U.S. Sup. Ct. 1987).

.50 **Compilations (Pre *Feist* Publications).** As a second compiler, the defendant was free to check its independent work against the publisher's maps, but by copying copyrighted maps and editing them, it did not make an independent production. *Rockford Map Publishers, Inc. v. Directory Service Company of Colorado, Inc.* (CA-7 1985) 1985 COPYRIGHT ...
denied ...
d 781. ...
ectory ...
ducing ...
intiff's ...
subse- ...
y list- ...
after a ...
start- ...
direc- ...
uri v. ...
D Mo. ...
4, 671 ...
F.Supp. 1514.

.503 A publisher's use of the plaintiff's copyrighted yellow pages directory as a source of information for its own prototype directory was without authorization. The defendant did not use the plaintiff's database, for which it may have been licensed, but instead copied the format and contents of an existing source of information. *Southwestern Bell Media, Inc. v. Trans Western Publishing, Inc.* (DC Kan. 1987) 1988 COPYRIGHT LAW DECISIONS ¶ 26,197, 670 F.Supp. 899.

.504 A publisher of a yellow pages directory used substantially the same format and headings as were contained in the plaintiff's copyrighted yellow pages directory. Such use was likely to constitute impermissible copying. *Southwestern Bell Media, Inc. v. Trans Western Publishing, Inc.* (DC Kan. 1987) 1988 COPYRIGHT LAW DECISIONS ¶ 26,197, 670 F.Supp. 899.

.505 The defendant's wholesale copying of mileage data from a publisher's copyrighted highway mileage guide books into its data base constituted infringement because the defendant did not merely check its independent work against the publisher's books, but copied all of the key point pair mileages from one guide book and at least 80 percent of the segment mileages. *Rand McNally & Co. v. Fleet Management Systems, Inc.* (DC ND Ill 1986) 1986 COPYRIGHT LAW DECISIONS ¶ 26,007, 634 F.Supp 604.

.506 Putting a publisher's copyrighted work into a computer violated the publisher's exclusive rights.

Starting with paragraph 2200 are digests of all cases dealing with the "Elements of Infringement." The specific reference 2202.48 leads to a case on point.

Be sure to read the relevant cases in their entirety. Notice how citations are given to both the CCH reporter and to the *National Reporter System.*

See next Illustration.

[Illustration 109]

PAGE FROM CUMULATIVE INDEX, CCH COPYRIGHT LAW REPORTER

9656   **Cumulative Index—Current Topical Index**   183   6-93
See also Cumulative Index on page 9701.

From Compilation
Paragraph No.

To New Development
Paragraph No.

2206	Three-step procedure based on abstractions test applied (CA-2)	26,931
	Total look and feel of posters were similar to illustrator's work (DC La)	26,897
	Use of expert's affidavit in infringement action was proper (CA-9)	26,896
	User manual referenced and explained infringed program (DC Mich)	26,972
	Virtual identity standard applied to software as a whole (DC Cal)	27,086
	When viewed in the entirety, communications programs were similar (DC Mich)	26,972
2208	Despite religious purposes, unlicensed broadcasts were willful (DC Tex)	26,916
	Lack of intent to infringe was not a defense to infringement (DC Ga)	26,839
	Subscriber was liable despite its lack of intent to infringe (DC Tex)	26,881
2210	Apparent authority defense unavailable for copyright infringement (CA-8)	27,037
	Assignment by licensee was material breach that was infringement (DC Ga)	27,018
	Distributing Cambodian video infringed underlying Chinese version (DC Mass)	26,949
	Extrinsic evidence showed distributor had limited rights (CA-9)	27,068
	First sale doctrine did not allow distribution in U.S. of imports (CA-9)	26,872
	Foreign distributions were illegally authorized in United States (CA-9)	27,068
	Future technology clause did not cover home video market (CA-9)	27,068
	Ignorance of true facts not established for estoppel (DC NY)	27,004
	License implicitly granted to copy and distribute programs (CA-9)	26,933

One must also ascertain if there are any relevant cases that were decided after those that appear in the main (compilation) volume. This can be accomplished by consulting the cross-reference tables in the volume that contains current materials.

2214		
	Bill would license video viewing of professional sports events	20,735
	Conditional foreign licenses did not authorize infringing uses (DC Cal)	26,856
	Decision on willfulness not required to award statutory damages (DC Minn)	27,057
	Defenses rejected and complaint's factual allegations not denied (CA-7)	27,079
	Disc jockey controlled performances and admissions fee charged (DC Fla)	27,060
	Equitable estoppel did not bar assertion of copyrights in song (DC NY)	26,934
	Insufficient malice made willful infringements dischargeable (Bankr Ct Me)	26,942
	Malice should have been implied from willful infringer's conduct (DC Me)	27,052
	Minimum damages awarded because infringement was not willful (DC NC)	26,941
	Motion picture studio's new use ouside of license agreement (DC NY)	26,934
	Music performed after license was terminated for unpaid fees (DC La)	27,066
	Music willfully performed after ASCAP license was terminated (DC Okla)	27,006
	No new facts to rebut ruling that country club infringed music (DC Ill)	26,837
	No showing that unreasonably high licensing fees were sought (DC Ga)	26,839
	Owner responsible although he did not hire bands that performed (DC Ohio)	26,913
	Proof of copyright ownership, unauthorized performances unrebutted (CA-5)	26,990
	Radio station payment did not permit performance at restaurant/bar (DC Ga)	26,839
	Radio station's unlicensed performances were willful infringement (DC SC)	27,040
	Radio stations willfully played music after license termination (DC Miss)	27,016
	Restaurant operators should have known of licensing requirement (DC Fla)	27,060
	Retransmitted simulcasts were not performed in the United States (DC Cal)	26,924
	Unauthorized perfomances of songs in ASCAP repertory enjoined (DC DofC)	27,014
	Unauthorized performance by musican at restaurant was infringement (DC Tex)	26,844
2220	Building designed from unauthorized copy of architectural plans (DC NJ)	27,025
	Program not similar to copyrightable portions of earlier software (DC Okla)	27,095
2222	Absence of primary infringement caused denial of contributory claim (DC Cal)	26,856
	Factual issues existed on direct infringement and knowledge (DC NY)	26,906
	Knowledge of distributor's infringement was not shown (DC Cal)	26,924
2235	Chip Act's reverse engineering did not bar other forms of copying (CA-9)	27,001
	Copyright Act provision does not preclude fair use defense (CA-9)	27,001
	House plan copied solely to complet construction of house (CA-4)	27,085
	Subscriber photocopied and faxed newsletters without authorization (DC Tex)	26,881
	Unlicensed radio retransmissions at restaurant/bar was not fair use (DC Ga)	26,839
	Use of material from management training model not fair use (DC Tex)	26,946
2240	Documents provided to expert witnesses to prepare their testimony (CA-9)	26,958
	Equitable rule of reason did not support photocopying journal (DC NY)	26,956
	Intermediate software copying for reverse engineering not excepted (DC Cal)	26,895
	News monitoring would be fair use under bill	20,720

[Illustration 110]

PAGE FROM CCH FOOD, DRUG, COSMETIC LAW REPORTER

1520   12-2-91   **10,025**

FOOD DEFINITIONS

¶ 10,011

"Food" is defined in most state food laws to mean: (1) articles used for food or drink for man or other animals, (2) chewing gum, and (3) articles used for components of any such article.

A few states impose special restrictions on the use of "food additives," "color additives," and "pesticide chemicals" in or on food and define these terms.

Definitions of "food," "food additive," "color additive," and "pesticide chemical" that appear in the basic laws are referred to in the chart below.

State	"Food"	"Food Additive"	"Color Additive"	"Pesticide Chemical"
Ala.	¶ 11,020			
Alas.	¶ 11,624			
Ariz.	¶ 12,011	¶ 12,011	¶ 12,011	¶ 12,011
Ark.	¶ 12,512			
Cal.	¶ 13,023	¶ 13,024	¶ 13,015	¶ 13,036
Colo.	¶ 13,512	¶ 13,512	¶ 13,512	¶ 13,512
Conn.	¶ 14,012	¶ 14,012	¶ 14,012	¶ 14,012
Del.	¶ 14,511			
D.C.[1]	¶ 15,012, 15,052			
Fla.	¶ 15,513	¶ 15,513	¶ 15,513	¶ 15,513
Ga.				
Ha·				
Ida				
Ill.				
Ind				

> Several looseleaf services include coverage for state laws. In some, the sections containing the full text of the state laws are preceded with a chart outlining where the laws on a topic may be found for the various states.

State	"Food"	"Food Additive"	"Color Additive"	"Pesticide Chemical"
Iowa	¶ 18,551			
Kan.	¶ 19,012	¶ 19,012	¶ 19,012	¶ 19,012
Ky.	¶ 19,512	¶ 19,512	¶ 19,512	¶ 19,512
La.	¶ 20,012			
Me.	¶ 20,542			
Md.	¶ 21,011	¶ 21,011	¶ 21,011	
Mass.	¶ 21,511			
Mich.	¶ 22,034	¶ 22,036	¶ 22,037	¶ 22,035
Minn.	¶ 22,511	¶ 22,511	¶ 22,511	¶ 22,511
Miss.	¶ 23,014			
Mo.	¶ 23,511			
Mont.	¶ 24,052	¶ 24,052	¶ 24,052	¶ 24,052
Neb.				

[1] Provisions of the Federal Act also are applicable to commerce within the District of Columbia.

Food Drug Cosmetic Law Reports   **¶ 10,011**

[Illustration 111]

PAGE FROM BNA MASTER INDEX TO LABOR RELATIONS REPORTER CONTAINING FAIR EMPLOYMENT PRACTICES (FEP) OUTLINE OF CLASSIFICATIONS

D-I 116   FEP Cases OUTLINE OF CLASSIFICATIONS

▶ **108.81—Contd.**

.8155	—Against EEOC, etc.
.8157	—Depositions
.8158	—Interrogatories
.8160	—Records, documents, etc. [For interrogatories, see ▶ 108.8158.]
.8162	—Requests for admission
.8163	—Ex parte interviews; access to employees and ex-employees [For cases prior to FEP Vol. 53, see ▶ 108.8151.]
	—Defenses
.8165	——In general [For relevancy defense cases after FEP Vol. 52, see ▶ 108.8170.]
.8166	——Privilege

> **Step 1**
>
> Consult the Outline of Classifications for Fair Employment Practices (FEP) in the Master Index to Labor Relations Reporter. Note how 108.8908 appears to be relevant. Consult this paragraph number for digests of cases in the Consolidated Index and Digest (CDI) in the Master Index. See next Illustration.
>
> Note: This search could have started in the FEP–Master Index using a subject approach rather than a classification approach.

.834	1866 Act
.836	Equal Pay Act
.837	Age Discrimination in Employment Act
.839	State FEP Acts [For cases prior to FEP Vol. 53, see ▶ 108.831.]

▶ **108.85 Sanctions**

[For sanctions in discovery proceedings, see ▶ 108.8175. For attorneys' fees for discovery proceedings, see ▶ 108.8937. For sanctions for appeals, see ▶ 108.781.]

.8501	In general
.8511	Fed.R.Civ.P. 11

▶ **108.87 Pattern-or-Practice Suits**

[For remedies, see ▶ 200.01 et seq.]

.871	In general
.873	Jurisdiction and procedure
.875	Evidence

▶ **108.89 Attorneys and Attorneys' Fees**

[For attorneys and attorneys' fees in the federal sector, see ▶ 110.8901 et seq.]

.8901	In general
.8903	Appointment [For petition for attorney, see ▶ 108.6915.]
.8905	Disqualification
.8908	Paralegals and law clerks
	Fees
.8911	—In general
.8912	—Factors in determining fees [For contingency fee cases after FEP Vol. 46, see ▶ 108.8920. For incentive fees, including bonuses, multipliers and upward adjustments of fees, see ▶ 108.8918. For delay in awarding fees, see ▶ 108.8919.]
.8914	—Discovery for purpose of determining fees
.8915	—Purpose of award
.8916	—Burden of proof
.8917	—Contingency fees [For cases before FEP Vol. 47, see ▶ 108.8912.]
.8918	—Incentive fee (bonus, multiplier, upward adjustment of fees, etc.) [For upward adjustment or multiplier due to delay in award after FEP Vol. 30, see ▶ 108.8919.]
.8919	—Delay in awarding fees [For cases prior to FEP Vol. 31, see ▶ 108.8912 and ▶ 108.8918.]
	Award; entitlement
.8921	—In general [Includes Equal Access to Justice Act cases]
.8922	—Discretion of court in awarding fees
.8924	—Discretion of court as to amount
.8926	—Rate of payment [For time spent in litigating fee issue, see ▶ 108.8938.]
.8927	—Calculation of hours
.8928	—Allocation of liability; award against attorneys
.8932	—Award against EEOC, US
.8933	—Award against state, local governments
.8935	—Appeals, fees for
.8937	—Discovery proceedings, fees for
.8938	—Time spent in litigating fee issue [For rate of payment, see ▶ 108.8926.]
.8940	Prevailing party
.8943	Interim award
.8950	Recovery by employer, union
.8960	1866 and 1871 Acts, availability of fees
.8965	Recovery by private non-profit corporation
.8967	Third parties; intervenors

[Illustration 112]

PAGE FROM BNA MASTER INDEX TO LABOR RELATIONS REPORTER CONTAINING FAIR EMPLOYMENT PRACTICES (FEP) CUMULATIVE DIGEST AND INDEX (CDI)

. Final CDI	61 FEP Cases	D-II A765

▶ **108.875** Employer has not engaged in pattern or practice of bias in job upgrades, even though women occupy lower job classifications than men with comparable seniority, where there is no evidence that women were told not to bid for jobs, that bids went unrecognized, or that jobs were so male-dominated that women did not seek to obtain them when they were available. —Jenson v. Eveleth Taconite Co. (DC Minn) 61 FEP Cases 1252

Policy and practice of bias by facility in providing training opportunities has not been shown, despite claim that women are not trained in duties of jobs other than own to same extent as men, where there was no evidence that training ...
de jure means of groo...
for promotion. *Id.*

Finding that employ...
or practice of exposin...
hostile environment d...
class member to pres...
sexually harassed, but ...
remains on individua...
show by preponderanc...
was as affected as rea...

▶ **108.8901** Reversit...
when one of protecte...
torneys testified as to l...
tion that employer ha...
ery to construct cha...
showed pattern of ag...
where chart was excl...
grounds. —Gusman v...
61 FEP Cases 382

Employee who asked firm to withdraw as counsel should not bear costs of retaining successor counsel and learning issues in case, where it is not unheard of that lengthy litigation generates ill will within camps of contending parties, and absent showing that plaintiff acted unreasonably to undermine attorney-client relationship, it would be mistake to craft rule binding party to lawyer in whom party has lost confidence by imposing cost on seeking new counsel. —Malarkey v. Texaco Inc. (DC SNY) 61 FEP Cases 407

▶ **108.8908** Counsel for claimants properly were awarded fees incorporating 1988 rates of $110 per hour for 1985 law school graduates to $235 per hour for 1969 law school graduates, in addition to $70 per hour for paralegals. —Davis v. San Francisco, City & County of (CA 9) 61 FEP Cases 440

▶ **108.8911** Discharged police officer could have obtained attorneys' fees award

under Rehabilitation Act in state-court proceeding, and failure to do so bars him, on ground of res judicata, from seeking fees in federal court following state-court decision awarding reinstatement and back pay. —Antonsen v. Ward (CA 2) 2 AD Cases 279

Lower court properly awarded attorneys' fees to ex-employees after finding that employer improperly removed state-court action, which was based on claims of age bias and breach of contract, on theory that action raised claims under ERISA because ex-employees, in depositions, expressed concern that decision to discharge them was motivated by potential for pension savings,
... to award fees if
... nd finding of im-
... ng removal is not
... rd of fees, which
... ble. —Morris v.
... c. (CA 6) 61 FEP

... can include reim-
... ket expenses like
... ing costs that are
... torney-client rela-
... Francisco, City &
... P Cases 440
... cation was timely,
... d within six weeks
... ere employer filed
... time, and counsel
... tion in reliance on
... uiring itemization
... g. —McKenzie v.
... Inc. (CA 11) 61
FEP Cases 1534

Firm that withdrew from case at request of employee should not be required to pay costs associated with retaining successor counsel and learning of issues in case, absent showing that it acted in way inconsistent with professional obligations and thus caused relationship with client to deteriorate. —Malarkey v. Texaco Inc. (DC SNY) 61 FEP Cases 407

▶ **108.8912** Billing rate that attorney can obtain from paying client is presumptive rate that should be used in determining fee award under 1964 CRA, and fact that there is different average rate in community is not reason to depart from presumptive rate. —Gusman v. Unisys Corp. (CA 7) 61 FEP Cases 382

Experienced attorney for handicapped ex-NIH employee is awarded $165 per hour and junior associates between $90 and $125 per hour, where claim was not difficult to litigate, senior counsel was quite able but

---

Step 2

Note how 108.8908 digests cases dealing with the question of awarding attorney's fees to non-lawyers employed by attorneys.

The search must be updated by consulting any supplemental indexes.

Full texts of the digested cases are in the volumes of *Fair Employment Practices* (FEP) cases. Note that the case located is in volume 61 of FEP Cases. It is first published in the looseleaf "Cases" binder of the FEP volumes and later in a bound volume.

See next Illustration.

[Illustration 113]

PAGE FROM A VOLUME OF BNA FAIR EMPLOYMENT PRACTICES CASES

61 FEP Cases 440   DAVIS v. CITY & COUNTY OF SAN FRANCISCO

lows: In footnote 3, line 9 [61 FEP Cases at 111, footnote 4, line 12], delete the phrase "he relied solely on federal precedent," the period following the phrase, and the following sentence, which begins "consequently, the district court's analysis. . ." Replace the deleted text with the following: "consequently the district court's analysis

4. Attorneys' fees — Time spent on fee petition ▸108.8938

Title VII claimants' counsel were properly compensated for time spent on fee petition, even though they hired additional lawyer to act as fee counsel, there being no claim that time spent by claimants' counsel on fee petition

---

Step 3

Read the full text of digested cases located through indexes. In the problem given, only one case was relevant. Note how the publisher provides headnotes that enable the researcher to go directly to the point in the case being researched, in this instance headnote 7.

See next Illustration.

---

into five subclasses because of potential conflicts of interest and that each subclass necessarily had to be represented by different attorney, and it found that hours claimed by additional attorneys with special expertise who were hired to help develop overall strategy and legal analysis reflected their contribution to case for most part.

6. Attorneys' fees — Hours ▸108.8927

Title VII claimants' counsel were properly awarded fees for time spent in press conferences and other public relations work that contributed directly and substantially to attainment of claimants' litigation goals.

DAVIS v. CITY & COUNTY OF SAN FRANCISCO

U.S. Court of Appeals, Ninth Circuit (San Francisco)

DAVIS, et al. v. CITY AND COUNTY OF SAN FRANCISCO, No. 91-15113, October 6, 1992

CIVIL RIGHTS ACT OF 1964

1. Attorneys' fees — Hours ▸108.8927

Federal district court properly allowed counsel for Title VII claimants to supplement their time sheets with additional documentation of their efforts; it did not abuse its discretion in finding that reconstructed records, which drew on agendas and summaries of meetings and notes and time sheets of co-counsel, were extensive.

2. Attorneys' fees — Hours ▸108.8927

Attorneys are not entitled to attorneys' fees for performing clerical matters, such as filing of pleadings and travel time associated with this task.

3. Attorneys' fees — Hours ▸108.8927

Title VII claimants' counsel were properly allowed to claim time spent traveling to co-counsel meetings, where counsel submitted evidence establishing that local attorneys customarily bill their clients for travel time to co-counsel meetings, and city did not introduce any contrary evidence.

7. Attorneys' fees — Rate ▸108.8908 ▸108.8926

Counsel for Title VII claimants properly were awarded fees incorporating 1988 rates of $110 per hour for 1985 law school graduates to $235 per hour for 1969 law school graduates, in addition to $70 per hour for paralegals.

8. Attorneys' fees — Rate ▸108.8926

Federal district court properly applied same hourly rate to each task performed by each attorney; private practitioners do not generally charge varying rates for different lawyerly tasks that they undertake on given case.

9. Attorneys' fees — Rate ▸108.8926

Federal district court properly applied 1988 billing rates to each hour claimed by counsel regardless of year in which work was actually performed.

10. Attorneys' fees — Contingency ▸108.8917

Federal district court should not have enhanced lodestar amount of attorneys' fees awarded to Title VII claimants' counsel to account for fact

[Illustration 114]

PAGE FROM A VOLUME OF BNA FAIR EMPLOYMENT PRACTICES CASES

---

61 FEP Cases 448   DAVIS v. CITY & COUNTY OF SAN FRANCISCO

fighting force. As of August 8, 1990 minority composition stood at 24%. In a department which hired no women before 1985 there are now 36, comprising 2.6% of the force. One of the women is a lieutenant. Minority men have registered even broader gains in the officer ranks. In a fire department that had no minority members in the ranks of lieutenant or above in 1985, there are presently 54 lieutenants, eight captains, five battalion chiefs, one assistant chief and one assistant deputy chief II." *Id.* The court also scrutinized the educational background, career history and community standing of each appellee's attorney and concluded that they possessed a "high level of experience, ability and reputation . . . ." *Id.*

[7] In light of these factors, the court turned to the evidence submitted by the appellees concerning the rates charged by San Francisco attorneys for work comparable to that performed in the SFFD litigation. We recently pronounced that declarations of

The City did not controvert this evidence below. The only evidence it presented concerning billing rates was a survey done of the California legal market as a whole which discussed a wide variety of practice areas. As the Supreme Court made clear in *Blum,* however, the proper reference point in determining an appropriate fee award is the rates charged by private attorneys in the same legal market as prevailing counsel, San Francisco in this instance, for work similar to that performed by such counsel, broad-based complex litigation here. The City's survey was properly dismissed by the district court as shedding no light on this matter.

Before this court, the City discusses several district court decisions which, in its estimation, establish that the rates claimed by appellees' counsel for work performed in the San Francisco market were excessive. In *Bernardi v. Yeutter,* 754 F.Supp. 743 [54 FEP Cases 1551] (N.D. Cal. 1990), *aff'd in part and rev'd in part,* 951 F.2d 971 [60 FEP

Bracketed numbers in the text of the cases, in this example [7], identify the location that served as the topic of the headnote.

Block, 940 F.2d 1211, 1235 [60 FEP Cases 1000] (9th Cir.), *cert. denied,* 112 S.Ct. 640 [60 FEP Cases 1896] (1991). Here, the appellees produced numerous affidavits declaring that the fees sought by appellees' counsel, which incorporated 1988 rates of $110 per hour for 1985 law school graduates to $235 per hour for 1969 law school graduates, in addition to $70 per hour for paralegals, were well within the bounds of the "prevailing market rates" that form the basis for a proper fee award. *Blum* at 895. The district court referred to several of those affidavits in granting appellees' counsel's requested rates. It pointed to the declaration of a "prominent Title VII class action attorney" in San Francisco that attorneys at his firm with credentials similar to those of appellees' counsel would, in 1988, have billed at rates ranging from $110 per hour for 1986 law school graduates to $250 per hour for 1969 graduates, with paralegal time billed at $50 to $85 per hour. It further noted the affidavit of an attorney at McCutchen, Doyle, Brown & Enersen, a well-respected San Francisco firm, that lawyers comparable to appellees' counsel at his firm would have billed at 1988 rates ranging from $150 per hour for 1985 graduates to $230 for 1971 graduates. It referred, finally, to an affidavit indicating that a third San Francisco firm billed at essentially the same rates. 748 F.Supp. at 1430-1431.

party in a sex discrimination case. One of those lawyers is also involved in this case. The court pointedly noted, however, that it did not consider "the case to have been complex litigation," 754 F.Supp. at 746, and therefore rejected evidence concerning the much higher rates which San Francisco attorneys charge for such litigation. By contrast, there is no claim here that the challenge to the SFFD's hiring and promotion policies did not amount to a complex class suit.

The City also points to the district court's decision in *Bucci v. Chromalloy,* 1989 W.L. 222441 [60 FEP Cases 405] (N.D. Cal. 1989), *aff'd* 927 F.2d 608 [61 FEP Cases 616] (9th Cir. 1991) (unpublished memorandum), where fees were awarded based on rates ranging from $175 per hour for an attorney of twenty years experience to $130 per hour for an attorney of nine years experience. While those rates are somewhat lower than the ones utilized by the district court in the present case, the district court in *Bucci* characterized the proceedings before it as having been quite simple. "This case was a straightforward discrimination action based on a flagrant pattern of abusive and insulting behavior on the part of plaintiff's supervisor. While the action vindicated significant civil rights, it did not involve complex fact patterns or novel and difficult legal questions. Indeed, plaintiff's counsel admitted in

Chapter 14

SHEPARD'S CITATIONS AND OTHER CITATOR SERVICES

Citators are sources, available in print and electronic format, that provide, through letter-form abbreviations or words, the subsequent history and interpretation of reported cases, and lists of cases and legislative enactments construing, applying, or affecting statutes. Citators also provide references to a variety of secondary sources. The most widely-used citators for research in the United States and its territories are the various units of *Shepard's Citations.*

SECTION A. INTRODUCTION TO SHEPARD'S CITATIONS

Some previous chapters were directed toward enabling one to locate court cases, statutory provisions, administrative documents, and secondary sources relevant to a particular point of law. In most instances, this research is a preliminary step toward a more concrete goal—preparation of a trial or appellate brief, an opinion letter, or an article. However, before relying on any primary authority that has been located as "good law," its current status must be determined.

For example, a case must be checked to make certain that it has not been reversed by a higher court, overruled by a subsequent case of the same court, or so eroded by criticism by the courts that its merit is questionable. Statutes must be checked to determine whether they have been ruled unconstitutional, amended, or repealed. Verification of the validity of authority is usually accomplished by the use of *Shepard's Citations,* and the process used is typically referred to as "Shepardizing."[1] Also, secondary authority relevant to the point of law being researched can frequently be located through Shepardizing.

Shepard's Citations consist of many units, and are available in book, online, and CD–ROM formats. These publications can be thought of as either "jurisdictional," *e.g.,* those covering a state or a grouping of states and those in the federal arena, or "topical," *e.g.,* those covering a specialized type of materials, such as law reviews or Restatements, or

[1] The term "Shepardizing" is the trademark property of Shepard's/McGraw–Hill, Inc. and is used here with reference to its publications only and with its express consent. The term is derived from the company's founder Frank Shepard, who in 1873 began the process of listing each time a case was cited or affected by a later case.

How to Shepardize: Your Guide to Complete Legal Research Through Shepard's Citations is a complimentary pamphlet issued periodically by the publisher and is an excellent source for additional detail about the technique of Shepardizing and the various units of *Shepard's Citations.* A separate pamphlet, *Questions and Answers,* with practice exercises, as well as a software tutorial, are also available.

those devoted to a particular subject, such as labor or tax law. The type of unit or units to use depends upon the type of research being conducted.

The distinguishing feature of *Shepard's Citations* is the combination of a unique citation style, *e.g.,* 833 F. Supp. 1028 would be shortened to 833FS1028, and editorial letters employed by the publisher, *e.g., q* for *questioned.* For the uninitiated, looking at a page of *Shepard's Citations* can seem as daunting as one's initial exposure to a logarithm table, but in actually the process of "Shepardizing" is relatively simple to master.

SECTION B.   CASE CITATORS

1.   Understanding Shepard's Citations' References, Abbreviations, and Arrangement

Shepard's Citations for cases provide a means to analyze whether any reported case has been cited by a later case and, if so, whether the case can be relied on as authority. A case being checked for its subsequent history, current status, and use by other courts is referred to as the "cited" case. If a case has been cited by later cases and other sources, these cases and other sources are referred to as "citing" references. In addition to providing references to sources citing your case, *Shepard's Citations* also provides a letter-form abbreviation preceding a citing reference if that citing reference somehow affects the case being researched.

These letter codes relate either to the *history* or the *treatment* of the case. The *history* letter-form abbreviations pertain specifically to what has happened to the case during the adjudication phase and generally involve the same parties, facts, and litigation. If, for example, a higher court has "affirmed" or "reversed" the case being Shepardized, the letter "a" or "r" precedes the citing reference.

The *treatment* letters, by contrast, relate to how courts in different litigation have evaluated the cited case. The value of precedent for any given case depends to a large extent on the assessment of the case by other courts, and these assessments can be of vital importance in determining the present value of the cited case as authority. For example, one court may have "criticized" the wisdom of the cited case or "followed" its soundness or reasoning. These citing references will be preceded either by the letter "c" or "f." If no letter precedes a citing reference, it simply means the citing source has included a reference to the cited case but that neither its history nor treatment was affected.

There is no need to try to learn these abbreviations as they are defined in the prefatory materials of every book. [See Illustration 115.] The *Shepard's Citations* in CALR systems use expanded citation styles that make them readily understandable.

[Illustration 115]

PAGE SHOWING ABBREVIATIONS—ANALYSIS AND ABBREVIATIONS—COURTS, SHEPARD'S NORTHWESTERN REPORTER CITATIONS

ABBREVIATIONS—ANALYSIS

History of Case

a	(affirmed)	Same case affirmed on appeal.
cc	(connected case)	Different case from case cited but arising out of same subject matter or intimately connected therewith.
D	(dismissed)	Appeal from same case dismissed.
m	(modified)	Same case modified on appeal.
r	(reversed)	Same case reversed on appeal.
s	(same case)	Same case as case cited.
S	(superseded)	Substitution for former opinion.
v	(vacated)	Same case vacated.
US	cert den	Certiorari denied by U. S. Supreme Court.
US	cert dis	Certiorari dismissed by U. S. Supreme Court.
US	reh den	Rehearing denied by U. S. Supreme Court.
US	reh dis	Rehearing dismissed by U. S. Supreme Court.

Treatment of Case

c	(criticised)	Soundness of decision or reasoning in cited case criticised for reasons given.
d	(distinguished)	Case at bar different either in law or fact from case cited for reasons given.
e	(explained)	Statement of import of decisions in cited case. Not merely a restatement of the facts.
f	(followed)	Cited as controlling.
h	(harmonized)	Apparent inconsistency explained and shown not to exist.
j	(dissenting opinion)	Citation in dissenting opinion.
L	(limited)	Refusal to extend decision of cited case beyond precise issues involved.
o	(overruled)	Ruling in cited case expressly overruled.
p	(parallel)	Citing case substantially alike or on all fours with cited case in its law or facts.
q	(questioned).	Soundness of decision or reasoning in cited case questioned.

ABBREVIATIONS—COURTS

Cir. DC–U.S. Court of Appeals, District of Columbia Circuit
Cir. (number)–U.S. Court of Appeals Circuit (number)
Cir. Fed.–U.S. Court of Appeals, Federal Circuit
CCPA–Court of Customs and Patents Appeals

A page similar to this can be found in each unit of *Shepard's Citations*. It should always be consulted if the meanings of the publisher's abbreviations are in doubt.

CuCt Customs Court
ECA–Temporary Emergency Court of Appeals
ML–Judicial Panel on Multidistrict Litigation
RRR–Special Court Regional Rail Reorganization Act of 1973

xviii

In 1993, Shepard's began systematically recompiling its case citators and reissuing them in a format different from the way they have appeared historically. Older volumes list citations in eight columns and do not contain the names of the cited cases. The volumes with the new format list citations in six columns and include the names of the cited cases. This new format, while providing an important enhancement and improving legibility, substantially increases the number of volumes in a unit.

The arrangement of references in *Shepard's Citations* is straightforward, regardless of whether an old or new version is being used. Case citations are arranged in numerical order, corresponding to the order of the citation in the reporter being Shepardized. These cited case references are listed by volume and page number in black letter (**bold**) type. Each cited reference is followed by "parallel" references to the same case in a different reporter, if such a parallel reference is available. Parallel references, if any, are enclosed in parentheses. Citing references follow immediately thereafter. [See Illustrations 120–124; compare Illustrations 123 and 124.] Once a parallel citation is included in a bound volume, it is not included in the supplementary pamphlets. *If no reference to a reported case is in Shepard's Citations, it means there are no parallel references and no citing references.*

A separate set of *Shepard's Citations* is published for each set of court reports. Consequently, there are sets of *Shepard's Citations* for each of the fifty states, the District of Columbia, and Puerto Rico; separate sets for each of the regional reporters of the *National Reporter System;* one set for the *Federal Reporter* and the *Federal Supplement;* and one for the reports of the Supreme Court of the United States.

Based on the foregoing discussion, an example can illustrate some of the ways *Shepard's Citations* can facilitate one's case law research. Assume the problem under research pertains to warrantless searches. During the course of the research, a Wisconsin Supreme Court case, *State v. Griffin,* 131 Wis. 2d 41, 388 N.W.2d 535 (1986) is found and is on point. [See Illustrations 116–118.] Before this case can be cited as authority, one must first determine if *Griffin* has been appealed to the Supreme Court of the United States and has either been affirmed or reversed. If it has been reversed, it is no longer controlling authority and must not be cited as if it were.

Another fact to ascertain is whether the Wisconsin Supreme Court in a subsequent case overruled its decision in the *Griffin* case (assuming it had not been reversed). If this case has been overruled, it can no longer be cited as authority.

These determinations, both as to history and treatment, are made by checking *Shepard's Wisconsin Citations* or *Shepard's Northwestern Reporter Citations.* Because these citators list every case subsequently decided in which the cited case was mentioned, it can be determined easily if the cited case has been affirmed, reversed, overruled, etc.

Since many court cases are reported in both official and unofficial sets of court reports, one has to determine which set of *Shepard's* to use in Shepardizing a case. For example, since the *Griffin* case was reported in both a set of state court reports and in a regional reporter, one must determine whether to Shepardize the case in the appropriate state or regional reporter unit of *Shepard's Citations*. Each bound volume and pamphlet supplement contains a cover page that lists the sources covered by that citator. [See Illustration 119.] Which citator unit to select is discussed *infra*.

2.   Shepard's Citations for the States and Territories

These are used in connection with state reports and are available for each of the fifty states, the District of Columbia, and Puerto Rico. They are available in print and online versions, and increasingly as CD–ROM products.

Because most reported cases cover more than one point of law, *Shepard's,* through the use of superscript figures, keys each citing case to the headnotes of the cited case. For example, the case of *State v. Griffin,* as published in the *Wisconsin Reports 2d,* has ten headnotes, each on a different point of law. A citing case may cite *Griffin* only for the point of law in its fourth headnote. Therefore, *Shepard's* adds the superscript *4* to the citing case. By this means, one can find in *Shepard's Wisconsin Citations* all subsequent cases that have cited *Griffin* for that point of law. [See Illustrations 116–117 and 120–121.]

The state *Shepard's* units give citing cases only from courts within the jurisdiction or cases that originated in the federal court within the state. A state *Shepard's* also gives citations to any legal periodical in the state (plus 20 national legal journals) that cite the cited case, as well as citations to Attorneys General's opinions of the state in question that cite the cited case.

The order of arrangement of citations to state cases is always as follows:[2]

a.   Those from state and federal courts showing a history relationship to the cited case.

b.   Those from state courts showing the treatment accorded the cited case.

c.   Those from federal courts showing the treatment accorded the cited case.

d.   Those in articles in legal periodicals.

e.   Those in annotations of *United States Supreme Court Reports, Lawyers' Edition* and *American Law Reports*.

f.   Those in selected legal texts.

[2] This listing is also is in the prefatory material for each state *Shepard's* volume.

State *Shepard's* also have a section or a separate volume arranged by the regional reporter citation. By this means, when only a state unit *Shepard's* is available, the case can be still Shepardized under both the state and regional reporter citation. In both instances, citing cases are given only for the courts within the state.

Separate companion volumes, *State Case Name Citators,* provide both plaintiff-defendant and reverse defendant-plaintiff listings for each case decided by courts within the state being covered.

3. Shepard's Citations for the Regional Reporters

In the example of *State v. Griffin,* this case also could be Shepardized in *Shepard's Northwestern Reporter Citations* under 388 N.W.2d 535. In such instances, that reporter volume has to be examined to determine which headnote or headnotes are of interest. In the *North Western Reporter 2d,* the *Griffin* case is given four headnotes, and each can be followed in the same manner as described *supra.* In our example, if the *Shepard's Wisconsin Citations* is used, all citing cases are to cases in the *Wisconsin Reports* as well as to federal cases in the jurisdictions covering Wisconsin.

By contrast, in the *Shepard's Northwestern Reporter Citations,* all citations to the same cases are to the *North Western Reporter* as well as to federal cases in the jurisdictions covering Wisconsin. The regional *Shepard's,* unlike the state *Shepard's,* also give citations to any case throughout the *National Reporter System.* Thus, if a Massachusetts case cited *State v. Griffin,* this citing reference can be found in *Shepard's Northwestern Reporter Citations.* The order of citing references is generally the same as described for state citators. [See Illustrations 122–123.]

4. Shepard's Citations for Federal Cases

a. *Shepard's United States Citations.* This voluminous unit is divided into four separate parts:

(1) *Cases.* The cases volumes consist of main volumes and bound and pamphlet supplements that contain citations to the *U.S. Reports,* the *U.S. Supreme Court Reports, Lawyers' Edition,* and *West's Supreme Court Reporter.* When a state court cites a Supreme Court of the United States case, it is listed only under the *U.S. Reports* citation if the state case was reported prior to the summer of 1986. For state cases reported after that time, the citations are listed under all three reporters. Recently, the publisher has begun to include references to *slip opinions* in the pamphlet supplements only. These references are listed by docket number.

Where there is no single majority opinion in a case, citing cases are listed separately under the name of the justice whose opinion is being cited and only in the *U.S. Reports* section. (Citations to the syllabus of the case are listed under the heading of "First.") In the *Lawyers'*

Edition and *West's Supreme Court Reporter* sections, citations to all parts of these fragmented cases are listed together.

(2) *Constitutions, Statutes, Treaties, and Court Rules.* These volumes include all cases citing the U.S. Constitution, the *United States Code,* the *U.S. Treaty Series,* and the court rules of the Supreme Court of the United States. This unit is discussed in Section E, *infra.*

(3) *Administrative.* These volumes show citations to the decisions and orders of selected federal administrative agencies, courts, boards, and commissions.

(4) *Patents and Trademarks.* These volumes of *Shepard's United States Citations* are a compilation of citations to U.S. patents, trademarks, and copyrights. [See Illustration 131.]

The patents section lists each patent by number and lists all citations to a patent by a court or administrative agency; the copyright section lists titles of copyrighted works and lists citations to all court cases and administrative decisions involving each title; and the trademark section lists all trademarks alphabetically and lists all citations to court cases and administrative decisions involving the trademark. A separate section contains all citations to cases published in the *United States Patent Quarterly* and *Decisions of the Commissioner of Patents.*

b. *Shepard's United States Supreme Court Case Name Citator.* This is a companion set to *Shepard's United States Citations* and is to be used in conjunction with it. It lists alphabetically both the plaintiff's and defendant's names with date of decision for all Supreme Court of the United States cases since 1900.

c. *Shepard's Federal Citations.* This multi-volume unit is divided into two separate parts:

(1) Citations to cases reported in *Federal Cases* and *Federal Reporter* (F., F.2d, F.3d).

(2) Citations to cases in *Federal Supplement, Federal Rules Decisions, Court of Claims Reports,* and *Claims Court Reporter* (now *Federal Claims Reporter*).

d. *Federal Case Names Citators.* This is a companion set to *Shepard's Federal Citations.* A separate volume or volumes is published for each of the federal circuits. Names can be checked by either plaintiff or defendant for references in the *Federal Reporter 2d* and *3d, Federal Supplement, Federal Rules Decisions,* and *Bankruptcy Reporter.*

e. *Federal Circuit Table.* This publication identifies the circuit or district of any reference shown in any edition of *Shepard's Citations* in terms of volume and page of the *Federal Reporter, Federal Supplement, Federal Rules Decisions,* and *Bankruptcy Reporter.* Each table lists for any page in such volumes the circuit or district in which that page originates. [See Illustration 132.]

f. *Shepard's Seventh Circuit Citations.* This set, published in 1992, lists every 7th Circuit Federal Court of Appeals and district court

case within the 7th Circuit as reported in the *Federal Reporter, Federal Reporter 2d* and *3d, Federal Rules Decisions,* and *Federal Supplement.* It is likely that citators for the other federal circuits will be published in the future.

5. Shepard's Case Citations in Electronic Format

a. *In General.* Many units of *Shepard's Citations* are available in the CALR services, WESTLAW and LEXIS. Coverage is comprehensive for cases. To access either service, type *sh* followed by the volume, reporter, and the beginning page of the case to be researched. The screen displays from the two vendors differ, but both customized displays consolidate the references from several citators and their supplements into an integrated whole. [See Illustration 125, Figures 1 and 2.]

b. *Shepard's PreView.* Shepard's PreView, available exclusively on WESTLAW, contains current citations to cases appearing in the advance sheets of the *National Reporter System.* It allows one to update citations located through the typical online search or through use of the print version. The citing references do not, however, contain history or treatment codes or headnote numbers. When Shepard's completes its analysis of a case, these citing references are incorporated into the online and print versions and the reference to that case in PreView is removed. Shepard's PreView can be updated by use of the Quick*Cite* feature discussed in Section J–3.

c. *CD–ROMs.* Shepard's is also in the process of producing case citations for selected citations in CD–ROM products, several of which are already available. These products allow Shepardizing without incurring online charges.

SECTION C. OTHER USES FOR SHEPARD'S CITATIONS—CASES

In addition to the traditional Shepardizing methods discussed *supra, Shepard's Citations* have several other important uses: [3]

1. Citations to Articles in Legal Periodicals

The state units of *Shepard's Citations,* in addition to indicating every time a cited case has been cited by a citing case, also indicate when the cited case has been cited in a legal periodical published within the state or in twenty national legal periodicals.[4]

---

[3] For a useful article discussing some of the ways *Shepard's* can be utilized, see Adolph J. Levy, *16 More Ways to Use Shepard's Citations,* TRIAL, Feb. 1992, at 69.

[4] These are: *ABA Journal; California Law Review; Columbia Law Review; Cornell Law Review; Georgetown Law Journal; Harvard Law Review; Law and Contemporary Problems; Michigan Law Review; Minnesota Law Review; New York University Law Review; Northwestern University Law Review; Stanford Law Review; Texas Law Review; UCLA Law Review; University of Chicago Law Review; University of Illinois Law Review; University of Pennsylvania Law Review; Virginia Law Review; Wisconsin Law Review;* and *Yale Law Journal.*

2. A.L.R. Annotations

When Shepardizing a case citation, the various *Shepard's* units indicate when the case has been cited by an *A.L.R. Annotation*, or when the case has been used as the subject of an *A.L.R. Annotation*. A separate publication, *Shepard's Citations for Annotations*, discussed in Chapter 7–B–4, lists annotations as both citing and cited references.

3. Using Shepard's Citations to Find Parallel Citations

In Chapter 5, it was pointed out how, given a state report citation, the *National Reporter System* regional citations can be found by using the *National Reporter Blue Book*. *Shepard's Citations* also can be used for this purpose, and in addition, to find the state citation from the regional citation. An entry in *Shepard's* always includes the parallel citation as the first citation under the page number the first time the case is listed.[5] When a case has also been reported in one of the *A.L.R.* series, that is also listed.

4. Using Shepard's Citations as Research Aids

Although *Shepard's Citations* are essential research aids, they should not be stretched beyond their intended function.

The editors' use of the letter-form abbreviations to indicate the treatment of cases is intelligently conservative. The essence of a citing case may go beyond its expressed language. The outcome of a case is not identified by the abbreviations unless its expression is clearly stated in the opinion. Therefore, a case that implicitly overrules a cited case will not be marked with the symbol *o* for *overruled*. This can be determined only by a careful reading of the case. In other words, although *Shepard's Citations* immeasurably facilitate research, there are no substitutes for reading and "squeezing the juices" from cases.

In addition, cases dealing with the same subject matter, which do not cite each other, are not covered by *Shepard's Citations*. On the other hand, since *Shepard's* are not selective, the citing cases may be so numerous as to create a formidable research problem. A further limitation is that *Shepard's Citations* perpetuate the inaccuracies created by judges who inappropriately cite cases. These, however, are minor defects that the general utility, comprehensiveness, and accuracy of the citators effectively overbalance.

---

[5] Because cases are frequently reported earlier in the units of the *National Reporter System* than in the official reports, the parallel state citation often is not available at the time a citation first appears in a regional *Shepard's*. When a parallel citation is not the first citation under the page number, check the subsequent volumes and pamphlets of the *Shepard's Citations* unit being used. If a parallel citation still does not appear, it is likely that the state citation is from a state that has discontinued its official state reports.

SECTION D. ILLUSTRATIONS: SHEPARD'S CITATIONS—CASES

Shepardizing State v. Griffin

[Illustration 116]

FIRST PAGE FROM STATE v. GRIFFIN IN WISCONSIN REPORTS 2d

OFFICIAL WISCONSIN REPORTS

State v. Griffin, 131 Wis. 2d 41

STATE of Wisconsin, Plaintiff-Respondent,

v.

Joseph G. GRIFFIN, Defendant-Appellant-Petitioner.

Supreme Court

No. 84–021–CR. Argued June 4, 1986.—Decided June 20, 1986.

(Affirming 126 Wis. 2d 183, 376 N.W.2d 62 (Ct. App. 1985).)
(Also reported in 388 N.W.2d 535.)

1. **Criminal Law and Procedure § 788.50*— constitutionality—question of law—deference to lower courts.**

First page of *State v. Griffin* as published in the official *Wisconsin Reports 2d.*

---

to decisions of trial court and court of appeals.

2. **Searches and Seizures § 29*—warrantless search of residence—exceptions to search warrant requirement.** Though person's home or residence is entitled to special dignity and sanctity, warrantless search is justified if recognized exceptions to search warrant requirement, which include consent, search incident to lawful arrest, hot pursuit, exigent circumstances and plain view, are present.

3. **Searches and Seizures § 29*—warrantless search of probationer's residence by probation officer—justification.** Where probationer appealed propriety of warrantless search of probationer's residence by probation officer which resulted in seizure of handgun used to convict probationer of possession

---

*See Callaghan's Wisconsin Digest, same topic and section number.

[Illustration 117]

SECOND PAGE FROM STATE v. GRIFFIN IN WISCONSIN REPORTS 2d

OFFICIAL WISCONSIN REPORTS

State v. Griffin, 131 Wis. 2d 41

of firearm by convicted felon and where prosecution did not rely on any recognized exception to justify such warrantless search, but rather, relied on accused's probationary status, court could conclude that, if there was to be such exception to search warrant requirement, its foundation was to be found in nature of probation since neither Wisconsin nor United States Supreme Court has declared such exception.

4. **Constitutional Law § 121*—rights of probationers—role of probation officer.**
Supreme Court has recognized limits on liberty and privacy interests of probationers based on nature of probation and application of less stringent standard for probation agent's search and seizure coincides with agent's dual role of assisting in rehabilitating probationer and protecting public.

5. **Searches and Seizures § 29*—warrantless search of probationer's residence by probation officer—possibility of police abuse.**
Probationer's argument on appeal that supreme court should

> This is the second page of *State v. Griffin*. The Wisconsin Supreme Court has provided a total of ten headnotes for this case in its official *Wisconsin Reports 2d*.
>
> *Shepard's Wisconsin Citations—Cases* are keyed to these headnotes and will show the treatment of a cited case by a citing case by reference to the headnotes.

reasonable search could not be deemed unlawful simply because police were source of information which led to search.

6. **Searches and Seizures § 29*—warrantless search of probationer's residence by probation officer—rights of innocent third persons.**
In considering propriety of warrantless search of probationer's residence by probation officer, court was unpersuaded by probationer's argument that warrant was necessary to protect rights of innocent third persons who may be living with probationer where court, in creating exception to search warrant requirement which allows probation officers to conduct warrantless search of residences of probationers, court was not

*See Callaghan's Wisconsin Digest, same topic and section number.

42

[Illustration 118]

FIRST PAGE FROM STATE v. GRIFFIN IN NORTH WESTERN REPORTER 2d

STATE v. GRIFFIN   Wis. **535**
Cite as 388 N.W.2d 535 (Wis. 1986)

131 Wis.2d 41
STATE of Wisconsin,
Plaintiff-Respondent,

v.

Joseph G. GRIFFIN,
Defendant-Appellant-Petitioner.

No. 84-021-CR.

Supreme Court of Wisconsin.

Argued June 4, 1986.

Opinion Filed June 20, 1986.

Defendant was convicted in the Circuit Court, Rock County, J. Richard Long, J., of

> First page of *State v. Griffin* as published in the unofficial *North Western Reporter 2d*. Note that the West editors have prepared four headnotes for this case and that these headnotes differ from those in *Wisconsin Reports 2d*.
>
> *Shepard's Northwestern Reporter Citations* are keyed to these headnotes.

Shirley S. Abrahamson, J., filed dissenting opinion.

Bablitch, J., filed dissenting opinion.

1. Criminal Law ⬅982.8

Probation agent who reasonably believes that a probationer is violating the terms of probation may conduct a warrantless search of probationer's residence, and evidence obtained in search may be used at a trial seeking new conviction of the probationer if the search is otherwise reasonable. U.S.C.A. Const.Amends. 4, 14.

2. Criminal Law ⬅982.8

Warrantless search of probationer's residence could be made by probation officer based on "reasonable grounds" to believe that probationer had contraband at

his residence, where probation officer was informed by police detective that there might be guns in probationer's apartment. U.S.C.A. Const.Amends. 4, 14.

3. Criminal Law ⬅982.8

Reasonable grounds standard contained in administrative code, which was less than probable cause standard needed to obtain warrant, was sufficient for searches and seizures conducted by probation officers of a probationer's residence. U.S.C.A. Const.Amends. 4, 14; W.S.A. 941.-29(2).

4. Criminal Law ⬅982.8

Probation officer had reasonable grounds to make warrantless search of probationer's residence on tip from police detective that there might be guns in probationer's apartment, where search was not a police search, purpose of police officers in going to probationer's residence was for protection of probation officers, and gun was discovered in drawer which was apparently broken in such a way as to allow gun to be seen in unopened drawer. U.S.C.A. Const.Amends. 4, 14; W.S.A. 941.29(2).

Alan G. Habermehl, Madison, argued, for defendant-appellant-petitioner; Kalal & Habermehl, Madison, on brief.

Barry M. Levenson, Asst. Atty. Gen., argued, for plaintiff-respondent; Bronson C. La Follette, Atty. Gen., on brief.

DAY, Justice.

This is a review of a published decision of the court of appeals, *State v. Griffin*, 126 Wis.2d 183, 376 N.W.2d 62 (Ct.App. 1985), affirming the judgment of the circuit court for Rock county, Honorable J. Richard Long, circuit judge, convicting Joseph G. Griffin, (Defendant) of possession of a firearm by a convicted felon contrary to Section 941.29(2), Stats.[1] Defendant was

1. Section 941.29(1) and (2), Stats., provides in part:

"**941.29 Possession of a firearm.** (1) A person is subject to the requirements and penalties of this section if he or she has been: "(a) Convicted of a felony in this state. . . .

[Illustration 119]

TITLE PAGE: SHEPARD'S WISCONSIN CITATIONS

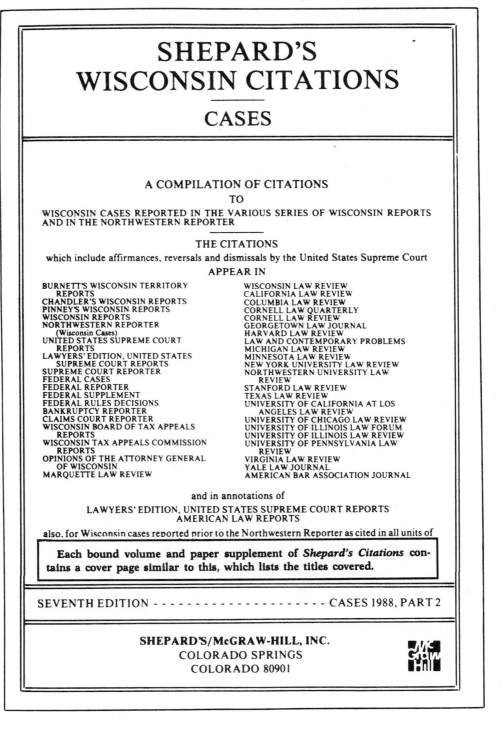

SHEPARD'S
WISCONSIN CITATIONS

CASES

A COMPILATION OF CITATIONS

TO

WISCONSIN CASES REPORTED IN THE VARIOUS SERIES OF WISCONSIN REPORTS
AND IN THE NORTHWESTERN REPORTER

THE CITATIONS

which include affirmances, reversals and dismissals by the United States Supreme Court

APPEAR IN

BURNETT'S WISCONSIN TERRITORY
   REPORTS
CHANDLER'S WISCONSIN REPORTS
PINNEY'S WISCONSIN REPORTS
WISCONSIN REPORTS
NORTHWESTERN REPORTER
   (Wisconsin Cases)
UNITED STATES SUPREME COURT
   REPORTS
LAWYERS' EDITION, UNITED STATES
   SUPREME COURT REPORTS
SUPREME COURT REPORTER
FEDERAL CASES
FEDERAL REPORTER
FEDERAL SUPPLEMENT
FEDERAL RULES DECISIONS
BANKRUPTCY REPORTER
CLAIMS COURT REPORTER
WISCONSIN BOARD OF TAX APPEALS
   REPORTS
WISCONSIN TAX APPEALS COMMISSION
   REPORTS
OPINIONS OF THE ATTORNEY GENERAL
   OF WISCONSIN
MARQUETTE LAW REVIEW

WISCONSIN LAW REVIEW
CALIFORNIA LAW REVIEW
COLUMBIA LAW REVIEW
CORNELL LAW QUARTERLY
CORNELL LAW REVIEW
GEORGETOWN LAW JOURNAL
HARVARD LAW REVIEW
LAW AND CONTEMPORARY PROBLEMS
MICHIGAN LAW REVIEW
MINNESOTA LAW REVIEW
NEW YORK UNIVERSITY LAW REVIEW
NORTHWESTERN UNIVERSITY LAW
   REVIEW
STANFORD LAW REVIEW
TEXAS LAW REVIEW
UNIVERSITY OF CALIFORNIA AT LOS
   ANGELES LAW REVIEW
UNIVERSITY OF CHICAGO LAW REVIEW
UNIVERSITY OF ILLINOIS LAW FORUM
UNIVERSITY OF ILLINOIS LAW REVIEW
UNIVERSITY OF PENNSYLVANIA LAW
   REVIEW
VIRGINIA LAW REVIEW
YALE LAW JOURNAL
AMERICAN BAR ASSOCIATION JOURNAL

and in annotations of

LAWYERS' EDITION, UNITED STATES SUPREME COURT REPORTS
AMERICAN LAW REPORTS

also, for Wisconsin cases reported prior to the Northwestern Reporter as cited in all units of

Each bound volume and paper supplement of *Shepard's Citations* contains a cover page similar to this, which lists the titles covered.

SEVENTH EDITION - CASES 1988, PART 2

SHEPARD'S/McGRAW-HILL, INC.
COLORADO SPRINGS
COLORADO 80901

[Illustration 120]

PAGE FROM SHEPARD'S WISCONSIN CITATIONS: CASE EDITION

WISCONSIN REPORTS, 2d SERIES

Vol. 129

—277—	—491—	—230—	—499—	134Wis2d⁵	—416—	—25—	—251—
(385NW161)	(385NW234)	(387NW98)	(388NW160)	[361	(388NW652)	(390NW74)	(392NW449)
US cert den				f135Wis2d⁴ ·			
in107SC148	—496—	—247—	—523—	[408	—422—	—29—	—262—
129Wis2d230	(385NW171)	(387NW106)	(388NW170)	f135Wis2d⁸	(388NW624)	(390NW575)	(392NW97)
d137Wis2d⁷55		cc122Wis2d	s133Wis2d33	[408			
		[673		135Wis2d498	—435—	—62—	—266—
—301—	**Vol. 130**	137Wis2d⁴			(389NW49)	(390NW79)	(392NW453)
(385NW196)		[208	**Vol. 131**	Cir. 7		d133Wis2d	cc83Wis2d239
	—1—			819F2d¹822	—446—	[368	
—308—	(385NW509)	—276—	—1—		(388NW927)		—289—
(384NW712)		(386NW519)	(388NW176)	—189—		—68—	(392NW98)
	—4—			(388NW553)	—451—	(389NW823)	
—310—	(386NW53)	—285—	—21—	—220—	(389NW366)	135Wis2d¹	—304—
(384NW709)	s125Wis2d224	(387NW118)	(388NW584)	(388NW601)		[226	(392NW461)
	135Wis2d369	132Wis2c ①	s125Wis2d418	s113Wis2d497	—459—	136Wis2d¹5	
—319—	137Wis2d²		Cir. 10	s125Wis2d111	(389NW359)	d137Wis2d⁵	—310—
(385NW510)	[231	—291—	647FS902	f131Wis2d¹⁰		[250	(392NW104)
		(387?)121) ②		[148		j137Wis2d263	
—331—	—18—		—41—	f131Wis2d⁹	—477—		—318—
(385NW200)	(386NW47)	—300—	(388NW535)	[148	(389NW54)	—74—	(392NW108)
	s125Wis2d272	(387NW124)	a107SC3164	134Wis2d⁹		(390NW76)	
—348—			a55USLW	[410	—492—	136Wis2d⁶22	—335—
(384NW713)	—29—	—308—	[5156	e136Wis2d¹⁰	(389NW59)	137Wis2d⁶	(392NW469)
L135Wis2d⁴	(386NW51)	(387? 51)	s126Wis2d183	[480		[209	133Wis2d²
[232		s128 ③ 1531	s93L E699		—507—		[159
	—34—		s93L E977	—246—	(390NW660)	—82—	
—357—	(387NW55)	—313—	s107SC643	(389NW12)	137Wis2d³	(390NW86)	—340—
(384NW717)	s83Wis2d601	(387NW128)	s107SC926	cc131Wis2d69	[206		(392NW115)
	131Wis2d⁷	r136Wis2d37	f135Wis2d⁶	cc131Wis2d		—145—	
—362—	[242		[409	[133	—515—	(389NW825)	—351—
(384NW719)	134Wis2d²	—327—	137Wis2d¹	133Wis2d³	(389NW73)		(392NW464)
	[251	(387NW291)	[183	[311		—153—	
—373—				133Wis2d²	—525—	(390NW81)	—364—
(385NW514)	—56—	—335—	—69—	[313	(389NW67)		(392NW119)
	(387NW245)	(387NW295)	(389NW1)	e133Wis2d⁹		—164—	
—377—	cc130Wis2d79		US cert den	[314	—525—	(389NW828)	—373—
(385NW208)			in107SC584	137Wis2d¹⁴	(389NW67)		(392NW123)
d134				Cir. 7	[168	f132Wis2d401	

This Illustration is from the bound 1988 Cases volume of *Shepard's Wisconsin Citations*.

1. Note under 131 Wis. 2d 41 (*State v. Griffin*) how the first citation in parentheses, *i.e.*, 388 N.W.2d 535, is to a case in another set of court reports. This is the parallel citation to the same case in a different reporter.

2. Note also that *State v. Griffin* has been affirmed by the Supreme Court of the United States. This case can therefore be cited as good authority.

3. Assume you are especially interested in knowing if other Wisconsin courts have followed the point of law covered in headnotes 4 and 6. Note that headnote 6 was followed in the case reported in 135 Wis. 2d. The reference to page 409 is a "pinpoint" cite directly to the page on which the reference to headnote 6 appears. Does this mean that no Wisconsin court has followed the point of law in headnote 4?

See next Illustration.

Cir. 7	133Wis2d⁴	—464—		(388NW645)	[600	—225—	(393NW116)
65BRW⁶442		(387NW751)	—147—			(392NW439)	
65BRW⁷443	[275	134Wis2d38	(388NW612)	—405—	—18—		
	—212—	j134Wis2d44		(388NW641)	(390NW572)	—243—	
—478—	(386NW512)	j134Wis2d55	—153—		135Wis2d²	(392NW445)	
(386NW59)	r134Wis2d260	61NYL1076	(388NW565)		[191	Cir. 7	
			US cert den			71BRW⁵279	
			in107SC583				
			e134Wis2d¹				
			[124				

[Illustration 121]

PAGE FROM SHEPARD'S WISCONSIN CITATIONS: ANNUAL CUMULATIVE SUPPLEMENT

WISCONSIN REPORTS, 2d SERIES

Vol. 130

Vol. 130	155Wis2d⁵	15COA723§	—376—	f160Wis2d¹	155Wis⑶	1989WLR609	916F2d1219
—4—	[699	[13	143Wis2d434	[396	[319		Cir. 8
j141Wis2d675	156Wis2d⁵	SCT§ 2.07	143Wis2d³	d161Wis2d¹	155Wis2d⁴	—69—	912F2d⁴1009
141Wis2d800	[718	52Æ900s	[844	[320	159Wis2d⁵89	US cert den	
142Wis2d²	156Wis2d⁶	53Æ270s	149Wis2d⁴	162Wis2d³19	165Wis2d664	in479US989	—133—
[847	[720		[336	f162Wis2d24	166Wis2d847	158Wis2d642	US cert den
143Wis2d858	159Wis2d158	—247—	160Wis2d822	163Wis2d239	36Æ900s	159Wis2d575	in479US1037
144Wis2d³15	e159Wis2d¹²	m139Wis2d	161Wis2d741	f166Wis2d⁵			in107SC891
d144Wis2d³15	[159	[112	162Wis2d¹	[693	—84—	f145Wis2d⁶	
d144Wis2d⁴15	159Wis2d¹³	150Wis2d141	[869	167Wis2d¹	141Wis2d²	[414	—147—
146Wis2d²	[159		d162Wis2d⁵	[353	147Wis2d⁵	156Wis2d²89	
[656	h165Wis2d⁶	—276—	[874	Cir. 7	148Wis2d⁵	[473	160Wis2d¹
146Wis2d²	[404	156Wis2d¹	165Wis2d¹	d847F2d¹438	147Wis2d³	[707	[633
[704	f166Wis2d519	[816	[707	d847F2d²438	d148Wis2d¹	[708	
154Wis2d262	c166Wis2d525	164Wis2d⁵	168Wis2d¹	f881F2d¹1413	[460	148Wis2d463	—153—
155Wis2d371	j166Wis2d550	[392	[331	Cir. 10			US cert den
j159Wis2c							9US989
159Wis2d							Wis2d⁵

When using *Shepard's Citations*, a researcher must always check not only the bound volumes but also the latest pamphlet supplement or supplements.

1. By checking the annual pamphlet supplement you find that headnote 4 was followed at 159 Wis. 2d 770.

2. Note also that since publication of the bound volume that *State v. Griffin* has also been cited by the First Circuit Court of Appeals.

3. Note that the *Wisconsin Law Review* has also cited the *Griffin* case.

143Wis2d²	—174—	Cir. 7	[360	141Wis2d800	157Wis2d593	148Wis2d848	149Wis2d342
[621	143Wis2d⁷	d834F2d¹629	144Wis2d⁴	142Wis2d712	Cir. 3	f149Wis2d⁸	150Wis2d⁴
144Wis2d²	[104	674FS¹1364	[361	144Wis2d135	912F2d623	[843	[724
[403	144Wis2d¹	ROP§ 8.11	144Wis2d⁵	144Wis2d141	f912F2d⁶624	153Wis2d⁶41	f151Wis2d⁴
144Wis2d²	[526		[361	144Wis2d⁵	Cir. 7	f154Wis2d338	[199
[825	q151Wis2d¹	—327—	d145Wis2d	[141	e859F2d505	155Wis2d425	j151Wis2d214
147Wis2d²	[245	149Wis2d¹	[170	f145Wis2d³	15COA723§	157Wis2d443	151Wis2d¹
147Wis2d⁸	155Wis2d¹	[539	d145Wis2d¹	[839	24COA575§	f160Wis2d⁶	[214
[211	[594	149Wis2d⁴	[170	f145Wis2d³	[31	[909	151Wis2d²
147Wis2d⁸	155Wis2d²	[539	d145Wis2d⁵	[839	SCT§ 5.44	f162Wis2d254	[214
[213	[599	8Æ16s	[170	e148Wis2d²38	84Æ322s		151Wis2d³
150Wis2d³	167Wis2d⁴		f145Wis2d¹	e148Wis2d³38		—123—	[214
[875	[406	—335—	[656	149Wis2d673		138Wis2d⁴	151Wis2d⁸
160Wis2d¹	167Wis2d⁴	149Wis2d¹	[656	151Wis2d⁶	—41—	[346	[214
[735	[407	[152	f145Wis2d¹	[333	a483US868	140Wis2d⁴	151Wis2d¹¹
	47Æ103¹s	149Wis2d946	d146Wis2d¹	153Wis2d²	a97LℤΞ709	[192	[214
—56—		150Wis2d¹	[686	[410	a107SC3164	f141Wis2d124	151Wis2d858
144Wis2d²	—187—	[182	d146Wis2d²	153Wis2d³	s479US1005	f141Wis2d¹	152Wis2d⁵
[436	140Wis2d¹	76WiAG22	[686	[411	s479US1053	[126	[304
167Wis2d³	[524		d146Wis2d⁵	157Wis2d253	f140Wis2d⁹	d148Wis2d	155Wis2d⁶
[598		—340—	[686	Cir. 10	[425	[610	[129
	—194—	53Æ190n	d146Wis2d¹	894F2d⁶1148	151Wis2d360	d148Wis2d⁴	155Wis2d⁶
—79—	m138Wis2d		[690		152Wis2d¹	[618	[226
141Wis2d⁹	[395	—357—	d146Wis2d²	—464—	158Wis2d¹⁰	148Wis2d²	155Wis2d⁵
[964		139Wis2d⁴	[690	142Wis2d432	[617	[623	[227
144Wis2d445	—206—	[735	146Wis2d⁵	143Wis2d⁶	159Wis2d¹	148Wis2d²	155Wis2d⁴
144Wis2d¹²	141Wis2d¹	d142Wis2d	[691	[214	[767	[625	
[900	[709	[304	f148Wis2d¹	149Wis2d⁶79	159Wis2d⁸	149Wis2d⁴	[232
d144Wis2d¹³		152Wis2d⁴	[634	152Wis2d123	[769	[395	f155Wis2d⁴
[903	—212—	[356	f148Wis2d²	160Wis2d361	159Wis2d⁹	151Wis2d³	[546
d144Wis2d¹³	153Wis2d⁶	WTA 88-1-	[634	73M⑴⁸	[769	[147	156Wis2d⁶
[909	[326	[533	f149Wis2d⁷25	8Æ37⑴	f159Wis2d⁴	f159Wis2d³	[137
144Wis2d¹¹		Cir. 7	f152Wis2d¹37		[770	[125	159Wis2d12
[911	—230—	132BRW²912	158Wis2d¹89	—499—	161Wis2d¹88	d163Wis2d¹	159Wis2d321
j144Wis2d923	148Wis2d349		159Wis2d¹	140Wis2d⁵55	h166Wis2d¹	[231	161Wis2d88
d145Wis2d¹	156Wis2d¹		[266	e141Wis2d176	[586	166Wis2d¹	163Wis2d130
[501	[200		f159Wis2d²	142Wis2d¹	166Wis2d760	[121	163Wis2d175
f149Wis2d⁷	156Wis2d327		[268	[867	166Wis2d769	d⑵Vis2d³	166Wis2d⁴80
[828	84NwL407		f160Wis2d¹	143Wis2d764	Cir. 1	[121	
155Wis2d⁵			[160	145Wis2d177	903F2d62	Cir. 7	*Continued*
[193							

94

[Illustration 122]

PAGE FROM SHEPARD'S NORTHWESTERN REPORTER CITATIONS: 1985–1990 BOUND SUPPLEMENT

NORTHWESTERN REPORTER, 2d SERIES

Vol. 388

> *State v. Griffin* can also be Shepardized in *Shepard's Northwestern Reporter Citations* under its unofficial citation.
>
> 1. Note that the parallel citation is given to the official reports. Note also how citations to all citing cases are to the *North Western Reporter 2d* and other West reporters.
>
> 2. The regional *Shepard's* not only give citations to citing cases within the state of the cited case, but also provide citations from any other states that cite the cited case. In this Illustration, a Massachusetts court has cited *State v. Griffin*.

—257—	—296—	416NW562	89A2.7s	—454—	64A4806n	—525—	418NW⁶12
(150McA91)	(150McA40)			(222Neb878)	64A4871n	393NW457	423NW825
404NW677	405NW143	—336—	—385—		65A4894n	394NW⁷717	d423NW¹¹
	413NW467	(150McA276)	394NW⁴211	—458—	65A4911n	e394NW721	[825
—259—	417NW¹601	lv app den	394NW⁵211	(223Neb92)	66A4430n	j394NW725	d423NW⁶826
(150McA97)	428NW327	in428Mch860	430NW⁴230	s382NW576	66A4436n	403NW⁷423	423NW¹829

(central explanatory box overlays several citation columns)

428NW	402NW⁸95	(150McA294)	410NW⁶413	421NW764	s334NW807	—535—	——
446NW³530	403NW¹102	lv app den	412NW¹46	424NW¹131	399NW¹796	(131Wis2d41)	(131Wis2d
31A2.1375s	406NW¹225	in426Mch881	d413NW⁸828	424NW²131	419NW⁴540	a97LE709	[322)
12A4.1062s	408NW¹430	418NW¹⁶719	424NW⁸583	424NW⁴132	e422NW²795	a55USLW	s373NW85
	413NW¹98	432NW⁸376	438NW⁶677	6A2.1008s	429NW¹729	[5156	432NW²616
—274—	418NW¹417	432NW⁹376	446NW193		431NW²639	s376NW62	433NW¹3
(150McA128)	419NW¹460	f438NW⁴627	89A2.7s	—477—	444NW⁸326	s93LE699	
lv app den	421NW¹558	f823F2d⁴992	100A3.1129s	(223Neb139)	444NW⁹326	s93LE977	—584—
in425Mch864	427NW¹581	PLPD§4.19		413NW¹301	Tex	f400NW⁴485	(131Wis2d21)
395NW¹291	428NW¹733	76A2.9s	—417—	428NW³507	774SW707	404NW74	s373NW65
411NW851	437NW¹644		412NW⁷91			f410NW⁴620	s394NW313
446NW300		—349—	416NW188	—479—	—515—	f410NW⁴620	e859F2d⁶505
446NW¹486	—306—	(150McA306)		(223Neb142)	(223? 02)	444NW435	859F2d⁶505
	(150McA65)	lv app den	—421—	s430NW273	394N Ω n	Mass	859F2d⁶506
—276—		in425Mch882	392NW³346	393NW⁶440	402N\ 3	525NE382	647FS902
(150McA194)	—312—	416NW418	415NW³701	416NW³7	416NW510		15COA723§7
r414NW706	(150McA78)	436NW⁹727	415NW⁴701	416NW⁷7		—546—	SCT§5.44
s364NW284	s347NW770	10MeLR253	d420NW³244	416NW⁸8	—516—	(131Wis2d84)	84A2.322s
	s377NW703	9PST695§39		416NW⁶512	Case 1	s378NW294	
—281—	400NW¹716	54A2.273s	—425—	434NW⁶308	(223Neb261)	f388NW¹914	—593—
(150McA205)		85A2.889s	392NW⁹723	442NW⁸863		f388NW²915	(131Wis2d
404NW²728	—315—		392NW³724	d445NW296	—516—	f427NW133	[101)
Mo	(150McA230)	—355—	408NW²214	d445NW¹296	Case 2	433NW296	s373NW450
740SW200	v414NW886	(150McA351)		447NW⁸233	(223Neb273)	433NW³297	407NW318
	s414NW886	v393NW176	—429—		388NW¹819	434NW859	f430NW⁵598
—284—	s425NW711		s413NW189	—483—	398NW⁶726	Minn	436NW920
(149McA394)	391NW³379	—358—		(223Neb150)	402NW⁶877	444NW⁴265	f440NW⁵350
v395NW239	403NW⁷175	(150McA358)	—432—	cc246NW594	423NW²491	444NW³268	
s296NW147	405NW⁸118	419NW599	88BRW²963	cc250NW867	429NW³369	MFLA§4.06	—601—
s332NW149	405NW¹⁰393	425NW131		cc303NW490	EDP§8.06	12PST475§	(131Wis2d
s406NW232	408NW⁹519	425NW²132	—434—	390NW²³532	56A4.104n	[26	[220)
	408NW¹⁰519		f399NW²08	391NW²⁵570	56A4.879n		s335NW376
—287—	411NW⁷821	—369—	d401NW¹437	391NW²⁵73	41A4.481s	—553—	s370NW827
(150McA212)	413NW³442	96A2.823s		391NW⁶574		(131Wis2d	f388NW⁶613
lv app den	413NW³499		—438—	394NW⁶641	—522—	[189)	388NW¹⁰615
in426Mch852	413NW⁵499	—370—	(222Neb806)	395NW¹566	406NW²673	s376NW868	397NW⁸150
403NW³127	431NW⁸64	s364NW900	422NW²549	398NW⁴704	419NW¹307	S D	402NW⁷735
	q431NW⁵469	403NW²680	74A3.854s	399NW²⁷263	419NW²168	cc319NW177	e402NW⁸736
—291—	437NW¹6375			399NW⁹264	413NW643	413NW643	436NW⁸913
(150McA29)	93A2.287s	—373—	—446—	404NW¹437	429NW¹447	87A3.93s	439NW137
401NW¹375	64A4.590n	390NW¹829	(222Neb850)	404NW²437	432NW¹874		
401NW⁴375		j390NW833	419NW246	408NW²⁷317	432NW⁸874	—565—	—612—
439NW¹271	—326—	414NW²536	419NW⁷156	430NW¹⁰288	435NW¹702	(131Wis2d	(131Wis2d
444NW³198	(150McA254)	430NW²260	419NW⁵666	442NW¹³200	436NW¹239	[153)	[147)
Pa	s418NW94		434NW²340	444NW649	437NW¹521	e396NW¹162	397NW⁸669
542A2d165	f408NW¹150	—376—	436NW510	665FS776	441NW⁹671	397NW⁹485	—615—
	429NW³228	401NW⁶111	442NW¹214	665FS790	Mich	f400NW⁸485	(131Wis2d
—294—	661FS¹310	409NW⁶530	W Va	Utah	442NW¹417	401NW180	[301)
(150McA35)	661FS¹313	Wis	375SE411	765P2d898		406NW⁸403	
58A3.1027s	q696FS¹526	j424NW202	31A2.1078s	39A3.550s		407NW312	
	f696FS535	19COA143§	43A3.699s	63A4.527n		418NW¹12	Continued
	Nebr	[17		64A4.801n			

[Illustration 123]

PAGE FROM SHEPARD'S NORTHWESTERN REPORTER CITATIONS: ANNUAL CUMULATIVE SUPPLEMENT

NORTHWESTERN REPORTER, 2d SERIES

Vol. 389

—206—	**—376—**	SCT§ 5.22	**—593—**	**—707—**	**—823—**	**—7—**	**—114—**
456NW399	Fla		449NW⁵270	460NW³309	Mich	US cert den	457NW¹169
456NW716	583So2d666	**—532—**	f453NW170	460NW²496	460NW526	in479US1037	917F2d264
Tex		447NW¹⁰50	455NW671		j460NW532	in107SC891	
816SW484	**—408—**		459NW884	**—713—**		D C	**—116—**
	SCT§ 2.32	**—535—**	f467NW166	Case 2	**—840—**	570A2d793	d465NW³34
—216—		a483US868	f469NW834	c449NW¹164	452NW²528		
451NW⁸869	**—412—**	a107SC3164		457NW¹738	CLH§ 15.01	**—12—**	**—141—**
457NW645	466NW767	s479US1005	**—601—**	465NW699		450NW⁴448	MMPC§ 2.06
466NW292	482NW⁷518	s479US1053	450NW⁸513		**—848—**	450NW790	
468NW¹535		s107SC643	450NW¹⁰513	**—717—**	459NW213	j464NW105	**—144—**
749FS736	**—429—**	s107SC926	453NW⁸129	470NW²719	481NW582	464NW843	931F2d416
	449NW¹754	449NW44	457NW306			d464NW²844	
—231—		463NW393	464NW⁴26	**—723—**	**—852—**	d464NW⁵844	**—149—**
454NW84	**—434—**	465NW246	942F2d1150	472NW¹⁰333	462NW457	469NW188	MMPC§ 2.12
480NW³282	d465NW¹410	465NW²247		472NW¹³334		469NW243	
	j465NW412	f465NW³247	**—612—**	472NW⁵336	**—857—**	f469NW⁴245	**—156—**
—263—		467NW566	457NW²306	481NW²90	f452NW⁸88	f477NW293	475NW433
454NW144	**—446—**	h480NW³448	467NW¹113	Ohio	453NW¹764	f477NW²295	Ariz
	Mass	480NW803		574NE499	454NW³315	478NW²299	786P2d1030
—267—	574NE1002	480NW808	**—615—**	JuS§ 3.01	456NW¹296	771FS277	
457NW105		903F2d62	442NW⁶545		f469NW¹570		**—159—**
480NW¹333	**—462—**	Ill	455NW890	**—732—**	477NW811	**—40—**	450NW⁸18
	PLU§ 9.16	577NE817	479NW⁶240	j451NW221	477NW816	d450NW³794	
—294—			Iowa	451NW900		d450NW⁴794	**—179—**
451NW¹622	**—467—**	**—546—**	e469NW⁹668	456NW273	**—860—**	d479NW⁴243	461NW⁶675
743FS¹523	464NW²178	f454NW36	Minn	460NW⁵926	453NW³764		i461NW679
118BRW							

> As mentioned previously, when using *Shepard's Citations* a researcher must always check not only the bound volumes but also the latest pamphlet supplement or supplements.
>
> By checking the annual pamphlet supplement even more citing sources may be located. Any later supplements should also be consulted.
>
> Compare the format used in this Illustration with Illustration 124.

	in481US1042		23COA521§ 3	**—770—**	TP§ 5.15	**—73—**	**—222—**
—326—	in107SC1987	**—565—**		451NW²224		468NW775	477NW¹540
m455NW1	f467NW¹⁵408	US cert den	**—652—**		**—908—**	RLPB§ 4.19	
N M	89A⅔718n	in479US989	468NW⁴775	**—774—**	f464NW²20		**—224—**
814P2d132	89A⅔771n	in107SC583	472NW⁴595	Case 2	f464NW³20	**—78—**	460NW¹81
		454NW⁸784		f472NW¹151	471NW³515	f453NW⁷252	741FS³764
		455NW621	**—660—**		471NW³515		
—336—	**—497—**	455NW⁸622	471NW⁴267	**—784—**		**—85—**	**—229—**
463NW459	457NW454	f455NW⁷624	S D	468NW³572	d479NW²564	Case 2	456NW255
480NW641	461NW⁸559	455NW⁹625	451NW³291		912F2d³1009	461NW²658	
Ariz	480NW216	455NW⁴625		**—787—**	916F2d1219	464NW¹902	**—236—**
810P2d606		f455NW904	**—665—**	Calif		Alk	N D
RPHP§ 4.20	**—510—**	456NW¹833	82A⅔609n	267CaR494	**—916—**	817P2d926	460NW²121
76A⅔320n	f449NW²554	464NW390			US cert den		
76A⅔327n	459NW⁴220	464NW405	**—677—**	**—795—**	in479US1034	**—89—**	**—244—**
78A⅔467n	477NW⁷11	467NW566	Case 16	480NW³154	in107SC883	Case 2	478NW⁸204
81A⅔167n	481NW⁷215	471NW193	945F2d1031		s450NW486	r463NW⁴27	
		471NW231		**—801—**	s464NW643	s468NW⁷902	**—257—**
—343—	**—516—**	471NW⁴233	**—680—**	449NW³770		455NW¹441	CLH§ 13.02
j462NW357	Case 2	479NW551	Case 1	451NW⁴699		456NW²400	
462NW¹²361	479NW¹795	480NW448	Nebr		**Vol. 389**	470NW³486	**—269—**
d475NW373		f482NW371	449NW542	**—807—**		Fla	927F2d332
	—522—		Ariz	466NW⁴78	**—1—**	564So2d568	927F2d¹²333
—358—	454NW¹729	**—580—**	804P2d1318	469NW⁴778	US cert den		
Kan	Calif	478NW389			in479US989	**—99—**	**—285—**
801P2d66	277CaR365		**—688—**	**—820—**	in107SC584	f931F2d1118	456NW768
		—584—	465NW⁸402	Ariz	462NW901		481NW³434
—373—	**—525—**	460NW⁶430	470NW⁸682	796P2d897	464NW845	**—111—**	
480NW²120	451NW737	912F2d623	471NW657			460NW¹303	
119BRW²691	454NW542	f912F2d⁷624	Kan			750FS¹250	
83A⅔271n	458NW³356	Kan	819P2d602			750FS²250	
	e477NW⁶602	827P2d1205					
	e477NW⁷602	24COA575§					
	930F2d⁷1335	[31					

[Illustration 124]

PAGE FROM SHEPARD'S ARKANSAS CITATIONS: CASE EDITION

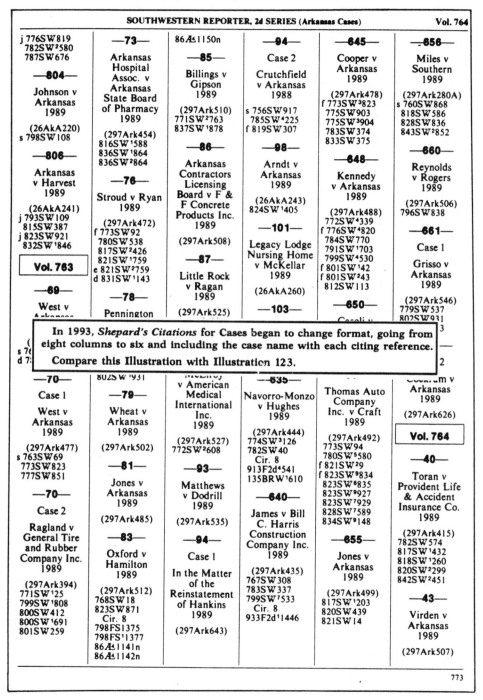

		SOUTHWESTERN REPORTER, 2d SERIES (Arkansas Cases)			**Vol. 764**

j 776SW819 782SW²580 787SW676	**—73—** Arkansas Hospital Assoc. v	86A41150n **—85—** Billings v	**—94—** Case 2 Crutchfield	**—645—** Cooper v Arkansas 1989	**—656—** Miles v Southern 1989
—804— Johnson v Arkansas 1989	Arkansas State Board of Pharmacy 1989	Gipson 1989 (297Ark510) 771SW²763	v Arkansas 1988 s 756SW917 785SW⁴225	(297Ark478) f 773SW³823 775SW903 775SW³904	(297Ark280A) s 760SW868 818SW586 828SW836
(26AkA220) s 798SW108	(297Ark454) 816SW¹588 836SW¹864	837SW¹878 **—86—**	f 819SW307 **—98—**	783SW374 833SW375	843SW²852 **—660—**
—806— Arkansas	836SW²864 **—76—**	Arkansas Contractors Licensing	Arndt v Arkansas 1989	**—648—** Kennedy	Reynolds v Rogers 1989
v Harvest 1989	Stroud v Ryan 1989	Board v F & F Concrete Products Inc.	(26AkA243) 824SW¹405	v Arkansas 1989	(297Ark506) 796SW838
(26AkA241) j 793SW109 815SW387	(297Ark472) f 773SW92	1989 (297Ark508)	**—101—** Legacy Lodge	(297Ark488) 772SW⁴339 f 776SW⁴820	**—661—**
j 823SW921 832SW¹846	780SW538 817SW²426 821SW¹759	**—87—**	Nursing Home v McKellar 1989	784SW770 791SW¹703 799SW⁴530	Case 1 Grisso v
Vol. 763	e 821SW²759 d 831SW¹143	Little Rock v Ragan 1989	(26AkA260)	f 801SW¹42 f 801SW²43 812SW113	Arkansas 1989
—69— West v Arkansas	**—78—** Pennington	(297Ark525) 	**—103—** Casali v	**—650—** Casali v	(297Ark546) 779SW537 802SW931

In 1993, *Shepard's Citations* for Cases began to change format, going from eight columns to six and including the case name with each citing reference.

Compare this Illustration with Illustration 123.

—70— Case 1 West v Arkansas 1989	802SW¹931 **—79—** Wheat v Arkansas 1989	McElroy v American Medical International Inc. 1989	**—635—** Navorro-Monzo v Hughes 1989	Thomas Auto Company Inc. v Craft 1989	Cook m v Arkansas 1989 (297Ark626)
(297Ark477) s 763SW69 773SW823 777SW851	(297Ark502) **—81—** Jones v	(297Ark527) 772SW²608 **—93—**	(297Ark444) 774SW³126 782SW40 Cir. 8	(297Ark492) 773SW94 780SW⁵580 f 821SW²9	**Vol. 764** **—40—**
—70— Case 2	Arkansas 1989 (297Ark485)	Matthews v Dodrill 1989	913F2d⁴541 135BRW¹610 **—640—**	f 823SW⁹834 823SW⁶835 823SW⁹927 823SW⁷929	Toran v Provident Life & Accident Insurance Co.
Ragland v General Tire and Rubber Company Inc.	**—83—** Oxford v Hamilton	(297Ark535) **—94—** Case 1	James v Bill C. Harris Construction Company Inc.	828SW⁷589 834SW⁹148 **—655—**	1989 (297Ark415) 782SW574
1989 (297Ark394) 771SW¹25	1989 (297Ark512) 768SW18	In the Matter of the Reinstatement	1989 (297Ark435) 767SW308	Jones v Arkansas 1989	817SW¹432 818SW¹260 820SW²299 842SW²451
799SW¹808 800SW412 800SW¹691 801SW259	823SW871 Cir. 8 798FS1375 798FS¹1377 86A41141n 86A41142n	of Hankins 1989 (297Ark643)	783SW337 799SW⁷533 Cir. 8 933F2d¹1446	(297Ark499) 817SW¹203 820SW439 821SW14	**—43—** Virden v Arkansas 1989 (297Ark507)

[Illustration 125]

SAMPLE SCREENS FROM WESTLAW AND LEXIS
SHOWING SHEPARDIZED CASE ONLINE

Figure 1. WESTLAW

```
FOR EDUCATIONAL USE ONLY       SHEPARD'S  (Rank 1 of 1)      Page 1 of 3
CITATIONS TO: 131 Wis.2d 41
CITATOR: WISCONSIN CITATIONS
DIVISION: Wisconsin Reports 2nd Series
COVERAGE: First Shepard's volume through Aug. 1993 Supplement
Retrieval                                     Headnote
   No.     --Analysis--- ------Citation------    No.
    1         Same Text ( 388 N.W.2d 535)
    2      A  Affirmed   483 U.S. 868
    3      A  Affirmed    97 L.Ed.2d 709
    4      A  Affirmed   107 S.Ct. 3164
           A  Affirmed    55 USLW 5156
    5     SC  Same Case  126 Wis.2d 183
          SC  Same Case  479 U.S. 1005
          SC  Same Case  479 U.S. 1053
          SC  Same Case   93 L.Ed.2d 699
          SC  Same Case   93 L.Ed.2d 977
          SC  Same Case  107 S.Ct. 643
          SC  Same Case  107 S.Ct. 926
    6      F  Followed   135 Wis.2d 406, 409     6
   > Insta-Cite  > Shepard's PreView  > QuickCite  > Commands  > SCOPE
Copyright (C) 1993 McGraw-Hill, Inc.; Copyright (C) 1993 West Publishing Co.
```

Cases can be Shepardized on both **WESTLAW** and **LEXIS**. These figures show the results when **131 Wis. 2d 41** is Shepardized. Note that the screen displays of the two vendors differ somewhat.

Figure 2. LEXIS

```
              (c) 1993 McGraw-Hill, Inc. - DOCUMENT 1 (OF 1)


CITATIONS TO: 131 Wis.2d 41
SERIES: Shepard's Wisconsin Citations
DIVISION: Wisconsin Reports, 2d Series
COVERAGE: All Shepard's Citations Through 08/93 Supplement.
NUMBER  ANALYSIS              CITING REFERENCE         SYLLABUS/HEADNOTE
------  ----------------      -------------------      ------------------

    1   parallel citation     (388 N.W.2d 535)
    2   affirmed              483 U.S. 868
    3   affirmed               97 L.Ed.2d 709
    4   affirmed              107 S.Ct. 3164
    5   affirmed               55 U.S.L.W 5156
    6   same case             126 Wis.2d 183
    7   same case             479 U.S. 1005
    8   same case             479 U.S. 1053
    9   same case              93 L.Ed.2d 699
   10   same case              93 L.Ed.2d 977
   11   same case             107 S.Ct. 643
----------------------------------------------------------------------
To see the text of a citing case, press the citing reference NUMBER and then
the TRANSMIT key.
For further explanation, press the H key (for HELP) and then the TRANSMIT key.
Press Alt-H for Help  or  .SO to End Session  or  Alt-Q to Quit Software.
```

[Illustration 126]

COVER FROM ANNUAL CUMULATIVE SUPPLEMENT,
SHEPARD'S WISCONSIN CITATIONS

VOL. 85   NOVEMBER, 1992   NO. 3

Shepard's
Wisconsin
Citations

ANNUAL CUMULATIVE SUPPLEMENT
CASES AND STATUTES

The cover of the latest pamphlet supplement or supplements always lists "What Your Library Should Contain." It indicates all of the units of a particular set of *Shepard's Citations.*

Complete Shepardizing always includes using all bound volumes and paper supplements relevant to your research.

**RECYCLE YOUR
OUTDATED
SUPPLEMENTS**

When you receive new supplements and are instructed to destroy the outdated versions, please consider taking these paper products to a local recycling center to help conserve our nation's natural resources. Thank you

(USPS 656270)

IMPORTANT NOTICE

Do not destroy the November, 1992 gold paper-covered Annual Cumulative Supplement until it is removed from the "What Your Library Should Contain" list on the front cover of any future supplement.

WHAT YOUR LIBRARY SHOULD CONTAIN

1988 Bound Volume, Cases (Parts 1 and 2)*
1988 Bound Volume, Statutes*
Supplemented with:
  –Nov., 1992 Annual Cumulative Supplement Vol. 85 No. 3
Subscribers to Shepard's Wisconsin EXPRESS Citations should retain the latest blue-covered issue.

DESTROY ALL OTHER ISSUES

SEE TABLE OF CONTENTS ON PAGE III

SEE "THIS ISSUE INCLUDES" ON
PAGE IV

SHEPARD'S
McGRAW-HILL

SECTION E.   STATUTE CITATORS

Statute Editions or Statute sections within multiple units of *Shepard's Citations* cover the various types of legislative enactments and court cases relating to this legislation. *It is important to note that if no reference is given for a particular statutory provision, it means that provision has not been cited by a court or affected by subsequent legislation.*

1.   Statutes

Statutes, both state and federal, are treated by *Shepard's Citations* in a manner similar to cases.   The notations cover the form and operation of the law by the legislature and the courts.   Its operation is identified by abbreviations denoting legislative changes (amendments, repeals, revisions, reenactments, etc.) and judicial interpretations (constitutional, unconstitutional, invalid, etc.).   There are statute citators for the United States and for each state, the District of Columbia, and Puerto Rico.   These citators are being added to WESTLAW but, unlike that for cases, coverage is by no means complete.

The several volumes in the *Statutes Edition* of *Shepard's United States Citations* provide citations to subsequent legislation and federal court cases for provisions in the U.S. Constitution, all editions of the *United States Code* and the two annotated editions, Tariff Schedules, *U.S. Statutes at Large* (not in the *U.S. Code*), *U.S. Treaties and Other International Agreements,* General Orders in Bankruptcy, and the various federal court rules.   A brief examination of the set will reveal its specific arrangement.   [See Illustration 128 for how to Shepardize the current *U.S. Code.*]   It is worth noting that the *U.S. Statutes at Large* section enables a researcher to locate cases citing statutes no longer in effect or that were never published in the *U.S. Code.*

The format used for publication of state statutes varies, depending on the plan adopted by a jurisdiction.   For example, one state may arrange statutes by Title and Section numbers; another by Chapter and Paragraph numbers.   The Table of Abbreviations in each state unit of *Shepard's Citations* should be examined specifically to determine the local scheme.   [See Illustration 127.]   In some state *Shepard's* units, especially the supplemental pamphlets, cases and statutes are in separate sections in the same volume; for others, a separate *Statute Edition* may be provided.

The information contained in the state statutes units is presented according to this arrangement: statutory amendments, repeals, etc., are listed first, followed by state and federal court citations and citations in the attorneys general opinions, legal periodicals, and acts of the legislature.   [See Illustration 129.]

In addition to the statutory coverage provided in the state statute citators, these units cover additional sources, which are described in the remainder of this section.

2. Constitutions

Citations to federal and state constitutions are included in the state *Statute Editions* or Statute sections of *Shepard's Citations*. A Constitution section within the *Statute Editions* or Statute sections is arranged under the articles and amendments to the constitution. Citing sources, from both state and federal courts, are listed under these provisions. [See Illustration 130.]

3. Court Rules

Citations to court cases interpreting court rules also are covered by the *Statute Editions* for *Shepard's Citations*. The *Court Rules* section is arranged by court (final, intermediate, and original jurisdiction), and is subdivided by rule number. A separate set, *Federal Rules Citations*, includes citations to the various federal rules, the corresponding state rules of the 50 states and Puerto Rico, as well as every reported state and federal case involving procedural issues.

4. Jury Instructions

A separate section in the *Statute Editions* includes citing references to jury instructions from the jurisdiction. Jury Instructions are discussed in Chapter 18.

5. City Charters and Ordinances

Municipal charters and ordinances are part of the *Statute Editions*. Reference should be made to the citator of the state in which a city is located for citations to its charter or ordinances.

The sections under *Municipal Charters* in the *Statute Editions* are arranged alphabetically by cities in many state editions and subdivided by topics. The units also have a separate "Index to Municipal Charters." The *Ordinances* section also may be arranged alphabetically by cities and subdivided by topics. It, too, has an "Index to Ordinances." In some citators, the citations to the ordinances of the larger cities are arranged separately. To meet editorial requirements, the citations to ordinances may be indexed by section numbers as well as by topic.

SECTION F. ILLUSTRATIONS: SHEPARD'S CITATIONS—STATUTES

[Illustration 127]

ABBREVIATIONS—ANALYSIS TABLE FROM SHEPARD'S WISCONSIN CITATIONS—STATUTES EDITION

ABBREVIATIONS—ANALYSIS
STATUTES

Form of Statute

Act	Act	p	Page
Adj.	Adjourned Session	¶	Paragraph
Amend.	Amendment	P.L.	Public Law
Art.	Article	§	Section
Ch. or C	Chapter	Sp.	Special Session
Cl.	Clause	St.	Statutes at Large
Ex. Ord.	Executive Order	Subch.	Subchapter
Intro. Par.	Introductory Paragraph	Subd.	Subdivision
J.R.	Joint Resolution	Subsec.	Subsection
Mem. Ch.	Memorial Chapter	Vet. Reg.	Veterans Regulations
No.	Number		

Operation of Statute

Legislative

A	(amended)	Statute amended.
Ad	(added)	New section added.
E	(extended)	Provisions of an existing statute extended in their application to a later statute, or allowance of additional time for performance of duties required by a statute within a limited time.
L	(limited)	Provisions of an existing statute declared not to be extended in their application to a later statute.
R	(repealed)	Abrogation of an existing statute.
Re-en	(re-enacted)	Statute re-enacted.
Rn	(renumbered)	Renumbering of existing sections.
Rp	(repealed in part)	Abrogation of part of an existing statute.
Rs	(repealed and superseded)	Abrogation of an existing statute and substitution of new legislation therefor.
Rv	(revised)	Statute revised.
S	(superseded)	Substitution of new legislation for an existing statute not expressly abrogated.
Sd	(suspended)	Statute suspended.
Sdp	(suspended in part)	Statute suspended in part.
Sg	(supplementing)	New matter added to an existing statute.
Sp	(superseded in part)	Substitution of new legislation for part of an existing statute not expressly abrogated.
Va	(validated)	

Judicial

C	Constitutional.		V	Void or invalid.
U	Unconstitutional.		Va	Valid.
Up	Unconstitutional in part.		Vp	Void or invalid in part.

> **Each volume and pamphlet of *Shepard's Citations—Statutes* has an Abbreviation—Analysis Table. It should always be consulted to check the meanings of abbreviations used in the citator.**

[Illustration 128]

PAGE FROM SHEPARD'S U.S. CITATIONS—
STATUTES, 1990–1992 SUPPLEMENT

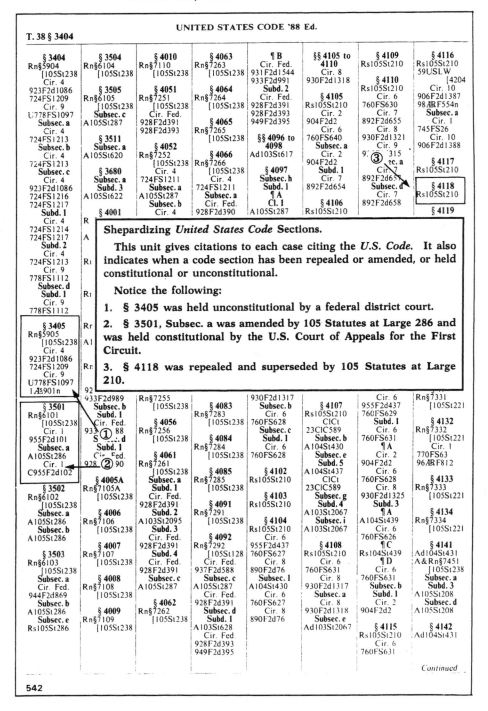

UNITED STATES CODE '88 Ed.

T. 38 § 3404

§ 3404	§ 3504	§ 4010	§ 4063	¶ B	§§ 4105 to 4110	§ 4109	§ 4116
Rn§5904	Rn§6104	Rn§7110	Rn§7263	Cir. Fed.	Cir. 8	Rs105St210	Rs105St210
[105St238	[105St238	[105St238	[105St238	931F2d1544	930F2d1318		59USLW
Cir. 4				933F2d991		§ 4110	[4204
923F2d1086	§ 3505	§ 4051	§ 4064	Subd. 2	§ 4105	Rs105St210	Cir. 10
724FS1209	Rn§6105	Rn§7251	Rn§7264	Cir. Fed.	Rs105St210	Cir. 6	906F2d1387
Cir. 9	[105St238	[105St238	[105St238	928F2d391	Cir. 2	760FS630	98ARF554n
U778FS1097	Subsec. c	Cir. Fed.		928F2d393	904F2d2	Cir. 7	Subsec. a
Subsec. a	A105St287	928F2d391	§ 4065	949F2d395	Cir. 6	892F2d655	Cir. 1
Cir. 4		928F2d393	Rn§7265		760FS640	Cir. 8	745FS26
724FS1213	§ 3511		[105St238	§§ 4096 to	Subsec. a	930F2d1321	Cir. 10
Subsec. b	Subsec. a	§ 4052		4098	Cir. 2	Cir. 9	906F2d1388
Cir. 4	A105St620	Rn§7252	§ 4066	Ad103St617	904F2d2	9.⑶ 315	
724FS1213		[105St238	Rn§7266			ec. a	§ 4117
Subsec. c	§ 3680	Cir. 4	[105St238	§ 4097	Subd. 1	Cir. 7	Rs105St210
Cir. 4	Subsec. a	724FS1211	Cir. 4	Subsec. h	Cir. 7	892F2d65	
923F2d1086	Subd. 3	Subsec. a	724FS1211	Subd. 1	892F2d654	Subsec. d	§ 4118
724FS1216	A105St622	A105St287	Subsec. a	¶ A		Cir. 7	Rs105St210
724FS1217		Subsec. b	928F2d390	Cl. 1	§ 4106	892F2d658	
Subd. 1	§ 4001	Cir. 4		A105St287	Rs105St210		§ 4119
Cir. 4							
724FS1214	R						
724FS1217							
Subd. 2	A						
Cir. 4							
724FS1213	R₁						
Cir. 9							
778FS1112							
Subsec. d	R₁						
Subd. 1							
Cir. 9							
778FS1112							

§ 3405	Rr
Rn§5905	
[105St238	A1
Cir. 4	
923F2d1086	
724FS1209	Rr
Cir. 9	
U778FS1097	
1A3901n	92

> **Sheparding *United States Code* Sections.**
>
> This unit gives citations to each case citing the *U.S. Code*. It also indicates when a code section has been repealed or amended, or held constitutional or unconstitutional.
>
> Notice the following:
>
> 1. § 3405 was held unconstitutional by a federal district court.
>
> 2. § 3501, Subsec. a was amended by 105 Statutes at Large 286 and was held constitutional by the U.S. Court of Appeals for the First Circuit.
>
> 3. § 4118 was repealed and superseded by 105 Statutes at Large 210.

	933F2d989	Rn§7255		930F2d1317	§ 4107	Cir. 6	Rn§7331
§ 3501	Subsec. b	[105St238	§ 4083	Subsec. b	Rs105St210	955F2d437	[105St221
Rn§6101	Subd. 1		Rn§7283	Cir. 6	ClCt	760FS629	
[105St238	Cir. Fed.	§ 4056	[105St238	760FS628	23ClC589	Subd. 1	§ 4132
Cir. 1	933⑴ 88	Rn§7256		Subsec. c	Subsec. b	Cir. 6	Rn§7332
955F2d101	S ...d	[105St238	§ 4084	Subd. 1	A104St430	760FS631	[105St221
Subsec. a	Subd. 1		Rn§7284	Cir. 6	Subsec. e	¶ A	Cir. 1
A105St286	Cir. Fed.	§ 4061	[105St238	760FS628	Subd. 5	Cir. 2	770FS63
Cir. 1	928⑵ 90	Rn§7261			A104St437	904F2d2	96ARF812
C955F2d102		[105St238	§ 4085	§ 4102	ClCt	Cir. 6	
		Subsec. a	Rn§7285	Rs105St210	23ClC589	760FS628	§ 4133
§ 3502	§ 4005A	Subd. 1	[105St238		Subsec. g	Cir. 8	Rn§7333
Rn§6102	Rn§7105A	Cir. Fed.		§ 4103	Subd. 4	930F2d1325	[105St221
[105St238	[105St238	928F2d391	§ 4091	Rs105St210	A103St2067	Subd. 3	
Subsec. a		Subd. 2	Rn§7291		Subsec. i	¶ A	§ 4134
A105St286	§ 4006	A103St2095	[105St238	§ 4104	A103St2067	A104St439	Rn§7334
Subsec. b	Rn§7106	Subd. 3		Rs105St210		Cir. 6	[105St221
A105St286	[105St238	Cir. Fed.	§ 4092	Cir. 6	§ 4108	760FS626	
		928F2d391	Rn§7292	955F2d437	Rs105St210	¶ C	§ 4141
§ 3503	§ 4007	Subd. 4	[105St128	760FS627	Cir. 6	Rs105St439	Ad104St431
Rn§6103	Rn§7107	Cir. Fed.	Cir. Fed.	Cir. 8	760FS631	¶ D	A&Rn§7451
[105St238	[105St238	928F2d391	937F2d588	890F2d76	Cir. 6	Rs105St210	[105St238
Subsec. a		Subsec. c	Subsec. c	Cir. 8	760FS631	Cir. 6	Subsec. a
Cir. Fed.	§ 4008	A105St287	A105St287	A104St430	930F2d1317	Subsec. b	Subd. 3
944F2d869	Rn§7108		Cir. Fed.	Cir. 6	Cir. 8	Subd. 1	A105St208
Subsec. b	[105St238	§ 4062	928F2d391	760FS627	Subsec. a	Cir. 2	Subsec. d
A105St286		Rn§7262	Subsec. d	Cir. 8	Cir. 8	904F2d2	A105St208
Subsec. e	§ 4009	[105St238	Subd. 1	890F2d76	930F2d1318		
Rs105St286	Rn§7109		A103St628		Subsec. e	§ 4115	§ 4142
	[105St238		Cir. Fed.		Ad103St2067	Rs105St210	Ad104St431
			928F2d393			Cir. 6	
			949F2d395			760FS631	

Continued

[Illustration 129]

PAGE FROM SHEPARD'S WISCONSIN CITATIONS—STATUTES EDITION

WISCONSIN STATUTES—WISCONSIN STATUTES ANNOTATED

1985-86 , 111.70

297NW824	**Subd. b**	746F2d1195	48WiAG291	38NW697	U95LE377	**111.57 to**	U340US388
305NW79	117Wis2d683	763F2d866	**Subd. a**	C42NW472	U71SC359	**111.60**	340US417
305NW103	134Wis2d380	577FS1557	Ad1979C221	C42NW477	**Subsec. 5**	25ChL121	U95LE372
330NW595	345NW449	627FS1312	**Subd. b**	C44NW547	**Subd. f**	**111.57**	95LE390
339NW352	396NW786	628FS1483	98Wis2d595	149NW669	132Wis2d417	C255Wis154	U71SC359
354NW225	**Subd. c**	652FS1484	297NW820	153NW606	**111.53**	C257Wis43	71SC374
385NW517	117Wis2d683	60WiAG43	**Subd. c**	U340US383	A1969C276	C257Wis53	90FS349
407NW515	345NW449	66WiAG30	1979C355	253Wis586	C258Wis1	**111.61**	A1969C276
407NW909	**111.345**	68WiAG404	[§118	356US645	C255Wis154	C38NW692	C255Wis154
412NW524	Ad1981C334	1938WLR244	91Wis2d115	374US80	C257Wis43	C42NW472	C257Wis43
339FS1363	131Wis2d212	42NYL1060	91Wis2d476	U95LE370	C257Wis53	C42NW477	C257Wis53
565FS221	388NW562	**Subsec. 1**	94Wis2d613	95LE387	C258Wis1	C44NW547	C257Wis53
577FS1555	**111.36**	A1977C29	101Wis2d620	2LE1038	34NW844	U340US388	C258Wis1
60WiAG44	Ad1981C334	A1979C319	117Wis2d757	10LE767	C38NW692	U95LE372	C38NW692
67W							

> **Sheparizing a State Statute.**
>
> **Notice the following:**
>
> 1. Wisconsin Statutes § 111.50 was held constitutional by the Wisconsin Supreme Court, but held unconstitutional by the Supreme Court of the United States.
>
> 2. Wisconsin Statutes § 111.39, Subsec. 3m was added by the Wisconsin Acts of 1977.

Subd. b	738F2d790	Ad1977C29	46WiAG123	**111.04**	34NW844	C255Wis154	C44NW547
619FS1311	**Subsec. 4**	**Subsec. 3**	**Subd. a**	68WiAG171	C38NW692	C257Wis43	U340US387
Subd. f	113Wis2d568	A1973C268	A1979C221	63McL752	C42NW472	C257Wis53	U95LE372
746F2d1195	335NW838	37Wis2d704	**Subd. b**	**111.50**	C42NW477	C258Wis1	71SC359
Subd. g	**111.375**	62Wis2d399	A1979C221	C255Wis154	C44NW547	109Wis2d25	90FS349
A1983Act538	A1979C319	66Wis2d67	A1983Act122	C257Wis43	240NW419	C38NW692	83FRD277
111.335	50Wis2d326	69Wis2d783	**Subd. c**	C257Wis53	U340US388	C42NW472	56McL612
Ad1981C334	68Wis2d688	86Wis2d396	91Wis2d474	C258Wis1	U95LE372	C42NW477	44MnL208
121Wis2d297	91Wis2d113	155NW545	283①504	82Wis2d344	U71SC359	C44NW547	42ABA420
134Wis2d381	101Wis2d341	215NW443	§.2.6	C38NW692	90FS349	325NW355	**111.63**
359NW177	184NW141	224NW396	A1979C319	C42NW472	51WiAG92	U340US388	A1969C276
396NW786	229NW598	233NW364	**111.395**	C42NW477	**111.55**	U95LE372	C255Wis154
Subsec. 1	280NW758	273NW207	A1977C29	C44NW547	A1969C276	U71SC359	C257Wis44
Subd. c	305NW70	46WiAG123	91Wis2d468	262NW227	253Wis589	1960WLR283	C257Wis53
¶1	746F2d1195	60WiAG44	95Wis2d400	U340US383	C255Wis154	**111.59**	C258Wis1
407NW906	627FS1312	35WiAG49	57WiAG179	95LE370	C257Wis43	A1969C276	C38NW692
716F2d1125	**111.337**	60WiAG44	53CaL778	U71SC359	C257Wis53	253Wis589	C42NW473
111.337	Ad1981C334	67WiAG175	**Subd. a**	113Wis2d201	C258Wis1	C255Wis154	C42NW547
Ad1981C334	**Subsec. 2**	42NYL832	A1977C29	25ChL122	**111.51**	72Wis2d274	C44NW547
Subsec. 2	**Subd. a**	68Wis2d354	120Wis2d365	C255Wis154	82Wis2d346	C257Wis43	U340US387
Subd. a	766F2d942	**Subsec. 1**	132Wis2d424	C257Wis43	34NW844	C257Wis53	U95LE371
766F2d942	A1983Act189	68Wis2d679	283NW604	C257Wis53	C38NW692	C258Wis1	U71SC359
Subd. b	305NW152	69Wis2d782	290NW555	C258Wis1	C42NW472	72Wis2d274	**111.64**
A1983Act189	68WiAG404	228NW650	291NW586	C258Wis1	C42NW472	34NW844	253Wis594
111.34	**Subsec. 2**	229NW593	297NW824	C38NW692	C42NW477	C38NW692	C255Wis154
Ad1981C334	A1979C221	233NW361	335NW414	C42NW474	C44NW547	C42NW472	C257Wis52
117Wis2d655	A1979C355	437FS103	354NW224	C42NW477	240NW419	C42NW477	C257Wis53
132Wis2d417	68WiAG404	66WiAG29	392NW845	C44NW547	262NW229	C44NW547	C258Wis1
134Wis2d379	**111.38 to**	**Subd. b**	437FS104	U340US388	U340US388	240NW419	34NW844
345NW435	**111.395**	66Wis2d53	627FS1312	U95LE382	340US411	U340US388	C38NW692
392NW842	42NYL824	68Wis2d347	660FS313	U71SC359	U95LE372	340US418	C42NW472
396NW785	**111.38**	224NW389	46WiAG123	**111.50**	95LE390	U95LE372	C42NW477
660FS313	275Wis528	228NW661	et seq.	A1969C276	U71SC359	95LE391	C44NW547
Subsec. 2	37Wis2d704	437FS103	1967C327	**Subsec. 4**	71SC374	U71SC359	340US387
117Wis2d654	82NW318	66WiAG29	1967C758	C257Wis48	90FS349	71SC375	95LE372
129Wis2d433	155NW548	**Subd. c**	[§13	C42NW475	137FS672	90FS349	71SC359
134Wis2d381	60②44	66WiAG30	1967C758②14	**Subsec. 5**	**111.56**	**111.60**	1961WLR604
345NW435	**Subsec. 6**	**Subsec. 3m**	253Wis594	C257Wis43	A1979C110	253Wis589	**111.70**
385NW517	101Wis2d354	Ad1977C29	254Wis349	C42NW474	C255Wis154	C255Wis154	et seq.
385NW521	305NW70	**Subsec. 4**	255Wis163	**111.52**	C257Wis53	C257Wis53	70Wis2d308
396NW786	**111.39**	A1979C319	37Wis2d704	C255Wis154	C257Wis53	C257Wis53	71Wis2d711
Subd. a	275Wis528	50Wis2d326	50Wis2d477	C257Wis43	C258Wis1	C258Wis1	81Wis2d90
129Wis2d441	50Wis2d325	91Wis2d477	C258Wis1	C257Wis43	C38NW692	72Wis2d274	83Wis2d106
134Wis2d380	101Wis2d342	155NW545	34Wis2d445	C38NW692	C42NW472	34NW844	86Wis2d255
396NW786	82NW318	184NW141	36Wis2d244	C42NW472	C42NW477	C38NW692	99Wis2d257
	184NW141	283NW605	34NW844	C42NW477	C44NW547	C42NW472	234NW290
	305NW65	728F2d929	36NW416	C44NW547	U340US400	C42NW477	
	738F2d793	46WiAG123	C38NW692	U340US398	U95LE378	C44NW547	*Continued*

[Illustration 130]

PAGE FROM WISCONSIN CONSTITUTION IN SHEPARD'S WISCONSIN CITATIONS—STATUTES EDITION

WISCONSIN CONSTITUTION, 1848

Art. 4

197Wis164	307NW663	**§ 1r**	85NW857	264NW622	**§ 1m**	284NW44	177NW899
198Wis332	36WiAG205	1971p1336	138NW249	267NW433	1965p899	339NW327	184NW683
222Wis69	1950WLR207	**§ 2**	301NW183	277NW687	1967p489	401NW795	186NW729
229Wis151	**§ 34**	200Wis540	19WiAG605	288NW454	1967p493	19WiAG535	187NW830
235Wis530	1959p940	228Wis656	20WiAG1201	289NW662	Ad1967p516	19WiAG598	192NW374
242Wis369	1961p694	228NW903	21WiAG1089	10NW180	1977p2120	29WiAG178	262NW629
265Wis336	Ad1961p737	280NW393	25WiAG480	11NW604	1979p646	31WiAG141	7NW378
34Wis2d191		**§ 3**	27WiAG92	126NW557	RApr3 1979	36WiAG576	13NW580
44Wis2d227	**Art. 5**	1965p868	27WiAG623	182NW482	**§ 1n**	43WiAG226	21NW381
59Wis2d412	70Wis2d867	1967p490	1946WLR283	208NW784	1965p899	61WiAG10	26NW260
61Wis2d555	136Wis2d143	1967p492	1956WLR95	235NW649	1967p489	63WiAG130	49NW415
70Wis2d466	236NW16	A1967p519	1959WLR422	237NW910	1967p493	1970WLR300	60NW353
101Wis2d71	401NW793	200Wis554	**§ 7**	264NW539	Ad1967p516	1974WLR729	98NW394
104Wis2d74	98F350	254W 06	1971p1336	28WiAG423	1977p2120	**§ 4**	115NW619
112Wis2d40	600FS765	228 1	1977p2120	29WiAG179	1979p646	1929p1066	182NW460
81NW869	54WiAG15	37N 476	1979p646	30WiAG250	RApr3 1979	A1929p1119	238NW510
84NW246	68WiAG109	48WiAG188	AApr3 1979	41WiAG207	**§ 1p**	1939p1044	263NW219
87NW815	1946WLR283	54WiAG13	228Wis646	43WiAG353	1965p899	1943p1005	291NW618
93NW265	**§ 1**	**§ 4**	242Wis42	52WiAG423	1967p489	1943p1035	292NW822
98NW954	1965p887	148Wis527	280NW393	55WiAG161	1967p493	1945p1144	316NW659
112NW432	1977p2120	170Wis237	7NW375	55WiAG198	Ad1967p517	1947C183	401NW801
121NW889	1979p646	183Wis154	32WiAG206	59WiAG94	1977p2120	1953p599	405NW727
137NW21	AApr3 1979	217Wis540	48WiAG191	60WiAG205	1979p646	1955p817	70US94
140NW79	141Wis628	22Wis2d557	54WiAG14	60WiAG247	RApr3 1979	1957p320	18LE33
142NW502	183Wis154	59Wis2d412	66WiAG185	62WiAG238	1974WLR732	1957p892	752F2d292
147NW226	196Wis493	70Wis2d485	66WiAG109	63WiAG163	**§ 2**	1959p939	769F2d1163
177NW34	228Wis656	71Wis2d131	62MqL538	63WiAG313	1943p1029	1959p949	821F2d451
181NW121	242Wis42	82Wis2d719	1944WLR79	63WiAG346	1945p1157	1961p693	648FS870
187NW218	83Wis2d816	83Wis2d816	**§ 8**	64WiAG20	A1947p1316	1961p727	20WiAG112
201NW385	106Wis2d42	136Wis2d124	1977p2120	66WiAG311	138Wis174	1961p736	21WiAG757
206NW908	111Wis2d180	134NW697	1979p646	70WiAG156	141Wis151	1963p670	22WiAG708

Sheperdizing a State Constitution.

Each state *Shepard's* has a part in its statute citators that includes a section on the state's constitution.

Notice the following:

1. **Article 5, § 5 was repealed in 1933.**

2. **Article 5, § 7 was amended on April 3, 1979.**

235NW630	30WiAG02	47WiAG355	**§ 9**	130Wi		131Wis500	45WiAG76
303NW629	54WiAG13	51WiAG4	1929p1085	130NW460	280NW701	132Wis462	45WiAG152
310NW630	34MqL1	61WiAG354	1931p936	401NW793	293NW163	148Wis459	48WiAG188
331NW668	66MqL276	63WiAG129	R1933p1297	20WiAG325	299NW45	154Wis297	48WiAG246
387NW278	1944WLR79	63WiAG238	1933C50	34MqL1	149NW615	154Wis297	48WiAG246
194F835	1950WLR234	60MqL886	25Wis2d137	1946WLR283	19WiAG529	171Wis521	50WiAG48
22WiAG36	1962WLR16	1962WLR16	130NW460	1977WLR941	22WiAG1045	176Wis107	50WiAG65
23WiAG289	1970WLR300	1962WLR330	22WiAG204	**§ 1**	34WiAG205	176Wis112	51WiAG202
26WiAG208	10 LR940	**§ 5**	**§ 10**	1977p2120	37WiAG84	177Wis295	52WiAG50
26WiAG275	1 76	1929p1084	1929p1079	1979p646	64WiAG49	179Wis407	58WiAG157
44WiAG152	**§ 1m**	1931p935	A1931p960	AApr3 1979	15MqL191	219Wis132	60WiAG87
52WiAG259	1965p899	R1933p1297	1939p948	101Wis646	1950WLR207	242Wis49	60WiAG503
54WiAG3	1967p489	149Wis86	1979p1845	183Wis154	**§ 3**	245Wis111	61WiAG117
60WiAG109	1967p493	25Wis2d137	160Wis389	248Wis256	101Wis646	248Wis248	61WiAG258
69WiAG154	Ad1967p515	34Wis2d485	183Wis154	234Wis606	102Wis514	250Wis21	61WiAG356
72WiAG138	1977p2120	112Wis2d267	218Wis302	78NW151	136Wis190	259Wis441	61WiAG444
74WiAG169	1979p646	136NW141	220Wis143	197NW832	149Wis86	265Wis3	62WiAG39
56MqL26	RApr3 1979	130NW460	221Wis551	21NW381	248Wis256	8Wis2d121	63WiAG199
1940WLR20	61WiAG46	149NW615	227Wis79	37NW476	19Wis2d577	17Wis2d27	63WiAG225
1944WLR96	**§ 1n**	332NW802	233Wis16	43WiAG220	34Wis2d485	49Wis2d506	63WiAG362
1949WLR312	1965p899	**§ 6**	233Wis442	48WiAG188	63Wis2d260	71Wis2d404	65WiAG134
1949WLR488	1967p489	176Wis539	243Wis459	1950WLR234	91Wis2d710	82Wis2d574	65WiAG247
1964WLR185	1967p493	177Wis303	244Wis8	1970WLR299	115Wis2d35	95Wis2d635	65WiAG294
1964WLR610	Ad1967p515	196Wis556	22Wis2d554	1970WLR	136Wis2d150	96Wis2d676	65WiAG304
57NwL286	1977p2120	200Wis330	49Wis2d320	[1043	78NW151	106Wis2d309	67WiAG3
§ 33	1979p646	2Wis2d240	59Wis2d412	1974WLR729	78NW757	136Wis2d163	67WiAG248
1943p1029	RApr3 1979	29Wis2d122	71Wis2d119	1977WLR947	116NW901	71NW800	67WiAG250
1945p1157		100Wis2d84	82Wis2d679		136NW141	97NW923	68WiAG45
Ad1947p1316		186NW722	152NW437		21NW381	111NW714	68WiAG63
265Wis210		187NW834	197NW832		120NW664	112NW475	68WiAG333
103Wis2d318		221NW611	260NW487		149NW615	134NW690	
60NW765		228NW593			217NW259	142NW639	*Continued*

SECTION G. OTHER UNITS OF SHEPARD'S CITATIONS

The *Shepard's Citations* described in the previous sections are all-inclusive, that is, each unit contains all cited cases, all statutes, and all citing cases irrespective of subject. The following units of *Shepard's Citations* contain citation information relevant only to a specific area or subject of law. This section omits the specialized or subject units previously discussed in this chapter.

1. Other Specific Shepard's Citators

a. *Acts and Cases by Popular Names, Federal and State.* [See Illustrations 40 and 68.]

b. *Code of Federal Regulations Citations.* Contains citing references from all courts, selected legal periodicals, and annotations for the *Code of Federal Regulations,* Presidential Proclamations, Executive Orders, and reorganization plans.

c. *Federal Law Citations in Selected Law Reviews.* This unit is discussed in Chapter 16.

d. *Law Review Citations.* This unit is discussed in Chapter 16.

e. *Professional and Judicial Conduct Citations.* This unit gives coverage of all citations to the Code of Professional Responsibility, the Model Rules of Professional Conduct, the Code of Judicial Conduct, and the Opinions and Rules of the American Bar Association's Committee on Ethics and Professional Responsibility.

f. *Restatement of the Law Citations.* This unit is discussed in Chapter 17.

2. Other Shepard's Citators, by Subject

Shepard's publishes numerous citators on particular subjects. New units are added periodically. Recently, several of these have started and then abruptly ceased publication. The listing below represents those of some duration and is not intended to be exhaustive.

a. *Bankruptcy Citations.* This unit includes citations to bankruptcy cases in *American Bankruptcy Reports,* in the various federal reporters, and in looseleaf services such as *Bankruptcy Court Decisions* (LRP), *Bankruptcy Law Reporter* (CCH), and *Collier Bankruptcy Cases* (Matthew Bender).

b. *Criminal Justice Citations.* The American Bar Association has adopted and published the *Standards Relating to the Administration of Criminal Justice* (1968–1973) and the *Revised ABA Standards for Criminal Justice,* 2d ed. (1980). While these *Standards* have no official status, they are frequently cited by courts. *Criminal Justice Citations* lists each of the *Standards* and then gives citations to those cases that have cited sections of the *Standards.* [See Illustration 132.]

c. *Employment Law Citations.* This unit covers all U.S. federal and state cases, published and unpublished, reported in BNA's *Federal Employment Practice Cases* and CCH's *Employment Practice Decisions,* as well as employment cases reported in numerous other sources.

d. *Environmental Law Citations (Federal).* This provides a comprehensive set of citations to federal environmental law cases, including the published and unpublished federal cases from the *Environmental Law Reporter,* and also provides statutory and regulatory coverage.

e. *Evidence Law Citations.* This source provides access to court citations to the cases that discuss the laws of evidence in the state and federal courts, including the ability to Shepardize Callaghan's *Federal Rules of Evidence Service,* as well as post–1975 state and federal cases in *Weinstein's Evidence* (Matthew Bender) and *Wigmore on Evidence* (Little, Brown).

f. *Federal Energy Law Citations.* This unit covers oil and gas, public utilities, natural resources, water, and environmental law. Citing sources include Supreme Court of the United States and lower federal court cases in selected energy cases, decisions and orders of the Federal Power Commission and the Federal Energy Regulatory Commission, and energy provisions in the *United States Code* and *Code of Federal Regulations.* Also included are cross references to reports of the same cases published in CCH's *Energy Management, Oil & Gas Reporter* (Matthew Bender), *Public Utilities Reports,* and CCH's *Utilities Law Reporter,* among others.

g. *Federal Labor Law Citations.* This multi-volume unit contains citations to the decisions and orders of the National Labor Relations Board. It also provides cross-reference tables to citations from labor law looseleaf services. The statutes volumes contain citations to the various federal statutes dealing with labor. A companion set, *Federal Labor Law Case Name Citator,* also is available.

h. *Federal Occupational Safety and Health Citations.* This unit contains citations to the cases of the Supreme Court of the United States and lower federal courts involving safety and health, to decisions of the Federal Occupational Safety and Health Review Commission and its administrative law judges, and to safety and health provisions in the *United States Code* and *Code of Federal Regulations.* Also included are cross references to any reports of the same cases as published in *Occupational Safety and Health Decisions* (CCH) and *Occupational Safety and Health Cases* (BNA).

i. *Federal Securities Law Citations.* This citator, prepared in cooperation with Commerce Clearing House, Inc., includes reference to cases and statutes, including those found in CCH's *Federal Securities Law Reporter.*

j. *Federal Tax Citations.* This unit covers tax decisions and is organized in a manner similar to the other *Shepard's Citations* units. It

is particularly useful for the cross-reference tables it provides to Commerce Clearing House and other looseleaf service citations.

k. *Immigration and Naturalization Citations.* This unit includes among its citing sources cases of the Supreme Court of the United States as reported in the three series of reporters, cases from the lower federal courts, articles in selected leading law reviews, and the provisions of the *U.S. Statutes at Large.* The cited sources include *Immigration & Nationality Decisions,* immigration and naturalization cases from all federal courts, provisions of the *United States Code,* and the immigration and naturalization parts of the *Code of Federal Regulations.*

l. *Labor Arbitration Citations.* This unit provides access to citations to federal and state case and statutory law relating to labor arbitration. The statute divisions begin with citations to the Federal Arbitration Act. A separate Case Name Table is included.

m. *Medical Malpractice Citations.* This citator covers cases involving medical professions.

n. *Military Justice Citations.* This unit covers citations to cases of the U.S. Court of Military Appeals and the Boards and Courts of Military Review and to the *Uniform Code of Military Justice,* the *Manual for Courts Martial,* and to military court rules and regulations. The citing material includes cases in the *Military Justice Reporter* and in other federal and state reporters, and references to Opinions of the Attorneys General of the United States.

o. *Products Liability Citations.* This citator includes as cited sources not only the usual federal and state court cases from the *National Reporter System,* but all CCH *Products Liability Reporter* cases, products liability provisions of the state statutes, warranty provisions of the U.C.C., and sections of the *Restatement of the Law—Torts.*

p. *Uniform Commercial Code Citations.* This unit is a compilation of citations of the Uniform Commercial Code as adopted by each state. The citing sources include cases from the *National Reporter System,* as well as law reviews and selected legal texts. The citator is arranged by U.C.C. section, then alphabetically by state, with the citation of the particular section in each state's statutory scheme given.

SECTION H. ILLUSTRATIONS: OTHER UNITS OF SHEPARD'S CITATIONS

131. Excerpts from Shepard's United States Citations: Patents and Trademarks

132. Excerpts from Federal Circuit Table and from Criminal Justice Citations

[Illustration 131]

EXCERPTS FROM SHEPARD'S UNITED STATES
CITATIONS: PATENTS AND TRADEMARKS

UNITED STATES PATENTS (Original)

No. 4,265,876

4,066,501	**4,103,189**	**4,134,402**	**4,158,676**	**4,176,324**	**4,203,158**	**4,226,737**	**4,251,033**
co1146OG720	Cir. Fed.	Cir. 7	Cir. 3	25PQ2d1389	1133OG20	Rx1144OG	Cir. 7
4,067,079	Va946F2d824	nd781FS1296	aj779FS1440	**4,178,654**	Rx1142OG	[560	aj976F2d702
Rx1133OG	Vnd20PQ2d	nd22PQ2d	**4,158,760**	Rx1135OG1		1132	aj24PQ2d1174
[1763	[1163	[1219	24PO2d1805	**4,180,539**	Rx1133	[TMOG(1)7	**4,251,331**
4,069,148	4,10						113JOG1I?

An excerpt from *Shepard's United States Citations: Patents and Trademarks.*

This is from the Patents section and illustrates how citations that have referenced a specific patent number can be located, *e.g.*, the "id" indicates that Patent No. 4,114,255 has been infringed.

4,076,645	**4,111,727**	[1929	[1134	aj20PQ2d1857	aj779FS1440	**4,230,899**	22PQ2d1131
Rx1136OG ·	1134OG7	aj22PQ2d1448	**4,159,933**	aj22PQ2d1352	**4,215,513**	24PQ2d1267	**4,253,615**
[673	**4,114,255**	**4,143,760**	Rx1138OG	**4,187,390**	Rx1138OG	**4,230,924**	co1132OG35
4,076,698	Cir. Fed.	Cir. Fed.	[699	Cir. Fed.	[2089	24PQ2d1805	**4,253,709**
Vp21PQ2d→	id946F2d821	aj947F2d471	**4,162,338**	aj975F2d860	**4,217,148**	**4,233,421**	Cir. 7
[1242	id20PQ2d	aj20PQ2d1242	Cir. 3	977F2d559	Cir. 3	df1142OG30	aj141FRD464
4,076,831	[1164	ndp20PQ2d	aj142FRD421	aj19PQ2d1622	Vi805FS256	**4,233,963**	aj21PQ2d1706
eg1134OG675	**4,116,387**	[1857	aj24PQ2d1955	aj24PQ2d1196	**4,217,901**	1132OG21	co1133OG106
eg1134	Cir. 7	aj22PQ2d1352	**4,163,028**	24PQ2d1451	1141OG8	1132	**4,254,045**
[TMOG(4)	aj976F2d702	**4,144,317**	Cir. 3	1143OG54	1141	[TMOG(2)21	co1139OG126
[679	aj24PQ2d1174	Cir. 3	aj779FS1440	eg1134OG675	[TMOG(1)8	**4,234,003**	**4,255,834**
4,079,584	**4,116,853**	795FS712	**4,164,464**	eg1134	1143	Cir. 7	Cir. 4
1142OG7	21PQ2d1084	23PQ2d1932	Rx1138OG		[TMOG(4)	aj805FS550	id794FS176

Levelite

TRADEMARKS

Levelite	Lewis	LG Land	Liberty Bowl	Li Chung	Life after	Life-Lite,	Life's
aj1138OGT(3)	**Game Strap**	**Grant &**	**Football**	**Shing Tong**	**Housework**	**The Long**	**Greatest**
[492	aj1132OGT(3)	**Company**	**Classic**	**(U.S.A.) Ltd.**	**Product, A**	**Lasting**	**Beach**
Level Lift	[264	aj1145OGT(3)	aj1135OGT(1)	aj1135OGT(4)	aj1138OGT(2)	**Disposable**	**Waikiki**
aj1138OGT(3)	**L'Executive**	[435	[193	[220	[460	**Flashlight**	aj1145OGT(3)
[493	aj1143OGT(4)						[501

An excerpt from *Shepard's United States Citations: Patents and Trademarks.*

This is from the Trademarks section and illustrates how sources involving specific trademarks can be located, *e.g.*, information on the Lexis/Nexis trademark can be located in 82 Trademark Reporter 620.

Levelline	[360					**Lifespan**	
aj1145OGT(3)	**Lex-Eze**					1340GT(4)	
[508	aj1139OGT(3)					[202	
Levels for	[575					**lifestarts**	
Living	**Lexis**					145OGT(3)	
aj1141OGT(1)	82TM798					[461	
[574						**Life's**	
Lever-	**Lexis/Nexis**					**'oo Short**	
agelease	82TM620	**LIAISON**	[682		**Manager**	**Ministry,**	aj1135OGT(3)
aj1139OGT(2)	**Lexitel**	aj1145OGT(3)		**Liberty**	aj1133OGT(5)	**Inc., The**	[322
[682	aj1135OGT(3)	[476		**Mint, The**	**LICOR DE**	[256	aj1139OGT(3)	**Lifestyle**
Leveron	[316	**Lia Long**	aj1133OGT(4)	**KAFIOLA**		[576	aj1146OGT(3)
aj1134OGT(4)	**LEXITEL**	**Island**	[222	aj1145OGT(5)	**Life**	**Lifepage**	[367
[203	aj1135OGT(3)	**Airlines Ltd.**		[385	**Expander**	aj1134OGT(2)	**Life Style**
Le Verrier	[316	aj1133OGT(3)	**Liberty**	**Licorice Ice**	aj1134OGT(2)	[233	aj1141OGT(4)
aj1144OGT(4)	**Lex-Soar**	[242	**Square**	aj1142OGT(2)	[215	**Lifeplus**	[566
[364	aj1144OGT(1)	**LIAR'S**	aj1145OGT(3)	[527	**LIFEFONE**	aj1138OGT(3)	**Lifestyle**
Lever 2000	[395	**POKER**	[454		aj1137OGT(1)	[489	**Connection**
aj1145OGT(3)	**Lextrack**	aj1132OGT(2)	**LIBERTY**	**Licorice**	[339		aj1133OGT(1)
[474	aj1145OGT(3)	[246	**SYSTEM**	**Pizza**	**Life Guard**	**Life's a**	[253
	[507	**Libby's**	aj1145OGT(5)	aj1135OGT(3)	aj1134OGT(2)	**Beach**	
			[382	[317	[215	aj1136OGT(5)	

[Illustration 132]

EXCERPTS FROM OTHER UNITS OF SHEPARD'S CITATIONS

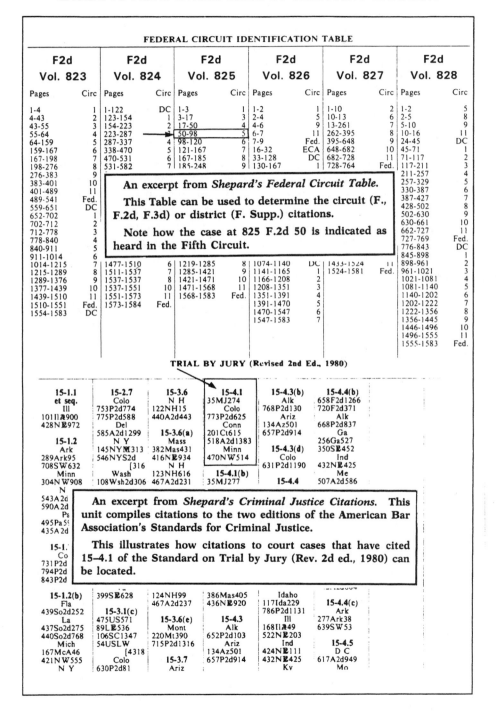

FEDERAL CIRCUIT IDENTIFICATION TABLE

F2d Vol. 823		F2d Vol. 824		F2d Vol. 825		F2d Vol. 826		F2d Vol. 827		F2d Vol. 828	
Pages	Circ	Pages	Circ	Pages	Circ	Pages	Circ	Pages	Circ	Pages	Circ
1-4	1	1-122	DC	1-3	1	1-2	1	1-10	2	1-2	5
4-43	2	123-154	1	3-17	3	2-4	5	10-13	6	2-5	8
43-55	3	154-223	2	17-50	4	4-6	9	13-261	7	5-10	9
55-64	4	223-287	3	50-98	5	6-7	11	262-395	8	10-16	11
64-159	5	287-337	4	98-120	6	7-9	Fed.	395-648	9	24-45	DC
159-167	6	338-470	5	121-167	7	16-32	ECA	648-682	10	45-71	1
167-198	7	470-531	6	167-185	8	33-128	DC	682-728	11	71-117	2
198-276	8	531-582	7	185-248	9	130-167	1	728-764	Fed.	117-211	3
276-383	9									211-257	4
383-401	10									257-329	5
401-489	11									330-387	6
489-541	Fed.									387-427	7
559-651	DC									428-502	8
652-702	1									502-630	9
702-712	2									630-661	10
712-778	3									662-727	11
778-840	4									727-769	Fed.
840-911	5									776-843	DC
911-1014	6									845-898	1
1014-1215	7	1477-1510	6	1219-1285	8	1074-1140	DC	1455-1524	11	898-961	2
1215-1289	8	1511-1537	7	1285-1421	9	1141-1165	1	1524-1581	Fed.	961-1021	3
1289-1376	9	1537-1537	8	1421-1471	10	1166-1208	2			1021-1081	4
1377-1439	10	1537-1551	10	1471-1568	11	1208-1351	3			1081-1140	5
1439-1510	11	1551-1573	11	1568-1583	Fed.	1351-1391	4			1140-1202	6
1510-1551	Fed.	1573-1584	Fed.			1391-1470	5			1202-1222	7
1554-1583	DC					1470-1547	6			1222-1356	8
						1547-1583	7			1356-1445	9
										1446-1496	10
										1496-1555	11
										1555-1583	Fed.

> An excerpt from *Shepard's Federal Circuit Table.*
>
> This Table can be used to determine the circuit (F., F.2d, F.3d) or district (F. Supp.) citations.
>
> Note how the case at 825 F.2d 50 is indicated as heard in the Fifth Circuit.

TRIAL BY JURY (Revised 2nd Ed., 1980)

15-1.1 et seq. Ill	15-2.7 Colo	15-3.6 N H	15-4.1 35MJ274	15-4.3(b) Alk	15-4.4(b) 658F2d1266
101Ill 900	753P2d774	122NH15	Colo	768P2d130	720F2d371
428NE972	775P2d588	440A2d443	773P2d625	Ariz	Alk
	Del		Conn	134Az501	668P2d837
15-1.2	585A2d1299	**15-3.6(a)**	201Ct615	657P2d914	Ga
Ark	N Y	Mass	518A2d1383		256Ga527
289Ark95	145NYM313	382Mas431	Minn	**15-4.3(d)**	350SE452
708SW632	546NYS2d	416NE934	470NW514	Colo	Ind
Minn	[316	N H		631P2d1190	432NE425
304NW908	Wash	123NH616	**15-4.1(b)**		Me
N	108Wsh2d306	467A2d231	35MJ277	**15-4.4**	507A2d586

> An excerpt from *Shepard's Criminal Justice Citations.* This unit compiles citations to the two editions of the American Bar Association's Standards for Criminal Justice.
>
> This illustrates how citations to court cases that have cited 15–4.1 of the Standard on Trial by Jury (Rev. 2d ed., 1980) can be located.

15-1.2(b) Fla	399SE628	124NH99	386Mas405	Idaho	
439So2d252	**15-3.1(c)**	467A2d237	436NE920	117Ida229	**15-4.4(c)**
La	475US571			786P2d1131	Ark
437So2d275	89LE536	**15-3.6(e)**	**15-4.3**	Ill	277Ark38
440So2d768	106SC1347	Mont	652P2d103	168Ill 49	639SW53
Mich	54USLW	220Mt390	Ariz	522NE203	
167McA46	[4318	715P2d1316	134Az501	Ind	**15-4.5**
421NW555	Colo		657P2d914	424NE111	D C
N Y	630P2d81	**15-3.7**		432NE425	617A2d949
		Ariz		Ky	Mo

Additional left-column entries (under 15-1.2 and 15-1.):

15-1.2 Ark
289Ark95
708SW632
Minn
304NW908
N
543A2d
590A2d
Pa
495Pa5
435A2d

15-1.
Co
731P2d
794P2d
843P2d

SECTION I. KEEPING SHEPARD'S CITATIONS CURRENT

1. Supplementation of Print Versions of Shepard's Citations

As with any set of law books, there must be a method of keeping the set up to date. Since *Shepard's Citations* are used to determine the current status of a case, statute, or administrative regulation or ruling, the method of supplementation is of utmost importance. Nearly every unit of *Shepard's* is published in at least one bound volume. In addition, each unit receives at least one, and sometimes as many as three, pamphlet supplements that cover all the cases since the date of the bound volume.

Typically, the cover of an annual supplement is gold. This annual supplement may then be supplemented by a red cover advance sheet pamphlet that is issued periodically throughout the year. At times, even this red cover pamphlet is sometimes supplemented with a thinner pamphlet without a cover. When the next red cover pamphlet is issued, the information from the non-covered pamphlet is incorporated into the red one. At the end of the year a new gold supplement is issued incorporating the existing advance sheets, or alternatively, the gold pamphlet and any other supplements are incorporated into newly-revised bound volumes and the supplementation process begins anew.

The frequency of the issuance of the pamphlet supplements varies among the different units. Some units are updated monthly; others, three times a year; still others, quarterly. Consequently, it is extremely important to ascertain that all bound volumes and pamphlet supplements of the unit being used are available during research. The cover of the latest pamphlet supplement prominently displays *What Your Library Should Contain*. [See Illustration 126.] This information should be examined carefully, and all the indicated bound volumes and pamphlet supplements should be consulted.

2. Supplementation of Online Versions of Shepard's Citations

The online CALR versions of *Shepard's Citations* are updated electronically as new print citators are issued. The online display always lists the latest coverage in the CALR service being used.

3. Shepard's EXPRESS Citations

Shepard's EXPRESS Citations, which is issued monthly or semimonthly depending upon the state, is a blue cover advance sheet supplement to a state's regular citator subscription, and is available for most states. It provides citation information that is faster than either the standard supplements or the online sources.

4. Shepard's Citations Telephone Update Service

Subscriber's to *Shepard's Citations* can call the publisher for the latest citations for the set to which a subscription exists. This service provides the most up-to-date information available.

SECTION J. OTHER CITATORS

Although *Shepard's Citations* are by far the most widely-used and diverse citators, other citators, particularly those available online, can also play an important role in one's research.

1. Auto–Cite and LEXCITE

Auto–Cite, a product of Lawyers Cooperative Publishing and available only on LEXIS, is a citation verification and case history service that can be accessed at any time during the online research process by entering *ac* and the case citation. This service provides the correct name of the case, parallel citations, year of decision, subsequent and prior history, references to cases that have had a negative impact on the precedential value of the case, and citations to *A.L.R.* and *Lawyers' Edition* articles citing the case under research. [See Illustration 133, Figure 1.]

LEXCITE, exclusive to LEXIS, enables a researcher to retrieve the most current cases within LEXIS case law documents that cite your case, including *id* and *supra* references, while automatically searching for all the parallel citations. It also locates references to other documents, such as law review articles and federal agency decisions.

2. Insta–Cite

Insta–Cite, West Publishing Company's verification and case history service on WESTLAW, can be accessed at any time during the online research process by entering *ic* and the case citation. It provides precedential history, citation verification, direct history, overruling information, and parallel citations. The direct history and citation verification are comprehensive for federal cases with coverage from 1754, but for state direct history coverage and citation verification is from 1879. Precedential history for both federal and state cases is from 1972. [See Illustration 133, Figure 2.] References to secondary sources are also retrieved using Insta–Cite.

3. WESTLAW and LEXIS as Citators

Both WESTLAW and LEXIS can be used as a citator after accessing a database or file. A search is constructed using information from the case title or statute citation. When this search is run, it retrieves the full text of the citing document. This type of search is particularly useful for retrieving very recent documents not yet covered by *Shepard's Citations*. The Quick*Cite* feature on WESTLAW, accessed by entering *qc,* makes use of WESTLAW as a citator automatic. Quick*Cite* updates Insta–Cite, Shepard's, and Shepard's PreView. The use of WESTLAW and LEXIS as citators is discussed in more detail in Chapter 22, J. Jacobstein, R. Mersky & D. Dunn, *Fundamentals of Legal Research* (6th ed.).

4. Looseleaf Service Citators

A few looseleaf services have citator volumes relating specifically to the subject matter of the service. Specialized looseleaf citators for federal taxation are discussed in Chapter 24, J. Jacobstein, R. Mersky & D. Dunn, *Fundamentals of Legal Research* (6th ed.).

SECTION K. ILLUSTRATIONS: AUTO–CITE AND INSTA–CITE

142. Screen Displays from Auto–Cite and Insta–Cite

[Illustration 133]

SCREEN DISPLAYS FROM INSTA–CITE AND AUTO–CITE

Figure 1. Insta-Cite

```
                          INSTA-CITE                      Only Page
CITATION: 388 N.W.2d 535
                         Direct History

     1  State v. Griffin, 126 Wis.2d 183, 376 N.W.2d 62
           (Wis.App., Sep 12, 1985) (NO. 84-021 CR)
        Review Granted by
     2  State v. Griffin, 127 Wis.2d 569, 383 N.W.2d 62 (Wis., Dec 11, 1985)
           (TABLE, NO. 84-021-CR)
        AND Decision Affirmed by
=>   3  State v. Griffin, 131 Wis.2d 41, 388 N.W.2d 535 (Wis., Jun 20, 1986)
           (NO. 84-021-CR)
        Certiorari Granted by
     4  Griffin v. Wisconsin, 479 U.S. 1005, 107 S.Ct. 643, 93 L.Ed.2d 699
           (U.S.Wis., Dec 08, 1986) (NO. 86-5324)
        AND Judgment Affirmed by
     5  Griffin v. Wisconsin, 483 U.S. 868, 107 S.Ct. 3164, 97 L.Ed.2d 709,
           55 USLW 5156 (U.S.Wis., Jun 26, 1987) (NO. 86-5324)
           ( > Additional Negative Indirect History)

     > Shepard's  > Shepard's PreView  > QuickCite  > Commands  > SCOPE
(C) Copyright West Publishing Company 1994
```

Both Insta-Cite and Auto-Cite can be used for citation verification and case history. In the two Auto-Cite screens not pictured are references to prior history and *A.L.R. Annotations* citing the case.

Figure 2. Auto-Cite

```
Auto-Cite (R) Citation Service, (c) 1993 Lawyers Cooperative Publishing

131 WIS 2D 41:                                    Screen 1 of 3

CITATION YOU ENTERED:

State v. Griffin, 131 Wis. 2d 41, 388 N.W.2d 535 (1986)

SUBSEQUENT APPELLATE HISTORY:

    cert. granted,  Griffin v. Wisconsin, 479 U.S. 1005, 93 L. Ed. 2d
  699, 107 S. Ct. 643 (1986)

      mot. granted, Griffin v. Wisconsin, 479 U.S. 1053, 93 L. Ed. 2d 977,
      107 S. Ct. 926 (1987)

    and aff'd,  Griffin v. Wisconsin*1, 483 U.S. 868, 97 L. Ed. 2d
    709, 107 S. Ct. 3164, 55 U.S.L.W. 5156 (1987)

----------------------------------------------------------------------------
Alternate presentation formats are available.
For further explanation, press the H key (for HELP) and then the ENTER key.
To return to LEXIS, press the EXIT SERV key.
Press Alt-H for Help  or  .SO to End Session  or  Alt-Q to Quit Software.
```

Chapter 15

LEGAL ENCYCLOPEDIAS

SECTION A. INTRODUCTION

In the previous chapters, discussion has focused on the primary
sources of the law: court cases; constitutions; statutes; legislative
histories; court rules; and various finding and verification aids for these
sources: indexes; digests; citators, and other legal materials that enable
a researcher to find both the source and status of the law. The mass of
primary source materials has reached such voluminous proportions that
secondary sources play significant roles in identifying and explaining the
law. In this and the next four chapters, discussion will focus on the
secondary sources of the law. The secondary sources to be discussed
consist of legal encyclopedias, periodicals, treatises, restatements, and
other miscellaneous sets of law books. As will be pointed out, it is
frequently a much better practice to start one's research with secondary
sources rather than initially consulting the sets containing the primary
sources studied in some previous chapters.

Sometimes a person beginning a research project will lack even the
most rudimentary knowledge necessary to identify and pursue the legal
issues involved. At other times, a refresher in broad concepts might be
needed. Legal encyclopedias are very useful for objective background
information and as sources of leads to other materials.

Legal encyclopedias are written in narrative form, are arranged by
subject, and contain footnote references to cases on point. In most
instances, they are noncritical in approach and do not attempt to be
analytical or evaluative. Instead, they simply state the propositions of
law, with introductory explanations of an elementary nature. These
features make legal encyclopedias popular and useful research tools.
Their utility as secondary sources, however, has frequently been abused
by both courts and attorneys. In particular, a legal encyclopedia is
sometimes cited as a final authoritative source rather than as an
expository introduction to case authority.

In many research problems, it is necessary to go beyond such
rudimentary sources. It is not wise to stop one's research without
reading the cases cited in the footnotes, because cited references frequently will not fully reflect the propositions for which they stand, or
because the facts of the immediate problem will be distinguishable from
those in the cited cases.

These criticisms should not be interpreted as being directed at the
function of legal encyclopedias. These publications are excellent index

and introductory guides to the law. As long as this is kept in mind, and legal encyclopedias are not relied upon as the final authority for a proposition of law, they are valuable publications to consult initially. In most instances, the cases cited should be read, analyzed, and Shepardized; statutory sources must be checked to ascertain whether the rules of law have changed in the particular jurisdiction under research.

SECTION B. CURRENT GENERAL ENCYCLOPEDIAS

1. Corpus Juris Secundum (C.J.S.)

Corpus Juris Secundum has been published by West Publishing Company since 1936 and includes both procedural and substantive law. As its original subtitle indicates, *C.J.S.* was intended initially to be "A Complete Restatement of the Entire American Law As Developed by All Reported Cases." It aimed at citing all reported cases in its footnotes. However, in the mid–1980s, West abandoned its attempt to cite every case and adopted a new subtitle reflecting a different scope of coverage for the revised volumes issued since that time—"A Contemporary Statement of American Law as Derived from Reported Cases and Legislation." This new subtitle indicates that *C.J.S.* is no longer attempting to reference every case and that it provides some discussion of federal and local statutory law, including court interpretation.

It will take a substantial amount of time before the revision is complete. Until then, the set will consist of volumes reflecting two different editorial philosophies. The volumes reflecting the new philosophy can be identified by the subtitle on the title page, and often by their narrower size and the labeling of the topics on the volume's spine running horizontally rather than vertically. *C.J.S.* is a massive set consisting of 101 numbered volumes (or over 150 actual volumes considering that some volumes are contained in more than one part) and supersedes its predecessor, *Corpus Juris.*[1]

Over 400 broad topics, which are listed preceding the text of each volume, are covered in *C.J.S.* Each topic is sub-divided into many sections. Preceding each discussion in a section within a topic is a brief summary of the prevailing rule of law. This "black letter" statement is followed by text expounding upon the topic of the section. Footnote references are arranged hierarchically by federal court and then alphabetically by state. [See Illustrations 134–135.]

C.J.S. includes cross references for its titles and sections to corresponding West Topics and Key Numbers, permitting easy entry into the *American Digest System.* The West Topics and Key Numbers and secondary authority sources are noted under "Library References," which precede the text of the section in the *C.J.S.* replacement volumes published since 1961 and in the annual cumulative pocket supplements.

---

[1] Although *Corpus Juris Secundum* supersedes the text of *Corpus Juris,* occasionally the footnotes in *Corpus Juris Secundum* refer to *Corpus Juris* rather than repeating the citations that appear in the set.

C.J.S. has a multi-volume, soft-cover General Index that is issued annually. Each volume also has a separate, more-detailed index to each of the topics contained in it. When a topic is covered in more than one volume, the topic index is at the end of the concluding volume of the topic.

Research in *C.J.S.* is similar to that described in Chapter 6 for digests. *C.J.S.*'s General Index uses the familiar descriptive-word approach, or, if one knows the Topic, research can commence immediately in the appropriate volume. For example, if one is interested in the law of copyright, the index volumes can be bypassed and the search started immediately by consulting the volume that contains the title *Copyright.* If the broad topic of the law under which the subject is included is not familiar to the researcher, *e.g.,* restrictive covenants, the search should start first in the index volumes. At the beginning of each Topic is an outline and classification for the organization of the Title, which facilitates using the topical approach. [See Illustration 134.]

The set is kept up to date by replacement volumes and annual cumulative pocket supplements. The pocket supplements may include rewritten text, citations to cases decided since the publication of the original volumes, and references to secondary sources. Replacement volumes are published when significant sections of the text require rewriting or when the pocket supplements become very extensive and unwieldy. Replacement volumes contain a "Table of Corresponding Sections" that enables one to find where a section in the older volume is discussed in the replacement volume. The three volumes covering *Internal Revenue* are issued annually. Because rules, regulations, and new court cases occur so frequently in tax law, the user of these volumes should always check for the most current materials in one of the looseleaf taxation services described in Chapter 24, J. Jacobstein, R. Mersky & D. Dunn, *Fundamentals of Legal Research* (6th ed.).

Judicial and other definitions of *words and phrases* and *legal maxims* are interfiled alphabetically with the essay topics. They also are listed in each appropriate volume preceding the index, with references to the pages containing the definitions.

2. American Jurisprudence 2d (Am. Jur. 2d)

American Jurisprudence 2d, published by Lawyers Cooperative Publishing, is a non-critical, textual statement of substantive and procedural law, arranged under more than 430 topics. It contains 83 numbered volumes and approximately 120 actual volumes and supersedes *American Jurisprudence.* The editorial philosophy consistently underlying publication of *Am. Jur. 2d* is for the editors to sift through the legal authorities and to provide discussions of points of law that are supported by controlling cases that interpret and construe the law. Citations to these selective cases are provided in footnotes, as are citations to *A.L.R. Annotations,* which provide additional access to case law.

Since *Am. Jur. 2d* is a part of the publisher's *Total Client–Service Library (TCSL)*, it also gives in its footnotes references to treatment of a topic in other sets in the *TCSL*, including *A.L.R.* The publishers describe *Am. Jur. 2d* as giving the law in breadth and *A.L.R.* as giving the law in depth. The former is very useful to obtain a quick answer to a problem that then may be explored in depth through the use of *A.L.R.*

Like *C.J.S.*, *Am. Jur. 2d* can be researched using either a topical or descriptive-word index approach. *Am. Jur. 2d* has a multi-volume, soft cover index that is issued biennially with an annual update and is more inclusive than the entries in the *ALR Index*. Separate indexes arranged by topics, with subheadings under each topic, are at the end of the concluding volume of the topic.

[See Illustrations 137–138.]

Some other features of *Am. Jur. 2d* are:

a. As compared to *C.J.S.*, greater emphasis is placed on statutory law, federal procedural rules, and uniform state laws. The federal statutory law germane to a topic is covered, while state statutory law is covered in general but without reference to the specific laws of each state. A separate volume, *Table of Statutes, Rules, and Regulations Cited* (2d ed. 1990), covers the *United States Code Service*, the Federal Rules of Procedure, the Federal Rules of Evidence, other federal rules, and uniform and model laws. When a citation to one of these statutes or rules is known, this *Table* can be consulted to find where the subject matter of such citations is discussed in *Am. Jur. 2d*.

b. Federal tax laws are covered in three volumes, which are replaced annually.

c. References to definitions of words and phrases are interfiled alphabetically in the index volumes.

d. Tne set is kept up to date by annual pocket supplements and periodically-revised volumes. In addition, the *American Jurisprudence 2d New Topic Service,* a looseleaf volume started in 1973, covers (1) new topics of law that have developed after the printing of the main volumes and (2) substantial changes in the already published encyclopedic articles. For example, this service contains articles on *Real Estate Time–Sharing* and the *Americans with Disabilities Act.* The annual index to *Am. Jur. 2d* includes references to this *Service.* In the process of periodically revising the bound volumes, these new topics are incorporated into the full set and removed from the looseleaf volume.

e. The *American Jurisprudence 2d Desk Book,* another feature of *Am. Jur. 2d,* functions as a legal almanac of miscellaneous data and information. It is discussed in more detail in Chapter 18.

3. American Jurisprudence: Related Encyclopedias

Once one has determined the state of the substantive law related to the problem under research, sets related to *Am. Jur. 2d* and that are also

a part of the publisher's *Total Client–Service Library,* will provide information required to prepare a case for trial. These sets are:

a. *American Jurisprudence Proof of Facts.* This set, now in its third series, collectively exceeds 100 volumes. The purpose of *Proof of Facts* is to provide a guide for a lawyer in the organization and preparation of materials for trial and in the examination of witnesses. It is designed to assist lawyers in obtaining information from clients, taking depositions, preparing briefs, and in other steps necessary in preparing for trial. Each article contains "Proofs," which are checklists and planning guides designed to assist in the establishment of the facts in issue. A separate soft cover index is provided. The set is kept current through annual pocket supplements and new volumes.

b. *American Jurisprudence Trials.* This multi-volume set is essentially a treatise on trial practice. The first six volumes cover matters that are common to all types of problems in trial practice. The remaining volumes are called *Model Trials* and deal with the handling of trials for a specific topic. Unlike *Am. Jur. 2d* and the other related sets, *Am. Jur. Trials* is not written by the editorial staff of the publisher. Rather, each topic in the set is written by an experienced trial lawyer. This set has a separate soft cover index and is kept up to date with annual pocket supplements.

c. *American Jurisprudence Legal Forms 2d* and *American Jurisprudence Pleading and Practice Forms Revised.* These two multi-volume sets contain forms needed in the conduct of a trial and for other aspects of a lawyer's practice. Form books are discussed in more detail in Chapter 18.

4. The Guide to American Law: Everyone's Legal Encyclopedia

As the title indicates, this encyclopedia, published by West in 1983, is directed toward the non-lawyer. It is in twelve volumes and contains over 5,000 topics. It is a useful set to consult when a nontechnical explanation of a point of law is needed. In 1987 a single yearbook was published and in 1990 the set began being updated by an annual bound supplement. These supplements provide discussions of events for the year covered.

SECTION C.   ILLUSTRATIONS: ENCYCLOPEDIAS

In earlier chapters, especially those dealing with digests, *A.L.R.*, looseleaf services, and *Shepard's Citations,* we discussed how these sources can be used for finding cases.   Another approach to researching a topic and finding cases and related sources is to start in either *Corpus Juris Secundum* or *American Jurisprudence 2d.*

Problem: Can punitive damages be awarded for civil rights violations pertaining to employment discrimination that arise under Title VII?

Corpus Juris Secundum

134.   **Page from Analysis to Topic: Civil Rights**
135.   **Page from Volume 14A (1991) covering Civil Rights**
136.   **Page from Volume 14 Supp. (1974) covering Civil Rights**

American Jurisprudence 2d

137.   **Page from General Index**
138.   **Page from Volume 15 covering Civil Rights**

[Illustration 134]

PAGE FROM C.J.S. TOPIC OUTLINE: CIVIL RIGHTS

The most common method of locating relevant sections in *C.J.S.* is by consulting the General Index volumes. Sometimes it may be easier to take a topical approach. In this instance, by consulting the Topic Outline or "Analysis" for Civil Rights, it quickly becomes apparent that the matter under research is covered in § 317.

See next Illustration.

See also General Index

[Illustration 135]

PAGE FROM TOPIC: CIVIL RIGHTS—14A C.J.S. (1991)

---

§ 316   CIVIL RIGHTS   **14A C.J.S.**

of reasonable diligence,[99] and a back pay award may be offset by amounts earned in other occupations during the time that back pay accrued.[1] No per se rule in employment discrimination cases requires the tolling of back pay during

> **A discussion of cases dealing with punitive damages awards under Title VII.**
>
> **Preceding each discussion in a section within a topic in bold type is a brief summary of the prevailing rule of law, which is followed by "Library References."**
>
> **C.J.S. is undergoing revision. This volume 14A was published in 1991 and is said to represent "A Contemporary Statement of American Law As Derived from Reported Cases and Legislation," which is West's current philosophy used in publishing revised C.J.S. volumes.**
>
> **Compare with next Illustration.**

its resources,[11] and for damage to its fair housing goals.[12]

§ 317.   —— Exemplary or Punitive Damages

   a. In general
   b. Civil Rights Act guaranteeing equal rights under the law

a.   In General

In civil rights cases, exemplary or punitive damages may be allowed where the wrongful act or conduct complained of is accompanied by aggravating circumstances, such as malice, wantonness, or willfulness.

► Library References
   Civil Rights ⟐275, 275(1, 2).

In civil rights cases, exemplary or punitive damages may be allowed where the wrongful act or conduct complained of is accompanied by certain aggravating circumstances, such as malice, wantonness, or willfulness,[13] evil motive or intent,[14] or reckless or callous indifference to the federally protected rights of others.[15] However, where such aggravating circumstances are lacking, punitive damages will be denied.[16]

The infliction and amount of punitive damages are within the discretion of the trier of fact.[17] The allowance of such damages involves an eval-

---

98. U.S.—Satterwhite v. Smith, C.A.Wash., 744 F.2d 1380.

99. U.S.—Huegel v. Tisch, E.D.Pa., 683 F.Supp. 123.

1. U.S.—Wulf v. City of Wichita, C.A.10(Kan.), 883 F.2d 842, rehearing denied—Figueroa-Rodriguez v. Aquino, C.A.1 (Puerto Rico), 863 F.2d 1037.

2. U.S.—Huegel v. Tisch, E.D.Pa., 683 F.Supp. 123.

3. 42 U.S.C.A. § 1981.

4. U.S.—Hunter v. Allis-Chalmers Corp., Engine Div., C.A.7(Ill.), 797 F.2d 1417.

5. U.S.—Johnson v. Railway Exp. Agency, Inc., Tenn., 95 S.Ct. 1716, 421 U.S. 454, 44 L.Ed.2d 295.

6. U.S.—Starrett v. Wadley, C.A.10(Okl.), 876 F.2d 808.
   Ross v. Beaumont Hosp., E.D.Mich., 678 F.Supp. 680, appeal dismissed 844 F.2d 789.

7. U.S.—Starrett v. Wadley, C.A.10(Okl.), 876 F.2d 808.

8. U.S.—Wulf v. City of Wichita, C.A.10(Kan.), 883 F.2d 842, rehearing denied.

9. U.S.—Wulf v. City of Wichita, C.A.10(Kan.), 883 F.2d 842, rehearing denied.

10. 42 U.S.C.A. § 3612(c).

11. Ascertainment of value
   Nonprofit fair housing corporation, which successfully challenged advertising brochure for apartment complexes as discriminating against blacks in violation of Fair Housing Act, was entitled to recover the $2,300 it expended in pursuing its claim; while those costs might not be recoverable per se, they represented reasonable guideline for ascertaining value of corporation's "diversion of resources" element of damage.
   U.S.—Saunders v. General Services Corp., E.D.Va., 659 F.Supp. 1042.

12. U.S.—Saunders v. General Services Corp., E.D.Va., 659 F.Supp. 1042.

Standard of measurement
   U.S.—Gunby v. Pennsylvania Elec. Co., C.A.3(Pa.), 840 F.2d 1108, certiorari denied 109 S.Ct. 3213, 492 U.S. 905, 106 L.Ed.2d 564.

13. U.S.—Wolfel v. Bates, C.A.Ohio, 707 F.2d 932—Lenard v. Argento, C.A.Ill., 699 F.2d 874, certiorari denied 104 S.Ct. 69, 464 U.S. 815, 78 L.Ed.2d 84.
   Ostroff v. State of Florida, Dept. of Health & Rehabilitative Services, M.D.Fla., 554 F.Supp. 347.

14. U.S.—Laskaris v. Thornburgh, C.A.Pa., 733 F.2d 260, certiorari denied 105 S.Ct. 260, 469 U.S. 886, 83 L.Ed.2d 196.
   Reeder-Baker v. Lincoln Nat. Corp., N.D.Ind., 649 F.Supp. 647, affirmed 834 F.2d 1373—Esposito v. Buonome, D.Conn., 647 F.Supp. 580.

15. U.S.—Gordon v. Norman, C.A.6(Tenn.), 788 F.2d 1194—Laskaris v. Thornburgh, C.A.Pa., 733 F.2d 260, certiorari denied 105 S.Ct. 260, 469 U.S. 886, 83 L.Ed.2d 196.
   Reeder-Baker v. Lincoln Nat. Corp., N.D.Ind., 649 F.Supp. 647, affirmed 834 F.2d 1373—Invisible Empire Knights of Ku Klux Klan v. City of West Haven, D.C.Conn., 600 F.Supp. 1427.

16. U.S.—Sostre v. McGinnis, C.A.N.Y., 442 F.2d 178, certiorari denied 92 S.Ct. 719, 404 U.S. 1049, 30 L.Ed.2d 740, certiorari denied Oswald v. Sostre, 92 S.Ct. 1190, 405 U.S. 978, 31 L.Ed.2d 254.
   Arunga v. New York City Dept. of Personnel, D.C.N.Y., 342 F.Supp. 983—U.S. ex rel. Motley v. Rundle, D.C.Pa., 340 F.Supp. 807.

332

[Illustration 136]

PAGE FROM TOPIC: CIVIL RIGHTS—14 SUPP. C.J.S. (1974)

14 C. J. S. Supp.　　　　　　　　　　　　　　　　　**CIVIL RIGHTS　§§ 172–173**

be excessive[26] or grossly inadequate.[27]

Nominal damages. Whether or not actual com-

> **A discussion of cases dealing with punitive damages awards under Title VII.**
>
> *C.J.S.* **is undergoing revision. This volume 14 Supp., published in 1974 and subsequently replaced in 1991, is said to represent "A Complete Restatement of the Entire American Law As Developed by All Reported Cases."** *C.J.S.* **once attempted to cite all reported cases in its footnotes. This is no longer the prevailing philosophy.**
>
> **Compare with previous Illustration.**

---

physical[32] and mental[33] pain and suffering, as well as humiliation, embarrassment, and discomfort,[34] and injury to reputation,[35] are proper elements of actual damages for which compensatory award may be made. Any matter which is inconclusive cannot properly be considered as an element of damages.[36]

§ 173. —— Exemplary or Punitive Damages

In civil rights cases, exemplary or punitive damages may be allowed where the wrongful act or conduct complained of is accompanied by aggravating circumstances, such as malice, wantonness, or willfulness.

Library References

Civil Rights ⬤＝13.17.

In civil rights cases, exemplary or punitive damages may be allowed where the wrongful act or conduct complained of is accompanied by certain aggravating circumstances, such as malice, wantonness, or willfulness,[37] but where such aggravating

---

on other grounds, C.A., 460 F.2d 126.

26. U.S.—Collum v. Butler, D.C.Ill., 288 F.Supp. 918, affirmed, C.A., 421 F.2d 1257.

27. U.S.—Jenkins v. Averett, C.A.N.C., 424 F.2d 1228.

28. U.S.—U. S. ex rel. Motley v. Rundle, D.C.Pa., 340 F.Supp. 807—Wilson v. Prasse, D.C.Pa., 325 F.Supp. 9—Cordova v. Chonko, D.C.Ohio, 315 F.Supp. 953—Washington v. Official Court Stenographer, D.C.Pa., 251 F.Supp. 945.

Denial of damages

In civil rights class action against all Alabama justices of the peace, and others, in behalf of all persons tried by justices of the peace for violations of state highway laws after date of United States Supreme Court affirmance of decision that justices could not constitutionally try traffic cases under statutory scheme giving them pecuniary interest in conviction, in which plaintiffs sustained no actual monetary loss other than fines which they were not entitled to recover, nominal damages would not be awarded where the cost of administering award of $1 each to over 50,-000 plaintiffs would far outweigh the miniscule benefit that would accrue to plaintiffs.

U.S.—Callahan v. Sanders, D.C.Ala., 339 F.Supp. 814.

29. U.S.—U. S. ex rel. Motley v. Rundle, D.C.Pa., 340 F.Supp. 807—Sexton v. Gibbs, D.C.Tex., 327 F. Supp. 134, affirmed, C.A., 446 F.2d 904, certiorari denied 92 S.Ct. 733, 404 U.S. 1062, 30 L.Ed.2d 751.

Tracy v. Robbins, D.C.S.C., 40 F. R.D. 108.

v. Orange County Bd. of Ed., C.A.N.C., 464 F.2d 536—Arkansas Ed. Ass'n v. Board of Ed. of Portland, Arkansas School Dist., C.A.Ark., 446 F.2d 763.

31. U.S.—Cooper v. Allen, C.A.Ga., 467 F.2d 836.

Lazard v. Boeing Co., D.C.La., 322 F.Supp. 343.

32. McArthur v. Pennington, D.C. Tenn., 253 F.Supp. 420.

33. U.S.—Smith v. Sol D. Adler Realty Co., C.A.Ill., 436 F.2d 344—Donovan v. Reinbold, C.A.Cal., 433 F. 2d 738.

Wilson v. Prasse, D.C.Pa., 325 F. Supp. 9, affirmed, C.A., 463 F.2d 109—Rhoads v. Horvat, D.C.Colo., 270 F.Supp. 307—McArthur v. Pennington, D.C.Tenn., 253 F.Supp. 420.

34. U.S.—Sexton v. Gibbs, D.C.Tex., 327 F.Supp. 134, affirmed C.A., 446 F.2d 904, certiorari denied 92 S.Ct. 733, 404 U.S. 1062, 30 L.Ed.2d 751—Wilson v. Prasse, D.C.Pa., 325 F.Supp. 9—Rhoads v. Horvat, D.C. Colo., 270 F.Supp. 307—McArthur v. Pennington, D.C.Tenn., 253 F. Supp. 120—Solomon v. Pennsylvania R. Co., D.C.N.Y., 96 F.Supp. 709.

35. U.S.—McArthur v. Pennington, D.C.Tenn., 253 F.Supp. 420.

36. Loss of salary

Alleged loss of salary by plaintiff teacher, in action against sheriff and deputy for alleged violation of teacher's civil rights, was so inconclusive that it could not be considered as an element of damages.

U.S.—Rhoads v. Horvat, D.C.Colo., 270 F.Supp. 307.

37. U.S.—McDaniel v. Carroll, C.A. Tenn., 457 F.2d 968, certiorari denied 93 S.Ct. 897, 409 U.S. 1106,

34 L.Ed.2d 687—Mansell v. Saunders, C.A.Fla., 372 F.2d 573—Basista v. Weir, C.A.Pa., 340 F.2d 74—Hague v. Committee for Industrial Organization, C.C.A.N.J., 101 F.2d 774, modified on other grounds 59 S.Ct. 954, 307 U.S. 496, 83 L.Ed. 1423.

Tramble v. Converters Ink Co., D.C.Ill., 343 F.Supp. 1350—Urbano v. McCorkle, D.C.N.J., 334 F.Supp. 161, opinion supplemented 346 F. Supp. 51—Gaston v. Gibson, D.C. Tenn., 328 F.Supp. 3—Sexton v. Gibbs, D.C.Tex., 327 F.Supp. 134, affirmed C.A., 446 F.2d 904, certiorari denied 92 S.Ct. 733, 404 U.S. 1062, 30 L.Ed.2d 751—Wilson v. Prasse, D.C.Pa., 325 F.Supp. 9, affirmed, C.A., 463 F.2d 109—Chubbs v. City of New York, D.C.N.Y., 324 F.Supp. 1183—Sostre v. Rockefeller, D.C.N.Y., 312 F.Supp. 863—Davis v. Board of Trustees of Ark. A & M College, D.C.Ark., 270 F. Supp. 528, affirmed C.A., 396 F.2d 730, certiorari denied 89 S.Ct. 401, 393 U.S. 962, 21 L.Ed.2d 375—Brooks v. Moss, D.C.S.C., 242 F. Supp. 531.

Arrest and prosecution of reservation Indian

$500 would be awarded reservation Indian for Indian police officer's denial of Indian's civil rights in arrest and prosecution of Indian for breach of peace, in view of willfulness of officer's conduct and of indignity and humiliation suffered by Indian.

U.S.—Antelope v. George, D.C.Idaho, 211 F.Supp. 657.

Eviction of white tenants for having Negro guests

White tenants who were evicted from apartment allegedly because they had Negro guests were entitled

[Illustration 137]

PAGE FROM INDEX TO AMERICAN JURISPRUDENCE 2d

AMERICAN JURISPRUDENCE 2d

CIVIL RIGHTS AND DISCRIMINATION
—Cont'd

Public officers and employees—Cont'd
- sex discrimination, Civ R §§ 154, 192, 295
- special provisions of Title VII of Civil Rights Act of 1964 applicable to, Civ R §§ 295-298
- state action, what constitutes, Civ R § 8
"Public pi
   § 43
Public po
   cation,
Public re
   employ
Public saf
Public securities, Pub Sec § 166
Public transportation. **Carriers** (this index)
Public Utilities (this index)
Public welfare. Welfare, infra
Public works. **Job Discrimination** (this index)
Punishment. Sentence and punishment, infra
Punitive damages
- actions under 42 USCS § 1983, punitive damages in, Civ R § 16
- back pay award in Title VII cases, non-punitive nature of, Civ R § 431
- civil conspiracy provisions, recoverability under, Civ R § 25
- federal housing legislation, private suits to enforce, Civ R § 497
- job discrimination, Civ R §§ 431, 445; Job Discrim §§ 1930, 2424, 2425, 2428, 2430-2434
- jury trial in housing discrimination cases, as affecting right to, Civ R § 493
- post-Civil War statutes, under, Civ R § 274
- state civil rights statutes, provided under, Civ R § 261
- Title II of Civil Rights Act of 1964, punitive damages under, Civ R § 457
- Title VII employment discrimination cases, recovery of punitive damages in, Civ R § 445
- violations of 42 USCS § 1982, remedy for, Civ R § 14
- pupils. Students, infra
Purpose
- equal protection, purposeful discrimination necessary to establish denial of, Civ R § 7
- "private club" exempted from public accommodations provisions of Civil Rights Act of 1964, Civ R § 38
Qualifications
- **Job Discrimination** (this index)
- **Judges** (this index)
- membership in private club exempted from public accommodations provisions of Civil Rights Act of 1964, Civ R § 36
- teachers, evaluation of in connection with desegregation of faculties, Civ R § 73
Quantity or quality of production
- **Job Discrimination** (this index)
- quotas, infra
Quotas
- desegregation of faculties, application of in, Civ R § 75
- job discrimination, Civ R §§ 135, 421, 422, 425, 427; Job Discrim §§ 942, 2348-2362
- sex discrimination in education involving numerical admissions limitations, Civ R § 85
Racetracks. Racing and racetracks, infra
Racial balance, transportation of students to achieve, Civ R § 69

CIVIL RIGHTS AND DISCRIMINATION
—Cont'd

Racial discrimination, generally, Civ R § 14
Racial intermarriage, Civ R § 135
"Racial steering" by realtor, Civ R § 250
Racing and racetracks
- discrimination involving racetracks, Civ R § 57

Rapport with pupils, teacher qualifications evaluated as to, Civ R § 73
Real property. Property, supra
Realtors. **Brokers** (this index)
"Reasonable accommodation" of employee religious practices, Civ R §§ 195-201, 205, 206
"Reasonable-man" test in determining existence of reasonable cause as to truth of charge of discrimination, Civ R § 329
Reasonableness of attorney's fee, Civ R § 278
"Reasonable time," filing of private suit in federal district court within, Civ R § 365
Recall of employees. **Job Discrimination** (this index)
"Receiving" of notice of right to sue, time limit for filing of private suit in federal district court as running from, Civ R § 365
Recreational areas or facilities
- generally. **Amusements and Exhibitions** (this index)
- **Parks, Squares, and Playgrounds** (this index)
- sports, infra
Recruiting for employment. **Job Discrimination** (this index)
Recruitment and admissions, sex discrimination in education involving, Civ R § 85
"Red circling" of wages, Civ R §§ 140, 337, 338, 426; Job Discrim § 733
Redress of grievances, criminal conspiracy provisions protecting right to petition for, Civ R § 24
Reducing salons, discrimination involving, Civ R § 49
Re-employment. **Job Discrimination** (this index)
Referendum authorizing closing of public schools to perpetuate segregation, Civ R § 68
Referrals
- Community Relations Service, Civ R § 456
- employment. **Job Discrimination** (this index)
Refreshment counters, public accommodations provisions of Civil Rights Act of 1964 applicable to, Civ R § 31
Regional offices of Equal Employment Opportunity Commission, Civ R § 290
Regular course of business, EEOC subpoena relating to records not kept in, Civ R § 326
Rehiring or reinstatement. **Job Discrimination** (this index)
Relation back. Retroactivity, infra
Relationship between charges filed with EEOC and subsequent Federal District Court suit, necessity of, Civ R § 358
Relatives. Family or marital status
Release of backpay claims, Civ R § 435

CIVIL RIGHTS AND DISCRIMINATION
—Cont'd

Relevancy
- investigation by EEOC to discover "relevant" information, Civ R § 319
- irrelevant matter, Civ R §§ 326, 400, 406
Reliance on state female protective statute, Civ R §§ 187, 435, 447

Religious discrimination, generally, Civ R § 14
Religious organizations
- private and parochial schools, supra
- sex discrimination by educational institutions receiving federal assistance, provisions as to, Civ R § 84
Relocation policies of city, class action by tenants challenging, Civ R § 285
Remedies. Enforcement, supra
Removal of actions
- federal court, permissibility of removal to, Civ R § 261
- job discrimination, Job Discrim §§ 1549, 1551, 1742, 2089
- jury selection, Jury § 188
- state criminal trespass prosecutions involving public accommodations, removal to federal court, Civ R § 452
Removal or dismissal from employment or office. **Job Discrimination** (this index)
Rental of housing. Leases, supra
Reporter of court. Court reporter, supra
Representative nature of applicant's sample chosen for employment test, Civ R § 126
Reputation, Civ R § 108; Job Discrim §§ 289, 326-330, 1991, 2015
Rescission of discriminatory policy, issuance of injunction under Title VII, Civ R § 418
Research staff, class-action determination in Title VII suits, Civ R § 388
Reservation of rights against employer in conciliation agreement, necessity of, Civ R § 333
Residence
- conciliation agreement provision as to elimination of residency requirements, Civ R § 337
- **Housing Laws and Urban Redevelopment** (this index)
- **Job Discrimination** (this index)
- municipal corporations and subdivisions, Const L §§ 203, 773
- nonresidents, Commerce § 87; Const L § 203
- racial restrictions on places of, Civ R § 253
- zoning, racial segregation in residential areas, Civ R § 52
Res judicata
- generally, Civ R § 287.7
- **Job Discrimination** (this index)
Respondeat superior doctrine, applicability in civil rights cases, Civ R §§ 20.5, 26
Restaurants
- generally, Civ R § 55
- cafeterias and lunchrooms, supra
- job discrimination, Job Discrim § 604
- municipal facilities, discrimination involving restaurants in, Civ R §§ 259, 260

1106

> The General Index to *Am. Jur. 2d* will lead the researcher to where the topic under research is covered in *Am. Jur. 2d.*
>
> See next Illustration.

[Illustration 138]

PAGE FROM VOLUME 15, AMERICAN JURISPRUDENCE 2d

15 Am Jur 2d   CIVIL RIGHTS   -   § 446

hand, a requested remedy of enhanced retirement benefits for retired train porters was denied despite arguments that racial discrimination against them prevented them from being permitted to transfer to brakeman jobs, and that had they been permitted to transfer, they would have been the recipients of enhanced retirement benefits.[58]

§ 445. Punitive damages.

Although several courts have allowed plaintiffs to include a claim for punitive damages in their Title VII complaint,[59] they have rarely been awarded.[60]

It has been held that an award of punitive damages should be reversed because the relief provisions of Title VII do not authorize an award of either compensatory or punitive damages for discrimination in employment practices.[61]

§ 446. Attorneys' fees; in general.

Under 42 USCS § 2000e-5(k), the court in any action under Title VII, may,

---

> Notice that *Am. Jur. 2d* contains fewer footnotes than *C.J.S.*, even after the change in *C.J.S.*'s editorial philosophy. But also notice the reference to *A.L.R.* where additional cases can be located. *Am. Jur. 2d* is a useful way to find *A.L.R. Annotations.*
>
> **Note:** Both *Am. Jur. 2d* and *C.J.S.* include annual pocket supplements. A researcher should always remember to check these supplements for references to later sources.

---

59. Tooles v Kellogg Co. (DC Neb) 336 F Supp 14; Gary v Industrial Indem. Co. (DC Cal) 7 CCH **EPD** ¶ 9224; Tidwell v American Oil Co. (DC Utah) 3 CCH **EPD** ¶ 8022, decision on merits (DC Utah) 332 F Supp 424; Walters v Heublein, Inc. (DC Cal) 8 **FEP** 908; Dessenberg v American Metal Forming Co. (DC Ohio) 6 **FEP** 159, 6 CCH EPD ¶ 8813, decision on merits issued (DC Ohio) 8 CCH EPD ¶ 9575.

Annotation: 14 ALR Fed 608, 622, § 9 (punitive damages in actions for violations of Federal Civil Rights Acts).

Note, Employment Discrimination in Title VII of the Civil Rights Act of 1964. 84 Harv L Rev 1109. This note argues that the award of exemplary or punitive damages has often explicitly served to provide an additional incentive for private parties to bring suit, and suggests that the punitive damages remedy would perform a significant deterrent function and would provide additional relief to cover "those intangible injuries which are otherwise uncompensated by the Act."

But one District Court has struck a claim for punitive damages from a complaint. See Van Hoomissen v Xerox Corp. (DC Cal) 368 F Supp 829.

ployment Opportunity Com. v Detroit Edison Co. (CA6) 515 F2d 301).

61. Howard v Lockheed-Georgia Co. (DC Ga) 372 F Supp 854; Van Hoomissen v Xerox Corp. (DC Cal) 368 F Supp 829; Jiron v Sperry Rand Corp. (DC Utah) 9 CCH **EPD** ¶ 9990; Guthrie v Colonial Bakery Co. (DC Ga) 6 CCH **EPD** ¶ 8849; Attkisson v Bridgeport Brass Co. (DC Ind) 5 **FEP** 919, 5 CCH EPD ¶ 8522.

The relief provisions of Title VII do not specifically authorize an award of either compensatory or punitive damages for discrimination in employment practices; backpay in such cases is considered a form of restitution, not an award of damages; damages are a legal, not an equitable, remedy, and the Seventh Amendment requires a jury trial in a statutory action if the statute creates legal rights and remedies, enforceable in an action for damages in ordinary courts of law; since all the defendants in a discrimination case against a Detroit utility company had demanded a jury trial, which was denied by the court, the court's award of $4 million in punitive damages at the close of the trial, awarded because the trial court found malice on the part of the defendant, was improper. Equal Employment Opportunity Com. v Detroit Edison Co. (CA6 Mich) 515 F2d 301.

1019

SECTION D.   STATE ENCYCLOPEDIAS

Some states have encyclopedias devoted to their own laws.   Lawyers Cooperative Publishing publishes eight encyclopedias that follow the format of *Am. Jur. 2d,* while covering only the laws of a specific state. These are:

California Jurisprudence 3d

Florida Jurisprudence 2d

Illinois Jurisprudence

Kentucky Jurisprudence

Massachusetts Jurisprudence

New York Jurisprudence 2d

Ohio Jurisprudence 3d

Texas Jurisprudence 3d

The BEGIN library on LEXIS contains the jurisprudence sets from Florida, New York, Ohio, and Texas.

Five states have encyclopedias published by West Publishing Company, and these follow the format of *Corpus Juris Secundum.*   These are:

Illinois Law and Practice

Indiana Law Encyclopedia

Maryland Law Encyclopedia

Michigan Law and Practice

Pennsylvania Law Encyclopedia

Encyclopedias for Georgia (Harrison), Virginia and West Virginia (Michie), and Tennessee (Michie) are also available.

SECTION E.   SPECIFIC SUBJECT ENCYCLOPEDIAS

Three smaller legal encyclopedias focus on broad legal subjects that are national in scope.   The four-volume *Encyclopedia of Crime and Justice* (The Free Press, 1983) contains almost 300 topical, encyclopedic essays by named scholars covering the range of issues affecting criminal behavior and society's responses to it.   The *Encyclopedia of the American Judicial System: Studies of the Principal Institutions and Processes of Law* (Charles Scribner's Sons, 1987) is a three-volume work containing 88 encyclopedic essays by named scholars that provide historical accounts and discussions of substantive law, institutions and personnel, the judicial process, and constitutional law.   The *Encyclopedia of the American Constitution* is discussed in Chapter 8, Section A–2.

Chapter 16

LEGAL PERIODICALS AND INDEXES

Legal periodicals are extremely valuable secondary sources in legal research. Their value typically lies in the depth to which they analyze and criticize a particular topic and the extent of their footnote references to other sources. During the nineteenth century, they greatly contributed to improving the image of the legal profession in America.[1] With the proliferation of legislation and court cases, legal periodicals in the twentieth century play an increasingly important role in keeping researchers current in developing areas of the law and in providing information on the specialized areas of the law.

The function of a legal periodical has been described as the "recording and criticism of doings of legislators and judges, discussion of current case law, narration of the lives of eminent lawyers, and the scientific study of native and foreign jurisprudence."[2] Legal periodicals can be classified into five types of publications: (1) law school; (2) bar association; (3) subject, special interest, and interdisciplinary (frequently by commercial publishers); (4) legal newspapers; and (5) newsletters.[3] A variety of specialized indexes provide access to these publications.

SECTION A. LEGAL PERIODICALS

1. Law School Reviews/Journals

A periodical published by a law school is most often called a *review*, although *journal* is also widely used, *e.g., Harvard Law Review, Michigan Law Review, Yale Law Journal*. The two terms are used inter-

---

[1] MAXWELL H. BLOOMFIELD, AMERICAN LAWYERS IN A CHANGING SOCIETY, 1776–1876 142–43 (1976). For a brief account of legal periodicals in nineteenth-century America, *see* LAWRENCE M. FRIEDMAN, A HISTORY OF AMERICAN LAW 630–31 (2d ed. 1985). Additional sources that deal with the early history of legal periodicals in the United States include Marion Brainerd, *Historical Sketch of American Legal Periodicals*, 14 LAW LIBR. J. 63 (1921); Roscoe Pound, *Types of Legal Periodical*, 14 IOWA L. REV. 257 (1929); *Digest of American Law Reports and American Legal Periodical*, 23 AM. JURIST. 128 (1840). For an extensive history of law school reviews, *see* Michael I. Swygert & Jon W. Bruce, *The Historical Origin, Founding, and Early Development of Student–Edited Law Reviews*, 36 HASTINGS L.J. 739 (1985).

For a list of legal periodicals of the last century and their dates of publication, *see* LEONARD N. JONES, AN INDEX TO LEGAL PERIODICAL LITERATURE vii-x (1988); 2 *id.* at vii-x (1899). These volumes are part of what is referred to as the *Jones–Chipman Index*, which is discussed in Section B–1.

[2] FREDERICK C. HICKS, MATERIALS AND METHODS OF LEGAL RESEARCH 210 (3d rev. ed. 1942).

[3] For additional breakdowns of categories and for recommendations as to the titles that should be in a broad-based legal periodical collection, *see* Donald J. Dunn, *Law, in* MAGAZINES FOR LIBRARIES 660–80 (Bill Katz & Linda Sternberg Katz eds., 7th ed., 1992).

changeably.   These publications play a unique role in legal research.
One distinctive feature is the control of editorial policy and management
by student editors.   The students forming the membership of law review
are typically chosen on the basis of their scholarship record, through a
writing competition, or a combination of the two.   These students "on
law review" write articles and edit each other's work, evaluate for
potential publication the writings submitted by those outside the school,
and then edit those pieces accepted for publication.   As one legal scholar
has noted:

> There is not so far as I know in the world an academic faculty
> which pins its reputation before the public upon the work of
> undergraduate students—there is none, that is, except in the
> American law reviews.[4]

The typical law review is published quarterly, although some are
issued only annually and others as often as eight times a year.   It is
usually subsidized by its parent institution and sold at a modest cost,
with its circulation almost exclusively limited to law libraries, its alum-
ni/ae, and members of the bar within the jurisdiction where it is
published.[5]   An issue averages around 200 pages.

These publications are generally in two or more sections.   The first
consists of "lead articles" on various topics, usually written by law
professors and occasionally by practitioners or academics from other
disciplines.   [See Illustration 145.]   These articles are typically lengthy,
scholarly in nature, and may have a substantial impact in changing the
law or in charting the course for newly-developing fields of law.[6]

The next section, which is written by law students, is most often
called "Notes and Comments," with the former devoted to critical
analyses of recent court cases or legislation and the latter to surveys or
critiques of selected subjects of contemporary importance.   [See Illustration 146.]   Sometimes these *notes* and *comments* are in two separate
sections.   Many journals also publish book reviews.   In this section are
critical, detailed expositions that frequently venture beyond an assessment of the book to include the reviewer's personal opinion about the
issues raised in the book.   These book reviews are frequently lengthy
and extensively documented.

A "Commentary" section is appearing with increasing frequency in
law reviews.[7]   These *commentaries,* which typically undergo little or no
student editing and therefore can be published more quickly than other

---

[4] KARL N. LLEWELLYN, THE BRAMBLE BUSH 105 (1931).

[5] The *Harvard Law Review* has the largest circulation at over 10,000.   Most have
circulations of less than 1,000.

[6] *See, e.g.,* Samuel D. Warren & Louis D. Brandeis, *The Right to Privacy,* 4 HARV. L. REV.
193 (1890); William L. Prosser, *The Assault upon the Citadel (Strict Liability to the
Consumer),* 69 YALE L.J. 1099 (1960); Donald R. Korobkin, *Rehabilitating Values: A
Jurisprudence of Bankruptcy,* 91 COLUM. L. REV. 717 (1991).

[7] For an examination of this practice, *see Commentary,* 24 CONN. L. REV. 1959 (1991),
which contains seven brief articles.

segments in the review, often involve a scholar taking a position on a controversial topic, followed in the same or a subsequent issue with responses from other scholars that challenge those views. Sections like the "Commentary" are sometimes entitled "Essays" or "Correspondence." Frequently, a law review issue will be devoted to a symposium on a particular subject or contain an annual review of the work of a particular court.

Much has changed in the world of law review publishing in recent years, most notably the proliferation of subject-oriented and interdisciplinary journals. In 1941, the number of reviews published by American law schools totaled 50.[8] Today, students at the more than 175 American Bar Association-accredited law schools publish in excess of 420 titles.[9] Obviously, many schools publish more than one journal, with Harvard leading the way with ten. While it could once be said that law reviews were general in nature with no emphasis on any specific subject, only a law school's so-called "flagship" review or journal typically will be true to the general-interest notion. "Secondary" reviews on specialized subjects, *e.g.*, civil rights, constitutional law, environmental law, international law, and taxation, or reviews that are interdisciplinary in nature, *e.g.*, law and medicine, law and economics, now predominate. A representative listing is set forth in Section I *infra*.

Law school reviews have had a high degree of success in providing students with a meaningful research and writing experience [10] while serving as a forum for the foremost legal scholars to contribute articles that have been instrumental in molding the course of many legal doctrines.[11] Increasingly, courts are citing law review articles and student notes and comments.[12] It is interesting that it was not until 1917 that the Supreme Court of the United States began citing legal journal articles in its opinions,[13] while presently most opinions by the Court cite to or quote from these sources.

[8] This number is derived from the listing of law reviews in HICKS, *supra* note 1, at 207–09.

[9] This number is obtained from a list of law reviews/journals maintained by the authors of this text.

[10] *See* articles on *Student–Edited Law Reviews*, 36 J. LEGAL EDUC. 1–23 (1986).

[11] *See, e.g.*, Fred R. Shapiro, *The Most–Cited Law Review Articles*, 73 CAL. L. REV. 1540 (1985); Fred R. Shapiro, *The Most–Cited Articles from* The Yale Law Journal, 100 YALE L.J. 1449 (1991). A book resulted from the first article: FRED R. SHAPIRO, THE MOST-CITED LAW REVIEW ARTICLES (1987), which collects and reprints the 24 law review articles that have been most cited in other law review articles. *See also Symposium: Review of Articles That Shaped the Law*, 21 U. MICH. J.L. REF. 509 (1988).

[12] Richard A. Mann, *The Use of Legal Periodicals by Courts and Journals*, 26 JURIMETRICS J. 400 (1986); Louis J. Sirico, Jr. & Jeffrey B. Margulies, *The Citing of Law Reviews by the Supreme Court: An Empirical Study*, 34 UCLA L. REV. 131 (1986); Louis J. Sirico, Jr. & Beth A. Drew, *The Citing of Law Reviews by the United States Courts of Appeals: An Empirical Analysis*, 45 U. MIAMI L. REV. 1051 (1991).

[13] Chester A. Newland, Comment, *The Supreme Court and Legal Writing: Learned Journals as Vehicles of an Anti–Antitrust Lobby?* 48 GEO. L.J. 105, 127 (1959).

Today, as a result of the dramatic increase in the number of published journals, it is much less difficult for writers to have their work accepted for publication by a law review somewhere. However, it has become a virtual contest to have one's work published in a source that increases the likelihood that it will be cited and to identify the "best" sources. An increasing amount of literature is being published that attempts to rate the reviews.[14]

There are some notable exceptions to the student-edited law review model—the faculty-edited reviews. These publications are "refereed," *i.e.*, selection of an article for inclusion is based on peer review, often with those participating in the evaluative process not knowing the author of the piece—the so-called "blind" review. These highly-respected journals include *The American Journal of Legal History, Journal of Legal Studies, Journal of Law and Economics, Law and History Review,* and *Law and Society Review.*

Although there are numerous virtues to law reviews, they are not without their critics,[15] and the debate as to their relative value continues.[16] The substance of the criticism is usually aimed at their pedantic style, excessive use of footnotes,[17] and their similarity to each other. Indeed, one member of Congress has even attacked law reviews as having an insidious influence on the Supreme Court of the United States.[18] In spite of these criticisms, law school law reviews serve as important vehicles for the publication of significant legal research, as valuable resources for references to additional sources of information, and as incisive and effective teaching tools.

[14] *See, e.g.*, Olavi Maru, *Measuring the Impact of Legal Periodicals,* 1976 Am.B.Found. Res.J. 227; (ranks law reviews by the frequency with which they have been cited); *Chicago–Kent Law Review Faculty Scholarship Survey,* 65 CHIC.-KENT L. REV. 195 (1989) (ranks the leading law reviews based on frequency of citation as well as the productivity of law school faculties in those leading reviews; published annually since 1989); Scott Finet, *The Most Frequently Cited Law Reviews and Legal Periodicals,* LEGAL REFERENCE SERVICES Q., No. 3/4 1989, at 227 (surveys the literature on frequency of citation and then develops a composite listing); James Leonard, *"Seein' the Cites" A Guided Tour of Citation Patterns in Recent American Law Review Articles,* 34 ST. LOUIS U. L.J. 181 (1990) (investigates why some law reviews are cited more often than others as scholarly authority in law reviews). *See also supra* note 12, which includes additional articles frequently used in attempting to rate law reviews.

[15] Among the foremost critics was Yale Law Professor Fred Rodell. *See* Fred Rodell, *Goodbye to Law Reviews,* 23 VA. L. REV. 38 (1936); Fred Rodell, *Goodbye to Law Reviews—Revisited,* 48 VA. L. REV. 279 (1962).

[16] *See, e.g.*, Roger C. Cramton, *"The Most Remarkable Institution": The American Law Review,* 36 J. LEGAL EDUC. 1 (1986); Phil Nichols, Note, *A Student Defense of Student Edited Journals: In Response to Professor Roger Cramton,* 1987 DUKE L.J. 1122; E. Joshua Rosenkranz, *Law Review's Empire,* 39 HASTINGS L.J. 859 (1988); Michael Vitiello, *Journal Wars,* 22 ST. MARY'S L.J. 927 (1991); E. Joshua Rosenkranz, *The Empire Strikes Back,* 22 ST. MARY'S L.J. 943 (1991); Max Stier et al., *Law Review Usage and Suggestions for Improvement: A Survey of Attorneys, Professors, and Judges,* 44 STAN. L. REV. 1467 (1992).

[17] The current record is 4,824 established by Arnold S. Jacobs, *An Analysis of Section 16 of the Securities Act of 1934,* 32 N.Y.L. SCH. L. REV. 209 (1987).

[18] 103 CONG. REC. 16,159–62 (1957) (statement of Rep. Patman) (characterizing legal writing as "an organized form of lobbying").

2. Bar Association Periodicals

All fifty states and the District of Columbia have bar associations. In some states, membership is voluntary; in other states, it is a prerequisite to the practice of law within the state. The latter is called an *integrated bar*. [19] In addition, many counties and large cities have their own local bar associations. Most national and state bar associations, sections within these associations, and many local and specialized bar groups publish periodicals. These publications vary in scope from such distinguished periodicals as the *ABA Journal* or the *Record of the Association of the Bar of the City of New York* to those that are little more than newsletters.

The primary purposes of bar association publications are to inform the membership of the association's activities, to comment on pending and recent legislation, and to review current local court cases. When they do publish articles, these tend to stress the more practical aspects of the law, with emphasis on problem solving, rather than the theoretical ones. [See Illustration 147.] They are concerned more with the law as it is rather than with what it should be. Thus, bar association publications perform different functions than the law school reviews, where the emphasis is on reform and scholarly legal research. As a consequence, bar association publications generally have less historical value, but are more useful when researching subjects of current interest to practitioners.

3. Subject, Special Interest, and Interdisciplinary Legal Periodicals

As the literature of the law grows and reflects the increasing complexity of society, it is ever more difficult for lawyers and researchers to keep current not only with the general development of the law but also with their particular legal interests. Concurrent with this law explosion, law practices are increasingly becoming more specialized and legal periodicals are targeting the interest of particular sub-groups within the legal profession. Some of these periodicals are published by law schools, edited by students or faculty members, and follow the format of the traditional law review; others are published by non-profit associations; and still others, in ever-increasing numbers, are published by commercial publishing companies. Another recent development is the publication of periodicals devoted to law and its interaction with some other discipline. These periodicals reflect the increasing emphasis many law schools and legal and non-legal scholars place on integrating the findings of the social and behavioral sciences with the legal process.

    a. *Subject Journals.* Journals devoted to one area of law vary in

---

[19] For a complete list of bar associations, see the latest *American Bar Association Directory,* which is published annually.

scope from the very practical to the very scholarly.[20]   *Taxes: The Tax Magazine* and *Trusts and Estates,* both published by private companies, are examples of periodicals aimed primarily at practicing attorneys specializing in particular fields of law.   These contain articles written by well-known practitioners interpreting the impact of recent legislation and court cases, and many contain reviews of books within their subject area.   The *American Journal of International Law* and *American Journal of Comparative Law* are examples of periodicals published under the auspices of learned societies, while *Ecology Law Quarterly,* published at the University of California at Berkeley School of Law, and *Review of Litigation,* published at the University of Texas School of Law, are typical of subject journals that are similar in format to traditional law school reviews.

b.   *Special Interest Periodicals.*   These periodicals are aimed at those members of the legal community who have similar interests and serve as a means to encourage writing and research within the special area of interest.   They include such journals as *Catholic Lawyer, Christian Lawyer, Elder Law Journal, Journal of Law & Sexuality, Judges Journal, National Black Law Journal, La Raza Law Journal, Scribes Journal of Legal Writing,* and *Women Lawyers Journal.*

c.   *Interdisciplinary Journals.*   Perhaps the most distinguished of this group is *Journal of Law and Economics,* published by the faculty of the University of Chicago School of Law.   Other representative titles are *Journal of Law and Health, Journal of Law & Politics, Journal of Law and Religion, Journal of Legal Medicine, Journal of Psychiatry and Law, Law and Psychology Review,* and *Yale Journal of Law and the Humanities.*

4. Legal Newspapers

Legal newspapers can be national, state, or local in focus and are frequently available online as well as in print form.[21]   There are two weekly legal newspapers that are national in scope—*Legal Times* and *National Law Journal,* both of which began in 1978.   These contain articles and regular columns that pertain to a variety of issues and are valuable sources for fast-breaking legal developments.   The monthly *American Lawyer,* which commenced in 1979 and is also national in scope, tends to focus on sensational events, although it is also developing a sound reputation for investigative journalism.   The *Corporate Legal Times,* launched in 1990, is an example of a weekly, national newspaper with a subject focus.   *Lawyers Weekly USA,* started in 1993, is a biweekly national newspaper that places special emphasis on the needs of the smaller law firm.

[20] A few publishers publish annual anthologies consisting of a collection of the best articles written on a particular subject and published over the course of each year. *Advertising Law* is an example of one such annual.

[21] A complete list of legal newspapers is available in the annual *Gale Directory of Publications* and in a separate volume of the annual *Ulrich's International Periodicals Directory.*

Legal newspapers are published for many states. These are typically published either weekly or monthly and concentrate on matters of particular importance in the state. They often contain articles of both state and national interest, synopses of cases, and reports of disciplinary proceedings. Examples include *Connecticut Law Tribune, Massachusetts Lawyers Weekly, New Jersey Law Journal,* and *Texas Lawyer.*

In a few larger cities are newspapers devoted to legal affairs of their metropolitan area. These are generally published daily, Monday through Friday, and primarily contain information on court calendars and dockets, changes in court rules, news about recent changes in legislation, new administrative rules, and stories about local judges and lawyers. Some of the larger ones, such as *New York Law Journal* and *Los Angeles Daily Journal,* also publish current court cases and articles on various legal topics.

5. Newsletters

While the number of subject-matter journals has grown rapidly, it is the area of the commercially-published topical newsletter that has expanded most dramatically. As law has become more specialized, subject-matter newsletters have flourished. One would be hard-pressed to find an area of the law that is not served by one, and often many, law-related newsletters on the topic under research. These publications, often quite expensive, are typically issued weekly or monthly, consist of only a few pages, and focus on the most recent trends and developments. Rarely do they contain an index and even more rarely are they indexed by the major indexing publications. Their value lies in providing the practitioner with current awareness information.

The best source for identifying these publications is the annual *Legal Newsletters in Print* of Infosources. It contains a Title List of over 1,400 newsletters published in the United States. It also includes a Publisher's Index and a Subject Index with over 300 subject entries.

SECTION B. COMPREHENSIVE PERIODICAL INDEXES

The usefulness of legal periodicals to legal research depends almost entirely on the researcher's ability to find what articles have been written and where they have been published. Generally, it is necessary to rely on indexes to legal periodical literature for this purpose.

1. Jones–Chipman Index to Legal Periodicals

This was the first index that attempted to provide a comprehensive and systematic index to English language periodicals. It is in six volumes and covers periodicals published between 1803 to 1937. The first three volumes, which cover to 1908, precede the more extensive *Index to Legal Periodicals* that began in 1908 and is discussed *infra.* Therefore, these first three volumes of the *Jones–Chipman Index* must be consulted to locate articles prior to 1908.

2. Index to Legal Periodicals (ILP)

This index, which began in 1908, is a product of the H.W. Wilson Company and until 1980 was the only extensive index of legal periodical articles. *ILP* indexes approximately 600 English language legal periodicals published in the United States, Canada, Great Britain, Ireland, Australia, and New Zealand, so long as they regularly publish legal articles of high quality and of permanent reference value.

An advisory committee composed of law librarians and practitioners serves as a consultant to the publisher on editorial policy and content. New periodical titles that meet the criteria for inclusion are added each October. Articles must be at least five pages in length to be included. Biographies, bibliographies, book reviews, and case notes must be at least two pages in length to be indexed. Triennial cumulations were published through 1979. The present publication schedule is monthly, except September, with quarterly and then annual cumulations. A listing of periodicals covered—from the abbreviation used in *ILP* to full title—is included in the front of each issue and each volume.

In 1994, *ILP* began to index books. Each month, approximately 2,500 law-related titles are extracted from Wilson's *Cumulative Book Index*. Thereafter, subject headings (typically two to three per book) are adapted to those used in *ILP* and then these entries are added at the end of periodical entries for those same subjects. The books indexed are from the same countries as those for periodicals.

ILP has four different access points:

a. *Author/Subject Index*. Authors and subjects are included in one alphabet. Prior to 1983, the author entry cross references the researcher to the subject(s) under which the author's article is indexed. The cross reference includes the first letter of the title of the article. Under the subject, a full citation to the article, including the title, is provided. Since 1983, authors and subjects include full title and citation under each entry. Beginning in 1982, these citations to the journals are in *Bluebook* form. A list of subject headings used in *ILP* is included in the front of each issue and volume. A separate *Index to Legal Periodicals Thesaurus* (1988), which includes the primary term as well as broader, narrower, and related terms, enables a researcher to focus a search with substantial accuracy.

Commencing in 1994, author entries for books are included in this section. The subject entries for books are at the end of each subject entry for articles.

b. *Table of Cases*. This lists the names of cases (for the time period of the issue or volume) that have had a note or comment written on them. The listing is alphabetical by case name.

c. *Table of Statutes*. This lists statutes by subject under each jurisdiction, with federal laws listed first.

d. *Book Review Index*. This lists by author the books reviewed in the periodicals indexed by *ILP*.

[See Illustrations 139–141 for sample pages from the *Index to Legal Periodicals.*]

The *Index to Legal Periodicals* also is available in a variety of electronic formats. WILSONLINE provides online access, updated twice weekly, to *ILP* from August 1981 and to over twenty other H.W. Wilson Company specialized databases. WILSONLINE is also available to commercial subscribers on both LEXIS and WESTLAW, but not to law schools because of the discounted rates they pay for these two CALR services. WILSONDISC, a CD–ROM product, covers *ILP* from August 1981, is updated and cumulated monthly, and can be accessed without online charges.

3. Current Law Index (CLI), Legal Resource Index (LRI), and LEGALTRAC

These three indexes, produced by Information Access Company, began in 1980 and are published under the auspices of the American Association of Law Libraries (AALL), with an advisory committee of AALL assisting with content selection. As will be described below, the three titles used for these indexes reflect their different formats and, in some instances, their slightly different coverage. These indexes cover substantially more titles than *ILP* and indexing is more extensive.

All titles indexed are in the English language, the exception being those in French from Canada, and coverage is worldwide. All materials of value are indexed without limitation as to the number of pages. Coverage begins with the 1980 imprint for each periodical. Subject headings of the Library of Congress are used. These products are computer-produced and each has the following features:

a. *Author/Title Index.* This section lists all articles by author with full title and periodical citation and by title, again with the full bibliographic citation.

b. *Book Reviews.* Book reviews that appear in the periodicals covered by the indexes are listed under both the author and title of the book in the *Author/Title Index* section. An interesting feature is the rating of books from A to F, recording the opinion of the reviewer.

c. *Table of Cases.* Cases that are the subject of case notes are listed under the names of both plaintiff and defendant.

d. *Table of Statutes.* This lists all statutes cited in articles, by both official and popular citation.

(1) *Current Law Index (CLI).* This is a printed index issued monthly with quarterly and annual cumulations. It indexes over 800 periodicals, and each issue contains a list of periodicals indexed with addresses. The first seven volumes are each in single books. Effective with volume 8 (1987), *CLI* is published in two parts: Part A is a subject index; Part B is an index by author/title, cases, and statutes. [See Illustrations 142–144.]

(2) *Legal Resource Index (LRI)*.   *LRI* is the online counterpart of *CLI*.   It includes all titles in *CLI*, plus several major legal newspapers, and articles selected from non-legal periodicals that are law-related. The database is used to produce a microfilm product that is read on a specially-designed motorized reader.   Each month a cumulated reel of microfilm is sent to the subscriber, thus regularly integrating the authors/titles, tables of cases, and tables of statutes each into single arrangements.   Because a roll of microfilm can no longer hold the complete contents of *LRI*, older material is removed to a companion set of microfiche when a new roll of microfilm is received.   Therefore, a complete retrospective search from 1980 requires using both the microfilm reel and the microfiche set of *LRI*.   In spite of this need to consult two sources, it is still easier than consulting the multiple volumes of *CLI* and coverage is more extensive.

LRI is accessible through both LEXIS, WESTLAW, and Dialog.   It is this online access, updated daily, that greatly facilitates access to legal periodical literature from 1980 forward.   It can be searched on LEXIS using Boolean logic, natural language, and segment searches, and on WESTLAW using Boolean logic, natural language, and field searches.   In addition, a tape version of *LRI* can be purchased and added to a law library's online catalog.

(3) LEGALTRAC.   LEGALTRAC is a CD–ROM version of the online *LRI*, covering the same time period and same materials as *LRI*.   Using a keyboard, a researcher can enter a subject or name and the search will bring one to that point in the database.   A search can be expanded to include more than one word.   For example, entering "jury," "disagreements," and "Howe" as an "expanded" search retrieves all citations in which all three words appear in the citation.   While rudimentary in terms of search logic and far less sophisticated than online searching of *LRI*, it offers great advantages over the microfilm *LRI* and the print *CLI*.   An attached printer enables a researcher to print out search results, rather than noting them manually.   LEGALTRAC is updated monthly by a newly-issued cumulative disc.   A separate program enables subscribers to this product to indicate whether their library subscribes to a periodical indexed in the database.

4. Current Awareness Publications

Several publications, including a number of in-house library publications, are designed to alert users to the most recent articles in legal periodicals.   Two that are national in scope are especially useful:

(a) *Current Index to Legal Periodicals (CILP)*.   Published weekly by the Marian G. Gallagher Law Library of the University of Washington, this index covers articles too new to be in either *Current Law Index* or *Index to Legal Periodicals*.   It can be thought of as an advance sheet to the monthly issues of these two publications.   *CILP* provides a subject index as well as the contents of the journals indexed.   Recent issues are available on WESTLAW in the CILP database.

(b) *Legal Contents.* Published by Management Contents, this monthly service reprints the tables of contents for most currently-issued legal periodicals and includes an index of articles by field of law.

5. Annual Legal Bibliography

Published by the Harvard Law Library from 1961 to 1981, this source indexed both the books and articles the Library received. Over 2,000 periodicals were covered.

SECTION C. ILLUSTRATIONS: LEGAL PERIODICALS AND INDEXES

[Illustration 139]

PAGE FROM SUBJECT AND AUTHOR INDEX—
INDEX TO LEGAL PERIODICALS

56 **INDEX TO LEGAL PERIODICALS**

Judicial ethics

Texas

Lawyers married to judges: a dilemma facing state judiciaries—a case study of the state of Texas. M. M. Brandsdorfer. 6 *Geo. J. Legal Ethics* 635-63 Wint '93

Judicial intervention *See* Judicial activism

Judicial restraint

See also

Judicial activism

Judicial review

See also

Judicial activism

Separation of powers

Balancing cultural integrity against individual liberty: civil court review of ecclesiastical judgments. M. G. Weisberg, student author. 25 *U. Mich. J.L. Ref.* 955-1008 Spr/Summ '92

Constitutional midrash: the rabbis' solution to Professor Bickel's problem. D. R. Dow. 29 *Hous. L. Rev.* 543-81 Fall '92

The curious case of the Virginia Military Institute: an essay on the judicial function. A. Ides. 50 *Wash. & Lee L. Rev.* 35-48 Wint '93

Dialogue and judicial review. B. Friedman. 91 *Mich. L. Rev.* 577-682 F '93

Great Britain

The black hole theory. R. Gordon, C. Barlow. 143 *New L.J.* 322-3 Mr 5 '93

Judicial review of administrative acts

Judi...

M...

'9...

Prec...

ag...

Na...

27...

60...

Som...

v...

C...

Wint '93

Australia

The justiciability of environmental administrative action. S. Rigney. 10 *Envtl. & Plan. L.J.* 61-9 Ap '93

Canada

Rules and discretion in the governance of Canada. B. McLachlin. 56 *Sask. L. Rev.* 167-79 '92

Great Britain

The Jockey Club and judicial review. N. Parpworth. 137 *Solic. J.* 252-3 Mr 19 '93

Judicial statistics

Ontario

The Ontario Court of Appeal and speedy justice. C. Baar, I. Greene, M. Thomas, P. J. McCormick. 30 *Osgoode Hall L.J.* 261-90 Summ '92

Judiciary *See* Courts

Jung, Heike

Criminal justice—a European perspective. 1993 *Crim. L. Rev.* 237-45 Ap '93

Juries

See also

Instructions to juries

Jury selection

Law and fact

Bias and prejudice against foreign corporations in patent and other technology jury trials. J. L. Lahr. 2 *Fed. Cir. B.J.* 405-10 Wint '92

Federal Rule of Evidence 606(b) and the problem of "differential" jury error. D. A. Christman, student author. 67 *N.Y.U. L. Rev.* 802-39 O '92

Jury fact-finding in criminal cases: constitutional limits on factual disagreements among convicting jurors. S. W. Howe. 58 *Mo. L. Rev.* 1-83 Wint '93

Georgia

The Georgia jury and negligence: the view from the bench. R. P. Sentell, Jr. 26 *Ga. L. Rev.* 85-178 Fall '91; 27 *Ga. L. Rev.* 59-120 Fall '92

Jurisdiction

See also

Admiralty jurisdiction

Civil procedure

Criminal procedure

Federal jurisdiction

Forum non conveniens

Indians—Tribal courts

Venue

The aftermath of Burnham v. Superior Court [110 S. Ct. 2105 (1990)]: a new rule of transient jurisdiction? C. M. Daleiden, student author. 32 *Santa Clara L. Rev.* 989-1019 '92

Federal preemption in the resolution of child custody jurisdiction disputes. R. M. Baron. 45 *Ark. L. Rev.* 885-912 '93

Locke as the key: a unifying and coherent theory of in personam jurisdiction. R. B. Cappalli. 43 *Case W. Res. L. Rev.* 97-159 Fall '92

One child's odyssey through the Uniform Child Custody Jurisdiction and Parental Kidnapping Prevention Acts. J. C. Murray, student author. 1993 *Wis. L. Rev.* 589-617 '93

Public utility underwriting costs and regulatory climate: an examination of PUC and SEC multiple jurisdictions. R. F. Gorman, M. F. Grace, G. Vora. 10 *Yale J. on Reg.* 17-61 Wint '93

Remarks before the Conference on International Business Practice on practice before the United States Court of International Trade. G. W. Carman. 2 *Fed. Cir. B.J.* 123-36 Summ '92

Missouri

The enforceability of forum selection clauses: Missouri finally joins the majority. High Life Sales Co. v.

...2)].

...ev.

...R.

...'93

...ler.

Jurisprudence

See also

Constitutional theory

Economic jurisprudence

Hermeneutics

Legal positivism

Legal realism

Legal scholarship

Medical jurisprudence

Natural law

Rule of law

Sociological jurisprudence

Electronic technology: law and the legal mind. R. G. Hammond. 26 *Cornell Int'l L.J.* 167-87 Wint '93

An essay on private remedies. E. L. Sherwin. 6 *Can. J.L. Juris.* 89-112 Ja '93

Global rights and regional jurisprudence. K. T. Jackson. 12 *Law & Phil.* 157-92 My '93

The internalization paradox and workers' compensation. K. N. Hylton, S. E. Laymon. 21 *Hofstra L. Rev.* 109-82 Fall '92

The inward turn in outsider jurisprudence. R. Delgado. 34 *Wm. & Mary L. Rev.* 741-68 Spr '93

Locke as the key: a unifying and coherent theory of in personam jurisdiction. R. B. Cappalli. 43 *Case W. Res. L. Rev.* 97-159 Fall '92

Theorizing about law. R. Case. 6 *Can. J.L. Juris.* 113-38 Ja '93

The theory and practice of American legal history. J. T. Kloppenberg. 106 *Harv. L. Rev.* 1332-51 Ap '93

Jurisprudence, Medical *See* Medical jurisprudence

Jury selection

See also

Peremptory challenges

Morgan v. Illinois [112 S. Ct. 2222 (1992)]: the defense gets the reverse-Witherspoon [Witherspoon v. Illinois, 88 S. Ct. 1770 (1968)] question. T. J. R. Archer, student author. 44 *Mercer L. Rev.* 997-1006 Spr '93

Jury trial right *See* Right to trial by jury

Justice, William Wayne

The two faces of judicial activism. 61 *Geo. Wash. L. Rev.* 1-13 N '92

A page from the *Index to Legal Periodicals*. Assume you are interested in the conduct of juries.

Note how entries for authors and for subjects are in one alphabet.

ILP is also available to commercial subscribers on WILSONLINE, LEXIS, and WESTLAW and on WILSONDISC.

[Illustration 140]

PAGE FROM TABLE OF CASES—INDEX TO LEGAL PERIODICALS

844   INDEX TO LEGAL PERIODICALS

Mu'Min v. Virginia, 111 S. Ct. 1899 (1991)
   82 *J. Crim. L. & Criminology* 920-54 Wint '92
   23 *Loy. U. Chi. L.J.* 557-79 Spr '92
   23 *St. Mary's L.J.* 541-61 '91

Municipal Court; Johnetta J. v., 267 Cal. Rptr. 666
   11 *N. Ill. U. L. Rev.* 445-79 Spr/Summ '91
Muniz; United States v. 23 M.J. 201
   1992 *Army Law.* 26-31 Ja '92
Munoz; Norwood Hosp. v., 564 N.E.2d 1017 (Mass.)
   25 *Suffolk U. L. Rev.* 821-8 Fall '91
Murphy v. Brentwood Dist. Council, [1990] 2 All E.R. 908
   20 *Can. Bus. L.J.* 164-79 My '92
   1991 *Conv. & Prop. Law. (n.s.)* 225-43 My/Je '91
   54 *Mod. L. Rev.* 561-70 Jl '91
   42 *N. Ir. Legal Q.* 26-37 Spr '91
   11 *Oxford J. Legal Stud.* 416-30 Aut '91
   12 *Oxford J. Legal Stud.* 112-28 Spr '92
Murphy v. Morgan, 914 F.2d 846
   29 *J. Fam. L.* 939-43 '90/'91
Murphy, Estate of v. Commissioner, 60 T.C.M. (CCH) 645
   15 *Rev. Tax'n Individ.* 291-301 Aut '91
   45 *Tax Law.* 609-20 Wint '92
Murphy ex rel. K.H. v. Morgan, 914 F.2d 846
   25 *Suffolk U. L. Rev.* 789-96 Fall '91
Murray v. Giarratano, 109 S. Ct. 2765

National Bellas Hess, Inc. v. Department of Revenue, 87 S. Ct. 1389
   23 *Conn. L. Rev.* 1087-124 Summ '91
National Corn Growers v. Canada (Canadian Import Tribunal), 74 D.L.R.4th 449
   13 *Advoc. Q.* 78-89 Ag '91
National Ctr. for Immigrants' Rights, Inc.; INS v., 112 S. Ct. 551
   6 *Geo. Immigr. L.J.* 167-71 Mr '92
National Ctr. for Immigrants' Rights, Inc. v. INS, 913 F.2d 1350
   14 *Fordham Int'l L.J.* 1069-102 '90/'91
   5 *Geo. Immigr. L.J.* 801-8 Fall '91
   6 *Geo. Immigr. L.J.* 345-67 Je '92
National Fed'n of Federal Employees v. United States, 688 F. Supp. 671
   10 *Mich. J. Int'l L.* 163-75 Wint '89
National Fed'n of the Blind; Riley v., 108 S. Ct. 2667
   10 *Cardozo Arts & Ent. L.J.* 101-25 '91
National Football League; Powell v., 888 F.2d 559
   8 *U. Miami Ent. & Sports L. Rev.* 121-39 Spr '91
National Solid Wastes Management Ass'n & Chem. Waste Management, Inc. v. Alabama Dep't of Envtl. Management, 910 F.2d 713
   37 *Loy. L. Rev.* 189-203 Spr '91
   64 *Temp. L. Rev.* 1141-59 Wint '91
   12 *Whittier L. Rev.* 635-74 '91
National Spa & Pool Inst., Inc.; King v., 570 So. 2d

> When you know that a particular case deals with the subject under research, *e.g., Mu'Min v. Virginia,* citations to law review notes written about the case can be located in the Table of Cases section of the *Index to Legal Periodicals.* Other issues and volumes of *ILP* should be consulted for additional notes on the same case.

   18 *Pepp. L. Rev.* 828-31 Ap '91

N

N.D. McLennan, Ltd.; Pink Panther Food Corp. v., 75 O.R.2d 651
   13 *Advoc. Q.* 264-72 O '91
N.N. v. Moraine Mut. Ins. Co., 450 N.W.2d 445 (Wis.)
   1991 *Wis. L. Rev.* 139-73 '91
Nabors; United States v., 901 F.2d 1351
   8 *Cooley L. Rev.* 411-23 '91
Nace; Commonwealth v., 571 A.2d 1389 (Pa.)
   64 *Temp. L. Rev.* 267-79 Spr '91
Napa Valley Wine Train, Inc. v. Public Utils. Comm'n, 787 P.2d 976 (Cal.)
   18 *Pepp. L. Rev.* 762-77 Ap '91
Napier City Council; Woolworths (NZ), Ltd. v., [1991] B.C.L. 782
   1991 *N.Z. L.J.* 380-1 N '91
NASA; New York Times Co. v., 920 F.2d 1002
   1991 *Duke L.J.* 753-801 Je '91
   19 *W. St. U. L. Rev.* 325-43 Fall '91
NASCO, Inc.; Chambers v., 111 S. Ct. 2123 (1991)
   105 *Harv. L. Rev.* 349-60 N '91
   37 *Loy. L. Rev.* 1043-55 Wint '92
   66 *Tul. L. Rev.* 591-603 D '91
   14 *U. Ark. Little Rock L.J.* 107-23 Fall '91
Nash Finch, Inc.; Stoner v., 446 N.W.2d 747 (N.D.)
   67 *N.D. L. Rev.* 541-52 '91
Nason Hosp.; Thompson v., 591 A.2d 703 (Pa.)
   30 *Duq. L. Rev.* 639-60 Spr '92
Nassif; City of Bismarck v., 449 N.W.2d 789 (N.D.)
   67 *N.D. L. Rev.* 123-53 '91
Nate Leasing Co. v. Wiggins, 789 P.2d 89 (Wash.)
   16 *Tul. Mar. L.J.* 213-24 Fall '91
National Audubon Soc'y; Edwards v., 556 F.2d 113
   20 *Cap. U. L. Rev.* 471-96 Spr '91
   86 *Nw. U. L. Rev.* 417-52 Wint '92
   65 *St. John's L. Rev.* 731-41 Summ '91
National Australia Bank, Ltd.; Bond Brewing Holdings, Ltd. v., [1990] 1 A.C.S.R. 445
   107 *Law Q. Rev.* 551-5 O '91

National Trust Co. v. Mead, 71 D.L.R.4th 488
   70 *Can. B. Rev.* 359-80 Je '91
   55 *Sask. L. Rev.* 429-40 '91
National Union Fire Ins. Co.; Aaron v., 876 F.2d 1157
   16 *Tul. Mar. L.J.* 235-50 Fall '91
National Union Fire Ins. Co.; Foster v., 902 F.2d 1316
   44 *Ark. L. Rev.* 865-93 '91
National Wildlife Fed'n; Lujan v., 110 S. Ct. 3177 (1990)
   54 *Alb. L. Rev.* 863-930 '90
   5 *B.Y.U. J. Pub. L.* 217-33 '91
   40 *Cath. U. L. Rev.* 443-74 Wint '91
   24 *Conn. L. Rev.* 293-361 Fall '91
   18 *Ecology L.Q.* 335-404 '91
   5 *J. Envtl. L. & Litig.* 99-126 '90
   68 *N.D. L. Rev.* 1-70 '92
   23 *Pac. L.J.* 223-66 O '91
   3 *Pace Y.B. Int'l L.* 363-94 '91
   62 *U. Colo. L. Rev.* 933-56 '91
   39 *U. Kan. L. Rev.* 997-1043 Summ '91
   66 *Wash. L. Rev.* 893-912 Jl '91
Nationwide; Cone v., 551 N.E.2d 92 (N.Y.)
   12 *Pace L. Rev.* 199-226 Wint '92
Native Village of Noatak; Blatchford v., 111 S. Ct. 2578
   26 *Val. U. L. Rev.* 639-69 Spr '92
Natural Resources Defense Council, Inc.; Chevron, U.S.A., Inc. v., 104 S. Ct. 2778 (1984)
   32 *B.C. L. Rev.* 757-834 Jl '91
   10 *Rev. Litig.* 695-712 Summ '91
   60 *UMKC L. Rev.* 27-66 Fall '91
   1991 *Wis. L. Rev.* 1275-99 '91
   101 *Yale L.J.* 969-1041 Mr '92
Natwest Wholesale Australia Pty., Ltd.; Gamer's Motor Centre (Newcastle) Pty., Ltd. v., [1987] 163 C.L.R. 236
   19 *Austl. Bus. L. Rev.* 261-80 Ag '91
Navarro; Skyywalker Records, Inc. v., 739 F. Supp. 578
   11 *Loy. LA. Ent. L.J.* 623-55 '91
   44 *Okla. L. Rev.* 513-35 Fall '91
   17 *T. Marshall L. Rev.* 113-46 Fall '91
NBC; Newton v., 913 F.2d 652
   22 *Golden Gate U. L. Rev.* 235-61 Spr '92
   11 *Loy. LA. Ent. L.J.* 717-48 '91
NCAA; Banks v., 746 F. Supp. 850
   20 *Cap. U. L. Rev.* 643-59 Summ '91
Near v. Minnesota, 51 S. Ct. 625
   13 *Comm. & L.* 43-59 Je '91

[Illustration 141]

PAGE FROM BOOK REVIEWS—INDEX TO LEGAL PERIODICALS

BOOK REVIEWS

The 1993 EC VAT system. 1992
    1993 *Brit. Tax Rev.* 180-2 '93. R. Pincher

A

Ackerman, B. A. The future of liberal revolution. 1992
    106 *Harv. L. Rev.* 1364-9 Ap '93
Ackerman, B. A. We the people. 1991
    1992 *B.Y.U. L. Rev.* 1035-54 '92. R. Berger
    26 *Ind. L. Rev.* 677-90 '93. J. W. Torke
Appleby, J. O. Liberalism and republicanism in the historical imagination. 1992
    10 *Const. Commentary* 258-66 Wint '93. C. Ward
Arnold, T. and others. Patent alternative dispute resolution handbook. 1991
    9 *Santa Clara Computer & High Tech. L.J.* 397-401 Mr '93. N. Yeend

B

Bakken, G. M. Practicing law in frontier California. 1991
    37 *Am. J. Legal Hist.* 96-100 Ja '93. V. A. Saker
Bell, D. A. Faces at the bottom of the well. 1992
    106 *Harv. L. Rev.* 1358-63 Ap '93
    45 *Stan. L. Rev.* 1133-60 Ap '93. R. Delgado
Bergh, G. C. J. J. van den. The life and work of Gerard Noodt, 1647-1725. 1988
    37 *Am. J. Legal Hist.* 106-8 Ja '93. A. J. Schmidt
Bodenhamer, D. J. Fair trial. 1991

Bou~~~ ~~~
or~~~

Burt~~~

~~~Zo Suffolk U. L. Rev. 925-33 Fall '92. P. G. Lannon, Jr.

> Each issue of *ILP* has a separate Book Reviews section. All books that have been reviewed in an issue are in one alphabet listing the book's author and the book's title.

C

Canadian perspective on legal theory. 1991
    6 *Can. J.L. Juris.* 175-8 Ja '93. J. E. Bickenbach
Carter, S. L. Reflections of an affirmative action baby. 1991
    10 *Const. Commentary* 211-17 Wint '93. D. R. Ortiz
Coquillette, D. R. The civilian writers of Doctors' Commons, London. 1988
    37 *Am. J. Legal Hist.* 106-8 Ja '93. A. J. Schmidt
Cornell, D. Beyond accommodation. 1991
    15 *Sydney L. Rev.* 101-11 Mr '93. P. Cheah
Cornell, D. The philosophy of the limit. 1992
    6 *Can. J.L. Juris.* 169-74 Ja '93. C. B. Gray
Corporate law in Canada. 2nd ed. 1991
    21 *Can. Bus. L.J.* 473-80 Mr '93. J. A. VanDuzer
The Critical lawyers' handbook. 1992
    14 *Liverpool L. Rev.* 215-21 '92. S. E. Salako

D

De Grazia, E. Girls lean back everywhere. 1992
    4 *Cardozo Stud. L. & Lit.* 289-304 Fall '92. Y. Hachamovitch
Drumbeat. 1989
    6 *Can. J. Women & L.* 215-18 '93. C. Rhinelander

E

Easterbrook, F. H. and Fischel, D. R. The economic structure of corporate law. 1991
    61 *Geo. Wash. L. Rev.* 272-98 N '92. F. S. McChesney
    24 *J. Mar. L. & Com.* 243-5 Ja '93. J. P. McMahon
The Economic and Commercial Implications of the Entry into Force of the Hamburg Rules and the Multimodal Transport Convention. 1991
Ellickson, R. C. Order without law. 1991
    81 *Cal. L. Rev.* 417-29 Ja '93. R. D. Cooter

    102 *Yale L.J.* 1787-801 My '93. B. Yngvesson
Ely, J. W. The guardian of every other right. 1992
    10 *Const. Commentary* 238-46 Wint '93. C. M. Rose
Enough is enough. 1987
    6 *Can. J. Women & L.* 211-14 '93. M. E. Turpel

F

Fishkin, J. S. Democracy and deliberation. 1991
    10 *Const. Commentary* 194-202 Wint '93. M. Fitts
Fritz, C. G. Federal justice in California. 1991
    37 *Am. J. Legal Hist.* 96-100 Ja '93. V. A. Saker

G

Gates, J. B. The Supreme Court and partisan realignment. 1992
    10 *Const. Commentary* 254-7 Wint '93. F. J. Sorauf
Gattini, A. Zufall und force majeure im System der Staatenverantwortlichkeit   anhand   der ILC-Kodifikationsarbeit. 1991
    87 *Am. J. Int'l L.* 339-41 Ap '93. C. Gray
Gelbspan, R. Break-ins, death threats, and the FBI. 1991
    20 *Am. J. Crim. L.* 177-90 Fall '92. W. Long
Goldstein, J. The intelligible Constitution. 1992
    10 *Const. Commentary* 167-74 Wint '93. T. E. Baker
Goldstein, P. Copyright. 1989
    9 *U. Miami Ent. & Sports L. Rev.* 297-9 Fall '92. I. F. Jacobson

Gore, A., Jr. Earth in the balance. 1992
    102 *Yale L.J.* 1719-61 My '93. R. W. Hahn
Gorton, L. and Ihre, R. A practical guide to contracts of affreightment and hybrid contracts. 2nd ed. 1990
    24 *J. Mar. L. & Com.* 246-7 Ja '93. R. Harris
Graber, M. A. Transforming free speech. 1991
    10 *Const. Commentary* 247-53 Wint '93. N. L. Rosenberg
Gray, C. S. House of cards. 1992
    7 *Emory Int'l L. Rev.* 249-57 Spr '93. B. L. McNamee
Greene, T. and Flexner, S. B. The language of the Constitution. 1991
    10 *Const. Commentary* 277-9 Wint '93. S. Thorpe

H

Hacker, A. Two nations. 1992
    81 *Cal. L. Rev.* 387-415 Ja '93. R. Delgado
Hall, K. and Rise, E. W. From local courts to national tribunals. 1991
    37 *Am. J. Legal Hist.* 91-2 Ja '93. J. E. Fennelly
Horwitz, M. J. The transformation of American law, 1870-1960. 1992
    106 *Harv. L. Rev.* 1332-51 Ap '93. J. T. Kloppenberg
Huber, P. W. Galileo's revenge. 1991
    21 *Hofstra L. Rev.* 183-204 Fall '92. J. L. Lewin
Human rights in cross-cultural perspectives. 1992
    87 *Am. J. Int'l L.* 345-8 Ap '93. D. L. Donoho

J

Jankowski, M. S. Islands in the street. 1991
    20 *Am. J. Crim. L.* 191-3 Fall '92. S. Calcote
Justice, ethics, and New Zealand society. 1992
    23 *Vict. U. Wellington L. Rev.* 11-17 F '93. I. Macduff

K

Kahlenberg, R. D. Broken contract. 1992
    73 *B.U. L. Rev.* 121-37 Ja '93. J. W. Barnard

[Illustration 142]

PAGE FROM SUBJECT INDEX—CURRENT LAW INDEX

[Illustration 143]

PAGE FROM AUTHOR/TITLE INDEX—CURRENT LAW INDEX

HOLTHOUSE, PHILIP J.   AUTHOR/TITLE INDEX

HOLTHOUSE, Philip J.
A hazardous ruling: the Service denies deductibility of asbestos mitigation costs.
20 Journal of Real Estate Taxation 261-268 Spring '93

HOLYOAK, Jon
Negligence in Building: Cases and Commentary. by Jon Holyoak rev by A.H. Hudson grade B
9 Professional Negligence 46(2) March '93

HOMBS, Mary Ellen
Recent developments affecting homeless people. (Thirteenth Annual Review of Poverty Law)
26 Clearinghouse Review 1205-1210 Jan '93
Homeless Young People in Scotland. rev by Richard Mays grade B   SCOLAG 63-64 April 30 '93

HONEYBALL, Simon
Employment Rights in Britain and Europe. rev by Simon Honeyball grade C
20 International Journal of the Sociology of the Law 363-364 Dec '92

HONNOLD, John O.
Ocean carriers and cargo; clarity and fairness - Hague or Hamburg?
24 Journal of Maritime Law and Commerce 75-109 Jan '93

HONORE, Tony
Honore's South African Law of Trust, 4th ed. by Tony Honore and Edwin Cameron rev by David M. Maclean grade B
67 Australian Law Journal 235-236 March '93
Justinian's codification: some reflections.
25 Bracton Law Journal 29-37 Annual '93
Honore's South African Law of Trust, 4th ed.

HORSFALL, Jan
The Presence of the Past: Male Violence in the Family. by Jan Horsfall rev by Ann Munster grade B
21 Journal of Criminal Justice 204-205 March-April '93

HORTEN, Monica
Technology briefing. (electronic communication software package called Notes) (United Kingdom)
137 Solicitors Journal 282(1) March 26 '93

HORVATH, Vivian
Bruce v. Legal Aid Board: legal aid - specialist providing welfare benefits advice to solicitor and his client. (United Kingdom)
23 Family Law 69-70 Feb '93
Croydon London Borough Council v. A (No. 3): care order - supervision order. (United Kingdom)
23 Family Law 70-72 Feb '93
Godwin v. Uzoigwe: child - defendants in loco parentis to child when brought into the jurisdiction. (United Kingdom)   *23 Family Law 65-66 Feb '93*
S v. Oxfordshire County Council. (United Kingdom)
23 Family Law 74-75 Feb '93

HORWITZ, Morton J.
The Transformation of American Law: 1870-1960, The Crisis of Legal Orthodoxy. by Morton J. Horwitz rev by James T. Kloppenberg grade B
106 Harvard Law Review 1332-1351 April '93

HORWOOD, Richard M.
Planning strategies when a client's death is imminent.
20 Estate Planning 168-174 May-June '93

HOSAY, Cynthia K.
National health care reform needed - but what kind?

HOWELL, Rosemary
Reducing overheads: make staff cuts a last resort. (New South Wales)
31 Law Society Journal 27(1) March '93

HOWELL, T.
Conflict Among Nations. by T. Howell rev by Edwin Vermulst grade A
30 Common Market Law Review 202-207 Feb '93

HUBBARD, Catherine
Are huge tax increases the way to balance the budget?   *59 Tax Notes 321-322 April 19 '93*
Facing complaints, Rostenkowski is committed to passing Clinton plan. (Dan Rostenkowski)
59 Tax Notes 11-15 April 5 '93

HUBER, Peter W.
Galileo's Revenge: Junk Science in the Courtroom. by Peter W. Huber rev by Michael A. McDermott grade A
7 Harvard Journal of Law & Technology 207-211 Fall '92
Galileo's Revenge: Junk Science in the Courtroom. by Peter W. Huber rev by Jeff L. Lewin grade A
21 Hofstra Law Review 183-204 Fall '92

HUBER, Stephen K.
International Efforts to Combat Money Laundering. rev by Stephen K. Huber grade A
27 International Lawyer 243-246 Spring '93

HUBER, William F.
Consolidated return prop. regs. revise income allocation and excess loss account rules. (part 2)
78 The Journal of Taxation 146-151 March '93

rev

HOO   '93
(/
HOO   ohn
R

A typical page from the Author/Title section of *Current Law Index*. This section serves as an index to articles by author and also as an index to book reviews. Note the following:

HOO
Bi

1. Authors are listed alphabetically with the complete title and citation.

2. Book reviews are listed under both the author and title of the book. Books are rated A–F according to the opinion of the reviewer.

HOP   Jan
'93

Stephanopoulos: VAT under consideration for health care reform. (George Stephanopoulos, value added tax) (Brief Article)
59 Tax Notes 393-394 April 19 '93
Clinton officially releases budget. (1994 budget)
59 Tax Notes 151-152 April 12 '93
House and Senate agree on budget; cap on itemized deductions out.   *59 Tax Notes 7(1) April 5 '93*
Senate adopts budget; Clinton will exempt ethanol from Btu tax.
58 Tax Notes 1687-1688 March 29 '93

HOPPER, Brett L.
The selling real estate broker and the purchaser: assessing the relationship.
1992 Brigham Young University Law Review 1135-1153 Fall '92

HORIGUCHI, Wataru
Securities malfeasance in Japan: the need for an independent organization to monitor insider trading, price manipulation, and loss compensation. (Nihon-Hastings Pacific Rim Conference)
16 Hastings International and Comparative Law Review 223-229 Wntr '93

HORN, Michael S.
New regulation allows existing export manufacturing facilities to become special customs zones. (Indonesia)
15 East Asian Executive Reports 8(3) April 15 '93

HORN, Norbert
Das Zivil -und Wirtschaftsrecht im neuen Bundesgebiet. by Norbert Horn rev by Joachim Rosengarten grade B
40 American Journal of Comparative Law 751-755 Summer '92

HORNE, William W.
What' sex got to do with it? The sexual harassment charges surrounding former Morgan Stanley GC Philip Lacovara are dubious at best. It was his assault on the firm's powerful bankers that proved his real undoing.
15 American Lawyer 42(10 ① 3

HORNIG, Christopher
May HUD give away what it doesn't own? (Public Housing Authorities and HOPE, part 1) (Homeownership and Opportunity for People Everywhere Programs)
25 The Urban Lawyer 69-95 Wntr '93

HORNSBY, William E.
States revamp their advertising rules - most carry more restrictions.
62 The Journal of the Kansas Bar Association 19(3) April '93

Commerce. (Natural Resources Issue)
64 University of Colorado Law Review 277-370 Spring '93
Environmental law. (Fifth Circuit Symposium)
38 Loyola Law Review 775-803 Fall '92

HOUSMAN, Robert F.
Making trade and environmental policies mutually reinforcing: forging competitive sustainability. (Trade and the Environment)
23 Environmental Law 545-573 April '93

HOUSTON, Douglas A.
A losing proposition for customers. (includes related article on Viroqua, Wisconsin) (Demand-side Management) (Cover Story)
131 Public Utilities Fortnightly 17(4) May 1 '93

HOVENKAMP, Herbert
The marginalist revolution in legal thought.
46 Vanderbilt Law Review 305-359 March '93

HOWARD, Brian E.
Spoliation of evidence. (Missouri)
49 Journal of the Missouri Bar 121(12) March-April '93

HOWARD, Hugh
One stop shop now. (Child Support Agency) (United Kingdom)
137 Solicitors Journal 295(1; ② '93

HOWARD, Jay M.
When two tax theories collide: a look at the history and future of progressive and proportionate personal income taxation.
32 Washburn Law Journal 43-76 Fall '92

HOWARD, Richard F.
Special education: past, present and future. (Massachusetts)
37 Boston Bar Journal 21(6) March-April '93

HOWARD, Tim
The Carriage of Goods by Sea Act 1992. (United Kingdom)
24 Journal of Maritime Law and Commerce 181-190 Jan '93

HOWARTH, William
'Poisonous, noxious or polluting': contrasting approaches to environmental regulation. (United Kingdom)
56 Modern Law Review 171-187 March '93

HOWE, Scott W.
Jury fact-finding in criminal cases: constitutional limits on factual disagreements among convicting jurors.   *58 Missouri Law Review 1-83 Wntr '93*

HOWELL, Jean
The priority of dealings with equitable interest in land: section 137 of the Law of Property Act 1925 or registration? (United Kingdom)
Conveyancer and Property Lawyer 22-38 Jan-Feb '93

HUFFAKER, John B.
Trustees' disclaimer could not create marital deduction.   *78 The Journal of Taxation 226-227 April '93*
Partial election of special-use valuation allowed.
78 The Journal of Taxation 162(1) March '93
Protective alternate valuation election could be made. (farm property)
78 The Journal of Taxation 158-159 March '93
QSST rules override trust law for sales of S corp. stock. (qualified Subchapter S trust)
78 The Journal of Taxation 159(2) March '93
Rules for valuing partial interests updated.
78 The Journal of Taxation 162-163 March '93

HUGHES, Elaine L.
Environmental offences and vicarious liability. (Canada)
3 Journal of Environmental Law and Practice 105-112 Dec '92

HUGHES, John
Legal and ethical implications of clinical research on human subjects.
22 Cambrian Law Review 5-25 Annual '91

HUGHES, Sarah
International Maritime Conventions. rev by Jonathan Lux and Sarah Hughes grade A
21 International Business Lawyer 147(1) March '93
Human Rights and the European Community: A Critical Overview.
by Andrew Clapham rev by Monika Lahiri grade A
18 The Yale Journal of International Law 442-443 Wntr '93
Human Rights in Cross-Cultural Perspectives: A Quest for Consensus.
by Abdullahi Ahmed Na'im rev by Douglas Lee Donoho grade A
87 American Journal of International Law 345-348 April '93
Human Rights in States of Emergency in International Law.
by Jaime Oraa rev by Robert McCorquodale grade A   *52 Cambridge Law Journal 163-164 March '93*

HUMBACH, John A.
What is behind the 'property rights' debate? (Lucas v. South Carolina Coastal Council: Colloquium)
10 Pace Environmental Law Review 21-42 Fall '92

HUMPHREYS, Gordon
Trading places: the need for reform in international trade dispute resolution.
21 International Business Lawyer 174(3) April '93
An overview of the implications of the Carriage of Goods by Sea Act 1992. (United Kingdom)
Journal of Business Law 61-66 Jan '93

[Illustration 144]

PAGE FROM TABLE OF CASES—CURRENT LAW INDEX

MORRIS, R. V.

TABLE OF CASES

MORPETH Ward Justices, R. v.,
Q.B. Div'l Ct. Feb. 20, 1991 Breach of the peace apprehended - magistrates' power to bind over to keep the peace. (Great Britain)
Criminal Law Review 497-499 July '92

MORRIS, R. v.,
Vict. June 22, 1992 The tax prosecution-led recovery. (Victoria)
21 Australian Tax Review 155-162 Sept '92
Substantial frauds - sentencing. (Victoria)
66 Law Institute Journal 780-781 Sept '92
93 Crim. App. 93 (C.A. 1991) Juror employed by company whose goods were stolen. (Great Britain)
56 Journal of Criminal Law 40-42 Feb '92
1984 A.C. 320 (H.L.) Rethinking appropriation. (Great Britain)
56 Journal of Criminal Law 87-100 Feb '92

MORRIS v. Sullivan,
897 F.2d 553 (D.C. Cir. 1990) The concept of implied reopening: shooting a hole through Califano v. Sanders. *1 The OHA Law Journal 14-19 Nov '90*

MORRISON, Payne v.,
Vict. Apr. 18, 1991 Vendors' statements. (conveyancing) (Victoria)
65 Law Institute Journal 1130-1131 Dec '91

MORRISON v. Olson,
487 U.S. 654 (1988) The structural Constitution: unitary executive, plural judiciary.
105 Harvard Law Review 1153-1216 April '92

MORRISTOWN, Kreimer v.,
958 F.2d 1242 (3d Cir. 1992) Constitutional law - First Amendment - public library may constitutionally deny access to patrons on the basis of personal hygiene. (Case Note)
22 Seton Hall Law Review 1567-1574 Fall '92

MORROW, Watts v.
(1991) 1 W.L.R.
property. (D
2) (Great Bri
8 P
(1991) 4 All E.R.
opportunities

MORTGAGE Servic
The Independent,
mortgage tra

MORTIER, Wiscon
111 S. Ct. 2476
13 Journal

Federal pree
the past, pr
Intervenor v.
11 Virginia Env
'91
Getting the bags out: the role of legislative history in determining the pre-emptive effect of FIFRA upon local regulation of pesticides in Wisconsin Public Intervenor v. Mortier. (Case Note)
15 Hamline Law Review 223-245 Fall '91

MORTON, Carlson v.,
745 P.2d 1133 (Mont. 1987) Ethics and malpractice. (Symposium on Professional Malpractice)
12 Mississippi College Law Review 151-160 Fall '91

MORTON International, Inc. v. Cardinal Chemical Co.,
No. 93-1174 (Fed. Cir. 1992) Morton, the dual loser patentee: frustrating Blonder-Tongue.
74 Journal of the Patent and Trademark Office Society 344(1) May '92

MORTON, R. v.,
Q.B. Div'l Ct. Aug. 23, 1991 Reckless driving - reckless driving not resulting in death - relative gravity in comparison with causing death by reckless driving. (Great Britain)
Criminal Law Review 70-71 Jan '92

MOSER v. DeSetta,
589 A.2d 679 (Pa. 1991) Estates and trusts - inter vivos gifts - mental competence - undue influence - confidential relationship - the burden of proof is initially on the donor to overcome the presumption of mental competence of the donor. (Case Note)
30 Duquesne Law Review 741-759 Spring '92

MOSLEY, Michigan v.,
423 U.S. 96 (1975) Rationale of right to counsel ruling necessitates reversal of Michigan v. Mosley's right to silence ruling. (Case Note)
27 Tulsa Law Journal 181-202 Winter '91

MOTOR Oil Hellas (Corinth) Refineries S.A. v. Shipping Corp. of India,
(1990) 1 Lloyd's Rep. 391 (H.L.) Waiver (of contractual rights) distributed. (Australia) (Great Britain)
4 Journal of Contract Law 59-74 March '91

MOUNT Isa Mines Ltd., Commissioner of Taxation v.,
91 A.T.C. 4154 (Austl. Fed. Ct. 1990) The treatment of demolition expenses under the Income Tax: the Mount Isa Mines case. (Australia)
13 Sydney Law Review 605-619 Dec '91

MOUNTAIN States Telephone & Telegraph Co. v. Garfield County,
811 P.2d 184 (Utah 1991) Upholding the constitutionality of Utah's Uniform Tax Rule. (Recent Developments in Utah Law) (Case Note)
1992 Utah Law Review 208-221 Wntr '92

1796

MOZERT v. Hawkins County Public Schools,
827 F.2d 1058 (6th Cir. 1987) Reasoning and results. (response to Hugh Breyer, Journal of Law and Education, vol. 20, p. 63, 1991)
21 The Journal of Law and Education 443(1) Summer '92
Mozert v. Hawkins County Public Schools, the Supreme Court, and Mr. Breyer: a comment. (response to Hugh Breyer, Journal of Law and Education, vol. 20, p. 63, 1991)
21 The Journal of Law and Education 445-452 Summer '92

MUEHLINS, Corgan v.,
574 N.E.2d 602 (Ill. 1991) Negligent infliction of emotional distress in air crash cases: a new flight path? (Illinois)
70 Washington University Law Quarterly 935-957 Fall '92

MUELLER Brass Co. v. Reading Industries,
352 F. Supp. 1357 (E.D Pa 1972) The muddy metaphysics of joint inventorship: cleaning up after the 1984 amendments to 35 U.S.C. s. 116.
5 Harvard Journal of Law & Technology 153-208 Spring '92

MUGLER v. Kansas,
123 U.S. 623 (1887) Back to basics: the South Carolina Supreme Court returns to the Mugler v. Kansas era of regulatory takings doctrine. (Case Note)
12 Journal of Energy Natural Resources & Environmental Law 237-259 Fall '92

MULDOON v. Herron,
1970 S.L.T. 228 (Sess.) Remembrance of things past. (corroboration of identity) (Scotland)
Scots Law Times 9(5) Jan 17 '92

MULHOLLAND v. United States,

The Table of Cases in the *Current Law Index* lists all cases commented on in articles in the reviews indexed and gives the citation of the case and full title of the case note. Again, note the case of *Mu'Min v. Virginia.*

All citations in *CLI*, plus additional citations, are in *Legal Resource Index* and LEGALTRAC. *Legal Resource Index* is available on WESTLAW, LEXIS, and other online services.

Souter.
11 Glendale Law Review 101-119 Wntr-Summer '92

MULLIKIN v. United States,
No. 90-6456 (6th Cir. Dec. 30, 1991) Penalty may be assessed at any time; IRS not limited by general assessment period.
8 Tax Management Financial Planning Journal 106-107 March 17 '92
6th Cir. Dec. 30, 1991 Split on S/L for aiding and abetting penalty.
76 The Journal of Taxation 202(1) April '92
69 A.F.T.R.2d (P-H) 92-376 (6th Cir. 1991) A gallows in the town square? Recent cases cast light on new taxpayer and return preparer penalty regs.
54 Tax Notes 573-576 Feb 3 '92

MU'MIN v. Virginia,
111 S. Ct. 1899 (1991) The Supreme Court's failure to establish adequate judicial procedures to counter the prejudicial effects of pretrial publicity. (Case Note)
23 Loyola University of Chicago Law Journal 557-579 Spring '92
Constitutional law - Sixth Amendment and Fourteenth Amendment - as a part of proper voir dire procedure, a criminal defendant may request that jurors reveal whether they have been exposed to any pretrial publicity surrounding the case. (Case Note)
69 University of Detroit Mercy Law Review 443-457 Spring '92
Sixth Amendment - the right to an impartial jury: how extensive must voir dire questioning be? (Supreme Court Review) (Case Note)
82 Journal of Criminal Law and Criminology 920-954 Wntr '92
Constitutional law - voir dire - a trial court's refusal to question prospective jurors about the specific contents of pretrial publicity which they had read or heard did not violate a defendant's Sixth Amendment right to an impartial jury, or Fourteenth Amendment to due process. (Case Note)
23 St. Mary's Law Journal 541-561 Fall '91
Sixth and Fourteenth Amendments do not compel content questions in assessing juror impartiality. (Case Note)
25 Akron Law Review 479-496 Fall '91

MUNGHOO v. The Queen,
(1991) 1 W.L.R 1351 (P.C.) Right to hearing within a reasonable time. (Mauritius, Great Britain)
56 Journal of Criminal Law 168-170 May '92

MUNICIPAL Court, Johnetta J. v.,
281 Cal. App. 3d 1255 (1990) Testing the hand that bites you: mandatory AIDS testing, and the Fourth Amendment. (Case Note)
11 Northern Illinois University Law Review 445-479 Spring-Summer '91

MUNIZ, Pennsylvania v.,
110 L. Ed. 528 (1990) 'Walking the line' between testimonial and real evidence with videotaped drunk drivers. (Case Note)
13 Criminal Justice Journal 357-366 Spring '92

MUNOZ, Norwood Hospital v.,
564 N.E.2d 1017 (Mass. 1991) Constitutional law - potential abandonment of minor child curtails adult's right to refuse life-saving medical treatment. (Case Note)
25 Suffolk University Law Review 821-828 Fall '91

MUNSINGWEAR, Inc., United States v.,
310 U.S. 34 (1950) On mootness, mergers, and misreading Munsingwear. (antitrust)
38 Federal Bar News & Journal 517-521 Nov-Dec '91

MURAKAMI, Adams v.,
813 P.2d 1348 (Cal. 1991) New judicially made rules affecting punitive damages in California. (Case Note)
25 Loyola of Los Angeles Law Review 1441-1481 June '92

MURPHY ex rel. K.H. v. Morgan,
914 F.2d 846 (7th Cir. 1990) Constitutional law - limitations on section 1983 protection for foster children. (Case Note)
25 Suffolk University Law Review 789-796 Fall '91

MURPHY, R. v.,
Vict. Ct. Crim. App. Apr. 7, 1992 Parties' failure to call
te Journal 571(2) July '92
uncil,
steps forward or one step
ads in Canada. (Sympos-
in the Law of Economic
Journal 164-179 May '92
the consumer protection
ntwood District Council)
tudies 112-128 Spring '92
ruction industry. (Great
egligence 86-87 June '91
for the construction
egligence 91-93 June '91
professional liability in
y. (Great Britain)
7 Professional Negligence 94-98 June '91
Concurrent liability after Murphy. (Great Britain)
7 Professional Negligence 20-22 March '91

MURPHY v. ISKCON of New England, Inc.,
571 N.E.2d 340 (Mass. 1991) Murphy v. I.S.K.Con. of New England, Inc. and intentional infliction of emotional distress: an alternative analysis under the free speech clause. (Case Note)
25 Loyola of Los Angeles Law Review 1409-1440 June '92
Constitutional law. - introduction of evidence of religious organization's scriptural text to support a child and mother's claims of intentional infliction of emotional distress and mother's claim in intentional interference with parental rights violated religious organization's constitutional right to free exercise of religion under the first amendment of the United States. (Case Note)
30 Journal of Family Law 687-693 May '92

MURRAY-GOULBURN Co-Operative, New South Wales Dairy Corp. v.,
171 C.L.R. 363 (Austl. 1991) Moove: the experiment that went wrong.
82 Trademark Reporter 341-408 May-June '92

MURRAY, Jones v.,
489 U.S. 602 (1989) Allowing the government to get blood from a stone. (search and seizure) (Case Note)
42 Case Western Reserve Law Review 635-657 Wntr '92

MURRAY, R. v.,
N.S.W. Ct. Crim. App. Apr. 6, 1992 Riotous assembly - inconsistent verdicts - summing up - general principles - judicial intervention in defences cross-examination - admissibility - doctrine of completeness. (New South Wales)
16 Criminal Law Journal 273-276 August '92

MURRAY v. City of Austin,
947 F.2d 147 (5th Cir. 1991) No stamp of approval. Austin's city seal and the establishment clause. (religious symbol in municipal seal) (Case Note)
12 Mississippi College Law Review 513-531 Spring '92

MURRAY v. Giarratano,
109 S. Ct. 2765 (1989) Execution of the unrepresented. (Case Note)
17 New England Journal on Criminal & Civil Confinement 211-231 Wntr '91

[Illustration 145]

PAGE FROM VOLUME 58—MISSOURI LAW REVIEW

MISSOURI
LAW REVIEW

VOLUME 58	WINTER 1993	NUMBER 1

Jury Fact-Finding in Criminal Cases: Constitutional Limits on Factual Disagreements Among Convicting Jurors

Scott W. Howe[*]

I. INTRODUCTION

Criminal juries have an uncertain task. While we tout their constitutional role[1] in our justice system as the central fact finder[2], we are unsure about their fact- | A typical leading article from a law school law review. | factual specificit[ ] e hand, we do not expect juries to reach a collective vision of past events in perfect detail. Jurors legitimately may find guilt though they disagree on the precise

---

[*] Associate Professor, Western New England College, School of Law; A.B., 1977, University of Missouri; J.D., 1981, University of Michigan.

I am indebted to Howard I. Kalodner, Dean, Western New England College, School of Law, for institutional and financial support, to Catherine Jones, Anne Goldstein and Randy Coyne for valuable comments on earlier drafts and to Barbara Falvo for secretarial and technical assistance.

1. The Sixth Amendment provides: "In all criminal prosecutions, the accused shall enjoy the right to a speedy and public trial, by an impartial jury of the State and district wherein the crime shall have been committed . . . ." U.S. CONST. amend. VI. The Supreme Court has held this requirement of jury trial applicable to the states through the Fourteenth Amendment. *See* Duncan v. Louisiana, 391 U.S. 145, 156 (1968).

The Seventh Amendment provides: "In Suits at common law, where the value in controversy shall exceed twenty dollars, the right of trial by jury shall be preserved, and no fact tried by a jury, shall be otherwise reexamined in any Court of the United States, than according to the rules of the common law." U.S. CONST. amend. VII. This provision is not applicable to the states through the Fourteenth Amendment. *See* Minneapolis & St. Louis R.R. v. Bombolis, 241 U.S. 211, 211 (1916); Walker v. Sauvinet, 92 U.S. 90, 93 (1876); Melancon v. McKeithen, 345 F. Supp. 1025, 1048 (E.D. La. 1972), *aff'd*, 409 U.S. 943 (1973).

2. Criminal juries are more than fact finders. Through their accepted authority to "nullify" a criminal law—to exonerate an indisputably guilty defendant—criminal jurors become judges of law itself. *See generally* Alan Scheflin & Jon Van Dyke, *Jury Nullification: The Contours of a Controversy*, 43 LAW & CONTEMP. PROBS., Autumn 1980, at 51. Yet, our unwillingness to tell jurors of this nullification power reveals ambivalence over the role of criminal jurors as lawmakers. *See id.* at 53-56.

[Illustration 146]

PAGE FROM VOLUME 23—ST. MARY'S LAW JOURNAL

CONSTITUTIONAL LAW—Voir Dire—A Trial Court's Refusal to Question Prospective Jurors About the Specific Contents of Pretrial Publicity Which They Had Read or Heard Did Not Violate a Defendant's Sixth Amendment Right to an Impartial Jury, or Fourteenth Amendment Right to Due Process.

Mu'Min v. Virginia, 500 U.S. __,
111 S. Ct. 1899, 114 L. Ed. 2d 493 (1991).

Dawud Majid Mu'Min escaped from a prison work detail[1] and went to a nearby shopping center where he murdered a store owner.[2] Substantial publicity preceded his trial, and on voir dire, eight of twelve venirepersons said

> A typical law review student note. The purpose of student notes or comments is to promote critical analysis of recent cases or topics of law.

heard about the case.[4] However, all of the jurors collectively swore they could be impartial.[5] After the trial court found Mu'Min guilty of capital murder,[6] he appealed claiming that the judge's preclusion of proposed voir

---

1. *Mu'Min v. Virginia*, 500 U.S. __, __, 111 S. Ct. 1899, 1901, 114 L. Ed. 2d 493, 501 (1991). Mu'Min was an inmate at the Haymarket Correctional Unit in Virginia serving a sentence of forty-eight years for first degree murder. He was assigned to the Virginia Department of Transportation (VDOT) on work detail supervised by an employee of VDOT. *Id.*

2. *Id.* After stepping over a small perimeter fence Mu'Min walked about a mile to a retail carpet store, where he asked the store owner about prices of oriental carpets. According to Mu'Min, they argued about prices and the store owner called him "nigger," spit in his face, and kicked him in the genitals. *Mu'Min v. Virginia*, 389 S.E.2d 886, 890 (Va. 1990), *aff'd*, 500 U.S __, 111 S. Ct. 1899, 114 L. Ed. 2d 493 (1991).

3. *Mu'Min*, 500 U.S. at __, 111 S. Ct. at 1902-03, 114 L. Ed. 2d at 502-03. Over forty-seven newspaper articles were submitted to the trial court in support of a motion for a change of venue. These articles included discussions of Mu'Min's alleged confession of murder, his rejection for parole six times, and alleged prison infractions. *Id.* at __, 111 S. Ct. at 1901, 114 L. Ed. 2d at 501.

4. *Id.* at __, 111 S. Ct. at 1902-03, 114 L. Ed. 2d at 502-03 (1991). *See* FED. R. CRIM. P. 24(a) (voir dire to be conducted as trial court "deems proper").

5. *Mu'Min*, 500 U.S. at __, 111 S. Ct. at 1903, 114 L. Ed. 2d at 503. Potential jurors were asked specific questions as to their ability to remain impartial and the judge removed four venirepersons for cause. *Id.*

6. *Id.* At the time, the Virginia Code § 18.2-31 defined Capital murder, punishable as a class one felony, as:

  (c) The willful, deliberate and premeditated killing of any person by a prisoner confined in a state or local correctional facility as defined in 53.1-1, or while in the custody of an employee thereof;

[Illustration 147]

PAGE FROM VOLUME 54—TEXAS BAR JOURNAL

C R I M I N A L   E V I D E N C E

Inquiring Jurors Want to Know: Can We Ask Questions?

By David Schlueter

This is a typical page from a state bar journal. Articles are usually brief, practitioner-oriented, and consider matters of contemporary interest.

Judge: Ladies and gentlemen of the jury. As I previously instructed you, if you have any questions for this witness you should write them out on the pieces of paper provided to you and pass them to the bailiff. I will then rule on the legality of the questions and if they are all right I will read the question to the witness.

Counsel: Your honor, we renew our objection to this entire procedure. Neither the Rules of Criminal Evidence nor the Code of Criminal Procedure address this matter.

Judge: Your objection is overruled, counsel.

Is the judge correct? May jurors ask questions of the witnesses? The jury is supposed to be a "fact-finder." Can it also be a "fact-getter"? According to recent caselaw, the jury may be permitted to submit questions to witnesses.

In *Allen v. State*[1] and *Buchanan v. State*[2] the Houston Court of Appeals concluded that the trial judge did not commit error in permitting the jurors to submit questions to the witnesses. In each case the trial judge

gave preliminary instructions to the jury concerning the procedure for submission of questions and cautioned them to keep in mind that counsel had prepared the case with an eye on what was important in the case and, further, not to put a "chilling effect" on their questions. After each witness had finished testifying, the judge asked for any written questions from the jurors who were then excused from the courtroom while counsel made any objections to the questions. If the questions were considered legally admissible, they were read verbatim to the witness, in the presence of the jury, by the trial judge. Counsel were then permitted to ask follow-up questions.

In both *Allen* and *Buchanan* several questions were asked of the prosecution's witnesses. Although defense counsel objected to the procedures used, no objections were lodged to the questions themselves.[3]

Noting that this was an issue of first impression in Texas, the court in *Allen* observed that of those "foreign authorities" which have considered the issue, there was virtual unanimity in approving the practice.[4] In particular, the court drew from the Fifth Circuit's observation that it makes good common sense to permit jurors to ask occasional questions which may clarify a point.[5] The court rejected defense arguments that permitting jurors to ask questions violated Article 36.27 of the Code of Criminal Procedure,[6] that Article 36.01 provided no support for the procedure,[7] and that Article 36.13 only permits the jury to be the exclusive judge of the facts.[8] The court also rejected the argument that the trial judge misdirected the jury as to its function in the trial. Judge Ellis dissented in both cases, noting that the process impermissibly relieved the prosecution of establishing the defendant's guilt beyond a reasonable doubt.[9]

As noted by the court, Rule of Criminal Evidence 610(a) gives the judge flexibility in controlling the mode of interrogating witnesses.[10] Nonetheless, the practice of permitting the jury to question witnesses has its pitfalls. Using the procedures outlined in the *Allen* and *Buchanan* cases, the following points may help avoid those pitfalls.

First, as with questions from the bench, questions from the jury should not be permitted if it appears that the questioner has become an "advocate." This is a thin line and the case law addressing questions by the bench should be helpful here.[11] The clearest case of permissible questions would probably be those which only seek clarification of testimony given by the witness and do not

explore theories of the case which have not been presented by either side.

Second, the jury should not be informed which counsel objected to the question nor the basis of the objection.[12]

Third, the questions should be written, preferably marked as court or appellate exhibits, and included with the record of trial.

Finally, the judge should read the questions to the witness. This form of *indirect* questioning provides the trial judge with control over the process, not only in determining beforehand the appropriateness of the question, but also in preventing direct confrontations between the witness and the juror who asked the question.[13]

---

1. 807 S.W.2d 639 (Tex. App. — Houston [14th Dist.] 1991).
2. 807 S.W.2d 644 (Tex. App. — Houston [14th Dist.] 1991).
3. 807 S.W.2d at 642; 807 S.W.2d at 645.
4. The *Allen* opinion contains a list of jurisdictions which have considered, and approved of the process (807 S.W.2d at 640-641). The court noted that the Court of Criminal Appeals had not condemned the practice but had observed that the practice would not appear harmful or improper when no objection had been made by the defendant. *Carr v. State*, 475 S.W.2d 755, 757 (Tex. Crim. App. 1972).
5. *United States v. Callahan*, 588 F.2d 1078, 1086 (5th Cir.), *cert. denied*, 444 U.S. 826 (1979).
6. Article 36.27 addresses jurors communicating with the court.
7. Article 36.01 addresses the general order of proceeding in a trial.
8. Article 36.13 simply indicates that the jury is the exclusive judge of the facts.
9. 807 S.W.2d at 642, 807 S.W.2d at 647.
10. *See* Tex. R. Crim. Evid. 610(a).
11. *See, e.g., Delaporte v. Preston Square, Inc.* 680 S.W.2d 561 (Tex. App. — Dallas 1984, writ ref. n.r.e.). *See also* Fed. R. Evid. 614 (Calling and Interrogation of Witnesses by Court).
12. In *Allen*, the judge instructed the jurors that if a question was not permitted they should put the "blame" on him, and not counsel.
13. This point was recognized by the court in *Allen*, 807 S.W.2d 642, and could be particularly important where the question indicates that the juror has abandoned his or her impartiality and is challenging the credibility of the witness.

David Schlueter is a professor of law at St. Mary's University where he teaches evidence and criminal procedure. He received his law degree from Baylor in 1971 and has written and lectured extensively on the topic of evidence.

SECTION D.   OTHER INDEXES TO
PERIODICAL LITERATURE

Several other periodical indexes, less comprehensive than those discussed in Section B, can often be useful in legal research.

1.   Index to Periodical Articles Related to Law

The *Index to Periodical Articles Related to Law* [22] began in 1958 in recognition of the importance that other disciplines have for the law.   It indexes articles of a legal nature in English that, in the judgment of the editors, are of research value and appear in periodicals not covered by the *Index to Legal Periodicals, Index to Foreign Legal Periodicals,* or *Legal Resource Index.*   It is issued quarterly and cumulated annually. Citations are arranged alphabetically by subject, with a separate author index.   A four-volume, thirty-year cumulation covering 1958–1988 consists of a two-volume subject index and a two-volume author index.   A one-volume, five-year cumulation covers 1989–1993.

Since legal subjects are assuming greater prominence in a variety of non-legal journals, this *Index* is particularly valuable in locating timely articles on newly-developing areas that often first appear in non-legal periodicals.   With fifteen or more different periodical indexes being brought together in this publication, it is useful as a companion to the comprehensive legal periodical indexes.

2.   Index to Foreign Legal Periodicals

The *Index to Foreign Legal Periodicals* began in 1960 and is published under auspices of the American Association of Law Libraries.   It covers a wide range of journals and collections of essays dealing with public and private international law, comparative law, and the municipal law of all countries of the world other than the United States, the British Isles, and nations of the British Commonwealth whose legal systems are based on the common law.   Subject headings are in English, but titles of articles using the Roman alphabet are printed in the language of publication.   Titles of articles using an alphabet other than Roman are translated into English, with an indication of the language of publication.   Translations of the English language subject headings are provided in separate sections for the French, German, and Spanish languages.

This *Index* is published quarterly.   Triennial cumulations were published until 1983; since 1984 annual cumulations have been published.   Articles less than four pages and book reviews less than two and one-half pages in length are generally excluded from indexing.

The *Index to Foreign Legal Periodicals* is divided into the following units: (1) subject index; (2) geographical index, grouping—by country or region—the topics of articles listed in the subject index; (3) book review

---

[22] Glanville Publishers, Inc., Dobbs Ferry, NY. 10522.   Edited by Roy M. Mersky, J. Myron Jacobstein, and Donald J. Dunn.

index; and (4) author index. The author index entries refer to the subject index where the citations are complete.

3. Index to Canadian Legal Periodical Literature

This index was started by the Canadian Association of Law Libraries in 1961 to cover the growing number of Canadian legal journals and give access to two systems of law, civil and common, in two languages, English and French. This index covering more than 125 titles is published by Index to Canadian Legal Periodical Literature of Montreal in quarterly and since 1986 in annual cumulative volumes. Four cumulative volumes cover 1961–70, 1971–75, 1976–80, and 1981–85.

4. Legal Journals Index

This index, which began in 1986, includes monthly parts and quarterly cumulations, plus an annual cumulative bound volume. It indexes all items in over 150 British legal journals and is published by Legal Information Sources Ltd. of Wheaton Bridge, England.

5. Current Australian and New Zealand Legal Literature

Published by the Law Book Company of Australia since 1973, this is a quarterly non-cumulating index of Australian and New Zealand legal periodicals.

6. Index to Indian Legal Periodicals

Since 1963 the Indian Law Institute of New Delhi, India, has issued this publication, which indexes periodicals (including yearbooks and other annuals) pertaining to law and related fields published in India. It is issued semi-annually with annual cumulations.

7. Index to Legal Periodicals in Israel

Published by Israel Bar Publishing and edited by Ester Mann Snyder, Director, Bar Ilan University, this publication consists of a bound volume covering 1982–1988 and a 1989–1990 supplement. Additional supplements are planned.

8. Legal Information Management Index

This index (Newton Highlands, Mass.), published since 1984, is issued bimonthly with an annual cumulation. It indexes approximately 120 periodicals published in the United States and abroad, including journals, newsletters, newspapers, and annuals. Substantive English-language articles, bibliographies, surveys, and reviews relating to legal information management and law librarianship are covered. It includes key word, author, and review indexes.

9. Annuals and Surveys Appearing in Legal Periodicals: An Annotated Listing

Begun in 1987, this looseleaf volume is divided into three sections: state surveys; federal court surveys; and subject-specific surveys. Each

listing contains the title of the survey, the name of the publication in which it appears, the author, descriptive notes, and citations. It is supplemented annually and is published by Fred B. Rothman & Company.

SECTION E.   INDEXES TO SPECIAL SUBJECTS

Several indexes provide access to periodical articles on particular legal or law-related subjects. These include:

1.   Index to Federal Tax Articles

This index, published by Warren, Gorham & Lamont, is a computer-produced bibliography first published in 1975. It covers the literature on federal income, estate, and gift taxation contained in legal, tax, and economic journals, as well as non-periodical publications. Consisting of separate subject and author indexes, entries are arranged in reverse chronological order under author's name. Three volumes provide retrospective coverage from 1913 to 1974. Since 1974 articles are in bound volumes, with the most recent articles in quarterly supplements.

2.   Federal Tax Articles

This looseleaf reporter of Commerce Clearing House, Inc. began in 1962 and is updated monthly. It contains summaries of articles on federal taxes (income, estate, gift, and excise) appearing in legal, accounting, business, and related periodicals. Proceedings and papers delivered at major tax institutes are also noted. The contents are arranged by Internal Revenue Code section numbers. Separate author and subject indexes are also provided. Cumulative bound volumes, with coverage dating from 1954, are published periodically to make room for current materials in the looseleaf volume.

3.   Criminal Justice Periodical Index

This quarterly index, published by University Microfilms International, covers over 100 criminal justice and law enforcement periodicals published in the United States, England, and Canada. There is an author index and a subject index, which includes case names.

4.   Kindex

Subtitled, *An Index to Legal Periodical Literature Concerning Children, Kindex* is published by the National Center for Criminal Justice and is issued six times each year with annual cumulations. The indexers emphasize practical information for those involved in the criminal justice system.

5.   Non–Legal Periodical Indexes

Since law impinges on all disciplines, it is sometimes necessary to turn to comprehensive indexes that are non-legal in nature to ascertain general information or to examine legal issues from a non-legal perspec-

tive. There are numerous indexes of this type, and they should not be overlooked when exhaustive research is required. For example, H.W. Wilson Company, publisher of *ILP*, also publishes several non-legal indexes, including the following: *Business Periodicals Index; Humanities Index; Reader's Guide to Periodical Literature*, which covers popular magazines; and *Social Science Index*. *PAIS International*, published by Public Affairs Information Service, Inc., focuses on economics and public affairs and includes several law reviews and government publications in its coverage.

The Information Access Company, publisher of *CLI, LRI*, and LEGALTRAC, also publishes a number of non-legal indexes, including the following: *Academic Index*, which covers scholarly publications from numerous disciplines; *Magazine Index*, an index somewhat comparable to *Reader's Guide; Business Index*, and *Trade and Industry Index*.

SECTION F.   PERIODICAL DIGESTS AND ABSTRACTS

1. Criminology and Penology Abstracts

This is a biweekly international abstracting service covering the etiology of crime and juvenile delinquency, the control and treatment of offenders, criminal procedure, and the administration of justice. Formerly *Excerpta Criminologica* (Volumes 1–8, 1961–68), *Criminology and Penology Abstracts* is prepared by the Criminologica Foundation in cooperation with the University of Leiden, The Hague, Netherlands.

2. Callaghan's Law Review Digest

This bimonthly digest, which began in 1950 and ceased in 1989, contains selected, condensed articles from the legal literature.

3. Monthly Digest of Tax Articles

This monthly periodical by Newkirk Products presents significant current tax articles in abridged form.

SECTION G.   OTHER SOURCES

References to legal periodical articles are frequently found in other reference books. Many state codes and the annotated editions of the *United States Code* cite relevant articles in the notes preceding the annotations. Most of the West digests will, under the Topic and Key number, give citations to pertinent law review articles. Similarly, various units of Lawyers Cooperative Publishing's *Total Client–Service Library* provide references to legal periodical articles. Both national legal encyclopedias provide law review article references.

In addition, *Shepard's Citations* provides, through several means, the ability to locate articles cited by courts and other legal periodicals and to locate articles that cite to cases, constitutions, statutes, and rules. These sources are:

1. Shepard's Law Review Citations

This citator, with coverage beginning in 1957, provides citations for almost 200 legal periodicals that have been cited in published reports of the state and federal courts. [See Illustration 148.]

2. Federal Law Citations in Selected Law Reviews

This citator lists each time any of the nineteen national law school law reviews covered by *Shepard's Citations*[23] cites to a case in the *U.S. Reports, Federal Reporter* (F., F.2d, F.3d), *Federal Cases, Federal Supplement, Federal Rules Decisions, Bankruptcy Reporter,* and other lower federal court reporters, and each time any of these reviews cite to the U.S. Constitution, any edition of the *United States Code,* or the various federal court rules. It also provides citations to each time any of the nineteen law reviews cite to a review in this group. Coverage is for articles published since 1973. [See Illustration 149.]

3. Legal Periodical Citations in Other Units of Shepard's Citations

The individual state citators provide citations to cases, statutes, constitutions, and court rules that have been cited in the law reviews and bar journals of the state unit being used, by the nineteen national law reviews, and by the *ABA Journal.* [See Illustration 121.] *Shepard's United States Citations* and *Shepard's Federal Citations* also provide citations to the *ABA Journal.*

SECTION H. ILLUSTRATIONS: LAW REVIEW CITATIONS IN SHEPARD'S CITATORS

148. Page from Shepard's Law Review Citations
149. Page from Shepard's Federal Law Review Citations in Selected Law Reviews

[23] This list of law reviews is provided in Chapter 15, Section B–1.

[Illustration 148]

PAGE FROM SHEPARD'S LAW REVIEW CITATIONS

STANFORD LAW REVIEW — **Vol. 35**

> This unit of *Shepard's* provides a means for "Shepardizing" law review articles cited since 1957. Through its use, one can find every time a law review article has been cited by another law review or in a court case.

36StnL1169
62TxL1279
63TxL234
71VaL75
7VtL273
1982WLR
[1071
1984WLR
[388
94YLJ6
94YLJ8
94YLJ279
94YLJ827

−447−
451US635
68LE505
101SC2064
50ChL655
52ChL644
1982DuL557
46PitL115
14SeHL53

−473−
667F2d859
71CaL878
7Day313
80McL362
15SMJ557
63TxL460

−591−
562FS398
73CaL1094
73CaL1192
31CLA1007
85CR901
34HLJ1035
10Hof742
96HLR563
97HLR705
37MiL391
68MnL537
130PaL1350
131PaL734
56SCL1192
35StnL677
36StnL211
36StnL255
36StnL301
36StnL427
71VaL197
19WFL357
94YLJ6
94YLJ345

−773−
16JMR16
43LJ671
12Mem570
132PaL453
24W&M207
10WmM199

−819−
741F2d1560
741F2d1562
568FS1547
17Akr429
71CaL1120
32CLA457
70Cor28
83CR250
84CR1147
1985DuL5
19GaL320

52GW672
52GW703
95HLR630
97HLR1355
21HUL111
30KLR493
45LJ526
80McL1175
43MdL257
56NYL661
58NYL947
59NYL279
38SLJ863
34StnL776
35StnL3
35StnL24
35StnL51
36StnL978
70VaL380
35VLR1089
28VR55
91YLJ8
93YLJ8

−97!
546FS1(
1982Az!
32KLR1
15LoyL1
132PaL!
132PaL!

73CaL1060
85CR462
23Duq95
34FLR369
11JCUL196
60NDL631
130PaL613
130PaL685
131PaL728
132PaL1331
36RLR29
55SCL1009
34StnL64
60TxL14
62TxL417
16UCD926
68VaL206
70VaL55
70VaL1236
36VLR1498
25W&M190

−275−
693F2d267
92YLJ771

−385−
461US490
76LE90
103SC1970
693F2d1105
566FS1382
582FS1144
51USLW
[4570
16Pcf106
32SR882
57TLQ589
57TuL1295
58TuL779
15UCD841

Vol. 34

−1−
32Buf546
29CLA72
32CLA505
67Cor1039
64MBJ283
12PLR3
37SLJ1100
36StnL300
37StnL611
59TxL705
1981WLR
[1126
1983WLR
[650
94YLJ295
94YLJ512

−113−
464US519

−513−
32EmJ187
69ILR122

−739−
83Mch1256
33Buf729
63BUR833
49ChL995
30CLA1200
32CLA37
83CR4
16Crt600
8Day634
8Day804
9Day211
10Day810
1984DuL
[1211
17GaL289
18GaL167
73Geo96

78NwL1446
131PaL790
133PaL550
58SCL76
58SCL165
58SCL279
58SCL566
58SCL604
34StnL766
35StnL241
36StnL207
36StnL279
36StnL490
36StnL721
36StnL1325
37StnL2
59TuL298
60TxL392
60TxL497
60TxL578
62TxL1240
62TxL1502
63TxL389
29VR672
92YLJ678
92YLJ1132
93YLJ1045
94YLJ4
94YLJ834

−765−
27AzL59
33Buf729
63BUR836
30CLA1203
32CLA37
83CR4
84CR1731
8Day708
8Day803
9Day175
1984DuL
[1211

17GaL289
73Geo96
96HLR803
69ILR101
82McL321
131PaL1351
133PaL550
133PaL698
58SCL279
58SCL624
35StnL241
36StnL248
37StnL4
59TuL292
60TxL395
60TxL578
62TxL1240
1985UtLR
[104
29VR674
92YLJ963
94YLJ837

35StnL3
35StnL48
35StnL61
70VaL614
28VR65

−957−
19GaL507
73KLJ476
37MiL424
58NYL518
15RLJ26
57SCL562
94YLJ10

−1017−
85CR941

−1133−
105SC3390
105SC3399
53USLW
[5091
724F2d1534
310NC70
NC
310SE307
33Buf360
53FR393
15ToI1399

−1183−
748F2d163
63BUR614
49ChL986
32CLA496
70Cor822
34DeP143
33EmJ718
69ILR54
47LCP(1)301
45LJ29

83McL1540
42MdL216
59NYL2
36StnL477
17UCD759
92YLJ594

Vol. 35

−1−
741F2d1562
40BL105
50ChL542
32CLA457
84CR1146
19GaL309
52GW678
52GW753
97HLR1363
80McL1175
43MdL271
30NYF28
58NYL995
59NYL279
38SLJ863
34SR979
35StnL23
35StnL51
36StnL983
70VaL654
70VaL670
35VLR1268
94YLJ271

−23−
741F2d1562
71CaL1100
50ChL542
32CLA457
84CR1147
52GW679
52GW752
97HLR1363
59NYL279
38SLJ863
34SR979
35StnL3
35StnL51
36StnL984
70VaL654
1984WLR
[637

−51−
50ChL542
32CLA457
84CR1147
19GaL311
52GW753
97HLR1363
80McL1175
59NYL279
38SLJ863
34SR979
35StnL3
35StnL24
36StnL983
37StnL366
70VaL604
70VaL654
94YLJ271

−69−
37AkL567
72CaL1045
69Cor70
84CR49
32DeP269
34DR390
36FLR707
52FR487
1982IlLR834
59NYL488

132PaL76
132PaL1309
17Suf597
71VaL515
86WVL1080

−175−
38BRW904
1983AzS385
64BUR95
50ChL1052
53FR953
98HLR1436
60ILJ78
68MnL921
133PaL992
36StnL733

−213−
35Mer841
37MiL493
69MnL299
133PaL550
58SCL285
29StLJ378
70VaL836

−387−
53USLW
[4407
14EnL358

−423−
61NY382
Alk
689P2d478
NY
462NE1146
474NYS2d
[428
63NbL731
70VaL903

−649−
29StLJ1077
29StLJ1163
36StnL299
70VaL1367

−681−
85LE439
105SC2087
53USLW
[4531
125NH64
Iowa
368NW73
NH
480A2d874
NY
489NYS2d
[828
1984BYU307
71VaL4
93YLJ614

−857−
757F2d169
40BL1454
52ChL107
52ChL645
73KLJ286
30NYF16
36StnL1007
70VaL629
Continued

[Illustration 149]

PAGE FROM SHEPARD'S FEDERAL LAW CITATIONS
IN SELECTED LAW REVIEWS

UNITED STATES SUPREME COURT REPORTS

Vol. 494

1991WLR462	—440—	—781—	100YLJ2319	59ChL203	—265—	—815—	—113—
100YLJ1580	79CaL719	79CaL915	101YLJ189	59ChL480	91McL647	Case 1	93CR312
101YLJ333	58ChL29	105HLR570	101YLJ1208	104HLR1367	140PaL120	91McL117	91McL329
101YLJ999	37CLA657	55LCP(1)30	102YLJ240	105HLR591			87NwL577
	105HLR1005	53LCP(3)200	102YLJ268	106HLR259	—307—	—819—	140PaL840
—223—	105HLR1175	91McL605		1991IILR927	77Cor728	Case 9	
79CaL740	105HLR1204	139PaL618	—408—	1992IILR419	90McL612	44StnL934	—152—
37CLA658	86NwL515	71TxL789	77MnL749	90McL517			76MnL1137
93CR340	87NwL128	102YLJ1298	86NwL1	77MnL367	—342—	—820—	87NwL59
101YLJ332	87NwL131			140PaL26	81Geo770	Case 5	87NwL67
	140PaL124	—905—	—469—	140PaL194	141PaL283	70TxL1563	87NwL79
—274—	44StnL396	Case 1	59ChL108	140PaL566	45StnL546		87NwL145
106HLR340	69TxL1095	1991IILR937	77MnL599	44StnL66		—832—	140PaL1376
70TxL867	69TxL1096		139PaL653	100YLJ1799	—365—	Case 8	44StnL102
	70TxL1074		140PaL2233	102YLJ1615	70TxL1745	102YLJ243	101YLJ987
—324—	70TxL1549	Vol. 492	71TxL755				101YLJ1035
92CR549	79VaL72		71TxL791	—905—	—378—	—846—	
80Geo21	1991WLR420	—1—	71TxL800	Case 5	59ChL128	Case 10	—210—
80Geo77	101YLJ405	93CR604		90McL1855	59ChL483	92CR509	92CR1655
91McL882	101YLJ1035	77MnL1017	—490—		90McL518		93CR317
91McL921			79CaL767	—937—	140PaL232	—882—	106HLR215
67NYL493	—490—	—33—	79CaL1538	Case 2	140PaL560	Case 1	76MnL266
	37CLA676	93CR330	80CaL1027	1992IILR9	79VaL53	86NwL662	
—350—		53LCP(4)155	80CaL1521	1992IILR37		66NYL1280	—259—
77Cor523	—524—	75MnL1367	81CaL46		—400—		77Cor728
	81CaL132	78VaL1496	59ChL30	Vol. 493	80CaL1244	—901—	92CR1690
—376—	59ChL261		59ChL218		92CR1938	Case 5	81Geo561
76MnL1135	77Cor133	—96—	59ChL410	—20—	93CR56	59ChL1296	105HLR1234
77VaL632	55LCP(1)57	80Geo755	38CLA87	1991IILR683	70TxL1808		91McL943
	55LCP(1)63	101YLJ409	77Cor512			—955—	91McL944
—397—	55LCP(2)					446	87NwL721
79CaL303	53LCP(3	This unit of *Shepard's* enables one to find when					141PaL816
79CaL731	140PaL9	any one of nineteen national law reviews cite to a				131	45StnL963
79CaL841	140PaL2:	federal court case, federal statute, federal court					70TxL1745
79CaL867	44StnL92	rule, or the U.S. Constitution. Coverage began in				3—	—325—
58ChL880	1992WLI	1973.				1.	77Cor728
59ChL60	[1					71	
59ChL226						39	—407—
59ChL320	—600—					8	92CR2015
59ChL356	79CaL66	101YLJ1035	91McL635	92CR1124	701xL1763		77MnL1024
37CLA926	37CLA658		91McL665	90McL1062		—1022—	45StnL581
38CLA87	93CR601	—257—	91McL940	86NwL504	—474—	Case 2	45StnL639
91CR1701	105HLR705	1992IILR174	91McL968	140PaL817	92CR731	1992WLR	101YLJ333
92CR1354	69TxL160	1992IILR422	76MnL249	70TxL1559	106HLR245	[1440	
81Geo302		75MnL1358	76MnL253		76MnL1154		—484—
81Geo371	—617—	77MnL1119	76MnL268	—120—		—1076—	92CR2007
105HLR1208	93CR601	77MnL1137	76MnL1174	77Cor9	—521—	Case 7	101YLJ333
106HLR124	104HLR1802	86NwL1130	77MnL1157	77Cor831	80Geo552	80CaL777	
106HLR133	105HLR671	140PaL1254	86NwL850	105HLR850	101YLJ1000		—516—
106HLR760	55LCP(1)239		139PaL574	76MnL1143	101YLJ1035	—1094—	67NYL638
106HLR946	76MnL923	—302—	140PaL67	140PaL753		Case 5	70TxL1608
1991IILR926	69TxL160	79CaL749	141PaL1030		—549—	55LCP(2)116	70TxL1633
1991IILR	70TxL934	92CR2095	141PaL1043	—132—	91McL592	55LCP(2)169	71TxL4
[1087		75MnL1443	44StnL262	101YLJ1035	1992WLR368	55LCP(2)192	
55LCP(1)28	—657—	77MnL1042	45StnL31				—596—
55LCP(2)100	140PaL488	45StnL581	71TxL201	—146—	—812—	Vol. 494	1991IILR683
53LCP(3)201		45StnL639	71TxL209	76MnL1139	Case 1		
91McL605	—701—	78VaL1554	71TxL1091		70TxL956	—26—	—624—
85NwL471	79CaL669	1991WLR936	78VaL1567	—165—		80Geo681	76MnL938
67NYL712	37CLA635	101YLJ189	79VaL1	1992IILR59	—812—	101YLJ1000	140PaL125
139PaL620	77Cor190	101YLJ333	79VaL8	141PaL489	Case 10	101YLJ1035	
139PaL1351	79Geo1731	102YLJ205	79VaL38		1991IILR		—638—
139PaL1369	91McL405	102YLJ228	79VaL46	—182—	[1098	—56—	101YLJ979
140PaL25	76MnL1148	102YLJ267	1991WLR853	59ChL1324		55LCP(4)255	101YLJ987
69TxL1005	140PaL757		1991WLR934	87NwL606	—813—	55LCP(4)347	101YLJ1035
71TxL781	43StnL992	—361—	1992WLR	140PaL8	Case 9	101YLJ1008	
71TxL787	69TxL1103	79CaL749	[1417	71TxL1002	77MnL755		—652—
71TxL1092		1992IILR9	102YLJ1621		77MnL785	—83—	59ChL44
77VaL868	—754—	1992IILR37		—215—		80Geo552	59ChL99
1990WLR	79CaL614	91McL602	—573—	55LCP(1)66		76MnL1143	59ChL229
[1549	79CaL741	76MnL1168	80CaL982	1991WLR707			80Geo1907
1992WLR725	67NYL270	86NwL1053	80CaL1613				106HLR288
100YLJ1405	101YLJ333	86NwL1057	81CaL294				1992IILR465
100YLJ2087		45StnL1018	59ChL116				
102YLJ1212		79VaL714	59ChL126				*Continued*
102YLJ1298							

SECTION I. ONLINE FULL-TEXT RETRIEVAL

The full text of many law review articles are available in the LAWREV Library of LEXIS and on WESTLAW in the TP–ALL database (Texts & Periodicals–All Law Reviews, Texts & Bar Journals) and in the JLR database (Journals & Law Reviews). This online access means articles can be searched on both systems using Boolean logic or natural language searches. Since the legal periodical indexes previously described cannot capture all the nuances of an article in the subject headings assigned to it, this online access greatly enhances one's ability to locate topics discussed within the articles. Both CALR services have specialized features used for searching these articles. Therefore, the vendors' guides should be consulted for details.

The philosophies of these two CALR vendors differ as to how legal periodical articles are added to their services. LEXIS identifies the specific law review and journal titles it considers most important and adds the full text of each issue to its LAWREV Library. Although WESTLAW also has the full-text of numerous law reviews online, it also uses a selective approach, identifying articles, notes, etc., from a much larger range of titles that are deemed significant and then adding the full text of these articles to its databases. In other words, LEXIS provides complete coverage for a select group of titles; WESTLAW has some complete coverage, but also provides selective coverage from a broader base of titles than LEXIS. Although coverage is by no means comprehensive in either WESTLAW or LEXIS, both continue to rapidly add law reviews and journals to their services.

SECTION J. LISTS OF SUBJECT LEGAL PERIODICALS

1. **Representative Subject Periodicals from American Law Schools**

Columbia University Law School:

> *Columbia Business Law Review*
> *Columbia Human Rights Law Review*
> *Columbia Journal of Environmental Law*
> *Columbia Journal of Gender and Law*
> *Columbia Journal of Law and Social Problems*
> *Columbia Journal of Transnational Law*
> *Columbia—VLA Journal of Law & the Arts*
> *Journal of Chinese Law*
> *Parker School Journal of East European Law*

Harvard University Law School:

> *Harvard Journal on Legislation*
> *Harvard Journal of Law and Public Policy*
> *Harvard BlackLetter Journal*
> *Harvard Civil Rights—Civil Liberties Law Review*

Harvard Environmental Law Review
Harvard Human Rights Journal
Harvard International Law Journal
Harvard Journal of Law & Technology
Harvard Women's Law Review

University of California School of Law at Berkeley:

Asian Law Journal
Ecology Law Quarterly
High Technology Law Journal
Berkeley Journal of Employment and Labor Law
International Tax and Business Lawyer
Berkeley Women's Law Journal
La Raza Law Journal

University of Texas School of Law:

Texas International Law Journal
American Journal of Criminal Law
Review of Litigation
Texas Journal of Women and the Law
Texas Intellectual Property Law Journal

Yale University Law School:

Yale Law & Policy Review
Yale Journal of Law and the Humanities
Yale Journal of International Law
Yale Journal of Law & Feminism
Yale Journal on Regulation

2. International Legal Periodicals from American Law Schools

American University Journal of International Law and Policy
Arizona Journal of International and Comparative Law
Asian Law Journal (University of California at Berkeley)
Boston College International and Comparative Law Review
Boston College Third World Law Journal
Boston University International Law Journal
Brooklyn Journal of International Law
California Western International Law Journal
Canada–United States Law Journal (Case Western Reserve University School of Law)
Case Western Reserve Journal of International Law
Colorado Journal of International Environmental Law & Policy
Columbia Journal of Transnational Law
Connecticut Journal of International Law

Cornell International Law Journal

Currents: International Trade Law Journal (South Texas College of Law)

Denver Journal of International Law and Policy

Dickinson Journal of International Law

Duke Journal of Comparative & International Law

East European Constitutional Review (University of Chicago)

Emory International Law Review

Florida Journal of International Law

Fordham International Law Journal

George Washington Journal of International Law and Economics

Georgetown International Environmental Law Review

Georgia Journal of International and Comparative Law

Harvard International Law Journal

Hastings International and Comparative Law Review

Houston Journal of International Law

Indiana International & Comparative Law Review (Indianapolis)

Indiana Journal of Global Legal Studies (Bloomington)

Journal of Chinese Law (Columbia University School of Law)

Journal of International Law and Practice (Detroit College of Law)

Journal of Space Law (University of Mississippi)

Journal of Transnational Law and Policy (Florida State University College of Law)

Law and Policy in International Business (Georgetown University Law Center)

Loyola of Los Angeles International & Comparative Law Journal

Maryland Journal of International Law and Trade

Michigan Journal of International Law

Minnesota Journal of Global Trade

New Europe Law Journal (Yeshiva University, Cardozo Law School)

New York Law School Journal of International and Comparative Law

New York University Journal of International Law and Politics

North Carolina Journal of International Law and Commercial Regulation

Northwestern Journal of International Law & Business

Pace Journal of International and Comparative Law

Pace Yearbook of International Law

Pacific Rim Law & Policy Journal (University of Washington School of Law)

Parker School Journal of East European Law (Columbia University School of Law)

Stanford Journal of International Law

Suffolk University Transnational Law Review

Syracuse Journal of International Law and Commerce

Temple International and Comparative Law Journal

Territorial Sea Journal (University of Maine School of Law)

Texas International Law Journal

Touro Journal of Transnational Law

Transnational Law & Contemporary Problems (University of Iowa College of Law)

Transnational Lawyer (University of the Pacific, McGeorge School of Law)

Tulane European and Civil Law Forum

Tulsa Journal of Comparative & International Law

UCLA Asian American Pacific Islands Law Journal

UCLA Pacific Basin Law Journal

United States–Mexico Law Journal (University of New Mexico)

University of Miami Inter–American Law Review

University of Miami Yearbook of International Law

University of Pennsylvania Journal of International Business Law

Vanderbilt Journal of Transnational Law

Virginia Journal of International Law

Willamette Bulletin of International Law and Policy

Wisconsin International Law Journal

Yale Journal of International Law

Chapter 17

TREATISES, RESTATEMENTS, UNIFORM LAWS, AND MODEL CODES

SECTION A.   TREATISES: IN GENERAL

Legal treatises are another important category of the secondary sources of the law.   Treatises can be defined as expositions by legal writers on case law and legislation pertaining to a particular subject and published in book form.[1]   This definition, of course, embodies a range of publications, including multi-volume works, textbooks, and shorter monographs.   Treatises are usually able to treat a subject in greater depth than a legal encyclopedia, but not to the extent found in a periodical article.

The first treatises were written by legal scholars during the early development of the common law.   Since there were few court cases available as precedent during the formative stages of our legal system, writers such as Lord Coke and William Blackstone played significant roles in the development of the law through their thoughtful, detailed *Commentaries*.   As the growth of the law resulted in an ever-increasing number of law reports, treatises were needed to organize the diffuse principles of case law.   One commentator has noted that treatises were first written because of the lack of precedents and then because there were too many of them.[2]

During the eighteenth and the early nineteenth centuries in the United States, English treatises were an integral part of an American lawyer's library.   Gradually, American lawyers and legal scholars, such as James Kent and Joseph Story, began publishing treatises devoted entirely to American law.[3]   Moreover, the American system of federalism has resulted in an increasing number of treatises dealing with the law of a particular state.

---

[1] Even this most basic definition is subject to some qualification, as many treatises published in book form are also available in electronic format.   In addition, work is underway to publish some legal treatises exclusively in electronic format.

[2] GEORGE PATON, A TEXTBOOK OF JURISPRUDENCE 264 (4th ed. 1972). *See* A.W.B. Simpson, *The Rise and Fall of the Legal Treatise and the Forms of Legal Literature*, 48 U. CHI. L. REV. 632 (1981).

[3] For a discussion of the development and influence of treatises on American law, see LAWRENCE M. FRIEDMAN, A HISTORY OF AMERICAN LAW 624–26 (2d ed. 1985). *See also* Erwin C. Surrency, *The Beginnings of American Legal Literature*, 31 AM. J. LEGAL HIST. 207 (1987).

1. The Nature of Treatises

Treatises can be broadly classified into six types: (1) critical; (2) interpretative; (3) expository; (4) textual (for law students); (5) practitioner-oriented; and (6) law for the layperson. In most instances, however, particular treatises do not fall neatly into such a classification, and they frequently may include some features of all types.

a. *Critical Treatises.* These examine an area of law in depth and constructively criticize, when necessary, rules of law as presently interpreted by the courts. They often include historical analyses in order to show that current rules actually had different meanings or interpretations than those presently given by the courts. The author may include a thoughtful examination of the policy reasons for one or more such rules.[4]

b. *Interpretative Treatises.* These provide an analysis and interpretation of the law. Authors of such works do not attempt to evaluate rules in relation to underlying policy, but rather to explain the terminology and meaning of the rules as they exist. Emphasis is placed upon understanding the law and not upon proposing what the law should be. [See Illustrations 150–151.]

c. *Expository Treatises.* These exist primarily as substitutes for digests and are principally used as case finders. They consist primarily of survey-type essay paragraphs arranged under conventional subject headings with profuse footnote citations. Usually minimal analysis and synthesis of conflicting cases are the most a researcher can expect to find in them.

A real danger exists if one relies exclusively upon the expository treatise or encyclopedia article without verifying the writer's synopses of the cases.

d. *Student Textbooks.* These may also be classified as expository because they are usually elementary treatments and omit comprehensive and critical features of other works. In fact, the term *hornbook*[5] *law,* frequently used by a judge to describe simple and well-settled points of law, comes from West Publishing Company's *Hornbook Series* of student treatises. [See Illustrations 152–153.] Student hornbooks, however, are useful as case finders because their references are usually selective and limited to landmark cases.

The titles in West's *Nutshell Series,* another group of student texts, are, as the name implies, non-sophisticated books that provide an overview of a topic without detailed analysis or extensive case references.

---

[4] For example, Professor Richard Powell, in his multi-volume treatise on real property, discussing the interests of a landlord and tenant in a condemnation proceeding, criticizes the current rule as follows: "*This rule is regrettable.* It embodies a rigidly conceptualistic survival of the historical idea that the tenant 'owns the land for the term'...." 2 RICHARD R. POWELL, THE LAW OF REAL PROPERTY ¶ 236[3][A] (1990) (emphasis added).

[5] For the derivation of the word *hornbook, see* 6 THE NEW ENCYCLOPEDIA BRITANNICA, MACROPEDIA 63–64 (15th ed. 1990).

Other leading publishers of student textbooks include The Foundation Press, Inc. and Little, Brown & Company.

e. *Practitioner–Oriented Books*. In recent years, continuing education for lawyers has become increasingly important. The American Law Institute and American Bar Association Joint Committee on Continuing Legal Education, the Practising Law Institute, and state bar associations hold seminars and symposia on many current subjects that are directed toward practicing lawyers and intended to keep them up to date on new developments in the law. Many states have their own continuing legal education institutes.[6] It is quite common for such institutes to publish handbooks and texts in conjunction with their programs.

These volumes, as well as a rapidly-increasing number of practice-oriented books by commercial publishers, usually furnish analyses of the law, practical guidance, forms, checklists, and other time-saving aids. Very frequently, these publications deal with such subjects as business transactions, personal injuries, commercial and corporate practice, probate practice, trial practice, and other subjects of primary interest to practicing attorneys. West Publishing Company, for example, has a *Practitioner Treatise Series*.

f. *Law for the Layperson*. Increasingly, non-lawyers are turning to so-called "self-help" books. These publications, which often are met with disdain by the legal community, are intended to enable the lay public to conduct some of their own legal affairs without the aid of an attorney, *e.g.,* preparation of a will.[7] Nolo Press of Berkeley, California, is the leading publisher of books of this genre. Oceana Publications' *Legal Almanac Series* attempts to describe basic legal issues in simple language. The American Civil Liberties Union has also published several titles targeted for the lay audience.

2. The Characteristics of Treatises

The fundamental characteristics of treatises are essentially the same. They contain the following elements:

a. *Table of Contents*. The table of contents shows the topical division of the treatise, which is usually arranged by chapters and subdivisions thereof.

b. *Table of Cases*. The table of cases provides references to where cases discussed by the author are cited in the text.

c. *Subject Matter*. The subject matter of the text is contained in the main body of the publication.

---

[6] For a listing of continuing legal education courses, see the bimonthly issues of *The CLE Journal and Register,* published by the ALI/ABA Committee on Continuing Professional Education.

[7] The best source for identifying these type materials is FRANK G. HOUDEK, LAW FOR THE LAYMAN: AN ANNOTATED BIBLIOGRAPHY (1991).

d. *Supplementation.* Supplementation of treatises is about evenly split between pocket parts in the back of the volume that indicate recent statutory and case developments, and looseleaf volumes, which provide for the addition of current material and the removal of that which is obsolete, usually by interfiling. In recent years, treatises are increasingly being published in the looseleaf format.

e. *Index.* The index, embodying an alphabetical arrangement of the topics, sub-topics, descriptive words, and cross references, is the last feature.

3. Locating Treatises

Because of the varied nature and characteristics of treatises, it is important to be able to identify and locate them with ease. Among the more useful sources are the following:

a. *Library Catalog.* The essential starting point in determining whether the library being used has a particular title, or publications on a particular subject, is its catalog. Either containing individual cards or providing information electronically, catalogs enable a researcher to locate materials by author, title, or subject. Most law libraries use the classification system and subject headings established by the Library of Congress. The electronic catalogs typically enable users to also access information by any word in the bibliographic record for that item or to combine two or more words in a search for even more refined results.

b. *New York University, School of Law Library, A Catalogue of the Law Collection of New York University* (Julius Marke ed. 1953). This is an excellent source for older treatises and includes book review annotations.

c. *Law Books Recommended for Libraries; Recommended Publications for Legal Research.* In the 1960s, the Association of American Law Schools (AALS) undertook a massive Library Studies Project designed to identify all published treatises and to provide a listing of those rated as either A, B, or C. Arranged under 46 subjects and entitled *Law Books Recommended for Libraries,* these lists were published separately in six notebook volumes during 1967–1970, with supplements issued for 42 of these subjects during 1974 to 1976. Actual coverage of titles extended only to approximately 1970. The project was then discontinued.

Subsequently, *Recommended Publications for Legal Research* (Oscar J. Miller & Mortimer D. Schwartz eds.), published by Fred B. Rothman, began in an effort to fill the gap left by the cessation of the AALS project. A separate volume for each year dating back to 1970 was prepared, and each year a new volume is issued covering titles published during the previous year. This publication also uses the A, B, and C ratings employed in the AALS project.

d. *Law Books in Print; Law Books Published. Law Books in Print,* a multi-volume bibliography first published in 1957, includes law books in the English language from publishers around the world. Sepa-

rate indexes for author/title, publisher, and subject are included. Each entry includes author, title, edition, publisher, date, pagination, number of volumes, subject, Library of Congress catalog number, and price. The 7th edition, with coverage through 1992, was published in late 1993. New editions are issued approximately every three years. The set, published by Glanville Publishers, Inc., is updated twice a year by cumulative supplements entitled *Law Books Published.*

d. *Catalog of Current Law Titles.* Published bimonthly by Ward and Associates, this source, which began in 1984 as *National Legal Bibliography* and assumed its present title in 1989, lists by subject and jurisdiction the titles cataloged by over sixty law libraries in the country during the intervening two months. A separate section lists those titles cataloged by at least one-fourth of those libraries. Each issue also includes an author index. An annual cumulation is published.

e. *Indexes Covering Treatises.* In 1994, the *Index to Legal Periodicals* added books to the scope of its coverage. Approximately 2,500 titles are included in each issue of *ILP*. Entries are listed under main entry (author or title) and under subject at the end of the subject entries for articles. *PAIS International* indexes some law-related titles, including government publications.

f. *Other Sources.* Numerous other sources provide information pertaining to treatises. Three of the more notable ones are: R.R. Bowker's annual, *Law Books and Serials in Print* and *Books in Print;* and the American Bar Association's *Recommended Law Books* (J.A. McDermott ed. 1986), which is an annotated, subject-arranged listing of books of special value to practitioners.

g. *Library Assistance.* If a source to satisfy your needs is not available in your library, remember to consult a librarian. Librarians likely have access to at least one of the two online bibliographic databases, OCLC and RLIN. These databases include many millions of records pertaining to titles. This information is merged to form a union catalog. Librarians may also have access to a vast array of other sources, both print and online, all of which can assist in locating materials. Once an item is identified that is not available in your library, it might be possible to obtain that item through interlibrary loan.

SECTION B. TREATISES: RESEARCH PROCEDURE

1. Case Method

If the name of a leading case on point is known, consult the table of cases of the treatise in use to ascertain whether this case is discussed in the book. If so, an examination of the cited pages in the text will reveal a discussion of the subject matter with additional cases on point.

2. Index Method

Consult the index in the back of the book if the name of a case is not known or if the research is in a particular aspect of a subject. Select an

appropriate descriptive or legal topic to use the index.   References will be to the text of the publication.

3. Topic Method

The Topic method can be used through the table of contents; however, its effectiveness in locating the pertinent text depends on the researcher's understanding of the structural subject subdivisions used in that treatise.

4. Definition Method

The index to the treatise may list words and phrases that are defined and explained in the text.

5. Electronic Format Method

Increasingly, treatises are becoming available in online and CD–ROM formats.   This electronic access enables a researcher to use search strategies unavailable in the print versions, and often to hypertext to and from sections in the treatise and perhaps even to sources cited by that treatise.   Researchers may want to determine if a treatise is available electronically and use it in that format.

SECTION C.   ILLUSTRATIONS: TREATISES

[Illustration 150]

INDEX PAGE FROM SCHOSHINSKI, AMERICAN LAW OF LANDLORD AND TENANT

INDEX

TERMINATION OF TENANCY —Cont'd

Federally assisted housing, § 13:8

Government interference with particular use, option of termination by tenant upon, § 5:17

Options to renew and purchase, § 9:11

Periodic tenancy, § 2:13

Public housing, generally, § 13:4

Subsidized housing, § 13:8

Tenancy at sufferance, § 2:21

Tenancy at will, § 2:18

Void or unenforceable lease, § 2:26

TERMS AND CONDITIONS OF LEASE

Holdover tenancy, terms and conditions carried over into new tenancy, § 2:23

THEATERS

Tort liability of landlord for injuries on premises used for public purpose, § 4:7

THIRD PARTIES

Criminal acts of third person, liability of landlord, §§ 4:13, 15

Exculpatory clause as affecting tort liability of landlord for injuries to third parties, effect of, § 4:11

Granting license to third person on covenant not to assign, § 8:16

Interference with right of possession by, § 3:2

Latent defects, tort liability of landlord for injuries from, § 4:3

Lessor as third party beneficiary to assignments, § 8:12

Options to renew and purchase, rights of third parties, §§ 9:9, 13

Public premises, tort liability of landlord for injuries on, § 4:7

Recordation statutes, protection of, § 2:6

Statutory lien of landlord on property of third parties found on premises of

TIME AND DATE—Cont'd

Pleading retaliation by landlord, time limitations attached to, § 12:6

Rent (this index)

Rent control, § 7:7

TITLE

Tenancy at will, termination by transfer or denial of landlord's title, § 2:18

TORT LIABILITY OF LANDLORD

Generally, §§ 4:1 to 15

Breach of covenant to repair, § 4:5

Criminal actions by third parties generally, §§ 4:14, 15

Damages (this index)

Exceptions. Immunity from liability, infra

Exculpatory clauses, generally, §§ 4:10 to 13

Family of tenant, injury to, §§ 4:1, 3, 11

Immunity from liability

generally, § 4:1

– exceptions to immunity
  generally, §§ 4:2 to 8

– – breach of covenant to repair, § 4:5

– – injuries sustained on premises control by landlord, § 4:4

– – latent defects, § 4:3

– – negligent repair, § 4:6

– – public purpose, premises used for, § 4:7

– – recent developments imposing liability, § 4:9

– – statutory obligation, liability predicated on, § 4:8

Indemnification based on tort liability, § 8:12

Invitees, liability for injuries to, §§ 4:1, 3 to 5, 11, 15

Injuries sustained on premises controlled by landlord, § 4:4

Latent defects, § 4:3

Negligent repair, § 4:6

PROBLEM

Is a landlord liable for injuries occurring to someone on property over which the landlord has retained control?

To locate a discussion of this issue and related cases, consult the Index to *American Law of Landlord and Tenant.*

Retaliatory action by landlord, proscribed conduct, § 12:4

TIME AND DATE

Conduct of landlord, time limitations attached to statutory prohibitions on, §§ 12:10, 11

Estate for years, § 2:7

Options to Renew and Purchase (this index)

Statutory obligation, liability predicated on, § 4:8

"TOUCH AND CONCERN"

Transfer of leasehold interests, requirement of touch and concern for covenant running the land, § 8:2

TRADE FIXTURES

Removal, right of tenant as to, § 5:29

[Illustration 151]

PAGE FROM SCHOSHINSKI, AMERICAN LAW OF LANDLORD AND TENANT

---

§ 4:3   CHAPTER FOUR

If the lessor fails to fulfill his obligations under these principles, he has been held liable for injuries incurred by the tenant,[27] his family,[28] or his guests and other invitees.[29] However, third parties have been denied recovery against the landlord if the tenant had notice of the defect.[30]

§ 4:4. Injuries sustained on premises controlled by landlord

Another exception to the lessor's tort immunity subjects him to potential liability for injuries sustained on parts of the premises over which he has retained control. The liability is predicated upon the existence of a duty of a possessor of land to exercise reasonable care to keep his property in reasonably safe condition for permissible entrants.[31] A large number of cases which have imposed liability on the landlord on the basis of retained control deal with injuries sustained when the landlord

> Note that the index leads to a relevant discussion of the issue under research. A typical treatise, such as this one, will contain text and then footnote references to cases and other pertinent materials. If supplementation is also provided, this material should be consulted for later information.

extended include stairways,[34] porches,[35] hallways and entrance

---

rill v Sinclair Refining Co. (1945) 225 NC 421, 35 SE2d 240, 243 ("known to the lessor, or which he should have known").

27. See, e.g., Wright v Peterson (1967) 259 Iowa 1239, 146 NW2d 617; Smith v Green (1970) 358 Mass 76, 260 NE2d 656.

28. See, e.g., Rahn v Beurskens (1966) 66 Ill App 2d 423, 213 NE2d 301; Knox v Sands (1967, Mo) 421 SW2d 497; Francis v Pic (1975, ND) 226 NW2d 654.

29. See, e.g., Kraus v Webber (1971) 359 Mass 565, 270 NE2d 789; Reckert v Roco Petroleum Corp. (1966, Mo) 411 SW2d 199.

30. For discussion and criticism of this rule see Webel v Yale University (1939) 125 Conn 515, 518–19, 7 A2d 215, 216, 123 ALR 863. See also 2 F. Harper & F. James, The Law of Torts, § 27.16, at 1509 (1956).

31. 2 F. Harper & F. James, The Law of Torts, § 27.17 (1956); W. Prosser, Handbook of the Law of Torts, § 63, at 405–08 (4th ed. 1971). See also Harkrider, Tort Liability of a Landlord, 26 Mich. L. Rev. 383, 401–04 (1928); Love, Landlord's Liability for Defective Premises: Caveat Lessee, Negligence, or Strict Liability?, 1975 Wis. L. Rev. 19, 65–68 (1975); Note, Control by the Landlord—How Much is Necessary to Hold Him Liable?, 21 Albany L. Rev. 87 (1957).

32. See, e.g., Harris v H. G. Smithy Co. (1970) 139 App DC 65, 429 F2d 744; Levine v Katz (1968) 132 App DC 173, 407 F2d 303; Geesing v Pendergrass (1966, Okla) 417 P2d 322.

33. See, e.g., Fitzpatrick v Ford (1963, Mo) 372 SW2d 844, 849.

34. See, e.g., Fantacone v McQueen (1961, 1st Dist) 196 Cal App 2d 477,

[Illustration 152]

PAGE FROM PROSSER AND KEETON ON THE LAW OF TORTS, FIFTH EDITION

Chapter 10

OWNERS AND OCCUPIERS OF LAND

Table of Sections

§ 57. Outside of the Premises

The largest single area in which the concept of "duty" has operated as a limitation upon liability has concerned owners and occupier: [Page from a treatise written primarily for law students. This particular title is part of West Publishing Company's *Hornbook Series*.] sons, t the co ed upon it, have been concerned chiefly with the possession of the land, and this has continued into the present day. This development has occurred for the obvious reason that the person in possession of property ordinarily is in the best position to discover and control its dangers, and often is responsible for creating them in the first place.[1] He has a privilege to make use of the land

for his own benefit, and according to his own desires, which is an integral part of our whole system of private property; but it has been said many times that this privilege is ... s of ... pos... inci... unreasonable risks of harm to others in the vicinity.[2]

His liability for a breach of this obligation may fall into any of the three categories into which tort liability has been divided. It may rest upon intent, as where he fills the air with poisonous fumes knowing that they are certain to damage the plaintiff's adjoining

---

§ 57

1. The obligation may arise from possession and control, even without legal ownership. Jacobs v. Mutual Mortgage & Investment Co., 1966, 6 Ohio St.2d 92, 216 N.E.2d 49; Trainor v. Frank Mercede & Sons, Inc., 1965, 152 Conn. 364, 207 A.2d 54. See Sprecher v. Adamson Companies, 1981, 30 Cal.3d 358, 178 Cal.Rptr.

783, 788, 636 P.2d 1121, 1126; Black v. City of Cordele, 1982, 163 Ga.App. 322, 293 S.E.2d 557 (operator-occupier of city-owned gas pipeline system).

2. Schulz v. Quintana, Utah 1978, 576 P.2d 855; Smith, Reasonable Use as a Justification for Damage to a Neighbor, 1917, 17 Col.L.Rev. 383.

386

[Illustration 153]

PAGE FROM PROSSER AND KEETON ON THE LAW OF TORTS, FIFTH EDITION

---

432   OWNERS AND OCCUPIERS OF LAND   Ch. 10

sonably be looked for.[50] A person who climbs in through a basement window in search of a fire or a thief does not expect any assurance that he will not find a bulldog in the cellar, and he is trained to be on guard for any such general dangers inherent in the profession.[51] But whether this requires a blanket rule limiting liability in every case is another question. One solution would be to require the occupier to take precautions only where it is reasonable to expect him to do so. On this basis, there is obvious merit in the position, taken by a small number of courts, that such visitors are entitled to the status of invitees, and to the full duty of reasonable care, when they come under the same circumstances as other members of the public to a part of the premises held open to the public.[52] This means that a policeman calling to make an inquiry at a business office is an invitee; and that the occupier must exercise ordinary care to see that the usual means of access to his premises are safe for a visiting fireman. The additional obligation in fa...

requ...   **Note the footnote references to court cases and to secondary sources.**   d for
state...   **Note also how this particular volume indicates how to frame an online**   .l, un-
firen...   **search for this issue using WESTLAW.**   prop-

ally as invitees, although there does not appear to be any trend in this direction nor sufficient reason on balance for moving the law this far.

50. See Boneau v. Swift & Co., Mo.App.1934, 66 S.W.2d 172, 173; Shypulski v. Waldorf Paper Products Co., 1951, 232 Minn. 394, 397, 45 N.W.2d 549, 551; Notes, 1926, 26 Col.L.Rev 116; 1938, 22 Minn.L.Rev. 898.

51. Steelman v. Lind, 1981, 97 Nev. 425, 634 P.2d 666; Walters v. Sloan, 1977, 20 Cal.App.3d 199, 142 Cal.Rptr. 152, 155, 571 P.2d 609; Malo v. Willis, 1981, 126 Cal.App.3d 543, 178 Cal.Rptr. 774 (dictum).

52. Mounsey v. Ellard, 1973, 363 Mass. 693, 297 N.E.2d 43; Nared v. School District of Omaha in County of Douglas, 1974, 191 Neb. 376, 215 N.W.2d 115. See also McCarthy v. Port of New York Authority, 1968, 30 A.D.2d 111, 290 N.Y.S.2d 255. Cf. Caroff v. Liberty Lumber Co., App.Div.1977, 146 N.J.Super. 353, 369 A.2d 983 (park ranger). This is the position taken in Second Restatement of Torts, § 345, Comment e.

53. See Murphy v. Ambassador East, 1977, 54 Ill. App.3d 980, 12 Ill.Dec. 501, 370 N.E.2d 124 (policeman; but no duty on particular facts); Strong v. Seattle Ste-

§ 62. Abolition of Categories

The traditional distinctions in the duties of care owed to persons entering land—based upon the entrant's status as a trespasser, li...

...ty.... In 1957, England by statute abolished the distinction between licensees and invitees, and imposed upon the occupier a "common duty of care" toward all persons who

vedore Co., 1970, 1 Wn.App. 898, 466 P.2d 545 (fireman); cf. Cameron v. Abatiell, 1968, 127 Vt. 111, 241 A.2d 310. But even in these jurisdictions, the underlying fireman's rule based on assumption of risk may bar recovery for the negligence in starting the fire or otherwise creating the need for professional assistance in the first place. Washington v. Atlantic Richfield Co., 1976, 66 Ill.2d 103, 5 Ill.Dec. 143, 361 N.E.2d 282 (Schaefer, J.) (5–2).

§ 62

1. See, e.g., 2 Harper & James, Law of Torts, 1956, 1430–1505; Hughes, Duties to Trespassers: A Comparative Survey and Revaluation, 1959, 68 Yale L.J. 633; McMahon, Conclusions on Judicial Behavior from a Comparative Study of Occupiers' Liability, 1975, 38 Mod.L.Rev. 39; Notes, 1977, 36 Md.L.Rev. 816; 1979, 33 Ark.L.Rev. 194.

For the modern status of these entrant classification rules, see Annot., 1983, 22 A.L.R.4th 294.

WESTLAW REFERENCES

di invitee
272k32(2 3)
376k6(3)
"public invitee"
restatement +s torts /s invitee* /s duty

Area of Invitation

area /3 invitation

Care Required

digest(invitee* /s reasonable /5 care /s duty)
digest(invitee* /p "standard of care")

Public Employees, Generally

272k32(2 17)
"garbage collector" garbagem'n "building inspector"
mailm'n "meter reader" "meat inspector" /s invitee*

Firemen and Policemen; "Fireman's Rule"

firem'n policem'n /s licensee*
"fireman's rule"

SECTION D.   RESTATEMENTS OF THE LAW

In the 1920s, prominent American judges, lawyers, and law professors were becoming concerned over two main defects in case law—its growing uncertainty and undue complexity.   As a result, in 1923, the American Law Institute (ALI) was founded by a group of these leaders to overcome the weaknesses apparent in case law.[8]   The objectives of the ALI focused on reduction of the mass of legal publications that had to be consulted by the bench and bar, on simplification of case law by a clear, systematic restatement of it, and on diminishing the flow of judicial decisions.   It was feared that the increasing mass of unorganized judicial opinions threatened to break down the common law system of expressing and developing law.[9]

To remedy these problems, the ALI undertook to produce a clear and precise restatement of the existing common law that would have "authority greater than that now accorded to any legal treatise, an authority more nearly on a par with that accorded the decisions of the courts." [10]

Procedurally, this is accomplished by the engagement of eminent legal scholars to be Reporters for the various subjects that are to be restated.   Each Reporter prepares tentative drafts, which are then submitted to and approved by the members of the ALI.   Often, numerous tentative drafts, with the work extending over many years, are prepared before final agreement can be reached and a Restatement adopted.

Between 1923 and 1944, Restatements were adopted for the law of agency, conflict of laws, contracts, judgments, property, restitution, security, torts, and trusts.   Since 1957, Restatements (Second) have been adopted for agency, contracts, conflict of laws, foreign relations law, judgments, property (landlord & tenant and donative transfers), torts, and trusts, and the process is not yet complete.

In 1986, a third series of the Restatements started with issuance of *Restatement (Third) of the Foreign Relations Law of the United States.* Since then a *Restatement (Third) of Trusts: Prudent Investor Rule* and

[8] This discussion of the Restatements is based on the following sources: (1) William Draper Lewis, *History of the American Law Institute and the First Restatement of the Law, in* AMERICAN LAW INSTITUTE, RESTATEMENT IN THE COURTS 1–23 (permanent ed. 1945); (2) HERBERT F. GOODRICH & PAUL A. WOLKIN, THE STORY OF THE AMERICAN LAW INSTITUTE, 1923–1961 (1961); (3) AMERICAN LAW INSTITUTE, THE AMERICAN LAW INSTITUTE 50TH ANNIVERSARY (1973); (4) AMERICAN LAW INSTITUTE, ANNUAL REPORTS.   *See also The American Law Institute Restatement of the Law and Codifications, in* 3 PIMSLEUR'S CHECKLISTS OF BASIC AMERICAN LEGAL PUBLICATIONS § V (Marcia S. Zubrow ed. & comp., looseleaf) [AALL Publication Series No. 4].   This checklist updates all previous checklists and lists all Restatements, including preliminary and tentative drafts.

[9] Lewis, *supra* note 8, at 1.

[10] *Report of the Committee on the Establishment of a Permanent Organization for the Improvement of the Law Proposing the Establishment of the American Law Institute, in* AMERICAN LAW INSTITUTE, THE AMERICAN LAW INSTITUTE 50TH ANNIVERSARY 34 (1973).

Restatement (Third) of the Law of Unfair Competition have been adopted. In addition, tentative drafts of additional topics for both the second and third series continue to be issued, likely resulting in additional Restatements in the future.

The status of the revision of specific Restatements and of proposed new Restatements can be ascertained from the latest ALI Annual Reports, which are issued separately and since 1988 are in ALI's annual *Proceedings,* and from its quarterly newsletter, *The ALI Reporter.*

It has been recommended that state legislatures be required to approve the Restatement, not as formal legislative enactments, but as aids and guides to the judiciary so that they will feel free to follow "the collective scholarship and expert knowledge of our profession," [11] but this proposal was not adopted by the ALI membership. Nevertheless, many courts began to give greater authority to the Restatements than that accorded to treatises and other secondary sources. In many instances, an authority is given to the Restatements nearly equal to that accorded to decided cases.[12]

The First Series of the Restatements reflected the desire of the ALI's founders that the Restatements be admired and adopted by the courts. To this end they deliberately omitted the Reporters' citations and reference to the tentative drafts upon which the Restatement rules were based.

With publication of the Second Series of the Restatements, a decision was made to abandon the idea of the Restatements serving as a substitute for the codification of the common law. The Second and Third Series at times indicate a new trend in the common law and attempt to predict what a new rule will or should be.[13] This change in policy is also reflected in the appearance of citations to court cases and to the Notes of the Reporters. Appendices contain citations to and brief synopses of all cases that have cited the Restatements. It should be noted that a new Restatement on the same topic as a existing one, does not supersede the older version. Some courts, in fact, continue to cite the earlier Restatements.

The frequency with which the Restatements are cited by the courts merits their study in legal research. As of March 1, 1991, the Restatements had been cited by the courts 114,451 times.[14] Therefore, they not only provide clear statements of the rules of the common law, which are operative in a great majority of the states, but also provide very valuable sources for finding cases on point.

[11] Alpheus Thomas Mason, *Harlan Fiske Stone Assays Social Justice, 1912–1923,* 99 U. PA. L. REV. 887, 915 (1951) (quoting from a speech given by Stone).

[12] For a discussion of the precedential authority of the Restatements, see James F. Byrne, *Reevaluation of the Restatements as a Source of Law in Arizona,* 15 ARIZ. L. REV. 1021, 1023–26 (1973).

[13] *Id.*

[14] AMERICAN LAW INSTITUTE, 68TH ANNUAL MEETING PROCEEDINGS 671 (1992).

Moreover, a comparison of the texts of the Restatements and the case law of the several states reveals that there are surprisingly few deviations from the common law as expressed in the Restatements. It has been suggested, therefore, that there is in fact a common law that transcends state lines and prevails throughout the nation.[15] However, the legal rules may at times be inaccurately and confusingly stated by the various courts. Thus, the objective of the Restatements is to clear away much of the verbal debris and bring the accepted rules to the forefront. To this extent, the Restatements are useful research aids in the law.

Further discussion over the value of the Restatements is best left to others.[16] As a legal researcher, however, one must be familiar with the publications of the American Law Institute and their method of use.[17]

1. The Features of the Restatements

The various Restatements are typically divided broadly into chapters, further subdivided into narrower titles, and then into numbered discrete sections. Each section begins with a "black letter" **(boldface)** restatement of the law, followed by comments that contain hypothetical illustrations. Reporters' Notes are at the end of each section.[18] [See Illustrations 155–157.] These Notes can serve as a legislative history of the section and will, if applicable, give the text of the section or sections of the earlier Restatements that are superseded by this later section.

The following additional features are included in the Restatements, Second and Third Series:

a. *Tables.* These list citations of court cases, statutes, and other authorities included in the Restatement being used.

b. *Conversion Tables.* These enable a user to find where a section in a Tentative Draft is included in the final Restatement.

c. *Cross-references.* These give references to West's *Key Number System* and to *A.L.R. Annotations.*

[15] Herbert F. Goodrich, *Restatement and Codification, in* DAVID DUDLEY FIELD: CENTENARY ESSAYS CELEBRATING ONE HUNDRED YEARS OF LEGAL REFORM 241–250 (Allison Reppy ed. 1949).

[16] An exhaustive list of articles on all aspects of the work of the American Law Institute is in the Annual Reports section of the Annual Meeting *Proceedings* under the title *The Institute in Legal Literature, A Bibliography.*

[17] THE AMERICAN LAW INSTITUTE ARCHIVE PUBLICATIONS IN MICROFICHE (William S. Hein & Co.) is the most exhaustive collection of documents on the ALI and its projects and covers from the ALI's founding in 1923 forward. It includes the ALI *Proceedings, Annual Reports,* minutes, the various drafts of the Restatements from inception to completion, the codifications together with their background sources for projects with which the ALI has been associated, and previously unreleased confidential documents. The set is updated either semi-annually or annually, thus covering newly-issued items. At the end of 1992, the collection contained over 2,900 documents. A hard copy guide provides access to these materials.

[18] For the first three Restatements (Second), namely agency, torts, and trusts, the Reporters' Notes are in the Appendix volumes accompanying these subjects.

2. Indexes

a. *Restatements, First Series.* A one-volume index to all the Restatements in the First Series has been published. Each Restatement also has its own subject index.

b. *Restatements, Second Series* and *Third Series.* Some of the older Restatements have their own subject index in each volume and covering only the materials in that volume. More recent Restatements contain an index in the last volume of the Restatement or in a separate volume. [*See* Illustration 154.] There is not a comprehensive index to all of these Restatements.

3. The Restatements As Cited By the Courts

As mentioned, the ALI maintains information pertaining to each time the Restatements are cited by the courts. Originally, this was accomplished by a set entitled *Restatements in the Courts.* Issued first as a Permanent Edition covering 1932–1944 and then updated with bound supplements covering from 1945–1975, this set recorded, with annotations, each time a court cited a section of the Restatement.

These annotations were subsequently recompiled and added to the individual Appendix volumes to the current Restatements. New Appendix volumes are published periodically. [See Illustrations 158–159.] These Appendices, prior to being cumulated into bound volumes, are updated either by cumulative pocket supplements or separate annual cumulative supplements, and by a semi-annual pamphlet entitled *Interim Case Citations.* This interim pamphlet only contains citations and does not include the case synopses found in the pocket supplements and cumulative volumes.

4. Online Access to the Restatements

The Restatements, including the current pocket parts, annual supplements, and interim case citation pamphlets, are available on WEST-LAW. All Restatements can be searched by accessing the *Restatements of the Law* database (REST). Each Restatement also is available in its own database. Restatements are available in LEXIS in the BEGIN library, RESTAT file.

5. Locating Legal Periodical Articles Concerning the ALI and the Restatements

The *Index to Legal Periodicals, Current Law Index,* and *Legal Resource Index* use the "American Law Institute" as a subject heading. While *ILP* lists articles about the Restatements only under a general subject heading, *CLI* and *LRI* include references by subject as well as under the name of the specific Restatement.

6. Shepardizing the Restatements

Shepard's Restatement of the Law Citations is devoted entirely to coverage of the Restatements. This set gives citations to all federal

court reports, all units of the *National Reporter System,* and all state
court reports that cite to a Restatement. It also includes articles citing
the Restatements in the nineteen leading law reviews and the *ABA
Journal.* [See Illustration 160.]

7. State Annotations

Some states have prepared annotations to court citations to the
Restatements, *e.g., The California Annotations to the Restatement of the
Law of Torts.* The law library catalog should be consulted to ascertain if
such annotations exist for a particular state.

8. Restatements in the American Law Institute Archive Publications in Microfiche

The *American Law Institute Archive Publications in Microfiche* [19]
(William S. Hein & Co.), a massive collection of ALI documents, includes
over 1,800 documents relating to all series of the Restatements. These
include the various tentative drafts, proposed final drafts, the adopted
Restatements, and previously unreleased confidential documents. A
hard copy guide provides access to this collection.

SECTION E. ILLUSTRATIONS: RESTATEMENT (SECOND) OF TORTS

**Problem: A, an inmate in a state prison, had suffered a severe
toothache. The Warden waited three days before
taking A to the dentist. As a result of the delay, all
of A's teeth had to be removed. Is the Warden,
acting as a custodian of A, subject to liability to A?**

[19] For additional information about the content of this collection, see *supra* note 17.

[Illustration 154]

PAGE FROM INDEX TO §§ 281 TO 503, RESTATEMENT (SECOND) OF TORTS

CONTROL OF THIRD PERSONS

CONTROL OF THIRD PERSONS
Generally, §§ 315–320.
Assumption of, liability as based on, § 302 B e F.
Contributory negligence in failure of,
   Negligent third person, conduct of, § 495.
   Parent's failure to control child, § 496.
Custodian of person, duty of,
   Dangerous person, control of, § 319.
   Third person, control of. § 320.

CRIMINAL MATTERS—Cont'd
Court's adoption of standard of conduct defined by criminal law, §§ 286 d., 287.
Foreseeability of indirect harm through criminal acts of others, § 302 B.
Knowledge that others may act criminally, standard of care as requiring, § 290 (a) m.
Legal cause, criminal acts of third person as affecting actor's negli-

> The index in each Restatement 2d volume only covers the topics addressed by that volume. Once the appropriate volume is located, typically by reference to the Table of Contents, that volume's index can be used to locate treatment of a custodian's duty to those in their care.
>
> See the following Illustrations for examples of how the Restatements are arranged.

causing, § 442 B c.

CO-OWNERSHIP
Imputed negligence as affected by co-ownership of automobile, § 491 h.

CORRELATION
Duty of, § 289 g.

CORROBORATION
Emotional disturbance, effect of lack of corroboration as to physical harm resulting from, § 436 g.

COUNTIES
See Government and Governmental Agencies.

COURT OR JUDGE
Direction of Verdict, see that title.
Functions of, generally, see Questions of Law and Fact.
Instructions to Jury, see that title.

COVENANTS
Lessee's covenant to repair as affecting lessor's liability to persons on the land, § 359 i.
Lessor's covenant to repair,
   Independent contractor employed pursuant to, liability for acts of, § 419 a–c.
   Persons on the land, basis of liability to, § 357.
   Persons outside the land, basis of liability to, § 378.

CRIMINAL MATTERS
Business visitor injured by criminal acts of third person, § 344 f.
Child, standard of care required of, as based on law as to criminal liability of child, § 283 A b.

CUMULATIVE CAUSES
Criminal acts done under opportunity afforded by actor's negligence as superseding cause as affected by, § 448 c.
Legal cause as affected by cumulative effect of other causes, § 433 (a) (d).

CUMULATIVE LIABILITY
Manufacturer and person under duty to inspect chattel, § 396 b.
Possessor of land and person taking over entire charge of land, § 387 c.
Supplier of chattels and third person under duty to inspect same, § 393 a.

CURIOSITY
Chattel unsafe for any use but preservation as, liability of supplier of, § 389 b.

CUSTODY AND CUSTODIANS
Affirmative duty of custodian to protect person in custody, § 314 A (4).
Animals deprived of custody, legal cause of harm by or to, § 438.
Control of Third Persons, see that title.
Helpless person, duty of one taking charge of, § 324.
Imputed negligence as affected by custody of child, § 488 (1) c, d.

CUSTOM AND USAGE
Animals customarily confined, legal cause of harm by or to, when at large, § 438 a.
Invitee status as based on, § 332 c.
Licensee status as affected by, § 330 e, f, h, l.

[Illustration 155]

PAGE FROM RESTATEMENT (SECOND) OF TORTS

§ 314   TORTS, SECOND   Ch. 12

is subject to liability for permitting the train to continue in motion with knowledge of A's peril.

e. Since the actor is under no duty to aid or protect another who has fallen into peril through no conduct of the actor, it is immaterial that his failure to do so is due to a desire that the other shall be harmed.

Illustration:

4. A, a strong swimmer, sees B, against whom he entertains an unreasonable hatred, floundering in deep water and obviously unable to swim. Knowing B's identity, he turns away. A is not liable to B.

The Restatement's "Black Letter" Rules immediately follow the section number.

condition of land or chattels owned or in the possession or custody of the actor, unless he stands in some relation to the other which carries with it the duty of preparing a safe place or thing for the other's reception or use, or of warning him of its dangerous condition. (See §§ 342–350.)

§ **314 A.** Special Relations Giving Rise to Duty to Aid or Protect

(1) A common carrier is under a duty to its passengers to take reasonable action

(a) to protect them against unreasonable risk of physical harm, and

(b) to give them first aid after it knows or has reason to know that they are ill or injured, and to care for them until they can be cared for by others.

(2) An innkeeper is under a similar duty to his guests.

(3) A possessor of land who holds it open to the public is under a similar duty to members of the public who enter in response to his invitation.

(1) One who is required by law to take or who voluntarily takes the custody of another under circumstances such as to deprive the other of his normal opportunities for protection is under a similar duty to the other.

See Reporter's Notes.

See Appendix for Reporter's Notes, Court Citations, and Cross References

118

[Illustration 156]

PAGE FROM RESTATEMENT (SECOND) OF TORTS

Ch. 12   STANDARD OF CONDUCT   § **314 A**

Caveat:

The Institute expresses no opinion as to whether there may not be other relations which impose a similar duty.

Comment:

a. An additional relation giving rise to a similar duty is that of an employer to his employee. (See § 314 B.) As to the duty to protect the employee against the conduct of third persons, see Restatement of Agency, Second, Chapter 14.

b. This Section states exceptions to the general rule, stated in § 314, that the fact that the actor realizes or should realize that his action is necessary for the aid or protection of another does not in itself impose upon him any duty to act. The duties stated in this Section arise out of special relations between the parties, which create a special responsibility, and take the case out of the general rule. The relations listed are not intended to be exclusive, and are not necessarily the only ones in which a

> **Following the "Black Letter" Rule or Rules is a Comment section explaining the purpose of the Rules.**

criminal law, but there have as yet been no decisions allowing recovery in tort in jurisdictions where negligence actions between husband and wife for personal injuries are permitted. The question is therefore left open by the Caveat, preceding Comment *a* above. The law appears, however, to be working slowly toward a recognition of the duty to aid or protect in any relation of dependence or of mutual dependence.

c. The rules stated in this Section apply only where the relation exists between the parties, and the risk of harm, or of further harm, arises in the course of that relation. A carrier is under no duty to one who has left the vehicle and ceased to be a passenger, nor is an innkeeper under a duty to a guest who is injured or endangered while he is away from the premises. Nor is a possessor of land under any such duty to one who has ceased to be an invitee.

d. The duty to protect the other against unreasonable risk of harm extends to risks arising out of the actor's own conduct, or the condition of his land or chattels. It extends also to risks arising from forces of nature or animals, or from the acts of third persons, whether they be innocent, negligent, intentional, or even criminal. (See § 302 B.) It extends also to risks arising from pure accident, or from the negligence of the plaintiff himself, as

See Appendix for Reporter's Notes, Court Citations, and Cross References

119

[Illustration 157]

PAGE FROM RESTATEMENT (SECOND) OF TORTS

over at a station to those who will do so. A continues to ride on the train in an unconscious condition for five hours, during which time his illness is aggravated in a manner which proper medical attention would have avoided. B Railroad is subject to liability to A for the aggravation of his illness.

3. A is a guest in B's hotel. Without any fault on the part of B, a fire breaks out in the hotel. Although they could easily do so, B's employees fail to call A's room and warn him to leave it. As a result A is overcome by smoke and carbon monoxide before he can escape, and is seriously injured. B is subject to liability to A.

4. A, a child six years old, accompanies his mother, who is shopping in B's department store. Without any fault on the part of B, A runs and falls, and gets his fingers caught

> Frequently, the Comment section includes hypothetical examples.

the escalator. As a result, A's injuries are aggravated in a manner which would have been avoided if the escalator had been shut off with reasonable promptness. B is subject to liability to A for the aggravation of his injuries.

5. A, a patron attending a play in B's theatre, suffers a heart attack during the performance, and is disabled and unable to move. He asks that a doctor be called. B's employees do nothing to obtain medical assistance, or to remove A to a place where it can be obtained. As a result, A's illness is aggravated in a manner which reasonably prompt medical attention would have avoided. B is subject to liability to A for the aggravation of his illness.

6. A is imprisoned in a jail, of which B is the jailor. A suffers an attack of appendicitis, and cries for medical assistance. B does nothing to obtain it for three days, as a result of which A's illness is aggravated in a manner which proper medical attention would have avoided. B is subject to liability to A for the aggravation of his illness.

7. A is a small child sent by his parents for the day to B's kindergarten. In the course of the day A becomes ill with scarlet fever. Although recognizing that A is seriously ill, B does nothing to obtain medical assistance, or to take the child home or remove him to a place where help can be obtained. As a result, A's illness is aggravated in a manner which proper medical attention would have avoided.

[Illustration 158]

PAGE FROM AN APPENDIX VOLUME, RESTATEMENT (SECOND) OF TORTS

§ **314**   TORTS, SECOND   Ch. 12

Duty of motor vehicle driver to sound warning in approaching place where children are playing or gathered. 30 A.L.R.2d 40.

Unsignaled stop or slowing of motor vehicle as negligence. 29 A.L.R.

> The Reporter's Notes contain information pertaining to the development of the Restatement and include references to cases and secondary authorities. These Notes are in the Appendix volumes for the Restatements (Second) of Agency, Torts, and Trusts. For all other Restatements 2d, these Notes are at the end of each section of the Restatement. Recent Restatements also include WESTLAW references.

person. 64 A.L.R.2d 1179.

Liability of one undertaking to care for child for injury to child. 27 A.L.R. 1018.

§ 314 A.   **Special Relations Giving Rise to Duty to Aid or Protect.**

⟶ REPORTER'S NOTES

This Section has been added to the first Restatement.

Illustration 1 is based on Yazoo & M. V. R. Co. v. Byrd, 89 Miss. 308, 42 So. 286 (1906); Layne v. Chicago & Alton R. Co., 175 Mo. App. 34, 157 S.W. 850 (1913); Cincinnati, H. & D. R. Co. v. Kassen, 49 Ohio St. 230, 31 N.E. 282, 16 L.R.A. 674 (1892); Yu v. New York, N. H. & H. R. Co., 145 Conn. 451, 144 A.2d 56 (1958); Continental Southern Lines, Inc. v. Robertson, 241 Miss. 796, 133 So. 2d 543, 92 A.L.R.2d 653 (1961), passenger injured through his own negligence.

Illustration 2 is taken from Middleton v. Whitridge, 213 N.Y. 499, 108 N.E. 192, Ann. Cas. 1916C, 856 (1915). Cf. Kambour v. Boston & Maine R. Co., 77 N.H. 33, 86 A. 624, 45 L.R.A. N.S. 1188 (1913); Jones v. New York Central R. Co., 4 App. Div. 2d 967, 168 N.Y.S.2d 927 (1957), affirmed, 4 N.Y.2d 963, 177 N.Y.S. 2d 492, 152 N.E.2d 519 (1958); Yu v. New York, N. H. & H. R.

Co., 145 Conn. 451, 144 A.2d 56 (1958).

Compare, as to the duty of a carrier to protect its passengers from dangers arising from the conduct of third persons: Hillman v. Georgia Ry. & Banking Co., 126 Ga. 814, 56 S.E. 68, 8 Ann. Cas. 222 (1906); Nute v. Boston & Maine R. Co., 214 Mass. 184, 100 N.E. 1099 (1913); Kuhlen v. Boston & N. St. R. Co., 193 Mass. 341, 79 N.E. 815, 7 L.R.A. N.S. 729, 118 Am. St. Rep. 516 (1907); Exton v. Central R. Co. of New Jersey, 62 N.J.L. 7, 42 A. 486, 56 L.R.A. 508 (1898), affirmed, 63 N.J.L. 356, 46 A. 1099, 56 L.R.A. 512; Kinsey v. Hudson & Manhattan R. Co., 130 N.J.L. 285, 32 A.2d 497, 14 N.C.C.A. N.S. 692 (Sup. Ct. 1943), affirmed, 131 N.J.L. 161, 35 A.2d 888 (Ct. Err. & App.); Harpell v. Public Service Coordinated Transport, 20 N.J. 309, 120 A.2d 43 (1955); Mulhause v. Monongahela St. R. Co., 201 Pa. 237, 50 A. 937 (1902); St. Louis, I. M. & S. R. Co. v. Hatch, 116 Tenn. 580, 94

See also cases under division, chapter, topic, title, and subtitle that includes section under examination.

[Illustration 159]

PAGE FROM AN APPENDIX VOLUME, RESTATEMENT
(SECOND) OF TORTS

Ch. 12   CITATIONS TO RESTATEMENT, SECOND   § 314A

the warnings, the owners of a mall complex and the lessees of a theater in that complex allowed patrons to leave the theater uninformed. Within two miles of the complex, flood waters struck the vehicle of a family that had just left the theater, drowning one child. The victim's estate sued the owner and the lessees. The trial court dismissed the action against the lessees and granted summary judgment to the owners. Affirming with respect to the owners and reversing and remanding with respect to the lessees, this court held that the lessees owed the family, as business visitor invitees, an affirmative duty to exercise reasonable care for their safety, including an obligation to warn them of reasonably foreseeable off-premises danger. A concurring and dissenting opinion argued that moral outrage was not necessarily a sound premise for adjusting legal relationships and that an actor's realization that an action on his part was necessary for another's protection did not of itself impose on him a duty to take such action. Mostert v. CBL & Associates, 741 P.2d 1090, 1100–1101.

Wyo.1991. Com. (c) cit. in diss. op. Af-

ries the inmate sustained after he slipped on a pillow that the deputy had left on a stairway. The inmate contended that the deputy's negligence deprived him of his interest in freedom from bodily harm, and violated his right to due process because the deputy's sovereign immunity barred state tort claims. The district court granted the deputy's motion for summary judgment, and the court of appeals affirmed. The Supreme Court affirmed, holding that the deputy's negligence was not deliberate conduct constituting an abuse of power for which the due process clause had been implemented. The Court noted that state tort law may establish a special duty of care for jailors, for which negligence would be a breach, but that it was not embraced by the Fourteenth Amendment. Daniels v. Williams, 474 U.S. 327, 335–36, 106 S.Ct. 662, 667, 88 L.Ed.2d 662 (1986).

C.A.2, 1988. Illus. 6 cit. in ftn. An FBI informant who failed to induce a casino developer to participate in an illegal scheme intentionally disrupted the developer's business interests. When the developer sued

---

> The Appendix volumes for the Restatements 2d include a synopsis of each case that has cited a Restatement rule, and further indicate whether the court supported or did not support the rule.

---

gent in failing to render first aid to the decedent. The trial court entered judgment on a jury verdict for the defendant. Affirming, this court held that the trial court properly instructed the jury that the defendant owed its customer a duty to summon medical assistance within a reasonable time but that it did not owe a duty to provide medical training to its food service personnel or medical rescue services to its customers. The dissent argued that, although there was no duty for a lay person trained in first aid who came upon an accident to stop and help injured persons, even though he might be able to help, an innkeeper who invited guests to his place of business could not refuse to give assistance to his patrons as was within his ability to provide. Drew v. LeJay's Sportsmen's Cafe, Inc., 806 P.2d 301, 307.

§ 314A. Special Relations Giving Rise to Duty to Aid or Protect

U.S.1986. Subsec. (4) cit. in disc. A prison inmate sued the prison deputy for inju-

torts exception to the Federal Tort Claims Act. Affirming, this court held that the mere fact that the plaintiff was the subject of an undercover investigation by the FBI gave rise to no special affirmative duty to protect the plaintiff independent of the government's duty to supervise its agents. Guccione v. U.S., 847 F.2d 1031, 1037, rehearing denied 878 F.2d 32 (2d Cir.1989).

C.A.3, 1985. Subsecs. (1)(a) and (2) cit. in sup. A tavern patron who had been stabbed brought a personal injury action against a tavern owner and the patron's assailant. This court reversed and remanded the district court's judgment against the defendants. The court held that the tavern owner was entitled to a new trial, since the assailant's deposition should have been admitted on the issue of whether the owner's negligence was the proximate cause of the patron's injury. The court ruled that summary judgment should not have been granted on the issue of the assailant's liability, since the assailant's plea to third-degree

---

Cit.—cited; com.—comment; fol.—followed; sup.—support.
A complete list of abbreviations precedes page 1.

[Illustration 160]

PAGE FROM SHEPARD'S RESTATEMENT OF THE LAW CITATIONS

§ 314				TORTS, SECOND				
151CA3d	Minn	17C3d435	36C3d806	429So2d1326	264A2d374	Comment d	649P2d1119
[1102	289NW483	30C3d367	38C3d124	470So2d20	SD	144Az11	Ill
157CA3d144	Mo	95Ill&154	47DC2d103	Haw	214NW788	81Ill&144	437NE935
173CA3d841	648SW885	168NJS484	60H564	592P2d825	368NW627	Ariz	Mich
173CA3d	650SW297	Calif	61H376	604P2d1202	So C	695P2d260	342NW604
[1208	ND	118CaR133	65H188	649P2d1119	238SE168	Ill	62CaL1027
174CA3d215	349NW642	131CaR23	104Ida385	Idaho	Utah	289NE221	46HLR712
15C3d49	Nev	148CaR808	108Ida24	659P2d139	697P2d243	Comment e	77McL1593
30C3d367	580P2d483	151CaR731	81Ill&144	696P2d875	Wash	573F2d438	
34C3d23	NJ	152CaR231	141Ill&99	Ill	562P2d267	63CA3d542	
65H188	403A2d509	178CaR788	361Ill&969	289NE221	Wis	107Ill&352	§ 315
55Ill&410	NY	185CaR398	521Ill&200	302NE208	270NW426	386Mas887	et seq.
3MaA753	426NYS2d	188CaR212	741Ill&925	328NE542	345NW448	Calif	73CA3d706
389Mas50	[934	190CaR312	761Ill&697	344NE538	W Va	134CaR33	Calif
66Mch1461	443NYS2d	191CaR710	95Ill&154	367NE281	271SE338	Ill	141CaR193
393Mch414	[143	199CaR527	105Ill&920	393NE584	62CaL1027	437NE935	
303Md242	Ohio	529P2d557	107Ill&352	395NE185	67Cor940	Iowa	
94Nev402	458NE1263	551P2d343	109Ill&886	419NE571	45LCP(3)75	294NW561	§§ 315
103NYM583	485NE291	636P2d1126	109Ill&980	435NE188	66McL1462	Mass	to 320
110NYM926	Pa	Ill	122Ill&408	437NE934	77McL1268	438NE349	78CA3d313
200&135	155A2d346	419NE571	137Ill&252	441NE370	77McL1593	Ohio	104CA3d819
9&S79	260A2d760	Minn	137Ill&643	441NE390	79A31214n	485NE291	123CA3d257
397Pa317	264A2d373	323NW25	137Ill&852	461NE619	Caveat	Comment f	135CA3d537
437Pa511	428A2d1357	NJ	60Il2d559	484NE471	168NJS484	386Mas887	138CA3d621
286PaS337	SD	403A2d509	364Mas710	484NE1212	200&135	120A149	143CA3d308
168NJS483	368NW626	Tex	386Mas887	485NE482	Ohio	200&135	13C3d186
139Vt641	Tex	526SW612	389Mas50	Iowa	485NE291	85Wis2d305	17C3d435
58Wis2d266	491SW485	Comment d	39McA275	294NW561	Comment a	Fla	27C3d751
85Wis2d303	526SW608	Tex	77McA523	334NW759	535FS59	401So2d1137	168NJS483

> **Each Section of the various Restatements and the related Comment, in this Illustration § 314A of the *Restatement (Second) of Torts*, can be Shepardized using *Shepard's Restatement of the Law Citations*.**

134CaR32	45LCP(3)87	566SW775	81NM738	Mass	70CA3d779	Wis	164CaR268
144CaR799	77McL1593	Comment f	41NY82	308NE476	79CA3d159	270NW427	167CaR75
178CaR787	21MnL266	30C3d367	59NY258	438NE349	104CA3d811	Illustra-	176CaR470
190CaR312	24MnL671	Calif	106NYM818	449NE334	153CA3d	tions	185CaR398
192CaR235	89PaL321	178CaR788	120A149	Md	[1143	1 to 7	188CaR212
196CaR304	96PaL590	636P2d1126	17&A85	492A2d1301	34C3d31	96CA3d522	191CaR710
197CaR923	124PaL1034	Ohio	200&A139	Mich	200&A135	Calif	199CaR527
199CaR192	9TxL234	485NE291	43OrA507	197NW493	Calif	157CaR824	529P2d557
203CaR580	20TxL772	Tex	437Pa512	224NW849	139CaR86	Illustra-	551P2d343
219CaR536	43YLJ887	678SW536	88SD25	258NW545	144CaR799	tion 1	614P2d733
219CaR677	70A31130n		269SoC482	308NW693	164CaR269	77McL1268	Minn
219CaR850	83A31202n	§ 314A	121NJS535	339NW217	192CaR241	Illustra-	323NW25
301P2d990	Comment a	54USLW	168NJS484	342NW606	200CaR783	tion 5	NJ
539P2d41	243CA2d461	[4092	17WAp242	345NW688	664P2d145	153CA3d382	403A2d508
636P2d1125	15C3d49	447F2d741	85Wis2d302	Mo	710P2d919	Calif	65Cor210
Colo	30C3d367	498F2d616	117Wis2d683	446SW140	Ohio	200CaR262	24MnL671
664P2d139	215Va158	545F2d283	Alk	Nev	485NE291	Illustra-	15TxL11
Fla	Calif	573F2d435	627P2d628	580P2d483	SD	tion 6	
282So2d178	52CaR525	592F2d46	Ariz	NJ	368NW627	153CA3d382	
390So2d156	123CaR473	680F2d1260	603P2d122	298A2d89	Comment c	Calif	§§ 315
428So2d376	178CaR788	721F2d869	695P2d259	403A2d509	722F2d222	200CaR262	to 319
429So2d1325	539P2d41	722F2d220	Calif	NM	448FS732	Fla	303Md243
Haw	636P2d1126	727F2d954	67CaR514	472P2d1001	153CA3d	429So2d1326	Minn
649P2d1119	Ore	759F2d1124	134CaR32	NY	[1143	Illustra-	338NW255
Ill	702P2d1141	727F2d954	144CaR799	359NE392	137Ill&253	tion 7	352NW781
371NE70	Va	448FS732	157CaR824	451NE205	137Ill&643	153CA3d382	62CaL1027
Ind	207SE844	535FS59	190CaR314	390NYS2d	264Md586	6MaA555	
433NE49	62CaL1493	566FS1231	199CaR189	[883	200&A135	Calif	§ 315
Iowa	Comment b	124Az230	200CaR783	435NYS2d	200CaR783	200CaR262	506F2d705
364NW231	561FS1134	144A710	205CaR845	[515	Calif	Mass	573F2d435
369NW415	Comments	260CA2d755	211CaR360	464NYS2d	710P2d919	285NE792	590F2d763
La	c to f	364Mas709	685P2d1196	[447	Ill	379NE1114	612F2d140
455So2d1371	Mass	63CA3d542	695P2d657	Ohio	484NE472		727F2d901
Mass	308NE471	79CA3d159	710P2d910	467NE897	484NE1212	§ 314B	759F2d1124
328NE528	Comment c	96CA3d522	Fla	477NE671	Md	596F2d560	773F2d187
449NE334	135CA3d537	141CA3d448	372So2d1147	485NE289	287A2d255	65Ill&88	776F2d822
Md	138CA3d621	151CA3d	401So2d1137	Ore	Ohio	107Ill&352	780F2d103
492A2d1300	141CA3d446	153CA3d	[1098	401So2d	485NE291	129McA543	
Mich	143CA3d308	[1143	421So2d195	[1367	Pa	Tex	*Continued*
224NW852					260A2d761	652SW569	Haw

356

SECTION F.   UNIFORM LAWS AND MODEL ACTS

1.   Uniform Laws

The Restatements, as mentioned, have as their aim the restating of the common law as developed by the courts. The movement of law reform also has focused on statutory law and the need, in many instances, for uniform statutes among the states. Toward this aim, the American Bar Association passed a resolution recommending that each state and the District of Columbia adopt a law providing for the appointment of Commissioners to confer with Commissioners of other states on the subject of uniformity in legislation on certain subjects. In 1892 the National Conference of Commissioners on Uniform State Laws was organized, and by 1912 each state had passed such a law. According to the National Conference's constitution, its object is to "promote uniformity in state law on all subjects where uniformity is desirable and practical." [20]

The National Conference will designate an act as a *Uniform Act* when it has a reasonable possibility of ultimate enactment in a substantial number of jurisdictions. The Conference meets once a year and considers drafts of proposed uniform laws. When such a law is approved, it is the duty of the Commissioners to try to persuade their state legislatures to adopt it. Of course, adoption by the Conference has no legal effect; only subsequent enactment by a state's legislature can achieve this result. The Conference has approved over 200 acts and over 100 have been adopted by at least one state. Perhaps the most notable example is the *Uniform Commercial Code.*

Laws approved by the National Conference of Commissioners on Uniform State Laws are published in the following forms:

a.   As separate pamphlets.

b.   In the annual *Handbook* of the National Conference.

c.   In *Uniform Laws Annotated, Master Edition.* The multi-volume *Uniform Laws Annotated, Master Edition,* published by West Publishing Company, contains over 160 laws. A law must have been adopted by at least one state to be included in this set. Volumes are revised periodically and pocket supplements and annual pamphlets are issued. [See Illustrations 161–163.]

After each section of a uniform law, pertinent official Comment of the Commissioners is given. This is followed by references to law review articles, related West digest Topics and Key Numbers, and *Corpus Juris*

---

[20] This document is published annually in the HANDBOOK OF THE NATIONAL CONFERENCE OF COMMISSIONERS ON UNIFORM STATE LAWS AND PROCEEDINGS OF THE ANNUAL MEETING. For a more detailed discussion of the National Conference, *see* WALTER P. ARMSTRONG, A CENTURY OF SERVICE: A CENTENNIAL HISTORY OF THE NATIONAL CONFERENCE OF COMMISSIONERS ON UNIFORM STATE LAWS (1991); Richard E. Coulson, *The National Conference of Commissioners on Uniform State Laws and the Control of Law-Making—A Historical Essay,* 16 OKLA. CITY U.L. REV. 295 (1991).

Secundum. In recently-revised volumes and the supplementation WESTLAW references are also provided. Each volume contains a detailed index to the laws it contains. Tables in both the bound volumes and the supplements list the states that have adopted each uniform law. [See Illustration 166.] The *Uniform Laws Annotated, Master Edition* is included in WESTLAW in the ULA database.

　　　d. *National Conference of Commissioners on Uniform State Law Archive Collection in Microfiche.* This collection, prepared by William S. Hein & Co. and containing over 700 documents, includes transcripts of the National Conference's annual meetings and Committee of the Whole meetings, the *Handbooks* from 1892 to date, and successive drafts of uniform laws up to and including the uniform law as adopted. A hard copy index to the set is provided. The collection is updated annually.

2. Model Acts

　　　An act that does not have a reasonable possibility of uniform adoption is designated as a *Model Act.* The expectation of the drafters is that parts, but not necessarily all of the act will be adopted, or modified and then adopted, by various states. The National Conference of Commissioners on Uniform State Laws occasionally drafts some model acts, but this work is most often left to the American Law Institute.[21] Among the more significant of these ALI works are the Model Business Corporation Act and the Model Penal Code. The National Conference and the ALI worked jointly on the Uniform Commercial Code.

3. Locating Uniform Laws and Model Acts and Related Publications

　　　a. *Handbook of the National Conference of Commissioners on Uniform State Laws.* This annual publication includes discussions of pending legislation, as well as the texts of all uniform laws adopted during that year. Through this *Handbook* a researcher can locate a uniform law, even if it has not been adopted by any state. A complete list of acts approved by the National Conference appears each year in the *Handbook's* Appendices. Charts are included that show which states have adopted specific Uniform Laws and Model Acts, and the date of adoption.

　　　b. *Directory of Uniform Acts and Codes.* This annual pamphlet, published as part of the *Uniform Laws Annotated, Master Edition,* shows in which volume of the *Master Edition* a particular law is published. [See Illustration 164.] This *Directory* also includes a state-by-state listing showing which laws each state has adopted, a list of the Commissioners by state, and a brief subject index to all acts in the set. [See Illustration 165.]

　　　c. *Martindale–Hubbell Law Directory.* One volume of this publication[22] includes, on a selective basis, the unannotated text of uniform laws and model acts.

---

[21] Documents pertaining to the uniform laws and model acts with which the ALI has been associated are contained in the source described in *supra* note 17.

[22] The *Martindale–Hubbell Law Directory* is discussed in Chapter 19.

d. *Legal Periodical Articles.* The *Index to Legal Periodicals, Current Law Index,* and *Legal Resource Index* index under subject the articles written about various uniform laws and model acts. In addition, *ILP* uses a separate heading for "Uniform laws," and *CLI* and *LRI* use the heading "Uniform state laws." These headings enable articles to be grouped collectively. *CLI* and *LRI* also list articles about model codes under the specific name of the act.

SECTION G. ILLUSTRATIONS: UNIFORM LAWS

[Illustration 161]

PAGE FROM VOLUME 8A, UNIFORM LAWS ANNOTATED, MASTER EDITION

UNIFORM ANATOMICAL GIFT ACT

An Act authorizing the gift of all or part of a human body after death for specified purposes.

1968 ACT

Sec.

1. Definitions.
2. Persons Who May Execute an Anatomical Gift.
3. Persons Who May Become Donees; Purposes for Which Anatomical Gifts May be Made.
4. Manner of Executing Anatomical Gifts.
5. Delivery of Document of Gift.
6. Amendment or Revocation of the Gift.
7. Rights and Duties at Death.
8. Uniformity of Interpretation.
9. Short Title.
10. Repeal.
11. Time of Taking Effect.

Be it enacted . . . .

Library References

Dead Bodies ⚎1.   C.J.S. Dead Bodies § 2.

§ 1. [Definitions]

(a) "Bank or storage facility" means a facility licensed, accredited, or approved under the laws of any state for storage of human bodies or parts thereof.

(b) "Decedent" means a deceased individual and includes a stillborn infant or fetus.

(c) "Donor" means an individual who makes a gift of all or part of his body.

(d)   approved   ated
by the   ere-
of, alth

> **This is an example of a typical Uniform Law adopted by the National Conference of Commissioners on Uniform State Laws.**

(e) "Part" means organs, tissues, eyes, bones, arteries, blood, other fluids and any other portions of a human body.

(f) "Person" means an individual, corporation, government or governmental subdivision or agency, business trust, estate, trust, partnership or association, or any other legal entity.

(g) "Physician" or "surgeon" means a physician or surgeon licensed or authorized to practice under the laws of any state.

[Illustration 162]

PAGE FROM VOLUME 8A, UNIFORM LAWS ANNOTATED, MASTER EDITION

ANATOMICAL GIFT ACT § 1

(h) "State" includes any state, district, commonwealth, territory, insular possession, and any other area subject to the legislative authority of the United States of America.

⟶ **COMMENT**

Subsection (f) is taken verbatim from the Uniform Statutory Construction Act, section 26(4). In any state that has adopted the Uniform Act or its equivalent, this subsection will be unnecessary.

Subsection (h) is taken from section 26(9) of the Uniform Statutory Construction Act.

Action in Adopting Jurisdictions

Variations from Official Text:

Alabama. Omits definition of "state" found in subsec. (h).

Alaska. In subsec. (d), inserts "a state" following "United States government,".

Omits definition in subsec. (f).

California. In "or her" following

In subsec. (e), substitutes "the cornea, sclera, or vitreous and other segments of, or the whole, eye" for "eyes".

Omits definition of "state" found in subsec. (h).

Connecticut. In subsec. (a), omits "licensed, accredited, or approved under the laws of any state", and makes other language changes in the section without affecting the substance.

Delaware. In subsec. (e), substitutes "includes" for "means" and adds "and 'part' includes 'parts' " at the end thereof.

District of Columbia. In subsec. (e), substitutes "includes" for "means" and adds "and 'part' includes 'parts' " at the end thereof.

In subsec. (h), inserts "the District of Columbia" after "insular possession".

Florida. Section reads:
"For the purpose of this part of this law:
"(1) 'Bank' or 'storage facility' means a facility licensed, accredited, or approved under the laws of any state for storage of human bodies or parts thereof.

"(2) 'Donor' means an individual who makes a gift of all or part of his body.

means a hospital li- or approved under tate and includes a l by the United :, a state, or a sub- although not required to be licensed under state laws.

"(4) 'Physician' or 'surgeon' means a physician or surgeon licensed to practice under chapter 458 or chapter 459, or similar laws of any state. 'Surgeon' includes dental or oral surgeon."

Illinois. In subsec. (g), adds "medicine in all of its branches" preceding "under the laws."

Adds definitions as follows:
" 'Death' means for the purposes of the Act, the irreversible cessation of total brain function, according to usual and customary standards of medical practice.

" 'Technician' means an individual trained and certified to remove tissue, by a recognized medical training institution in the State of Illinois."

Iowa. In subsec. (d), inserts "under the laws of this state, or licensed" following "licensed" where first appearing.

In subsec. (e), substitutes "includes" for "means" and adds "and 'part' includes 'parts' " at the end thereof.

After each Section of the Uniform Law the official Comment of the Commissioners explaining each Section is given.

31

[Illustration 163]

PAGE FROM VOLUME 8A, UNIFORM LAWS ANNOTATED, MASTER EDITION

§ 1   ANATOMICAL GIFT ACT

Heart transplants: Legal obstacles to donation. 45 Chicago-Kent L.Rev. 78 (1968).

Liability and the heart transplant. 6 Houston L.Rev. 85 (1968).

Medico-legal problems of organ transplantation; gifts of bodies or parts thereof. Victor Richards, M. D. 21 Hast.L.J. 77 (1969).

Need for a redefinition of "death". 45 Chicago-Kent L.Rev. 202 (1968).

Planning for the disposition of human remains. 52 Ill.Bar J. 870 (1964).

Problem of death under Uniform Anatomical Gift Act. 5 Gonzaga L. R. 33.

Procurement of organs for transplantation. David W. Louisell. 64 N.W.L.Rev. 607 (1969).

Statute relating to disposition of a dead man's body. Richard M. Gudeman. 41 Chicago Bar Rec. 310 (1960).

Supplying organs for transplantation. Jessie Dukeminier, Jr. 68 Mich.L.Rev. 811 (1968).

Uniform Anatomical Gift Act of Missouri. H. Elvin Knight, Jr. 26 J. of Mo.Bar 420 (1970).

When does a person die? Fred L. Bardenwerper. 31 Gavel No. 2, p. 14 (1970).

Notes of Decisions

1. Death

Context in which term "death" is used within provisions of Public Health Law governing anatomical gifts upon death implies a definition consistent with the generally accepted medical practice of doctors primarily concerned with effectuating purposes of provisions. New York City Health & Hospitals Corp. v. Sulsona, 1975, 367 N.Y.S.2d 686, 81 Misc.2d 1002, 76 A.L.R.3d 905.

§ 2.   [Persons Who May Execute an Anatomical Gift]

(a) Any individual of sound mind and 18 years of age or more may give all or any part of his body for any purpose specified in section 3, the gift to take effect upon death.

(b) Any of | At the end of each Section, | of priority stated,
when persons | references are given to addi- | le at the time of
death, and in | tional research aids. | itrary indications
by the decede | | by a member of
the same or a | Also, annotations are pro- | part of the dece-
dent's body for | vided to all court cases citing |
     | the Section. |

    (1) the spo | The supplementation should

    (2) an adul | be checked for later informa-

    (3) either | tion.

    (4) an adult brother or sister,

    (5) a guardian of the person of the decedent at the time of his death,

    (6) any other person authorized or under obligation to dispose of the body.

(c) If the donee has actual notice of contrary indications by the decedent or that a gift by a member of a class is opposed by

[Illustration 164]

PAGE FROM UNIFORM LAWS ANNOTATED—DIRECTORY OF UNIFORM ACTS AND CODES

DIRECTORY OF UNIFORM ACTS

List of Uniform Acts or Codes, in alphabetical order, showing where each may be found in Uniform Laws Annotated, Master Edition.

The designation "Pocket Part" under the page column indicates that the particular Act or Code is complete in the Pocket Part. The designation "Pamphlet" under the page column indicates that the particular Act is complete in a Supplementary or Special Pamphlet. The user should always, of course, consult the Pocket Part or Pamphlet for changes and subsequent material when an Act or Code appears in the main volume.

Title of Act	Uniform Laws Annotated Volume	Page
Abortion Act, Revised	9, Pt. I	1
Absence as Evidence of Death and Absentees' Property Act	8A	1
Acknowledgment Act	12	1
Notarial Acts, Uniform Law on	14	125
Administrative Procedure Act, State (1981) (Model)	15	1
Administrative Procedure Act, State (1961) (Model)	15	137
Adoption Act	9, Pt. I	11
Aircraft Financial Responsibility Act	12	21
Alcoholism and Intoxication Treatment Act	9	79
Anatomical Gift Act (1987 Act)	8A	Pocket Part
Anatomical Gift Act (1968 Act)	8A	15
Ancillary Administration of Estates Act	8A	69
Antitrust, State Antitrust Act	7B	711
Arbitration Act	7	1
Attendance of Witnesses From Without a State in Criminal Proceedings, Act to Secure	11	1

> **This Table lists all Uniform Laws contained in the set and shows in which volume the text of the Uniform Law can be located. Similar information can also be found in the annual *Handbook* of the National Conference of Commissioners on Uniform State Laws.**

Children and minors,		
Abortion Act, Revised	9, Pt. I	1
Adoption Act	9, Pt. I	11
Child Custody Jurisdiction Act	9, Pt. I	115
Civil Liability for Support Act	9, Pt. I	333
Gifts to Minors Act (1966 Act)	8A	181
Gifts to Minors Act (1956 Act)	8A	225
Interstate Family Support Act	9, Pt. I	Pocket Part
Juvenile Court Act	9A	1
Parentage Act	9B	287
Paternity Act	9B	347
Putative and Unknown Fathers Act	9B	Pocket Part
Reciprocal Enforcement of Support Act (1968 Act)	9B	381
Reciprocal Enforcement of Support Act (1950 Act)	9B	553
Revised Abortion Act	9, Pt. I	1
Status of Children of Assisted Conception	9B	Pocket Part
Transfers to Minors Act	8A	Pocket Part

1

[Illustration 165]

PAGE FROM UNIFORM LAWS ANNOTATED—DIRECTORY OF UNIFORM ACTS AND CODES, TABLE (BY JURISDICTIONS) LISTING UNIFORM ACTS ADOPTED

TABLE OF JURISDICTIONS LISTING UNIFORM ACTS ADOPTED

List of jurisdictions, in alphabetical order, listing the Uniform Acts or Codes adopted by that particular jurisdiction, and where each may be found in Uniform Laws Annotated, Master Edition.

Each Uniform Act or Code in the Master Edition contains a Table showing the statutory citations of each of the adopting jurisdictions.

ALABAMA

Title of Act	Uniform Laws Annotated Volume	Page
Anatomical Gift Act (1968 Act)	8A	15
Attendance of Witnesses From Without a State in Criminal Proceedings, Act to Secure	11	1
Brain Death Act	12	Pocket Part
Certification of Questions of Law Act	12	49
Child Custody Jurisdiction	9, Pt. I	115
Commercial Code[1]	1 to 3A	
Common Trust Fund Act	7	401
Condominium Act	7	421
Controlled Substances Act	9, Pt. II	1
Criminal Extradition Act	11	51
Declaratory Judgments Act	12	109
Disclaimer of Property Interests Act	8A	85

This Table lists all states alphabetically and indicates under each state which uniform laws or model codes have been adopted by that state.

Enforcement of Foreign Judgments Act (1964 Act)	13	149
Federal Lien Registration Act	7A	359
Fiduciaries Act	7A	391
Fraudulent Transfer Act	7A	639
Guardianship and Protective Proceedings Act	8A	437
Insurers Liquidation Act	13	429
Limited Partnership Act (1976 Act)	6	Pocket Part
Mandatory Disposition of Detainers Act	11	321
Motor Vehicle Certificate of Title and Anti-Theft Act	11	421
Parentage Act	9B	287
Partnership Act (1914 Act)	6	1
Photographic Copies of Business and Public Records as Evidence Act	14	185
Principal and Income Act (1931 Act)	7B	183
Reciprocal Enforcement of Support Act (1950 Act)	9B	553
Securities Act (1956 Act)	7B	509
Simplification of Fiduciary Security Transfers Act	7B	689
Simultaneous Death Act (1940 Act)	8A	557
State Administrative Procedure Act (1961) (Model)	15	137
Trade Secrets Act	14	433
Transfers to Minors Act	8A	Pocket Part

1 Adopted 1972 Revision of Article 9.

9

[Illustration 166]

PAGE FROM VOLUME 8A, UNIFORM LAWS ANNOTATED, MASTER EDITION—TABLE OF JURISDICTIONS ADOPTING THE UNIFORM ANATOMICAL GIFT ACT

UNIFORM ANATOMICAL GIFT ACT

Table of Jurisdictions Wherein Act Has Been Adopted

Jurisdiction	Laws	Effective Date	Statutory Citation
Alabama [1]	1969, Sp.Sess., No. 164	5–14–1969 [2]	Code 1975, §§ 22–19–40 to 22–19–47, 22–19–60.
Alaska	1972, c. 78	1–1–1973	AS 13.50.010 to 13.50.090.
Arizona	1970, c. 147, § 3	8–11–1970	A.R.S. §§ 36–841 to 36–848.
Arkansas	1969, Act 4	1–23–1969	Ark.Stats. §§ 82–410.4 to 82–410.14.
California	1970, c. 1006, § 3	11–23–1970	West's Ann.Cal. Health & Safety Code, §§ 7150 to 7158.
Colorado	1969, c. 239	4–24–1969	C.R.S. 1973, 12–34–101 to 12–34–109.
Connecticut	1969, P.A. 425	1–1–1970	C.G.S.A. §§ 19a–272 to 19a–279.
Delaware	57 Del.L. c. 445, § 2	5–20–1970	24 Del.C. §§ 1780 to 1789.
District of Columbia	P.L. 91–268, §§ 1 to 8	5–26–1970	D.C.Code 1981, §§ 2–1501 to 2–1508.
Florida	1969, c. 69–88	6–14–1969	West's F.S.A. §§ 732.910 to 732.921.
Georgia	1969, No. 82	6–14–1969	O.C.G.A. §§ 44–5–140 to 44–5–148.
Hawaii	1969, No. 81	6–23–1969	HRS §§ 327–1 to 327–9.
Idaho	1969, c. 98	3–11–1969	I.C. §§ 39–3401 to 39–3411.
Illinois	P.A. 76–1209	10–1–1969	S.H.A. ch. 110½, ¶¶ 301 to 311.
Indiana	1969, c. 166	3–13–1969 [2]	West's A.I.C. 29–2–16–1 to 29–2–16–9.
Iowa	1969 (63 G.A.) c. 137	7–1–1969	I.C.A. § 142A.1 et seq.
Kansas	1969, c. 301	7–1–1969	K.S.A. 65–3209 to 65–3217.
Kentucky	1970, c. 68	6–18–1970	KRS 311.165 to 311.235.

> **A Table preceding the start of each Uniform Law indicates the jurisdictions that have adopted Act, its effective date, and where it can be located in the state's code and session laws.**

Mississippi	1970, c. 413	4–6–1970	Code 1972, §§ 41–39–11, 41–39–31 to 41–39–53.
Missouri	1969, S.B. No. 43	5–28–1969	V.A.M.S. §§ 194.210 to 194.290.
Montana	1969, c. 340	3–13–1969	MCA 72–17–101 to 72–17–210.
Nebraska	1971, LB 799, § 12	8–27–1971	R.R.S.1943, §§ 71–4801 to 71–4812.
Nevada	1969, c. 119	3–17–1969	N.R.S. 451.500 to 451.585.
New Hampshire	1969, c. 345	8–29–1969	RSA 291–A:1 to 291–A:9.
New Jersey	1969, c. 161	9–9–1969	N.J.S.A. 26:6–57 to 26:6–65.
New Mexico	1969, c. 105	3–29–1969	NMSA 1978, §§ 24–6–1 to 24–6–9.
New York	1970, c. 466	5–5–1970	McKinney's Public Health Law §§ 4300 to 4307.
North Carolina	1969, c. 84	10–1–1969	G.S. §§ 90–220.1 to 90–220.8.
North Dakota	1969, c. 255	3–5–1969 [2]	NDCC 23–06.1–01 to 23–06.1–09.
Ohio	1969, p. 1796	11–6–1969	R.C. §§ 2108.01 to 2108.10.
Oklahoma	1969, c. 13	7–29–1969	63 Okl.St.Ann. §§ 2201 to 2209.
Oregon	1969, c. 175	8–22–1969	ORS 97.250 to 97.295.
Pennsylvania	1972, P.L. 508, No. 164	7–1–1972	20 Pa.C.S.A. §§ 8601 to 8607.
Rhode Island	1969, c. 248	5–16–1969	Gen.Laws 1956, §§ 23–18.5–1 to 23–18.5–7.
South Carolina	1969, No. 356	7–1–1969	Code 1976, §§ 44–43–310 to 44–43–400.
South Dakota	1969, c. 111	3–14–1969	SDCL 34–26–20 to 34–26–41.
Tennessee	1969, c. 35	3–25–1969	T.C.A. §§ 53–42–101 to 53–42–109.
Texas	1969, c. 375	5–29–1969	Vernon's Ann.Texas Civ.St. art. 4590—2.
Utah	1969, c. 64	5–13–1969	U.C.A.1953, 26–28–1 to 26–28–8.
Vermont	1969, No. 53	4–10–1969	18 V.S.A. §§ 5231 to 5237.
Virginia	1970, c. 460	4–3–1970	Code 1950, §§ 32.1–289 to 32.1–297.

15

Chapter 18

OTHER RESEARCH AIDS

Attorneys General and Office of Legal Counsel Opinions, Dictionaries, Directories, Abbreviations, Quotations, General Legal Reference Sources, Research on the Supreme Court of the United States, Forms, Jury Instructions and Verdicts/Settlements, Briefs and Records on Appeal, and Professional Responsibility

This chapter covers a variety of types of law books that are useful in legal research, but which do not fit into any of the categories discussed in previous chapters.

SECTION A. OPINIONS OF THE ATTORNEYS GENERAL

The formal opinions of the attorneys general have the characteristics of both primary and secondary authority.[1] As the legal adviser to the executive officials of the government, the attorney general renders requested legal advice to them generally in the form of written opinions. Although these opinions are official statements of an executive officer, issued according to his or her authority, they are merely advisory statements and are not mandatory orders. Therefore, the inquirers and other officials are not bound to follow such recommendations and conclusions. However, the opinions are strongly persuasive and are generally followed by executive officers. Also, they have significant influence on the courts in their deliberations.

The opinions, as a general rule, relate to (1) interpretation of statutes or (2) general legal problems. Some attorneys general limit their advice and will not render opinions as to the constitutionality of proposed legislation.

1. Attorneys General of the United States Opinions

The opinions of the Attorneys General of the United States have been published in forty-two volumes covering 1789–1974, with each volume containing the opinions covering several years, *e.g.,* volume 42 covers 1961 through 1974. Over the last two decades, there has been a precipitous decline in the number of formal opinions selected for publica-

---

[1] Formal opinions are those written and signed by the Attorney General. For additional information on the role of the attorneys general, *see State Attorneys General Powers and Responsibilities* (Lynne M. Ross ed. 1990) (prepared for the National Association of Attorneys General); *200th Anniversary of the Office of the Attorney General* (1989); Peter E. Heiser, Jr., *The Opinion Writing Function of Attorneys General*, 18 IDAHO L. REV. 9 (1982); William H. Thompson, *Transmission or Resistance: Opinions of State Attorneys General and the Impact of the Supreme Court*, 9 VAL. U. L. REV. 55 (1974).

tion.[2] Those that have been published since volume 42 are included in the annual *Opinions of the Office of Legal Counsel.*[3] This publication is discussed in Section B, *infra.*

The full text of the Attorneys General opinions are available on WESTLAW in the USAG database, and on LEXIS in the GENFED Library, USAG file. The *United States Code Annotated* and the *United States Code Service* include digests of U.S. Attorney General opinions in their annotations. Citations are included in the United States and federal units of *Shepard's Citations* when these opinions are cited in a court case.

2. State Attorneys General Opinions

Almost every state publishes the opinions of its attorney general.[4] They are included in the annotations of many annotated state codes, and the state units of *Shepard's Citations* indicate when a state attorney general opinion has been cited by a court.

WESTLAW and LEXIS also include attorneys general opinions for the states, but coverage is not comprehensive. These vendors' listings should be checked for the scope of coverage.

SECTION B. OPINIONS OF THE OFFICE OF GENERAL COUNSEL

Pursuant to 28 U.S.C. § 510, the United States Attorney General has delegated to the Office of Legal Counsel the duties of preparing formal opinions of the Attorney General, rendering informal opinions to the various federal agencies, assisting the Attorney General in the performance of his or her function as adviser to the President, and rendering opinions to the Attorney General and the various organizational units of the Department of Justice.[5]

The *Opinions of the Office of Legal Counsel* have been published annually since 1977 and include the memorandum opinions, which are written by various attorneys in the Office on matters referred to the Office for response, as well as the formal Attorney General Opinions. Only a small portion of the memorandum opinions rendered are actually published, since the addressee of the opinion must agree to publication.

---

[2] For example, from 1909 through 1912, an average of 58 opinions were published each year. From 1937 through 1940, the average was 37. During the 1950s the average number of published opinions declined to 7. A total of only 13 opinions were published during 1970 through 1974. Irwin S. Rhodes, *"Opinions of the Attorney General" Revised,* 64 A.B.A. J. 1374 (1978).

[3] Volume 4A (1980) contains 11 opinions, the first to be issued since 1974. An additional 12 opinions have been published through 1992. While there may someday be a volume 43 of Attorney General opinions, the present rate at which these opinions are published suggests that its publication date is in the distant future.

[4] A checklist of published opinions of state attorneys general is in 3 PIMSLEUR'S CHECKLISTS OF BASIC AMERICAN LEGAL PUBLICATIONS § III (Marcia S. Zubrow ed. & comp., looseleaf) [AALL Publication Series No. 4].

[5] *See* 28 C.F.R. § 0.25.

Like the opinions of the Attorney General, the opinions of the Office of Legal Counsel are merely advisory statements and are not mandatory orders. Complete coverage of these opinions is in WESTLAW's USAG database.

SECTION C.   LAW DICTIONARIES

Law dictionaries are useful for identifying the definitions of words in their legal sense or use. For each word or phrase a short definition is given. Some legal dictionaries also provide a citation to a court case or other reference tracing the source of the word or phrase. The multi-volume set *Words and Phrases,* discussed in Chapter 6, Section L–1, includes digests from court cases in which a word or phrase has been judicially interpreted. *Words and Phrases* can also be used as a dictionary; but since it is limited to those words that were involved in litigation, it is not a true dictionary.[6] Moreover, most dictionaries are much more compact and are published in one or two volumes. Listed below are some of the more commonly-used American and English law dictionaries.

1.   American Law Dictionaries

a.   *Ballentine's Law Dictionary, with Pronunciations,* 3d ed., Lawyers Cooperative Publishing, 1969, 1429p. This volume often provides citations to *A.L.R. Annotations* and *American Jurisprudence 2d.*

b.   *Black's Law Dictionary,* 6th ed., West Publishing Company, 1990, 1657p. The most widely-used of all law dictionaries, this volume includes a Guide to Pronunciations of Latin Phrases and a Table of Abbreviations. It is on WESTLAW in the DI database. An abridged, paperback version is also available.

c.   *Bouvier's Law Dictionary and Concise Encyclopedia* (3d revision), 8th ed., West Publishing Company, 1914, 3 volumes; reprinted in 1984 by William S. Hein & Co., Inc. This edition is out of date in some respects. It is a particularly scholarly work, however, and many of its definitions are encyclopedic in nature. It is still very useful for many historical terms.

d.   William C. Burton, *Legal Thesaurus,* 2d ed., Macmillan Publishing Company, 1992, 1011p. This volume consists of legal words, words used by the legal community, and words that will enhance legal communication. It includes "associated concepts" and translations of many foreign words and phrases. An index provides references from secondary words to main words.

e.   Bryan Garner, *A Dictionary of Modern Legal Usage,* Oxford University Press, 1987, 587p. Including definitions, spelling rules, and grammar guidelines, this volume is perhaps most valuable for its "authoritative guidance on many matters of usage that are unique to legal

[6] The British counterpart to *Words and Phrases* is the four-volume *Words and Phrases Legally Defined* (3d ed. 1988), which includes both judicial and statutory definitions.

writing." [7] This dictionary is available on LEXIS in the LEXREF library, DMLU file.

f. Steven H. Giffis, *Law Dictionary,* 3d ed., Barron's, 1991, 537p. Among the better of the "pocket" dictionaries, this one includes reference to treatises and legal periodical articles.

g. Wesley Gilmer, *The Law Dictionary: Pronouncing Edition: A Dictionary of Legal Words and Phrases with Latin and French Maxims of the Law Translated and Explained,* rev. 6th ed., Anderson Publishing Company, 1986, 426p.

h. David Mellinkoff, *Mellinkoff's Dictionary of American Legal Usage,* West Publishing Company, 1992, 703p. This dictionary provides definitions, which are often followed by illustrative examples of the words' meanings.

i. Daniel Oran, *Oran's Dictionary of the Law,* 2d ed., West Publishing Company, 1991, 500p. Written for a wide audience, the definitions are concise and contemporary. Common abbreviations are identified and explained in the alphabetical arrangement.

j. Kenneth R. Redden & Gerry W. Beyer, *Modern Dictionary of the Legal Profession,* William S. Hein & Co., Inc., 1993, 802p. This volume, updated annually, focuses on modern legal terms and concepts selected from a wide array of professions.

k. William P. Statsky, *West's Legal Thesaurus/Dictionary: A Resource Guide for the Writer and Computer Researcher,* West Publishing Company, 1985, 813p. This volume includes in one alphabet definitions as well as alternative words to be used.

2. English Law Dictionaries

a. William A. Jowitt & Clifford Walsh, *Jowitt's Dictionary of English Law,* 2d ed. by John Burke, Sweet & Maxwell, 1977, 2 vols.

b. *Mozley and Whiteley's Law Dictionary,* 10th ed. by E.R. Hardy Ivamy, Butterworths, 1988, 510p.

c. Percy G. Osborn, *Osborn's Concise Law Dictionary,* 8th ed. by Leslie Rutherford & Shelia Bone, Sweet & Maxwell, 1993, 392p.

d. *Stroud's Judicial Dictionary of Words and Phrases,* 5th ed. by Frederick Stroud & John S. James, Sweet & Maxwell, 1986, 5 vols., with cumulative supplements.

3. Special Law Dictionaries

There are also dictionaries devoted to specific subjects, such as labor law, environmental law, and taxation. These can be located by checking the library's catalog under the subject and then subdivision, *e.g.,* Taxation—United States—Dictionaries. An unusual hybrid is Richard Sloane, *The Sloane–Dorland Annotated Medical Legal Dictionary,* West

---

[7] Charles Alan Wright, Book Review, TOWNES HALL NOTES, Spring 1988, at 5.

Publishing Company, 1987, 787p., which, according to its preface at v, "combines the established definitions of medical terms with judicial interpretations of the same terms." A dictionary that explains the use of Latin terminology with respect to the broader context in which it occurs is Russ VerSteeg, *Essential Latin for Lawyers,* Carolina Academic Press, 1990, 166p. Several bilingual and multilingual law dictionaries are available, such as Portuguese–English, English–Japanese, and English–French–German. These can be identified through the library catalog.

SECTION D. LAW DIRECTORIES

Law directories vary in the scope of their coverage. Some of them attempt to list all lawyers; others are limited to a region, state, municipality, or a speciality. Law directories are useful in locating information about a particular lawyer or law firm and are used by many lawyers when they have to refer a case to a lawyer in another city.

1. General Directories

a. *Martindale–Hubbell Law Directory.* This 26 volume set, consisting of two separate units with different colored bindings, is the most comprehensive directory of lawyers and is published annually in two distinct units.

One unit consists of 16 numbered and three unnumbered volumes, each with maroon and beige bindings. The first 15 volumes of this unit are arranged alphabetically by state. Each of these volumes is in three color-coded sections. Practice Profiles (blue pages) consist of two alphabetical lists, one of the cities within each state, and a second of the lawyers or law firms within each city. All lawyers admitted to the bar of any jurisdiction are eligible for a general listing without cost.

For each listed attorney, information is given for date of birth, date of admission to the bar, college and law school attended, American Bar Association membership, and speciality. At the end of this section are Practice Profiles for patent and trademark attorneys. Confidential ratings [8] also are given, which estimate legal ability and provide general recommendations. Listings of United States Government Lawyers located in Washington, D.C. are grouped by departments, agencies, commissions, etc. and follow the regular listing for that city.

The second section, Professional Biographies (white pages), is another double alphabetic arrangement, this time done by cities within the state and law firms within each city. Each entry may include the address and telephone number of the firm, names and short biographies of its members, representative clients, areas of practice, and references. Since this section requires a charge for inclusion, the list is not comprehensive. Section three, Services and Suppliers (yellow pages), is ar-

---

[8] A key to the ratings is included in the preliminary pages to each volume, along with the numeric codes for the List of Colleges, Universities, and Law Schools.

ranged alphabetically by cities within the state, then by category of service provided, and then by company name.

Volume 16 is devoted to Corporate and Other Law Departments and includes a Corporation Index, a Corporate Attorney Index, and a Corporate Professional Biographies section. This volume also contains a law school section that includes address, phone number, and key contacts, descriptions about the institution and its academic programs, and professional biographical summaries about the law faculty. This law school section is not comprehensive.

Three unnumbered volumes complete this first unit. Two of these volumes contain a national, alphabetically-arranged listing of individual's names together with the city where they practice, and a national index to the cumulative content for the Services and Suppliers, arranged by category. A separate, unnumbered volume is for "Areas of Practice" and requires a payment of a fee for inclusion. It is arranged alphabetically by area of practice and within that alphabetically by cities within the alphabetically-arranged states.

Six unnumbered volumes, in blue and beige bindings, comprise the second unit. These volumes consist of the following: a two-volume Law Digest for the fifty states, the District of Columbia, Puerto Rico, and the Virgin Islands, with the second volume also containing Uniform and Model Acts as well as an American Bar Association Codes section; a Canadian and International Lawyers and Firms volume; an International Law Digest with digests of laws from almost 60 foreign countries and the European Communities; a Europe, Asia, Australasia, Middle East & Africa volume; and a North American & The Caribbean and Central & South American volume.

Martindale–Hubbell also is available in CD–ROM. In addition, the first 16 volumes are available on LEXIS in the MARHUB library.

b. *West's Legal Directory.* This is an online directory available on WESTLAW (WLD). It contains profiles of law firms, branch offices, and biographical records from all states, Puerto Rico, the Virgin Islands, the District of Columbia, and Canada. While by no means as comprehensive as *Martindale–Hubbell,* the number of entries is increasing rapidly with frequent updating. Numerous topical directories are available within the larger database, all including the same specialized search features.

c. *Who's Who in American Law.* This biannual compilation contains biographical information on over 27,000 attorneys selected for their prominence as judges, educators, or practitioners. Despite the large number of entries, there is no claim to comprehensiveness in any areas of the profession. In fact, the content is influenced greatly by one's willingness to complete the paperwork necessary for inclusion. The format is similar to that used in other Marquis *Who's Who* publications.

d. *The American Bar, The Canadian Bar, The International Bar.* These are annual biographical directories of ranking United States and foreign lawyers. The first two directories provide sketches of the North

American law offices listed and individual biographical data. The third unit is a professional international directory of the "finest lawyers in the world."

e. *Other International Directories.* Many other companies publish directories that are used to locate a recommended attorney in a particular country and city to deal with general legal questions. Included in these are *The Canadian Law List, The International List, The International Lawyers, Kime's International Law Directory,* and *Waterlow's Solicitors' & Barristers' Directory.*

2. State and Regional Directories

Many states have directories of the attorneys in their states. Legal Directory Publishing Co.[9] covers all states except New York and Alaska and lists attorneys by county and city. These directories also contain some biographical data.

3. Specialty Directories

Some directories are published that list only the attorneys who practice law in a particular specialty. These are useful for those who want reference to a lawyer in a specific city on a legal problem common to the specialty. Examples of these directories include *American Bank Attorneys, Lawyer's Register International By Specialities and Fields of Law, Markham's Negligence Counsel, The Probate Counsel,* and Prentice Hall Law & Business' *Directory of Corporate Counsel.* The latter title is available on WESTLAW (CORP–DIR).

4. Judicial Directories and Biographies

a. *Directories*

(1) *BNA's Directory of State & Federal Courts, Judges, and Clerks* (Washington, D.C.)

(2) *Judicial Staff Directory* (Congressional Staff Directory, Ltd., Mount Vernon, VA)

(3) *United States Court Directory* (Administrative Office of the United States Courts)

(4) *Want's Federal–State Court Directory* (Want Publishing Co., Washington, D.C.)

(5) Iris J. Wildman & Mark Handler, *Federal Judges and Justices: A Current Listing of Nominations, Confirmations, Elevations, Resignations, Retirements* (Fred B. Rothman & Co., Littleton, CO)

b. *Biographical Directories*

(1) *Historic*

(a) *Biographical Dictionary of the Federal Judiciary, 1789–1974* (Gale Research Company, Detroit, MI)

---

[9] 9111 Garland Rd., Dallas, TX 75218.

(b) *Judges of the United States,* 2d ed., 1983 (Bicentennial Committee of the Judicial Conference of the United States; covers 1780–1982)

(2) *Current*

(a) *The American Bench* (Forster–Long, Inc., Sacramento, CA), annual.

(b) *The Almanac of the Federal Judiciary* (Prentice Hall Law & Business), 2 vols., looseleaf.

5. Academic Directories

Certain directories are compiled to serve the academic legal community. The Association of American Law Schools' *AALS Directory of Law Teachers* allows one to find addresses for and biographical information on law school faculty, as well as indexing by subject or specialty. This publication can be searched on WESTLAW (WLD–AALS).

The *Directory of Legal Academia* is an electronic directory maintained by the Legal Information Institute at Cornell University. It can be accessed by telnet to gopher—law.cornell.edu. This information is also available on diskette.

The American Association of Law Libraries' *AALL Directory and Handbook* lists geographically the law libraries in the United States and Canada and the law librarians employed in those law libraries. A separate alphabetical listing of law library personnel is also included.

SECTION E. MISCELLANEOUS LEGAL
REFERENCE SOURCES

1. Abbreviations

Many of the legal dictionaries and legal research texts contain tables of abbreviations, *see, e.g.,* Appendix A. In addition to these sources, the following are especially useful:

a. Mary Miles Prince, *Bieber's Dictionary of Legal Abbreviations,* 4th ed., William S. Hein & Co., Inc., 1993, 791p. This volume gives the abbreviation followed by the word or words represented by that abbreviation.

b. Mary Miles Prince, *Bieber's Dictionary of Legal Citations,* 4th ed., William S. Hein & Co., Inc., 1992, 371p. This provides examples of statutes, reporters, and legal periodicals in *Bluebook* form.

c. Donald Raistrick, *Index to Legal Citations and Abbreviations,* 2d ed., Professional Books, 1993, 497p. While the focus of this publication is British, it includes references to sources to the United States and other countries.

d. *World Dictionary of Legal Abbreviations,* Igor I. Kavass & Mary Miles Prince, General Editors, William S. Hein & Co., Inc., 1991 (looseleaf). Abbreviations and acronyms from the English, French, Italian, Portuguese, and Spanish legal literature are covered.

2. Quotations

Often use of an apt quotation can enhance a legal document or an oral presentation. Several sources focus on providing information about law-related quotations. Examples of more recent ones are:

a. Eugene C. Gerhart, *Quote It! Memorable Legal Quotations,* Clark Boardman Co., 1969, 766p.; Eugene C. Gerhart, *Quote It II: A Dictionary of Memorable Legal Quotations,* William S. Hein & Co., Inc., 1988, 553p. Collectively these two volumes contain over 5,000 quotations arranged under subject. Both include author and word indexes.

b. Simon James & Chantal Stebbins, *A Dictionary of Legal Quotations,* Macmillan Publishing Company, 1987, 209p. This volume is arranged under 160 key words and includes indexes for authors and sources and for key words.

c. M. Frances McNamara, *2,000 Famous Legal Quotations,* Aqueduct Books, 1967, 718p. This includes a subject arrangement and a general index.

d. Diana V. Pratt, *Respectfully Quoted: A Dictionary of Quotations Requested from the Congressional Research Service,* Library of Congress, 1989, 520p. This volume contains 2,100 statements, a significant number of which are law-related, gathered in response to Congressional inquiries for quotations addressed to the Congressional Research Service.

e. Fred R. Shapiro, *The Oxford Dictionary of American Legal Quotations,* Oxford University Press, 1993, 582p. The most scholarly of the quotation books, this source contains 3,500 quotations by Americans about law or foreigners about American law. It is arranged alphabetically by subject and chronologically within each subject and includes cross references and author and key-word indexes.

f. David S. Shrager & Elizabeth Frost, *The Quotable Lawyer,* Facts on File Publications, 1986, 373p. In this volume are almost 2,600 quotations arranged under 140 major subject headings. An author and subject index are included.

g. Quotations can also be located in WESTLAW, LEXIS, and NEXIS either using the actual language of the quotation or through a formulated search strategy.

3. General Legal Reference Sources

Often researchers will need information that is not purely law, such as statistics, maps, information on state and federal agencies, compound interest and annuity tables, abbreviations, and addresses and telephone numbers for various groups and organizations. At other times, quick reference may be needed to the U.S. Constitution, the Model Rules of Professional Conduct, correct grammar and usage, biographies, bibliographies, and succinct discussions of legal concepts and legal issues. While no single source can respond to all ready-reference needs, those described below collectively fill the most frequent ones.

a. *American Jurisprudence 2d Desk Book,* Lawyers Cooperative Publishing, 2d ed., 1992, 1290p. This volume, with an annual pocket supplement, is in four parts: federal matters; international matters; national and state matters; and research and practice aids. It includes such items as federal agency organization charts, court rules, consumer price indexes, a statute of limitations table by state and subject, medical charts, compound interest and annuity tables, and weights and measures.

b. *Encyclopedia of Legal Information Sources,* Brian L. Baker & Patrick J. Petit eds., 2d ed., Gale Research Inc., 1993, 1083p. This is a bibliographic guide to approximately 29,000 citations for publications, organizations, and other sources of information on 180 law-related subjects.

c. *Law and Legal Information Directory,* Seven Wasserman et al. eds., Gale Research Inc., 6th ed. 1991, 2 vols. This is a guide to national and international organizations, services, programs, and miscellaneous other information, consisting primarily of addresses, telephone numbers, and frequent annotations.

d. *The Lawyers Almanac,* Prentice Hall Law & Business, 1980 to date. This annual volume is in five main sections: (1) The Legal Profession, which provides information on the nation's largest 500 law firms and 50 legal departments, as well as information on law school enrollments and admissions, state mandatory continuing legal education requirements, and ABA leadership; (2) The Judiciary; (3) Government Departments and Agencies; (4) Statutory Summaries and Checklists; and (5) Commonly Used Abbreviations.

e. *Lawyers Desk Book,* 9th ed., Prentice Hall, 1989, 764p. This volume contains over forty topical discussions on such matters as commercial paper, landlord and tenant, and estate planning. Its appendices include incorporating fees by state, self-liquidating mortgage payment tables, a garnishment guide, and various tax tables.

f. *Legal Researcher's Desk Reference,* Infosources Publishing, 1990 to date, biennial. This volume includes addresses and phone numbers for agencies, elected officials, clerks, U.S. attorneys, law publishers, etc., plus finding aids to federal laws and regulations and historical tables on presidents and Supreme Court justices.

g. William P. Statsky *et al., West's Legal Desk Reference,* West Publishing Company, 1991, 1564p. This volume combines many types of publications into one source: a dictionary; a style and grammar guide; a bibliography of primary and secondary sources by subject and country; and a collection of litigation documents, plus numerous charts and tables, addresses and telephone numbers, and abbreviations.

h. David M. Walker, *Oxford Companion to Law,* Oxford University Press, 1980, 1366p. Although primarily British in focus, this volume is a combination dictionary and concise encyclopedia. It describes words, terms, and individuals, often including bibliographic references. Appen-

dices list holders of various offices since 1660 and bibliographic notes used in compiling the volume.

SECTION F. FORMS

Much of a lawyer's time is spent in drafting legal documents, *e.g.,* wills, trusts, leases. To assist lawyers in this aspect of their practice, many different form books have been published to enable lawyers to model documents after examples and to tailor them to their particular needs. Today, most practitioners store electronically the documents that have been created from form books for subsequent revision and reuse. When using form books, it should be kept in mind that they are all general in nature and that before using a form, extreme care should be exercised to make sure that the language is entirely suitable for the purpose for which it is to be used. Books of forms may be classified as follows:

1. General Form Books

This type provides forms for all aspects of legal practice and varies from one volume to multi-volume sets. They are generally annotated, and each form contains references to cases that have favorably construed provisions within the form. Editorial comment is also frequently given. Examples are:

a. *American Jurisprudence, Legal Forms, 2d* (Lawyers Cooperative Publishing), 20 numbered volumes in multiple books, with annual pocket supplements. A two-volume soft-cover index provides access to the set. Two separate volumes, *Federal Tax Guide to Legal Forms* is a companion to the larger set. This set is a part of the publisher's *Total Client–Service Library.*

b. *American Jurisprudence, Pleading and Practice Forms, Revised* (Lawyers Cooperative Publishing), 25 numbered volumes in multiple books, with annual pocket supplements. A two-volume soft-cover index provides access to the set. This set is part of the publisher's *Total Client–Service Library.*

c. Marvin Hyman, *Basic Legal Forms With Commentary,* 2d ed. (Warren, Gorham & Lamont), 1 volume, looseleaf.

d. *Nichols Cyclopedia of Legal Forms, Annotated* (Clark Boardman Callaghan), 10 numbered volumes in multiple books, with annual pocket supplements.

e. Jacob Rabkin & Mark Johnson, *Current Legal Forms with Tax Analysis* (Matthew Bender), 10 numbered volumes in multiple books, looseleaf.

f. *West's Legal Forms, 2d* (West Publishing Company), 29 volumes in multiple books, with annual pocket supplements. A soft-cover index is provided separately.

2. Federal Forms

Bender's Federal Practice Forms, Nichols Cyclopedia of Federal Forms, West's Federal Forms, and *Federal Procedural Forms, Lawyers Edition,* all of which relate to conducting matters in the federal courts, are discussed in Chapter 12, Section B–7, J. Jacobstein, R. Mersky & D. Dunn, *Fundamentals of Legal Research* (6th ed.).

3. Subject Form Books

Many form books are devoted to a particular subject or to a particular phase of the litigation process. These are similar to the general form books, but contain more forms on the subject covered than will usually be found in those of a general nature. Examples are:

a. *National*

(1) Alvin L. Arnold, *Modern Real Estate Mortgage Forms Series* (Warren, Gorham & Lamont), looseleaf.

(2) F. Lee Bailey & Kenneth J. Fishman, *Complete Manual of Criminal Forms,* 3d ed. (Clark Boardman Callaghan), 3 volumes, looseleaf.

(3) *Bender's Forms of Discovery* (Matthew Bender), 16 numbered volumes in multiple books, looseleaf.

(4) *Fletcher Corporation Forms Annotated* (Clark Boardman Callaghan), 7 volumes in multiple books, with pocket supplements.

(5) Robert P. Wilkins, *Wills & Trust Agreements: A Systems Approach,* 2d ed. (Shepard's/McGraw–Hill), 2 volumes, looseleaf.

b. *State*

Most states also have form books that are keyed to local practice. These are published both by commercial publishers and by state bar associations. They contain the same features as the form books discussed above, but since they are designed for local use, may be more useful for the practitioner. Examples are:

(1) *California Legal Forms, Transaction Guide* (Matthew Bender), multi-volume, looseleaf.

(2) *Legal Forms Manual for Real Estate Transactions* (State Bar of Texas), multi-volume.

4. Other Sources of Forms

a. *Forms in Treatises.* Many multi-volume sets of treatises will include forms, either integrated within the text or in separate volumes.

b. *State Codes.* Some state codes include both substantive and procedural forms. For any particular state code, consult the general index under *Forms.*

SECTION G.   JURY INSTRUCTIONS AND VERDICT AND SETTLEMENT AWARDS

1.   Jury Instructions

Before juries begin their deliberations the judge instructs them on the applicable law.   Often the attorneys have the opportunity to submit proposed instructions to the judge in advance, tailoring these instructions to the pleadings and evidence in the particular case.   It is at the judge's discretion whether to use these instructions or to use his or her own or those from other sources.   The instructions given to a jury are often pivotal to the outcome of its deliberations.

A number of publications are available that contain instructions characterized as "pattern" or "model" instructions.   Some of these are prepared for use in specific states;   others relate to particular subjects, *e.g.,* antitrust, damages in torts, employment discrimination, and medical issues;   and still others are for use in the various federal circuits.   These federal circuit instructions, both civil and criminal, are published in pamphlet form.   The Federal Judicial Center, the Judicial Conference of the United States, and committees of the various circuits are often instrumental in preparing these instructions.   These sources can be identified in a library's catalog under "Instructions to Juries." [10]   Two commercially-published sets that contain extensive collections of instructions for use in the federal courts, together with commentary and case references, are:

a.   Edward J. Devitt et al., *Federal Jury Practice and Instructions: Civil and Criminal,* 4th ed., West Publishing Company, multi-volume with annual pocket supplements.   This set began in 1992 and is currently replacing the third edition.

b.   Leonard B. Sand et al., *Modern Federal Jury Instructions,* Matthew Bender, 1985 to date, multi-volume, looseleaf.   Both civil and criminal instructions are provided along with commentary and case references.

2.   Verdict and Settlement Awards

It is often instructive to have a sense about the measure of damages that might be awarded in a particular type of case.   Having this information available can potentially influence whether to take a case, whether to go to trial and let the case be decided by a judge or jury, or to settle.

The multi-volume *Personal Injury Valuation Handbooks* (Jury Verdict Research, Inc.) are arranged by type of injury, by recovery probabilities, and by psychological factors affecting verdicts.   *Jury Verdict and Settlement Summaries* by LRP Publications is available on WESTLAW

[10] Also useful in locating jury instructions are Cheryl Nyberg & Carol Boast, *Jury Instructions: A Bibliography Part I: Civil Jury Instructions,* LEGAL REFERENCE SERVICES Q., Spring/Summer 1986, at 5; Cheryl Nyberg et al., *Jury Instructions: A Bibliography Part II: Criminal Jury Instructions,* LEGAL REFERENCE SERVICES Q., Fall/Winter 1986, at 3.

in the LRP–JV database.   These summaries cover, among other things, case type, geographical area, factual information about the case, and the verdict or settlement amounts.   LEXIS has a VERDCT Library with several files containing case information on verdict and settlement amounts, expert witnesses, case summaries, and counsel data.

SECTION H.   RESEARCHING THE SUPREME COURT OF THE UNITED STATES *

In Chapter 4 we discussed how to research the opinions of the Supreme Court of the United States.   In this Section various sources are discussed that help in researching the Court as an institution.   No effort has been made to be exhaustive.   For general works on the Court and extensive biographies on individual Justices, consult the catalog in your library.   In addition, the extensive periodical literature about the Court, none of which is included in this Section, can be found using standard indexes to legal periodicals.

1.   Biographies and Profiles

Several works provide varying levels of biographical information about the Justices.   Perhaps the most comprehensive work is Leon Friedman & Fred L. Israel, *The Justices of the United States Supreme Court: Their Lives and Major Opinions* (Chelsea House, 5 vols., 1969–1978).   Henry Flanders' *The Lives and Times of the Chief Justices of the Supreme Court of the United States* (T. & J.W. Johnson & Co., 1881), while dated, is still a good source of information on early Chief Justices.

For briefer entries, one can consult *Men of the Supreme Court: Profiles of the Justices,* by Catherine A. Barnes (Facts on File, 1978) and *The Supreme Court Justices: Illustrated Biographies, 1789–1993,* by Clare Cushman (Congressional Quarterly, 1993).   For a more eulogistic treatment of selected Justices, see *Memorials of the Justices of the Supreme Court of the United States,* edited by Roger F. Jacobs (Fred B. Rothman & Co., 1981), which reprints the speeches given at the Bar of the Supreme Court to mark the death of a Justice.

2.   Nominations

One can gain insight into the ideological and philosophical beliefs of a particular Justice by examining transcripts of the hearings held during the confirmation process.   *The Supreme Court of the United States: Hearings and Reports on Successful and Unsuccessful Nominations of Supreme Court Justices by the Senate Judiciary Committee,* compiled by J. Myron Jacobstein & Roy M. Mersky (William S. Hein & Co., Inc., 1975–), is an ongoing, multi-volume set that contains the text of confirmation hearings and any related Committee Reports.   Coverage begins with the 1916 nomination of Louis D. Brandies and runs, to date, through the 1990 nomination of David H. Souter.   Compilations pertain-

---

* David Gunn, Head of Reference Services at the University of Texas at Austin, Jamail Center for Legal Research, Tarlton Law Library, assisted with preparation of this section.

ing to the Clarence Thomas and Ruth Bader Ginsburg confirmation hearings are in preparation.

3. Personal Papers

If one needs to research the papers of the Justices, the leading source of information about them is Alexandra K. Wigdor, *The Personal Papers of the Supreme Court Justices: A Descriptive Guide* (Garland Pub., 1986).

4. Ratings and Statistical Studies

The seminal work in this area is Albert P. Blaustein & Roy M. Mersky, *The First One Hundred Justices: Statistical Studies on the Supreme Court of the United States* (Archon Books, 1978). More recently, William D. Pederson and Norman W. Proxier have edited *Great Justices of the U.S. Supreme Court: Ratings and Case Studies* (P. Lang, 1993).

5. History

A large number of histories have been written about the Court. The classic work is Hampton L. Carson's *The Supreme Court of the United States: Its History* (John W. Huber, 1891), written to commemorate the one hundredth anniversary of the Supreme Court. The most scholarly and complete history of the Courts is *The Oliver Wendell Holmes Devise: History of the Supreme Court of the United States*, edited by Paul A. Freund and Stanley Katz (1971–). Eleven of the projected fourteen volumes are now available.

An equally impressive work is the four-volume *The Documentary History of the Supreme Court of the United States, 1789–1800*, under the editorship of Maeva Marcus and James R. Perry (Columbia University Press, 1985), which attempts to gather together all the original materials necessary to reconstitute the record of the first eleven years of the Court. Bernard Schwartz has authored the most current single-volume work, *A History of the Supreme Court* (Oxford University Press, 1993).

For less scholarly, more accessible approaches, consult *The Illustrated History of the Supreme Court of the United States*, by Robert Shnayerson (Harry N. Abrams, 1986), or *The Supreme Court of the United States: Its Beginnings & Justices, 1790–1991*, issued by the Commission on the Bicentennial of the United States Constitution.

The *Journal of Supreme Court History*, 1990 to date (formerly the *Yearbook*, 1976–1990), both published by the Supreme Court Historical Society, are good sources of interesting articles on former Justices and their Courts. *The Docket*, 1959 to date, which is published quarterly by the Supreme Court's Public Information Office, includes a wealth of Supreme Court trivia and other items on more esoteric aspects of the Court.

6. Reference and Research Guides

Congressional Quarterly, Inc. (CQ) seems to have cornered the market on reference and research guides to the Court. The following four titles are published by it. *How to Research the Supreme Court,* by Fenton S. Martin and Robert U. Goehlert (1992) is a good introduction to materials on the Court. These authors have also compiled the invaluable *The U.S. Supreme Court: A Bibliography* (1990), which provides a comprehensive listing of works about the Court. *The Supreme Court A to Z: A Ready Reference Encyclopedia,* edited by Elder Witt (1993), is a single-volume work with typically brief, alphabetical entries. The final CQ title, also by Elder Witt, is *Congressional Quarterly's Guide to the United States Supreme Court* (1990), which provides a narrative overview of the workings of the Court.

Other sources include: *The Supreme Court at Work* (Congressional Quarterly, 1990); *A Reference Guide to the United States Supreme Court,* edited by Stephen P. Elliott (Facts on File, 1986); and *The Supreme Court: A Citizen's Guide,* by Robert J. Wagman (1993). Not to be overlooked is Kermit Hall's *The Oxford Companion to the Supreme Court of the United States* (Oxford University Press, 1992), a single volume, encyclopedic compilation of relatively brief, alphabetical entries.

7. Case Selection and Decisionmaking

For works on the forces that determine Supreme Court decisionmaking, see *Deciding to Decide: Agenda Setting in the United States Supreme Court,* by H.W. Perry, Jr. (Harvard University Press, 1991); *The Transformation of the Supreme Court's Agenda: From the New Deal to the Reagan Administration,* by Richard L. Pacelle, Jr. (1991); *Case Selection in the United States Supreme Court,* by Doris M. Provine (University of Chicago Press, 1980); and *Supreme Court Decision Making,* by David W. Rohde and Harold L. Spaeth (W.H. Froeman & Co., 1976).

SECTION I. BRIEFS, RECORDS, AND ORAL ARGUMENTS ON APPEAL

After a case has been decided by a trial court or an intermediate court of appeals, the case may be appealed to a higher court. If an appeal is granted, the attorneys for each side submit written briefs in which they set forth the reasons why the appellate court should either affirm or reverse the decision of the lower court. These various briefs contain the theories upon which arguments hinge and discussion and analysis of the law, with citation to authority. At times, and quite often for cases being heard by the Supreme Court of the United States, *amicus curiae* ("friends of the court") briefs are also filed by groups or individuals in support of one side of the case.

Where available, the record of trial court action is submitted with the brief. This record usually contains forms of the preliminary motions and pleadings in the case, examination and cross examination of witness-

es, the instructions to the jury, the opinion of the lower court, and various other exhibits.

Briefs and records can potentially provide attorneys who have a similar case with much of their research and a list of arguments that have or have not impressed an appellate court.[11] Oral arguments show the focus of the attorneys and judges during the in-person courtroom dynamics.

1. Supreme Court of the United States

A small number of libraries receive copies of the briefs and records that are submitted to the Supreme Court of the United States. Most law school libraries and larger bar association libraries also have these briefs and records available in microform.[12] Summaries of some attorneys' briefs are included in the *United States Supreme Court Reports, Lawyers' Edition.*

a. *Computer–Assisted Legal Research.* Briefs and records for cases argued beginning with the October 1979 Term are available on LEXIS in the GENFED library, BRIEFS file. Commencing with the 1990–91 Term, these sources are available on WESTLAW in the SCT–BRIEFS database. These records and briefs do not become available in the online services until after the oral argument in the case.

b. *Oral Arguments.*

(1) *Audiotapes.* Oral arguments presented before the Supreme Court have been recorded since 1955. These tapes are available from the National Archives. They will be duplicated at no charge if a tape is provided; otherwise they are available for purchase at a nominal charge.[13]

---

[11] For a composite listing of the locations where the various records and briefs can be located, see the following four articles by Gene Teitlebaum: *United States Supreme Courts Records and Briefs: An Updated Union List,* LEGAL REFERENCE SERVICES Q., Fall 1982, at 9; *United States Courts of Appeals Briefs and Records: An Up-dated Union List,* LEGAL REFERENCE SERVICES Q., Fall 1983, at 67; *State Courts of Last Resort's Briefs and Records: An Up-dated Union List,* LEGAL REFERENCE SERVICES Q., Summer/Fall 1985, at 187; *Intermediate Appellate State Courts' Briefs and Records: An Updated Union List,* LEGAL REFERENCE SERVICES Q., Spring/Summer 1988, at 159.

[12] The *CIS US Supreme Court Records & Briefs,* a microfiche collection, includes all argued cases since 1987 and, since 1975, all non-argued cases in which one or more justices wrote a dissent from the *per curiam* decision to deny review.

[13] Until late 1993, tapes were not available until three years after the oral arguments, could only be used for educational or instructional purposes, and could not be copied and disseminated. However, the Supreme Court's policy changed following publication of MAY IT PLEASE THE COURT: THE MOST SIGNIFICANT ORAL ARGUMENTS MADE BEFORE THE SUPREME COURT SINCE 1955 (Peter Irons & Stephanie Guitton eds. 1993). This publication by The New Press consists of a 370 page book and six 100–minute cassettes, which include 23 edited live recordings of oral arguments, with a voice-over narration by Irons. Publication of these materials created a furor, with charges levied by the Supreme Court that one of the editors (Irons) violated contractual arrangements by duplication and dissemination of the tapes. *See, e.g.,* Tony Mauro, *Tapes Project Sparks Clash: Supreme Court to Legal Scholar: Keep Oral Arguments to Yourself,* LEGAL TIMES, at 1, Aug. 16, 1993; Maro Robbins,

(2) *Transcripts.* Starting with the 1953 Term, transcripts of oral arguments are available from Congressional Information Service in a microfiche set entitled *Oral Arguments of the US Supreme Court.* The *U.S. Law Week* frequently provides brief excerpts of oral arguments in its weekly releases.

c. *Landmark Briefs and Arguments of the Supreme Court of the United States: Constitutional Law.* This series from University Publications of America covers 1793 to date. The period 1793–1973 is in 80 volumes. Annual supplements published from 1974 forward average approximately eight volumes each. As the title indicates, coverage is selective.

d. *Antitrust Law: Major Briefs and Oral Arguments of the Supreme Court of the United States, 1955 Term–1975 Term.* This 36 volume set, published by University Publications of America, has not been supplemented.

2. Other Courts of Appeals

Most large law libraries receive the briefs and records for the federal court of appeals for the circuit in which they are located. In addition, Microform, Inc. provides a microfiche collection of the records and briefs from all circuits. Some law libraries also receive the briefs and records of the state's appellate court or courts. Briefs and records from other circuits and other state appellate courts can frequently be obtained from law libraries in those states through interlibrary loan.

SECTION J. PROFESSIONAL RESPONSIBILITY

Codes of conduct developed by the American Bar Association have governed the conduct of lawyers since the *Canons of Professional Ethics* was adopted in 1908. The *Canons* was replaced in 1969 by the *Model Code of Professional Responsibility.* The 1969 *Code* was widely-adopted by the states. In 1983, the *Model Rules of Professional Conduct* were promulgated, and it is these *Model Rules* that are supposed to constitute the national standard of conduct for lawyers.[14] The format is similar to that used in the Restatements discussed in Chapter 17.

These *Model Rules* and their related Comments have been amended numerous times since their original promulgation over twenty years ago. It is up to each state to adopt the *Model Rules* as its state standard. While over two-thirds of the states have adopted the *Model Rules,* some have only adopted portions of them, still others follow the 1969 *Code,* and still others have rules specific to the particular state.

"May It Please the Court" Doesn't Please the Court, NAT'L L.J., at 47, Oct. 11, 1993. Its ultimate result, however, was to cause the Supreme Court to change its existing policy and to make the tapes readily and immediately available to the public through the National Archives. *See* Linda Greenhouse, *Supreme Court Eases Restrictions On Use of Tapes of Its Arguments,* N.Y. TIMES, at A22, col. 1, Nov. 3, 1993.

[14] For information pertaining to the development of the *Model Rules,* see CENTER FOR PROFESSIONAL RESPONSIBILITY, AMERICAN BAR ASSOCIATION, THE LEGISLATIVE HISTORY OF THE MODEL RULES OF PROFESSIONAL CONDUCT (1987).

The ABA has also promulgated rules of conduct for the judiciary, beginning with the *Canons of Judicial Ethics* in 1922. In 1972 the *Code of Judicial Conduct* was adopted, and in 1990 it was replaced by the *Model Code of Judicial Conduct*. These current codes are published as separate pamphlets and are included in one of the unnumbered volumes of the *Martindale–Hubbell Law Directory*.[15]

Enforcement of these rules and the power to discipline lawyers and judges is the responsibility of the state legislature or the highest court in the state, since the ABA, as a voluntary association, has no such authority. The procedure for the discipline of lawyers varies from state to state. The rules governing discipline can be located by consulting the indexes of the state codes. The common practice is for the highest court of the state to appoint a committee of lawyers to hear complaints and to make recommendations to the court. Disciplinary actions are frequently reported in state legal newspapers and in bar association journals.

1. Opinions on Legal Ethics

The American Bar Association has a Standing Committee on Ethics and Professional Responsibility, which is charged with interpreting the professional standards and recommending appropriate amendments and clarifications. Lawyers and judges can describe to this Committee a situation they are facing and request an opinion as to the propriety of their action. These opinions interpret the *Model Rules* and the *Model Code of Judicial Conduct,* continuing to include references to the 1969 *Model Code* and the 1972 *Code of Judicial Conduct.*

These opinions are published in *Opinions on Professional Ethics* (1967), the two-volume *Informal Ethics Opinions* (1975), *Formal and Informal Ethics Opinions* (1984), and a current looseleaf service, *Recent Ethics Opinions.* These opinions are also available on WESTLAW (LS–ABAEO) and in LEXIS, in various files in the ETHICS Library. New opinions are published in the *ABA Journal.*

Most state bar associations have committees similar to the ABA Standing Committee. The opinions of these committees, along with other information on professional responsibility, can be located in the following sources:

a. *ABA/BNA Lawyer's Manual on Professional Conduct.* A joint project of the American Bar Association and the Bureau of National Affairs, Inc., this multi-volume looseleaf set is the most comprehensive source for a wide range of materials dealing with the legal profession. It includes court cases on the discipline of lawyers and the text of state ethics opinions.

b. *National Reporter on Legal Ethics and Professional Responsibility* (University Publications of America). This multi-volume looseleaf

---

[15] An annotated version of the *Model Rules* is available as a separate book, *i.e.,* CENTER FOR PROFESSIONAL RESPONSIBILITY, AMERICAN BAR ASSOCIATION, ANNOTATED RULES OF PROFESSIONAL CONDUCT (2d ed. 1992).

service includes the full text of court cases on legal ethics and the full text of ethics opinions from state and local bar associations.

c.   Eugene M. Wypski, *Opinions/Committees of Professional Ethics.* Volumes 1–3 contain the opinions of the Association of the Bar of the City of New York and the New York County Bar Association; Volume 4 and subsequent volumes contain the opinions for other states.

d.   *State and Local Bar Journals.*   These publications often print the new opinions of state and local ethics committees.

e.   *State Ethics Sources Online.*   WESTLAW has ethics opinions online for some states.   These can be searched collectively in the MLS–EO database or in separate databases by state.   LEXIS has an ETHICS library, which includes state case law relevant to ethical concerns.

2.   Shepard's Professional and Judicial Conduct Citations

This citator is devoted to coverage of citations by the state and federal courts and secondary sources to the various codes of conduct and the ABA's formal and informal opinions.

Chapter 19

INTERNATIONAL LAW *

SECTION A. INTRODUCTION

1. International Law in United States Law

International law is part of our law, and must be ascertained and administered by the courts of justice of appropriate jurisdiction as often as questions of right depending upon it are duly presented for their determination.[1]

International law and international agreements of the United States are law of the United States and supreme over the law of the several States. Cases arising under international law or international agreements of the United States are within the Judicial Power of the United States, and subject to Constitutional and statutory limitations and requirements of justiciability, are within the jurisdiction of the federal courts.[2]

Despite some recently expressed doubts,[3] these quotations, one classic and one contemporary, accurately state the relation between international law and the law of the United States. The Supremacy Clause of the Constitution (Art. VI, § 2) declares:

This Constitution, and the Laws of the United States which shall be made in Pursuance thereof, *and all Treaties made, or which shall be made, under the Authority of the United States,* shall be the supreme Law of the Land; and the Judges in every State shall be bound thereby, any Thing in the Constitution or Laws of any State to the Contrary notwithstanding.[4]

---

* This chapter was written by Jonathan Pratter, Foreign and International Law Librarian, University of Texas School of Law.

[1] The Paquete Habana, 175 U.S. 677, 700 (1900).

[2] RESTATEMENT (THIRD) OF THE FOREIGN RELATIONS LAW OF THE UNITED STATES §§ 111(1), (2) (1987).

[3] The controversy over the Supreme Court's decision in United States v. Alvarez–Machain, 112 S. Ct. 2188 (1992), raises the issue of the application of the rule in The Paquete Habana. *See, e.g.,* Keith Highet *et al., Criminal Jurisdiction—Extradition Treaties—U.S. Government-sponsored Abduction of Mexican Citizen,* 86 AM. J. INT'L L. 811 (1992); Monroe Leigh, *Is the President Above Customary International Law?,* 86 AM. J. INT'L L. 736 (1992); Malvina Halberstam, *In Defense of the Supreme Court Decision in Alvarez–Machain,* 86 AM. J. INT'L L. 736 (1992); Michael J. Glennon, *State Sponsored Abduction: a Comment on United States v. Alvarez–Machain,* 86 AM. J. INT'L L. 746 (1992); Richard Pregent, *Presidential Authority to Displace Customary International Law,* 129 MIL. L. REV. 77 (1990).

[4] Emphasis added.

To give practical impact to these broad statements of law, consider the fact that since 1988 an agreement for the sale of goods (probably the most common of all commercial transactions) between a seller in the United States and a buyer in any of over thirty other countries will be governed by a treaty—the United Nations Convention on Contracts for the International Sale of Goods [5]—unless the parties provide otherwise. In an increasingly transnational world, lawyers practicing anywhere in the United States should consider an understanding of international law and of how to research it to be standard equipment.

2. Definition of International Law

"International law ... consists of rules and principles of general application dealing with the conduct of states and of international organizations and with their relations *inter se,* as well as with some of their relations with persons, whether natural or juridical." [6] Two points arise from this definition. First, the focus is on the legal relations among sovereign states. For this reason the subject is sometimes known as the law of nations, and sometimes as *public* international law. The latter term is often used in contrast to the field known as *private* international law, or more commonly in the United States, conflict of laws. This subject concerns the legal relations of individuals where the law of more than one state may be involved.

The second point to be made about the definition of international law is that sovereign states are not the only actors on the scene. Obviously, international organizations such as the United Nations or the Organization of American States are not nations. But their structure, powers, and relations are a significant topic of international law. Moreover, the individual is by no means excluded from participation, although the understanding of exactly how persons, either natural or legal, participate in international law is not a well-settled question. Nevertheless, it is clear that a topic like international human rights is centrally concerned with the position of the individual.

3. The Sources of International Law

International law lacks the formal machinery for making law that is an obvious characteristic of a national legal system. There is no duly constituted legislature, executive or judiciary, although more or less distant analogs of each of these can be found. In the absence of such a machinery the question of where international law comes from has to receive a lot of attention. This is the question of the *sources* of international law.

Article 38(1) of the Statute of the International Court of Justice [7] is generally considered to be an authoritative statement of the sources of international law. Article 38(1) provides:

---

[5] UN Doc. A/Conf. 97/18 (Annex I) (1980), 52 Fed. Reg. 6262 (1987), *reprinted in* 19 I.L.M. 671 (1980).

[6] RESTATEMENT (THIRD) OF FOREIGN RELATIONS LAW OF THE UNITED STATES § 101 (1987).

[7] 59 Stat. 1055 (1945), T.S. No. 993.

The Court, whose function is to decide in accordance with international law such disputes as are submitted to it, shall apply:

(a) international conventions, whether general or particular, establishing rules expressly recognized by the contesting states;

(b) international custom, as evidence of a general practice accepted as law;

(c) the general principles of law recognized by civilized nations;

(d) . . . judicial decisions and the teachings of the most highly qualified publicists of the various nations, as subsidiary means for the determination of rules of law.

We can then identify five main categories of sources:

a. *International Conventions.* This includes treaties and other international agreements of all kinds. ("Convention" here is a synonym for agreement.) It also includes bilateral agreements (between two parties) and multilateral agreements (having three or more parties).

b. *Customary International Law.* These are rules that arise by virtue of the general and consistent practice of states acting out of a sense of legal obligation.

c. *General Principles of Law.* Examples of such general principles "common to the major legal systems" (to use the contemporary formulation) include the doctrine of laches or the passage of time as a bar to a claim, principles of due process in the administration of justice, and the doctrine of *res judicata.*

d. *Judicial Decisions.* This category includes the decisions of international tribunals and of national courts, when the latter deal with questions of international law. An international tribunal covers various kinds of judicial fora, ranging from the International Court of Justice to an ad hoc arbitral panel constituted to decide a particular international dispute.

e. *Writings of International Law Scholars.* This is current usage for the archaic language found in Article 38 ("teachings of the most highly qualified publicists"). This category covers treatises and textbooks of leading scholars, the draft conventions and reports of the International Law Commission of the United Nations, which was formed "for the Purpose of encouraging the progressive development of international law and its codification," and the reports and resolutions of such non-governmental groups as the American Society of International Law, the International Law Association, and the Institut de Droit International.

Law librarians often use the term "secondary sources" to describe such materials because they are commentaries or discussion of the law rather than formal sources of law. This description is consistent with the usage of Article 38(1), which calls such materials "subsidiary means." The difference comes in the case of judicial decisions, which

under Article 38(1) are also "subsidiary means" rather than primary sources of law.[8]

SECTION B. INTERNATIONAL AGREEMENTS: UNITED STATES SOURCES

1. Introduction

A treaty is "an international agreement concluded between States in written form and governed by international law ... whatever its particular designation."[9] This basic definition makes the important point that the terminology describing a particular international agreement does not affect its legal status as an agreement binding in international law. There is an entire catalog of terms used in connection with various kinds of international agreement: treaty, convention, protocol, covenant, charter, statute, act, declaration, concordat, exchange of notes, agreed minute, memorandum of agreement, and memorandum of understanding, for example.

The subject is further complicated in the practice of the United States by the frequent use we make of the *executive agreement*. Under the Constitution, the President has the "Power, by and with the Advice and Consent of the Senate, to make Treaties, provided two thirds of the Senators present concur ..."[10] But this formal treaty-making power does not exhaust the President's authority to negotiate international agreements. In fact, there are far more executive agreements in force between the United States and other countries than there are treaties. The difference between the two kinds of agreement is a subject for the substantive course in international law.[11] For our purposes it is enough to know that both constitute binding international agreements.

2. Current Sources

a. *T.I.A.S. and U.S.T.* Since 1945, the State Department has published the international agreements of the United States in a series of pamphlets called *Treaties and Other International Acts Series (T.I.A.S.)*. The series began with number 1501 and as of this writing has reached T.I.A.S. 11629, an agreement concluded in December 1988. Since 1950, the State Department has published the agreements that first appear in *T.I.A.S.* in a series of bound volumes entitled *United States Treaties and Other International Agreements (U.S.T.)*. *U.S.T.* is up to 35 volumes and a volume may have as many as five or six

---

[8] To avoid confusion, the reader should note that in discussions of researching international law the word "sources" can have two different senses. The first sense refers to the formal sources of international law as described in Article 38(1). The other sense refers to published sources, that is, the publications and other resources described in this chapter that make up the documentation of international law.

[9] Vienna Convention on the Law of Treaties, concluded at Vienna, May 23, 1969, art. 2 § 1(a), 1155 U.N.T.S. 331.

[10] U.S. CONST. art. II, § 2.

[11] *See generally*, BARRY E. CARTER & PHILLIP TRIMBLE, INTERNATIONAL LAW 134–208 (1991); LOUIS HENKIN ET AL., INTERNATIONAL LAW: CASES AND MATERIALS 198–240 (3d ed. 1993).

separately bound parts. [See Illustration 169.] Volume 35, part 1, the most recently issued as of this writing, ends with T.I.A.S. 10726, an agreement concluded in June 1983. By statute, both *U.S.T.* and *T.I.A.S.* are authoritative sources for the text of agreements published there.[12]

b. *U.S.C., U.S.C.A., U.S.C.S. and Federal Register.* There is a tendency to think that U.S. treaties might be found in one of these places. In general, that is *not* true. *U.S.C.* does not have treaties. The annotated codes, *U.S.C.A.* and *U.S.C.S.*, publish a few treaties of general interest. For example, the United Nations Convention on Contracts for the International Sale of Goods appears in the Appendix volume to Title 15 of *U.S.C.A. U.S.C.S.* has an unnumbered volume, the second half of which is devoted to "U.S.C.S. Conventions," containing the text of, and annotations to, seven multilateral treaties to which the United States is a party. The *Federal Register* rarely publishes U.S. international agreements. Therefore, research for the text of U.S. international agreements *should not* begin with one of these sources. On the other hand, they *should* be consulted to find implementing legislation and judicial interpretation, as noted below in Section B–7.

c. *Commercial Sources.* The reader should note the substantial delay in the publication of both official series. *U.S.T.* and *T.I.A.S.* run 10 and 5 years behind, respectively. Obviously, such delays cause problems for researchers. These are primary sources of law containing binding international agreements of the United States, most of which are *currently in force.*

Two commercial publishers recently began services that go some way to resolving the difficulty. Since 1991, Hein's *United States Treaties and Other International Agreements—Current Microfiche Service* and Oceana's *Consolidated Treaties & International Agreements—Current Service* have made available documents that the State Department has not yet released for publication. At the time of writing, the Oceana series is current to DOS 92–193,[13] and the Hein series, to DOS 93–89. Many of these documents eventually will appear in *T.I.A.S.* Until the State Department remedies the time lag in its publishing program, the commercial services will be the only comprehensive source for recent international agreements of the United States.

Another recent development is the availability, beginning in mid–1993, of a full-text database of U.S. international agreements on WEST-LAW. The database has the identifier USTREATIES. Coverage is spotty. It is supposed to begin with 1979 but it is actually very uneven and inconsistent until 1990, when coverage improves significantly. At the time of writing, the USTREATIES database was current to DOS 93–99, an agreement concluded in March 1993.

---

[12] 1 U.S.C. §§ 112a, 113 (1988).

[13] The Department of State Number (DOS) is the preliminary number assigned to an international agreement pending publication.

3. Earlier Publications

a. *United States Statutes at Large.* Treaties of the United States were published in *United States Statutes at Large* from volume 8 through volume 64 (1949). Volume 8 collected together treaties entered into between 1776 and 1845. Beginning with volume 47, executive agreements were included. Volume 64, part 3 (1950–51) contains an index of all the agreements in *United States Statutes at Large*.

b. *T.S. and E.A.S.* The current pamphlet series, *T.I.A.S.*, was preceded by the *Treaty Series (T.S.)* and the *Executive Agreement Series (E.A.S.).* *Treaty Series* reached number 994 and *Executive Agreement Series* went to number 506, for a total of 1500. Thus, *T.I.A.S.* begins at 1501.[14]

c. *Bevans.* A useful collection published by the State Department is *Treaties and Other International Agreements of the United States of America, 1776–1949,*[15] known as *Bevans* from the name of the compiler. It collects together in 13 volumes the international agreements of the United States up to the beginning of *U.S.T.* Multilateral treaties are arranged chronologically in volumes 1–4. Bilateral treaties are arranged alphabetically by the name of the other country in volumes 5–12. Volume 13 is a general index. Two other collections published by the State Department are also known by the names of their respective compilers: *Treaties, Conventions, International Acts, Protocols, and Agreements Between the United States of America and Other Powers*[16] (Malloy) and *Treaties and Other International Acts of the United States of America*[17] (Miller). For most purposes *Bevans* supersedes both of these earlier collections.

4. United States Treaties in Congressional Documents

a. *Senate Treaty Documents and Senate Executive Reports.* Once a treaty for which the advice and consent of the Senate will be sought has been negotiated and signed, the President submits it to the Senate in a Message from the President, with the text of the agreement annexed to it. The proposed treaty is referred to the Committee on Foreign Relations for hearings and a recommendation to the full Senate. Until the 97th Congress (1981–82), the Senate printed the proposed treaty under the name *Senate Executive Document* with a letter designation.

Beginning with the 97th Congress, the printed treaties are called *Treaty Documents* and receive a number. For example, the Message from the President Transmitting the Income Tax Convention with the Russian Federation, signed in Washington on 17 June 1992, is Treaty Document 102–39. The Committee on Foreign Relations makes its

---

[14] For detailed information on these series and on the bibliography of the early publication of United States international agreements, *see* 1 HUNTER MILLER, TREATIES AND OTHER INTERNATIONAL ACTS OF THE UNITED STATES OF AMERICA 35–138 (1931).

[15] Compiled by Charles I. Bevans (U.S.G.P.O. 1968–1976).

[16] Compiled by William M. Malloy (U.S.G.P.O. 1910–1938).

[17] Edited by Hunter Miller (U.S.G.P.O. 1931–1948).

recommendation in a report printed in the numbered series of *Senate Executive Reports*. Beginning in 1970, the references to both Treaty Documents and Executive Reports, with a descriptive abstract, are found in the annual volumes of *CIS—Abstracts,* under the heading "Senate Committees—Foreign Relations—Executive Reports and Executive Documents" (S384 and S385).[18] The *Monthly Catalog of United States Government Publications* also indexes these documents.

b. *Congressional Index.*[19] Treaties submitted to the Senate for advice and consent can, unlike bills, be held over from year to year. Some international agreements can remain pending in the Senate for a long time. Volume 1 (Senate) of the *Congressional Index* has a "Treaties" tab that is useful for tracking down treaties pending in the Senate. There is a subject index and a section of summaries of all pending treaties with a chronology of actions relating to each one.

5. Other Publications

a. *Unperfected Treaties of the United States, 1776–1976.*[20] This multi-volume set is an annotated collection of the treaties to which the United States was a signatory, but which never went into force.

b. *Extradition Laws and Treaties of the United States.*[21] This looseleaf set contains extradition treaties currently in force between the United States and other countries, arranged alphabetically by the name of the other country.

c. *Indian Affairs: Laws and Treaties.*[22] Volume 2 contains treaties made by the United States with Indian tribes between 1778 and 1883. It was reprinted under the title *Indian Treaties.*[23] Volume 7 of *United States Statutes at Large* also has a compilation of Indian treaties. Treaties concluded with Indian tribes before the independence of the United States are in *Early American Indian Documents: Treaties and Law, 1607–1789.*[24]

d. *Tax Treaties,*[25] *Federal Tax Treaties.*[26] Both of these looseleaf publications give comprehensive coverage with annotations and background material of the income and estate tax treaties of the United States currently in force and pending ratification.

[18] For earlier documents, *see* MARIANA G. MABRY, CHECKLIST OF SENATE EXECUTIVE DOCUMENTS AND REPORTS, 1947–1970 (1970).

[19] (Commerce Clearing House 1938–).

[20] Edited by CHRISTIAN L. WIKTOR (Oceana Publications 1976).

[21] Edited by IGOR I. KAVASS & ADOLPH SPRUDZS (W.S. Hein 1979–).

[22] Compiled and edited by CHARLES J. KAPPLER (U.S.G.P.O. 1903–1941).

[23] (Interland Publishing 1972).

[24] Edited by ALDENT T. VAUGHN (U.P.A. 1979–1989).

[25] (Commerce Clearing House 1952–).

[26] (Prentice–Hall 1958–).

6. Finding United States International Agreements and Verifying their Status

The process of locating international agreements requires the use of methods with which the researcher will not be familiar from having done research in other U.S. legal materials. In addition, there is an essential second step to take after finding the text of an agreement. International agreements, like other primary sources of law, must be verified as to their current status. Multilateral agreements do not come into force once they are negotiated. A minimum number of countries has to agree to join a multilateral treaty before it becomes binding. That may take years.

Moreover, only those countries that agree to become parties to a multilateral agreement are bound by it, thus making it essential to know who the states party are. States may accede to (join) a multilateral treaty long after it is first negotiated, and as a final complication, they may denounce (terminate) their participation in either a multilateral or bilateral agreement at any time. Obviously then, the process of verification is crucial. The finding tools noted in this section refer to the location of the text of international agreements; they also provide critical additional information for verification.

a. *Treaties in Force.*[27] The full title is *Treaties in Force: A List of Treaties and Other International Agreements in Force on January 1, 199__* It is published annually by the State Department, but usually appears several months after the date on the cover. It is divided into bilateral and multilateral sections. The bilateral section is organized alphabetically by the name of the other country and subdivided by subject matter; the multilateral section is organized alphabetically by subject matter and chronologically within each subject heading. Each entry begins with the name of the agreement, followed by the place and date it was concluded, the date it entered into force (if multilateral, the date of entry into force in general and for the United States, in particular), the citation (with parallel citations), a list of the other states party to the agreement (if multilateral), and brief notes regarding such points as whether a state entered a reservation or declaration to a multilateral agreement. [See Illustrations 167 and 168.]

Thus, *Treaties in Force* can answer several questions: a) What international agreements does the United States currently have with a particular country or in a particular subject matter?; b) Is a particular international agreement in force for the United States?; c) Where can the text be found?; and d) What other countries are parties to a multilateral agreement? *Treaties in Force* is current to the date on the cover and needs updating to catch developments that have occurred since it was last issued. The foreword to *Treaties in Force* mentions that further inquiries regarding U.S. international agreements may be made to the Office of Treaty Affairs, Department of State, Washington, DC 20520.

---

[27] (U.S.G.P.O. 1944–).

b. *US Department of State Dispatch.*[28] Since 1939 the State Department has published a journal of information of some kind, either weekly or monthly. Until 1989, it was titled *Department of State Bulletin.* In 1990, after complaints from lawyers and the academic community concerning the termination of the *Bulletin,* the State Department began publication of the weekly *Dispatch.* Every month the *Dispatch* carries a section called "Treaty Actions." This department keeps track of world treaty developments in which the United States participates or which affect the international relations of the United States. By checking the "Treaty Actions" section for the period following the cover date of the current *Treaties in Force,* it is possible to update the status of a U.S. international agreement to within approximately one month to six weeks.

c. *A Guide to the United States Treaties in Force.*[29] This commercial publication contains essentially the same information as that found in *Treaties in Force.* However, as it is more heavily indexed, it can be used to find references to agreements that might be hard to locate in *Treaties in Force.*

d. *United States Treaty Index: 1776–1990 Consolidation.*[30] This is a comprehensive index of all documented international agreements of the United States entered into from 1776 through 1990. This 12–volume set supersedes the various components of the *UST Indexing Service,* formerly from the same publisher. The set consists of a "master guide" in numerical order, a chronological guide, a country index, and a subject index. The final volume is a "geographical subject index," which provides added indexing by country.

e. *Current Treaty Index.*[31] This is the semi-annual supplement to the *United States Treaty Index: 1776–1990 Consolidation.* It is organized along the same lines as the consolidation and updates it to within approximately the last six months. Note that this index takes note of many documents that have not appeared in the official U.S. treaty publications. Therefore, the researcher must use this index in conjunction with one of the commercial sources for recent U.S. international agreements.

7. Implementation and Judicial Interpretation of United States Treaties

a. *U.S.C., U.S.C.A., U.S.C.S., C.F.R., Federal Register.* Often the terms of a U.S. international agreement require implementing legislation to become effective as part of U.S. law. For example, the Convention on the Recognition and Enforcement of Foreign Arbitral Awards[32] is enact-

---

[28] (U.S.G.P.O. 1990–).

[29] Compiled and edited by IGOR I. KAVASS (W.S. Hein 1983–).

[30] Compiled and edited by IGOR I. KAVASS (W.S. Hein 1991).

[31] Compiled and edited by IGOR I. KAVASS (W.S. Hein 1982–).

[32] 21 U.S.T. 2517, 330 U.N.T.S. 38.

ed as chapter 2 of the Federal Arbitration Act.[33]   In addition, when a branch of the federal executive is charged with carrying out various responsibilities of the United States under a treaty and its implementing legislation, then there will be implementing administrative regulations to be found.   For example, under the UNESCO Convention on the Means of Prohibiting and Preventing the Illicit Import, Export and Transfer of Ownership of Cultural Property [34] and its implementing legislation,[35] the U.S. Customs Service makes regulations for the emergency restriction on the import of various kinds of cultural property. These regulations are first published in the *Federal Register* and later summarized in a list at 19 C.F.R. § 12.104g.   Therefore, when researching a U.S. international agreement, it is essential to check for federal legislation and administrative regulations on point.

b.   Finding cases decided under and interpreting U.S. international agreements requires creative research along various lines.   Four lines of inquiry are suggested here.

(1) The West digests include a topic, "Treaties," that collects cases involving the interpretation and application of U.S. international agreements.

(2) *U.S.C.S.* has a volume called "Annotations to Uncodified Laws and Treaties," which collects case notes to various multilateral, bilateral, and Indian treaties of the United States.

(3) The "Statute Edition" of *Shepard's United States Citations* collects cases in federal court citing to U.S. international agreements published in *U.S.T.* and *T.I.A.S.*   To find state cases citing U.S. treaties, the various state editions of Shepard's have to be consulted.   Note that treaties published before 1950 have to be "shepardized" using the section for *United States Statutes at Large,* where treaties were published up to that time.

(4) The WESTLAW and LEXIS databases are probably the best way to find U.S. cases arising under or interpreting U.S. international agreements.   The search query can be formulated by using key words from the formal and popular name of the treaty, e.g., (convention +3 prevention +3 pollution +3 ships) or marpol.[36]   When doing thorough research for U.S. cases none of these four avenues of research should be relied upon to the exclusion of the others.

[33] 9 U.S.C. §§ 201 *et seq.* (1988).

[34] 823 U.N.T.S. 231.

[35] Convention on Cultural Property Implementation Act, 19 U.S.C. §§ 2601 *et seq.* (1988).

[36] This search will retrieve the International Convention for the Prevention of Pollution from Ships, 12 I.L.M. 1319 (1973), and its Protocol, 17 I.L.M. 546 (1978).   The popular name for these agreements is "MARPOL."

SECTION C. INTERNATIONAL AGREEMENTS: ADDITIONAL SOURCES (OTHER THAN UNITED STATES PUBLICATIONS)

1. General Treaty Collections

a. *United Nations Treaty Series (U.N.T.S.).* Under Article 102 of the United Nations Charter, every member of the UN is required to register its international agreements with the Secretariat, which is required to publish them. The idea of compulsory registration and publication is in part to prevent secret diplomacy. Begun in 1946, *U.N.T.S.* now has over 1,350 volumes and contains thousands of agreements. [See Illustration 170.] However, *U.N.T.S.* runs about eight years behind. Its index volumes also run behind and are difficult to use. The researcher should note that the formal title by which libraries catalog this source is *Treaty Series (United Nations).*

b. *League of Nations Treaty Series (L.N.T.S.).* This is the predecessor of *U.N.T.S.,* having been published under the auspices of the League of Nations. In 205 volumes covering the period 1920–1946, it published the treaties registered with the Secretariat of the League. The formal title under which the researcher should look in library catalogs is *Treaty Series (League of Nations).*

c. *Consolidated Treaty Series (C.T.S.).* This commercially published series is in 243 volumes covering the period 1648–1919. It is good for locating the text of historically important international agreements. Note that the three treaty series mentioned above (*C.T.S., L.N.T.S.,* and *U.N.T.S.*) cover a continuous period of time from 1648 to the present.

2. Other Treaty Collections

a. *European Treaty Series.* The Council of Europe, an international organization of 25 European nations, has as one of its main purposes the drafting and sponsoring of multilateral agreements on subjects of mutual benefit. The most significant treaty sponsored by the Council of Europe is the European Convention for the Protection of Human Rights and Fundamental Freedoms.[37] The Council of Europe's treaties are first published as individual documents in the *European Treaty Series.* They have also been collected and republished (through 1989) in the five volumes of *European Conventions and Agreements.*[38]

b. *International Legal Materials (I.L.M.).* Published since 1962 by the American Society of International Law, this is a leading source for the text of recent international agreements of note. *I.L.M.* appears six times a year and is probably the best place to look for the publication of recent international documents of significance, including international agreements. *I.L.M.* contains many other kinds of documents besides, including judicial decisions, arbitral awards, and the documents of inter-

[37] E.T.S. No. 5, 213 U.N.T.S. 221.

[38] (Council of Europe 1971–).

national organizations, for example.   It is available online through LEXIS (INTLAW library, ILM file).

    c. *O.A.S. Treaty Series.* Like the Council of Europe, the Organization of American States drafts and sponsors multilateral agreements of mutual interest to member states.   These are published in the *O.A.S. Treaty Series.*[39] Its formal title under which it will be cataloged in libraries is *Treaty Series (Organization of American States).*

    d. *National Treaty Series.* Like the United States, many other countries publish their international agreements in a special series. Examples are the United Kingdom *Treaty Series* and *Recueil des Traités et Accords de la France.* A useful listing of many of these national collections is compiled at Simone–Marie Kleckner, *Public International Law and Organization: International Law Bibliography* 6–13, which is found in *A Collection of Bibliographic and Research Resources.*[40]

    e. *Subject Compilations.* Many publishers, both official and commercial, have put together collections of international agreements. These collections can be very useful because they bring together in one place documents that otherwise are often difficult to find.   There are too many of these collections to list comprehensively here, but some leading examples are mentioned.

    The Hague Conference on Private International Law publishes its 32 multilateral agreements on various aspects of conflict of laws and international judicial assistance in a one-volume book titled *Collection of Conventions (1951–1988).* The recent explosion of interest in international environmental law has produced several collections of international agreements, including: *Basic Documents of International Environmental Law,*[41] *International Environmental Law,*[42] and *Selected Multinational Treaties in the Field of the Environment.*[43] In the field of human rights, another topic of current interest, useful collections include: *Basic Documents on Human Rights*[44] and *Human Rights: A Compilation of International Instruments.*[45]

3. Finding International Agreements (When the United States May Not Be a Party)

    In addition to the finding tools mentioned in Section B–6 *supra,* there are several sources that serve to locate international agreements, whether or not the United States is a party.

---

[39] THE BLUEBOOK, 15th ed., mistakenly continues to use the former title, *Pan–American Treaty Series.*

[40] (Oceana 1984–).

[41] Edited by HARALD HOHMANN (Graham and Trotman 1992).

[42] Edited by W.E. BURHENNE (E. Schmidt 1974).

[43] (United Nations Environment Program, 1983–1991) (Volume 2 is published by Grotius Publications).

[44] Edited by IAN BROWNLIE (3d ed. Oxford 1992).

[45] (United Nations 1988).

a. *Multilateral Treaties Deposited With the Secretary–General.* This annual publication from the United Nations tracks the status of 273 international agreements drafted under the auspices of the United Nations and League of Nations.   The entry for each treaty gives complete information (as of 31 December) regarding the states party to the treaty and the relevant dates.   This is one of the few sources that publishes the text of various declarations and reservations entered by states at the time of becoming a party.

b. *Multilateral Treaties: Index and Current Status.*[46]   This useful volume provides current information on about 1000 treaties.   Each entry gives an indication of the date of conclusion, the citation to the location of the text, the date of entry into force, the states party to the treaty, and the states signatory.   There is a notes section describing the agreement and making reference to related documents.   The latest cumulative supplement brings matters up to 1 January 1991.

c. *World Treaty Index.*[47]   The advantage of this five-volume index is that it covers bilateral as well as multilateral agreements.   The disadvantage is that it does not go beyond 1980.   This limits its usefulness substantially.

SECTION D.   CUSTOMARY INTERNATIONAL LAW

1. Introduction

Article 38 of the Statute of the International Court of Justice speaks of "international custom, as evidence of a general practice accepted as law."   Several questions arise from this formulation.   The first must be, "*Whose* custom?"   For those who believe that international law is preeminently the law of *interstate* relations, the focus will be on the custom of state actors and their governmental representatives.   For those who believe that international law is *transnational* law, the perspective takes in all actors on the international scene, including international organizations, multinational corporations, and even people.   The next question has to be, "*What* is international custom?"   The text of Article 38 gives the germ of an answer: "a general practice accepted as law."   Customary international law, then, has a dual character.   It derives 1) from the general practice of states and other subjects of international law 2) acting from a sense of legal obligation.   A leading treatise thus distinguishes customary international law from an international usage because the latter "is a general practice which does *not* reflect a legal obligation." [48]

Unfortunately for research in international law, the definition of international custom simply pushes the difficulty back a step.   Now the question becomes, "How does the researcher go about establishing the

---

[46] Edited by M.J. Bowman & D.J. Harris (Butterworths 1984).

[47] Edited by Peter H. Rohn (2d ed. ABC–Clio Information Services 1983).

[48] Ian Brownlie, Principles of Public International Law 5 (4th ed. Oxford 1990) (emphasis added).

existence of something that by definition is unwritten and the evidence for which might be found in any number of sources?"

> Brownlie suggests the following list of possible documentary sources: diplomatic correspondence, policy statements, press releases, the opinions of official legal advisers, official manuals on legal questions, e.g., manuals of military law, executive decisions and practices, orders to naval forces, etc., comments by governments on drafts produced by the International Law Commission, state legislation, international and national judicial decisions, recitals in treaties and other international instruments, a pattern of treaties in the same form, the practice of international organs, and resolutions relating to legal questions in the United Nations General Assembly.[49]

This list makes the point that the search for evidence of state practice as an element of customary international law must go forward on several fronts. Despite the difficulties there are some well-established sources with which the researcher can begin the process.

2. Digests of Practice: United States Publications

The United States leads the world in the publication of what are known generally as digests of international law or digests of practice in international law. The first of these was published in 1877.[50] Digests of practice bring together references and quotations from a huge array of sources and organize them according to the main topics of public international law. Sometimes a digest will focus on the practice of a particular nation. However, the digests produced in the United States (under the auspices of the State Department) draw their material from a broad range of international sources.

a. *Digest of International Law.*[51] Whiteman's is the most recent of the U.S. digests. It is in 14 volumes plus an index volume.

b. *Digest of International Law.*[52] Hackworth's digest, in eight volumes, covers the period 1906–1939.

c. *A Digest of International Law as Embodied in Diplomatic Discussions, Treaties and other International Agreements, International Awards, the Decisions of Municipal Courts, and the Writings of Jurists....*[53] Moore's digest, in eight volumes, set the pattern for its successors and supersedes Wharton's.

d. *A Digest of the International Law of the United States Taken from Documents Issued by Presidents and Secretaries of State, and from*

---

[49] *Id.* (footnotes omitted).

[50] JOHN L. CADWALADER, DIGEST OF THE PUBLISHED OPINIONS OF THE ATTORNEYS-GENERAL, AND OF THE LEADING DECISIONS OF THE FEDERAL COURTS, WITH REFERENCE TO INTERNATIONAL LAW, TREATIES AND KINDRED SUBJECTS (U.S.G.P.O. 1877).

[51] Prepared by MARJORIE M. WHITEMAN (U.S.G.P.O. 1963–1973).

[52] Compiled by JOHN B. MOORE (U.S.G.P.O.).

[53] Compiled by JOHN B. MOORE (U.S.G.P.O. 1906).

Decisions of Federal Courts and Opinions of Attorneys–General.[54] Wharton's digest in three volumes was the first to adopt a subject arrangement according to the main topics of international law.

e. *Updating the U.S. Digests.* Whiteman's digest completed publication in 1973. The next year the State Department began a new project of preparing an annual *Digest of United States Practice in International Law.*[55] A total of eight annual volumes were issued, covering the period 1973–1980.[56] Unfortunately, nothing has appeared since. However, beginning with volume 53 (1959) and continuing to the present, the *American Journal of International Law* has published a section titled, "Contemporary Practice of the United States Relating to International Law." It follows the arrangement of the annual *Digest of United States Practice in International Law.* In contrast to Whiteman's digest and its predecessors, the focus is on the practice of the United States.

3. Digests of Practice from Other Countries

Several other digests relating to the practice of particular countries in international law are available. Two leading examples are given here.

a. *A British Digest of International Law.*[57] This was to be a major project in two phases. Five volumes of the first phase, covering the years 1860–1914, were published but nothing has appeared since 1967. Fortunately, the *British Yearbook of International Law* carries a section called, "United Kingdom Materials on International Law."

b. *Répertoire de la Pratique Française en Matière de Droit International Publique.*[58] This digest of practice from France can be supplemented with the sections of the *Annuaire Français de Droit International* titled, "Pratique Française du Droit International" and "Chronologie des Faits Internationaux d'Intérêt Juridique."

4. Additional Sources Documenting State Practice

a. *Foreign Relations of the United States.*[59] This multi-volume series prepared by the State Department constitutes the official record of the foreign policy and diplomacy of the United States. It now has over 350 volumes. Supplemental documents in this series are now published in microform.

b. *American Foreign Policy: Current Documents.*[60] This is an annual series prepared by the State Department since 1956. The last volume published was for 1986. Each volume is organized into topical

[54] Edited by FRANCIS WHARTON (U.S.G.P.O. 1886).

[55] ((U.S.G.P.O. 1974–).

[56] The last volume (1980) was published in 1986.

[57] Edited by CLIVE PARRY (Stevens & Sons 1967–).

[58] Edited by ALEXANDRE C. KISS (C.N.R.S. 1962–1972).

[59] (U.S.G.P.O. 1861–).

[60] (U.S.G.P.O. 1956–).

and regional chapters. These collections published by the government can be supplemented with the privately or commercially-published series, *The United States in World Affairs*,[61] *Documents on American Foreign Relations*,[62] and *American Foreign Relations*.[63]

c. *British and Foreign State Papers*.[64] The British equivalent of *Foreign Relations of the United States*, it covers the period 1812–1968. For the period 1945–1950, *Documents on British Policy Overseas*[65] provides supplemental coverage, as does *Documents on International Affairs*[66] for the period 1926–1963.

d. *United Nations Legislative Series*. This is the overall title for a group of materials published by the United Nations in which are collected national legislation and other elements of state practice in areas of interest to the United Nations. The series includes: *Laws Concerning Nationality; Laws and Regulations Regarding Diplomatic and Consular Privileges and Immunities; Legislative Texts and Treaty Provisions Concerning the Legal Status, Privileges and Immunities of International Organizations; Legislative Texts and Treaty Provisions Concerning the Utilization of International Rivers for Purposes Other than Navigation; Materials on Succession of States; National Legislation and Treaties Relating to the Territorial Sea, the Contiguous Zone, the Continental Shelf, the High Seas, and to Fishing and Conservation of the Living Resources of the Sea; Materials on Succession of States in Respect of Matters other than Treaties; National Legislation and Treaties Relating to the Law of the Sea; Materials on Jurisdictional Immunities of States and their Property.*

e. *Repertory of Practice of United Nations Organs*.[67] In several volumes updated with supplements this is an article-by-article digest of UN practice under the Charter of the United Nations.

SECTION E. GENERAL PRINCIPLES OF LAW

This source of law, the third main source set out in Article 38 of the Statute of the International Court of Justice, presents some of the same kinds of difficulties as those encountered in researching customary international law. There is no authoritative collection of general principles. The evidence for the existence of a general principle of law has to be developed from a variety of authorities. Some of these may be primary sources, but more likely, the first approach to discovering a general principle will be a discussion of the subject in an authoritative secondary source, such as a leading treatise.

[61] (Council on Foreign Relations 1931–1971).

[62] (Council on Foreign Relations 1939–1970).

[63] (New York University Press 1971–1978).

[64] (H.M.S.O. 1928–1977).

[65] (H.M.S.O. 1984–1989).

[66] (O.U.P. 1929–1973).

[67] (United Nations 1955–).

There is a conceptual difficulty that has to be resolved before research can even begin. Does this source have to do with general principles of law as found in *national* legal systems or does it refer to general principles that are peculiar to *international* law? No doubt, there is substantial overlap, for example, where ideas such as good faith in the performance of agreements or the duty to compensate for causing harm are concerned. There is some disagreement, but the prevailing opinion is that the idea refers to those general principles common to the major *domestic* legal systems. Therefore, the phrase has to be distinguished from another one, "general principles of *international* law," which for most purposes are principles derived from customary international law.[68]

Given the emphasis on domestic law, it becomes apparent that someone wanting to do original research on general principles of law would have to know *comparative* law—the comparative study of national legal systems. Fortunately, the secondary literature of international law has already performed a lot of this work with respect specifically to establishing general principles applied in the international arena.[69] However, there is nothing to prevent the researcher from enlisting the assistance of virtually this entire book on the fundamentals of legal research, as part of a project to discover a general principle of law common to the major legal systems, starting with the United States.

SECTION F. ADJUDICATIONS

States might settle their differences in a variety of hopefully peaceful ways, ranging from diplomatic negotiation to compulsory submission of a dispute to the World Court,[70] with such mechanisms as mediation, conciliation, and binding arbitration in between.[71] Article 38 of the Statute of the International Court of Justice accepts "judicial decisions" as a "subsidiary means for the determination of rules of law." The phrase "subsidiary means" does not capture the significance for the contemporary development of international law of the analysis and application of international legal norms in various kinds of international adjudication. Moreover, the phrase "judicial decisions" is too narrow because it does not indicate that the decisions of international arbitral tribunals and the decisions of national courts on international legal

---

[68] *See generally* RESTATEMENT (THIRD) OF THE FOREIGN RELATIONS LAW OF THE UNITED STATES § 102 cmt. 1, reporter's note 7 (1987); IAN BROWNLIE, PRINCIPLES OF PUBLIC INTERNATIONAL LAW 15–19 (4th ed. 1990). *Compare* Herman Mosler, *General Principles of Law, in* 7 ENCYCLOPEDIA OF PUBLIC INTERNATIONAL LAW 89 (Rudolf Bernhardt ed. 1984).

[69] In addition to the references already noted, *see generally* BIN CHENG, GENERAL PRINCIPLES OF LAW AS APPLIED BY INTERNATIONAL COURTS AND TRIBUNALS (Stevens 1953); Arnold D. McNair, *The General Principles of Law Recognized by Civilized Nations,* 33 BRIT. Y.B. INT'L L. 1 (1957).

[70] This is the informal name of the International Court of Justice and of the Permanent Court of International Justice.

[71] *See generally* J.G. MERRILLS, INTERNATIONAL DISPUTE SETTLEMENT (2d ed. Grotius Publications 1991).

questions are also included in the category.[72] This section focuses on the leading documentary sources for the decisions of the main international tribunals. It then discusses the ways of finding United States court cases dealing with questions of international law.

1. International Court of Justice

The International Court of Justice (I.C.J.) is the principal judicial organ of the United Nations. It was founded in 1945 at the same time as the United Nations itself. The seat of the Court is the Peace Palace at the Hague, Netherlands. It is composed of 15 judges elected by the General Assembly and Security Council of the United Nations. Only states may be parties in a proceeding before the I.C.J. The I.C.J. takes jurisdiction of a dispute either by agreement of the parties, or because the parties have made a declaration under Art. 36(2) of the Statute of the International Court of Justice that they accept the "compulsory jurisdiction" of the Court in any legal dispute involving a state that has made the same declaration. The Court also has the authority to give advisory opinions on legal questions to the General Assembly and Security Council. Without a doubt, the judgments of the I.C.J. are the single most significant component of the source of international law known as judicial decisions. The publications of the I.C.J. are described below.

a. *Reports of Judgments, Advisory Opinions and Orders.* The final decisions (judgments on the merits) of the Court are published in this series. [See Illustration 171.] The text of a final judgment including separate and dissenting opinions may reach several hundred pages. Judgments appear even longer because the English and French text are printed together on facing pages. Decisions are first published separately; then the collected decisions for each year are published together in a single volume. The researcher should take note that the documents of the I.C.J. as published in this series are available in full text on WESTLAW in the INT–ICJ database. [See Illustration 172.]

b. *Pleadings, Oral Arguments, Documents.* Volumes in this series are published after the end of a case, sometimes years after the judgment. They contain the pleadings, the briefs (memorials), the record of oral proceedings, and other documents, such as maps, that may be submitted to the Court. For each case, several volumes may be published in this series.

c. *Acts and Documents Concerning the Organization of the Court.* This is a single volume that has been updated, most recently in 1978. It is a useful place to find the United Nations Charter and the Statute and Rules of Court.

d. *Yearbook.* This annual publication has chapters on the organization of the Court, its work during the year, and useful biographies of the judges.

---

[72] *See generally* IAN BROWNLIE, PRINCIPLES OF PUBLIC INTERNATIONAL LAW 19, 20 (4th ed. 1990).

e. *Bibliography of the International Court of Justice.* Each year the Registry of the Court issues this bibliography listing works relating to the Court.

f. The secondary literature (books and journal articles) on the Court is extensive. It can be researched using the heading "International Court of Justice" in library catalogs and journal indexes. Recommended secondary reading on the I.C.J. includes: *Documents on the International Court of Justice,*[73] *The World Court: What It Is and How It Works,*[74] and *The International Court of Justice at a Crossroads.*[75]

g. The predecessor to the I.C.J. was the Permanent Court of International Justice (P.C.I.J.), which was established under the League of Nations. It sat to hear cases from 1922 to early 1940 and was dissolved in 1946 when the I.C.J. was inaugurated. Many decisions of the P.C.I.J. are of continuing significance in international law. The publications of the P.C.I.J. were issued in series much like those of the I.C.J.:

Series A. *Collection of Judgments* (up to 1930);

Series B. *Collection of Advisory Opinions* (up to 1930);

Series A/B. *Judgments, Orders and Advisory Opinions* (after 1930);[76]

Series C. *Acts and Documents Relating to Judgments and Advisory Opinions* (up to 1930)/*Pleadings, Oral Statements and Documents* (after 1930);

Series D. *Acts and Documents Concerning the Organization of the Court;*

Series E. *Annual Reports;*

Series F. *Indexes.*

2. Digests of I.C.J. and P.C.I.J. Decisions

The use of the digests noted below facilitates research by providing detailed references and extensive excerpts from those parts of often very lengthy I.C.J. and P.C.I.J. judgments dealing with particular points of international law.

a. *The Case Law of the International Court.*[77]

b. *Digest of the Decisions of the International Court of Justice.*[78]

---

[73] Compiled and edited by SHABTAI ROSENNE (3d ed. M. Nijhoff 1991).

[74] By SHABTAI ROSENNE (M. Nijhoff 1989).

[75] Edited by LORI F. DAMROSCH (Transnational 1987).

[76] The judgments of the P.C.I.J. are also available in WORLD COURT REPORTS: A COLLECTION OF THE JUDGMENTS, ORDERS AND OPINIONS OF THE PERMANENT COURT OF INTERNATIONAL JUSTICE (Manley O. Hudson ed. Carnegie Endowment for International Peace 1934–1943).

[77] Edited by EDVARD HAMBRO (A.W. Sijthoff 1952–1976).

[78] Edited by RUDOLF BERNHARDT (Springer 1931–). Earlier volumes deal with the P.C.I.J. Beginning in 1993 this series is retitled, WORLD COURT DIGEST.

c. *A Digest of the Decisions of the International Court.*[79]

3. International Arbitrations: Collections and Digests of Decisions

Finding published decisions of international arbitral tribunals is notoriously troublesome.   Several circumstances contribute to this situation.   Most international arbitrations are ad hoc.   The tribunal is constituted to resolve the particular dispute, and there is no sponsoring institution to deal with publication....
It has fallen to scholars working in their private capacity to prepare collections and digests.   The result is that the documentation in this field is widely scattered.[80]

The difficulties of finding international arbitral decisions should not discourage the researcher.   The sources noted below and in the following section make the task less frustrating.

a. *Reports of International Arbitral Awards* (R.I.A.A.).[81] Published by the United Nations, this is probably the leading current source for the text of *selected* international arbitral awards.   Volume XIX, the most recent, contains decisions rendered as long ago as 1972, but also contains the ruling from 1986 by the Secretary–General in the Rainbow Warrior Affair between France and New Zealand.   Each volume is indexed, but there is no overall index or table of cases.   This means that R.I.A.A. must be used together with one of the finding tools noted in the next section.

b. *International Law Reports.*[82]   Because it contains the reports of many kinds of international adjudications, this series could be mentioned under any of several headings.   It appears here because it is particularly valuable for its publication of substantial extracts from arbitral decisions that would be very difficult to find elsewhere.

c. *International Legal Materials* (I.L.M.).[83]   Significant arbitral awards often are published first in I.L.M.

d. *History and Digest of the International Arbitrations to which the United States Has Been a Party.*[84]   The United States has long been an active participant in the process of international arbitration.   In fact, a leading commentator notes that "modern arbitration begins with the Jay

[79] Edited by KRYSTYNA MAREK (M. Nijhoff 1974–1978).

[80] Jonathan Pratter, Book Review, 26 TEX. INT'L L.J. 597, 603 (1991).   On the substantive law of international arbitration, see generally J. GILLIS WETTER, THE INTERNATIONAL ARBITRAL PROCESS: PUBLIC AND PRIVATE (Oceana Publications 1979).

[81] (United Nations, 1948–).

[82] (Grotius Publications 1932–).   Until 1949 the title was ANNUAL DIGEST AND REPORTS OF PUBLIC INTERNATIONAL CASES and the publisher was Butterworth.

[83] See the main discussion of I.L.M. at Section C.2.B.

[84] By JOHN B. MOORE (U.S.G.P.O. 1898).

Treaty of 1794 between the United States and Great Britain....''[85] In many cases, the government would publish the results of the early arbitrations in which the United States participated. But these books are very difficult to find today. Therefore, Moore's *History and Digest* in six volumes continues to be a valuable source for reports of arbitrations of the United States from the late 18th to the end of the 19th century.

e. *International Adjudications: Ancient and Modern: History and Documents.*[86] This ambitious project never was completed, but six volumes were issued between 1929 and 1936.

f. *The Hague Court Reports*[87] and *The Hague Arbitration Cases.*[88] The title refers to an institution known formally as the Permanent Court of Arbitration. It is not a court, but a mechanism for establishing arbitral panels. Between 1900 and 1932 twenty cases were heard, but none since then. The decisions, some of them still significant in international law, are published in these collections.

g. *Iran–United States Claims Tribunal Reports.*[89] Following the resolution of the Iran Hostage Crisis in late 1980, an arbitral tribunal was set up to decide outstanding claims between United States citizens and companies and the government of Iran. Although its work now is winding down, the Iran–United States Claims Tribunal probably has been the most notable arbitral institution in recent years. To date, its decisions are reported in the 27 volumes of this series.[90]

4. Finding Tools for International Arbitrations

Research in international arbitration would be virtually impossible without the use of the finding tools noted here.

a. *Survey of International Arbitrations, 1794–1989.*[91] This book covers approximately 600 international disputes that resulted in an agreement to arbitrate, although in some cases an award was never rendered. The one-page entries for each case give all the critical information, including the parties, a brief description of the dispute, a note on the agreement to arbitrate and where to find it if available, and

[85] IAN BROWNLIE, PRINCIPLES OF PUBLIC INTERNATIONAL LAW 709 (4th ed. 1990). The arbitrations under the Jay Treaty had to do with both boundaries and claims for compensation following the Revolutionary War. The work of the various arbitral commissions is reported in the first volume of MOORE'S HISTORY AND DIGEST.

[86] Edited by JOHN B. MOORE (Oxford University Press 1929–1936).

[87] Edited by JAMES B. SCOTT (Oxford University Press 1916–1932).

[88] Compiled by GEORGE G. WILSON (Ginn 1915).

[89] (Grotius Publications 1983–).

[90] Two collections of arbitral decisions, both in French, deserve mention in a footnote: A. DE LAPRADELLE & N. POLITIS, RECUEIL DES ARBITRAGES INTERNATIONAUX (Pedone 1905–1954); HENRI LA FONTAINE, PASICRISIE INTERNATIONALE: HISTOIRE DOCUMENTAIRE DES ARBITRAGES INTERNATIONAUX (Stämpfli 1902).

[91] Edited by A.M. STUYT (3d ed. M. Nijhoff 1990).

notes on the disposition with citations to the text of the award if it has been published.

b. *Repertory of International Arbitral Jurisprudence.*[92] This is a comprehensive collection of excerpts from hundreds of arbitral decisions organized according to a detailed outline of international law. Each extract refers to a table of awards where the researcher will find the essential information about the decision, including a citation to the publication of the full text.[93] In three volumes, the *Repertory* covers the period 1794–1988.

5. International Law in U.S. Courts

a. Using the fundamental techniques of legal research introduced in this book, the researcher can find cases of United States courts, usually federal courts, on questions of international law. For example, the West digests have two topics, "International Law" and "Treaties" that collect cases on several points of international law as it is applied in the courts of this country. The first topic is useful for such questions as the sources of international law and its relation to United States law, territorial sovereignty, foreign sovereign immunity, the act of state doctrine, and extraterritoriality. The second topic deals with the negotiation, operation, and interpretation of international agreements in United States law. Another topic on point in a specialized area is "Ambassadors and Consuls."

American Law Reports, Federal (A.L.R. Fed.) offers another example of how to apply the fundamentals of legal research to finding United States cases on international law. Here can be found annotations on subjects such as "Giving United States District Courts Jurisdiction of Action by Alien for Tort Only, Committed in Violation of Law of Nations or Treaty of United States"[94] and "United Nations Resolution as Judicially Enforceable in United States Domestic Courts."[95]

In this area of research, the significance of using WESTLAW and LEXIS cannot be overstated. The fact of the matter is that cases in a United States court raising a question of international law might crop up in almost any field of law. Significant cases having international legal implications could start life as a suit on a bill of lading[96] or promissory note.[97] Obviously, the digests will not deal adequately with this possibility. A well-designed search on WESTLAW or LEXIS is an indispensable

---

[92] Edited by VINCENT COUSSIRAT-COUSTÈRE & PIERRE M. EISEMANN (M. Nijhoff 1989–1991).

[93] The researcher should be aware that sometimes the text of arbitral awards is never published in completely unabridged form. Instead, for example, lengthy extracts will appear in one of the leading journals of international law.

[94] 34 A.L.R. Fed. 388.

[95] 42 A.L.R. Fed. 577.

[96] *See, e.g.,* Banco Nacional de Cuba v. Sabbatino, 376 U.S. 398 (1964) (act of state doctrine).

[97] *See, e.g.,* Gau Shan Co., Ltd. v. Bankers Trust Co., 956 F.2d 1349 (6th Cir. 1992) (injunction against suit in a foreign court and international comity).

step in the research process when looking for cases with an international legal component.

b. *American International Law Cases.*[98] This set of reports, now in a third series, reprints cases originally published in the West reports.[99]

SECTION G. SECONDARY SOURCES

Article 38 of the Statute of the International Court of Justice expressly acknowledges secondary sources ("the teachings of the most highly qualified publicists") as means for the "determination of rules of law."[100] A strong case can be made for the view that the researcher in international law, especially the beginner, should *start* work with a good secondary source, such as a leading textbook. The reason is that the beginner has not yet learned what are the significant primary sources of law for a specific question. It is the task of a good secondary source to refer to (with citations) and to analyze the crucial primary sources as part of the discussion of an issue. Therefore, a good secondary source can efficiently orient and give direction to research. The secondary literature of international law is massive and expanding rapidly. Moreover, it is multilingual. This section can give only a brief overview of the available resources with indications of specific titles that will be particularly useful to the international law researcher in the United States.

1. Textbooks and Treatises

a. It is possible to mention only some of the more recent books that discuss general international law. This by necessity excludes the many titles that focus on one aspect of the subject, such as the law of the sea, or human rights. Of course, textbooks and treatises on various aspects of international law are found by consulting the appropriate subject heading in the law library catalog. Mentioned here are four of the most current one-volume introductory texts in English: *Principles of Public International Law* by Ian Brownlie,[101] *An Introduction to International Law* by Mark W. Janis,[102] *International Law* by Malcolm N. Shaw,[103] and *Introduction to International Law* by Joseph G. Starke.[104] Two general, though not comprehensive, works by Louis Henkin, a leading international law scholar in the United States, are *How Nations Behave: Law and Foreign Policy*[105] and *Foreign Affairs and the Constitution.*[106] The

---

[98] (Oceana Publications 1971–).

[99] In-depth discussion of finding international law cases in the national courts of other countries is beyond the scope of this chapter. However, the following English-language sources deserve mention: COMMONWEALTH INTERNATIONAL LAW CASES (Oceana Publications 1974–); DECISIONS OF GERMAN COURTS RELATING TO PUBLIC INTERNATIONAL LAW (Springer 1978–).

[100] *See* the discussion in Section A–3, *supra.*

[101] (4th ed. Oxford University Press 1990).

[102] (2d ed. Little, Brown 1993).

[103] (3d ed. Grotius Publications 1991).

[104] (10th ed. Butterworth 1989).

[105] (2d ed. Columbia University Press 1979).

[106] (Foundation Press 1972).

multi-volume treatise on international law, well-known in France and Germany, is rare in English. An exception is Charles Cheney Hyde's *International Law: Chiefly as Interpreted and Applied by the United States.*[107]

b. *Restatement of the Law: The Foreign Relations Law of the United States.*[108] Usually known as the *Restatement, Third,* this is probably the secondary source in the United States that can claim the greatest influence and authority in the field of international law. Its "black-letter rules" give a clear and concise statement of the contemporary view of the leading international law scholars in the United States on a wide range of issues. The comments and reporter's notes add background, depth, and copious citations to the primary sources and secondary literature.

c. *Collected Courses of the Hague Academy of International Law.*[109] Every summer the Hague Academy of International Law offers a series of advanced courses on both public and private international law. This extensive series of collected monographs (lengthy articles devoted to a particular subject) is usually known by its title in French, *Recueil des Cours.* It is true that not all contributions are in English, but many are and they can be valuable secondary sources on many aspects of international law. Unfortunately, the indexing for the *Recueil des Cours* is not current, though some recent volumes contain a listing of article titles back to the last time an index was produced (for the volumes through 1976).

2. Dictionaries and Encyclopedias

a. *Encyclopedia of Public International Law.*[110] Together with the *Restatement, Third,* this encyclopedia offers one of the better starting points for research. Published initially in twelve installments according to broad subjects, it is now being reissued with updated articles in a strictly alphabetical arrangement. To date, the first volume (A–D) of the new edition has appeared.

b. *Encyclopaedic Dictionary of International Law.*[111] There are several dictionaries of international law, some of dubious quality. The one mentioned here is accurate and useful.

3. Journals

There are many journals devoted to international law. The advantage of using journals is that they keep track of the latest developments and of current opinion in the field. Of course, law journal articles are

---

[107] (2d ed. Little, Brown 1945).

[108] (American Law Institute Publishers 1987).

[109] (M. Nijhoff, 1923–).

[110] (North–Holland 1992–).

[111] Edited by CLIVE PARRY ET AL. (Oceana Publications 1986).

filled with footnotes containing copious citations to primary sources or to other secondary authority on point. The explanation for the proliferation of law journals in international law can be traced in part to the phenomenon of law school publication of student-edited law journals in the United States. There are over 60 of these currently in publication.[112] Leading examples are the *Harvard International Law Journal*,[113] *Columbia Journal of Transnational Law*,[114] and the *Texas International Law Journal*.[115]

The most important journal of international law in the United States is the *American Journal of International Law* [116] published by the American Society of International Law. Also worthy of note is *The International Lawyer* [117] published by the Section of International Law and Practice of the American Bar Association. Of course, many outstanding international law journals are published outside the United States. The leading example in English is the *International and Comparative Law Quarterly* [118] published by the British Institute of International and Comparative Law.

Quite possibly the most prestigious journals of international law are not published in English. (International law remains one of the few fields in which a working knowledge of more than one language is a valuable asset.) Candidates for the position include the *Journal du Droit International* [119] and the *Zeitschrift für ausländisches öffentliches Recht and Völkerrecht*.[120]

4. Yearbooks

As indicated in the term describing it, the yearbook of international law is an annual publication, generally sponsored and edited by a national association of international law, by a university institute of international law, or by an editorial committee of international law scholars from one country. Unfortunately, no yearbook is produced in the United States. The usual format of a yearbook is to begin with lead articles followed by shorter notes and book reviews. Almost invariably, a yearbook will have sections covering developments in international law in the courts of the country and in the practice of the government. These sections make yearbooks very useful for keeping up with the latest developments as surveyed by the leading scholars. There are roughly 15 yearbooks from various countries. Three of the most prestigious are:

---

[112] A listing of these student-edited international law journals is in Chapter 16, Section I–2.

[113] (1967–).

[114] (1961–).

[115] (1965–).

[116] (1907–).

[117] (1966–).

[118] (1955–).

[119] (Editions Techniques 1874–).

[120] (Kohlhammer 1929–).

British Yearbook of International Law,[121] *Annuaire Français de Droit International,*[122] and *German Yearbook of International Law.*[123]

5. Indexes and Bibliographies

The standard periodical indexes in law, the *Current Law Index* and *Index to Legal Periodicals,* work satisfactorily as far as concerns articles on international law published in the United States. In addition, they will capture a fair percentage of articles on international law published in British law reviews. However, a substantial amount of writing on international law *in English* is done in sources published in Europe, Asia, and other parts of the world not covered by the usual indexes. Therefore, in-depth research requires the use of some creativity and unfamiliar resources.

a. *Public International Law: A Current Bibliography of Books and Articles.*[124] This is the only source that can make a claim to comprehensive coverage. It is prepared at the Max Planck Institute for Comparative Public Law and International Law in Heidelberg, Germany. References are entered under 26 topics of international law. The bibliography is published twice a year, but unfortunately is running about two years behind.

b. *Public International Law: A Guide to Information Sources.*[125] This is the most recent book-length guide to the subject. However, it goes into more detail about sources of borderline utility than the average researcher will find beneficial. It is organized in a way that will appeal more to law librarians than to lawyers, and it is not written from the perspective of a practicing lawyer in the United States.

c. *Subject Bibliographies.* There is a large number of bibliographies on particular aspects of international law. The selection given here concentrates on recent titles in selected areas of interest. The researcher should always check to find recent bibliographies on a particular topic; those mentioned here are for illustrative purposes only: *Bibliography on the Peaceful Settlement of International Disputes;* [126] *Peaceful Settlement of Disputes between States: a Selective Bibliography;* [127] *Bibliography of International Humanitarian Law Applicable in Armed Conflicts;* [128] *Human Rights: a Reference Handbook;* [129] *Interna-*

[121] (O.U.P. 1921–).

[122] (C.N.R.S. 1956–).

[123] (Duncker & Humblot 1954–).

[124] (Springer 1975–).

[125] By ELIZABETH BEYERLY (Mansell 1991).

[126] By CATHERINE BOULERY (Henry Dunant Institute 1990).

[127] Prepared by DAG HAMMARSKJÖLD LIBRARY (United Nations 1991).

[128] Prepared by INTERNATIONAL COMMITTEE OF THE RED CROSS & HENRY DUNANT INSTITUTE (2d ed. International Committee of the Red Cross 1987).

[129] By LUCILLE WHALEN (ABC–CLIO 1989).

tional Environmental Law: International Law Bibliography; [130] *The Law of the Sea: A Bibliography on the Law of the Sea, 1968–1988: Two Decades of Law–Making, State Practice, and Doctrine;* [131] *Marine Affairs Bibliography: A Comprehensive Index to Marine Law and Policy Literature;* [132] *World Wide Space Law Bibliography;* [133] *World Wide Space Law Bibliography, 1977–1986.* [134]

SECTION H. DOCUMENTS OF INTERNATIONAL ORGANIZATIONS

1. Introduction

The term international organization refers to an association of states established by a treaty. The organization pursues the common aims of its member states as set out in the founding treaty. An international organization has a legal personality separate from its member states and the founding treaty provides for decision-making and administrative structures to allow the organization to carry out its work. There can be "universal" international organizations such as the United Nations. Its purposes are wide-ranging and membership is open to any state. Or there can be international organizations devoted to special purposes, *e.g.,* the World Health Organization, or to particular regions of the world, *e.g.,* the Organization of American States. [135] The organizations we are concerned with here are sometimes known as international *governmental* organizations (IGOs) to distinguish them from international *non-governmental* organizations (NGOs) such as Amnesty International or Greenpeace.

For our purposes, the significance of international organizations lies in the fact that they produce documents of great interest in international law. Documents of international organizations are interesting because the constitution and law of international organizations, and their methods of deliberations and modes of action, are themselves part of the study of international law. Their documentation is significant because the substantive issues international organizations deal with are at the forefront of contemporary international law.

Even experienced researchers have difficulty with the documents of international organizations. There are several reasons for this. First, there is a surprisingly large number of international organizations.

---

[130] By ROBERT J. MUNRO (Oceana Publications 1990) (published in COLLECTION OF BIBLIOGRAPHIC AND RESEARCH SOURCES [Oceana Publications 1984–]).

[131] (United Nations 1991).

[132] (University of Virginia Law Library 1980–) (Earlier material is cumulated in MARINE AFFAIRS BIBLIOGRAPHY, 1980–1985 [M. Nijhoff 1987]).

[133] By KUO LEE LI (Institute and Center of Air and Space Law, McGill University 1978).

[134] By KUO LEE LI (De Daro 1987) (with annual updates to 1990).

[135] *See generally* FREDERIC L. KIRGIS, JR., INTERNATIONAL ORGANIZATIONS IN THEIR LEGAL SETTING (2d ed. West 1993); 5 ENCYCLOPEDIA OF PUBLIC INTERNATIONAL LAW (North–Holland 1983) (Titled "International Organizations in General/Universal International Organizations and Cooperation").

Within the UN system alone there are 20 affiliated international organizations known collectively as *specialized agencies,* each autonomous, with its own founding treaty and membership. The *Yearbook of International Organizations* [136] requires three volumes and several thousand pages to catalog and describe all the various international organizations, both IGOs and NGOs, currently in existence. Next, each IGO has its own publishing program and method of organizing its documents. Then, there may be deficiencies in distribution. Finally, libraries may have trouble organizing collections and providing access. Thus, it can be hard to find a particular document of a particular international organization.

The researcher can mitigate frustration by going to work armed with an accurate citation (reference) that includes the name of the document or a clear indication of its subject matter, the document "symbol" or number assigned by the organization, and the date the document was issued. A good overview of issues concerning the use of documents produced by international organizations is *International Information: Documents, Publications, and Information Systems of International Governmental Organizations.* [137]

2. United Nations

a. *Introduction.* The UN carries out its work through a complex organizational structure. The wide range of UN concerns has led to the establishment of an equally wide range of commissions, committees, and conferences, etc. The key to understanding UN documentation is to understand both how the UN is organized and how it carries out its work. This is because most of its documentation is the product of the UN's official work, combined with the fact that documents are identified with the particular body within the UN structure that produced them. Those unfamiliar with the UN should consult *Everyone's United Nations,* [138] *Basic Facts About the United Nations,* [139] *Guide to United Nations Organization, Documentation & Publishing for Students, Researchers, Librarians,* [140] and *Encyclopedia of the United Nations and International Agreements.* [141]

b. *United Nations Charter.* The Charter is the constitutive document of the UN, as well as a binding international agreement that is acknowledged to state fundamental principles of international law. The text of the Charter can be found in many places. Likely sources are 1

---

[136] (K.G. Saur 1948–).

[137] Edited by PETER I. HAJNAL (Libraries Unlimited 1988).

[138] (10th ed. United Nations 1986).

[139] (United Nations 1989).

[140] By PETER I. HAJNAL (Oceana 1978). Researchers should also be aware of UNITED NATIONS DOCUMENTATION: A BRIEF GUIDE (UN 1981), available on request from Dag Hammarskjöld Library, United Nations, New York, NY 10017.

[141] By EDMUND J. OSMANCZYK (2d ed. Taylor & Francis 1990).

U.N.T.S. xiv, *Basic Documents in International Law 2,*[142] *Yearbook of the United Nations,* or in any of the documentary supplements to the leading casebooks on international law. There are excellent recent commentaries on the Charter in French [143] and German.[144] The only article-by-article commentary in English is somewhat out of date, but still useful.[145]

c. *UN Document Symbols.* The UN uses a system of document symbols to identify and organize its documentation. The ruling idea is the *issuing body.* This means that the symbol is designed to identify the document by its source in the UN hierarchy of organization. A typical document symbol is E/CN.4/1984/WG.1/42. The forward slash is a distinguishing feature. This example denotes a document (number 42) produced during 1984 by the Working Group on the Draft Convention on the Rights of the Child (WG.1) under the Commission on Human Rights (CN.4), which is itself a subsidiary organ of the Economic and Social Council (E).

The components of the system of UN document symbols are:

(1) *Leading elements,* denoting the five major UN organs that use the system (the International Court of Justice does not):

A/–	General Assembly
E/–	Economic and Social Council
S/–	Security Council
T/–	Trustee Council
ST/–	Secretariat

(2) *Special leading symbols* have been created for other bodies. Some important examples are:

CCPR/–	Human Rights Committee (under the International Covenant on Civil and Political Rights)
CERD/–	International Convention on the Elimination of All Forms of Racial Discrimination
TD/–	United Nations Conference on Trade and Development (UNCTAD)
UNEP/–	United Nations Environment Programme

(3) Elements denoting the *subsidiary organ:*

–/AC./–	Ad hoc committee
–/C./–	Standing or main sessional committee
–/CN./–	Commission
–/CONF./–	Conference

---

[142] Edited by Ian Brownlie (3d ed. O.U.P. 1983).

[143] Jean-Pierre Cot & Alain Pellet, La Chartes des Nations Unies: Commentaire Article par Article (Economica 1985).

[144] Bruno Simma. ed., Charta der Vereinten Nationen: Kommentar (Beck 1991).

[145] Leland M. Goodrich et al., Charter of the United Nations: Commentary and Documents (3d ed. Columbia University Press 1969).

–/WG./–   Working Group

(4) Elements denoting the *nature of the document:*

–/PV.__   Verbatim records of meetings ("procès verbaux")
–/RES/–   Preliminary text of adopted resolutions
–/SR.__   Summary records of meetings

(5) Elements indicating a *change in an earlier document:*

–/Add.__   Addendum
–/Corr.__   Corrigendum
–/Rev.   Revision

(6) Elements indicating *distribution:*

–/L.__   Limited
–R.__   Restricted

Detailed information on UN document symbols is in *United Nations Document Series Symbols, 1946–1977* [146] and *United Nations Document Series Symbols, 1978–1984.* [147] Recently created document symbols are covered in *UNDOC: Current Index* (discussed in f–1 of this Section).

d. *UN Working Documents and Official Records.* The various bodies of the UN produce vast amounts of documents relating to their work. Some of these documents receive the name *official records.* The main organs of the UN—the General Assembly and its seven committees, the Security Council, the Economic and Social Council, and the Trustee Council—issue official records. Both working documents and official records are issued with a document symbol as described above. A complicating factor is that official records and many working documents come out in both *provisional* and *final* form.

In provisional form, working documents and official records appear individually on plain white paper. Official records are later collected together and republished in bound form, with tan paper covers for the General Assembly, yellow for the Security Council, and light blue for the Economic and Social Council. In final form, official records contain meeting records, annexes, and supplements. Note that significant working documents reappear in the annexes and supplements to the official records.

Obviously, provisional documents appear first. Therefore, they prove more useful for contemporaneous research. The official records in final form are easier to use, but are published late. The experienced researcher doing contemporaneous research learns how to find significant documents by knowing what kind of symbol they are likely to carry.

e. *Sales Publications.* The UN has an active publishing program through which it offers a wide array of publications for sale. This

[146] (United Nations 1978).
[147] (United Nations 1986).

includes subscriptions to working documents and official records. However, it also includes many titles in the fields of international relations, population issues, environmental policy, international trade and economics, and statistics. Sales publications receive a sales number, *e.g.,* 90.II.A.5, which is used only for ordering and should not be confused with the document symbol.[148]

    f. *Tools for Researching UN Documents.*

    (1) *UNDOC: Current Index.* This is the main index of UN documents and must be used for thorough research. It is published quarterly in two parts, a main part of document descriptions with name and title indexes, and a second part containing a subject index. [See Illustration 173.] There is an annual cumulation, but since 1984 it is available only on microfiche. Use of *UNDOC* can start with the indexes, or if one knows the UN body or document symbol of interest, the researcher can go straight to the document descriptions and scan for documents of note. [See Illustration 174.] *UNDOC* continues two earlier indexes produced by the UN, *UNDEX*[149] and *United Nations Document Index: Cumulative Index,*[150] which will be of interest for the years before 1979.

    (2) *Index to Proceedings of the General Assembly, Index to Proceedings of the Security Council, Index to Proceedings of the Economic & Social Council.* The indexes are not as easy to use as *UNDOC,* but they are valuable resources that would have to be consulted for in-depth research.

    (3) *Yearbook of the United Nations.*[151] The *Yearbook* covers the activities of both the UN and the specialized agencies. It is organized in broad subject categories such as Political and Security Questions, Regional Questions, Economic and Social Questions. Under each sub-topic the action of UN organs is summarized and important resolutions are reproduced. Particularly valuable are the references (by document symbol) to UN documents relating to the points discussed.

3. European Community

    a. *Introduction.* The European Community (EC) is an international organization of twelve European countries—Belgium, France, German, Italy, Luxembourg, The Netherlands, Denmark, Ireland, United Kingdom, Greece, Portugal, and Spain. The EC is sometimes called a *supranational* organization because it has the authority under its founding treaties to make law binding on the member states. A source of confusion is the similarity between the names of the EC and of the Council of Europe, a different organization. The Council of Europe is responsible, among other things, for the administration of the European

---

[148] The annual UN sales catalog is useful for reference and can be requested free from United Nations Publications, Sales Section, 2 United Nations Plaza, Room DC2–853, New York, NY 10017.

[149] (UN 1970–1978).

[150] (UN 1950–1973).

[151] (UN 1947–).

Convention for the Protection of Human Rights and Fundamental Freedoms.[152] The European Court of Human Rights is an arm of the Council of Europe, *not* of the EC.[153]

Again, the interest of the EC for our purposes is that it produces a large amount of documents of significance for the study of the EC itself and of subjects with which the EC is concerned. The EC carries out its work through four main institutions—the Council, the Commission, the European Parliament, and the Court of Justice. Of lesser importance for research are the Economic and Social Committee, the Court of Auditors and the newly-created Committee of the Regions. Each institution produces documentation. It can appear in a variety of forms. As in the case of the UN, the researcher will gain by knowing the institutional structure and law-making process of the EC. For this purpose, a leading treatise on the law and institutions of the EC is indispensable.[154]

b. *EC Documents.* There is room in this chapter to touch on only the most notable publications of the EC. Researchers needing in-depth information should consult *The Documentation of the European Communities: a Guide.*[155] The text of the founding treaties can be located in several places. Likely sources are *Treaties Establishing the European Communities,*[156] *Encyclopedia of European Community Law,*[157] and *Basic Community Laws.*[158]

(1) *Official Journal of the European Communities.*[159] The *Official Journal* is the central gazette of EC legal information. It is published every business day in all Community languages. The *Official Journal* has more than one part. Most important are the "L" series (containing final legislative acts such as amendments to the founding treaties, directives, regulations, decisions, opinions, and recommendations) and the "C" series (containing information and notices, including proposals for legislation, European Parliament resolutions, opinions of the Economic and Social Committee, and excerpts from the judgments of the Court of Justice). Every issue of the *Official Journal* is numbered separately. You cannot find something unless you have this number. Thus, a typical reference might be "*OJ* **L291**/10 (1992)." This refers to

---

[152] E.T.S. No. 5, 313 U.N.T.S. 221.

[153] *See generally* THE COUNCIL OF EUROPE: A GUIDE (Council of Europe 1986); A.H. ROBERTSON & J.G. MERRILLS, HUMAN RIGHTS IN EUROPE: A STUDY OF THE EUROPEAN CONVENTION ON HUMAN RIGHTS (3d ed. Manchester University Press 1993).

[154] *See, e.g.,* DERRICK WYATT & ALAN DASHWOOD, WYATT AND DASHWOOD'S EUROPEAN COMMUNITY LAW (3d ed. Sweet & Maxwell 1993); GEORGE A. BERMANN ET AL., CASES AND MATERIALS ON EUROPEAN COMMUNITY LAW (West 1993); STEPHEN WEATHERILL & PAUL BEAUMONT, EC LAW (Penguin 1993); RALPH H. FOLSOM, EUROPEAN COMMUNITY LAW IN A NUTSHELL (West 1992).

[155] By IAN THOMSON (Mansell 1989).

[156] (EC 1987).

[157] (Sweet & Maxwell 1973–).

[158] Edited by BERNARD RUDDEN & DERRICK WATT (4th ed. O.U.P. 1993).

[159] (1973–). The OFFICIAL JOURNAL was not published in English before 1973. There is an OFFICIAL JOURNAL SPECIAL EDITION (1972–73) of translations of EC law enacted before the UK and Ireland became members.

issue 291 of the L series for 1992, page 10. There are monthly and annual indexes.

(2) *Bulletin of the European Communities.*[160] This is a monthly bulletin that reports on the work of the Community institutions. It is good for starting research on current developments in the EC. There are numerous references to EC documents on point. There is an irregular *Supplement to the Bulletin* that republishes documents published in the *Official Journal.*

(3) *General Report on the Activities of the European Communities.*[161] This is an annual account of the work of the EC. It too is useful for researching current developments across the full range of EC activity. The footnotes refer to documents published in the *Official Journal.*

(4) *Directory of Community Legislation in Force.*[162] EC law as published in the *Official journal* is *not* later compiled in a set of "statutes in force." Therefore, a research tool like the *Directory* is essential in verifying and updating the status of EC legislation. It is published twice a year, but many libraries in the United States receive it annually in microfiche. There are commercial research tools that perform essentially the same function: *European Communities Legislation: Current Status* [163] and *Guide to EEC Legislation.*[164]

(5) *Reports of Cases Before the Court.* This is the official name of the reports of the European Court of Justice. However, the informal name is *European Court Reports* and they often cited *E.C.R.* Several parts are issued each year. Delays caused by the requirement of translating the *Reports* into all community languages have put them behind. Few libraries receive the advance text. Therefore, researchers should know about the commercial editions that appear much faster than *E.C.R.* These are the *Common Market Law Reports* [165] and *European Community Cases.*[166]

(6) *COM Documents.* The European Commission has what is known as the "right of initiative," *i.e.,* the power to make proposals for EC legislation. Only some of this proposed legislation is published in the "C" series of the *Official Journal,* and even then, without the accompanying report of the Commission. To see much important documentation from the Commission it is necessary to consult it in the form of a COM document, or document from the Commission. These documents are published individually in the hundreds each year. Some

[160] (1968–).

[161] (1968–).

[162] (1984–).

[163] (Butterworth 1988–).

[164] (North–Holland 1979–).

[165] (Sweet & Maxwell 1962–). There is a companion series called C.M.L.R. Antitrust Reports (Sweet & Maxwell 1991–).

[166] (Commerce Clearing House (C.C.H.) 1989–). This series replaces the reports of the E.C.J. decisions collected in transfer binders of the C.C.H. Common Market Reporter.

libraries, usually EC depository libraries in the United States, will have COM documents available on microfiche. These documents have a title followed (or preceded) by a document number of the type "COM(93)207."

c. *Publications about the EC.* There is a mass of secondary literature about the EC. Much of it deals specifically with legal issues. There is also a large literature on the EC from the perspective of political science and international relations. The Library of Congress subject headings for general works are: "European Economic Community," "European Economic Community Countries," and "European Federation." Works on EC law receive the subject heading "Law—European Economic Community Countries." The subject *subheading* used in the last example can be transferred to narrow a search on any field of law, *e.g.,* "Antitrust Law—European Economic Community Countries."

Journal articles on EC law will appear in virtually any of the law reviews published in the United States and Britain. Therefore, research in the standard journal indexes will prove fruitful. There are several English-language journals devoted to EC law: *Common Market Law Review,*[167] *European Law Review,*[168] *Legal Issues of European Integration,*[169] *New Europe Law Review.*[170] A journal from the perspective of political science is *Journal of Common Market Studies.*[171] Two annuals of interest are *Yearbook of European Law* [172] and *Collected Courses of the Academy of European Law.*[173]

d. *EC Information Online.* Both LEXIS and WESTLAW carry extensive databases of EC law and general information. The CELEX database of EC law in force is available on both systems.[174] CELEX is a legal database developed by the EC. On LEXIS and WESTLAW it can be searched using the standard commands of the two systems. CELEX is sometimes described as a full-text database. This is incorrect. References on CELEX to recent EC legislation do not have the text of the law, but only a brief description with a citation to the *Official Journal.* Judgments of the European Court of Justice are on both systems. On WESTLAW they are part of the CELEX database; on LEXIS they are in the EUROPE library, CASES file.

Both systems have other EC information of interest. LEXIS has a file of EC press releases (EUROPE library, RAPID file). WESTLAW has a well-written, up-to-date newsletter of EC information called *European*

[167] (Nijhoff 1963–).

[168] (Sweet & Maxwell 1975–).

[169] (Kluwer 1974–).

[170] (Yeshiva University 1992–).

[171] (Blackwell 1962–).

[172] (O.U.P. 1982–).

[173] (Nijhoff 1991–).

[174] On LEXIS, the EUROPE library, ECLAW file; on WESTLAW, the CELEX databases.

Update (EURUPDATE). These are only samples. For more information, consult the current editions of the *LEXIS/NEXIS Library Contents* and of the *WESTLAW DataBasics*.

SECTION I. ILLUSTRATIONS

[Illustration 167]

PAGE FROM BILATERAL SECTION OF TREATIES IN FORCE

MEXICO (Cont'd)

ENVIRONMENTAL COOPERATION (See also **BOUNDARY WATERS; POLLUTION**)

Agreement on cooperation for the protection and improvement of the environment in the border area. Signed at La Paz August 14, 1983; entered into force February 16, 1984. TIAS 10827; 1352 UNTS 67.

Annexes:
Agreement of cooperation for solution of the border sanitation problem at San Diego, California-Tijuana, Baja California. Signed at San Diego July 18, 1985; entered into force July 18, 1985. TIAS 11269.
Agreement of cooperation regarding pollution of the environment along the inland international boundary by discharges of hazardous substances, with appendices. Signed at San Diego July 18, 1985; entered

transboundary air pollution caused by copper smelters along their common border. Signed at Washington January 29, 1987; entered into force January 29, 1987. TIAS 11269.
Agreement of cooperation regarding international transport of urban air pollution, with appendix. Signed at Washington October 3, 1989; entered into force August 22, 1990. TIAS 11269.

Agreement on cooperation for the protection and improvement of the environment in the metropolitan area of Mexico City. Signed at Washington October 3, 1989; entered into force August 22, 1990. TIAS

EXTRADITION

Extradition treaty, with appendix. Signed at Mexico May 4, 1978; entered into force January 25, 1980. 31 UST 5059; TIAS 9656.

FINANCE

Agreement regarding the consolidation and rescheduling of certain debts owed to, guaranteed or insured by the United States through the Export-Import Bank of the United States.

Signed at Mexico March 7, 1984; entered into force May 2, 1984. TIAS 10961.

Agreement regarding the consolidation and rescheduling of certain debts owed to, guaranteed by, or insured by the United States Government and its agencies, with annexes. Signed at Washington April 9, 1987; entered into force May 21, 1987. TIAS

Swap agreement between the United States Treasury and the Banco de Mexico/Government of Mexico, with memorandum of understanding. Signed at Washington and Mexico September 14, 1989; entered into force September 14, 1989. TIAS

Exchange stabilization agreement among the United States Treasury and the Banco de Mexico/Government of Mexico. Signed at Washington and Mexico January 12, 1990; entered into force January 12, 1990. TIAS

Agreement regarding the consolidation and re-

ment of Mexico, with memorandum of understanding. Signed at Washington and Mexico March 23, 1990; entered into force March 23, 1990. TIAS

HEALTH

Memorandum of understanding concerning exchange of information on, and control of, products involved in commerce between the United States and Mexico which are regulated on behalf of the United States by the Food and Drug Administration. Signed at Mazatlan August 13, 1974; entered into force August 13, 1974. 28 UST 1622; TIAS 8522.

Agreement for scientific cooperation on alcohol-related problems. Signed at Washington March 11, 1982; entered into force March 11, 1982. TIAS 10491.

Memorandum of understanding regarding cooperation in the scientific and regulatory fields of health. Signed at Mexico February 22, 1988; entered into force February 22, 1988. TIAS

Memorandum of understanding regarding cooperation in ensuring the safety and wholesomeness of fresh and fresh frozen oysters, clams and mussels exported to the United States from Mexico. Signed at Acapulco No-

vember 12, 1988; entered into force November 12, 1988. TIAS

Memorandum of understanding regarding mutual cooperation in the regulation of raw agricultural products involved in commerce between Mexico and the United States, with annex. Signed at Mexico November 28, 1988; entered into force November 28, 1988. TIAS

HOUSING

Agreement for cooperation in the field of housing and urban development. Signed at Mexico February 16, 1979; entered into force February 16, 1979. 30 UST 5865; TIAS 9523; 1180 UNTS 255.

JUDICIAL ASSISTANCE

Procedures for mutual assistance in the administration of justice.

2153; TIAS 8930).
May 31 and June 1, 1978 (29 UST 3200; TIAS 9005; 1124 UNTS 433).
November 17 and December 5, 1978 (30 UST 2177; TIAS 9322).
August 25 and November 9, 1981 (33 UST 4353; TIAS 10305).
November 10 and 25, 1981 (33 UST 4353; TIAS 10305).

Treaty on cooperation for mutual legal assistance. Signed at Mexico December 9, 1987; entered into force May 3, 1991. TIAS

MAPPING

Memorandum concerning cooperation and mutual assistance in mapping, charting and geodesy. Signed at Mexico July 25, 1975; entered into force July 25, 1975. 27 UST 1083; TIAS 8248.

MARITIME MATTERS

Treaty for the sending of vessels for purposes of assistance and salvage. Signed at Mexico June 13, 1935; entered into force March 7, 1936. 49 Stat. 3359; TS 905; 9 Bevans 1015; 168 LNTS 135.

Question: Does the United States have an extradition treaty with Mexico?

Answer: Use Part 1 of the current edition of *Treaties in Force*. Part 1 is organized by the name of the other country and subdivided by topic. Note the parallel citation to *U.S.T.* and *T.I.A.S.*

[Illustration 168]

PAGE FROM MULTILATERAL SECTION OF TREATIES IN FORCE

310   TREATIES IN FORCE

CULTURAL PROPERTY (Cont'd)

Convention on the means of prohibiting and preventing the illicit import, export and transfer of ownership of cultural property. Done at Paris November 14, 1970; entered into force April 24, 1972; for the United States December 2, 1983.
TIAS   ; 823 UNTS 231.
States which are parties:
Algeria
Angola
Argentina
Australia [1]
Belarus [2]
Belize
Bolivia
Brazil
Bulgaria
Burkina Faso
Cambodia
Cameroon
Canada
Central African Rep.
Colombia
Cote d'Ivoire
Croatia
Cuba
Cyprus
Czechoslovakia [3]
Dominican Rep.
Ecuador
Egypt
El Salvador
Georgia
German Dem. Rep. [4]
Greece
Grenada
Guatemala
Guinea
Honduras
Hungary
India
Iran
Iraq
Italy
Jordan
Korea, Dem. People's Rep.
Korea, Rep.
Kuwait
Lebanon
Libya
Madagascar
Mali
Mauritania
Mauritius
Mexico
Mongolia
Nepal
Nicaragua
Niger
Nigeria
Oman
Pakistan
Panama
Peru
Poland
Portugal
Qatar
Saudi Arabia
Senegal

Spain
Sri Lanka
Syrian Arab Rep.
Tajikistan
Tanzania
Tunisia
Turkey
Ukraine [2]
Union of Soviet Socialist Reps. [2][5]
United States [1]
Uruguay
Yugoslavia [6]
Zaire
Zambia

NOTES:
[1] With reservation and understandings.
[2] With declaration.
[3] See note under CZECHOSLOVAKIA in bilateral section.
[4] See note under GERMANY, FEDERAL REPUBLIC OF in bilateral section.
[5] See note under UNION OF SOVIET SOCIALIST REPUBLICS in bilateral section.
[6] See note under YUGOSLAVIA in bilateral section.

CULTURAL RELATIONS

(See also WORLD HERITAGE)

Treaty on the protection of artistic and scientific institutions and historic monuments. Signed at Washington April 15, 1935; entered

Convention providing for creation of the Inter-American Indian Institute. Done at Mexico City November 1, 1940; entered into force December 13, 1941.
56 Stat. 1303; TS 978; 3 Bevans 661.
States which are parties:
Bolivia
Brazil
Chile
Colombia
Costa Rica
Ecuador
El Salvador
Guatemala
Honduras
Mexico
Nicaragua
Panama
Paraguay
Peru
United States
Venezuela

Agreement for facilitating the international circulation of visual and auditory materials of an educational, scientific and cultural character, with protocol. (Beirut agreement) Done at Lake Success July 15, 1949; entered into force August 12, 1954; for the United States January 12, 1967.
17 UST 1578; TIAS 6116; 197 UNTS 3.
States which are parties:
Brazil
Cambodia
Canada
Congo
Costa Rica
Cuba [1]

Costa Rica
Dominican Rep.
El Salvador
Guatemala
Haiti
Honduras
Mexico
Nicaragua
Panama
Peru
United States
Venezuela

NOTES:
[1] With reservation.
[2] See note under YUGOSLAVIA in bilateral section.

Agreement on the importation of educational, scientific and cultural materials, with protocol. (Florence agreement) Done at Lake Success November 22, 1950; entered into force May 21, 1952; for the United States November 2, 1966.
17 UST 1835; TIAS 6129; 131 UNTS 25.

> **Question: Is the United States a party to the UNESCO Cultural Property Convention concluded in Paris on November 14, 1970? What other countries are also parties to the Convention?**
>
> **Answer: Use Part 2 of the current edition of *Treaties in Force*. Part 2 is organized by topic; treaties within a topic are arranged chronologically by the date they were concluded ("done"). The citation to *T.I.A.S.* is blank, indicating that this treaty has not yet been published in an official U.S. Treaty source. Note the parallel citation to *U.N.T.S.* The entry is followed by the list of the other states party to the treaty.**

[Illustration 169]

FIRST PAGE OF EXTRADITION TREATY WITH MEXICO AS FOUND IN U.S.T.

MEXICO

Extradition

Treaty signed at Mexico City May 4, 1978;
Ratification advised by the Senate of the United States of America
* November 30, 1979;*
Ratified by the President of the United States of America Decem-
* ber 13, 1979;*
Ratified by Mexico January 31, 1979;
Ratifications exchanged at Washington January 25, 1980;
Proclaimed by the President of the United States of America
* February 6, 1980;*
Entered into force January 25, 1980.

BY THE PRESIDENT OF THE UNITED STATES OF AMERICA

A PROCLAMATION

CONSIDERING THAT:

The Extradition Treaty between the United States of America and the United Mexican States was signed at Mexico City on May 4, 1978, the text of which, in the English and Spanish languages, is hereto annexed;

The Senate of the United States of America by its resolution of

> **The treaty document as published in *U.S.T.* is prefaced with the chronological data and the Proclamation of the treaty by the President. The text of the treaty appears on the following pages. Note the parallel citation to *T.I.A.S.***

States;

It is provided in Article 23 of the Treaty that the Treaty shall enter into force on the date of exchange of the instruments of ratification;

The instruments of ratification of the Treaty were exchanged at Washington on January 25, 1980; and accordingly the Treaty entered into force on that date;

Now, THEREFORE, I, Jimmy Carter, President of the United States of America, proclaim and make public the Treaty, to the end that it be observed and fulfilled with good faith on and after January 25,

(5059)   TIAS 9656

[Illustration 170]

FIRST PAGE OF UNESCO CULTURAL PROPERTY
CONVENTION AS FOUND IN U.N.T.S.

---

232   *United Nations — Treaty Series*   · 1972

CONVENTION[1] ON THE MEANS OF PROHIBITING AND PREVENTING THE ILLICIT IMPORT, EXPORT AND TRANSFER OF OWNERSHIP OF CULTURAL PROPERTY

The General Conference of the United Nations Educational, Scientific and Cultural Organization, meeting in Paris from 12 October to 14 November 1970, at its sixteenth session,

Recalling the importance of the provisions contained in the Declaration of the Principles of International Cultural Co-operation, adopted by the General Conference at its fourteenth session,

Considering that the interchange of cultural property among nations for scientific, cultural and educational purposes increases the knowledge of the

> **U.N.T.S. publishes the convention text in all four of its official languages: English, Spanish, French, and Russian.**

civilization and national culture, and that its true value can be appreciated only in relation to the fullest possible information regarding its origin, history and traditional setting,

Considering that it is incumbent upon every State to protect the cultural property existing within its territory against the dangers of theft, clandestine excavation, and illicit export,

Considering that, to avert these dangers, it is essential for every State to become increasingly alive to the moral obligations to respect its own cultural heritage and that of all nations,

Considering that, as cultural institutions, museums, libraries and archives should ensure that their collections are built up in accordance with universally recognized moral principles,

---

[1] Came into force on 24 April 1972 with respect to the following States, i.e. three months after the deposit of the third instrument of ratification or acceptance with the Director-General of the United Nations Educational, Scientific and Cultural Organization, in accordance with article 21 :

State	*Date of deposit of the instrument of ratification or acceptance (a)*
Ecuador	24 March 1971a
Bulgaria	15 September 1971
Nigeria	24 January 1972

Subsequently, the Convention came into force with respect to the following State three months after the deposit of its instrument of ratification, in accordance with article 21 :

Central African Republic . . . .   1 February 1972
(To take effect on 1 May 1972).

No. 11806

[Illustration 171]

**FIRST PAGE OF A DECISION OF THE INTERNATIONAL
COURT OF JUSTICE**

INTERNATIONAL COURT OF JUSTICE

REPORTS OF JUDGMENTS,
ADVISORY OPINIONS AND ORDERS

CASE CONCERNING MILITARY AND PARAMILITARY ACTIVITIES IN AND AGAINST NICARAGUA

(NICARAGUA *v.* UNITED STATES OF AMERICA)

MERITS

JUDGMENT OF 27 JUNE 1986

1986

The decision of the International Court of Justice are published in the series *Reports of Judgments, Advisory Opinions and Orders.* Note that this is a judgment on the *merits*, as distinguished from an order or judgment on an interlocutory matter (such as a question of jurisdiction), which are published in the same series.

AFFAIRE DES ACTIVITÉS MILITAIRES ET PARAMILITAIRES AU NICARAGUA ET CONTRE CELUI-CI

(NICARAGUA c. ÉTATS-UNIS D'AMÉRIQUE)

FOND

ARRÊT DU 27 JUIN 1986

[Illustration 172]

TEXT OF I.C.J. DECISION AS RETRIEVED
ON WESTLAW'S INT–ICJ DATABASE

AUTHORIZED FOR EDUCATIONAL USE ONLY   PAGE   1

Citation	Rank(R)	Database	Mode
1986 I.C.J. 14	R 1 OF 20	INT-ICJ	Page

189. As regards the United States in particular, the weight of an expression of opinio juris can similarly be attached to its support of the resolution of the Sixth International Conference of American States condemning aggression (18 February 1928) and ratification of the Montevideo Convention on Rights and Duties of States (26 December 1933), Article 11 of which imposes the obligation not to recognize territorial acquisitions or special advantages which have been obtained by force. Also signifcant is United States acceptance of the principle of the prohibition of the use of force which is contained in the declaration on principles governing the mutual relations of States participating in the Conference on Security and Co-operation in Europe (Helsinki, 1 August 1975), whereby the participating States undertake to 'refrain in their mutual relations, as well as in their international relations in general,' (emphasis added) from the threat or **use** of **force**. Acceptance of a text in these terms confirms the existence of an opinio juris of the participating States **prohibiting** the **use** of **force** in international relations.

190. A further confirmation of the validity as **customary international law** of the principle of the **prohibition** of the **use** of **force** expressed in Article 2, paragraph 4, of the Charter of the United Nations may be found in the fact that it is frequently referred to in statements by State representatives as being not only a principle of **customary international law** but also a fundamental or cardinal principle of such **law**. The **International Law** Commission, in the course of its work on the codification of the law of treaties, expressed the view that 'the law of the Charter concerning the **prohibition** of the **use** of **force** in itself constitutes a conspicuous example of a rule in **international law** having the character of jus cogens' (paragraph (1) of the commentary of the Commission to Article 50 of its draft Articles on the Law of Treaties, ILC Yearbook, 1966-II, p. 247). Nicaragua in its Memorial on the Merits submitted in the present case states that the principle prohibiting the use of force embodied in Article 2, paragraph 4, of the Charter of the United Nations 'has come to be recognized as jus cogens'. The United States, in its Counter-Memorial on the questions of jurisdiction and admissibility, found it material to quote the views of scholars that this principle is a 'universal norm', a 'universal international law', a 'universally recognized principle of

---

Judgments of the I.C.J. can be lengthy, which makes it difficult to find text on point within a case. Using the INT–ICJ database on WESTLAW the researcher can discover specific discussion within the opinion. For example, a search on the prohibition on the use of force in customary international law recovers paragraphs 189 and 190 of the judgment in *Nicaragua v. United States of America* (1986). Note the highlighted terms.

---

which may refer to aggression, this text includes others which refer only to less grave forms of the use of force. In particular, according to this resolution:

'Every State has the duty to refrain from the threat or use of force to violate the existing international boundaries of another State or as a means

WESTLAW

[Illustration 173]

PAGE FROM SUBJECT INDEX IN UNDOC: CURRENT INDEX

SUBJECT INDEX - UNDOC: Current Index January 1993

ENVIRONMENTAL IMPACT ASSESSMENT (continued)
----Points of contact regarding notification in accordance with article 3 of the Convention on Environmental Impact Assessment in a Transboundary Context. [E/ECE/]ENVWA/WG.3/R.5 (001885)
----Population, resources and the environment. (002070)
----Situation of human rights in Iraq. A/47/367 (000268)
----Statement to the plenary by the Chairman of Special Commission 3 on the progress of work in that Commission : Preparatory Commission for the International Seabed Authority and for the International Tribunal for the Law of the Sea, Special Commission 3. LOS/PCN/L.108 (002111)
----World investment report. 1992. ST/CTC/130 (002892)

ENVIRONMENTAL INDICATORS.
See also: ENVIRONMENTAL ACCOUNTING; ENVIRONMENTAL POLICY
----Guidelines on the ecosystem approach in water management. [E/ECE/]ENVWA/WP.3/R.28 (001896)

ENVIRONMENTAL LAW.
See also: ENVIRONMENT; ENVIRONMENTAL MANAGEMENT; ENVIRONMENTAL POLICY; ENVIRONMENTAL PROTECTION; FISHERY LEGISLATION; FORESTRY LEGISLATION; INTERNATIONAL LAW; POLLUTION CONTROL; TOXIC WASTE MANAGEMENT; TRANSBOUNDARY WASTE DISPOSAL; WASTE DISPOSAL
----Costs and benefits for the developing countries of becoming parties to environmental treaties. (003222)
----The environment in Europe and North-America : annotated statistics 1992. (002681)
----Environmental conventions elaborated under the auspices of the United Nations Economic Commission for Europe (UN-ECE). (002785)
----Human rights and the environment. E/CN.4/Sub.2/1992/7 (001437)
----International legal instruments. [E/ECE/]ENVWA/WG.5/R.4 (001889)
----Outcome of the United Nations Conference on Environment and Development : implications for European environmental policies. [E/ECE/]ENVWA/WG.5/R.1 (001887)
----Protection of the environment in times of armed conflict : draft resolution. A/C.6/47/L.2 (000385)
----United Nations Decade of International Law. A/47/384 (000277)

ENVIRONMENTAL MANAGEMENT.
See also: COASTAL ZONE MANAGEMENT; ECODEVELOPMENT; ENVIRONMENT; ENVIRONMENTAL IMPACT ASSESSMENT; ENVIRONMENTAL LAW; ENVIRONMENTAL MONITORING;

----Report and proceedings of the United Nations/International Astronautical Federation/Canada Workship on Space Technologies for Development, organized in cooperation with the Government of Canada, Montreal, Canada, 2-5 October 1991. A/AC.105/520 (000424)
----Report of the Chairman of the Drafting Group to the Plenary : Governing Council of the United Nations Development Programme, 39th session, 4-29 May 1992, Geneva. DP/1992/L.13/Add.15 (000950)
----Report of the United Nations Technical Conference on Practical Experience in the Realization of Sustainable and Environmentally Sound Self-development of Indigenous Peoples, Santiago, Chile, 18 to 22 May 1992. E/CN.4/Sub.2/1992/31/Add.1 (001458)
----Report on the Secretariat's activities in support of the implementation in the ESCAP region of the Programme of Action for the Least Developed Countries for the 1990s. E/ESCAP/874 (001974)
----Report on the 1st African Regional Conference on Environment and Sustainable Development held in Kampala, Uganda, 12-16 June 1989. E/ECA/CM/16/19 (001764)
----Report on the 2nd United Nations Conference on the Least Developed Countries, Paris, 3-14 September 1990. E/ESCWA/DPD/1992/2 (001990)
----Saving our planet : challenges and hopes. (003235)
----Third country programme for Antigua and Barbuda. DP/CP/ANT/3 (000998)
----Third country programme for Saint Kitts and Nevis. DP/CP/STK/3 (001046)
----Women and the environment. E/CN.6/RES/36/8 (001821)

ENVIRONMENTAL MONITORING.
See also: POLLUTANT LEVELS; POLLUTION CONTROL
----Activities and future funding of International Cooperative Programmes, the Pilot Programme and the Coordination Center for Effects. [E/ECE/]EB.AIR/R.72 (001859)
----Conclusions and draft recommendations of a Workshop on Measurements of Nitrogen-containing Compounds. [E/ECE/]EB.AIR/GE.1/R.72 (001863)
----Draft mandates for the Task Force on Mapping and for the Coordination Center for Effects. [E/ECE/]EB.AIR/WG.1/R.76 (001867)
----Draft work-plan for the implementation of the Convention on Long-Range Transboundary Air Pollution. [E/ECE/]EB.AIR/R.68 (001855)
----Financial requirements for the implementation of the Convention on Long-Range Transboundary Air Pollution. [E/...858)
...ent.
...oring
...c of
...R.27
...onment
...tion 572)
...water

> **Question:** What recent documents has the UN produced concerning its action in the field of environmental law?
>
> **Answer:** The researcher goes to the subject index of *UNDOC* and looks under "Environmental Law" and related headings. The researcher notes the reference number on documents of interest. For example, the document on "Human rights and the environment" has the reference number "(001437)."

----Fifth country programme for Brazil. DP/CP/BRA/5 (001009)
----Fifth country programme for the Dominican Republic. DP/CP/DOM/5 (001021)
----Fifth country programme for the Niger. DP/CP/NER/5 (001042)
----Fourth country programme for Belize. DP/CP/BZE/4 (001012)
----Fourth country programme for Seychelles. DP/CP/SEY/4 (001045)
----Fourth country programme for the Czech and Slovak Federal Republic. DP/CP/CZE/4 (001019)
----A framework for an evolving Environmental Programme for Europe. [E/ECE/]ENVWA/WG.5/R.3 (001888)
----Integration of environment and development in Asia and the Pacific. E/ESCAP/838 (001949)
----Our planet : the magazine of the United Nations Environment Programme. Vol. 4, no. 1, 1992. (003232)
----Outcome of the United Nations Conference on Environment and Development : implications for European environmental policies. [E/ECE/]ENVWA/WG.5/R.1 (001887)
----Public administration and finance matters. E/1992/13 (001189)
----Regional cooperation and coordination in remote sensing and geographic information systems for sustainable natural resources development and environmental management. E/ESCAP/851 (001959)

Commission for Europe, Executive Body for the Convention on Long-Range Transboundary Air Pollution. [E/ECE/]EB.AIR/R.67 (001854)
----Progress of the International Cooperative Programme for Assessment and Monitoring of Acidification of Rivers and Lakes. [E/ECE/]EB.AIR/WG.1/R.79 (001869)
----Progress of the International Cooperative Programme for Assessment and Monitoring of Air Pollution Effects on Forests. [E/ECE/]EB.AIR/WG.1/R.77 (001868)
----Progress of the International Cooperative Programme for Research on Evaluating Effects of Air Pollutants and Other Stresses on Agricultural Crops. [E/ECE/]EB.AIR/WG.1/R.81 (001871)
----Progress of the International Cooperative Programme on Effects of Air Pollution on Materials, including Historic and Cultural Monuments. [E/ECE/]EB.AIR/WG.1/R.80 (001870)
----Report and proceedings of the United Nations/International Astronautical Federation/Canada Workship on Space Technologies for Development, organized in cooperation with the Government of Canada, Montreal, Canada, 2-5 October 1991. A/AC.105/520 (000424)
----Report of the Committee on Natural Resources and Energy on its 18th session. E/ESCAP/847 (001956)
----Report of the 11th session : Economic Commission for Europe, Executive Body for the Convention on Long-Range Transboundary Air Pollution, Working Group on Effects. [E/ECE/]EB.AIR/WG.1/18 (001865)

-551-

[Illustration 174]

PAGE FROM DOCUMENT DESCRIPTIONS
IN UNDOC: CURRENT INDEX

DOCUMENTS AND PUBLICATIONS - UNDOC: Current Index January 1993

* Economic and Social Council. Commission on Human Rights.
* Subcommission on Prevention of Discrimination and
* Protection of Minorities, 44th session, Geneva, 3-28 August
* 1992.

E/CN.2/1992/1/Add.1/Corr.1 (001431)
Annotations to the provisional agenda : Commission on Human
Rights, Sub-Commission on Prevention of Discrimination and
Protection of Minorities, 44th session : corrigendum /
prepared by the Secretary-General. - Geneva : UN, 7 Aug.
1992.
[1] p.
Corrects "Annex: Members and alternates of the
Sub-Commission on Prevention of Discrimination and
Protection of Minorities".
Language versions: A, C, E, F, R, S.
Photo-offset.

E/CN.4/Sub.2/1992/3 (001432)
Review of the work of the Subcommission. - Report of the
Inter-sessional Working Group on the Methods of Work of the
Sub-Commission established pursuant to Commission on Human
Rights Resolution 1992/66. - Geneva : UN, 22 June 1992.
20 p.
Includes draft decision containing guidelines on the
methods of work of the Subcommission.
Language versions: A, C, E, F, R, S.
Photo-offset.

E/CN.4/Sub.2/1992/3/Add.1 (001433)
Review of the work of the Subcommission. - Report of the
Inter-sessional Working Group on the Methods of Work of the
Sub-Commission established pursuant to Commission on Human
Rights resolution 1992/66. - Geneva : UN, 22 June 1992.
2 p.
Contents: Draft proposal on the methods of consideration
of violations of human rights in the Sub-Commission /
submitted by Mr. Chernichenko.
Language versions: A, C, E, F, R, S.
Photo-offset.

E/CN.4/Sub.2/1992/4 (001434)

E/CN.4/Sub.2/1992/7/Add.1 (001438)
Review of further developments in fields with which the
Subcommission has been concerned. - Human rights and the
environment : progress report / prepared by Fatma Zohra
Ksentini, Special Rapporteur, in accordance with
Sub-Commission resolution 1991/24. - Geneva : UN, 14 Aug.
1992.
7 p.
Includes excerpts from Rio Declaration on Environment and
Development.
Contents: ch. 4. United Nations Conference on Environment
and Development.
Language versions: A, C, E, F, R, S.
Photo-offset.

E/CN.4/Sub.2/1992/9 (001439)
Review of further developments in fields with which the
Subcommission has been concerned. - The right to freedom of
opinion and expression : final report / by Danilo Türk and
Louis Joinet, Special Rapporteurs. - Geneva : UN, 14 July
1992.
ii, 35 p.
Includes bibliographical references.
Language versions: A, C, E, F, R, S.
Photo-offset.

E/CN.4/Sub.2/1992/9/Add.1 (001440)
Review of further developments in fields with which the
Subcommission has been concerned. - The right to freedom of
opinion and expression : final report / prepared by Danilo
Türk and Louis Joinet, Special Rapporteurs. - Geneva : UN,
14 July 1992.
3 p.
Contents: Conclusions and recommendations.
Language versions: A, C, E, F, R, S.
Photo-offset.

E/CN.4/Sub.2/1992/10 (001441)
Review of further developments in fields with which the
Subcommission has been concerned. - Discrimination against
HIV-infected people or people with AIDS : final report /
submitted by Mr. Varela Quirós, Special Rapporteur. - Geneva
: UN, 28 July 1992.
ii, 43 p.

> In the section of document descriptions, the reference number from the
> index appears in the right of each column. The document symbol appears
> in the left. Note that documents are organized by issuing body, so that if
> the research interest was in the work of the Subcommission on Prevention
> of Discrimination and Protection of Minorities, the researcher could go
> directly to that part of the descriptions and browse through the entries.

Reviews ILO activities during 1991-1992.
Language versions: A, C, E, F, R, S.
Photo-offset.

E/CN.4/Sub.2/1992/8 (001436)
Review of further developments in fields with which the
Subcommission has been concerned. - Unesco activities
concerning prevention of discrimination and protection of
minorities : report / submitted by Unesco. - Geneva : UN,
24 July 1992.
4 p.
Language versions: A, C, E, F, R, S.
Photo-offset.

E/CN.4/Sub.2/1992/7 (001437)
Review of further developments in fields with which the
Subcommission has been concerned. - Human rights and the
environment : progress report / prepared by Fatma Zohra
Ksentini, Special Rapporteur, in accordance with
Sub-Commission resolution 1991/24. - Geneva : UN, 2 July
1992.
ii, 33 p.
Includes extracts from the constitutions of 49 countries
relating to environmental protection, as well as
decisions and comments of human rights bodies. - Includes
bibliographical references.
Language versions: A, C, E, F, R, S.
Photo-offset.

Concerns mainly the situation in Europe, North America
and Australia. - Prepared on the basis of replies from
Governments, specialized agencies, intergovernmental and
non-governmental organizations. - "Bibliography": p.
42-44.
Language versions: A, C, E, F, R, S.
Photo-offset.

E/CN.4/Sub.2/1992/12/Add.1 (001443)
Elimination of racial discrimination. Adverse consequences
for the enjoyment of human rights of political, military,
economic and other forms of assistance given to the racist
and colonialist régime of South Africa. - Updated report /
prepared by Ahmad M. Khalifa, Special Rapporteur. - Geneva :
UN, 3 June 1992.
206 p.
Consists of updated list of banks, insurance companies
and other enterprises giving assistance to South Africa.
Language versions: E.
Photo-offset.

SECTION J. SUMMARY

This section summarizes the essential sources mentioned in this chapter. References in parentheses are to the sections of this chapter where fuller information will be found.

1. **The sources of international law (see Article 38(1) of the Statute of the International Court of Justice) (A.3)**

   a. international agreements

   b. customary international law

   c. general principles of law

   d. judicial decisions

   e. writings of international law scholars (secondary sources)

2. **International Agreements of the United States (B.1–7)**

   a. Current Sources (B.2)

   (1) *Treaties and Other International Acts Series* (T.I.A.S.)

   (2) *United States Treaties and Other International Agreements* (U.S.T.)

   (3) *United States Treaties and Other International Agreements— Current Microfiche Service* (Hein)

   (4) *Consolidated Treaties & International Agreements—Current Service* (Oceana)

   (5) WESTLAW *USTREATIES* database

   b. Earlier Publications (B.3)

   (1) *United States Statutes at Large* (STAT.), volumes 8 through 64 (1949)

   (2) *Treaty Series* (T.S.) and *Executive Agreement Series* (E.A.S.), the predecessors to T.I.A.S.

   (3) *Treaties and Other International Agreements of the United States of America, 1776–1949* (Bevans)

   c. Finding and Verifying United States International Agreements (B.6)

   (1) *Treaties in Force: A List of Treaties and Other International Agreements in Force on January 1, 199___,* published annually by the State Department

   (2) *US Department of State Dispatch,* "Treaty Actions" section

   (3) *A Guide to the United States Treaties in Force*

   (4) *United States Treaty Index: 1776–1990 Consolidation*

   (5) *Current Treaty Index*

3. Additional Sources for International Agreements (C.1–3)

a. General Treaty Collections (C.1)

(1) *Consolidated Treaty Series,* covering the period 1648–1919

(2) *League of Nations Treaty Series,* covering the period 1920–1946

(3) *United Nations Treaty Series,* covering the period 1946–present

b. Other Treaty Collections (C.2)

(1) *European Treaty Series*

(2) *International Legal Materials*

(3) *O.A.S. Treaty Series*

c. Additional Tools for Finding and Verifying International Agreements (C.3)

(1) *Multilateral Treaties Deposited with the Secretary–General*

(2) *Multilateral Treaties: Index and Current Status*

(3) *World Treaty Index,* 2d edition

4. Customary International Law (D.1–4)

a. Digests of Practice: United States Publications (D.2)

(1) Whiteman, Hackworth, Moore, and Wharton [175]

(2) *Digest of United States Practice in International Law,* eight volumes covering the period 1973–1980

(3) "Contemporary Practice of the United States Relating to International Law" in each quarterly issue of *American Journal of International Law*

b. Additional Sources Documenting State Practice (D.4)

(1) *Foreign Relations of the United States*

(2) *American Foreign Policy: Current Documents*

(3) *British and Foreign State Papers*

(4) *United Nations Legislative Series*

5. General Principles of Law (E)

a. Consult a leading treatise discussing the idea of general principles of law as it is applied in international law, *e.g.,* Ian Brownlie, *Principles of Public International Law* 15–19 (4th ed. 1990).

b. Apply the method of comparative law and the fundamental techniques of legal research as described in this book to discover a general principle of law common to the major legal systems.

---

[175] *See* section D.2, *supra,* for fuller discussion of the U.S. digests of practice, which are informally known by the names of their editors and compilers.

6. Adjudications (Judicial Decisions and International Arbitrations) (F.1–5)

    a.   International Court of Justice (I.C.J.) (F.1)

    (1) *Reports of Judgments, Advisory Opinions and Orders*

    (2) INT–ICJ database on WESTLAW

    (3) *Pleadings, Oral Arguments, Documents*

    b.   Permanent Court of International Justice (P.C.I.J.) (F.1.g)

    (1) *Collection of Judgments* (Series A, to 1930)

    (2) *Collection of Advisory Opinions* (Series B, to 1930)

    (3) *Judgments, Orders and Advisory Opinions* (Series A/B, after 1930)

    (4) *Acts and Documents Relating to Judgments and Advisory Opinions* (to 1930); *Pleadings, Oral Statements and Documents* (after 1930) (Series C)

    c.   International Arbitrations (F.3)

    (1) *Reports of International Arbitral Awards* (R.I.A.A.)

    (2) *International Law Reports*

    (3) *International Legal Materials*

    (4) *Survey of International Arbitrations, 1794–1989*

    (5) *Repertory of International Arbitral Jurisprudence*

7. Secondary Sources (G.1–5)

    a.   *Restatement of the Law: the Foreign Relations Law of the United States (Restatement, Third)*

    b.   *Collected Courses of the Hague Academy of International Law ("Recueil des Cours")*

    c.   *Encyclopedia of Public International Law*

    d.   Journals such as *American Journal of International Law*

    e.   Yearbooks such as *British Yearbook of International Law*

8. Documents of International Organizations (H.1–3)

    a.   *Yearbook of International Organizations*

    b.   United Nations (H.2)

    (1) *UNDOC: Current Index*

    (2) *Yearbook of the United Nations*

    c.   European Community (H.3)

    (1) *Official Journal of the European Communities*, "L" and "C" series

    (2) *Bulletin of the European Communities*

(3) *Directory of Community Legislation in Force*

(4) *Reports of Cases Before the Court* (official reports of the European Court of Justice

(5) *Common Market Law Reports* and *European Community Cases*

(6) EC information on LEXIS and WESTLAW, especially CELEX, the database of EC law.

Appendix A

STATE GUIDES TO LEGAL RESEARCH

As discussed in Chapter 1, the United States consists of 51 major legal systems, one for each state and the federal government. While the state systems have much in common, each is the product of a unique history and legal background. Methods of legislating, codifying, and court reporting vary from state to state. Where possible, a researcher should take the time to learn the unusual aspects of legal research in each state's materials in which extended research is conducted.

In many states, law librarians and others who are familiar with legal research, have written guides detailing the history and organization of their states. The list below is a compilation of these guides. It includes books as well as shorter bibliographic sources from the American Association of Law Libraries (AALL) Occasional Papers Series, but excludes sources that may appear in legal periodicals. A researcher contemplating or beginning any research in one of the states listed below is advised to consult the guides first. Such a first step could save much time and effort in the endeavor.

Alabama	George D. Schrader, *Alabama Law Bibliography* (Barrister Press, 1990). Hazel L. Johnson & Timothy L. Coggins, *Guide to Alabama State Documents and Selected Law–Related Materials* (AALL, 1993).
Alaska	Aimee Ruzicka, *Alaska Legal and Law–Related Publications: A Guide for Law Libraries* (AALL, 1984).
Arizona	Kathy Shimpock–Vieweg & Marianne Sidorski Alcorn, *Arizona Legal Research Guide* (Hein, 1992). Richard Teenstra et al., *Survey of Arizona Law–Related Documents* (AALL, 1984).
Arkansas	Lynn Foster, *Arkansas Legal Bibliography: Documents and Selected Commercial Titles* (AALL, 1988).
California	Karla Castetter, *Locating the Law: A Handbook for Non–Librarians*, 2d ed. (Southern California Association of Law Libraries, 1989). Dan F. Henke, *California Law Guide*, 2d ed. (Parker & Son, 1976 and 1985 cum. supp.) Verona Mackay & Laura Peritore, *California Government Publications and Legal Resources* (AALL, 1991).
Colorado	Gary Alexander et al., *Colorado Legal Resources: An Annotated Bibliography* (AALL, 1987).
Connecticut	Shirley R. Bysiewicz, *Sources of Connecticut Law* (Butterworth, 1987). Lawrence G. Cheeseman & Arlene C. Bielefield, *Connecticut Legal Research Handbook* (Connecticut Law Book Company, 1992).

David R. Voisinet et al., *Connecticut State Legal Documents: A Selective Bibliography* (AALL, 1985).

District of Columbia   Carolyn P. Ahearn et al., *Selected Information Sources for the District of Columbia,* 2d. ed. (AALL, 1985).

Florida   Harriet L. French, *Research in Florida Law,* 2d ed. (Oceana, 1965).

Mark E. Kaplan, *Guide to Florida Legal Research,* 3d ed. (Florida Bar, 1992).

Niki L. Martin, *Florida Legal Research and Source Book* (D & S Publishers, 1990).

Carol A. Roehrenbeck, *Florida Legislative Histories: A Practical Guide to Their Preparation and Use* (D & S Publishers, 1986).

Georgia   Leah F. Chanin & Suzanne L. Cassidy, *Guide to Georgia Legal Research and Legal History* (Harrison Company, 1990).

Rebecca Simmons Stillwagon, *Georgia Legal Documents: An Annotated Bibliography* (AALL, 1991).

Hawaii   Jerry Dupont & Beverly D. Keever, *The Citizens Guide: How to Use Legal Materials in Hawaii* (1983).

Richard F. Kahle, *How to Research Constitutional Legislative and Statutory History in Hawaii* (Hawaii Legislative Reference Bureau, 1986).

Idaho   Patricia A. Cervenka et al., *Idaho Law–Related State Documents* (AALL, 1989).

Illinois   Bernita J. Davies & Francis J. Rooney, *Research in Illinois Law* (Oceana, 1954).

Roger F. Jacobs et al., *Illinois Legal Research Sourcebook* (Illinois Institute for Continuing Legal Education, 1977).

Cheryl R. Nyberg et al., *Illinois State Documents: A Selective Annotated Bibliography for Law Librarians* (AALL, 1986).

Laurel Wendt, *Illinois Legal Research Manual* (Butterworth, 1988).

Indiana   Linda K. Fariss & Keith A. Buckley, *An Introduction to Indiana State Publications for the Law Librarian* (AALL, 1982).

Iowa   Angela K. Secrest, *Iowa Legal Documents Bibliography* (AALL, 1990).

Kansas   Fritz Snyder, *A Guide to Kansas Legal Research* (Kansas Bar Association, 1986).

Martin E. Wisneski, *Kansas State Documents for Law Libraries: Publications Related to Law and State Government* (AALL, 1984).

Kentucky   Paul J. Cammarata, *Kentucky State Publications: A Guide for Law Librarians* (AALL, 1990).

Wesley Gilmer, Jr., *Guide to Kentucky Legal Research 2d: A State Bibliography* (State Law Library, 1985).

Louisiana   Win–Shin S. Chiang, *Louisiana Legal Research,* 2d ed. (Butterworth, 1990).

Madeline Hebert, *Louisiana Legal Documents and Related Publications* (AALL, 1990).

Kate Wallach, *Louisiana Legal Research Manual* (LSU Law School, 1972).

Maine	William W. Wells, Jr., *Maine Legal Research Guide* (Tower Publishing, 1989).
Maryland	Lynda C. Davis, *An Introduction to Maryland State Publications* (AALL, 1981). Michael S. Miller, *Ghost Hunting: Finding Legislative Intent in Maryland* (Maryland State Law Library, 1984).
Massachusetts	Margot Botsford et al., *Handbook of Legal Research in Massachusetts,* rev. ed. (Massachusetts Continuing Legal Education, Inc., 1988). Anthony J. Burke & Mary McLellan, *Guide to Massachusetts Legislative and Government Research* (Legislative Service Bureau, 1981). Leo McAuliffe & Susan Z. Steinway, *Massachusetts State Documents Bibliography* (AALL, 1985).
Michigan	Richard L. Beer & Judith J. Field, *Michigan Legal Literature: An Annotated Guide,* 2d ed. (Hein, 1991). Nancy L. Bosh, *Research Edge: Finding Law and Facts Fast* (Institute of Continuing Legal Education, 1993). John Doyle, *Michigan Citation Manual* (Hein, 1986). Michigan Association of Law Libraries, *Legal Research Guide for Michigan Libraries* (1982). Stuart D. Yoak & Margaret A. Heinen, *Michigan Legal Documents: an Annotated Bibliography* (AALL, 1982).
Minnesota	Marsha L. Baum & Mary Ann Nelson, *Guide to Minnesota State Documents and Selected Law–Related Publications* (AALL, 1985). Arlette M. Soderberg & Barbara L. Golden, *Minnesota Legal Research Guide* (Hein, 1985).
Mississippi	Ben Cole, *Mississippi Legal Documents and Related Publications: A Selected Annotated Bibliography* (AALL, 1987).
Missouri	Mary Ann Nelson, *Guide to Missouri State Documents and Selected Law–Related Materials* (AALL, 1991).
Montana	Stephen R. Jordan, *Bibliography of Selective Legal and Law Related Montana Documents* (AALL, 1990).
Nebraska	Mitchell J. Fontenot et al., *Nebraska State Documents Bibliography* (AALL, 1988). Paul F. Hill, *Nebraska Legal Research and Reference Manual* (Mason, 1983).
Nevada	Katherine Henderson, *Nevada State Documents Bibliography* (AALL, 1984).
New Jersey	Cameron Allen, *A Guide to New Jersey Legal Bibliography and Legal History* (Rothman, 1984). Paul Axel–Lute, *New Jersey Legal Research Handbook* (New Jersey Institute for Continuing Legal Education, 1985). Christina M. Senezak, *New Jersey State Publications, A Guide for Law Libraries* (AALL, 1984).
New Mexico	Arie W. Poldervaart, *Manual for Effective New Mexico Legal Research* (Univ. of New Mexico Press, 1955). Patricia Wagner & Mary Woodward, *Guide to New Mexico State Publications,* 2d ed. (AALL, 1991).
New York	Robert Allan Carter, *New York State Constitution: Sources of Legislative Intent* (Rothman, 1988).

Susan L. Dow & Karen L. Spencer, *New York Legal Documents: A Selective Annotated Bibliography* (AALL, 1985).

Ellen M. Gibson, *New York Legal Research Guide* (Hein, 1988).

North Carolina   Igor I. Kavass & Bruce A. Christensen, *Guide to North Carolina Legal Research* (Hein, 1973).

Thomas M. Steele & Donna Diprisco, *Survey of North Carolina State Legal and Law–Related Documents* (AALL, 1987).

Ohio   Christine A. Corcas, *Ohio Legal and Law–Related Documents* (AALL, 1986).

David M. Gold, *A Guide to Legislative History in Ohio* (Ohio Legislative Service Commission, 1985).

Ohio Regional Association of Law Libraries, *Ohio Legal Resources—An Annotated Bibliography and Guide,* 2d ed. (1984).

Susan Schaefgen & Melanie K. Putnam, *Ohio Legal Research* (Professional Education Systems, 1988).

Oklahoma   Christine A. Corcas, *Oklahoma Legal and Law–Related Documents and Publications: a Selected Bibliography,* (AALL, 1983).

Oregon   Leslie Ann Buhman et al., *Bibliography of Law Related Oregon Documents* (AALL, 1984).

Pennsylvania   Joel Fishman, *Bibliography of Pennsylvania Law: Secondary Sources* (Pennsylvania Legal Resources Institute, 1992).

Joel Fishman, *An Introduction to Pennsylvania State Publications for the Law Librarian* (AALL, 1985).

Caroll C. Moreland & Erwin C. Surrency, *Research in Pennsylvania Law,* 2d ed. (Oceana, 1965).

Rhode Island   *Legal Research in Rhode Island* (Rhode Island Law Institute, 1989).

South Carolina   Robin K. Mills & Jon S. Schultz, *South Carolina Legal Research Handbook* (Hein, 1976).

South Dakota   Delores A. Jorgensen, *South Dakota Legal Documents: A Selective Bibliography* (AALL, 1988).

Delores A. Jorgensen, *South Dakota Legal Research Guide* (Hein, 1988).

Tennessee   Lewis L. Laska, *Tennessee Legal Research Handbook* (Hein, 1977).

D. Cheryn Picquet & Reba A. Best, *Law and Government Publications of the State of Tennessee: A Bibliographic Guide* (AALL, 1988).

Texas   Malinda Allison & Kay Schleuter, *Texas State Documents for Law Libraries* (AALL, 1983).

Karl T. Gruben & James E. Hambleton, *A Reference Guide to Texas Law and Legal History,* 2d ed. (Butterworth, 1987).

Paris Permenter & Susan F. Ratliff, *Guide to Texas Legislative History* (Legislative Reference Library, 1986).

Vermont   Virginia Wise, *A Bibliographic Guide to the Vermont Legal System,* 2d ed. (AALL, 1991).

Virginia   John D. Eure, *A Guide to Legal Research in Virginia* (Virginia Law Foundation, 1989).

	Jacqueline Lichtman & Judy Stinson, *A Law Librarian's Introduction to Virginia State Publications* (AALL, 1988).
Washington	Scott F. Burson, *Washington State Law–Related Publications: A Selective Bibliography with Commentary* (AALL, 1984).
West Virginia	Sandra Stemple et al., *West Virginia Legal Bibliography* (AALL, 1990).
Wisconsin	Richard A. Danner, *Legal Research in Wisconsin* (University of Wisconsin, Extension Law Department, 1980). Janet Oberla, *An Introduction to Wisconsin State Documents and Law Related Materials* (AALL, 1987).
Wyoming	Nancy S. Greene, *Wyoming State Legal Documents: An Annotated Bibliography with Commentary* (AALL, 1985).

Appendix B

LEGAL RESEARCH IN TERRITORIES
OF THE UNITED STATES

The United States has sovereignty over a relatively small number of territories that are not among the fifty states. Each of these territories enjoys some degree of local autonomy, and researchers interested in the law of any of these areas must examine certain locally-originated materials as well as those portions of the general body of federal law that apply to the territory. The following is a listing of the more important local sources of law in these territories.

AMERICAN SAMOA

American Samoa was annexed by the United States pursuant to a treaty with Britain and Germany in 1899. It has a popularly-elected governor and a bicameral legislature. It is administered under the United States Department of the Interior, which publishes the annual reports of the governor and other information about the territory.

Statutes

American Samoa Code Annotated, Book Publishing Company, Seattle, Wash., 1981–.

The code is in looseleaf format, updated annually by replacement pages. It has a general index and tables showing the location of sections by legislative act and from the 1949, 1961, and 1973 codifications of American Samoa statutes.

Legislative Material

Fono Journal, American Samoa Legislature, Pago Pago, American Samoa, 1948–1952.

The annual Fono was a predecessor of the present legislature. It began as an advisory board made up of selected Samoa title holders who met once a year to discuss items placed on its agenda by the government.

House Journal, American Samoa Legislature, 1953–; *Senate Journal,* American Samoa Legislature, 1953–.

The official journals of the legislature.

Session Laws and Digest, American Samoa Legislature, 1976–.

This service contains most of the available material for legislative history as well as the text of new statutes.

Court Reports

American Samoa Reports, the Government of American Samoa, Equity Publishing Corporation, Orford, N.H.

There are only four volumes in this set, covering the period from the beginning of American sovereignty in 1900 until 1974. Each volume contains headnotes and a digest, and has tables of lands and Matai titles considered as well as the more common tables of cases and of statutes and regulations cited or construed.

American Samoa Reports, 2d series.

This is issued biennially and contains selected opinions of the Trial and Appellate Divisions of the High Court from 1975.

Administrative Rules and Regulations

American Samoa Administrative Code, Book Publishing Company, Seattle, Wash., 1981–.

The administrative code is in looseleaf format, updated annually by replacement pages. It has a general index.

Law Review

The Samoan Pacific Law Journal, American Samoa Bar Association, Pago Pago, American Samoa, 1973–1981.

In addition to the more usual law review articles, this journal published case summaries and digests for recent cases that were not yet contained in the *American Samoa Reports.*

GUAM

Guam, like Puerto Rico, was ceded to the United States by Spain in the 1898 Treaty of Paris. It has a popularly-elected governor and a unicameral legislature, and it sends one non-voting delegate to the United States House of Representatives. Guam is under the jurisdiction of the Department of the Interior, which publishes annual reports of the Governor and other information on the island.

Statutes

Guam Code Annotated, Guam Law Revision Commission, Agana, Guam, 1993.

In 1993, the *Guam Code Annotated* was published in a new edition with amendments. There are 21 titles in 17 looseleaf volumes, plus an index.

Legislative Materials

Public Laws and Executive Orders, Guam Law Revision Commission, Agana, Guam, 1975–.

This service is published as a looseleaf. The public laws are available in the William S. Hein & Co. microfiche collection of state session laws.

Court Reports

Guam Reports, Equity Publishing Corporation, Orford, N.H., 1979–.

The one bound volume of this set is supplemented by a looseleaf service.

Administrative Rules and Regulations

Administrative Rules and Regulations of the Government of Guam, Secretary of the Legislature, Agana, Guam.

A looseleaf set with annual supplementation.

Journal

Guam Bar Journal, Guam Bar Association, Agana, Guam, 1981–.

Computer Databases

WESTLAW has a database (GU–CS) that carries decisions from the U.S. District Court of Guam, Appellate Division. Many of these decisions are not reported in the *Federal Supplement.*

NORTHERN MARIANA ISLANDS

This island group included in the Trust Territory of the Pacific Islands has essentially completed the process of becoming a United States Commonwealth. Under its Covenant with the United States and its Constitution, the Commonwealth of the Northern Mariana Islands has a substantial amount of governmental autonomy that includes legislative, executive and judicial powers. In 1986 the United Nations Trusteeship Council declared that it was appropriate for the trusteeship to terminate. In December 1990, the Security Council voted to terminate trusteeship status.

Statutes

Commonwealth Code. Saipan, Mariana Islands: Commonwealth Law Revision Commission, 1983–.

This is a three-volume looseleaf updated approximately semi-annually. It contains legislation enacted by the commonwealth legislature.

Administrative Rules and Regulations

Commonwealth Register. Saipan, Mariana Islands: Registrar of Corporation, Office of the Attorney General.

Judicial Decisions

Commonwealth Reporter, Saipan, Northern Mariana Islands: Law Revision Commission.

The Commonwealth Judicial Reorganization Act of 1989 reestablished the trial-level court and renamed it the Superior Court of the Commonwealth. As noted below, the act made major changes in appellate jurisdiction as well. Both trial-level and appellate decisions formerly were published in the *Commonwealth Reporter.* It now only reports trial-level cases.

Northern Mariana Islands Reports, Saipan, Northern Mariana Islands, Saipan Press, 1991–.

The Commonwealth Judicial Reorganization Act of 1989 also created the Supreme Court of the Commonwealth to hear appeals in cases decided in the Northern Mariana Islands. From the Supreme Court appeal lies to the United States Court of Appeals for the Ninth Circuit. The *Northern Mariana Islands Reports* publishes, unofficially, the decisions of the Supreme Court.

Computer Databases

WESTLAW has a database (MP–CS) which, beginning in 1990, carries the decisions of the Supreme Court of the Commonwealth. Before 1990, decisions are reported from the Appellate Division of the former U.S. District Court for the Northern Mariana Islands.

PUERTO RICO *

Puerto Rico was ceded by Spain to the United States under the 1898 Treaty of Paris. Since 1917 its citizens have been citizens of the United States, and since 1952 it has had approximately the same control over its internal affairs as do states of the United States, exercised through a governor and a bicameral legislature. Puerto Rico currently has *commonwealth status* with only non-voting representation in the United States Congress.

Statutes

Leyes de Puerto Rico/Laws of Puerto Rico, 1900–, Equity Publishing Corporation, Orford, N.H.

The session laws are published in separate Spanish and English series. They are also available on microfiche in the William S. Hein & Co. series of state session laws. Because of the substantial delay in the publication of bound session law volumes, private publishers have started advance session law services. There are currently three competing services: *Servicio Legislativo de Puerto Rico, Leyes Aprobadas,* and *Leyes Selladas.*

* The authors thank Lcda. María M. Otero, Director of the Legislative Library of Puerto Rico, for her assistance in updating the Puerto Rico section of Appendix B.

Laws of Puerto Rico Annotated, Butterworth of Puerto Rico, San Juan, Puerto Rico, 1965–.

This is the standard English-language compilation of the Puerto Rican statutes. It is updated with pocket parts and replacement supplements. The annotations include not only court cases but also cross-references to *Rules and Regulations of Puerto Rico.* There are historical notes to trace the development of various sections. *Laws of Puerto Rico Annotated* is published in separate English and Spanish editions, as both languages are official.

Court Reports

Puerto Rico Reports, Equity Publishing Corporation, Orford, N.H., vols. 1–100.

This English-language set includes all cases from the Supreme Court of Puerto Rico from 1900–1972. The English version suspended publication with volume 100. The decisions of the Supreme Court since 1972 are available in translation, but unpublished, from the Court. Certified or plain copies of translations prepared by the Court can be requested from Secretaría del Tribunal Supremo, Negociado de Traducciones, Apartado 2392, San Juan, Puerto Rico 00902–2392.

Decisiones de Puerto Rico, Equity Publishing Corporation, Orford, N.H., vols. 1–.

The Spanish version of the reports of the Supreme Court of Puerto Rico continues to be published, but there is approximately a two-year delay before a volume of decisions is published.

Jurisprudencia del Tribunal Supremo de Puerto Rico. Publicaciones JTS, San Juan, Puerto Rico, 1977–.

These are weekly advance sheets of the decisions of the Supreme Court, published only in Spanish, with quarterly indexes and case tables.

Digests

Digesto de Puerto Rico. Butterworth de Puerto Rico, San Juan, Puerto Rico, 1974–.

This is the topical digest to the decisions of the Supreme Court of Puerto Rico. It is published in Spanish only. Organization is analogous to the West digests. Updating is by cumulative annual pocket parts.

Administrative Rules and Regulations

Rules and Regulations of Puerto Rico, Commonwealth of Puerto Rico, Department of State, San Juan, Puerto Rico, 1957–1972.

This looseleaf service contained the codification of all regulations adopted by the executive branch of Puerto Rico. This set is no longer kept current.

Puerto Rico Register, Commonwealth of Puerto Rico, Department of State, San Juan, Puerto Rico, 1957–1982.

This looseleaf service was published periodically (about seven times a year), and contained new regulations and amendments to existing regulations, thus keeping the *Rules and Regulations of Puerto Rico* up to date. It is not currently published in either Spanish or English.

Catalog of Regulations of Puerto Rico. Escrutinio Legislativo, San Juan, Puerto Rico, 1991–.

This is a looseleaf compilation of Puerto Rican administrative regulations in force. Updating is by replacement pages. At present, it is the only published source for current regulations.

Executive Opinions

Opiniones del Secretario de Justicia de Puerto Rico, Puerto Rico Department of Justice, San Juan, Puerto Rico, 1903–.

The *Opiniones* are more or less equivalent to attorney general's opinions. They come out irregularly but are kept up to date. They are published in the William S. Hein & Co. microfiche set of attorneys general opinions.

Law Reviews

Revista De Derecho Puertorriqueño. Quarterly publication of the Universidad Catolica de Puerto Rico, School of Law, Ponce, Puerto Rico, 1961–.

Revista del Colegio de Abogados de Puerto Rico. Quarterly publication of the Colegio de Abogados de Puerto Rico, San Juan, Puerto Rico, 1939–.

Revista Jurídica de la Universidad de Puerto Rico. Quarterly publication of the Escuela de Derecho de la Universidad de Puerto Rico, Rio Piedras, Puerto Rico, 1932–.

Revista Jurídica de la Universidad Interamericana de Puerto Rico. A triannual publication of the Universidad Interamericana de Puerto Rico, Santurce, Puerto Rico, 1964–.

Citation Index

Shepard's Puerto Rico Citations, Shepard's/McGraw–Hill, Colorado Springs, Colo., 1968–.

This is a complete citation system showing all citations by the Puerto Rico and federal courts to the Puerto Rico cases reported in the various series of Puerto Rico reports and all citations by the Puerto Rico and federal courts to the Constitution of the Common-

wealth of Puerto Rico, the Organic Acts, and codes and laws, acts, ordinances, and court rules. All citations by the Puerto Rico courts to the United States Constitution and federal statutes are also shown.

Computer Databases

WESTLAW has a Puerto Rico database that contains the Puerto Rico statutes, the rules of court, and a legislative service that purports to have the text of recently passed laws, though it does not appear to contain anything more recent than the other statute databases. There is another database of decisions from the 1st Circuit and from the U.S. District Court for the District of Puerto Rico. It contains many decisions from the District Court that are not published in the *Federal Supplement.*

LEXIS has a Puerto Rico library that contains a file for the annotated statutes and a file that purports to have the text of recently passed laws, though it does not appear to contain anything more recent than the other statute databases. There is no separate cases file, though the same results on WESTLAW can be obtained in the GENFED cases library by running a search that includes the words Puerto Rico.

Neither LEXIS nor WESTLAW carries the decisions of the Puerto Rico Supreme Court, and that has to count as a major deficiency in both systems.

Compuclerk—LPRA. Compact Disc Technologies, San Juan, Puerto Rico, 1992–.

This is a database in CD–ROM format containing the full text in Spanish of *Leyes de Puerto Rico Anotadas (Laws of Puerto Rico Annotated).*

Compuclerk—DPR. Compact Disc Technologies, San Juan, Puerto Rico, 1989–.

This is a database in CD–ROM format containing the full text of the decisions (in Spanish) of the Supreme Court of Puerto Rico, from 1899 to the present.

Legal Research Guide

Gorrín Peralta, Carlos I. *Fuentes y Proceso de Investigación Juridica.* (Orford, NH: Butterworth Legal Publishers, Equity Publishing Division, 1991).

This is the only current and generally available guide to legal research in Puerto Rico, in either Spanish or English. It doubles as the only good guide in Spanish to U.S. legal research in general.

VIRGIN ISLANDS

Formerly the Danish West Indies, the Virgin Islands of the United States were purchased by the United States in 1917. A local govern-

ment consisting of a governor and a 15–member unicameral legislature has existed since 1954. The territory sends a non-voting delegate to the United States House of Representatives. Past efforts to draft a formal constitution securing a greater measure of self-government have been unsuccessful.

Statutes

Session Laws of the Virgin Islands, Office of the Government Secretary, Charlotte Amalie, Saint Thomas, Virgin Islands: Equity Publishing Corporation, Orford, New Hampshire, 1955–.

Published annually, this publication contains the complete text of all laws and resolutions enacted by the legislature and approved by the governor. It also contains a resume of legislative activities, which gives a short summary of action taken on every bill introduced in the legislature for that year. The messages of the governor (mainly veto messages) can be found in the appendix of each volume. Each volume contains a table showing bill numbers of acts and resolutions, a table showing the corresponding sections of the *Virgin Islands Code* to the new acts, and a topical index. The Session Laws of the Virgin Islands are also contained in the series of state session laws published in microfiche by William S. Hein & Co.

Virgin Islands Code Annotated, Butterworth Legal Publishers, Equity Publishing Division, Orford, N.H., (3d ed.), 1970–.

Annotated and updated annually with pocket parts, this set contains the complete text of documents and acts having historical and current significance to the Virgin Islands (*i.e.,* the Danish Colonial Law of 1906; the 1916 Convention between the United States and Denmark providing for the cession of the Danish West Indies; and the Organic Acts). There are distribution tables showing where provisions of prior laws were carried into the *Code.* An index is also included.

Court Reports

Virgin Islands Reports, the Government of the Virgin Islands, Equity Publishing Corporation, Orford, N.H., 1959–.

Beginning in 1917, the *Reports* contain opinions of the District Court of the Virgin Islands, the Territorial Court, and of the United States Court of Appeals for the Third Circuit and the Supreme Court of the United States in cases originating in the Virgin Islands. Also included are opinions of the District Court Commissioners (if not reversed), opinions of the police (now municipal) courts if they discuss questions of the law, opinions of the Tax Court of the United States in Virgin Islands cases, and opinions of the Attorney General of the United States with respect to matters concerning the Virgin Islands. Each opinion has headnotes, and each volume has a table of cases reported and tables of statutes, treaties, executive orders,

court procedural rules, and other resources cited or construed, and a topical digest of the cases found in that volume.

The *Reports* are kept up to date by a looseleaf service containing current cases, but the update service is more than a year behind.

Digests

Butterworths Virgin Islands Digest. Butterworth Legal Publishers, Equity Publishing Division, Orford, NH, 1991–.

The *Virgin Islands Digest* gives topical access to decisions published in the *Virgin Islands Reports.* Coverage in the current bound volumes is through 1990 and updating is done by means of pocket parts.

Administrative Rules and Regulations

Virgin Islands Rules and Regulations, Government Secretary for the Government of the Virgin Islands, Equity Publishing Corporation, Orford, N.H., 1959–.

Contained in looseleaf binders for easy updating, this service provides an official record of all departmental regulations filed with the Government Secretary. The regulations are classified by subject matter and arranged and numbered to correspond to the pertinent titles and chapters of the *Virgin Islands Code.* A source note under the first section of each regulation or group of regulations shows the office or agency that issued it, and the approval and effective dates. The set contains a topical index and a table of agencies showing which regulations have been adopted by each agency or department. The *Virgin Islands Rules and Regulations* are kept up to date by the *Virgin Islands Register.*

Virgin Islands Register, Government Secretary for the Government of the Virgin Islands, Equity Publishing Corporation, Orford, N.H., 1960–.

Each issue of the *Register* is published in two parts. Part 1 (called *Temporary and Special Materials*) contains gubernatorial proclamations, executive orders and reorganization plans, documents, or classes of documents that the governor determines to have general applicability and legal effect, and documents required by the legislature to be published. Part 2 (called *Amendments and Additions to Rules and Regulations*) contains supplementary looseleaf pages that are interfiled into the *Virgin Islands Rules and Regulations* to keep it current. Volumes for 1960–1970 were issued by the Government Secretary for the Government of the Virgin Islands; those for 1971 to the present are issued by the Lieutenant Governor of the Virgin Islands.

Attorney General Opinions

Opinions of the Attorney General of the Virgin Islands, the Lieutenant Governor for the Government of the Virgin Islands, Equity Publishing Corporation, Orford, N.H., 1965–.

This service contains all important opinions of general significance rendered from 1935 by the chief legal officer of the Government of the Virgin Islands, variously designated as Government
Attorney, the District Attorney, the United States Attorney, and the
Attorney General of the Virgin Islands. Each volume contains
headnotes at the beginning of the opinions (summarizing the legal
points therein) and a digest of legal points at the end of the volume.
Also included are tables listing federal, and local laws; federal, state
and local judicial opinions; and regulations and executive orders
cited throughout the opinions.

Appendix C

STATE REPORTS

A. YEAR OF FIRST REPORTED CASE DECIDED IN THE STATES' APPELLATE COURTS

Many of the states were territories or colonies at the time of their first appellate decision. Pennsylvania was a commonwealth. In 1840, what is now the state of Texas was an independent republic.

While printing began in the Colonies in 1638, the first case reported appears to be the *Trial of Thomas Sutherland* for murder, printed in 1692. About 30 of the 150 English reports were being used in this country prior to the American Revolution as the written case law, because only about 35 to 40 legal books or pamphlets had been printed here.

Connecticut was the first state to publish an official law report after a 1784 statute entitled *An Act Establishing the Wages of the Judges of the Superior Court* was passed requiring judges of the supreme and superior courts to file written opinions. The first volume, known as *Kirby's Reports,* was published in 1789 by Ephraim Kirby in Litchfield, Connecticut, and includes as its first case one from 1785. In 1790 came Dallas' *Pennsylvania Cases;* in 1792 followed Hopkinson's *Admiralty Reports;* and Chipman's *Vermont Reports* in 1793. Through the early 1800s reports followed in North Carolina, Virginia, Kentucky, New Jersey, Maryland, Louisiana, New York, and Tennessee. Some of these early reports gathered and published cases much older than the publication date of the reporter. For example, the *Harris & McHenry Reports* from the General Court of Maryland contains a case decided in 1658.

State	Date	State	Date
Alabama	1820	Indiana	1817
Alaska	1869	Iowa	1839
Arizona	1866	Kansas	1858
Arkansas	1837	Kentucky	1785
California	1850	Louisiana	1809
Colorado	1864	Maine	1820
Connecticut	1785	Maryland	1658
Delaware	1792	Massachusetts	1804
District of Columbia	1801	Michigan	1805
Florida	1846	Minnesota	1851
Georgia	1846	Mississippi	1818
Hawaii	1847	Missouri	1821
Idaho	1866	Montana	1868
Illinois	1819	Nebraska	1860

State	Date	State	Date
Nevada	1865	Rhode Island	1828
New Hampshire	1796	South Carolina	1783
New Jersey	1789	South Dakota	1867
New Mexico	1852	Tennessee	1791
New York	1791	Texas	1840
North Carolina	1778	Utah	1855
North Dakota	1867	Vermont	1789
Ohio	1821	Virginia	1729
Oklahoma	1890	Washington	1854
Oregon	1853	West Virginia	1864
Pennsylvania	1754	Wisconsin	1839
		Wyoming	1870

B. STATES THAT HAVE DISCONTINUED PUBLISHING OFFICIAL STATE REPORTS

State	Last Published Volume	Year	First Volume Only in National Reporter System
Alabama	295	1976	331 So. 2d
Ala. App.	57	1976	331 So. 2d
Colorado	200	1980	616 P.2d
Colo. App.	44	1980	616 P.2d
Delaware	59	1966	220 A.2d
Florida	160	1948	37 So. 2d
Indiana	275	1981	419 N.E.2d
Ind. App.	182	1979	366 N.E.2d
Iowa	261	1968	158 N.W.2d
Kentucky	314	1951	237 S.W.2d
Louisiana *	263	1972	270 So. 2d
Maine	161	1965	215 A.2d
Minnesota	312	1977	254 N.W.2d
Mississippi	254	1966	183 So. 2d
Missouri	365	1956	295 S.W.2d
Mo. App.	241	1952	274 S.W.2d
North Dakota	79	1953	60 N.W.2d
Oklahoma	208	1953	265 P.2d
Okla. Crim.	97	1953	265 P.2d
Rhode Island	122	1980	501 A.2d
South Dakota	90	1976	245 N.W.2d
Tennessee	225	1972	476 S.W.2d
Tenn. App.	63	1971	480 S.W.2d
Tenn. Crim. App.	4	1970	475 S.W.2d
Texas *	163	1962	358 S.W.2d
Tex. Crim. App.*	172	1963	363 S.W.2d
Tex. Civ. App.*	63	1911	134 S.W.
Utah (2d Series)	30	1974	519 P.2d
Wyoming	80	1959	346 P.2d

* These states have discontinued their official reports, but have not adopted the *National Reporter System* Reports as official. Alaska has used the *Pacific Reporter* as its official reporter since being admitted to statehood.

Appendix D

COVERAGE OF THE NATIONAL
REPORTER SYSTEM

The entire system, with its coverage, is outlined below:

Reporter	Began in	Coverage
Atlantic Reporter	1885	Conn., Del., Me., Md., N.H., N.J., Pa., R.I., Vt., and D.C.
California Reporter	1959	Calif. Sup. Ct., Courts of Appeal and Appellate Department of the Superior Court.
Illinois Decisions	1976	Ill. (all state courts).
New York Supplement	1888	N.Y. (all state courts). Since 1932, the N.Y. Court of Appeals opinions are published here as well as in the North Eastern Reporter.
North Eastern Reporter	1885	Ill., Ind., Mass., N.Y., and Ohio.
North Western Reporter	1879	Iowa, Mich., Minn., Neb., N.D., S.D., and Wis.
Pacific Reporter	1883	Alaska, Ariz., Cal. to 1960, Calif. Sup. Ct. since 1960, Colo., Hawaii, Idaho, Kan., Mont., Nev., N.M., Okla., Or., Utah, Wash., and Wyo.
South Eastern Reporter	1887	Ga., N.C., S.C., Va., and W.Va.
South Western Reporter	1886	Ark., Ky., Mo., Tenn., and Tex.
Southern Reporter	1887	Ala., Fla., La., and Miss.
Supreme Court Reporter	1882	Supreme Court of the United States.
Federal Reporter	1880	From 1880 to 1912: United States Circuit Court (abolished in 1912). From 1880 to 1932: District Courts of the United States (coverage transferred to Federal Supplement). 1891 to date: United States Court of Appeals (formerly U.S. Circuit Court of Appeals). 1912 to 1913: Commerce Court of the United States (abolished in 1913). 1929 to 1932 and 1960 to 1982: United States Court of Claims (abolished in 1982). 1929 to 1982: United States Court of Customs and Patent Appeals.[1] 1943 to 1961: United States Emergency Court of Appeals. 1972 to date: Temporary Emergency Court of Appeals.

[1] Since 1983, jurisdiction of the U.S. Court of Customs and Patent Appeals and the appellate division of the U.S. Court of Claims transferred to U.S. Court of Appeals for the Federal Circuit.

Reporter	Began in	Coverage
Federal Supplement	1932	1932 to date: United States District Courts. 1932 to 1960: United States Court of Claims. 1956 to 1980: United States Customs Court (replaced by United States Court of International Trade). 1980 to date: United States Court of International Trade. 1969 to date: Judicial Panel on Multidistrict Litigation. 1974 to date: Special Court under the Regional Rail Reorganization Act of 1973.
Federal Claims Reporter	1983	1983 to 1992: formerly United States Claims Court Reporter through vol. 26, covering United States Claims Court.[2] 1992 to date: United States Court of Federal Claims. Commences with vol. 27.
Federal Rules Decisions	1940	District Courts of the United States.
Military Justice Reporter	1975	U.S. Court of Military Appeals and Court of Military Review of the Army, Navy–Marine Corps, Air Force and Coast Guard.
Bankruptcy Reporter	1979	Bankruptcy cases from U.S. Bankruptcy Courts, U.S. District Courts, U.S. Courts of Appeals, and U.S. Supreme Court.
Veterans Appeals Reporter	1991	Veterans appeals cases from the United States Court of Veterans Appeals, U.S. District Courts, U.S. Courts of Appeals, and U.S. Supreme Court.

[2] This court changed its name in 1992 to the United States Court of Federal Claims.

Appendix E *

FUNDAMENTAL LAWYERING SKILLS
§ 3 LEGAL RESEARCH

In order to conduct legal research effectively, a lawyer should have a working knowledge of the nature of legal rules and legal institutions, the fundamental tools of legal research, and the process of devising and implementing a coherent and effective research design:

3.1 *Knowledge of the Nature of Legal Rules and Institutions.* The identification of the issues and sources to be researched in any particular situation requires an understanding of:

(a) The various sources of legal rules and the processes by which these rules are made, including:

(i) Caselaw. Every lawyer should have a basic familiarity with: (A) The organization and structure of the federal and state courts of general jurisdiction; general concepts of jurisdiction and venue; the rudiments of civil and criminal procedure; the historical separation between courts of law and equity and the modern vestiges of this dual court system; (B) The nature of common law decisionmaking by courts and the doctrine of *stare decisis;* (C) The degree of "authoritativeness" of constitutional and common law decisions made by courts at the various levels of the federal and state judicial systems;

(ii) Statutes. Every lawyer should have a basic familiarity with: (A) The legislative processes at the federal, state, and local levels, including the procedures for preparing, introducing, amending, and enacting legislation; (B) The relationship between the legislative and judicial branches, including the power of the courts to construe ambiguous statutory language and the power of the courts to strike down unconstitutional statutory provisions;

(iii) Administrative regulations and decisions of administrative agencies. Every lawyer should have a basic familiarity with the rudiments of administrative law, including: (A) The procedures for administrative and executive rulemaking and adjudication; (B) The relationship between the executive and judicial branches, including the power of the courts to construe and pass on the validity and constitutionality of administrative regulations and the actions of administrative agencies;

(iv) Rules of court;

* Reprinted by permission of the American Bar Association.

(v) Restatements and similar codifications (covering non-official expositions of legal rules that courts tend to view as authoritative);

(b) Which of the sources of legal rules identified in § 3.1(a) *supra* tend to provide the controlling principles for resolution of various kinds of issues in various substantive fields;

(c) The variety of legal remedies available in any given situation, including: litigation; legislative remedies (such as drafting and/or lobbying for new legislation; lobbying to defeat pending legislative bills; and lobbying for the repeal or amendment of existing legislation); administrative remedies (such as presenting testimony in support of, or lobbying for, the adoption, repeal, or amendment of administrative regulations; and lobbying of an administrator to resolve an individual case in a particular way); and alternative dispute-resolution mechanisms (formal mechanisms such as arbitration, mediation, and conciliation; and informal mechanisms such as self-help);

3.2 *Knowledge of and Ability to Use the Most Fundamental Tools of Legal Research:*

(a) With respect to each of the following fundamental tools of legal research, a lawyer should be generally familiar with the nature of the tool, its likely location in a law library, and the ways in which the tool is used:

(i) Primary legal texts (the written or recorded texts of legal rules), including: caselaw reporters, looseleaf services, and other collections of court decisions; codifications of federal, state, and local legislation; collections of administrative regulations and decisions of administrative agencies;

(ii) Secondary legal materials (the variety of aids to researching the primary legal texts), including treatises, digests, annotated versions of statutory compilations, commentaries in looseleaf services, law reviews, and Shepard's Compilations of citations to cases and statutes;

(iii) Sources of ethical obligations of lawyers, including the standards of professional conduct (the Code of Professional Responsibility and the Model Rules of Professional Conduct), and collections of ethical opinions of the American Bar Association and of state and local bar associations;

(b) With respect to the primary legal texts described in § 3.2(a)(i) *supra*, a lawyer should be familiar with:

(i) Specialized techniques for reading or using the text, including:

(A) Techniques of reading and analyzing court decisions, such as: the analysis of which portions of the decision are holdings and which are *dicta;* the identification of narrower and broader possible formulations of the holdings of the case; the evaluation of a case's rela-

tive precedential value; and the reconciliation of doctrinal inconsistencies between cases;

   (B) Techniques of construing statutes by employing well-
   accepted rules of statutory construction or by referring to secondary sources (such as legislative history);

   (ii) Specialized rules and customs permitting or prohibiting
   reliance on alternative versions of the primary legal texts
   (such as unofficial case reporters or unofficial statutory
   codes);

(c) With respect to the secondary legal materials described in
§ 3.2(a)(ii) *supra,* a lawyer should have a general familiarity
with the breadth, depth, detail and currency of coverage, the
particular perspectives, and the relative strengths and weaknesses that tend to be found in the various kinds of secondary
sources so that he or she can make an informed judgment
about which source is most suitable for a particular research
purpose;

(d) With respect to both the primary legal materials described in
§ 3.2(a)(i) *supra,* and the secondary legal materials described
in § 3.2(a)(ii) *supra,* a lawyer should be familiar with alternative forms of accessing the materials, including hard copy,
microfiche and other miniaturization services, and computerized services (such as LEXIS and WESTLAW);

3.3 *Understanding of the Process of Devising and Implementing a
Coherent and Effective Research Design:* A lawyer should be
familiar with the skills and concepts involved in:

(a) Formulating the issues for research:

   (i) Determining the full range of legal issues to be researched
   (*see* Skill § 2.1 *supra*);

   (ii) Determining the kinds of answers to the legal issues that
   are needed for various purposes;

   (iii) Determining the degree of confidence in the answers that
   is needed for various purposes;

   (iv) Determining the extent of documentation of the answers
   that is needed for various purposes;

   (v) Conceptualizing the issues to be researched in terms that
   are conducive to effective legal research (including a consideration of which conceptualizations or verbalizations of
   issues or rules will make them most accessible to various
   types of search strategies);

(b) Identifying the full range of search strategies that could be
used to research the issues, as well as alternatives to research, such as, in appropriate cases, seeking the information
from other people who have expertise regarding the issues to
be researched (for example, other attorneys or, in the case of
procedural issues, clerks of court);

(c) Evaluating the various search strategies and settling upon a
research design, which should take into account:

(i) The degree of thoroughness of research that would be necessary in order to adequately resolve the legal issues (*i.e.,* in order to find an answer if there is one to be found, or, in cases where the issue is still open, to determine to a reasonable degree of certainty that it is still unresolved and gather analogous authorities);

(ii) The degree of thoroughness that is necessary in the light of the uses to which the research will be put (*e.g.,* the greater degree of thoroughness necessary if the information to be researched will be used at trial or at a legislative hearing; the lesser degree of thoroughness necessary if the information will be used in an informal negotiation with opposing counsel or lobbying of an administrator);

(iii) An estimation of the amount of time that will be necessary to conduct research of the desired degree of thoroughness;

(iv) An assessment of the feasibility of conducting research of the desired degree of thoroughness, taking into account:

(A) The amount of time available for research in the light of the other tasks to be performed, their relative importance, and their relative urgency;

(B) The extent of the client's resources that can be allocated to the process of legal research; and

(C) The availability of techniques for reducing the cost of research (such as, for example, using manual research methods to gain basic familiarity with the relevant area before using the more expensive resource of computerized services);

(v) If there is insufficient time for, or the client lacks adequate resources for, research that is thorough enough to adequately resolve the legal issues, a further assessment of the ways in which the scope of the research can be curtailed with the minimum degree of risk of undermining the accuracy of the research or otherwise impairing the client's interests;

(vi) Strategies for double-checking the accuracy of the research, such as using different secondary sources to research the same issue; or, when possible, conferring with practitioners or academics with expertise in the area;

(d) Implementing the research design, including:

(i) Informing the client of the precise extent to which the scope of the research has been curtailed for the sake of time or conservation of the client's resources (*see* § 3.3(c)(v) *supra*); the reasons for these curtailments; and the possible consequences of deciding not to pursue additional research;

(ii) Monitoring the results of the research and periodically considering:

(A) Whether the research design should be modified;

(B) Whether it is appropriate to end the research, because it has fully answered the questions posed; or, even though it has not fully answered the questions posed, further research will not produce additional information; or the information that is likely to be produced is not worth the time and resources that would be expended;

(iii) Ensuring that any cases that will be relied upon or cited have not been overruled, limited, or called into question; and that any statutes or administrative regulations that will be relied upon or cited have not been repealed or amended and have not been struck down by the courts.

In 1989 the American Bar Association Section of Legal Education and Admissions to the Bar created the Task Force on Law Schools and the Profession: Narrowing the Gap. Its purpose was to study and improve the processes by which new members of the profession are prepared for the practice of law. In August 1992, the Task Force issued its final report, *Legal Education and Professional Development—An Educational Continuum.* That report includes within it a "Statement of Fundamental Skills and Values," identifying "Legal Research" as one of the ten fundamental skills a lawyer should possess. The Task Force was chaired by former ABA President Robert MacCrate. We are grateful to Mr. MacCrate and to the American Bar Association for granting permission to reprint § 3 Legal Research.[1]

JMJ
RMM
DJD

[1] For additional information on § 3 Legal Research of the Task Force report, see Donald J. Dunn, *Legal Research: A Fundamental Lawyering Skill,* 1 PERSPECTIVES: TEACHING LEGAL RES. & WRITING 2 (1992); Donald J. Dunn, *Are Legal Research Skills Essential? "It Can Hardly Be Doubted . . .",* 1 PERSPECTIVES: TEACHING LEGAL RES. & WRITING 34 (1993).

CHART ON LEGAL RESEARCH PROCEDURE

RESEARCH PROBLEM	GENERAL BACKGROUND	MORE CRITICAL & DETAILED STUDIES	ANNOTATIONS	TEXT OF LAW OR CASE	LEGISLATIVE HISTORY	INTERPRETATION	SHEPARDIZING	ADDITIONAL CARDS	OTHER
CASE LAW									
1. Federal	1. C.J.S 2. Am. Jr. 2d	1. Treatises 2. Periodicals: Index Leg. Per.; Leg. Res. Index; Cur. Law Index; LegalTrac 3. Restatements	ALRs	1. S. Ct.: U.S. Rpts; U.S. Sup. Ct. Rpts (L. Ed.); Sup. Ct. Rpts. (West) 2. Fed. Rptr.; F.2d; F.3d 3. Fed. Supp.			1. Shepard's U.S & Fed. Citator	1. U.S. Sup. Ct. Dige. 2. West's various sets of lower court federal digests 3. Looseleaf Services	1. WESTLAW 2. LEXIS 3. Records & Briefs, if available
2. State	1. State Ency. 2. C.J.S. or Am. Jr. 2d	1. Treatises 2. Periodicals: Index Leg. Per.; Leg. Res. Index; Cur. Law Index; LegalTrac	ALRs	1. National Reporter System 2. State Reports			1. Shepard's State or Regional Citator 2. Nat'l Rptr. Blue Book	1. Am. Dig. System 2. National Reporter Blue Book	1. WESTLAW 2. LEXIS 3. Records & Briefs, if available 4. Restatements
STATUTORY LAW									
1. Federal	C.J.S. or Am. Jr. 2d	1. Treatises 2. Periodicals: Index Leg. Per.; Leg. Res. Index; Cur. Law Index; LegalTrac	1. ALRs 2. L. Ed.	1. U.S.C. 2. U.S.C.A. 3. U.S.C.S.	1. Pre-1970: See Chap. 10 2. Post-1970: C.I.S. 3. Pub. Legis. Histories	1. U.S.C.A 2. U.S.C.S. 3. U.S. Att'y Gen. Opinions	1. Provisions & Cases: U.S. 2. Cases: Fed. 3. Provisions: State or Regional Citator	1. U.S. Sup. Ct. Digests 2. West's various sets of lower court federal digests 3. Looseleaf Services	1. WESTLAW 2. LEXIS
2. State	1. State Ency. 2. C.J.S. or Am. Jr. 2d	1. State Treatises 2. Periodicals: Index Leg. Per.; Leg. Res. Index; Cur. Law Index; LegalTrac	ALRs	1. State Code 2. State Code Annotated	1. Citations: State 2. Intent: See Chap. 11	1. State Code Annotated 2. State Att'y Gen. Opinions	Provisions & Cases: State or Regional Citator	1. State or Regional Digests 2. Other State Codes Annotated 3. Uniform Laws Annotated	1. WESTLAW 2. LEXIS 3. Legal research guide for the state, where available
3. Local		Treatises		1. Mun. Code 2. Mun. Ordinances 3. Appropriate city official		State Digest	Provisions & Cases: State Citator	Shepard's Ordinance Law Annotations	1. WESTLAW 2. LEXIS

[GS784]

RESEARCH PROBLEM	GENERAL BACKGROUND	MORE CRITICAL & DETAILED STUDIES	ANNOTATIONS	TEXT OF LAW OR CASE	LEGISLATIVE HISTORY	INTERPRETATION	SHEPARDIZING	ADDITIONAL CASES	OTHER
CONSTITUTIONAL LAW									
1. Federal	1. C.J.S 2. Am. Jr. 2d	1. Treatises 2. *Periodicals:* Index Leg. Per.; Leg. Res. Index; Cur. Law Index; LEGALTRAC 3. Restatements	1. ALR Fed. 2. U.S. Sup. Ct. Rpts, L. Edition 3. LC Const.	1. U.S.C. 2. U.S.C.A. 3. U.S.C.S.	1. Citations: U.S.C.A.. U.S.C.S. Shepard's U.S., U.S.C. Stat. at Large 2. *Intent:* Federalist, etc.	1. U.S.C.A. 2. U.S.C.S. 3. LC Constitution 4. U.S. Att'y Gen. Opinions	1. *Provisions:* U.S., State 2. *Cases:* Fed., U.S., State	1. U.S. Sup. Ct. Dig. 2. West's various sets of lower court federal digests 3. Am. Dig. System	1. WESTLAW 2. LEXIS 3. Records & Briefs, if available
2. State	1. State Ency. 2. C.J.S. or Am. Jr. 2d	1. *Periodicals:* Index Leg. Per.; Leg. Res. Index; Cur. Law Index; LEGALTRAC	ALRs	1. State Code 2. State Code Annotated	1. State Const. Convention a. Proceedings b. Reports 2. Locally pub'd legis. rpts, H. & S. Jrnls, etc.	1. State Code Annotated 2. State Digest 3. State Att'y Gen. Opinions	1. *Provisions:* State Citator 2. *Cases:* State or Regional Citator	1. Am. Dig. System 2. Constitution of the U.S. National and State, Index	1. WESTLAW 2. LEXIS 3. Records & Briefs, if available
ADMINISTRATIVE LAW									
1. Federal	C.J.S. or Am. Jr. 2d	1. Pike & Fischer 2. Treatises 3. *Periodicals:* Index Leg. Per.; Leg. Res. Index; Cur. Law Index; LEGALTRAC	1. ALRs 2. L. Ed.	1. *Fed. Regs. & CFR:* Rules & Decisions 2. *Agency Rpts:* Decisions 3. *Looseleaf Services:* Rules & Decisions		1. Looseleaf Services 2. U.S. Sup. Court Digests 3. West's various sets of lower ct. federal digests	1. *CFR:* Citator 2. *Agency Cases:* U.S. Admin. Citator 3. *Court Cases:* U.S. & Fed. Citator		1. WESTLAW 2. LEXIS
2. State	State Ency.	1. State Treatises 2. *Periodicals:* Index Leg. Per.; Leg. Res. Index; Cur. Law Index; LEGALTRAC	ALRs	1. Adm. Code, if published 2. Register of agency regs. & rulings, if pub. 3. Agency: Rules & Decisions 4. Looseleaf service, if available		1. State or Regional Dig. 2. State Atty. Gen. Ops.	*Cases:* State or Regional Citator	1. Other state or regional digests 2. American Digest System	
3. Local				1. Local Adm. Dept. 2. Pamphlets		State Digest	*Cases:* State Citator	Other state digests	1. WESTLAW 2. LEXIS

(GS PW)

INDEX *

References are to Pages; italic type indicates Titles of Publications

* Prepared by Bonnie L. Koneski-White, Associate Law Librarian, Western New England College, School of Law.

References are to Pages; italic type indicates Titles

References are to Pages; italic type indicates Titles

†